The Case of Wagner
Twilight of the Idols
The Antichrist
Ecce Homo
Dionysus Dithyrambs
Nietzsche Contra Wagner

Based on the edition by
Giorgio Colli & Mazzino Montinari

First organized by Ernst Behler

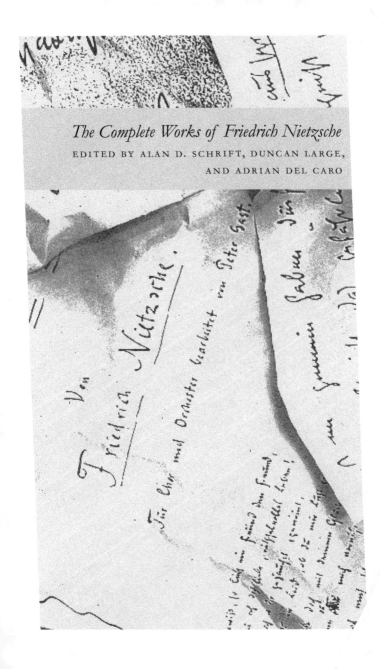

The Complete Works of Friedrich Nietzsche

EDITED BY ALAN D. SCHRIFT, DUNCAN LARGE,
AND ADRIAN DEL CARO

Friedrich Nietzsche

The Case of Wagner
Twilight of the Idols
The Antichrist
Ecce Homo
Dionysus Dithyrambs
Nietzsche Contra Wagner

Translated by Adrian Del Caro, Carol Diethe,
Duncan Large, George H. Leiner, Paul S. Loeb,
Alan D. Schrift, David F. Tinsley, and Mirko Wittwar

Afterword by Andreas Urs Sommer

STANFORD UNIVERSITY PRESS
STANFORD, CALIFORNIA

Stanford University Press
Stanford, California

Translated from Friedrich Nietzsche, *Sämtliche Werke: Kritische Studienausgabe*, ed. Giorgio Colli and Mazzino Montinari, in 15 vols. This book corresponds to Vol. 6, pp. 7–458, and Vol. 14, pp. 383–528.

Critical edition of Friedrich Nietzsche's *Sämtliche Werke* and unpublished writings based on the original manuscripts.

CIP data appears at the end of the book.

Contents

The Case of Wagner
A Musicians' Problem

Twilight of the Idols
or How to Philosophize with a Hammer

The Antichrist
Curse upon Christianity

Ecce Homo
How One Becomes What One Is

Dionysus Dithyrambs

Nietzsche Contra Wagner
Documents of a Psychologist

A Note
on This Edition

This is the first English translation of all of Nietzsche's writings, including his unpublished fragments, with annotation, afterwords concerning the individual texts, and indexes, in nineteen volumes. The aim of this collaborative work is to produce a critical edition for scholarly use. Volume 1 also includes an introduction to the entire edition, and Volume 19 will include a detailed chronology of Nietzsche's life. While the goal is to establish a readable text in contemporary English, the translation follows the original as closely as possible. All texts have been translated anew by a group of scholars, and particular attention has been given to maintaining a consistent terminology throughout the volumes. The translation is based on *Friedrich Nietzsche: Sämtliche Werke. Kritische Studienausgabe in 15 Bänden* (1980), edited by Giorgio Colli and Mazzino Montinari. The still-progressing *Nietzsche Werke: Kritische Gesamtausgabe,* which Colli and Montinari began in 1963, has also been consulted. The Colli-Montinari edition is of particular importance for the unpublished fragments, comprising more than half of Nietzsche's writings and published there for the first time in their entirety. Besides listing textual variants, the annotation to this English edition provides succinct information on the text and identifies events, names (except those in the Index of Persons), titles, quotes, and biographical facts of Nietzsche's own life. The notes are numbered in the text and are keyed by phrase. The Afterword presents the main facts about the origin of the text, the stages of its composition, and the main events of its reception. The Index of Persons includes mythological figures and lists the dates of birth and death as well as prominent personal characteristics. Since the first three volumes appeared, important corrections to the 1980 edition of the *Kritische Studienausgabe* have been noted, and these corrections have been incorporated into the translation that appears here.

ERNST BEHLER AND ALAN D. SCHRIFT

A Note
on This Translation

The genealogy of this translation requires some explanation. Carol Diethe prepared an initial draft translation of the entire manuscript. Before the editorial review of that manuscript could be completed, Carol's health situation made it impossible for her to continue working on the translation. As a consequence, additional translators were required to complete the editorial review of each of the texts included in this volume: Adrian Del Caro took over and completed the translations of *The Antichrist* and *Nietzsche Contra Wagner*; Duncan Large took over and completed the translation of *The Case of Wagner*; and Duncan Large, Adrian Del Caro, and Alan D. Schrift collaborated on revising and completing the translations of *Twilight of the Idols* and *Ecce Homo*, as well as Giorgio Colli's "Afterword" and Mazzino Montinari's editorial apparatus in the notes. Because many of the poems that appear in *Dionysus Dithyrambs* also appear in *Thus Spoke Zarathustra* (*Complete Works*, vol. 7), it was decided that the translators of that volume — Paul S. Loeb and David F. Tinsley — would do their own translation of this work to ensure consistency between the two versions of the poems as well as the other poems in *Dionysus Dithyrambs*. Loeb and Tinsley also provide the translations from their forthcoming translation of *Zarathustra* of the many passages from that work that Nietzsche cites in *Ecce Homo*. Similarly, because Mazzino Montinari's essay "Nietzsche's Unpublished

Writings 1885–1888 and the 'Will To Power'" will also appear in
Complete Works, vol. 17: *Unpublished Fragments: Summer 1886–
Fall 1887*, it was decided that the translator of that volume —
George H. Leiner — would provide the translation also published in this volume. And the translation of the "Afterword"
by Andreas Urs Sommer was provided by Mirko Wittwar and
Alan D. Schrift. Although Carol Diethe provided a first draft
translation of most of the translation of this volume, the responsibility for the published translation belongs to the team of editors and translators mentioned above.

The Case of Wagner
Twilight of the Idols
The Antichrist
Ecce Homo
Dionysus Dithyrambs
Nietzsche Contra Wagner

The Case of Wagner.

A Musicians' Problem.

Contents.

Foreword.

I am making things a little easier for myself. It is not just pure malice if I praise Bizet in this piece at Wagner's expense. With many a joke I am raising a matter that is no joke. Turning my back on Wagner was fate for me; it was a victory to like anything at all after that. Perhaps nobody was more dangerously entwined with Wagnerism, nobody has fought harder against it, nobody has been more pleased to be rid of it. A long story![1] — Do we want a word for it? If I were a moralist, who knows what I would call it! Perhaps *self-overcoming.* — But a philosopher dislikes a moralist . . . he also dislikes pretty words . . .

What is the first and last thing a philosopher demands of himself? To inwardly overcome his times, to become "timeless." Then what does he have to struggle hardest with? With whatever it is that makes him the child of his times. Well then! I am the child of these times just as much as Wagner, in other words a *décadent:*[2] except that I realized this, except that I fought against it. The philosopher in me fought against it.

The thing that preoccupied me most deeply was in fact the problem of *décadence* — I had my reasons for that. "Good and evil" is just a variation of that problem. If you have a trained eye for the signs of decline, then you understand morality as well — you understand what lurks beneath its most sacred names and evaluations: *impoverished* life, will to extinction, great fatigue. Morality *denies* life . . . I needed self-discipline for such a task: — to take sides *against* all that was sick in myself, including Wagner, including Schopenhauer, including the whole of modern "humaneness." — A deep estrangement, aloofness, guardedness toward everything coeval and timely: and as supreme wish the eye of *Zarathustra*: an eye that from a huge distance looks over the whole of human reality — and sees it *beneath* itself . . . For such a goal — what sacrifice would not be fitting? What "self-overcoming?" What "self-denying"?

My greatest experience was a *convalescence*. Wagner just ranks among my illnesses.

Not that I want to be ungrateful toward this illness. If, in this work, I uphold the thesis that Wagner is *harmful*, I shall propound with no less zeal *to whom* he is nonetheless indispensable — to the philosopher. Otherwise one can perhaps get by without Wagner: but the philosopher is not at liberty to avoid Wagner. He must be the bad conscience of his times[3] — for which he must have the best understanding. But where would he find for the labyrinth of the modern soul a more practiced guide, a more articulate expert on the soul, than Wagner? Modernity speaks its most *intimate* language through Wagner: it hides neither its good nor its evil, having discarded all shame. And the other way round: you have nearly made a final reckoning as to the *value* of the modern if you have achieved clarity on good and evil with Wagner. — I completely understand if a musician today says: "I hate Wagner but I can't stand any other music any longer." But I would also understand a philosopher who declared: "Wagner *sums up* modernity. It's no use, you have to be a Wagnerian first . . . "

The Case of Wagner.

Letter from Turin of May 1888.

ridendo dicere severum . . .[1]

Yesterday — would you believe it? — I heard *Bizet's* master-piece for the twentieth time. Once again I sat through it with tranquil reverence, I did not run away. This victory over my impatience surprises me. How such a work creates perfection! You yourself are turned into a "masterpiece" by it. And actu-ally, every time I heard *Carmen* I thought myself more of a philosopher, a better philosopher, than otherwise: I had become so forbearing, so happy, so Indian, so *settled* . . . five hours seated: first level of holiness! — Dare I say that Bizet's orchestral sound is practically the only one I can still bear? That *other* orchestral sound, now predominant, the Wagne-rian, at once brutal, artificial and "innocent," thus speaking to the modern soul's three senses all at once — how detrimental this Wagnerian orchestral sound is to me! I call it sirocco. I break out in an unpleasant sweat. Gone is *my* good weather.[2]

I find this music perfection. Light and pliant, it politely wafts along. It is pleasant, it does not *sweat*. "What is good is light, everything divine moves on delicate feet": first proposi-tion of my aesthetics. This music is evil, refined, fatalistic: at the same time it remains popular — it has the refinement of a race, not that of an individual. It is rich. It is precise. It con-structs, organizes, comes to an end: this makes it the opposite of the polyp in music, of "unending melody."[3] Has one ever

heard more painful tragic accents on the stage? And how are
these achieved! Without a grimace! Without counterfeiting!
Without the *lie* of grand style! — At last: this music takes the
listener to be intelligent, even a musician — *that* also makes it
the antithesis to Wagner, who, whatever else he might be, was
at any rate the most *impolite* genius in the world (Wagner
always takes us, so to speak, as though — —, he repeats a
thing until you despair — until you believe it).

And again: I become a better human being when this Bizet
speaks to me. A better musician, too; a better *listener.* Can one
possibly listen any better? — I still bury my ears *under* this
music, I hear its source. It seems to me that I experience its
emergence — I tremble at dangers that accompany some sort
of risk, I delight in serendipities of which Bizet is innocent. —
And strangely, I don't think about it, or don't *know* how much
I think about it. For meanwhile quite other thoughts run
through my head . . . Have you noticed that music *frees* the
mind and gives wings to thought? That the more you become a
musician, the more you become a philosopher? — As though
lightning flashed across the gray sky of abstraction; the light
sufficiently strong for all the filigree in things; the great problems within grasp; the world as though surveyed from a mountain. — I have just defined philosophical pathos. — And all of
a sudden the *answers* drop into my lap, a little hail of ice and
wisdom, of *solved* problems . . . Where am I? — Bizet makes
me fertile. Everything good makes me fertile. I have no other
gratitude, nor any other *proof,* for what is good. —

2.

This work, too, brings redemption: Wagner is not the only
"redeemer."[4] With it, you take your leave of the *damp* North,
of all the steam of the Wagnerian ideal. Just the plot saves you
from them. It still has that logic in passion of Mérimée's, the
shortest line, the *harsh* necessity; above all it has, as befits the
torrid zone, the dryness of the air, the *limpidezza*[5] in the air;
in every respect the climate here is different. Here speaks a

different sensuousness, a different sensibility, a different cheer-fulness. This music is cheerful; but not with a French or German cheerfulness. Its cheerfulness is African; it has disaster looming over it, its happiness is short, sudden, without mercy. I envy Bizet for having had the courage for this sensibility, which up till then had not yet had a language in the cultured music of Europe — for this more southerly, browner, more scorched sensibility . . . How the flaxen afternoons of its happiness do us good! At the same time we look around: did we ever see the sea *smoother*? — And how soothingly the Moorish dance speaks to us! How, in its lascivious melancholy, even our insatiability learns to be satisfied for once![6] Finally love — love translated back into *nature*! *Not* the love of a "higher virgin"! No Senta-sentimentality![7] Instead of that, love as fate, as *fatality*, cynical, innocent, cruel — and precisely, as such, *nature*! The love that is in its methods, war, and in its essence, the *deadly hatred* of the sexes! — I know of no instance where the tragic joke that characterizes love expresses itself so strictly, or so terribly turns into a formula, as in Don José's last cry with which the work ends:

"Yes, *I* have killed her!

I — my adored Carmen!"

— Such a conception of love (the only one worthy of the philosopher) is rare; it makes a work of art stand out among thousands. For on average, artists are like everyone else, or even worse — they *misunderstand* love. Even Wagner misunderstood it. They think they are selfless in love because they want another being's interest, often against their own interest. But in exchange they want to *possess* that other being . . . Even God is no exception here. He is far from thinking, "What has it to do with you if I love you?"[8] — He becomes terrible if you don't love him in return. "*L'amour*" — with this saying you are right, whether among gods or humans — "*est de tous les sentiments le plus égoïste, et, par conséquent, lorsqu'il est blessé, le moins généreux.*" (B. Constant.)[9]

3.

You already see how much this music *improves* me? — *Il faut méditerraniser la musique*:[10] I have reasons for this formula (*Beyond Good and Evil*, p. 220).[11] The return to nature, health, cheerfulness, youth, *virtue*! — And yet I was one of the most corrupt Wagnerians . . . I was in a position to take Wagner seriously . . . Oh, this old magician, how he tried to fool us! The first thing his art offers us is a magnifying glass: you look through it and cannot believe your eyes — everything becomes big, *even Wagner becomes big* . . . What a clever rattlesnake! All our lives it has rattled on to us about "devotion," about "loyalty," about "purity," retiring from the *depraved* world with a panegyric on chastity! And we believed it . . .

— But you are not listening to me? You even prefer the *problem* of Wagner to that of Bizet? Even I do not underestimate it: it has its charm. The problem of redemption is itself a venerable problem. Wagner thought about nothing so deeply as redemption: his opera is the opera of redemption. With him, somebody or other always wants to be redeemed: now a little man, now a little lady — that is *his* problem. And how richly he varies his leitmotif! What rare, what profound evasions! Who, if not Wagner, would teach us that innocence prefers to redeem interesting sinners? (The case in *Tannhäuser*.[12]) Or that even the wandering Jew is redeemed, becomes *settled*, when he marries? (The case in *The Flying Dutchman*.) Or that depraved old women prefer to be redeemed by chaste youths? (The case of Kundry.[13]) Or that beautiful young girls prefer to be redeemed by a knight who is a Wagnerian? (The case in *The Mastersingers*.[14]) Or that married women, too, like being redeemed by a knight? (The case of Isolde.[15]) Or that "the old God," after having morally compromised himself in every respect, is finally redeemed by a free spirit and immoralist? (The case in *The Ring*.[16]) Admire especially this last profundity! Do you understand it? I — guard against understanding it . . .[17] I would prefer to demonstrate rather than contest the fact that

still further lessons can be drawn from the works cited. That
you can be reduced to despair by a Wagnerian ballet — *and* to
virtue! (Again, the case of *Tannhäuser*). That there can be
disastrous consequences if you do not go to bed at the right
time (again the case of *Lohengrin*[18]). That you should never
know too precisely to whom you are actually getting married
(for the third time, the case of *Lohengrin*). — Tristan[19] and
Isolde extol the perfect husband who, in a given case, has only
one question: "But why didn't you tell me that before? Nothing is simpler!" Answer:

> "I cannot tell you that;
> And what you ask
> You never will find out."[20]

Lohengrin contains a solemnly declared ban on exploration
and enquiry. Wagner thereby represents the Christian concept: "You shall and you must *believe*." To be scientific is a
crime against the highest and the holiest . . . *The Flying Dutchman* preaches the exalted doctrine that woman can stabilize,
or to speak Wagnerian, "redeem," the most unsettled man.
Here we permit ourselves a question. For even assuming this
to be true, would that also make it desirable? — What becomes
of the "wandering Jew"[21] whom a woman adores and *stabi-
lizes*? He simply stops wandering and gets married, he is of no
concern to us anymore. — Translated into reality: the danger
for artists, for geniuses — and of course, that is what the
"wandering Jews" are — lies in woman: doting women are
their ruination. Practically none has character enough not to
be ruined — "redeemed" — when he feels treated like a god:
— he immediately *condescends* to the woman.[22] Man is a coward toward everything to do with the eternal-feminine: the
little women know that.[23] In many cases of womanly love, and
perhaps precisely in the most famous, love is just a more
refined *parasitism*, a nestling into a stranger's soul, now and
then even into a stranger's flesh — and oh! Always very much
at the expense of "the host!" — —

Everyone is familiar with the fate of Goethe in moraline-sour,[24] old-maidish Germany. He always offended the Germans, he had honest admirers only among Jewesses.[25] Schiller, the "noble" Schiller, who assaulted their ears with grand words — *he* was a man after their own hearts.[26] What was their complaint against Goethe? The "Mount of Venus," and that he had written the Venetian Epigrams.[27] Klopstock sermonized him early on;[28] there was a time when Herder liked to use the word "Priapus" when he spoke about Goethe.[29] Even *Wilhelm Meister*[30] was only rated as a symptom of decline, a moral version of "going to the dogs." The "menagerie of tame cattle" and the "worthlessness" of the hero angered Niebuhr, for example, who finally broke into a lament that *Biterolf*[31] could have sung: "Hardly anything could make a more painful impression than when a great mind deprives itself of its wings and seeks its virtuosity in something vastly inferior, *while renouncing higher things*"[32] . . . Above all, however, the genteel maiden was affronted: all the minor courts, every type of "Wartburg"[33] in Germany crossed itself in the presence of Goethe, especially the "unclean spirit"[34] in Goethe. — *This* is the story Wagner set to music. He *redeems* Goethe, it goes without saying; but in such a way that he craftily champions the genteel young maiden at the same time. Goethe is saved — a prayer saves him, a genteel maiden *draws him aloft . . .*[35]

— What would Goethe have thought about Wagner? — Goethe once presented himself with the question as to the danger that hovered over all the Romantics: the Romantics' doom. His answer is: "suffocation by ruminating on ethical and religious absurdities."[36] More briefly: *Parsifal*[37] — — The philosopher adds a further epilogue. *Sanctity* — perhaps the last thing of higher values that the people and women get to see, the horizon of the ideal for everything by nature myopic.[38] But among philosophers, as with every horizon, it is a mere failure of understanding, a kind of barrier at the point where *their* world just *begins* — *its* danger, *its* ideal, *its* desirability . . .

To put it more politely: *la philosophie ne suffit pas au grand nombre. Il lui faut la sainteté.* — [39]

4.

— I shall now tell the story of the *Ring*. It belongs here. This too is a tale of redemption: except that this time it is Wagner who is redeemed. — For half his life, Wagner believed in the *Revolution* as any old Frenchman did. — He sought it in the runic script of myth, he believed he had found the typical revolutionary in *Siegfried*. — "Where do all the disasters in the world come from?" Wagner asked himself. "From old contracts," he answered, like all ideologues of revolution. In plain language: from customs, laws, moral codes, institutions, everything on which the old world, the old society rested. "How does one rid the world of disaster? How does one abolish the old society? Only by declaring war on "contracts" (on custom, on morality). *Siegfried does that.* He starts early, very early: even his coming into being is a declaration of war on morality — he is born of adultery and incest . . . *Not* the saga but Wagner is the inventor of this radical trait; at this point he *corrected* the saga . . . Siegfried continues as he has begun: he just follows his first impulse, he throws to the wind anything traditional, all reverence, all *fear*. He stabs to death whatever he doesn't like. He irreverently runs his sword through ancient deities. His chief undertaking, however, aims to *emancipate woman* — "to redeem Brünnhilde" . . . Siegfried *and* Brünnhilde; the sacrament of free love; the advent of the golden age; twilight of the gods for old morality — *misfortune is abolished* . . . For a long while, Wagner's ship merrily ran along *this* course. Doubtless, Wagner sought in it *his* highest goal. What happened? A mishap. The ship struck a reef; Wagner was aground. The reef was Schopenhauer's philosophy; Wagner ran aground on a *contrary* worldview. What had he set to music? Optimism. Wagner was ashamed. Worse still, it was an optimism for which Schopenhauer had created an unkind epithet — *wicked* optimism.[40] Once more, he was ashamed. He deliberated for ages, his situation seemed desperate . . . At last, a way out dawned on him: what if he interpreted the reef on which he had been wrecked as a *goal*, as an ulterior motive, as the actual point of his journey? To be wrecked *here* — that was a goal, too. *Bene navigavi, cum naufragium feci*[41] . . . And he translated the *Ring* into Schopenhauerian. Everything goes wrong, everything is destroyed, the new world is as bad as the old: *nothingness*, the Indian Circe,[42] beckons . . . Brünnhilde, who was originally supposed to take her leave with a paean to free love, consoling the world with the promise of a socialist utopia where "everything will be fine," is now given something else to do. First, she must study Schopenhauer; she must put the fourth book of *The World as Will and Representation*[43] into verse. *Wagner was redeemed . . .* In all seriousness, this *was* a redemption. The good deed Wagner owes to Schopenhauer is immeasurable. Only the *philosopher of décadence* gave to the artist of *décadence his own self* — —

5.

To the *artist of décadence* — that's the word. And this is where I begin in earnest. I have no intention of looking on harmlessly whenever this *décadent* ruins our health — and music to boot! Is Wagner actually a human? Isn't he a sickness instead? He makes everything he touches sick — *he has made music sick* —

A typical *décadent* who feels indispensable in his depraved taste and with it claims a higher taste, knowing how to make his depravity count as law, as progress, as fulfillment.[44]

And people don't defend themselves. His power to seduce rises to monstrous levels, incense swirls around him, the misunderstanding of him goes by the name of "gospel," — he has certainly not just converted *the poor in spirit*![45]

I would like to open the windows a little. Air! More air![46]

— —

I am not surprised by the fact that people in Germany deceive themselves about Wagner. The opposite would surprise me. The Germans have constructed for themselves a Wagner whom they can revere: they have never been psychologists, they express their gratitude by misunderstanding. But that they deceive themselves about Wagner even in Paris, where nowadays hardly anybody is anything but a psychologist! And in St. Petersburg,[47] where people manage to guess things that even in Paris nobody guesses! How related to the whole of European *décadence* Wagner must be if he is not perceived by it as a *décadent*! He belongs to it: he is its protagonist, its biggest name . . . People exalt themselves when they praise *him* to the skies. — For it is already a sign of *décadence* that they do not defend themselves against him. Instinct is weakened. People are attracted to what they ought to shun. They put to their lips what will drive them faster into the abyss. — Would you like an example? Well, all you need to do is observe the régime that sufferers from anemia or gout or diabetes prescribe for themselves. Definition of the vegetarian: a being who needs a corroborating diet. To perceive the harmful as causing harm and *to be able* to forbid oneself something harmful is still a sign of youth and vitality. The exhausted are *lured* by that which is harmful: the vegetarian by vegetables. Sickness itself can be a stimulant to life: except that one has to be healthy enough for this stimulant! Wagner increases exhaustion: *for that reason* he attracts the weak and exhausted. Oh, the rattlesnake-pleasure of the old master, accustomed to seeing the "little children" come unto him! — [48]

I give this viewpoint precedence: Wagner's art is sick. The problems that he puts on stage — nothing but hysterics' problems — the convulsiveness of his affects, his overexcited sensibility, his taste, demanding ever sharper spices, his instability cloaked as principle, not least his choice of heroes and heroines, to be viewed as physiological types (— a gallery of invalids! —): all this together portrays a tableau of sickness that leaves no room for doubt. *Wagner est une névrose.*[49] Perhaps nothing is better known today, at any rate nothing is better studied, than the Protean nature of degenerescence,[50] in this case wrapped up as art and artist. Our doctors and physiologists have their most interesting case in Wagner, or at least a very complete one. Precisely because nothing is more modern than this total invalidity, this sluggishness and oversensitivity of the nervous system, Wagner is the *modern artist par excellence*, the Cagliostro[51] of modernity. Intermingled in his art in the most seductive way is what the whole world most needs today — the three great *stimulantia* of the exhausted: the *brutal*, the *artificial* and the *innocent* (idiotic).[52]

Wagner is a great ruination of music. He guessed in it the means to excite tired nerves — and with that, he made music sick. He has no little gift for invention in the art of goading on the most exhausted and coaxing the half-dead back to life. He is the master of hypnotic holds, he throws even the strongest down like bulls. Wagner's *success* — his success with nerves and therefore with the ladies — has turned the whole ambitious world of musicians into disciples of his secret art. And not just the ambitious, the *clever*, too . . . Nowadays, you only make money with sick music; our great theaters live off Wagner.

6.

— Again, I permit myself some amusement. I imagine what would happen if Wagner's *success* came alive, took physical form, if it mingled among young artists disguised as a benevolent scholar of music. How would it make itself known there, do you think? —

My friends, he would say, let's have a few words among ourselves. It is easier to make bad music than good. What if, besides that, it were to be even more advantageous? More effective, more persuasive, more inspiring, more reliable — more *Wagnerian*?[53] . . . *Pulchrum est paucorum hominum.*[54] Bad enough! We understand Latin, perhaps we also understand what is to our advantage. What is beautiful has a sting in its tail: we know that. So why beauty? Why not prefer something great, sublime, gigantic, that which moves the *masses*? — And again, it is easier to be gigantic than beautiful: we know that . . .

We know the masses, we know the theater. The best of those sitting there — German youths, horned Siegfrieds[55] and other Wagnerians — need the sublime, the profound, the overwhelming. That much we can still do. And the others seated there as well, the cultural cretins, the blasé nobodies, the eternally feminine, those happily digesting their food — in short, the *folk* — also need the sublime, the profound, the overwhelming just as much. The logic to all this is the same. "He who bowls us over is strong; he who raises us up is divine; he who keeps us guessing is profound." Gentlemen musicians, let us make up our minds: we want to bowl them over, we want to raise them up, we want to keep them guessing. That much we can still do.

With regard to keeping them guessing: that is the starting point for our concept of "style." Above all, not one thought! Nothing is more compromising than a thought! Instead, the state *before* thought, the jostle of embryonic thoughts, the promise of future thoughts, the world as it was before God created it — a recrudescence of chaos . . . Chaos keeps you guessing . . .

To speak in the Master's idiom: endlessness, but without melody.

Second,[56] with regard to bowling over, this already partly belongs to physiology. Above all, let's examine the instruments. A few of them even coax our bowels (they *open* the gates, as Handel would say),[57] others send shivers down our spine. The color of the sound is decisive here: *what* makes the sound is almost irrelevant. Let us be more precise on *this* point! Otherwise, why squander ourselves? With sound, let us be characteristic to the point of folly! People put it down to our intellect if we keep them guessing with sounds! Let's set the nerves on edge, let's slaughter them, let's get hold of thunder and lightning — that bowls people over . . .

Above all, however, *passion* bowls people over. — Let us be clear about passion. Nothing is cheaper than passion! You can dispense with all the virtues of counterpoint, you don't need to have learned anything — you can always be passionate! Beauty is difficult — let's be wary of beauty! . . . And, of course, *melody*! Let us slander, my friends, let us slander, if we are at all serious about our ideal, let us slander melody! Nothing is more dangerous than a tuneful melody! Nothing is more certain to spoil our taste! We shall be lost, my friends, if people ever like tuneful melodies again! . . .

Maxim: melody is immoral. *Proof:* Palestrina. *Practical application: Parsifal.* The lack of a melody even sanctifies . . .

And this is the definition of passion. Passion — or the gymnastics of the ugly on the rope of enharmonic modulation. — My friends, let us dare to be ugly! Wagner dared! Undaunted, let us roll out in front of us the mud of the most hideous harmonies! Let us not spare our hands! Only then will we be *natural* . . .

One final piece of advice! It might sum it all up in one. — *Let us be idealists!* — This is the wisest, if not the cleverest, thing we can do. In order to elevate humankind, we ourselves must be sublime. Let us wander over clouds, let us harangue infinity, let us place huge symbols all around us! *Sursum!*[58] Boom boom! — There is no better piece of advice. The "uplifted bosom" will be our argument, the "beautiful sentiment" our advocate. Virtue holds its own even against counterpoint. "Surely someone who improves us must be good himself?" that is what humanity has always concluded. So let us improve humanity![59] — That is how you become good (that way you can even become a "classic": Schiller became a "classic"). The snatching at base sensual excitement, at so-called beauty, has unnerved the Italian: let's stay German! Even Mozart's relationship to music — Wagner has told *us* as consolation! — was fundamentally frivolous . . . Let us never admit that music "serves as relaxation"; that it "cheers us up"; that it "gives pleasure." *Let us never give pleasure!* — We shall be lost if people ever think of art hedonistically again . . . that is bad eighteenth century . . . By the way, nothing should be more advisable than a dose of — *bigotry, sit venia verbo.*[60] That affords respect. — And let us pick the fitting moment to give black looks, to sigh in public, Christian sighs, putting great Christian compassion on show. "The human is depraved: who will redeem him? *What will redeem him?*" — Let's not answer. Let's be circumspect. Let's combat our ambition, which would like to found religions. But nobody must doubt that *we* will redeem him, that *our* music alone redeems . . . (Wagner's essay "Religion and Art."[61])

7.[62]

Enough! Enough! I fear you will have recognized only too clearly the sinister reality beneath my cheerful strokes — the picture of a decline in art, a decline in artists, too. The latter, a decline in character, could perhaps be provisionally expressed with this formula: the musician now becomes an actor, his art increasingly develops as a talent for *lying*. I shall have the opportunity to show in greater detail (in a chapter of my chief work bearing the title "On the Physiology of Art"[63]) how this total transformation of art into theatricality is just as clearly an expression of physiological degenerescence (more accurately, a form of hysteria) as each ruination and frailty in the art inaugurated by Wagner: for example, its visual restlessness that forces you to change position in front of it every moment. You know nothing of Wagner as long as you see in him just natural playfulness, arbitrary, capricious, incidental. He was neither a "flawed" nor "failed" nor "contradictory" genius, as people have said. Wagner was something *perfect*, a typical *décadent* in whom all "free will" is lacking and every trait is essential. If anything is interesting in Wagner it is the logic with which a physiological defect, point for point and step by step, proceeds as practice and procedure, as originality in terms of principle and as crisis in terms of taste.

I shall just dwell on the question of *style* this time. — What characterizes every *literary décadence*? The fact that life no longer dwells in the whole. The word becomes sovereign and leaps from the sentence, the sentence spreads out and obscures the meaning of the page, the page gains life at the expense of the whole — the whole is no longer a whole. But that is symbolic for every style of *décadence*:[64] every time anarchy of atoms, disgregation of the will, "freedom of the individual," morally speaking — broadened into a political theory, "*equal* rights for all." Life, *uniform* liveliness, the throb and exuberance of life squashed into the smallest forms, the rest *poor* in life. Everywhere paralysis, adversity, torpor, *or* animosity and chaos: both increasingly eye-catching in whatever higher forms of organization one climbs to. The whole no longer lives at all: it is put together, calculated, artificial, an artifact. —

In the beginning[65] was the hallucination for Wagner: not of sounds but gestures. He then seeks the semiotics of sound for them. If you want to admire him, then observe him in action here: how he makes a division, how he produces little units, how he enlivens these, drives them out and makes them visible. But this exhausts his strength: the rest is no good. How pathetic, how awkward, how amateurish is his method of "development," his attempt to at least mix up whatever has not grown apart. His manners meanwhile are reminiscent of the *frères* de Goncourt, who are germane to Wagner's style as well: in a way, one can commiserate with so much distress.[66] The fact that Wagner dressed up his incompetence for organic structure as principle, that he held up his "dramatic style" as an example where we would hold up his inability for any style at all as an example, is in accordance with an audacious habit that accompanied Wagner throughout life: he posits a principle where he lacks ability (— in this, by the way, he differs greatly from old Kant, who was fond of *another* audacity: namely, wherever he lacked a principle, he posited a "faculty" for it in humans . . .[67]). I repeat: Wagner is admirable and charming only in inventing what is most small, in thinking up the *détail* — here you do have right on your side in proclaiming him as a master of the first rank, as our greatest musical *miniaturist* who compresses an infinity of sense and sweetness into the smallest space.[68] His wealth of colors, of half-shadows, of secrets of dying light spoils us to such a degree that afterwards we find almost all other musicians too robust. — Believe me if you will, you cannot understand the highest conception of Wagner from what pleases people today. That has been invented to fool the masses, people like us recoil from it as from an all-too-saucy fresco.[69] What do *we* care about the *agaçant*[70] brutality of the Overture to *Tannhäuser*? Or the *Valkyrie* circus? Everything of Wagner's music that has become popular, even apart from the theater, is of questionable taste and ruins one's taste. I find the March in *Tannhäuser* smacks of bourgeois respectability;[71] the Overture to *The Flying Dutchman* is "an ado about nothing";[72] the *Lohengrin* Prelude provided the first, only-too-dangerous and only-too-polished example of how music can also be used to hypnotize[73] (— I dislike all music that aspires to nothing beyond persuading the nerves). But apart from the *magnétiseur*[74] and fresco-painter Wagner, there is another Wagner who lays up little gems: our greatest melancholic of music, full of glances, sweet nothings and words of consolation, in which nobody had anticipated him, that master of the sounds of wistful and sleepy happiness . . .[75] A lexicon of Wagner's most intimate words, nothing but short pieces of five to fifteen measures, nothing but music *nobody knows* . . . Wagner possessed the virtue of *décadents*: compassion — — — [76]

8.

— "Very well! But how *can* you lose your taste for this *décadent* if you do not happen to be a musician and do not happen to be a *décadent* yourself?" — The reverse! How can you *not*! Just try it! — You don't know who Wagner is: a very great actor! Is there any more profound or *weightier* effect in the theater? Just look at these young men — stiff, pale, breathless! They are Wagnerians: they don't know a thing about music — and nevertheless, Wagner lords it over them. Wagner's art pressurizes like a hundred atmospheres: just bend down, you can do no other.[77] The actor Wagner is a tyrant, his pathos casts

aside every taste, every resistance. — Who else has this com-
pelling power with gestures, who else can envision the gesture
so precisely, right from the start! This Wagnerian pathos holding its breath, this not-wanting-to-let-go of an extreme feeling,
this terrifying *length* in situations where even a moment could
strangle us! —

Was Wagner a musician at all? In any event he was something different *again*: namely, an incomparable *histrio*,[78] the
greatest mime, the most astonishing theater genius the Germans have ever had, our *stage-manager* par excellence. He
belongs elsewhere than in the history of music: he ought not
to be confused with its great authentic practitioners. Wagner
and Beethoven — that is a blasphemy — and actually an
injustice even to Wagner . . . As a musician he was only what
he was in general: he *became* a musician, he *became* a poet
because the tyrant in him, his theatrical genius, drove him to
it. Nobody can fathom Wagner until his domineering instinct
has been fathomed.

Wagner was *not* a musician by instinct. He proved this by
surrendering all lawfulness and, more precisely, all style in
music, in order to make out of it what was necessary for him, a
theatrical rhetoric, a means of expression, of reinforcing gesture, of suggestion, of the psychologically picturesque. Here,
Wagner ought to be classed as an inventor and innovator of the
first rank — *he has increased the linguistic capacity of music
immeasurably* — : he is the Victor Hugo of music as language.[79] Providing always that you first accept that music
might, under certain circumstances, not be music, but language, tool, *ancilla dramaturgica*.[80] Wagner's music, when *not*
protected by theatrical taste, a very tolerant taste, is simply bad
music, perhaps the very worst that has been made. When a
musician can no longer count to three, he becomes "dramatic,"
he becomes "Wagnerian" . . .

Wagner almost discovered what magic can be produced
with even a diffuse music made as it were *elementary*. His

awareness of that borders on the uncanny, like his instinct that he did not need the supreme lawfulness, *style*, in the least. What is elementary is *enough* — sound, movement, color, in short, the sensuousness of music. Wagner never calculates as a musician, out of some sort of musician's compunction: he wants the effect, he wants nothing but the effect. And he knows whom he has to impress! — In this, he has the lack of consideration that Schiller had, that every impresario has, he also has their contempt for the world he lays at his feet! . . . What makes you into an actor is having one more insight than the other humans: what should appear as true must not be true. Talma[81] formulated the premise: it contains the whole psychology of the actor, it contains — let us be in no doubt! — the actor's morality as well. Wagner's music is never true.

— But *people think it is*: and that makes it alright.

As long as you are still childlike and Wagnerian to boot, you consider Wagner himself as rich, even a model of prodigality, even a major landowner in the realm of sound. You admire in him what French youths admire in Victor Hugo, "regal generosity." Later you admire them both for opposite reasons: as masters and models of economy, *prudent* hosts. Nobody is their equal in depicting a princely feast with modest outlay. — The Wagnerian, with his believer's stomach, is even sated by the fare that his master conjures up for him. The rest of us, demanding *substance* above all in books as in music, and hardly satisfied by feasts merely "depicted," are much worse off. In plain language: Wagner does not give us enough to get our teeth into.[82] I have christened his *recitativo* — not much meat, a bit more bone and plenty of broth — *"alla genovese,"*[83] whereby I am not trying to flatter the Genoese, but rather the *older recitativo*, the *recitativo secco*.[84] As for the Wagnerian "leitmotif," I lack all culinary appreciation of it.[85] If you pressed me I would perhaps let it pass for an ideal toothpick, as an opportunity to get rid of *scraps* of food. Which leaves us with Wagner's "arias." — And now I shall not say another word.

9.

Even in devising his plot, Wagner is above all an actor. What occupies him first is a scene of guaranteed effect, a true *actio**) with a *haut-relief* of gesture, a scene that *bowls you over* — he ponders this deeply and only then extracts the characters from it. The whole of the rest follows from this, in accordance with a technical economy that has no reasons to be subtle. It is *not* Corneille's public that Wagner has to spare: just the nineteenth century. Wagner would probably think about "the one thing needful"[87] as any other actor today would do: a series of strong scenes, one stronger than the other — and, in between, much *shrewd* stupidity. He first tries to guarantee the effect of his work to himself, he begins with the third act, he *proves* his work to himself by its ultimate effect. With such a concept of the theater as guide, there is no danger of inadvertently creating a drama. Drama demands *hard* logic, but anyway, what did Wagner care about logic! To repeat: it was *not* Corneille's public that he had to spare, just Germans! We know which technical problem the dramatist has to tackle with all his power, often sweating blood: to make the knots in the plot *essential* and the dénouement as well, so that both are only possible in one single way and both create the impression of freedom (principle of the least expenditure of energy). Well, here Wagner is at his furthest from sweating blood; certainly he expends the least amount of energy on plot and dénouement. Put any "plot" of Wagner's under the microscope

---

*) {Nietzsche's} Note:[86] It has been a real misfortune for aesthetics that the word "drama" has always been translated as "action" [*Handlung*]. Wagner is not alone in making this mistake; everyone makes it; even philologists, who ought to know better. Ancient drama envisaged great *scenes of pathos* — it even precluded action (set it *before* the beginning or *behind* the scene). The word "drama" is of Doric descent and according to Doric linguistic usage it means "event," "story," both words in the hieratic sense. The oldest drama portrayed the local legend, the "holy story" on which the foundation of the cult rested (— so it was not a doing, but a happening: δϱᾶν does not mean "doing" in Doric at all).

— and you will have to laugh, I promise. Nothing is more amusing than the plot of *Tristan* unless it is the plot of *The Mastersingers*. Wagner is *not* a dramatist, have no illusions about that. He loved the word "drama": that's all — he always loved fine words. Even so, the word "drama" in his writings is just a misunderstanding (— *and* a clever trick: Wagner always turned up his nose at the word "opera" —); rather as the word "spirit" in the New Testament is plainly a misunderstanding.[88] — He was simply not enough of a psychologist for drama; he instinctively avoided psychological motivation — and how? By replacing it with idiosyncrasy . . . Very modern, isn't it? Very Parisian! Very *décadent*! . . . By the way, the *knotted plots* that Wagner actually unravels with the help of dramatic inventions are of quite another kind. I shall give an example. Take the case where Wagner needs a female voice. A whole act *without* a female voice — that's not on! But none of the "heroines" are free at that moment. What does Wagner do? He emancipates Erda,[89] the oldest woman in the world: "Arise, venerable grandmother! You have to sing!" Erda sings.[90] Wagner's object is achieved. He gets rid of the old lady again at once. "Why actually did you come? Clear off! Pray go back to sleep!" — *In summa*: a scene full of mythological horrors filling the Wagnerians with *foreboding* . . .

— "But the *content* of the Wagnerian texts! Their mythical content, their everlasting content!" — Question: how do we test this content, this everlasting content? The chemist answers: translate Wagner into the real, into the modern — let's be even more cruel — into the bourgeois! What happens to Wagner then? — Between ourselves, I've tried it. There is nothing more entertaining or more highly recommended if you are going for a walk, than to retell Wagner in an *updated* version: for example, Parsifal as a theology student with a grammar school education (— the latter being essential for *pure folly*). What surprises you have on the way! Would you believe it, the minute you strip off their heroic coating, Wagnerian heroines, one and all, could be taken for Madame Bovary![91] — And by the same token, you realize that *it was open to* Flaubert to translate his heroine into Scandinavian or Carthaginian and then offer her, mythologized, to Wagner as a libretto. Indeed, on the whole, Wagner seems to have taken no interest in any problems except for those that interest petty Parisian *décadents* today. Always five steps away from the hospital! Nothing but thoroughly modern, thoroughly *civic* problems! Have no doubts about it! . . . Have you noticed (it belongs to this association of ideas) that Wagnerian heroines never have any children? — They *can't* . . . The desperation with which Wagner tackled the problem of getting Siegfried born at all shows *how* modern he felt on this issue. — Siegfried "emancipates woman" — and yet with no hope of progeny. — Finally, a fact that leaves us stunned: Parsifal is Lohengrin's father! How did he do that? — Is it necessary to recall at this point that "chastity works *miracles*"? . . .

Wagnerus dixit princeps in castitate auctoritas.[92]

10.[93]

Incidentally, another word on Wagner's writings: they are, among other things, a lesson in *cleverness*. The system of procedures that Wagner handles can be applied in a hundred other ways — whoever has ears to hear, let him hear.[94] Perhaps I shall have a claim to public recognition if I give precise expression to the three most valuable procedures.

Whatever Wagner can*not* do is reprehensible.

Wagner could do a lot more: but he does not want to — strictly on principle.

Whatever Wagner *can* do, nobody will replicate, nobody has anticipated, nobody *should* replicate . . . Wagner is divine . . .

These three propositions are the quintessence of Wagner's literature: the rest is — just "literature."

— Not every kind of music has needed a literature up till now: in this case, we had better seek a sufficient reason. Is it

that Wagner's music is too difficult to understand? Or did he
fear the opposite — that it could be understood too easily —
that people would find it *not difficult enough*? — Actually, he
just repeated one proposition his whole life long: that his
music signified not just music, but more! Infinitely more! . . .
"*Not just* music" — no musician talks like that. To repeat:
Wagner could not create from the whole, he had no choice at
all but to make a patchwork, "motifs," gestures, formulas,
repeating things twice, a hundredfold; as a musician he was
still a rhetorician, therefore he absolutely *had* to emphasize the
"it signifies." "Music is only ever a means":[95] that was his theory, that was, above all, the only possible *praxis* for him. But
no musician thinks like that. — Wagner needed literature to
convince the world to take his music seriously, to find it profound, "because it *signified* infinity": throughout his life, he
was a commentator on "the idea." — What does Elsa mean?
Without a doubt: Elsa is "the unconscious *spirit of the people*"
(— "recognition of this made me become, of necessity, a complete revolutionary"[96] —).

Let us remind ourselves that Wagner was young at the time
when Hegel and Schelling were seducing minds; that he
guessed, that he seized hold of the only thing the German
takes seriously — "the idea," that is to say, something that is
abstruse, uncertain, full of foreboding; that clarity to Germans is objectionable and logic a contradiction. Schopenhauer
sternly accused the epoch of Hegel and Schelling of dishonesty — sternly and also wrongly: he himself, the pessimistic
old counterfeiter, was not a bit "more honest" than his more
famous contemporaries. Setting morality aside: Hegel is a *taste*
. . . And not just a German taste but a European one! — A
taste that Wagner understood — that he felt he could cope
with! That he immortalized! — He merely applied it in practice to music — he invented a style for himself that "signifies
infinity" — he became *Hegel's heir* . . . Music as "idea" — —

And how they understood Wagner! — The same kind of
human that raved about Hegel now raves about Wagner; those

in his set even *write* in Hegelian. — More than anyone else, a German youth could understand him. The two words "infinite" and "signification" already sufficed: they made him happy in an inimitable way. It is *not* the music with which Wagner conquered young men, it is the "idea": — it is the enigmatic nature of his art, its game of hide-and-seek among a hundred symbols, its polychromy of the ideal, that leads and lures these young men to Wagner; it is Wagner's genius for creating clouds, reaching, ranging and roaming through the ether, his being everywhere and nowhere, exactly the same things with which Hegel in his day seduced and enticed them! — In the midst of Wagner's versatility, richness and despotism, they feel as if they are self-justified — "redeemed" —. They tremble to hear how, in his art, the *great symbols* become audible out of the hazy distance with muffled thunder; they do not wax indignant if things are temporarily gray, grim and cold. Ultimately they are one and all, like Wagner himself, *related* to this bad weather, this German weather! Wotan is their god, but Wotan is the god of bad weather . . . From their angle, these German youths are right: how *could* they miss what we others, *we halcyons*, miss in Wagner — *la gaya scienza*; light feet; wit, fire, grace; grand logic; the dance of the stars; high-spirited intellectuality; the glimmering light of the South; the *smooth* sea— perfection . . . [97]

II.

— I have explained where Wagner belongs — *not* in the history of music. What significance does he nevertheless have in its history? *The advent of the actor in music:* a capital event that makes us think and perhaps fear as well. The formula is: "Wagner and Liszt." Never before has the integrity of musicians, their "sincerity," been put to the test in such a dangerous fashion. It is manifestly obvious: great success, success with the masses, is no longer on the side of the sincere — you have to be an actor for that! — Victor Hugo and Richard Wagner — they signify one and the same thing: that in declining cultures and wherever decisions are delegated to the masses, sincerity becomes super-fluous, disadvantageous, recessive. Only the actor still awakens *great* enthusiasm. — With that comes the *golden age* of the actor — for him and for everything related to his kind. Wagner marches with pipe and drum at the head of all artists skilled in performance, portrayal, virtuosity; first he won over the con-ductors, machinists and stage singers. Not to forget the orches-tra musicians: — he "redeemed" them from boredom . . . This movement that Wagner created even stretches into the realm of knowledge: whole related sciences slowly rise up from cen-turies of scholasticism. To give an example, I expressly com-mend *Riemann's*[98] services to rhythmics, the first to make the major concept of punctuation applicable to music as well (unfortunately by means of an ugly word: he calls it "phras-ing"). — All these are, and I say it with gratitude, the best and the worthiest of respect among Wagner's "admirers" — they are quite simply right to admire Wagner. The same instinct binds them to one another, they see in him their highest type, they feel transformed into a power, even a great power, ever since he ignited them with his own passion. In fact here, if anywhere, Wagner's influence has been truly *beneficial*. Never before in this sphere has so much been pondered, desired, worked over. Wagner installed a new conscience in all these artists: what they now demand of themselves *and achieve* was something they never demanded of themselves before Wagner — earlier, they were too modest for this. Another spirit has ruled in the theater since Wagner's spirit took charge there: people demand the most difficult things, they criticize harshly and seldom praise — the good and the excellent count as the rule.[99] Taste is no longer necessary; not even a voice. Wagner is only sung with a ruined voice: the effect is "dramatic." Even talent is excluded. *Espressivo*[100] at any price, as demanded by the Wagner-ideal, the *décadence*-ideal, does not get on well with talent. It requires merely *virtue* — by which I mean dres-sage, automatism, "self-denial." Neither taste, nor voice, nor talent: Wagner's stage needs only one thing — *Teutons!* . . .

Definition of the Teuton: obedience[101] and long legs . . . It is full of deep significance that the advent of Wagner coincides chronologically with the advent of the "Reich": both facts prove one and the same thing — obedience and long legs. — People have never obeyed better and have never been better commanded. Wagnerian conductors in particular are worthy of an age that posterity, with awed respect, will dub *the classical age of war*. Wagner knew how to command; that also made him a great teacher. He commanded as the inexorable will to himself, as the lifelong self-disciplinarian: Wagner, who perhaps provides the grossest example of self-violation in the history of art (— even Alfieri,[102] otherwise his closest relative, is surpassed. Note by a Turinese).

12.

Given the insight that our actors are more venerable than ever, the threat they pose is not to be conceived as any less . . . But who can still doubt what I want — which *three requirements* have this time prompted my wrath, my solicitude, my love of art, to speak?

That the theater should not gain control of the arts.
That the actor should not lead the sincere astray.
That music should not become an art of lying.

FRIEDRICH NIETZSCHE.

Postscript.[1]

—The seriousness of those last words permits me to disclose a few sentences here from an unpublished essay that at least leave no doubt as to my seriousness on the subject. The essay is entitled *What Wagner costs us.*[2]

Being in Wagner's entourage takes its toll. A dark feeling about this lingers even today. Even Wagner's success, his *victory*, could not tear this feeling out by the root. But back then, it was strong, it was dreadful, it was like an obscure hatred — for nearly three-quarters of Wagner's life. The resistance he encountered among us Germans cannot be too highly prized and esteemed. People defended themselves against him as against a disease — *not* with reasons — a disease cannot be refuted —, but with inhibition, mistrust, irritation, disgust, with a grim seriousness, as though a great danger lurked in him. The learned aestheticians from three schools of German philosophy showed themselves up when, with "ifs" and "thens," they carried out an absurd war against Wagner's principles — as if he cared about principles, even his own! — The Germans themselves had enough instinctive good sense here to refuse to allow themselves any "ifs" and "thens." An instinct is weakened when it rationalizes itself: because *by* rationalizing itself, it weakens itself. If there are signs that, in spite of the collective nature of European *décadence*, a trace of health, a hint of instinct for what is harmful and threatening still lives in the German character, I would want least of all for this *subdued* resistance to Wagner to be underestimated among them. It does us proud, it even allows us to hope: France would not have that much health at its disposal any more. The Germans, history's *procrastinators par excellence*, are nowadays the most backward civilized people in Europe: this does have an advantage, — which is that this makes them relatively the *youngest*.[3]

Being in Wagner's entourage takes its toll. Only quite recently did the Germans discard a sort of fear of him — the desire *to be rid of him* came over them at every opportunity.*) — Do you recall yet another curious circumstance when, quite late, quite unexpectedly, that old feeling made another appearance? At Wagner's burial, the first Wagner Association in Germany, founded in Munich, laid a wreath at his grave with an *inscription* that immediately became famous. "Redemption to the Redeemer!"[7] — it read. Everyone admired the lofty inspiration that had prompted this inscription, everyone admired the taste that is the preserve of Wagner's acolytes; many, however (strangely enough!), made the same small correction: "Redemption *from* the Redeemer!" — They breathed a sigh of relief. —

Being in Wagner's entourage takes its toll. Let's measure it against its effect on culture. Who was actually brought to the fore in this movement? What did it continually breed and cultivate? — Above all, the presumptuousness of amateurs, of art-idiots. Nowadays they organize associations, want their "taste" to catch on, and would like to pass judgment even *in rebus musicis et musicantibus*.[8] Second: an ever greater indifference to every

---

*) {Nietzsche's} Note: — Was Wagner a German at all? There are several reasons to ask. It is difficult to discover a single German trait in him. Great learner that he was, he learned how to imitate much that was German — that is all. His personality even *contradicts* what had been regarded as German hitherto: to say nothing of the German musician! — His father was an actor by the name of Geyer. A vulture[4] is practically an eagle.[5] What has been disseminated till now as "Wagner's Life" is a *fable convenue*,[6] if not worse. I confess to mistrust on every point where there is no other witness but Wagner. He did not have sufficient pride for any truth about himself, nobody was less proud; just like Victor Hugo, he remained true to himself even in things biographical — he remained an actor.

rigorous, noble, conscientious schooling in the service of art; in its place, the belief in genius; in plain speech: impertinent dilettantism (— the formula for that is found in *The Mastersingers*). Third and worst of all: *theatrocracy*[9] — the nonsense of a belief in the preeminence of the theater, in the theater's right to *control* over the arts, over art . . . But one ought to tell Wagnerians a hundred times to their face *what* the theater is: only ever something *inferior* to art, only ever something secondary, something vulgarized, something fabricated fraudulently for the masses! Even Wagner did not change any of that: Bayreuth is grand opera — and not even *good* opera . . . The theater is a form of *demolatry*[10] in matters of taste, the theater is a revolt of the masses, a plebiscite *against* good taste . . . *The case of Wagner proves precisely this:* he won the crowd — he ruined taste, he ruined our taste even for opera! —

Being in Wagner's entourage takes its toll. What does it do to the spirit? *Does Wagner free the spirit?* — He possesses every ambiguity, every double meaning, in fact, everything that persuades those who are uncertain without making them realize what they have been persuaded *about.* This makes Wagner a seducer in the grand style. There is nothing weary, decrepit, nothing life-threatening and world-calumniating in affairs of the spirit that has not been secretly taken into protection by his art — he hides the blackest obscurantism in the airy swathes of the ideal. He flatters every nihilistic (— Buddhistic) instinct and cloaks it in music, he flatters everything Christian, every religious expression of *décadence.* Open your ears: everything that ever grew in the soil of *impoverished* life, all the counterfeiting of transcendence and the beyond,[11] has its most sublime advocate in Wagner's art — *not* in formulas: Wagner is too clever for formulas — but in a persuasion to sensuousness which, in its turn, again renders the spirit worn down and weary. Music as Circe . . . His last work is his greatest masterpiece in this respect. *Parsifal* will hold its rank in the art of seduction forever as seduction's *stroke of genius* . . . I admire this work, I would like to have done it myself; failing that, *I understand*

it[12] . . . Wagner was never better inspired than at the end.
Here, the finesse in combining beauty and sickness goes so far
that it casts a shadow, so to speak, over Wagner's earlier art:
— it appears too bright, too healthy. Do you understand that?
Health and brightness working as shadows? Almost as an
objection? That's how far we are already *pure fools* . . . There
never was a greater master in musty hieratic fragrances —
there never lived a like authority on all *small* infinities, all that
trembles and is effusive, all femininisms[13] in the *idiotikon*[14] of
happiness! — And so, my friends, just drink the philters of
this art! Nowhere will you find a more congenial way of ener-
vating your spirit, of forgetting your manhood under a rose
bush . . . Oh, this old wizard! This Klingsor[15] of all Klingsors!
That's how he makes war on *us*! Us, the free spirits! How he
cajoles every cowardliness of the modern soul with the tones of
magic maidens.[16] There never was such a *deadly hatred* toward
knowledge! — Here, you must be a cynic so as not to be
seduced, you must be able to bite to avoid being adulatory. Well
then, you old seducer! The cynic warns you — *cave canem* . . . [17]

Being in Wagner's entourage takes its toll. I observe the
youths who have had long-term exposure to his infection. The
first, relatively innocent effect is the ⟨debasement of⟩[18] taste.
The effect of Wagner is like continual alcohol abuse. He stupe-
fies, he causes inflammation of the stomach. Specific effect:
degeneration of the feeling for rhythm. In the end, the Wagnerian calls rhythm what I myself, after a Greek saying, call
"moving the swamp." But the debasement of concepts is much
more dangerous. The youth becomes a mooncalf — an "idealist." He has gone beyond science; in this way he stands level
with the master. By contrast, he turns philosopher; he writes
for the *Bayreuther Blätter*;[19] he solves all problems in the name
of the Father, the Son, and the Holy Maestro. Certainly, the
strangest thing is the way nerves are wrecked. Walk through a
large town at night, you will hear all round you the sound of
instruments being tortured with ceremonial rage — inter-
spersed with wild howls. What is happening? — Youths are

paying homage to Wagner . . . Bayreuth rhymes with cold-water clinic.[20] — A typical telegram from Bayreuth: *betimes bemoaned.* —[21] Wagner is bad for youths; he is disastrous for womankind. What, medically speaking, is a female Wagnerian? — It seems to me that no doctor can be too serious in presenting young women with this alternative for the conscience: one *or* the other.[22] — But they have chosen already. No one can serve two masters[23] if one of them is called Wagner. Wagner has redeemed woman; in return, woman has built Bayreuth for him. Complete sacrifice, complete devotion: there is nothing she would not give him. Woman impoverishes herself on the Maestro's behalf; how touching she is, standing before him quite naked. — The female Wagnerian, the most pleasant form of ambivalence today: she *incorporates* the Wagnerian cause — in her sign, his cause *conquers* . . . Oh, this old robber! He robs us of the youths, and then he even robs us of our women and drags them into his den . . . Oh, this old Minotaur! How much he has cost us already! Every year, processions of the loveliest maidens and youths are led into his labyrinth so he can devour them — every year, all Europe chants "Off to Crete! Off to Crete!" . . . [24]

Second Postscript.

It seems that my letter is open to misunderstanding. Certain brows are furrowed in gratitude; I even hear modest rejoicing. — I would prefer, here as in many things, to be understood. — But since a new bug took up residence in the vineyards of the German spirit, the Reich-worm, the famous *Rhinoxera*,[1] nobody has understood a word of mine anymore. The *Kreuz-zeitung*[2] itself demonstrates this to me, to say nothing of the *Literarisches Zentralblatt*.[3] — I have given the Germans the deepest books they possess — reason enough for the Germans not to understand a word in them . . . If, in *this* work, I make war on Wagner — and on a German "taste" at the same time —, if I have harsh words for the cretinism at Bayreuth, I do not in the least want to celebrate any *other* musicians. *Other* musicians do not come into consideration when set against Wagner. In general, things are bad. Decline is widespread. The sickness lies deep. If Wagner remains the name for *the ruin of music*, like Bernini[4] for the ruin of sculpture, he really is not its cause. He merely speeded up its tempo — admittedly in such a way that you confront this almost precipitate down-slide into the abyss with horror. He had the naivety of *déca-dence*: that was his superiority. He believed in it, no logic of *décadence* made him pause. The others *hesitate* — that is what marks them out. Nothing else! . . . that Wagner and "the oth-ers" have in common — I shall spell it out: a deterioration of organizing powers; misuse of handed-down methods without the ability to provide a *justification* or purpose; counterfeiting in imitation of grand forms for which nobody nowadays is strong, proud, confident, *healthy* enough; over-boisterousness in the smallest things; emotion at any price; sophistication as expression of *impoverished* life; more and more nerves in place of flesh. — I know only one musician[5] today who is capable of carving an overture from a *single piece of wood*: and nobody knows him . . . Those who are famous today make music that is not "better" in comparison to Wagner, but merely more indecisive, more mediocre — more mediocre because any half measure has been abolished now *that the whole is there*. But Wagner was whole; but Wagner was whole ruination; but Wagner was courage, will, *conviction* in ruination — who cares about Johannes Brahms now! . . . His good luck was a German misunderstanding: people took him to be Wagner's antagonist, they *needed* an antagonist! That does not make for *necessary* music, it mainly makes for too much music! He who is not rich should be proud enough to be poor! . . . The rapport Brahms undeniably arouses here and there, quite apart from that partisan interest, partisan misunderstanding, puzzled me for a long time: until, almost by accident, I realized that he has an effect on a certain type of human. He has the melancholy of incapacity; he does *not* create out of fullness, he *thirsts after* fullness. If you discount what he copies, what he borrows from grand old or exotic-modern stylistic forms[6] — he is a master of imitation — only *longing* remains as his, alone . . . All those who are prone to longing, the unfulfilled of every kind, have guessed as much. He is too little of a character, too little of a center of attraction . . . those who are "impersonal," peripheral, understand that — they love him for it. In particular, he is the musician for a certain type of unsatisfied woman. Fifty paces further: and you have the female Wagnerian — exactly as you find Wagner fifty paces beyond Brahms —, the female Wagnerian, a more marked, more interesting, above all more *charming* type. Brahms is touching as long as he has secret raptures or mourns over himself — in that, he is "modern" —;

he goes cold and is irrelevant to us as soon as he *inherits* from the classical musicians . . . People like to call Brahms Beethoven's heir: I don't know of a more cautious euphemism. — Everything that makes a claim to "great style" in music today is therefore *either* false toward us *or* false toward itself. This alternative is thought-provoking enough: for it contains within itself casuistry as to the value of the two cases. "False toward *us*": most people's instinct protests against this — they do not want to be deceived —; admittedly I myself would always prefer this type to the other ("false toward *itself*"). That is *my* taste. To express this more clearly for the "poor in spirit":[7] Brahms — *or* Wagner . . . Brahms is *not* an actor. — One can subsume a large section of *other* musicians under the concept "Brahms." I shall not say a word about Wagner's clever apes, for example, Goldmark:[8] with his *Queen of Sheba*, he belongs in the zoo — we can all make exhibitions of ourselves. — What can be done well today, to the level of masterpiece, can only be something small. Only here is integrity still possible. But nothing can cure music *in* the main, *from* the main matter, from the fatality of being the expression of a physiological contradiction — of being *modern*. The best instruction, the most conscientious training, a fundamental intimacy, yes, even isolation in the company of the old masters — all that remains palliative, or more accurately, *illusory*, because we no longer have the predisposition for it in our bellies: whether it be the strong spirit of a Handel or the overflowing animality of a Rossini.[9] — Not everyone has the *right* to every teacher: that applies to whole ages. — Certainly, the possibility is not to be ruled out that somewhere in Europe there are still *remnants* of stronger races, of typically untimely humans: from them, a *belated* beauty and perfection could still be hoped for in music as well. What we can yet experience are exceptions at best. No god can save music from the *rule* that debasement is on top, that debasement is fatal. —

Epilogue.

— In order to heave a sigh of relief, let us withdraw for a moment at the last from the narrow world to which every question as to the value of *persons* condemns the spirit. A philosopher needs to wash his hands after he has been occupied with the "Case of Wagner" for so long. — I shall present my concept of the *modern*. Every era has, in its measure of strength, also a measure of those virtues that are permitted to it and those that are forbidden. Either it has the virtues of *ascending* life: then it will resist the virtues of descending life from the profoundest depths. Or the era itself represents descending life — then it also needs the virtues of descent and hates everything that justifies itself simply through fullness or superabundance of strength. Aesthetics is indissolubly bound to these biological prerequisites: there is an aesthetics of *décadence* and there is a *classical* aesthetics — something "beautiful in itself" is a phantasm, as is the whole of idealism. — In the narrower sphere of so-called moral values, no greater contrast can be found than that between *master morality* and the morality of *Christian* concepts of value: the latter having grown on ground that is morbid through and through (— the gospels present us with exactly the same physiological types as Dostoevsky's novels portray),[1] while on the other hand master morality ("Roman," "heathen," "Classical," "Renaissance") is the sign language of successful development, of *ascending* life, of the will to power as the principle of life. Master morality *affirms* just as instinctively as

Christian morality *denies* ("God," "the beyond," "self-effacement" nothing but negations). The former gives to things from its fullness — it transfigures, beautifies, makes *sense* of the world —, the latter impoverishes, makes the value of things pale and ugly, it *negates* the world. "World" is a Christian term of abuse. — These opposing points of view on values are *both* necessary: they are ways of seeing that cannot be dealt with through reasons and refutations. Christianity is not to be refuted any more than an eye condition is. The fact that pessimism was attacked like a philosophy was the pinnacle of scholarly idiocy. I assume the concepts "true" and "untrue" have no meaning in optics. — The only thing one should resist is falsity, the double-tongued instinct that *will* not perceive these opposites as opposites: an example is Wagner's will, which had no small mastery of such falsity. To eye up master morality, *noble* morality (— the Icelandic saga is practically its most important document —), and at the same time mouth the contrary doctrine of the "gospel of the humble,"[2] of the *necessity* for salvation! . . . By the way, I admire the modesty of the Christians who go to Bayreuth. I myself would not endure certain words from the mouth of a Wagner. There are concepts that do *not* belong in Bayreuth . . . Such as? A Christianity tailored for female Wagnerians, perhaps *by* female Wagnerians — for Wagner was formerly completely *feminini generis* —?[3] I say again, in my view Christians today are too modest . . . If Wagner was a Christian, well then, Liszt was perhaps a Church Father! — The need for *redemption*, the quintessence of all Christian necessities, has nothing to do with such clowns: it is the most honest expression of *décadence*, the most convinced and painful Yes-saying to the latter in sublime symbols and practices. The Christian wants to *get rid* of himself. *Le moi est toujours haïssable.*[4] — By contrast, noble morality, master morality is rooted in a triumphant Yes-saying to *itself* — it is self-affirmation, self-glorification of life, likewise needing sublime symbols and practices, but only "because the heart is too full."[5] The whole of *beautiful* and *great* art belongs here: essential to both is *gratitude*. On the other hand, one cannot discount its instinctive aversion *against* the *décadents*, its mockery of, even horror of, their symbolism: such things are practically its proof. The noble Roman looked on Christianity as *foeda superstitio*:[6] I remind you how the last German of noble taste, Goethe, reacted to the cross.[7] One seeks in vain for more valuable, more *necessary* opposites . . .*)[8]— But such a falsity as that of the Bayreuthers is not uncommon today. We all know the unaesthetic concept of the Christian *Junker*. This *innocence* between opposites, this "good conscience" while lying, is just *modern par excellence*, with it one can almost define modernity. The modern human represents, biologically, a *contradiction of values*, falling between two stools and saying Yes and No with the same breath. Is it any wonder that precisely in our times falsity itself became flesh and even genius? That *Wagner* "dwelt among us"?[9] I did not dub Wagner the Cagliostro[10] of modernity for no reason . . . But all of us have in our bodies, unconsciously and involuntarily, values, words, formulas and moralities of *conflicting* lineage — psychologically speaking, we are *false* . . . A *diagnosis of the modern soul* — where would that begin? With a resolute incision into this instinctive contradiction, with a disentangling of its opposite values, with vivisection carried out on its most *instructive* case. — The Case of Wagner is a *stroke of luck* for the philosopher — this piece is inspired by gratitude, as you can hear . . . [11]

*) {Nietzsche's} Note: My *Genealogy of Morality* gave the first instruction on the opposition between "noble morality" and "Christian morality": there is perhaps no more decisive turn in the history of religious and moral knowledge. This book, my touchstone for what belongs to me, has the good fortune to be accessible only to the highest and severest of minds: the *rest* lack ears for it. You have to dedicate your passion to things that nobody else is doing today . . .

Twilight of the Idols

or
How to Philosophize with a Hammer.

Contents

Foreword.[1]

To maintain one's cheerfulness when embroiled in a gloomy matter that is responsible beyond measure is no mean feat: yet what is more necessary than cheerfulness? Nothing can succeed where high spirits have no part. A surplus of strength is the only proof of strength. — A *revaluation of all values*, this question mark so black, so immense that it casts a shadow over the one who raises it — such a destiny of a task forces one to charge into the sun each moment to shake off a seriousness that has become heavy, all too heavy. Every means of doing that is justified, every "case" a case of luck.[2] *War* above all. War has always been the brainchild of all minds that have become too introspective, too deep; even in the wound there still lies healing power. A saying, the provenance of which I withhold from scholarly curiosity, has long been my motto:

increscunt animi, virescit volnere virtus.[3]

A different convalescence, my preference in certain circumstances, is *to sound out idols* . . . There are more idols than realities in the world: that is *my* "evil eye" for this world, as well as my "evil *ear*" . . . Here for once, to ask questions with the *hammer* and perhaps hear in answer that famous hollow tone that speaks of bloated guts — what delight for someone with ears even behind his ears — for me, old psychologist and Pied Piper that I am, in whose presence precisely what would like to remain silent *must become audible* . . . [4]

Even this work — as the title betrays[5] — is primarily a recreation, a sunspot, a sidestep into a psychologist's leisure. Perhaps also a new war? And are new idols being sounded out? . . . [6] This small work is a *grand declaration of war*, and as far as sounding out idols goes, this time they are not contemporary idols, but *eternal* idols, to be tweaked here with a hammer as with a tuning fork — there are certainly no idols more ancient, more entrenched, more puffed up . . . And none more hollow . . . That does not prevent them from being the *most believed in*; and, especially in the most distinguished case, they are absolutely not called idols.

> *Turin*, 30 September 1888,
> on the day when the first book of the *Revaluation*
> *of all Values* was completed.

FRIEDRICH NIETZSCHE.

Sayings and Arrows.[1]

1.[2]

Leisure is the beginning of all psychology. What? could psychology be a — vice?

2.

Even the most courageous among us rarely has the courage for what he actually *knows* . . .

3.

To live alone you must be an animal or a god — says Aristotle.[3] The third case is missing: you must be both — a *philosopher* . . .

4.

"All truth is simple."[4] — Is this not a twofold lie? —

5.

Once and for all, there is much I do *not* wish to know. — Wisdom sets boundaries even to knowledge.

6.[5]

In your wild nature you recover best from your un-nature, from your spirituality . . .

7.

What? Is the human just a mistake of God's? Or God just a mistake of the human's? — [6]

8.

From life's school of war. — What does not kill me makes me stronger.[7]

9.

Help yourself: then everyone else will help you. The principle of loving thy neighbor.[8]

10.

Do not act cowardly in regard to your actions! Do not let them down in retrospect! — The pang of conscience[9] is unseemly.

11.

Can an *ass* be tragic? — Perishing under a burden you can neither carry nor cast off? . . . The case of the philosopher.[10]

12.

If you have your *why?* of life, you can put up with almost every *how?* — The human being does *not* strive for happiness; only the Englishman does that.

13.[11]

Man created woman — but from what? From a rib of his God — of his "ideal" . . .

14.[12]

What? you are searching? you want to multiply yourself by ten, by a hundred? you are searching for supporters? — Search for *zeros*! —

15.

Posthumous humans — like me, for instance — are understood less well than timely ones, but are *heard* better. More strictly: we are never understood — and *hence* our authority . . . [13]

16.

Among women. — "The truth? Oh, you don't know the truth! Is it not an assassination attempt on all our *pudeurs*?"[14] —

17.

That's how I like an artist to be, modest in his needs: in fact, he wants only two things, his bread and his art — *panem et Circen* . . . [15]

18.

Someone unable to instill his will into things at least invests them with a *meaning*: this is to say he believes a will to be in them already (principle of "belief").

19.

What? You chose virtue and the lofty breast, and at the same time you squint at the advantages of being unscrupulous? — But with virtue you *renounce* "advantages" . . . (laid at the door of an anti-Semite.)

20.

The perfect woman carries out literature as she carries out a small sin: to try it out, in passing, looking around to see whether anyone is noticing and *so that* someone notices . . . [16]

21.[17]

Place yourself only in those situations where you cannot have sham virtues, where, on the contrary, like the tightrope walker on his wire, you either fall or stand — or get away . . .

22.

"Evil people have no songs."[18] — How come the Russians have songs?

23.

"German intellect":[19] a *contradictio in adjecto*[20] for eighteen years.[21]

24.

Searching for the beginnings turns you into a crab. The historian looks backwards; finally, he also *believes* backwards.

25.

Satisfaction protects even against colds. Has a woman who knew she was well dressed ever caught cold? — In which case, I presume she was scantily clad.

26.

I mistrust all systematizers and avoid them. The will to a system is a lack of integrity.

27.

People think woman has depth — why? because one can never get to the bottom of her. Woman[22] is not even shallow.

28.

When a woman has manly virtues, she needs running away from; and when she has no manly virtues, she herself does the running away.

29.

"How much did the conscience have to bite on in the past? what good teeth did it have? — And today? what is lacking?" — A dentist's question.

30.

Rarely does one commit a rash act alone. In the first rash act, one always does too much. For that reason, one usually commits a second — and then one does too little . . .

31.

The trodden worm turns. That is clever. That way it reduces the likelihood of being trodden on anew. In the language of morality: *humility.* —

32.

There is a hatred of lying and dissembling that stems from a touchy concept of honor; there is just such a hatred that stems from cowardice, to the extent that the lie is *forbidden* by divine order. Too cowardly to lie . . .

33.

How little is required for happiness![23] The sound of bag-pipes. — Without music, life would be an error.[24] The German imagines even God singing songs.[25]

34.

On ne peut penser et écrire qu'assis[26] (G. Flaubert). — I have you there, nihilist! To be steadfast[27] is precisely the *sin* against the Holy Spirit. Only thoughts that *come on the move* have value.

35.

There are cases where we are like horses, we psychologists, and become restless: we see our own shadows sway up and down ahead of us. The psychologist must look away from *himself* in order to see at all.[28]

36.[29]

Do we[30] immoralists do *harm* to virtue? — Just as little as anarchists do to princes. Only since the latter were shot at have they sat securely on their thrones again. Moral: *one must shoot at morality.*

37.

You are running *ahead*? — Are you doing this as a shepherd? or as an exception? A third case would be the fugitive . . . *First* question of conscience.

38.

Are you genuine? or just an actor? A representative? or what is represented? — In the end, you are nothing but a copy of an actor . . . *Second* question of conscience.

39.

The *disappointed one speaks.* — I was looking for great humans, but I only ever found the *apes* of their ideal.

40.[31]

Are you a bystander? or one who lends a hand? — or do you look away and step aside? . . . *Third* question of conscience.

41.[32]

Do you want to come along? or go ahead? or go alone? . . . One must know *what* one wants and *that* one wants. *Fourth* question of conscience.

42.

Those were steps for me, I climbed up over them — I had to go beyond them as well. But they thought that was where I wanted to retire . . .

43.

What does it matter whether *I* am proved right! I *am* right too often. — And he who laughs best today also laughs last.

44.[33]

Formula for my happiness: a Yes, a No, a straight line, a *goal* . . .

The Problem of Socrates.[1]

I.

The wisest have at all times reached the same conclusion about life: *it is good for nothing* . . . Always and everywhere we have heard the same sound from their lips — a sound full of doubt, full of melancholy, full of the tiredness of life, full of resistance to life. Even Socrates said as he died: "Living — that means being sick for a long time: I owe the savior Asclepius a cock."[2] Even Socrates had had enough. — What does this *prove*? What does this *indicate*? Formerly people would have said (— oh, people did say it, and loudly enough, our pessimists leading the way): "Something here must be true! The *consensus sapientium*[3] proves the truth!" — Will we talk like this today? is that our *prerogative*? "Something here must be *sick*" — is *our* reply: those wisest of all times,[4] one ought first to take a close look at them! Were they all perhaps unsteady on their legs? late? shaky? *décadents*? Would wisdom perhaps manifest itself on earth as a raven that a faint whiff of carrion can excite? . . . [5]

2.

I myself first came across this unpalatable fact, that the great wise men are *types in decline*, precisely in a case where learned and unlearned prejudice stands most strongly opposed: I recognized Socrates and Plato as symptoms of decay, as tools of Greek dissolution, as pseudo-Greek, as anti-Greek (*Birth of Tragedy*, 1872). That *consensus sapientium* — I understood this better and better — certainly does not prove that they were right over what they agreed on, rather it proves that they themselves, those who are most wise, were in agreement in some *physiological* way, so that they took — *had* to take — a negative stance toward life in the same way. Judgments, value judgments about life for and against, can in the last resort never be true: they have value only as symptoms, they can only be considered as symptoms — in themselves such judgments are stupidities.[6] One really has to stretch out one's fingers and make the attempt to grasp this astonishing finesse, *that the value of life cannot be estimated*. Not by someone alive, because they are an interested party, even an object of contention and no judge; and not by someone dead, for another reason. — If, for his part, a philosopher sees a problem in the *value* of life, this even raises an objection to him, a question mark against his prudence, an imprudence. — What? and all these great wise men — would not just have been simply *décadents*, they would not even have been wise? — But I return to the problem of Socrates.

3.

Socrates belonged by his descent to the lowest class of people: Socrates was rabble. You know, you can even still see how ugly he was. But ugliness, objectionable in itself, is practically a refutation with the Greeks. Was Socrates a Greek at all? Ugliness is often enough the expression of crossbred development, *inhibited* by crossbreeding. Otherwise it manifests itself as *degenerative* development. The anthropologists among criminologists tell us that the typical lawbreaker is ugly: *monstrum in fronte, monstrum in animo.*[7] But the lawbreaker is a *décadent*. Was Socrates a typical lawbreaker? — At the very least this would not be contradicted by the well-known judgment of a certain physiognomist that caused such disgust among Socrates' friends. A foreigner who knew about faces was walking through Athens, and told Socrates to his face that he *was* a *monstrum*

— he harbored all bad defects and desires within himself. And Socrates just answered: "You know me, dear sir!"[8] —

4.

Indicators of *décadence* in Socrates are not just the acknowledged depravity and anarchy of his instincts: a superfetation of logic and that *rickety malice* that marks him out indicate this too. Not to forget those auditory hallucinations that, in the guise of "Socrates' *daimon*,"[9] have been interpreted in a religious direction. Everything in him is exaggerated, *buffo*,[10] caricature, at the same time everything is hidden, undisclosed, underground. — I am trying to understand which idiosyncrasy it is that gave rise to that Socratic equivalence of reason = virtue = happiness: the most bizarre equivalence there is and which had in particular all the instincts of the ancient Hellenes against it.[11]

5.[12]

With Socrates, Greek taste is reversed in favor of dialectics: what is really going on there? Primarily, a *noble* taste is thereby vanquished; with dialectics, the rabble ends up on top. Before Socrates, those in good society rejected dialectical manners: these counted as bad manners, they showed them up. Youth was warned against them. People also mistrusted any such presentation of reasons. Honest things, like honest people, do not show their hand like that. It is indecent to reveal all five fingers. What must first be demonstrated is of little value. Everywhere that authority is still regarded as good manners, where people give commands rather than "give reasons," the dialectician is a type of clown: people laugh at him, they don't take him seriously. — Socrates was the clown who *made people take him seriously*: what was really going on there? —

6.

People only choose dialectics when they have no other means available. They are aware that it arouses mistrust, that it does little to convince. Nothing is easier to wipe away than the effect of a dialectician: the experience at every gathering where there are speeches proves that. It can only be used for *self-defense* in the hands of those who have no other weapons. You must be obliged to *enforce* your right: otherwise you would not enlist dialectic. The Jews were dialecticians because of that; Reynard the Fox[13] was one; and what? and Socrates was, too? —

7.

— Is Socratic irony an expression of revolt? of the rabble's *ressentiment*? does he, as one suppressed, savor his own ferocity in the knife-thrusts of the syllogism? does he *avenge* himself on the nobles he fascinates? — As a dialectician you have a ruthless tool in your hand; you can play the tyrant with it; you can show people up by winning. The dialectician leaves it to his opponent to prove he is not an idiot: he simultaneously renders people furious and helpless. The dialectician *impairs the potency* of his opponent's intellect. — What? is dialectic just a form of *revenge* with Socrates?

8.

I have intimated what made Socrates arouse revulsion: it is all the more necessary to explain the fact *that* he aroused fascination. — That he discovered a new form of *agon*,[14] in which he was the first fencing master for the noble circles of Athens, is one reason. He aroused fascination by touching on the agonistic drive of the Hellenes — he introduced a variation into the wrestling match between young men and youths. Socrates was also a great *eroticist*.

9.

But Socrates guessed even more. He saw *through* his noble Athenians, he understood that *his* case, his idiosyncratic case, was already no exception. The same kind of degeneracy was quietly preparing to emerge everywhere: the old Athens was coming to its end. — And Socrates understood that all the world had *need* of him — his method, his cure, his personal ploy of self-preservation . . . Everywhere, instincts were in anarchy; everywhere, people were five paces from excess: the *monstrum in animo* was the general danger. "The instincts want to play the tyrant; we must invent a *counter-tyrant* who is stronger" . . . When that physiognomist had revealed to Socrates who he was, a pit of all evil lusts, the great ironist spoke another word that provides the key to him. "This is true," he said, "but I became master of them all." *How* did Socrates become master of *himself*? — Basically, his case was only the extreme case, only the most eye-catching case of what was starting to become the general plight at the time: that no one was master of himself anymore, that the instincts were turning *against* one another. He was fascinating as this extreme case — his awe-inspiring ugliness was testimony for all eyes: he was fascinating, it goes without saying, even more as an answer, as a solution, as the semblance of a *cure* for this case. —

10.

If one finds it necessary to make a tyrant of *reason*, as Socrates did, there must be no small danger that something else will play the tyrant. Rationality was supposed to be the *savior* in those days, neither Socrates nor his "patients" were free to be rational — it was *de rigueur*, it was their *last* resort. The fanaticism with which the whole of Greek thinking hurls itself on rationality betrays an emergency: they were in danger, they only had one choice: either to perish or — to be *absurdly rational* . . . The moralism of Greek philosophers from Plato onwards is pathologically determined; likewise their esteem for dialectics. Reason = virtue = happiness means merely: Socrates must be imitated and permanent *daylight* created to counter the dark desires — the daylight of reason. One must be clever, clear, bright at any cost: any yielding to the instincts, to the unconscious, leads *downwards*.

11.

I have intimated what made Socrates fascinating: he appeared to be a physician, a savior. Is it still necessary to point out the error inherent in his belief in "rationality at any cost"? — It is self-deception on the part of philosophers and moralists to think they sidestep *décadence* just by conducting a war against it. It is beyond their power to step aside: what they choose as a means, as salvation, is itself yet again no more than an expression of *décadence* — they *change* its expression, they do not remove the thing itself. Socrates was a misunderstanding; *the whole morality of improvement, including the Christian one, was a misunderstanding* . . . The most blinding daylight, rationality at any cost, life bright, cold, cautious, conscious, without instinct, in opposition to the instincts, was itself only a sickness, a different sickness — and certainly no way back to "virtue," to "health," to happiness . . . *Having* to fight against the instincts — that is the formula for *décadence*: as long as life *ascends*, happiness equals instinct. —

12.

— Did he himself understand that, this cleverest of all those who outwit themselves? Did he admit this to himself at the end, in the *wisdom* of his courage for death? . . . Socrates *wished* to die: — not Athens, *he* gave himself the poisoned chalice, he forced Athens to the poisoned chalice . . . "Socrates is not a physician," he said quietly to himself: "here, death alone is the physician . . . Socrates himself was just sick for a long time . . ."

"Reason" in Philosophy.[1]

I.

You ask me what is all the idiosyncrasy with philosophers? . . .
For example, their lack of historical sense, their hatred of the
very idea of becoming, their Egyptianism. They believe they
are conferring an *honor* on something when they dehistoricize
it, *sub specie aeterni*[2] — when they make a mummy out of it.
For millennia, all the things philosophers have manipulated
were mummified concepts; nothing really alive came from
their hands. These gentlemen concept-idolaters kill and stuff
the corpse when they idolize — they become mortally dangerous to everything when they idolize. Death, change, age, as
well as procreation and growth, are objections for them —
indeed, refutations. What is, does not *become*; what becomes,
is not . . . Now they all believe in beings, to the point of desperation. But because they cannot get hold of one, they look
for reasons why it is being withheld from them. "It must be an
illusion, a deception, that we cannot perceive the being: where
has the deceiver got to?" — "We have it," they shout happily,
"it is sensuality! These senses, *which in any case are so immoral*,
deceive us as to the *true* world. Moral: away from sensual delusion, from becoming, from history, from the lie — history is
nothing but belief in the senses, belief in the lie. Moral: say
"no" to everything that lends credence to the senses, to the
whole of the rest of humanity: that is all "the people." Be a philosopher, be a mummy, represent monotono-theism by mimicking

gravediggers! — And above all, get rid of the *body*, this pitiful *idée fixe* of the senses! tainted by all the errors of logic that there are, refuted, impossible even, although it is rude enough to behave as though it were real!" . . .

2.

With great deference I single out the name of *Heraclitus*. When other plebeian philosophers rejected the evidence of the senses because these showed variety and variability, he rejected their evidence because it showed things as though they had duration[3] and unity.[4] Even Heraclitus did the senses an injustice. For these lie neither in the way the Eleatics[5] believed, nor as he believed — they do not lie at all. What we *make* of their evidence inserts the lie, for example, the lie of unity, the lie of materiality, substance, duration . . . "Reason" is the cause of our falsifying the evidence of the senses. In so far as the senses show becoming, passing away, change, they do not lie . . . But Heraclitus will be permanently in the right to hold that being is an empty fiction. The "apparent" world is the only one: the "true world" is just *a lie added on* . . .

3.

— And what fine tools of observation we have in our senses! This nose, for example, which as yet no philosopher has spoken of with admiration and gratitude, is actually the most delicate instrument at our disposal; it can detect minuscule differences in movement that even a spectroscope does not detect. Today, we possess science precisely to the extent that we decided *to accept* the evidence of the senses — to the extent that we learned to sharpen them, arm them, think them through to the end. The rest is a monstrosity and not-yet-science: by which I mean metaphysics, theology, psychology, epistemology. *Or* science of forms, doctrine of signs: like logic and that applied logic, mathematics. In these, reality does not exist, not even as a problem: just as little as does the question about what value in general a sign-convention like logic might have. —

4.

The *other* idiosyncrasy philosophers have is no less danger-ous: it consists in confusing the last with the first. They put what comes at the end — unfortunately! for it should not come at all — the "highest concepts," in other words the most gen-eral, emptiest concepts, the last fumes of a vaporizing reality,[6] at the beginning, *as* beginning. Again, this is just an expression of their way of venerating something: the higher *should* not grow out of the lower, absolutely *should* not have grown at all . . . Moral: everything of first rank must be *causa sui*.[7] The descent out of something different counts as an objection, as casting a doubt on value. All uppermost values are first rate, all the high-est concepts, existence, the absolute, the good, the true, the perfect — all of that cannot have become, therefore it *must* be *causa sui*. But none of these can be unequal to one another, nor be in contradiction with themselves . . . Therefore they have their stupendous concept "God" . . . The last, slightest, empti-est is placed first, as cause in itself, as *ens realissimum*[8] . . . To think that humanity had to take seriously the mental illness of sick cobweb-spinners! — And it has paid dearly for it! . . .

5.

— In contrast, let us finally present the different way *we* (— I say "we" out of politeness . . .) face up to the problem of error and appearance. Formerly, people used to take alter-ation, change, becoming in general as proof of appearance, as a sign that something must be there leading us astray. Today, on the other hand, precisely to the extent that our prejudice for reason forces us to posit unity, identity, duration, sub-stance, cause, materiality, being, we see ourselves, so to speak, embroiled in error, *forced* into error; so certain are we, on the basis of our strict reckoning, *that* the error is here. It is no dif-ferent with the motions of the great star: there, error has our eye as constant advocate while here it has our *language*. In terms of its emergence, language belongs to the time of the most

rudimentary form of psychology: we enter into a coarse fetish-
ism when we bring to mind the basic assumptions of the metaphysics of language, in plain language: of *reason*. *That* sees
doer and deed everywhere: that completely believes in the will
as cause; that believes in the "I," in the I as being, in the I as
substance and *projects* belief in the I-substance onto all things
— only in this way does it *create* the concept "thing" . . .
Everywhere, being as cause is insinuated, *smuggled in*; from
the conception "I," the concept "being" then follows as a
derivative . . . At the beginning stands the great fateful error
that the will is something that *functions* — that the will is a
faculty . . . Today we know it is just a word . . . Very much
later, in a world a thousandfold more enlightened, the philosophers with some surprise became aware of the *surety*, the
subjective *certainty* in dealing with categories of reason: they
decided that these could not stem from the empirical world
— in fact, the whole empirical world stood to contradict
them. *So where did they stem from?* — And in both India and
Greece, people made the same mistake: "we must have already
been at home in a higher world (— instead of *in a very much
lower one*: which would have been the truth!), we must have
been divine, *for* we have reason!" . . . Indeed, nothing has so
far had a more naïve power to persuade than the error of
being, for example as it was formulated by the Eleatics: it has
every word, every sentence that we speak on its side! — Even
the Eleatics' enemies succumbed to the temptation of their
concept of being: Democritus among others when he invented
his *atom* . . . "Reason" in language: oh, what a treacherous old
hag! I fear we shall not get rid of God because we still believe
in grammar . . . [9]

6.

People will thank me for compressing an insight so essential, so new, into four theses: by this means, I facilitate understanding and invite contradiction.

First proposition. The reasons for which "this" world has been designated as apparent establish on the contrary its reality — any *other* form of reality is absolutely indemonstrable.

Second proposition. The characteristics that have been given to the "true being" of things are the characteristics of non-being, of *nothingness* — the "true world" has been fashioned out of contradiction to the actual world: an apparent world indeed, in so far as it is but a *moral-optical* illusion.

Third preposition. To tell tales about an "other" world than this one makes no sense, unless we possess a powerful instinct for calumny, belittlement, suspicion against life: in the latter case, we take our *revenge* on life with a phantasmagoria of an "other," a "better" life.

Fourth proposition. To divide the world into "true" and "apparent," be it in the manner of Christianity or in the manner of Kant (a *deceitful* Christian, when all is said and done), is just a suggestion of *décadence* — a symptom of *declining* life . . . That the artist prizes appearance more highly than reality is not an objection to this proposition. For "appearance" here means reality *once again*, but selected, strengthened, corrected . . . The tragic artist is *not* a pessimist — he just says *Yes* to everything questionable and even dreadful, he is *Dionysian* . . .

How the "True World" Finally Became a Fable.[1]

History of an Error.

1. The true world, attainable for one who is wise, devout, virtuous — he lives in it, *he is it.*

   (Oldest form of the idea, relatively clever, simple, convincing. Paraphrase of the proposition, "I, Plato,[2] *am* the truth."[3])

2. The true world, unattainable for now, but promised to one who is wise, devout, virtuous ("to the sinner who does penance").

   (Progress of the idea: it becomes more refined, trickier, more incomprehensible — *it becomes woman*, it becomes Christian . . .)

3. The true world, unattainable, unproved, unpromised, but the mere thought of it a consolation, an obligation, an imperative.

   (Basically the same old sun, but through fog and skepticism; the idea become sublime, pale, northern, Königsbergian.[4,5])

4. The true world — unattainable? In any case, unattained. And, as unattained, also *unknown.* Consequently not a consolation, redemption, obligation: how could something unknown be obligatory? . . .

   (Gray morning. First yawn of reason. Cock-crow of positivism.[6])

5. The "true world" — an idea that is no longer of any use, no longer even obligatory — a useless idea that has become superfluous, *consequently* a refuted idea: let's get rid of it!

> (Broad daylight; breakfast; return of *bon sens*[7] and cheerfulness; Plato's[8] blush of shame; devilish noise from all free spirits.)

6. We have abolished the true world: which world was left? Perhaps the apparent one? . . . But no! *along with the true world we have also abolished the apparent one!*

> (Midday: moment of the shortest shadow; end of the longest error; high point of humanity; INCIPIT ZARATHUSTRA.[9])

Morality as Anti-Nature.[1]

All passions have a time when they are just disastrous, when they drag their victims down with the weight of stupidity — and a later, very much later time when they wed the spirit, "spiritualize" themselves. People used to make war on passion itself on account of the stupidity in passion: they swore to destroy it — all the old morality monsters are unanimous that "*il faut tuer les passions*."[2] The most famous formula for this is found in the New Testament in that Sermon on the Mount where, by the way, things are really not viewed *from on high*. It is even said there, for example, with reference to sexuality, "If thine eye offend thee, pluck it out":[3] fortunately no Christian obeys this command. To *destroy* the passions and desires, simply in order to curb their stupidity and its unwelcome consequences, seems to us today to be itself no more than an acute form of stupidity. We no longer admire dentists who *extract* teeth to stop them from aching . . . In fairness, on the other hand, let it be admitted that within the soil where Christianity grew, the notion "*spiritualization* of passion" could not possibly be conceived. Certainly, as is well known, the early Church fought *against* the "intelligent" in favor of the "poor in spirit":[4] how would one expect of it an intelligent war against passion? — The Church fights passion with excision in every sense: its practice, its "cure," is *castratism*. It never asks: "how do you spiritualize, beautify, deify a desire?" — in all ages, it has placed the emphasis for discipline on extermination (of sensuality, of pride, of desire for mastery, of greed, of thirst for revenge). — But to attack the passions at their roots means to attack life at its root: the practice of the Church is *hostile to life* . . .

2.

The same device, castration, extermination, is the instinctive choice of those battling with a desire who are too weak-willed, too degenerate, to hold it in check: those natures who need *la Trappe*,[5] put figuratively (and not so figuratively —), some sort of decisive declaration of hostility, a *cleft* between themselves and a passion. Only the degenerate find radical means indispensable; weakness of will, to put it more specifically, the incapacity *not* to react to a stimulus, is itself just another form of degeneration. Radical hostility, deadly hostility toward sensuality remains a thought-provoking symptom: we are entitled to have reservations about the overall condition of anyone zealous to such an extent. — Furthermore, that hostility, that hatred, only peaks when such natures are no longer robust enough even for the radical cure, the renunciation of their "devil." Just take stock of the whole history of priests and philosophers, artists included: it is *not* the impotent who say the most poisonous things about the senses, *nor* the ascetics, but those failed ascetics, the kind who really ought to have been ascetics . . .

3.

The spiritualization of sensuality is called *love*: it is a great triumph over Christianity. Another triumph is our spiritualization of *enmity*. This means people being deeply aware of what value there is in having enemies: in short, acting and deciding in the opposite way to how people formerly acted and decided. At all times, the Church wanted the destruction of its enemies: we, we immoralists and anti-Christians, see our advantage in the existence of the Church . . . Even in the realm of the political, enmity has now become more spiritual

— much cleverer, much more reflective, much more *lenient*. Nearly every party understands that its interest for self-preservation lies in the opposing party's maintaining strength; the same is true for grand politics. Especially a new creation, like the new Reich, needs enemies more than it needs friends: it only feels itself necessary when in opposition, only in opposition does it *become* necessary . . . We conduct ourselves no differently against the "inner foe": there too we have spiritualized enmity, and there too we have grasped its *value*. One is *fruitful* only at the cost of being rich in contradictions; one stays *young* only on condition that the soul does not stretch itself, does not long for peace . . . Nothing has become more alien to us than that desideratum of former times, "peace of soul," the *Christian* desideratum; nothing arouses our envy less than the morality-cow and the fat complacency of the good conscience. You have renounced *great* life if you renounce war . . . In many cases, of course, "peace of soul" is just a misunderstanding — something *different* that just does not know how to designate itself more honestly. A few instances, without digression or prejudice. "Peace of soul" can, for example, be the gentle radiation of a rich animality into what is moral (or religious). Or the onset of fatigue, the first shadow cast by the evening, any kind of evening. Or a sign that the air is damp, that south winds are approaching. Or unconscious gratitude for a good digestion (occasionally called "love of humanity"). Or the convalescent's loss for words, to whom all things taste new, and who waits . . . Or the state that follows a strong fulfillment of our dominant passion, the satisfaction of a rare satiety. Or the geriatric weakness of our will, of our desires, of our vices. Or laziness persuaded by vanity to put on moral garb. Or the entrance of certainty, even terrible certainty, after the long suspense and torture of uncertainty. Or the expression of maturity and mastery in the midst of doing, creating, effecting, willing, a quiet breathing, "freedom of will" *attained* . . . *Twilight of the Idols*: who knows? perhaps just another kind of "peace of soul" . . . [6]

4.[7]

— I formulate a principle. All naturalism in morality, that is, every *healthy* morality is dominated by an instinct of life — one or other of life's commands is fulfilled by a certain canonical "should" and "should not," some inhibition and animosity on life's way is removed by that. *Anti-natural* morality, that is, almost every morality yet taught, revered and preached, by contrast turns precisely *against* the instincts of life — it is a *condemnation* of these instincts, one moment almost a secret and the next moment almost loud and coarse. By saying "God examines the heart,"[8] it says no to the lowest and highest desires in life and takes God to be an *enemy of life* . . . The saint in whom God takes his pleasure is the ideal castrate[9] . . . Life ends where the "kingdom of God" *begins* . . .

5.

Assuming you have grasped the sacrilege of such a revolt against life, which has become almost sacrosanct in Christian morality, you will have fortunately understood something else as well: the uselessness, illusoriness, absurdity, *mendaciousness* in such a revolt. A condemnation of life on the part of somebody still alive remains, at the end of the day, just a symptom of a certain kind of life: the question, whether it is right or wrong, has not even been raised. You would have to be placed *outside* life, yet on the other hand know it as well as one, as many, as all who have lived it, before you even dared to touch on the problem of the *value* of life:[10] sufficient grounds to understand that the problem is inaccessible for us. When we speak of values we speak under the inspiration and from the viewpoint of life: life itself forces us to set values, life itself evaluates through us, *when* we set values . . . It follows from this that even the *anti-nature of morality* which construes God as contradiction and condemnation of life is just a value judgment of life — *which* life? *what* kind of life? — But I have already given the answer: of declining, weakened, fatigued, condemned life. Morality as it has been understood until now

— as finally formulated by Schopenhauer as "denial of the will to life" — is the *décadence-instinct*[11] itself, turning itself into an imperative: it says, *"Be destroyed!"* — it is a condemnation by the condemned . . .

6.

Let us also consider what utter naïveté it is to say, "the human *should* be so and so!" Reality presents us with a delightful array of types, the abundance of an extravagant play and change of forms: and some wretched loafer of a moralist comments: "No! the human should be *different*"? . . . He even knows what he should be like, this poor wretch of a bigot, he paints himself on the wall and then says *"ecce homo!"*[12] . . . But even when the moralist just turns to the individual and says to him: *"you* should be so and so!" he does not cease from making himself ridiculous. The individual is a piece of fate from head to toe, one more law, one more necessity for all that is coming and will be. To say to him, "change yourself," would be to demand that everything should change, even in retrospect . . . And really, there have been resolute moralists who wanted the human to be different, namely virtuous, they wanted him in their image, namely as a bigot: that is why they *denied* the world! No small folly! Not a modest kind of immodesty! . . . Morality, in so far as it *condemns*, as such, *not* with regard to the ways, means, and intent of life, is a specific error with which nobody should have compassion, a *degenerates' idiosyncrasy* that has caused an unspeakable amount of harm! . . . We others, we immoralists, have, in contrast, opened our hearts wide to every kind of understanding, comprehending, *approval.* We do not easily deny, we seek honor in being *affirmative.* Our eyes have been increasingly opened to an economy that can use and exploit all that is rejected by the priest's pious nonsense, by the *sick* reason of the priest, to that economy of the law of life that takes advantage of even the revolting species of bigot, priest, prig — *what* advantage? — But we ourselves, we immoralists, are the answer here . . .

The Four Great Errors.[1]

I.

Error of confusing cause and consequence. — There is no more dangerous error than *to mistake consequence for cause*: I call it the actual ruination of reason. Nevertheless, this error belongs to humanity's oldest and most recent habits: it is even venerated among us, going by the name of "religion," "morality." *Every* proposition formulated by religion and morality contains it; priests and moral lawgivers are the originators of that ruination of reason. — To take an example: everyone knows the book by the famous Cornaro[2] where he recommends his abstemious diet as a recipe for a long and happy — as well as virtuous — life. Few books have been so widely read; even today, thousands of copies are still printed in England every year. I do not doubt that scarcely a book (the Bible excepted, in fairness) has instigated so much harm, *shortened* so many lives, as this well-intentioned curiosity. The reason for this: the mistaking of consequence for cause. The upright Italian saw his diet as the *cause* of his long life, while the prerequisites for long life, extraordinarily slow metabolism, meager consumption, were the cause of his abstemious diet. He did not have the choice of eating a little *or* a lot, his frugality was *not* that of "free will": he was ill if he ate more. Whoever is not a carp, however, does well, indeed needs, to eat *properly*. A scholar of *our* time, with his rapid consumption of nervous energy, would kill himself with Cornaro's *régime. Crede experto.*[3] —

2.

The most common formulation at the heart of every religion and morality runs: "Do that and that, give up that and that — and you will be happy! If you don't . . . " Every morality, every religion *is* this imperative — I call it the great original sin of reason, *immortal unreason*. In my mouth, every formulation changes into its opposite — *first* example of my "revaluation of all values": a human who has turned out well, somebody "happy," *must* do certain acts and instinctively recoils from other acts, he transfers the orderliness that he represents physiologically into his relations with humans and things. In a formula: his virtue is the *consequence* of his happiness . . . Long life, plentiful progeny are *not* the reward for virtue, rather, virtue itself is the slowing down of the metabolism which also, among other things, has a long life, plentiful progeny, in short, *Cornarism* as its consequence. — The Church and morality say: "a race, a people perishes through vice and luxury." My *recovered* reason says: when a physiologically degenerate people dies out, vice and luxury *follow* from this (that is, the need for ever stronger and more frequent stimuli, as every exhausted nature knows). This young man became pale and limp before his time. His friends say: such and such an illness is to blame. I say: *that* he became ill, *that* he did not withstand the illness, was already the consequence of an impoverished life, a hereditary exhaustion. The newspaper reader says: this party will destroy itself with such a mistake. My *higher* politics says: a party that makes such mistakes is finished — it is no longer secure in its instincts. Every mistake in every sense is the consequence of instinct-degeneration, disgregation of the will: we are thereby practically defining the *bad*. Everything *good* is instinct — and, consequently, easy, necessary, free. Toil is an objection, the god is typically differentiated from the hero (in my language: *light* feet the first attribute of divinity).[4]

3.

Error of a false causality.[5] — We have at all times believed we
knew what a cause is, but where did we get our knowledge, or
more precisely, our faith in this knowledge? From the realm of
the famous "inner facts," none of which has actually proved to
be factual. We believed ourselves to be causal in the act of
willing; we thought that there at least causality *could be caught
in the act.* In the same way, people had no doubt that all *antecedentia*[6] of an action, its causes, were to be sought in consciousness and could be retrieved if sought — as "motives":
otherwise one would not be free *to* act, nor responsible *for* it.
Finally, who would have disputed that a thought is caused?
that the I caused the thought? . . . Of these three "inner facts,"
with which causality appeared to authenticate itself, the first
and most convincing is that of the *will as cause*; the conception of a consciousness ("mind") as cause and still later of the
I (of the "subject") as cause were simply appended after the
causality of the will had been established as given, as *empirical*
. . . In the meantime, we have had second thoughts. Today, we
do not believe a single word of all that. The "inner world" is
full of chimeras and will-o'-the-wisps: the will is one of them.
The will no longer moves anything, nor, in consequence, does
it explain anything — it just accompanies proceedings, it can
also be absent. The so-called "motive": another error. Just a
superficial phenomenon of consciousness, a side effect of the
deed that is more likely to conceal the *antecedentia* of a deed
than expose them. And then the I! This has become a fable, a
fiction, a play on words: it has completely ceased to think, feel
and will! . . . What follows from this? There are no such things
as mental causes! All the alleged empirical evidence for them
went to the devil! *That* is what follows from this! — And we
had carried out a canny abuse with that "empirical evidence,"
on its basis we had *created* the world as a world of cause, a
world of will, a world of mind. The oldest and longest-lasting
psychology was at work here, it did nothing else at all: every

event was to it a deed, every deed the consequence of a will, the world became a multiplicity of doers, a doer (a "subject") sneaked into every event. Human beings had projected from within themselves their three "inner facts," those they believed in most firmly, the will, the mind, the I — they merely extracted the concept of being[7] from their concept of I, they posited the "thing" as being[8] after their own image, according to their concept of the I as cause. Is it any wonder that they later rediscovered in things only *what they had invested them with*? — The thing itself, to repeat, the concept thing, is but a reflex of the belief in the I as cause . . . And indeed even your atom, my gentlemen mechanists and physicists, how much error, how much rudimentary psychology still resides in your atom! — To say nothing of the "thing in itself," the *horrendum pudendum*[9] of metaphysicians! The error of confusing mind as cause with reality![10] And making that the measure of reality![11] And calling it *God*! —[12]

4.

Error[13] *of imaginary causes*. — Taking the dream as a starting point: a specific sensation, for example following a distant cannon shot, has a cause subsequently imputed to it (often a whole short novel in which the dreamer himself is the protagonist). Meanwhile, the sensation lasts as a sort of resonance: biding its time, so to speak, until the drive for causality permits it to step into the foreground — now no longer as a coincidence, but as "meaning." The cannon shot manifests itself in a *causal* fashion, in an apparent reversal of time. What comes later, the motivation, is experienced first, often with a hundred details flashing past like lightning, the shot follows . . . What has happened? The ideas *produced* by a certain condition have been misunderstood as its cause. —[14] In fact, we do the same awake. Most of our general feelings — every kind of inhibition, pressure, tension, explosion in the play and counterplay of the organs, as in the state of the *nervus sympathicus*[15] in particular — arouses our drive for causality: we want to have a *reason* for feeling *such and such* — for feeling bad or feeling good. It is never enough for us merely to establish the fact *that* we feel such and such: we only concede this fact — become *conscious* of it — *when* we have given it a sort of motivation. In such a case, memory without our knowing it steps into action, introducing earlier circumstances of the same kind together with their interwoven causal interpretations — *not* their causality. Naturally, the belief that these ideas, the accompanying processes in consciousness, were the causes is also produced by memory. Thus arises a *habituation* toward a certain causal interpretation that in truth inhibits and even precludes an *inquiry* into the cause.

5.

Psychological explanation for this. — To trace something unknown back to something known relieves, calms, satisfies, as well as giving a feeling of power. With the unknown is the attendant danger, disquiet, worry — the first instinct goes toward *removing* these unpleasant conditions. First principle: any explanation is better than none. Because it is fundamentally only a matter of wanting to get rid of oppressive ideas, people are not too fussy about the means of getting rid of them: the first idea whereby the unknown announces itself as known is so soothing that people "hold it to be true." Proof of *pleasure* ("of strength") as criterion of truth. So the drive for causes is dependent on and aroused by the feeling of fear. Whenever possible, the "why?" should not give the cause for its own sake, but rather a *kind of cause* — a calming, liberating, alleviating cause. That something already *known*, experienced, inscribed in memory, is put forward as cause is the first consequence of this requirement. That which is new, unexperienced, strange, is excluded as cause. Thus not only are explanations of some kind sought as cause, but the explanations of a *select* and *preferred* kind, those by which most speedily and frequently the feeling of the strange, the new, the unexperienced, has been removed — the *most usual* explanations. — Result: one kind of cause-designation increasingly predominates, distills itself into a system and finally emerges *dominant*, that is, simply excluding *other* causes and explanations. — The banker immediately thinks of "business," the Christian of "sin," the girl of her love.

6.[16]

The whole realm of morality and religion belongs within this concept of imaginary causes. — "Explanation" of *unpleasant* general feelings. The latter are occasioned by beings hostile toward us (evil spirits: the most famous case — mistaking hysterics for witches). They are occasioned by actions that cannot be sanctioned (the feeling of "sin," of "sinfulness," grafted onto physiological discomfort — one can always find reasons to be dissatisfied with oneself). They are invoked as punishments, as retribution for something that we ought not to have done, ought not to have *been* (impudently generalized by Schopenhauer into a proposition in which morality appears for what it actually is, a venomous calumniator of life: "Every great pain, whether physical, whether mental, tells us what we deserve; because it could not befall us, unless we deserved it." *World as Will and Representation* 2, 666).[17] They are conditioned as consequences of ill-considered actions that ended badly (— the affects, the senses, are designated as cause, as "culpable"; physiological states of distress are presented, with help from *other* states of distress, as "deserved"). — "Explanation" of *pleasant* general feelings. They are conditioned by trust in God. They are conditioned by the consciousness of good actions (so-called "good conscience," a physiological condition that can sometimes be confused with good digestion, it is so similar). They are occasioned by a happy outcome in affairs (— a naïve misconception: the happy outcome of affairs gives neither a hypochondriac nor a Pascal pleasant general feelings). They are conditioned by faith, love, hope[18] — the Christian virtues. — In truth, all these alleged explanations are *resulting* conditions and, so to speak, translations of feelings of pleasure or displeasure into a false dialect: you are in a condition to hope *because* the underlying physiological feeling is strong and rich again;

you trust in God *because* the feeling of fullness and strength gives you peace. — Morality and religion completely belong to the *psychology of error*: in every single case, cause and effect are mixed up; or truth is confused with the effect of what is *believed* to be true; or a state of consciousness is confused with the causation of this state.[19]

7.

Error of free will. — Today we no longer have compassion for the concept of "free will": we know only too well what it is — the most disreputable theologians' artifice there is, intent on making humanity "answerable" in their sense, that is, *making it dependent on them* . . . Here I am just giving the psychology of all such "making answerable." — Everywhere that responsibilities are looked for, it tends to be the instinct of *wanting to punish and judge* that is doing the looking. Becoming has been stripped of its innocence whenever any state of being is traced back to will, intentions, acts of responsibility: the doctrine of the will was essentially invented for the purpose of punishment, that is to say, of *wanting to find guilty.* All the old psychology, the psychology of will, is predicated on the fact that the prime movers, the priests at the head of ancient communities, wanted to create for themselves a *right* to decree punishments — or wanted to create a right for God to do that . . . [20] Humans were thought of as "free" so they could be judged and punished — so they could become *guilty*: consequently every action *had to be* thought of as desired, the origin of every action as lying in consciousness (— whereby the most *fundamental* fraud *in psychologicis*[21] was made the very principle of psychology . . .) Today, when we have begun to move in the *opposite* direction, when we immoralists in particular try with all our strength to remove the concepts of guilt and punishment from the world again and to purge psychology, history, nature, societal institutions and their sanctions of them, there is in our eyes no more radical enmity than that of the theologians, who continue to contaminate the innocence of becoming with "punishment" and "guilt" by means of the concept of a "moral world order." Christianity is a metaphysics of the hangman . . . [22]

8.

But what can *our* doctrine be? — That nobody *gives* a human their characteristics, neither God, nor society, nor parents and ancestors, nor they *themselves* (— this last nonsensical idea, here rejected, was taught as "intelligible freedom" by Kant, perhaps also by Plato earlier). *Nobody* is responsible for the fact that they are there at all, that they are created in such and such a way, that they are in these circumstances and in this environment. The fatality of our nature is not to be construed from the fatality of all that has been and will be. We are *not* the consequence of an intention, a will, a purpose; with us the attempt is *not* made to achieve an "ideal human" or "ideal happiness" or "ideal morality" — it is absurd to want to *pass off* our nature as a purpose of some sort. *We* have invented the concept "purpose": in reality, purpose is *lacking* . . . You are necessary, a piece of fate, you belong to the whole, you *are* in the whole — there is nothing that could judge, measure, compare, condemn our being, for that would mean judging, measuring, comparing, condemning the whole . . . *But there is nothing except for the whole!* That nobody is held responsible anymore, that a form of being may not be traced back to a *causa prima*,[23] that the world is neither a unity of sensation nor of "mind" — *this alone is the great liberation* — only with this is the *innocence* of becoming restored . . . The concept "God" has hitherto been the greatest *objection* to existence . . . We repudiate God, we repudiate responsibility in God:[24] only *with that* do we redeem the world. —

The "Improvers" of Humanity.[1,2]

I.

People know my demand for philosophers to place them-selves *beyond* good and evil — to have the illusion of moral judgment *beneath* them. This demand results from an insight first formulated by myself:[3] *that there are no moral facts at all.* Moral judgment has this in common with religious judgment, that it believes in nonexistent realities. Morality is just an inter-pretation of certain phenomena, or more precisely, a *mis*inter-pretation. Moral judgment, like religious judgment, belongs to a level of ignorance where even the concept of the real, the dis-tinction between the real and the imaginary, is lacking: so that "truth" at such a level indicates nothing but things that today we call "fantasies." To that extent, moral judgment is never to be taken literally: as such it always contains nothing but non-sense. But it is invaluable as a *semiotic*: it reveals, at least for the knowledgeable, the most valuable realities of cultures and inner moods that did not *know* enough to "understand" themselves. Morality is just sign language, just symptomatology: one must already know *what* it is about in order to make use of it.

2.[4]

A first example and quite provisional. At all times, people have wanted to "improve" humans: this is above all what moral-ity has meant. But concealed within the same word are com-pletely divergent tendencies. Both the *taming* of the human beast as well as the *breeding* of a certain category of human have been termed "improvement": these zoological terms alone express the realities — admittedly, realities of which the typical "improver," the priest, knows nothing — *wants* to know nothing . . . To call the taming of an animal its "improvement" is almost a joke to our ears. Whoever knows what happens in menageries doubts that the beast is "improved" there. It is weakened, it is made less dangerous, it is rendered a *sick* beast through the depressive affect of fear, through pain, through wounds, through hunger. — It is just the same with the tame human whom the priest has "improved." In the early Middle Ages, when in fact the Church was above all a menagerie, people everywhere hunted down the choicest examples of the "blond beast"[5] — the noble Teutons, for example, were "improved." But what did such an "improved" Teuton, lured into the cloister, look like afterwards? Like a caricature of a human, like a freak: he had become a "sinner," he was stuck in a cage, behind bars that were nothing but terrifying concepts . . . There he now lay, sick, wretched, bearing malice toward himself: full of hatred toward the impulses of life, full of suspicion toward everything that was still strong and happy. In brief, a "Christian" . . . To put it physiologically: in the battle with the beast, rendering sick *can* be the only means of rendering it weak. The Church understood that: it *wrecked* the human, weakened him — but it claimed to have "improved" him . . .

3.

Let us take the other case of so-called morality, the case of *breeding* a certain race and kind. The greatest example of this is provided by Indian morality, sanctioned into a religion as "the law of Manu."[6] Here the task is set of breeding no less than four races at the same time: a priestly race, a warrior race, a trading and agrarian race, and finally a race of servants, the Sudras. Obviously we are not among animal trainers here: a type of human a hundred times gentler and more sensible is required even to conceive of such a breeding plan. One can breathe, stepping out into this healthier, higher, *wider* world from the sickly Christian air of incarceration. How paltry the "New Testament" is alongside Manu, how bad it smells! — But even this organization found it necessary to be *fearsome* — not, this time, in the battle with the beast, but with *its* opposite concept, the nonbred human, the mishmash human, the chandala.[7] And again it had no other means of making him harmless and weak than to render him *sick* — it was the fight with the "greatest number." Perhaps nothing is more repugnant to our feelings than *these* protective measures of Indian morality. The third edict, for example, that of "unclean vegetables" (Avadana-Sastra I) ordains that the only food allowed to chandalas shall be garlic and onions, in consideration of the fact that the holy scripture forbids them to be given grain or fruits with seeds, or *water* or fire. The same edict ordains that the water they need may not be taken from rivers, springs, or ponds, but only from the approaches to swamps and puddles created by the tread of animals. Similarly, they are forbidden to wash their clothes or *even wash themselves*, since any water given to them out of charity may only be used to quench their thirst. Finally, a veto on Sudra women helping chandala women in childbirth, and with regard to the latter, another prohibition *on helping each other . . .* [8] — The success of such a sanitary policing was manifest: murderous plagues, dreadful sexual diseases, as well as the "law of the knife," ordaining circumcision for male children and the removal of the *labia minora* for female children. — Manu himself says: "The chandalas are the fruit of adultery, incest and crime (— this the *necessary* consequence of the concept of breeding). For clothing they should just have the rags from corpses, for dishes they should have broken pots, for jewelry, old iron, for worship, only evil spirits; they should wander without rest from place to place. They are forbidden to write from left to right, and to use the right hand for writing: the use of the right hand and of writing from left to right is reserved only for the *virtuous*, the people of *pedigree*." —[9]

4.[10]

These decrees are instructive enough: we have in them once and for all completely pure and original *Aryan* humanity — we learn that the concept of "pure blood" is the antithesis of a harmless concept. On the other hand, it becomes clear in *which* people the hatred, the chandala-hatred toward this "humanity" immortalized itself, where it turned into religion and *genius* . . . From this point of view, the Gospels are a document of the first rank; even more so, the Book of Enoch.[11] Christianity, with Jewish roots and only comprehensible as an outgrowth of this soil, represents the *opposite movement* to every morality of breeding, race, privilege: — it is the *anti-Aryan* religion par excellence: Christianity, the revaluation of all Aryan values, the victory of chandala-values, the Gospel preached to the poor, the lowly, the united uprising of everything downtrodden, miserable, ill-formed, ill-used, against "pedigree" — undying chandala-revenge as *religion of love* . . .

5.

The morality of *breeding* and the morality of *taming* are, in their methods of proving themselves, fully worthy of one another: we may state as a first principle that in order to *make* morality, one must have the unreserved will to its opposite. This is the great, *uncanny* problem I have pursued the longest: the psychology of the "improvers" of humankind. A small and basically modest fact, that of the so-called *pia fraus*,[12] provided me with the first access to this problem: *pia fraus*, the legacy of all philosophers and priests who "improved" humanity. Neither Manu nor Plato nor Confucius nor the Jewish and Christian teachers have ever doubted their *right* to lie. They did not have doubts as to *quite different rights* . . . Expressed in a formula, one might say: *all* means that hitherto have been intended to make humanity moral have been fundamentally *immoral*. —[13]

What the Germans Lack.[1]

Among Germans today it is not enough to have intellect: they have to take it and *take liberties* with it . . . [2]

Perhaps I know the Germans, perhaps I have the prerogative to tell even them a few truths. The new Germany represents a great quantity of inherited and inculcated industriousness, so that for a while it may even be lavish in expending its accumulated hoard of strength. It is *not* high culture that accompanied its rise to mastery, still less a delicate taste, a noble "beauty" of the instincts; but *more manly* virtues than any other land in Europe can boast. — A good deal of geniality and self-respect, of reliability in one's dealings, in the reciprocity of duties, a great deal of hard work and endurance — and an inborn restraint that needs to be spurred on rather than hobbled. Added to which people still obey here without being humiliated . . . And nobody despises their opponent . . .

You can see that it is my wish to be fair to the Germans: I do not wish to be untrue to myself in this — so I must also outline my objections. Coming to power takes its toll: power *stultifies* . . . The Germans — people once called them the race of thinkers:[3] do they still think at all today? — The Germans are now bored by intellect, the Germans now mistrust the intellect, politics swallows all gravity for truly intellectual things — "Germany, Germany above all"[4] was, I fear, the end of German philosophy . . . "Are there German philosophers? Are there German

poets? Are there *good* German books?" people ask me abroad.
I blush, but with the courage I possess even in desperate cases I
answer: "Yes, *Bismarck*!" — Would I really even admit which
books people read today? . . . Cursed instinct of mediocrity! —[5]

2.

— What the German mind *could* be, who has not already
had lugubrious thoughts over that! But this nation has made
itself deliberately stupid for nearly a thousand years: nowhere
else have the two great European narcotics, alcohol and Christianity, been more wantonly misused. A third has even been
added recently which can single-handedly cause havoc with all
fine and bold mobility of the intellect, music, our constipated,
constipating German music. — How much tedious heaviness,
lameness, dampness, lounging around,[6] how much *beer* there is
in the German intellect! How is it actually possible that young
men who devote their being to the most intellectual goals do
not feel within them the first instinct of intellectuality, *the
intellect's instinct for self-preservation* — and drink beer? . . . The
alcoholism of educated young people is perhaps not a question
mark with regard to their erudition — one can even be a great
scholar without intellect — but in every other respect it remains
a problem. — Where do you not find it, the gentle degeneration that beer produces in the intellect! I once[7] put my finger
on just such a degeneration in a case that almost became
famous — the degeneration of our first German freethinker,
the *clever* David Strauss, into the author of a beer-house gospel
and "new faith" . . . Not for nothing did he make his vow to
the "fair brown" in verse[8] — true unto death . . .

3.

— I spoke of the German mind: that it is becoming more
vulgar and superficial. Is that enough? — At bottom, I am
alarmed by something else: the way that with German seriousness, German depth, German *passion* in intellectual things
there is increasing decline. The pathos has altered, not just the

intellectuality. — Here and there I come into contact with German universities: what kind of atmosphere dominates among their scholars, what intellectuality turned arid, complacent and lukewarm! It would be a profound mistake if people wanted to object to me about German science here — and proof besides that they have not read a word by me. For seventeen years I have tirelessly exposed the *anti-intellectualizing* influence of our present-day pursuit of science. The hard helotry to which the immense expanse of science condemns each individual today is one of the main reasons why natures characteristically fuller, richer, *deeper* can no longer find a suitable education *and educators*. Nothing makes our culture suffer *more* than a surfeit of arrogant loafers and human debris; our universities are, *against* their will, the very hothouses for this kind of instinct-impoverishment of the intellect. And the whole of Europe already has an inkling of it — grand politics deceive nobody . . . Increasingly, Germany counts as Europe's *flatland.*[9] — I am still *searching* for a German with whom *I* can be serious in my way — all the more so for one with whom I might be cheerful! *Twilight of the Idols:* ah, who today would comprehend *the type of seriousness* from which a recluse here is recovering! Cheerfulness is the most unintelligible thing about us . . .

4.

Let us make a rough calculation: it is not just obvious that German culture is in decline, there is no lack of sufficient reason for it. Nobody can spend more than they have — that applies to individuals as well as to peoples. If you spend yourself on power, grand politics, economic activity, affairs of the world, parliamentarianism, military interests — if you give away in *this* direction the quantum of understanding, seriousness, will, self-overcoming that you are, there will be a lack in the other direction. Culture and the state — do not deceive yourself about this — are antagonists: the "cultural state" is merely a modern idea. The one lives off the other, the one thrives at the expense of the other.

All great periods of culture are politically times of decline: what is great in the sense of culture has been nonpolitical, even *antipolitical*. — Goethe's heart opened up to the phenomenon Napoleon — it *shut* with the "Wars of Liberation"[10] . . . In the same moment that Germany is becoming a great power, France is acquiring a different importance as a *cultural power*. A lot of new seriousness and *passion* of the intellect has already emigrated to today's Paris; the question of pessimism, for example, the question of Wagner, nearly all psychological and artistic questions are considered there in an incomparably finer and more thorough fashion than in Germany — the Germans are even *incapable* of this sort of seriousness. In the history of European culture, the rise of the "Reich" means one thing above all: a *displacement of the center of gravity*. People know this everywhere already: in the main — and that still means culturally — the Germans no longer come into consideration.[11] People ask: can you indicate just one intellectual who *counts* for Europe? As your Goethe, your Hegel, your Heinrich Heine, your Schopenhauer counted? — That there is no longer one single German philosopher left, there is no end of astonishment at that. —[12]

5.

The whole system of higher education in Germany has lost the main thing: the *end* as well as the *means* to the end. The fact that upbringing, *education* itself, is an end — and *not* "the Reich" — that *educators* are needed for this end — and *not* grammar-school masters and university scholars — people forgot that . . . Educators are needed *who themselves are educated*,[13] superior, noble intellects, borne out at every moment, borne out by speech or silence, ripe cultures grown *sweet* — *not* the learned louts that high schools and universities provide as "higher wet-nurses"[14] for the young. Aside from the most exceptional of exceptions, educators, the *foremost* prerequisite of education, are *lacking*: *hence* the decline of German culture. — One of those isolated exceptions is my worthy friend Jakob

Burckhardt[15] in Basel: Basel has him to thank primarily for its preeminence in the humanities. — What Germany's "higher schools" actually achieve is brutal training to make a huge number of young men useful, *exploitable* for service to the state with least expenditure of time. "Higher education" and *huge number* — a contradiction in terms. Every higher education ranks as an exception: one must be privileged to have a right to such high privilege. No great or beautiful things can ever be common property: *pulchrum est paucorum hominum*.[16] — What *determines* the decline of German culture? That "higher education" is no longer a *privilege* — the democratism of "general education" that has become *commonplace* . . . [17] Not to forget that military privileges formally require *excessive attendance* at higher schools, which amounts to their destruction. Nobody in Germany today is free to give their children a noble education: our "higher" schools, every last one of them, are designed for the most questionable mediocrity with teachers, curricula, learning goals. And everywhere indecent haste holds sway, as if something had been omitted if a young man[18] aged twenty-three is not yet "ready" and cannot yet answer the "main question": *which* calling? — If I may say so, a higher type of human dislikes a "calling" precisely because he knows himself to be "called" . . . He has time, takes his time, he does not in the least think of being "ready" — at the age of thirty one is a beginner, a child with regard to "high" culture. — Our overcrowded high schools, our overburdened, stultified high-school teachers, are a scandal: perhaps there are *motives* for defending this state of affairs, as the Heidelberg professors recently did — but there are no reasons for doing so.

6.

— In order to preserve my practice, which is *Yes-saying* and occupied with contradiction and criticism only indirectly and reluctantly, I shall present the three tasks that justify the need for educators. You have to learn to *see*, learn to *think*, learn to *speak* and *write*: the goal of all three is a noble culture. — To learn to *see* — to accustom the eye to tranquility, patience, letting things come to it; to delay making a judgment, to learn to examine and grasp the individual case from all sides. That is the *first* preliminary training for intellectuality: *not* to react at once to a stimulus but to take in hand the instincts that can check or lead to a conclusion. To learn to *see*, as I understand it, is almost what nonphilosophical parlance dubs a strong will: the essential thing about it is precisely *not* "willing," *being able* to defer a decision. All lack of intellect, all vulgarity stems from the inability to withstand a stimulus — one *must* react, one follows every impulse.[19] In many cases such compulsion is already sickliness, decline, a symptom of exhaustion — almost everything that unphilosophical coarseness designates with the name "vice" is simply the physiological incapacity *not* to react. — A useful application of having learnt to see: as a *learner* in general you have become slow, suspicious, reluctant. You let the strange and the *new* of any kind approach you, with an initial hostile composure — you will pull your hand away from it. The open door approach, submissive prostration when faced with any insignificant fact, in perennial readiness to intrude, to *leap* among other people and other affairs, in short, that famous modern "objectivity" is bad taste, is *ignoble par excellence*. —

7.

To learn *to think*: in our schools, nobody has a concept of this anymore. Even at the universities, indeed among the very scholars of philosophy, logic as theory, as practice, as *trade* is beginning to die out. Read German books: not the remotest recollection that to think requires a technique, a teaching plan, a will to mastery — that thinking needs to be learned, as dancing needs to be learned, *as* a form of dancing . . . Who among Germans can still recognize from experience that delicate shudder that *light feet*[20] in intellectual matters convey to every muscle! — The stiff awkwardness of intellectual gestures, the *clumsy* hand in grasping — this is German to such an extent that abroad, people confuse it with the German character in general. The German has no *finger* for nuances . . . The fact that the Germans have tolerated their philosophers, especially that most deformed concept-cripple that ever existed, the *great* Kant, gives no small insight into German charm.[21] — For *dancing* of any kind cannot be excluded from *noble education*, being able to dance with the feet, with concepts, with words; do I need to say with a *quill* as well — that you must learn to *write*? — But at this point I would become a complete riddle to German readers . . .

Forays of an Untimely One.[1]

I.[2]

My impossibles. — *Seneca*: or the toreador of virtue. — *Rousseau*: or the return to nature *in impuris naturalibus.*[3] — *Schiller*: or the morality-trumpeter of Säckingen.[4] — *Dante*: or the hyena *poeticizing* in graves. — *Kant*, or cant as intelligible character. — *Victor Hugo*: or the Pharos by the sea of nonsense. — *Liszt*: or the School of Velocity — after women.[5] — *George Sand*: or *lactea ubertas*,[6] in plain language: the milk cow with a "nice style." — *Michelet*: or the enthusiasm that takes off its jacket . . . *Carlyle*: or pessimism as lunch repeated. — *John Stuart Mill*: or insulting clarity. — *Les frères de Goncourt*:[7] or the two Ajaxes[8] in contest[9] with Homer. Music by Offenbach. — *Zola*: or "the joy of stinking." —[10]

2.[11]

Renan. — Theology, or the ruination of reason through "original sin" (Christianity). Witness Renan, who, whenever he risks a Yes or No of a general kind, goes off on a tangent with painful regularity.[12] For example, he wants to connect *la science* and *la noblesse*: but *la science* belongs to democracy, that much is palpably plain. He wishes, with no small ambition, to present an aristocracy of the mind:[13] but at the same time he goes down on his knees, and not just his knees, before the opposite teaching, the *évangile des humbles* . . . [14] What use is all freethinking, modernity, mockery and turncoat-pliability if in your heart of hearts you have remained a Christian, a Catholic and indeed, a priest! Renan has his ingenuity for seduction, just like a Jesuit or father confessor; his intellectuality does not lack the broad priestly grin — like all priests, he only becomes dangerous when he loves. Nobody can equal his deadly method of adoration . . . [15] Renan's mind, a mind that *debilitates*, is one more stroke of doom for poor, sick, sickly willed France. —

3.[16]

Sainte-Beuve. — Nothing manly about him; replete with petty fury at all masculine traits. Drifts about, refined, curious, bored, listening in — by nature a woman, with a woman's urge for revenge and a woman's sensuality. As a psychologist, a genius of *médisance*;[17] with an inexhaustible supply of methods for it; nobody understands better how to mix poison with praise. Plebian in his lowest instincts and related to Rousseau's *ressentiment*: *consequently*, a Romantic — for beneath all *romantisme* there grunts and grinds Rousseau's instinct for revenge. A revolutionary, yet tolerably held in check by fear. Not free in the face of anything with any strength (public opinion, the academy, court, even Port-Royal[18]). Embittered toward anything great in a human or thing, toward anything with self-belief. Poet and half-woman enough still to perceive greatness as power; constantly hunched, like the celebrated worm, because he constantly feels trodden under foot.[19] As a critic, without any standard, scruple and spine, with the eloquence of a cosmopolitan libertine for many things but without the courage to own up to his own libertinage. As a historian, without philosophy, without the *power* of the philosophical view — therefore he declines the task of taking a stance in anything major, holding up "objectivity" as a mask. He deals differently with everything where a delicate, debilitated taste is of prime importance: there he really does have the courage to be himself, the pleasure in himself — there he is a *master*. — In some aspects, an early version of Baudelaire. —[20]

4.

The *Imitatio Christi*[21] belongs to the books I cannot hold in my hand without physiological repugnance; it wafts out a perfume of the eternal-feminine[22] for which one simply has to be French — or a Wagnerian . . . This Saint has a way of speaking about love that would make even a Parisienne curious. — I am told that the *shrewdest* Jesuit, A. Comte, who wanted to lead his French people to Rome by the *roundabout route* of science, took his inspiration from this book. I believe it: "the religion of the heart" . . .

5.[23]

G. Eliot. — They have got rid of the Christian God and now believe even more strongly that they must hold on to Christian morality: that is an *English* deduction, we do not want to blame moralizing little women *à la* Eliot for it. In England, they have to compensate for any small emancipation from theology in the most formidable way, as morality-fanatics.[24] That is the *penance* they do there. — For people like us, it is different. If we give up the Christian faith, we pull the *right* to Christian morality from under our feet. The latter is absolutely *not* self-evident: you must constantly throw light on this point, in spite of the English idiots. Christianity is a system, a coherent and *whole* vision of things. If we break off a main tenet, the belief in God, we thereby break up the whole: nothing essential is left in our hands. Christianity presupposes that the human does not know, *cannot* know what is good for him, what is evil: he believes in God, who alone knows. Christian morality is a command; its origin is transcendental; it is beyond all criticism, all right to criticize; it only has truth if God is truth — it stands and falls with this belief in God. — If the English actually believe they themselves know, "intuitively," what is good and bad, if they consequently imagine they no longer need Christianity as a guarantee for morality, this itself is just a *consequence* of the dominance of Christian value judgments and an expression of the *strength* and *depth* of that dominance: with the result that the origin of English morality has been forgotten, and the highly conditional nature of its right to existence is no longer felt. For the English, morality is not yet a problem . . .

6.[25]

George Sand. — I read the first *Lettres d'un voyageur*:[26] like everything that stems from Rousseau, false, made up, full of wind, exaggerated. I cannot stand this colorful tapestry-style; as little as I can stand the plebian ambition for generous feelings. Of course, the worst is her feminine coquetry with masculinity, with the manners of a badly brought up youth. — How cold she must have been all the while, this unbearable woman artist! She wound herself up like a clock — and wrote[27]. . . coldly, like Hugo, like Balzac, like all the Romantics the minute they started writing! And how complacently she must have lain there, this prolific writing-cow,[28] who had something German about her in the bad sense, like Rousseau himself, her master, and who in any case was only possible with the decline of French taste! — But Renan admires her . . . [29]

7.[30]

Morality for Psychologists. — Do not peddle colportage-psychology! Never observe *in order* to observe! It produces a false perspective, a squint, something forced and exaggerated! To experience out of a *desire* for experience — that does not work. You *must* not eye yourself up during an experience or each look will become an "evil eye." A born psychologist instinctively avoids looking in order to see; the same is true of the born artist. He never works "from nature"[31] — he leaves to his instinct, his *camera obscura*, the sifting and expressing of a "case," of "nature," of "experience" . . . Only the *general* penetrates his consciousness, the conclusion, the result: he has no knowledge of that random abstraction from the individual case. — What becomes of this when it is done differently? For example, if colportage-psychology is peddled in the manner of Parisian novelists great and small? *That* as it were lies in wait for a real event, *that* brings home a handful of curiosities every evening . . . But just look at what finally transpires — a heap of daubs, a mosaic at best, in every case something cobbled together, busy, loud with color. The worst offenders are the Goncourts: they cannot put three sentences together that do not simply pain the eye, the *psychologist's* eye. — Nature, artistically evaluated, is no model. It exaggerates, distorts, leaves gaps. Nature is *chance*. Study "from nature" seems to me a bad sign: it betrays submission, weakness, fatalism — this lying in the dust before *petits faits*[32] is unworthy of a *complete* artist. To see *what is* — that belongs to a different, *anti-artistic*, factual category of mind. You must know *who* you are . . .

8.[33]

On the psychology of the artist. — For there to be art, for there to be any kind of aesthetic doing and seeing, there is one indispensable condition: *intoxication*. Intoxication must first have increased the excitability of the whole machine: otherwise no art will be forthcoming. All forms of intoxication, however different their origin, have the capacity to do this: above all, the intoxication of sexual excitement, this oldest and most primordial form of intoxication. Similarly, intoxication that comes in the wake of all great desires, all strong affects; the intoxication of the feast, the contest, the feat of bravery, of victory, of all extreme movement; the intoxication of cruelty; the intoxication of destruction; intoxication under certain meteorological conditions, for example, the intoxication of spring; or when under the influence of narcotics; finally, the intoxication of the will, the intoxication of an accumulated and swollen will. — The essential thing about intoxication is the feeling of an increase in strength and fullness. Out of this feeling we hand over to things, we *force* them to take from us, we violate them — we call this process *idealizing*. Let us rid ourselves of a prejudice here: idealizing does *not* consist of withdrawing or discounting what is small and irrelevant, as commonly supposed. Rather, a tremendous *driving out* of the main traits is the decisive thing, so that the others just disappear.

9.

In this state, you enrich everything from your own abundance: what you see, what you want, is visibly swollen, urgent, strong, laden with force. The human in this state transforms things until they reflect his power — until they reflect his perfection. This *compulsion* to transform into perfection is — art. Even everything that he is not still contributes to his pleasure in himself; in art, the human relishes himself as perfection. — Allow me to imagine a contrasting state, a specific anti-artistry of the instinct — a manner of being that would impoverish and attenuate things, render them consumptive. And in fact, history has a wealth of such anti-artists, life's starvelings: who necessarily still have to take things to themselves, consume them, make them more *meager*. This is for example the case with the genuine Christian, Pascal, for instance: a Christian who is an artist at the same time *never happens* . . . Do not be so childish as to cite Raphael to me or any nineteenth-century homeopathic Christians: Raphael said Yes, Raphael *did* Yes, therefore Raphael was not a Christian . . .

10.[34]

What meaning attaches to the antithetical concepts *Apollonian* and *Dionysian*[35] that I introduced into aesthetics, both conceived as forms of intoxication? — Apollonian intoxication chiefly holds the eye aroused so that it receives the power of vision. The painter, sculptor, epic poet are visionaries par excellence. By contrast, in the Dionysian state the whole system of affects is aroused and heightened: so that it unleashes all its methods of expression at once, and at the same time drives out the power of representation, reproduction, transfiguration, transformation, every kind of mimicry and playacting. The essential thing remains the ease of metamorphosis, the inability *not* to react (— similar to the case of certain hysterics, who slip into *any* role at a given sign). It is impossible for the Dionysian human not to respond to any suggestion, he ignores no signal from the affects, he has the highest level of instinct for understanding and conjecture, just as he possesses the art of communicating to the highest level. Everywhere, he gets under the skin and slips into the mood: he transforms himself constantly. — Music as we understand it today is likewise a complete arousal and unleashing of the affects, but even so, it is just the leftovers of a much fuller realm of emotional expression, a mere *residuum* of Dionysian histrionics . . . To make music possible as a special art form, a number of senses had to be immobilized, above all the muscular sense (relatively, at least: for to a certain extent all rhythm still speaks to our muscles): so that the human no longer physically imitates and acts out immediately everything he feels. However, *that* is actually the normal Dionysian state, at least the original state; music is the specialization of this, arrived at slowly at the expense of closely related faculties.

II.

The actor, mime, dancer, musician, lyric poet are at heart related by instinct and in principle all one, but have gradually specialized and drawn apart — to the point of contradiction. The lyric poet remained united with the musician the longest, the actor with the dancer. — The *architect* represents neither a Dionysian nor an Apollonian state: here is the great act of will, the will that moves mountains, the intoxication of the great will that craves for art. The mightiest humans have always inspired the architect; the architect was always prone to the suggestion of power. An edifice is intended to display pride, victory over gravity, the will to power; architecture is a kind of power-eloquence in forms that are now persuasive, even flattering, now simply imperative. The highest feeling of power and security is expressed in whatever has *grand style*. Power that no longer needs any excuse; that scorns giving pleasure; that answers gravely; that does not need to be corroborated; that exists without being conscious that it is contradicted; that reposes within *itself*, fatalistically, a law among laws: *that* speaks of itself as grand style. —

12.[36]

I read the life of *Thomas Carlyle*,[37] this farce that flies in the face of knowledge and will, this heroic-moralistic interpretation of dyspeptic circumstances. — Carlyle, a man of strong words and attitudes, a rhetorician from *necessity*, constantly piqued by the craving for a strong faith *and* the feeling of being incapable of it (— in that, a typical Romantic!). The craving for a strong faith is *not* proof of a strong faith, rather the contrary. *Having that*, one can indulge in the splendid luxury of skepticism: one is secure enough, firm enough, sufficiently attached to it. Carlyle deafens something in himself by his *fortissimo*[38] admiration of humans of strong faith and by his fury against those less credulous: he *needs* noise. A continual, passionate *dishonesty* toward himself — that is his *proprium*, that is what makes and keeps him interesting. — Admittedly, he is admired in England just now for his honesty . . . Well, that is English; and in view of the fact that the English are the people of thorough-going cant,[39] it is even proper and not just understandable. Basically, Carlyle is an English atheist seeking to gain distinction for *not* being one.

13.

Emerson. — Much more enlightened, far-sighted, versatile, refined than Carlyle, above all, happier . . . Such a one who by instinct feeds exclusively on ambrosia and eschews things that are indigestible. A man of taste when set against Carlyle. — Carlyle, who loved him very much, said about him nevertheless: "he does not give *us* enough to bite on": which might rightly be said, but not to Emerson's disadvantage. — Emerson has that good-natured and witty cheerfulness that discourages all seriousness; he has no idea at all of how old he is or how young he might be — he could say of himself, in Lope de Vega's words, *"yo me sucedo a mi mismo."*[40] His spirit constantly finds reasons to be content and even grateful; and now and then he verges on the cheery transcendence of that upright citizen who returned from an assignation *tamquam re bene gesta.*[41] *"Ut desint vires,"* he said gratefully, *"tamen est laudanda voluptas." —*[42]

14.

Anti-Darwin. — Regarding the famous {"}struggle for *life*," it seems to me for the present that this is more a declaration than a proven fact. It happens, but as an exception; the situation of life as a whole is *not* a state of distress and starvation, but rather wealth and abundance, even absurd extravagance — where there is struggle, it is a struggle for *power* . . . One should not confuse Malthus with nature. — Assuming, however, that this struggle exists — and in fact, it does happen — it unfortunately turns out to be the reverse of what the Darwin school wishes, of what we possibly *might dare* to wish as well: namely the defeat of the strong, the more privileged, the fortunate exceptions. Species do *not* grow in perfection: repeatedly, the weak become master over the strong — that means they are the majority, they are also *cleverer* . . . Darwin forgot the intellect (that is English!), *the weak have more intellect* . . . you have to need intellect in order to acquire it — you lose it if you no longer need it. Anyone strong gets rid of his intellect (— "Let it go!" people think in Germany today — "the *Reich* must nevertheless remain with us"[43]). As you see, I interpret intellect to mean caution, patience, dissembling, great self-control and all that is mimicry[44] (a great deal of the so-called virtues belong to the latter).

15.[45]

Psychologist's casuistry. — Here we have a connoisseur of humans: why does he actually study humans? He wants to snatch a small advantage over them, or perhaps even a big one

— he is a *politico*! . . . Over there we have another connoisseur of humans: and you say he desires nothing for himself, he is completely "impersonal." Look closer! Perhaps he would even like a *worse* advantage: to feel himself superior to humans, to have a prerogative to despise them, to avoid confusing himself with them. This "impersonal one" is a *despiser* of humans: the former is the more humane species, in spite of appearances. At least he sees himself as an equal and *joins in* . . .

16.

The Germans' *psychological tact*, it seems to me, is called into question by a whole series of cases that modesty forbids me to list. In one particular instance I am not without an excellent reason to substantiate my thesis: I hold it against the Germans that they misjudged *Kant* and his "backdoor philosophy," as I call it — that was *not* a model for intellectual integrity. — The other thing I don't like to hear is the notorious "and": the Germans say "Goethe *and* Schiller" — I fear they say "Schiller and Goethe" . . . Do they not yet *know* this Schiller? — There are even worse "ands"; I have heard with my own ears, admittedly only among university professors, "Schopenhauer *and* Hartmann" . . . [46]

17.

The most intellectual humans, providing that they are also the bravest, also experience by far the most painful tragedies: but precisely because of this they honor life, since it presents them with its greatest opposition.

18.[47]

Concerning the "*intellectual conscience*." — To my mind, nothing is rarer today than genuine hypocrisy. I have a strong suspicion that the soft ambience of our culture is inimical to this plant. Hypocrisy belongs to periods of strong belief: in which people did not surrender their belief even when *required* to fake a different belief. Today they just give in; or, as is more common, they get themselves a second belief — remaining *honest* in every case. Doubtless, the number of possible convictions is much larger today than formerly: possible, that means allowed, that means *harmless*. From this arises tolerance toward yourself. — Tolerance toward yourself allows for a number of convictions: these coexist agreeably well — they avoid compromising themselves, as does everyone nowadays. How is a person compromised today? By being single-minded. By going in a straight line. By having fewer than five meanings.[48] By being genuine . . . I fear very much that modern humans are simply too complacent for a number of vices: so that the latter are virtually dying out. Everything evil that is conditioned by a strong will — and perhaps nothing can be evil without strength of will — degenerates to a virtue in our mild air . . . The few hypocrites I have met were impersonating hypocrisy: they were, like almost one in every ten today, actors. —

19.[49]

Beautiful and ugly. — Nothing is more conditioned, let us say *more restricted*, than our feeling for the beautiful. Whoever might want to think of it as detached from a human's pleasure in what is human would at once lose the ground underfoot. The "beautiful in itself" is just a phrase, not even a concept. In the beautiful, the human sets himself up as the measure of perfection; in selected cases, he worships himself in it. A species *cannot* help saying Yes to itself alone in this way. Its *most basic* instinct of self-preservation and self-enlargement still shines through in such sublimities. The human believes the world itself is heaped with beauty — *forgetting* that he is himself the cause. He alone has bestowed it with beauty, alas! only with a very human, all-too-human beauty . . . Fundamentally, the human mirrors himself in things, counting anything that reflects the mirror image as beautiful: the verdict "beautiful" is his *vanity of the species* . . . In fact, a small suspicion may whisper the question in the skeptic's ear: is the world really embellished just because the human takes it for beautiful? He has *humanized* it: that is all. But nothing, absolutely nothing, guarantees that the human alone is the model for beauty. Who knows how the human would look in the eyes of a higher authority on taste? Perhaps daring? perhaps even amusing? perhaps somewhat capricious? . . . "Oh Dionysus, divine one, why do you pull my ears?" Ariadne asked her philosophical lover in one of those famous *Dialogues on Naxos*: "I find your ears rather amusing, Ariadne: why are they not even longer?"[50]

20.

Nothing is beautiful, only the human is beautiful: all aesthetics rests on this naïveté, it is its *first* truth. Let us immediately add its second: nothing but the *degenerating* human is ugly — with that, the realm of aesthetic judgment is delineated. — Calculated physiologically, everything ugly weakens and distresses the human. It reminds him of decay, danger, powerlessness; he really does sacrifice strength through this. The effect of the ugly can be measured with the dynamometer. Wherever the human is oppressed, he senses that he is in the presence of something "ugly." His feeling of power, his will to power, his courage, his pride — all of this declines with the ugly and rises with the beautiful . . . In either case, *we reach a conclusion*: the required premises have accumulated in the instinct in great profusion. The ugly is understood as a sign and symptom of degeneration: whatever remotely reminds us of degeneration brings about in us the verdict of "ugly." Every hint of exhaustion, difficulty, age, fatigue, lack of freedom of every kind, whether as cramp or paralysis, above all the smell, the color, the shape of dissolution, decay, even in its last attenuation into a symbol — all that calls forth the same reaction, the value judgment "ugly." A *hatred*[51] springs out of this: who then does the human hate? Without a doubt: the *decline of his type*. The hatred springs from the deepest instinct of the species; in this hatred there is horror, caution, depth, farsightedness — it is the deepest hatred there is. For its sake, art is *deep* . . . [52]

21.

Schopenhauer. — Schopenhauer, the last German to be taken seriously (to be a *European* event like Goethe, like Hegel, like Heinrich Heine, and *not just* local, "national"), is a first-rate case study for the psychologist: namely as a fiendishly clever attempt to favor a nihilistic overall evaluation of life while fielding contrary examples, the great self-affirmations of the "will to life" and exuberant manifestations of life. One after the other he interpreted *art*, heroism, genius, beauty, great compassion, knowledge, will to truth, tragedy as after-effects of the "denial" or the need to deny the "will" — the greatest psychological fraud in history, with the exception of Christianity. On closer examination, this just makes him the heir to Christian interpretation: except that what Christianity had *rejected*, the great cultural achievements of humanity, he could also *validate* in a Christian, that is to say, nihilistic way (— namely as a route to "redemption," as prefatory forms of "redemption," as stimulants to the need for "redemption" . . .)

22.

I shall take an individual case. Schopenhauer speaks of *beauty* with melancholy passion — why, at the end of the day? Because in it he sees a *bridge* that people can use to go further or acquire the thirst to go further . . . For him, it is a momentary redemption from the "will" — it beckons toward everlasting redemption . . . In particular, he prizes it as a redemption from the "focal point of the will," sexuality — in beauty, he sees the drive to procreate *denied* . . . Strange saint! Somebody is contradicting you; I fear, it is nature. *For what purpose* is beauty in tone, color, scent, rhythmic movement displayed in nature at all? what *drives out* beauty? — Fortunately, a philosopher also contradicts him. No less an authority than the divine Plato[53] (— as Schopenhauer himself calls him[54]) upholds a different thesis: that all beauty instigates procreation — that this is precisely the *proprium* of its effect, from the most sensual right up to the most spiritual . . .

23.

Plato goes further. With an innocence for which you must be a Greek and not a "Christian," he says there would no longer be any Platonic philosophy at all if there were not such beautiful youths in Athens: the sight of them was what first spurred the philosopher's soul into an erotic spin and allowed no peace until it had sown the seed of all high things in such beautiful terrain.[55] Yet another strange saint! — you can hardly trust your own ears, even assuming you trust Plato. At least you can guess that in Athens, people philosophized *differently*, above all in public. Nothing is less Greek than the concept-cobweb-spinning of a hermit, *amor intellectualis dei*[56] in Spinoza's manner. Philosophy in Plato's manner would be better defined as an erotic competition, as a development and internalization of ancient agonal gymnastics and their *premises* . . . What finally blossomed from this philosophical eroticism of Plato's? A new art form of the Greek *agon*, the dialectic. — Let me point out, *against* Schopenhauer and to Plato's credit, that the whole of higher culture and literature in *classical* France, too, flourished in the soil of sexual interest. Everywhere in it you can look for gallantry, the senses, sexual competition, "woman" — you will never look in vain . . .

24.[57]

L'art pour l'art.[58] — The struggle against the purpose of art is always the struggle against the *moralizing* tendency in art, against its subordination to morality. *L'art pour l'art* means: "the devil take morality!" — But even this antagonism betrays the superior force of prejudice. When we have excluded the purpose of preaching morality and improving humanity from art, it by no means follows that art is completely without purpose, goal, meaning, in short, *l'art pour l'art* — a worm[59] biting its tail. — "Rather no purpose at all than a moralizing purpose!" — that is how mere passion talks. A psychologist asks on the other hand: what does all art do? does it not praise? does it not glorify? does it not make choices? does it not have preferences? With all these things it *strengthens* and *weakens* certain value judgments . . . Is this just incidental? a coincidence? Something where the artist's instinct was not engaged? Or rather: is it not the necessary precondition that *enables* the artist . . . ? Doesn't his basic instinct pursue art, or rather the meaning of art, *life*? a *desideratum of life*? — Art is the great stimulant to life: how could we understand it as purposeless, goalless, as *l'art pour l'art*? — One question remains: art also reveals much that is ugly, hard, questionable in life — does this not seem to put us off life? — And in fact, there have been philosophers who attributed this meaning to it: Schopenhauer taught "liberation of the will" as the whole purpose of art, he revered "attuning to resignation" as the great usefulness of tragedy. — But this — I have already indicated — is a pessimist's perspective and "evil eye" — : we must appeal directly to the artists themselves. *What does the tragic artist communicate of himself?* Is it not that he shows precisely the state of being *without* fear in the face of what is fearful and questionable? — This state itself is greatly to be desired; whoever knows it, esteems it with the highest veneration. He communicates it, he *must* communicate it, providing that he is an artist, a genius of communication. The courage and composure when faced with mighty foes, sublime hardship, a problem that arouses dread — it is this *victorious* state that the tragic artist selects and glorifies. In the face of tragedy, the bellicosity in our soul celebrates its Saturnalia; whoever is inured to suffering, whoever seeks it out, the *heroic* human lauds his existence with tragedy — to him alone the tragedian offers a draft of this sweetest cruelty. —

25.[60]

To make do with humans, to keep open house with one's heart, that is liberal, but nothing more than liberal. We recognize the hearts capable of *noble* hospitality by their windows with drawn curtains and closed shutters: they keep their best rooms empty. Why, though? — Because they are expecting guests with whom you do *not* have to "make do" . . .

26.

We no longer value ourselves enough when we communicate. Our actual experiences are not at all garrulous. They could not communicate themselves if they wanted to. For the reason that they are without words. We have long ago gone beyond what we have words for. In all speech there is a grain of contempt. It seems that language was only invented for the average, the middling, the communicative. With speech, the speaker has already *vulgarized* himself. — From a morality for the deaf and dumb and other philosophers.

27.[61]

"This picture is enchantingly beautiful!"[62] . . . The literary woman, unsatisfied, excitable, desolate of heart and soul, listening all the while with painful curiosity to the command that whispers from the depths of her constitution, "*aut liberi aut libri*":[63] the literary woman, sufficiently educated to understand the voice of nature even when it speaks Latin, and on the other hand, vain and enough of a goose to secretly speak French to herself as well: "*je me verrai, je me lirai, je m'extasierai et je dirai: Possible, que j'aie eu tant d'esprit?*" . . . [64]

28.[65]

The "impersonal" hold forth. — "We find nothing easier than to be wise, patient, superior. We drip with the oil of indulgence and compassion, we are impartial, absurdly so, we pardon everything. Precisely because of that, we ought to behave with rather more severity; precisely because of that, we should *cultivate* a little affect from time to time, a vicious little affect. It might gall us; and among ourselves we might laugh at the spectacle we create. But what is the use! We no longer have any alternative way of self-overcoming: this is *our* asceticism, *our* penance" . . . *Becoming personal* — the virtue of the "impersonal" . . .

29.

From a doctoral defense. — "What is the task of all higher education?" — To make the human into a machine.[66] — "What is the means to that?" — He must learn to be bored. — "How is that achieved?" — Through the concept of duty. — "Who is the model for that?" — The philologist: he teaches *cramming.* — "Who is the perfect human?" — The civil servant. — "Which philosophy provides the highest formula for the civil servant?" — That of Kant: the civil servant as thing in itself placed as judge over the civil servant as appearance. —

30.

The right to stupidity. — The fatigued and slow-breathing worker, who looks good-naturedly, who lets things take their course: this typical figure that one currently meets in this era of work (*and* of the "Reich"! —) in all classes of society lays claim today to *art*, no less, including books, above all journals — and even more to the splendor of nature, Italy . . . The evening person with the "dormant wild drives" mentioned by Faust[67] needs the freshness of summer, the seaside resort, the glacier, Bayreuth . . . In such eras, art has the right to *pure folly*[68] — as a sort of holiday for spirit, wit and mood. Wagner understood that. *Pure folly* is a tonic . . .

31.[69]

Another problem of diet. — The means by which Julius Caesar kept indisposition and headaches at bay: immense marches, the simplest lifestyle, conducted completely in the open air, continual feats — this is, in sum, the chief measure to maintain and protect from extreme vulnerability that subtle machine, working under the greatest stress, that is called genius. —

32.[70]

The immoralist speaks. Nothing offends the taste of a philosopher *more* than the human *insofar as it desires* . . . If he merely sees the human in action, if he sees this bravest, shrewdest, toughest of animals stray into even labyrinthine difficulties, how admirable the human appears to him! He even encourages him . . . But the philosopher despises the desiring human, as well as the "desirable" human — and all the desirable things, to boot, all the human's *ideals*. If a philosopher could be a nihilist, it would be because he finds the nothingness behind all the human's ideals. Or indeed, not even nothingness — but just the good-for-nothing, the absurd, the sick, the cowardly, the tired, dregs of all kinds from the *drained* chalice of his life . . . How does it come about that the human, so venerable as a reality, deserves no respect insofar as he desires? Does he have to atone for the fact that he is so proficient as a reality? Does he have to compensate for his doings, for the exertion of head and will in all his doings, by stretching his limbs in the imaginary and the absurd? — Up till now, the story of his desirable things was the human's *partie honteuse*:[71] we should be wary of reading too much into this. What justifies the human is his reality — it will always justify him. How much more valuable is the actual human, compared with some merely desired, dreamed-up, stinking and lying human? with some kind of *ideal* human? . . . And only the ideal human offends the philosopher's taste.

33.

Natural value of egoism. — Selfishness is worth only as much as the physiological value of the one who possesses it: it can have great value or it can be worthless and despicable. Every individual can be seen as representing an ascending or descending line of life. Having decided which it is, one also has a canon for the value of one's selfishness. The person representing an ascending line is indeed of enormous value — and for the sake of the whole of life, which takes a step *forward* with him, the worry about supporting him, about creating the optimum conditions for him, may well be extreme. The one singled out, the "individual," as understood by peoples and philosophers hitherto, is of course an error: he is nothing alone, not an atom, not a "link in the chain," nothing merely inherited from former times — he is the whole unified human line up to and including himself . . . If he represents descending development, decay, chronic degeneration, disease (— on the whole, diseases are already the results of decay, *not* its cause), little value is attached to him and, in all fairness, he should *take away* as little as possible from the privileged. He is still just their parasite . . .

34.

Christian and Anarchist. — If the anarchist, as the mouthpiece for *declining* echelons of society, demands with fetching indignation "law," "justice," "equal rights,"[72] he merely succumbs thereby to the pressure of his lack of culture, which has no idea how to grasp *why* he is actually suffering — in *what* way he is poor, in life . . . He has a mighty drive for causes: someone must be held responsible for making him feel bad . . . Already, his "fetching indignation" does him good, to scold is a pleasure for all poor devils — it gives a modest intoxication of power. Even complaint, making a complaint, can give life a thrill for the sake of which we can bear it: there is a rather fine dose of revenge in every complaint; people lay the blame for their discomfort, in certain circumstances even their wrong-doings, on those who are different, as if it were an injustice, a *forbidden* privilege. "If I am *canaille*[73] then you should be, too": people create a revolution with this logic. — Making a complaint never gets anywhere: it stems from weakness. Whether a person imputes his discomfort to others or *himself*— the socialist does the former, the Christian, for example, does the latter — really makes no difference. What they have in common, shall we also say what is *unworthy* about it all, is that somebody must be blamed for the fact that we suffer — in short, that the sufferer prescribes for himself the honey of revenge for his pain. The objects of this requirement for revenge as a requirement for *pleasure* are circumstantial causes: the sufferer finds occasions everywhere to cool his petty revenge — if he is a Christian, to repeat, he finds them in *himself*... The Christian and the anarchist — both are *décadents*. — But even when the Christian condemns, slanders, besmirches the "world," he does it with the same instinct with which the socialist worker condemns, slanders, besmirches *society*: the "Last Judgment" itself is still the sweet consolation of revenge — the same revolution as that expected by the socialist worker, only somewhat further off... The "beyond" itself — why have a beyond, if not as a means of besmirching this world?...

35.

Critique of décadence-*morality*. — An "altruistic" morality, a morality in which selfishness *atrophies* — remains a bad sign whatever the circumstances. This applies to individuals and especially to peoples. When selfishness starts to be lacking then the best is lacking. To instinctively choose what will harm one's *self*, to be *attracted* by "disinterested motives," almost provides the formula for *décadence*. "Not to pursue one's *own* purpose" — that is just a moral fig leaf for a quite different, namely physiological state of affairs: "I cannot *find* my purpose anymore"... Disgregation of the instincts! — When the human turns altruistic it is all over with him. — Instead of saying naïvely "*I* am not worth anything anymore," the moral lie in the mouth of the *décadent* says: "Nothing is worth anything — *life* is worth nothing"... In the end, such a verdict remains a great danger, and it is catching — on the whole morbid ground of society it will soon grow luxuriantly to tropical heights of concept-vegetation, now as religion (Christianity), now as philosophy (Schopenhauerism). In some instances, the miasma of just such poison-tree vegetation, rooted in decay, can contaminate *life* for ages, for millennia...

36.[74]

Morality for doctors. — The invalid is a parasite on society. In a certain state, it is bad form to continue to live. To vegetate

away in cowardly dependence on doctors and procedures after
the meaning of life, the *right* to life has disappeared, ought to
incur society's deep contempt. In addition, doctors ought to be
the instigators of this contempt — not prescriptions, but a new
dose of *disgust* toward their patients every day . . . To create a
new accountability, that of the doctor, for all cases where the
highest interest of life, of *ascending* life, demands the ruthless
suppression and dismissal of *degenerating* life — for example,
for the right to procreate, for the right to be born, for the right
to live . . . To die in a proud manner when it is no longer possible to live in a proud manner. Death chosen freely, death at the
right time, with brightness and joy, accomplished while surrounded by children and witnesses: so that a genuine farewell
is still possible, while the person saying farewell *is still there*, at
the same time a genuine reckoning of what has been achieved
and desired, a *summing-up* of life — all in contrast to the pitiable and horrifying comedy that Christianity has carried on
with the deathbed scene. We should not forget that it was
Christianity that debased the dying person's weakness into a
violation of the conscience, turning the very manner of death
into a value judgment on humans and their past life! — Here,
despite all cowardliness of prejudice, we should uphold above
all the proper, that is, physiological consideration of so-called
natural death: which in the end is just the "unnatural" one, a
suicide. You never come to grief through anyone else but yourself. Yet this is death in the most despicable circumstances, not
feely chosen, death at the *wrong* time, a coward's death. One
should, out of love for *life* — desire a different death, free, deliberate, not by chance and not by ambush . . . Finally, advice for
gentlemen pessimists and other *décadents*. We are not at liberty
to avoid being born: but we can rectify this mistake — for occasionally it is a mistake. — If you *do away* with yourself, you do
the most admirable thing possible: you almost deserve to live . . .
Society, what am I saying! *life* itself gains a greater advantage
through this than any "life" of denial, anemia and other merit
— you have freed others from having to look at you, you have

freed life of an *objection* . . . Pessimism, *pur, vert,*[75] *only proves itself* through the self-refutation of gentleman pessimists: we must go a step further into its logic, not just denying life with "will and representation," as did Schopenhauer — we must *first deny Schopenhauer* . . . By the way, pessimism, infectious as it is, does not, however, increase the morbidity of an age or race as a whole: it is the expression of these. You succumb to it as you do to cholera: you have to have a morbid enough proclivity for it already. Pessimism itself does not produce a single extra *décadent*; I recall the statistical evidence that during the years when cholera raged, there was no difference from other years in the number of deaths.[76]

37.

Whether we have become more moral. — As was to be expected, the whole *ferocity* of moral stultification that, as we all know, passes for morality itself in Germany was mobilized against my concept of "beyond good and evil" — : I could tell some pretty tales about that. Above all, I was asked to reflect on the "undeniable superiority" of our time in its ethical judgment, the genuine *progress* we have made here: in comparison with *us*, a Cesare Borgia should not be presented as a "superior human being" at all, as a kind of superhuman, as I present him . . . A Swiss editor of *Der Bund*,[77] having expressed his respect for the courage of such a venture, went so far as to "understand" the meaning of my works as being my attempt, through them, to abolish all decent sentiments. Much obliged![78] In reply I allow myself to pose the question *whether we have really become more moral.* The fact that the whole world believes this is already an objection . . . We modern humans, very tender, very fragile, taking and giving heed a hundredfold, actually do imagine that the delicate humanity we portray, this *achieved* unanimity in tolerance, helpfulness, mutual trust, is a positive advance that puts us far beyond Renaissance humans. But every era thinks like that, it *has to*. Certainly, we must not presume to put ourselves in Renaissance circumstances, even in thought:

our nerves could certainly not bear that reality, to say nothing of our muscles. With this incapacity, however, no progress is proved, but only another, later condition, weaker, more delicate, more fragile, out of which emerges by necessity a morality *rich in paying heed*. If we think away our delicacy and tardiness, our physiological aging, our "humanizing" morality would immediately lose its value as well — in itself, no morality has any value — : it would lower our estimation of ourselves. On the other hand, there is no doubt that we moderns, with our thick padding of humanity to avoid causing offence, would present a comedy to Cesare Borgia's contemporaries that would have them laughing themselves to death. In fact, we are inadvertently hugely amusing with our modern "virtues" . . . The reduction in instincts of animosity and mistrust — and presumably that is "progress" for us — represents just one of the results of our general reduction in *vitality*: it takes a hundred times more effort, more caution, to carry on so conditioned and late an existence. So there is mutual help and everyone is to a certain extent both a patient and nurse. Then that is called "virtue" — : among humans who knew life when it was different, fuller, more extravagant, more luxuriant, people would have had other words for it, "cowardice" perhaps, "wretchedness," "old wives' morality" . . . Our tempering of custom — that is my proposition, it is, if you like, my *innovation* — is a result of decline: on the other hand, the harshness and dreadfulness of custom can be a result of superfluity of life: for then much can also be risked, much can be demanded, much can also be *squandered*. What was once the spice of life would be *poison* for us . . . To be indifferent — even that is a form of strength — for that, we are likewise too old, too late: our morality of sympathy, which I have been the first to warn against and which one could term *l'impressionisme morale*,[79] is one further expression of the physiological overexcitability that characterizes all things *décadent*. The movement that tried to parade as scientific with Schopenhauer's *morality of compassion* — a most inauspicious attempt! — is the true *décadence* movement in morality, and as such it is closely connected to Christian morality. Strong eras, *noble* cultures see something despicable in compassion, in loving thy neighbor, in the lack of selfhood and self-reliance. — Epochs are to be measured according to their *positive strengths* — with the result that the period of the Renaissance, so extravagant and so portentous, is established as the last *great* epoch, and we, we moderns with our anxious care for the self and our loving thy neighbor, with our virtues of work, modesty, fairness, scientific method — acquisitive, economical, mechanical — appear as a *weak* epoch . . . Our virtues are conditioned, are *provoked* by our weakness . . . "Equality," a certain factual rapprochement that merely finds expression in the theory of "equal rights," is essentially part of the decline: the gulf between one human and another, one class and another, the profusion of types, the will to be oneself, to stand out, what I call the *pathos of distance*, characterizes every *strong* epoch. The tension and range between extremes is becoming less and less nowadays — in the end the extremes themselves blur into similarity . . . All our political theories *and* state constitutions, with the "German Reich" as no exception, are consequences, necessary results of decline: the unconscious effect of *décadence* has become master right down to the ideals of individual sciences. My objection to the whole of sociology in England and France is still that it knows from experience only the *model of decay* for society and, completely innocently, takes its own decaying instincts as the *norm* for sociological value judgments. The *declining* life, the removal of all organizing powers that partition, create a gulf, and form upper and lower ranks, is formulated into an *ideal* by the sociology of today . . . Our socialists are *décadents*, but even Mr. Herbert Spencer is a *décadent* — he sees something desirable in the victory of altruism! . . .

38.[80]

My concept of freedom. — The value of a thing sometimes lies not in what can be achieved with it but in how much has been paid for it — what it *costs* us. I shall give an example. Liberal institutions immediately stop being liberal once they have been achieved: in time, there is nothing worse and more detrimental to freedom than liberal institutions. We all know *what* they set in motion: they undermine the will to power, they are the leveling of hill and dale exalted to a morality, they make everything small, cowardly and pleasurable — the herd animal triumphs with them every time. Liberalism: in plain language *herd-animalization* . . . While people campaign for them, these institutions produce quite different effects; they do indeed greatly promote freedom. On closer inspection, it is war that produces these effects, the war *for* liberal institutions which, as war, lets the *illiberal* instincts persist. And war fosters freedom. For what is freedom! That we have the will to self-accountability. That we maintain the distance separating us. That we are increasingly indifferent to toil, hardness, renunciation, even to life. That we are prepared to sacrifice human beings to our cause, not excluding ourselves. Freedom means that the manly instincts, joyous in war and victory, hold mastery over other instincts like, for example, "happiness." The human being *who has become free*, and much more so the *spirit* that has become free, tramples underfoot the despicable brand of complacency dreamed up by shopkeepers, Christians, cows, women, the English and other democrats. The free human being is a *warrior*. — How does freedom gauge itself, in the individual or in a people? By the resistance that must be overcome and the effort it takes to remain *on top*. The highest type of free human being should be sought where the highest resistance is continually overcome: five paces from tyranny, right at the threshold of the danger of bondage. This is psychologically true if we understand by the term "tyrants" the most ruthless and terrible instincts that call forth the maximum of authority and discipline toward oneself — the finest type is Julius Caesar — ; this is politically true, too, if you just take a stroll through history. The peoples who were worth something, *became* worthy, never did so under liberal institutions: *great danger* made them into something worthy of respect: danger teaching us only then to know our resources, our virtues, our weapons of defense, our *spirit* — forcing us to be strong . . . *First* principle: you must need to be strong: or you never will be. — Those great hothouses for strong, for the strongest kind of human being there has ever been, the aristocratic communities after the fashion of Rome and Venice, understood freedom in exactly the same sense as I understand the word: as something that you have and have *not*, that you *want*, that you *conquer* . . .

39.

Critique of modernity. — Our institutions are no longer any good: everyone is unanimous on that. But that lies not with them, rather with *us*. Now that we have lost all instincts from which institutions grow, we lose the institutions themselves, because *we* are no longer any good for them. Democratism has always been the declining form of organizing force: in *Human, All Too Human* I, 318 {§472}, I have already characterized modern democracy, together with its half measures like the "German Reich," as a *declining form of the state*. For there to be institutions, there must be a kind of will, instinct, imperative, antiliberal to the point of malice: the will to tradition, to authority, to responsibility for centuries to come, to *solidarity* in chains of generations forwards and backwards *in infinitum*. If this will is there, something like the *imperium Romanum* is founded: or like Russia, the *only* power that nowadays incorporates permanence, that can wait, that can still promise something — Russia, the antithesis to the miserable European penchant for small states and nervousness that has entered a critical stage with the foundation of the German Reich . . . The entire West no longer has the instincts from which institutions grow, from which the *future* grows: perhaps nothing goes so much against the grain of its "modern spirit." One lives for today, one lives at great speed — one lives very irresponsibly: and precisely this is dubbed "freedom." What *makes* institutions out of institutions is despised, hated, rejected: everyone perceives a danger of new enslavement every time the word "authority" is said out loud. The *décadence* in the value-instincts of our politicians, of our political parties, has gone as far as this: *they instinctively prefer* whatever disintegrates, whatever accelerates the end . . . witness *modern marriage*. Clearly, all rationality has vanished from modern marriage: however, that does not provide an argument against marriage, but against modernity. The rationale for marriage — legally, this lay in the sole responsibility of the husband: with that the marriage had stability, whereas today it is lame in both legs. The rationale for marriage — that lay in its principle of indissolubility: through this it achieved an emphasis that, set against the fortuity of sentiment, passion and moment, knew *how to make itself heard*. Likewise the choice of spouse lay within the responsibility of families. With the growing indulgence toward the *love*-match, the actual basis of marriage, that which *makes* it into an institution, has been eliminated. An institution is never, ever founded on an idiosyncrasy, and marriage is *not*, as I said, founded on "love" — it is founded on the sexual drive, on the drive for property (wife and child as property), on the *drive for control*, which constantly organizes the smallest structure of control, the family, and which *needs* children and heirs in order to retain, physiologically, an achieved amount of power, influence, wealth, in order to prepare long-term tasks and instinctive solidarity down the centuries. Marriage as an institution already comprises approval for the greatest and most enduring form of organization: if society as a whole cannot *guarantee* itself as far as the most distant generations, then marriage has absolutely no meaning. — Modern marriage has *lost* its meaning — therefore, it is being abolished. —

40.[81]

The labor question. — The stupidity, basically the degeneration of instincts that lies at the heart of *all* stupidity today, lies in the fact that there is a labor question. *One does not ask* about certain things: instinct's first imperative. — I really do not see

what anyone can want to do with the European worker now
that he has been turned into a question. He is far too well off
not to ask for more, and to ask more presumptuously, every
step of the way. In the end, he has numbers on his side. The
hope is long gone that a modest and self-sufficient kind of human
of the Chinese type might develop here into a class: and this
would have made sense, it would almost have been a necessity.
And what did people do? — Everything to nip in the bud even
the possibility for that — we have, through our most irresponsible thoughtlessness, entirely destroyed the instincts by means
of which the worker is made possible as a class, possible *to
himself.* The worker has been deemed fit for military service, he
has been given the right to organize, the political right to vote:
hardly surprising, is it, if the worker today construes his existence as a state of distress (expressed morally as *injustice* —)?
But I ask again, what do we *want*? If we want an end, we must
want the means as well: if we want slaves, we are fools to raise
them to be masters. —

41.

"Freedom that I do *not* mean . . ."[82] — In such times as
now, to be delivered over to one's instincts is just one more
catastrophe. These instincts contradict, interfere with, destroy
one another: I have already defined the *modern* as a physiological self-contradiction. The rationale of education would want
at least one of these instinct-systems to be *paralyzed* by an iron
pressure in order to allow another to come into force and
become strong, become master. Today you would first have to
make the individual possible by *paring down*: possible, that
means *whole* . . . The exact opposite happens: the claim to
independence, to free development, to *laisser aller*[83] is most
vehemently made by precisely those for whom no rein *would
be too tight* — this applies *in politicis*, this applies in art. But
that is a symptom of *décadence*:[84] our modern concept "freedom" is one more proof of the degeneration of instincts. —

42.

Where faith is needed. — Nothing is rarer among moralists and saints than uprightness; perhaps they say the opposite, maybe they *believe* it themselves. For when a belief is more useful, effective, convincing than *conscious* hypocrisy, then hypocrisy instinctively becomes *innocent* straight away: first principle for an understanding of great saints. Even with philosophers, another kind of saint, their whole craft has the result that they only allow certain truths: namely, those for which their craft has *public* sanction — truths of *practical* reason, to speak Kantian. They know what they *must* prove, they are practical in that — they recognize each other by the fact that they agree upon "the truths." — "Thou shalt not lie" — in plain language: Mr. Philosopher, *beware* of speaking the truth . . .

43.

Said into the conservatives' ear. — What people did not know earlier, what they do know today, could know — a *regression*, a turnaround in any shape or form is completely impossible. At least we physiologists know that. Yet all priests and moralists have believed in it — they *wanted* to steer humanity back, to *screw* it back to an *earlier* stage of morality. Morality has always been a bed of Procrustes.[85] In this, even the politicians have emulated the preachers of virtue: even today there are still parties who dream as their goal the *crabwalk*[86] of all things. But nobody is at liberty to be a crab. We have no choice: we *must* move forward, which means progressing *step by step further into décadence* (— this is *my* definition of modern "progress" . . .). One can *obstruct* this development, and by means of the obstruction, stem and accumulate *décadence* itself, making it more vehement and *sudden*: more cannot be done. —

44.

My concept of genius. — Great men, like great times, are explosives in which immense energy is accumulated; their precondition, historical and physiological, is that a long time passes while they are collected, heaped up, saved up and preserved for — that a long time passes with no explosion.[87] If tension becomes too great within the mass, the most random stimulus is sufficient to call forth into the world the "genius," the "deed," the great destiny. Then the context, era, "Zeitgeist," "public opinion" are irrelevant! — Take the case of Napoleon. France during the Revolution, and prerevolutionary France even more, would have produced the most antithetical type to Napoleon: it *did* produce that type. And because Napoleon was *different*, the heir of a stronger, longer, older civilization than the shattered France that was going up in smoke, he became master there, he alone *was* master there. Great men are necessary, but chance dictates the timing of their appearance; that they almost always master their time is only because they are stronger, they are older, their preparation has taken longer. There is a connection between the hero and his epoch like that between strong and weak or old and young: the epoch is, relatively speaking, always much younger, thinner, more immature, less certain, more childish. — The fact that thinking on this in France today is *very different* (in Germany, too: but that is not important), that there, the theory of milieu,[88] truly a neurotic's theory, has become sacrosanct and virtually scientific, finding credence even among physiologists, all of this "has a bad smell," it makes one's spirits low. — In England, people think in the same way, yet nobody will mind that.[89] For the English, there are two ways to accommodate genius and "the great man": either the *democratic* way in the fashion of Buckle or the *religious* way in the fashion of Carlyle. — The *danger* that lies in great humans and great times is extraordinary; exhaustion of every kind and sterility dogs their steps. The great human is an end; the great era, the Renaissance for example, is an end. The genius — in work, in deed — is necessarily a squanderer: *that he expends himself* is what makes him great . . . The instinct of self-preservation is, as it were, shelved; the overwhelming pressure on him while

his energy flows out prohibits any such restraint or foresight.
People call that "self-sacrifice"; they praise his inherent "heroism," his indifference toward his own welfare, his devotion to
an idea, a great thing, a fatherland: all misunderstandings . . .
He streams out, he overflows, he uses himself up, he does not
spare himself — with fatality, doom-laden, involuntarily, just
as the river overflows its banks involuntarily. But because we
owe much to such explosives, we have given them much in
return: for example, a form of *higher morality* . . . For that is the
nature of human gratitude: it *misunderstands* its benefactors. —

45.[90]

The criminal and matters related to him. — The criminal
type: that is the type of the strong human in unfavorable circumstances, a strong human rendered sick. He lacks the wilderness, a certain freer and more dangerous nature and form of
existence where everything to do with attack and defense in
the strong human's instinct *is valid.* Society proscribes his *virtues*; his most vigorous drives, those that he has brought with
him, immediately intermingle with oppressive affects, with
suspicion, fear, dishonor. But this is almost the *recipe* for physiological degeneration. Whoever must do in secret the thing he
can do best and likes most, with prolonged tension, caution,
cunning, becomes anemic; and because he always reaps danger, persecution, catastrophe from his instincts, his feelings
also turn against these instincts — he feels them fatalistically.
It is our society, our tame, mediocre, castrated society that
necessarily debases the natural human, hailing from the mountains or from adventures at sea, into a criminal. Or almost
necessarily: for there are cases where such a human proves to be
stronger than society: the Corsican Napoleon is the most
famous instance. For the problem before us here, the evidence
of Dostoevsky[91] is relevant — Dostoevsky, by the way the only
psychologist from whom I had something to learn: he is one of
the most beautiful serendipities of my life, even more than the

discovery of Stendhal. This *deep* human, who was right ten times over to place little value on the superficial Germans, found the Siberian prisoners, in whose midst he lived for a long period, hardened criminals one and all for whom there was no way back into society, very different from what he expected — rather as though they had been carved from the best, hardest and most valuable wood that could possibly grow on Russian soil. Let us generalize the case of the criminal: let us think of natures who, for whatever reason, fall foul of public approval, who know they are not looked upon as beneficial and useful — that chandala-feeling that one does not count as an equal but as an unworthy, polluting outcast. All such natures have a subterranean color to their thoughts and deeds; everything about them becomes paler than it does for those whose existence basks in light of day. But nearly all forms of existence we find excellent today have formerly lived in this semi-sepulchral atmosphere, the scientific character, the artist, the genius, the free spirit, the actor, the merchant, the great discoverer . . . As long as the *priest* rated as the supreme type, *every* valuable kind of human was devalued . . . The time will come — I guarantee that— when he will rate as the *lowest*, as *our* chandala, as the most false, unprincipled human . . . I direct attention to how even now, under the mildest regime of customs that has ever held sway on earth, in Europe at least, every deviation, every lengthy, all-too-lengthy *submergence*, every unusual, opaque form of existence brings us closer to the type of which the criminal is the perfect instance. All innovators of the spirit have borne for a time the pallid and fatalistic sign of the chandala on their brow: *not* because they were seen as that, but because they themselves felt the dreadful chasm dividing them from all that is established and in good standing. Nearly every genius as part of their development experiences the "Catilin-arian existence,"[92] a feeling of hatred, revenge and rebellion against everything that already *is*, that no longer *becomes* . . . Cataline — the pre-existing form of *every* Caesar. —

46.

Here the view is free.[93] — It can be elevation of soul when a philosopher remains silent; it can be love when he contradicts himself; a politeness that tells lies is possible in one who knows. Not without delicacy has it been said: *il est indigne des grands cœurs de répandre le trouble, qu'ils ressentent:*[94] only one must add that not to be afraid *of the unworthiest things* can likewise be greatness of soul. A woman who loves, sacrifices her honor; a knower who "loves," perhaps sacrifices his humanity; a God who loved, became a Jew . . .

47.[95]

Beauty no accident. — Even the beauty of a race or family, its grace and goodness in all gestures, has to be worked at: like genius, it is the end result of the accumulated work of generations. People must have made great sacrifices to good taste, they must have done many things and left many things undone for its sake — France in the seventeenth century is admirable in both — it must have been their selective principle for society, place, clothing, sexual gratification, they must have preferred beauty to advantage, habit, opinion, lethargy. Supreme guideline: even in their own eyes, people should not "let themselves go." — Good things are immeasurably expensive: and the rule always applies that whoever *has* them is a different person from the one who *acquires* them. Everything good is legacy: anything that is not inherited is imperfect, is a beginning . . . In Athens at the time of Cicero, who expressed his surprise at the fact, men and youths were vastly superior to women in beauty: but what work and effort the male sex had demanded of itself for centuries there in the service of beauty! — We really should not misunderstand their method for this: a mere training of feelings and thoughts is practically nothing (— herein lies the great mistake of German education, which is completely illusory): first, the *body* must be talked round. A strict maintenance of significant, chosen gestures, a pact to live only among humans who do not "let themselves go," is quite sufficient to attract notice and selection: in two, three generations, everything has been *internalized*. It is decisive for the destiny of peoples and humanity that culture should begin at the *correct* point — *not* in the "soul" (as was the fateful superstition of priests and half-priests): the correct point is the body, gesture, diet, physiology, the *rest* follows from these . . . For that reason, the Greeks remain the *foremost cultural event* in history — they knew, they *did* what was necessary; Christianity, which has despised the body, has up till now been the greatest misfortune of humanity. —

48.

Progress in my sense. — I too speak of a "return to nature," although it is not actually a going back, rather a *coming up* — up to high, free, even dreadful nature and naturalness, the kind that plays with great tasks, *is entitled* to play . . . To speak through an *image*: Napoleon was an example of a "return to nature" as I understand it (for instance, *in rebus tacticis*,[96] still more in strategy, as the military knows). — But Rousseau — where did *he* actually want to go back to? Rousseau, the first modern human, idealist and *canaille* in a single human; who needed moral "dignity" to survive the sight of himself; sick with unbridled vanity and unbridled self-loathing. Even this monster who took up position at the threshold of the new age wanted a "return to nature" — I ask again, where did Rousseau want to go back to? — I still hate Rousseau *in* the Revolution, it is the world-historical expression of this duality of idealist and *canaille*. The bloodstained farce with which this Revolution took its course, its "immorality," does not concern me much: what I hate is its Rousseauesque *morality* — the so-called "truths" of the Revolution with which it still exerts an effect and persuades anything flat and mediocre over to its side. The doctrine of equality! . . . But there is no more poisonous venom: for it *seems* to be preached by justice itself, whereas it is actually the *end* of justice . . . "Equality to equals, inequality to unequals" — *that* would be the true speech of equality: and, following from this, "never make unequals equal."[97] — The fact that everything surrounding the doctrine of equality has been so horrifying and bloodstained has given a sort of glory and glow to this "modern idea" par excellence, so that the Revolution as a *spectacle* has seduced even the noblest minds. Yet in the end, that is no reason to show it more respect. — I see only one person who experienced it as it should be experienced, with *disgust* — Goethe . . .

49.[98]

Goethe — not a German event, but a European one: a magnificent attempt to overcome the eighteenth century through a return to nature, through raising himself *up* to the naturalness of the Renaissance, a sort of self-overcoming on the part of that century. — He bore its strongest instincts in himself:[99] the sensibility, the nature-idolatry, the antihistorical, the idealistic, the unreal and the revolutionary (— the latter is just a manifestation of the unreal). He was able to muster history, natural science, antiquity, likewise Spinoza, and practical activity above all; he surrounded himself with clearly defined horizons; he did not break off his connections with life, he took part in it; undaunted, he took as much as was possible upon himself, above himself, within himself. What he wanted was *totality*; he fought against the separation of reason, sensuality, feeling, will (— preached with alarming scholasticism by *Kant*, the antipode to Goethe), he disciplined himself into wholeness, he *created* himself . . . In the midst of a century inclined to unreality, Goethe was a convinced realist: he said Yes to everything related to him in this respect — he had no greater experience than that *ens realissimum*[100] by the name of Napoleon. Goethe conceived of a human who is strong, highly cultured, skilled in all physical functions, holding himself in check, paying himself respect, who has the prerogative to grant himself the whole range of wealth and naturalness, being strong enough for this freedom; the human of tolerance, not from weakness but from strength, because he knows how to turn to advantage what would destroy the average nature; the human for whom nothing else is forbidden than *weakness*, whether it goes by the name of vice or virtue . . . Such a spirit *who has become free* stands with joyful and trusting fatalism in the midst of the universe, in the *belief* that only what is isolated is to be shunned, and that in the whole, everything is redeemed and affirmed — *he no longer negates* . . . But such a belief is the highest of all possible beliefs: I have baptized it with the name of *Dionysus*. —

50.

One could say that in a certain sense, the nineteenth century *also* strove for all that Goethe in person strove for: universality of understanding, of acceptance, openness to all and sundry, a reckless realism, a respect for all facts. How did it happen that the end result was not Goethe but chaos, a nihilistic sigh, an I-am-completely-lost, an instinct for lethargy that *in praxi* continually produces *a harking back to the eighteenth century*? (— for example, as Romanticism of feeling, as altruism and hypersentimentality, as feminism in taste, as socialism in politics). Is not the nineteenth century, especially at its close, merely a reinforced, *brutalized* eighteenth century, in other words a century of *décadence*?[101] So that Goethe was just incidental, not just for Germany but for the whole of Europe, something beautiful in vain? — But we misunderstand great humans if we view them from the miserable perspective of public benefit. That no benefit can be derived from them, *even that belongs perhaps to greatness* . . .

51.[102]

Goethe is the last German for whom I have any respect: he would have felt three things the same way as I do — we also agree on the "Cross"[103] . . . People often ask me why I actually write in *German*: nowhere am I read worse than in my fatherland. But in the end who knows whether I even *want* to be read today? — To create things for the epoch to try its teeth on in vain; in form, *in substance* to strive for some tiny eternity — I have never been modest enough to demand any less of myself. The aphorism, the apothegm, in which among Germans I am the first to be a master, are the forms of "eternity"; it is my ambition to say in ten sentences what anyone else says in a book — what anyone else does *not* say in a book . . .

I have given humanity the deepest book in its possession, my *Zarathustra*:[104] soon, I shall give it its most independent one. —

What I Owe the Ancients.[1]

Finally, a word about that world to which I sought access, to which I have perhaps found a new point of access — the ancient world. Here again my taste, which might well be the opposite of a tolerant taste, is far removed from saying Yes indiscriminately: it says Yes reluctantly, preferably No, best of all, nothing . . . The same goes for whole cultures, the same goes for books — the same goes for places and landscapes. Basically, only a small number of books from antiquity count in my life; the most famous are not among them. My sense of style, of the epigram as style, awoke almost the moment I encountered Sallust. I have not forgotten my worthy teacher Corssen's astonishment when he had to give his worst Latin scholar the highest grade — at one stroke I had done the lot. Concise, severe, with as much substance as possible at the core and a chill malice toward "fine words" and "fine feelings" — I understood myself in all this. You can recognize in me a very serious attempt at *Roman* style, at "*aere perennius*"[2] in style, even in my *Zarathustra*. — And it was no different when I encountered Horace. No poet up to this day has given me the same artistic delight as I felt from the outset with an ode by Horace. In some languages what is achieved there is not even *desirable*. This mosaic of words where every word pours out its force as sound, as place, as concept, right and left and all around, this minimum in range and number of signs, this maximum of energy in the signs thereby achieved — all this is Roman and, if you will believe it, *noble par excellence*. Set against it, all the rest of poetry is rather too popular — just talkativeness about feelings . . .

2.

I do not owe the Greeks anything like such strong impressions; and, just to emphasize the point, they *cannot* be what the Romans are to us. One does not *learn* from the Greeks — their manner is too foreign, as well as being too fluid to have an imperative, "classical" effect. Who could ever have learned to write from a Greek! Who could ever have learned that *without* the Romans! . . . Please do not object by citing Plato. With regard to Plato, I am a thorough skeptic and have always been incapable of admiring the *artist* Plato, as is customary among scholars. At the end of the day, among the ancients themselves I have the most refined arbiters of taste on my side. To me, it seems that Plato throws together every form of style, by which he is the *first décadent* of style: he has something on his conscience similar to the Cynics, who invented the *satura Menippea*.[3] For Platonic dialogue, this dreadfully complacent and childish form of dialectic, to act as a stimulus, you must never have read good French writers — Fontenelle, for example. Plato is boring. — When all is said and done, my mistrust of Plato goes deep: I find him so detached from all the basic instincts of the Hellenes, so unfortunately moralistic, so preexistent-Christian — he already uses the concept "good" as the highest concept — that in preference to any other I would prefer to use the tough phrase "higher swindle," or idealism if people like that better — for the whole phenomenon of Plato. We have paid dearly for the fact that this Athenian went to school with the Egyptians (— or with the Jews in Egypt? . . .). In the great disaster of Christianity, Plato is the ambiguity and fascination dubbed "ideal," that made it possible for nobler natures of antiquity to be mistaken about themselves and go over the *bridge* leading to the "Cross" . . .

And how much of Plato there still is in the concept "Ch[...] in the construction, system, practice of the Church! — [...] relaxation, my preference, my *cure* for all Platonism has always been *Thucydides*. Thucydides and, perhaps, Machiavelli's *principe*[4] are chiefly related to myself through the absolute determination not to be taken in and to see reason in *reality* — *not* in "reason," still less in "morality" . . . Nothing is so thorough a cure as Thucydides for the Greeks' miserable embellishment of things into an ideal that the "classically educated" young man carries off with him into life as reward for his grammar-school dressage. Thucydides must be turned line by line and his ulterior motives divined as well as his words: there are few thinkers so rich in ulterior motives. In him, the *culture of sophists*,[5] meaning the *culture of realists*, reaches its perfect expression: that invaluable movement amid the moral- and ideal-swindling of the Socratic school just then breaking out everywhere. Greek philosophy as the *décadence*[6] of Greek instinct; Thucydides as the great sum, the last revelation of that strong, stern, hard actuality lying in the ancient Hellenes' instincts. In the end, *courage* in the face of reality decides between such natures as Thucydides and Plato: Plato is a coward in the face of reality — *consequently* he flees into the ideal; Thucydides has control over *himself*, consequently he retains control over things as well . . .

3.

Teasing out "beautiful souls,"[7] "the golden mean" and other perfections in the Greeks such as admiring their composure in greatness, their ideal cast of mind and high simplicity[8] — I was preserved from this "high simplicity," ultimately a *niaiserie allemande*,[9] by the psychologist within me. I saw their strongest instinct, the will to power, I saw them shudder at the unbridled force of this drive — I saw all their institutions sprout from protective measures designed to render them mutually safe from the *explosive* within them. The immense internal tension then released itself externally as dreadful and reckless enmity:

each other apart so that the citizens of each
wn peace. People needed to be strong: dan-
— it lurked everywhere. The splendidly sup-
1e foolhardy realism and immoralism that
Hellene, is a *necessity*, not a "nature." It came as
, it was not there at the beginning. And at feasts
nobody wanted anything but to feel they were *on
top*, to show themselves to be on top: these are means of glorifying oneself, in some circumstances of making oneself feared
. . . Judging the Greeks by their philosophers in a German
manner, perhaps making use of the philistinism[10] of the Socratic schools for information about *what* Hellenism was at its
core! . . . Philosophers really were the *décadents* of Hellenism,
the countermovement to ancient, noble taste (— against the
agonal instinct, against the polis, against the value of race,
against the authority of descent). The Socratic virtues were
preached *because* the Greeks had lost them: hot-tempered,
timorous, changeable, comedians one and all, they had a few
too many reasons to allow morality to be preached to them.
Not that it would have helped at all: but grand words and
postures suit *décadents* so well . . .

4.

I was the first who, in appreciation of the more ancient
instinct of the Hellenes, still prolific and even overflowing, took
that wonderful phenomenon seriously that bears the name of
Dionysus: it is only explicable from a *surplus* of energy. Whoever examines the Greeks, like that most distinguished expert
on their culture alive today, Jakob Burckhardt[11] in Basel,
immediately recognized something special afoot: Burckhardt
appended to his *Culture of the Greeks*[12] a section of his own on
the said phenomenon. If you want the antithesis, take a look at
the almost entertaining poverty of instinct among German
philologists when they approach the Dionysian. Especially the
celebrated Lobeck who, with the commendable reliability of a

desiccated bookworm, crept into this world of mysterious states and convinced himself he was being scientific when all the time he was being nauseatingly superficial and childish — Lobeck, with all the trappings of erudition, gave one to understand that there was no substance in all these curiosities. Actually, the priests might have communicated something of value to participants of such orgies, for example, that wine stimulates pleasure, that if need be, the human can live on fruit, that plants bloom in spring, wither in autumn. Concerning that disconcerting wealth of rites, symbols and myths of orgiastic origin with which the ancient world is quite literally overgrown, Lobeck finds here the occasion to be a degree more contrived. He writes in *Aglaophamus* I, 672: "When the Greeks had nothing better to do they laughed, jumped, rushed round, or, as is sometimes the human's wont, sat down and wept and lamented. *Others* later joined them and sought a reason of some kind for their conspicuous conduct; and thus the myriad legends and myths emerged as an explanation for these customs. On the other hand, people believed that the *comical antics* which now took place on feast days necessarily belonged to those festivals, and retained them as an indispensable part of the worship."[13] — That is despicable twaddle, nobody will take a man like Lobeck seriously for a moment. We are affected quite differently when we examine the concept "Greek" as envisaged by Winckelmann and Goethe and find it incompatible with that other element out of which Dionysian art emanated — with the orgiastic. Actually I do not doubt that Goethe completely excluded anything of that nature from the possibilities of the Greek soul. *Consequently, Goethe did not understand the Greeks.* For only in the Dionysian mysteries, in the psychology of the Dionysian state, does the Hellenic instinct express its *fundamental fact* — its "will to life." *What* did the Hellene vouch for with these mysteries? *Eternal* life, the eternal return of life; the future promised and sanctified in the past; the triumphant Yes to life beyond death and change; *true* life as collective continuation through procreation, through the mysteries of sexuality. Therefore, the Greeks regarded the *sexual* symbol as the quintessential symbol to worship, the really deep significance within the whole of antique piety. Every single detail of the act of procreation, pregnancy, birth, aroused the highest and most ceremonious feelings. In the lore regarding mysteries, *pain* is sanctified: "birth pangs" sanctify pain in general — all development and growth, everything that pledges the future, *presupposes* pain . . . For there to be eternal joy in creation, for the will to life to affirm itself eternally, there *must* be eternal "birth torment" as well . . . The word Dionysus signifies all this: I know of no higher symbolism than this *Greek* symbolism, that of the Dionysian. In it, the deepest instinct of life, that of the future of life, of the eternity of life, is experienced as religion — even the path to life, procreation, as the *sacred* path . . . Only Christianity, with its fundamental *ressentiment against* life, rendered sexuality something unclean: it threw *filth* at the beginning, at the precondition, of our life . . .

5.

The psychology of the orgiastic as an outpouring of the feeling for life and energy, within which even pain works as a stimulus, gave me the key to the concept of *tragic* feeling that has been misunderstood by Aristotle as well as, in particular, by our pessimists. Tragedy is so far from being something to prove the pessimism of the Hellenes in Schopenhauer's sense that it can actually be viewed as constituting a decisive repudiation of it and its *contrary case*. Saying Yes to life even in its strangest and hardest problems; the will to life, rejoicing in its own inexhaustibility through the *sacrifice* of its highest types — *that* is what I called Dionysian, *that* is what I discovered as the bridge to the psychology of the *tragic* poet. *Not* in order to break free from horror and compassion, not in order to be purged of a dangerous emotion by vehemently discharging it — as Aristotle understood it — : but, beyond horror and compassion, *to be oneself* that eternal joy in becoming — this joy that also even incorporates the *joy in destruction* . . . And with that, I touch again on my former point of departure — the *Birth of Tragedy* was my first revaluation of all values: with that, I put myself back into the soil from which grow my will, my *ability* — I, the last disciple of the philosopher Dionysus[14] — I, the teacher of the eternal recurrence . . .

The Hammer Speaks.

Thus Spoke Zarathustra, III.[1]

"Why so hard!" — *the charcoal once said to the diamond:
"for are we not close relatives?"*

*Why so soft? Oh, my brothers, and so I ask you: are you not
— my brothers?*

*Why so soft, so pliable and yielding? Why is there so much
denial, renunciation in your hearts? so little destiny in your gaze?*

*And if you do not want to be destinies, if you do not want to
be unrelenting: how could you ever — conquer with me?*

*And if your hardness does not want to flash and cut and
shred: how could you ever — create with me?*

*For indeed, all those who create are hard. And you must think
it bliss to imprint your hand upon millennia as upon wax —*

*— Bliss to write on the will of millennia as on bronze —
harder than bronze, nobler than bronze. Only that which is
noblest is completely hard.*

*I place this new tablet over you, oh my brothers: become
hard!* — —

The Antichrist.[1]

Curse upon Christianity.

Foreword.[2]

This book belongs to the very few. Perhaps not a single one of them is alive yet. It might be those who understand my Zarathustra: how could I mistake myself for those for whom ears are growing already today? — Only the day after tomorrow belongs to me. Some are born posthu⟨mously⟩.[3]

The circumstances under which people understand me and then understand by necessity ⟨—⟩ I know them only too well. One must be righteous to the point of being harsh in intellectual matters just to withstand my gravity and passion. One must be practiced in living on mountains — in seeing the pathetic contemporary prattle about politics and national selfishness beneath oneself. One must have grown indifferent, never asking whether truth has a use, whether it will become someone's doom . . . A predilection of strength for questions no one has the courage to tackle today; courage for the forbidden; a predestination to the labyrinth.[4] An experience out of seven solitudes. New ears for new music. New eyes for the most distant. A new conscience for truths that have remained mute hitherto. And the will to economy of grand style: keeping one's strength, one's enthusiasm together . . . Respect for oneself; love of oneself; unconditional freedom toward oneself . . .

Well then! These alone are my readers, my true readers, my predestined readers: who cares about the rest? — The rest is mere humanity. One must be superior to humanity through strength, through loftiness of soul — through contempt . . .

FRIEDRICH NIETZSCHE.

1.[1]

— Let us look each other in the face. We are Hyperboreans[2] — we know well enough how remotely we live. "Neither by land nor sea will you find the way to the Hyperboreans": Pindar[3] already knew that about us. Beyond the North, the ice, death — *our* life, *our* happiness . . . We discovered happiness, we know the way, we found the exit out of entire millennia of the labyrinth. Who *else* found it? Perhaps the modern human? "I am at my wit's end;[4] I am everything that is at its wit's end" — sighs the modern human . . . We were sick at *this* modernity — at lazy peace, cowardly compromise, the whole virtuous uncleanliness of the modern Yes and No. This tolerance and *largeur*[5] of heart that "pardons" all because it "understands" all[6] is a sirocco for us. Better to live in ice than among modern virtues and other south winds! . . . We were brave enough, we spared neither ourselves nor others: but we still had no idea *what to do* with our bravery. We became gloomy, we were called fatalists. *Our* fate — that *was* fullness, tension, damming of forces. We thirsted for lightning and deeds, we kept ourselves as distant as possible from the happiness of weaklings, from "humility" . . . There was a thunderstorm in our air, the nature that we are turned dim — *for we had no way*. Formula of our happiness: a Yes, a No, a straight line, a *goal* . . . [7]

2.[8]

What is good? — Everything that heightens the feeling of power,[9] the will to power, power itself in humans.

What is bad? All that stems from weakness.[10]

What is happiness? The feeling that power is *growing*, that resistance is being overcome.[11]

Not contentment but more power, *not* peace at all but war; *not* virtue but proficiency (virtue in Renaissance-style, *virtù*, moraline-free virtue).[12]

The weak and deformed should perish: first principle of *our* love of humanity.[13] And we should even help them.

What is more harmful than any vice? — The act of compassion toward all who are deformed and weak — Christianity . . .

3.[14]

The problem I am posing here is not what should succeed humanity in the sequence of life forms (— the human is an *end* —): but which type of human we should *breed*, should *will*, as being of higher value, worthier of life, more certain of a future.

This higher-valued type has existed often enough before: but as a stroke of luck, as an exception, never as *willed*. Instead, *he* was precisely the thing most feared, up to this point he was practically *the* fearful; — and out of fear, the opposite type was willed, bred, *achieved*: the household pet, the herd animal, the human as sick animal — the Christian . . .

4.[15]

Humanity does *not* represent a development for the better or the stronger or the superior in the way this is believed today. "Progress" is merely a modern idea, that is, a false idea. The European of today remains,[16] in terms of value, deeply[17] inferior to the European of the Renaissance; further development is absolutely *not*, by any form of necessity, enhancement, intensification, strengthening.

In another sense, in individual cases there is continual success in the most diverse places in the world and from the most diverse cultures where[18] a *superior type* does in fact present itself: something that is a kind of superhuman in relation to humanity as a whole. Such serendipities of great success have always been possible and perhaps will always be possible. And even whole families, tribes, peoples can in certain circumstances represent just such a *lucky hit*.

5.[19]

One ought not to decorate and embellish Christianity: it has conducted a *war to the death* against this *superior* type of human, it has proscribed all the basic instincts of this type, from these instincts it has distilled evil, *the* evil one — the strong human as the typical reprehensible one, the "reprobate human." Christianity took the side of everything weak, lowly, deformed, it made an ideal out of *antagonism* toward the survival instincts of strong life; it debased the good sense of even the intellectually strongest natures by teaching people to perceive the supreme values of intellectuality as sinful, as deceptive, as *temptations*. The most lamentable example — the corruption of Pascal,[20] who believed in the corruption of his reason through original sin, whereas it was only corrupted by his Christianity! —

6.

It is a painful, horrid spectacle that has opened up before me: I have drawn back the curtain on the *corruption* of the human. This word, in my mouth, is at least shielded from one suspicion: that it contains a moral accusation of the human. It is — I want to stress again — *moraline-free* in intent: to the point where I perceive that corruption to be at its strongest precisely where people have aspired most consciously toward "virtue," toward "Godliness." One will have guessed already, I understand corruption in the sense of *décadence*: my assertion is that all values in which humanity today encapsulates its supreme desirability are *décadence-values*.

I call an animal, a species, an individual corrupted when it loses its instincts, when it chooses, when it *prefers* what is disadvantageous to it. A history of the "loftier feelings," of the "ideals of humanity" — and it is possible I shall have to tell it — would practically also be an explanation of *why* humans are so corrupt.

I regard life itself as instinct for growth, for duration, for accumulation of forces, for *power*: where the will to power is lacking, there will be decline. My assertion is that this power is *lacking* in all the supreme values of humanity — that values of decline, *nihilistic* values, hold sway under the holiest of names.

7.[21]

Christianity is called the religion of *compassion*. —[22] Compassion stands in opposition to the tonic affects that heighten[23] the energy of the feeling of life: it has a depressive effect. One loses strength when one is compassion⟨ate⟩. Through compassion,[24] the losses of strength that suffering in itself already br⟨ings⟩[25] to life are increased and multiplied. Suffering itself becomes infectious through compassion; under[26] certain circumstances a total loss of life and vital energy can thereby be reached that stands in an absurd relationship to the quantum of its cause (— the Nazarene's death a case in point).[27] That is the first standpoint; but there is another, more important one. If we were to measure compassion according to the value of the reactions it tends to produce, its life-threatening character appears in a much clearer light. On the whole, compassion cancels out the law of development, which is the law of *selection*. It preserves what is ripe for destruction, it resists in favor of life's dispossessed and condemned, it gives life itself, through the abundance of failures of every kind whose life it *sustains*, a gloomy and questionable aspect. We have been so bold as to call compassion a virtue (— in every *noble* morality it counts as weakness —);[28] we have gone further, we have made it *the* virtue, the ground and origin of all virtues — but of course, as we must constantly bear in mind⟨,⟩ only from the standpoint of a philosophy that was nihilistic, that ⟨wr⟩ote *denial of life* on its shiel⟨d⟩.[29] Here, Schopenhauer was within his rights: life is denied though com⟨passion⟩, made more *wo⟨rthy⟩ of denial* — compassion is the *praxis* of nihilism. To repeat: this depressive and contagious instinct[30] cancels out those instincts that are bent on supporting and raising the value of life: both as a *multiplier* of misery and *conservator* of all that is miserable, it is a major instrument[31] in the increase of *décadence*[32] — compassion persuades us to *nothingness*! . . . One does not[33] say "nothingness": instead, one says "the beyond"; or "God"; or "the *true* life"; or nirvana, redemption, bliss . . . This innocent rhetoric from the realm of religio-moral idiosyncrasy immediately appears *much less innocent* when one grasps *which* tendency swathes itself here in the mantle of sublime words: the tendency *hostile to life*. Schopenhauer was hostile to life: *therefore* compassion became a virtue for him . . . As we know, Aristotle[34] saw in compassion a sickly and dangerous condition for which one did well to take a purgative now and then:[35] he understood tragedy as a purgative. In fact, the instinct for life should make us search for a means to lance so sickly and dangerous a buildup of compassion as that[36] represented by the case of Schopenhauer (and unfortunately our whole literary and artistic *décadence* too, from St. Petersburg to Paris, from Tolstoy[37] to Wagner): so that it *bursts* . . . Nothing is unhealthier, within our unhealthy modernity, than Christian[38] compassion. To be a physician *here*, to be inexorable *here*, to wield the scalpel *here* — that belongs to *us*, that is *our* kind of love for humanity,[39] with that *we* are philosophers,[40] we Hyperboreans! — — —

8.[41]

It is necessary to say *who* we perceive as our opposite — the theologians and everything with theologian-blood in its veins — our whole philosophy . . . One needs to have seen the catastrophe at close quarters, or better still, experienced it oneself, one needs to have been almost destroyed by it, in order to no longer take a joke here (the freethinking of our gentlemen naturalists and physiologists is in my view a *joke* — they lack passion in these things, they do not *suffer* from them —). This poisoning reaches much further than one thinks: I rediscovered the theologian-instinct of arrogance wherever anyone today feels himself to be an "idealist," — wherever, thanks to a higher lineage,[42] anyone claims the right to look on reality with a superior and alienated glance . . .[43] The idealist has, just like the priest, all the great concepts in his hand (and not just in his hand!), he plays them off with a benevolent contempt against "understanding," the "senses," "honors," the "good life," "science," he sees such things as being *beneath* him, as damaging and seductive forces over whi⟨ch⟩ "the spirit" hovers in pure for-itself-ness: — as if humility, chastity, poverty, in one word, *holiness*, had not done unspeakably more harm hitherto than horrors and vices of any kind . . . The pure spirit is a pure lie . . . As long as the priest, this denier, slanderer, poisoner of life by *profession*, continues to be seen as a *superior* kind of human, there will be no answer to the question: what *is* truth?[44] We *have* already turned truth on its head if the conscious advocate of nothingness and denial is regarded as the representative of "truth" . . .

9.

I wage war on this theologian-instinct: I found its trace everywhere. Whoever has theologian-blood in his veins takes a crooked and dishonest stance on all things from the start. The pathos that develops out of this dubs itself *faith*: eyes closed to itself once and for all so as not to suffer from the sight of incurable falseness. A morality, a virtue, a holiness are fashioned for oneself out of this flawed optics on all things, *good* conscience is linked to *false* viewing — one demands that no *other* sort of optics may be of more value once they have made their own sacrosanct with the name "God," "redemption," "eternity." I continued to dig out the theologian-instinct everywhere: it is the most widespread, the genuinely *subterranean* form of falseness there is on earth. What a theologian perceives to be true *must* be false: in this we practically have a criterion for truth. It is his most fundamental self-preservation instinct that forbids reality to be honored at any point or even to get a word in edgewise. As far as theologian-influence reaches, *value-judgment* is stood on its head, the concepts "true" and "false" are necessarily[45] reversed: whatever is most damaging to life is here called "true," whatever raises it, intensifies, affirms, justifies and renders it triumphant, that is called "false" . . . If on occasion theologians, through the "conscience" of the rulers (*or* peoples —), reach out for *power*, let us not doubt *what* is happening at bottom each time: the will to the end, the *nihilistic* will wants power . . .

10.

Among Germans, it is immediately understood when I say that philosophy is ruined by theologian-blood. The Protestant pastor is the grandfather of German philosophy, Protestantism itself their *peccatum originale*.[46] Definition of Protestantism: half-sided paralysis of Christianity — *and* of reason . . .[47] One only has to say the words "Tübingen Seminary"[48] to realize *what* German philosophy at bottom is — an *insidious* theology. The Swabians are the best liars in Germany, they lie innocently . . . What caused the rejoicing at the arrival of *Kant* that went through the German scholarly world, three-quarters of which consists of the sons of pastors and teachers — what caused the German conviction, still finding an echo today, that with Kant a turn for the *better* had begun? Theologian-instinct in the German scholar guessed *what* was now possible again . . . A secret path to the old ideal stood open, the concept *"true* world," the concept of morality as *essence* of the world (these two most malicious errors[49] that ever existed!) were once again, thanks to a craftily clever[50] skepticism, if not provable, then at least no longer *refutable* . . . Reason, the *right* to reason, does not stretch that far . . . Reality had been turned into an "appearance"; a completely *mendacious* world, that of being, had been turned into reality . . . The success of Kant is merely theologian-success: Kant was, like Luther, like Leibniz, one more obstacle for a none-too-steady German integrity — —[51,52]

11.

One more word against Kant as *moralist*. A virtue must be *our* invention, *our* most personal self-defense and basic need: in every other sense it is merely a danger. What does not condition our life, *harms* it: to want a virtue just out of a feeling of respect for the concept "virtue," as Kant wanted, is harmful. "Virtue," "duty," "good in itself," the good characterized by impersonality and universal validity — are figments of the imagination in which decline, the last debilitation of life, the

Königsbergian Chineseness[53] find expression. The opposite is
demanded by the deepest laws of preservation and growth: that
each should invent for himself *his* virtue, *his* categorical imperative. A people will perish if it confuses *its* duty with the general concept of duty. Nothing causes deeper, more intimate
ruin than any "impersonal" duty, any sacrifice to the Moloch
of abstraction. — That Kant's categorical imperative was not
perceived as *life-threatening*! . . . The theologian-instinct alone
protected it! — An action to which one is compelled by the
instinct for life has its proof of being a *right* action by the pleasure it brings: and that nihilist with Christian-dogmatic bowels
interpreted pleasure as an *objection* . . . What destroys quicker
than working, thinking, feeling without inner necessity, without a deep personal choice, without *pleasure*? as an automaton
of "duty"? It is practically a *recipe* for *décadence*, even for idiocy[54] . . . Kant became an idiot. And that was the contemporary of *Goethe*! This disaster of a spider was considered as the
German philosopher — and is still! . . . I am wary of saying
what I think of the Germans . . . Did Kant not see in the French
Revolution the transition from the inorganic form of a state to
the *organic*? Did he not ask himself whether there might be a
circumstance that cannot be explained otherwise than by a predisposition for morality in humanity, such that with this, the
"tendency of humanity toward the good" could be *proved*, once
and for all? Kant's answer: "that is the Revolution." Mistake-
prone instinct in all and everything, anti-nature[55] as instinct,
German *décadence* as philosophy — *that is Kant!* — [56]

12.[57]

I set to one side a few skeptics, the decent type in the history
of philosophy: but the rest do not know the basic demands of
intellectual integrity. All these great enthusiasts and prodigies
act like little women — they consider "beautiful feelings" to be
already an argument, the "heaving bosom" to be a bellows for
the Godhead, conviction to be a *criterion* of truth. Then finally
Kant, in his "German"[58] innocence, tried[59] to organize this form

of corruption, this lack of intellectual conscience, into a science under the concept "practical reason": he invented a form of reason just for those cases in which one need not be concerned about reason, namely when morality, when the sublime command "thou shalt" makes itself heard. If we reflect that in almost all peoples, the philosopher is just a further development of the priestly type, then this legacy of the priest, this *counterfeiting before oneself,* is no longer[60] a surprise. If one has holy tasks, for example, improving, saving, redeeming humanity, if one bears the Godhead in one's bosom, is a mouthpiece for imperatives from the hereafter, then with such a mission one already stands[61] outside[62] mere rational valuations — already hallowed in oneself by such a task, already in oneself the type of a superior order! . . . What does a priest care about *science*? He stands too high for that! — And the priest has *ruled* up till now! He *determined* the concepts "true" and "untrue"! . . . [63]

13.[64]

Let us not underestimate this: *we ourselves,* we free spirits, already constitute a "revaluation of all values," an *incarnate* declaration of war and victory against all the old concepts of "true" and "untrue." The most valuable insights are discovered last; but the most valuable insights are *methods. All* methods, *all* prerequisites of our present-day scientism, have been for millennia subjected to the deepest contempt, on their account, people were excluded from "honest" society — branded as the "enemy of God," a despiser of truth, as one "possessed." Whoever had a scientific character was chandala . . . We have had the whole pathos of humanity against us — their concept of what truth *ought* to be, what the service of truth *ought* to be: every "thou shalt" has hitherto been directed *against* us . . . Our aims, our practices, our quiet, careful, mistrustful manner — to them it all seemed completely unworthy and contemptible. In the end, we are entitled to ask, with some justification, whether or not it was an aesthetic taste that kept humanity in blindness for so long: they demanded of truth a

picturesque effect, likewise they demanded that the connoisseur's knowledge should have a strong effect on the senses.
Our *modesty* was what offended their taste for longest . . . Oh,
how they figured it out, these turkey cocks of God — —

14.

We have learned different. We have become more modest in
every respect.[65] We no longer trace the human from the "spirit,"
from the "Godhead," we have put the human back among the
animals. We regard the human as the strongest animal because
the most cunning: one consequence of this is his spirituality.
On the other hand, we guard against an[66] arrogance that seeks
to make itself heard even here: as though the human had been
the great ulterior motive of animal evolution. The human is not
at all the crown of creation, every being has reached the same
stage of perfection alongside him . . . And in asserting this, we
are still asserting too much: relatively speaking, the human is
the most deformed animal, the sickliest, the one that has
strayed most perilous⟨ly⟩ from its instincts — of course, with
all that, also the *most interesting*! — Concerning animals, Descartes was the first who, with admirable courage, hazarded the
thought of viewing the animal as a *machina*:[67] our whole physiology labors to prove this proposition. And logically, we do
not exempt humans, as Descartes did: whatever we understand
of humans today is[68] understood precisely to the extent that
they are understood mechanically. Formerly one gave humans
"free will" as dowry from a higher order: today we have even
taken away the will in the sense that it must no longer be
understood as a faculty. The old word "will" serves only to
indicate a resultant, a sort of individual reaction that necessarily follows from a multitude of partly contradictory, partly
compatible stimuli: — the will no longer "effects," no longer
"moves" . . . In former times, one used to see in human consciousness, in the "mind," the proof of a higher lineage, of
divinity; in order to *perfect* humans, the advice given was to
draw the senses in, turtle-like, to cease to have contact with

earthly things, to shed the mortal shroud: then the main thing remained, the "pure spirit." We have thought better[69] of this too: we count the act of coming to consciousness, the "mind," as precisely a symptom of a relative imperfection of the organism, as testing, touching, making mistakes, as a tribulation that uses up an unnecessary amount of nervous energy — we deny that anything perfect at all can be produced so long as it is still produced consciously. "Pure spirit" is pure folly: if we discount the nervous system and the senses, the "mortal shroud," then *we miscount*[70] — nothing more! . . .

15.[71]

In Christianity, neither morality nor religion has any point of contact with reality. Nothing but imaginary *causes* ("God," "soul," "ego," "spirit," "free will" — or even "unfree"); nothing but imaginary *effects* ("sin," "redemption," "mercy," "punishment," "forgiveness of sins"). A traffic between imaginary *beings* ("God," "spirits," "souls"); imaginary *natural* science (anthropocentric; complete lack of the concept of natural causes); an imaginary *psychology* (nothing but self-misunderstandings, interpretations of pleasant or unpleasant general feelings, for example of the conditions of the *nervus sympathicus* with the aid of the sign language of religio-moral idiosyncrasy — "repentance," "pang of conscience," "temptation by the devil," "the nearness of God"); an imaginary *teleology* ("the kingdom of races," "the Last Judgment," "eternal life"). — This purely *fictional world* distinguishes itself from the dream world, much to its disadvantage, in that the latter *mirrors* reality, whereas the *former* falsifies, devalues, denies reality. Once the concept "nature" had been invented as the counterconcept to "God," "natural" had to be the word for "reprehensible," — this entire fictional world has its root in *hatred* of all that is natural (— reality! —), it is the expression of a deep uneasiness with reality . . . *But this explains everything.* Who alone has reason to *lie his way* out of reality? Anyone who *suffers* from it. But to suffer from reality means being a *failed* reality ... The preponderance of feelings of displeasure over feelings of pleasure is the *cause* of this fictitious morality and religion: but such a preponderance also provides the *formula* for *décadence* ...

16.[72]

A critique of the *Christian concept of God* demands the same conclusion. — A people that still believes in itself also still has its own god. In him, it honors the conditions through which it rises to the top, its virtues — it projects its pleasure in itself, its feeling of power into a being to whom it can be grateful. Whoever is rich wants to give away; a proud people needs a god in order to *make sacrifices* ... Religion, within such presuppositions, is a form of gratitude. One is grateful for oneself: for this one needs a god. — A god like this must be able to help and hinder, must be able to be friend and foe — one admires him in good and bad alike. The *anti-natural* castration of a god into a god of good alone would lie beyond all desirability here. People need the bad god as much as they need the good: after all, one does not exactly owe one's own existence to tolerance and human kindness ... What would a god matter who did not know anger, vengeance, envy, mockery, cunning, violence? who perhaps even knew nothing of the delightful *ardeurs*[73] of victory and annihilation? Nobody would understand such a god: why should anyone have him? — Of course: when a people is perishing; when it feels its belief in the future, its hopes for freedom, disappearing forever; when it becomes aware of subjugation as the prime benefit, of the virtues of the subjugated as conditions of survival, then its god *must* change as well. Now he becomes a sneak, fearful, modest, advocating for "peace of the soul," for no-more-hating, for consideration, even for "love" toward friend and foe. He continually moralizes, creeping into the cave of every private virtue, becomes god for everyman, becomes a private person, a cosmopolitan ... Formerly he represented a people, the strength of a people, all that was aggressive and thirsty for power in the soul of a people: now

he is merely the good god . . . In fact, there is no other alternative for gods: *either* they are the will to power — in which case
they remain gods of a people — *or* else the impotence to power
— and then they necessarily become *good* . . .

17.[74]

Wherever the will to power in any form whatsoever declines,
there is also a physiological regression every time, *décadence*.
The godhead of *décadence*, gelded in its manly virtues and
drives, now necessarily turns into the god of the physiologically
regressive, of the weak. They do not call themselves the weak,
they call themselves "the good" . . . One can understand, without needing a nod and a wink, in which moments of history
the dualistic fiction of a good and bad god first becomes possible. With the same instinct that the subjugated use to degrade
their god to "good in itself," they erase the good characteristics
from the god of their conquerors; they take revenge on their
masters by *demonizing* their god. — The *good* god, just like the
devil: both spawns of *décadence*. — Who today can still yield
to the simplicity of the Christian theologians to the point of
declaring, with them, that the development of the concept of
god from the "God of Israel," from god of a people into Christian God, into the quintessence of everything good, is *progress*?
— But even Renan does that.[75] As if Renan had a right to
simplicity! Yet the very opposite is plain as day. When the presuppositions for *ascending* life, when everything strong, brave,
masterful, proud, has been eliminated from the concept of
God, when he sinks, step by step, to being the symbol of a
crutch for the weak, a sheet anchor for all who are drowning,
when he becomes God-of-the-poor, God-of-sinners, God-of-
the-sick par excellence, and the predicate "Savior," "Redeemer,"
is all that *remains* as it were of the godly predicate as such: *what*
does such a transformation tell us? such a *reduction* of the
Godly? — To be sure: "the kingdom of God" has been enlarged
thereby. Formerly he just had his people, his "chosen" people.
Meanwhile, just like his people themselves, he went abroad, began

wandering, and since then he never sat still anywhere: until finally he became at home everywhere, the great cosmopolitan — until he got "the great number" and half the earth on his side. But the God of the "great number," the democrat among the Gods, nevertheless did not become a proud heathen God: he remained a Jew, he remained God of the nook, the God of all dark corners and places, of all unhealthy quarters in the whole world! . . . His earthly kingdom is and remains an underground kingdom, a hospital, a subterranean kingdom, a ghetto kingdom . . . And he himself so pale, so weak, so *décadent* . . . Even the palest of the pale, the gentlemen metaphysicians, the concept-albinos, became master over him. The latter spun their webs round him for so long that, hypnotized by their movements, he himself turned into a spider, a *metaphysicus*. Now he spun the world anew from out of himself — *sub specie Spinozae*[76] — now he transfigured himself into something thinner and paler, became an "ideal," became "pure spirit," became "*absolutum*," became "thing in itself" . . . *Decline of a God*: God became "thing in itself" . . .

18.

The Christian concept of God — God as God of the sick, God as a spider, God as spirit — is one of the most corrupt concepts of God ever arrived at on earth; perhaps it even represents the low-water mark in the descending development of the God-type. God degenerated into a *contradiction of life* instead of being its transfiguration and eternal *Yes*! In God, hostilities have been declared against life, nature, the will to life! God the formula for every slander of "this world," for every lie about the "hereafter"! In God nothingness deified, the will to nothingness sanctified! . . . [77]

19.

The fact that the strong races of northern Europe did not reject the Christian God really brings no honor to their religious talent, to say nothing of their taste. They really *ought* to have finished up with such a sickly and decrepit spawn of *déca-dence*. But there is a curse upon them for not finishing up with him: they have absorbed sickness, old age, contradiction into all their instincts — since that time they have not *created* any new god! Nearly two millennia and not a single new god! Instead, still surviving as though justified, like an *ultimatum* and *maximum*[78] of god-creating energy, of the *creator spiritus* in humans, this pitiful God of Christian monotono-theism! this hybrid anomaly of decay consisting of nullity, concept and contradiction, in which all *décadence*-instincts, all cowardices and exhaustions of the soul find sanction! — —

20.[79]

With my condemnation of Christianity I would not wish to have been unjust toward a related religion that, according to its number of believers, even predominates, namely toward *Buddhism*. Both belong together as nihilistic religions — they are *décadence*-religions[80] — yet both are separate in the most remarkable way. That one can *compare* them today is something for which the critic of Christianity is deeply thankful to India scholars. — Buddhism is a hundred times more realistic than Christianity — it embodies the inheritance of an objective and cool posing of problems, it arrives *after* a philosophical movement lasting hundreds of years, the concept of god is already done away with when it arrives. Buddhism is the only genuinely *positivistic* religion revealed to us by history, even in its epistemology (a strict phenomenalism —), it no longer speaks of the "struggle against *sin*," but instead, nodding fully to reality, of the "struggle against *suffering*." It has — and this differentiates it sharply from Christianity — the self-deception of moral concepts already behind it — in my parlance it stands *beyond* good and evil. — The *two* physiological facts on which it rests and keeps its eye are: *first* an excessive sensitivity that expresses itself as a refined capacity for pain, *and then* over-spiritualization, too long a life spent in concepts and logical procedures, during which the person-instinct has been damaged, to the advantage of the "impersonal" (— both states that at least a few of my readers, the "objective ones" like myself, will know from experience). Based on these physiological conditions, a *depression* arose: it is against it that Buddha takes hygienic measures. His countermeasures are life in the open air, the wandering life, moderation and selectivity with food; caution toward any *spirituosa*;[81] likewise caution with any gall-inducing affects that might heat the blood; no *worries*, neither for oneself nor others. He calls for ideas that either bring calm or good cheer — he invents methods to wean oneself from the rest. He understands kindness, being kind, as health-promoting. *Prayer* is excluded, as is *asceticism*; no categorical imperative, no *compulsion* at all, not even within a monastic community (— one can leave —). All these would be ways to strengthen that aforementioned excessive sensitivity. This is precisely why he also does not promote struggle against those who think differently; there is nothing his teaching guards against more than the feeling of revenge, aversion, *ressentiment* (— "animosity will not end animosity":[82] the touching refrain through the whole of Buddhism . . .). And justifiably so: precisely these affects would be completely *unhealthy* with regard to the dietetic main purpose. He combats the spiritual fatigue he detects, and which expresses itself in excessive "objectivity" (that is, a weakening of individual interest, loss of center of gravity, of "egoism"), by firmly redirecting even spiritual interests to the *person*. In the Buddha's teaching, egoism becomes a duty: the "one thing is needful,"[83] the "how do *you* free yourself of suffering" regulates and delimits the whole spiritual diet (— perhaps one should recall that Athenian who waged war on pure "scientism," Socrates, who raised personal egoism to morality even in the realm of problems).[84]

21.

The precondition for Buddhism is a very mild climate, great gentleness and liberalness in customs, *no* militarism; and that it is within the higher and even learned classes that the movement has its seat. One wants to have cheerfulness, silence, absence of desire as the highest goal, and one *achieves* the goal. Buddhism is not a religion where one merely aspires to perfection: perfection is the norm. —

In Christianity, the instincts of the subjects and the oppressed are in the foreground: it is the lowest classes that seek their "salvation" in it. Here, as an *occupation*, the casuistry of sin, self-criticism, conscience-inquisition are practiced as a remedy for boredom; here, the affect toward *someone mighty*, named "God," is continually upheld (through prayer); here, what is highest is seen as unattainable, as a gift, as "grace." Here openness is lacking as well; the hideaway, the dark room is Christian. Here, the body is despised, hygiene is rejected as sensuality; the Church even resists cleanliness (— the first Christian measure after driving out the Moors was the closure of the public baths, of which Cordoba alone had 270). Christian is a certain sense of cruelty[85] toward oneself and others; hatred toward those who think differently; the will to persecute. Gloomy and inciting thoughts are in the foreground; the most coveted states, designated with the highest names, are like epilepsy; the diet is sustained in such a way as to favor morbid manifestations and to overexcite the nerves. Christian is the deadly enmity toward the masters of the earth, the "noble" — and at the same time a covert secret competition (— leaving them the "body," *only* the "soul" is wanted . . .). Christian is the hatred of the *intellect*, of pride, courage, freedom, libertinage of the intellect; Christian is the hatred of the *senses*, of the pleasures of the senses, of any pleasure at all . . .

22.

This Christianity, when it left its native soil, the lowest classes, the *underworld* of antiquity, when it went forth for power among barbarian peoples, no longer presupposed *weary* humans here, but those who were internally feral and self-mutilating — the strong human being, but deformed. Dissatisfaction with oneself, suffering from oneself is here *not* excessive sensitivity and a capacity for pain, as with the Buddhists, but conversely, an overpowering compulsion to hurt, to release inner tension by hostile actions and ideas. Christianity needed *barbaric* concepts and values in order to gain mastery over the barbarians: such as the sacrifice of the firstborn, drinking blood at communion, contempt for intellect and culture; torture in all its forms, sensual or not; the great pomp of the cult. Buddhism is a religion for *late* humans, for kind, gentle races grown overspiritual, who feel pain too easily (— Europe is a long way from being ripe for it —): for these people, it is a leading back to peace and good cheer, to a diet in matters spiritual, to a certain hardening up in matters physical. Christianity desires mastery over *beasts of prey*; its means is to render them *sick* — weakening is the Christian recipe for *taming*, for "civilization." Buddhism is a religion for the final stage and weariness of civilization, while Christianity does not yet even find civilization present — in certain circumstances it will ground it.

23.

Buddhism, to repeat, is a hundred times more cold, truthful, objective. It no longer needs to make its suffering, its capacity for suffering, *respectable* by its interpretation as sin — it simply says what it thinks "I suffer." For the barbarian, on the other hand, suffering in itself is not respectable: he first needs an interpretation in order to admit to himself *that* he suffers (his instinct sooner impels him to denial of suffering, to bearing it in silence){.} Here, the word "devil" was a boon: there was an exceedingly powerful and terrible enemy — one did not need to be ashamed of suffering from such an enemy. —

Christianity has a few refinements at its core that belong to the Orient. Above all it knows that it is actually irrelevant whether something ⟨is⟩ true, but of the highest importance *insofar* as it is believed to be true. Truth and the *belief* that something is true: two quite disparate worlds of interest, almost *contrary* worlds — one reaches the one or the other by fundamentally different routes. To be knowledgeable about this — that practically *constitutes* a sage in the Orient: the Brahmans

CURSE UPON CHRISTIANITY   153

understood it so, as did Plato and every student of esoteric wisdom.[86] If, for example, any *happiness* lies in believing oneself to
be redeemed of sin, then it is *not* necessary to presume that the
human is sinful but that he *feels* sinful. But generally when *faith*
is necessary above all, then reason, knowledge, research must
be discredited: the path to truth becomes a *forbidden* path. —
Strong *hope* is a much greater stimulus to life than any single
happiness that actually happens. Those suffering must be sustained by a hope that cannot be countermanded by reality —
that fulfillment cannot *do away with*: a hope for the hereafter.
(Precisely because of this capacity for stringing along the unfortunate, the Greeks regarded hope as the evil of evils, as the
genuinely *devious* evil, it stayed behind in the barrel of evils.[87])
So that *love* is possible, God must be a person; so that the basest
instincts can have a say, God must be young. To cater to wom-
en's ardor, a handsome saint must be placed in the foreground, a
Mary for that of the men. This under the premise that Christianity desires mastery over a terrain where the cults of Aphrodite
or Adonis have already determined the *concept* of the cult. The
requirement of *chastity* strengthens the vehemence and intro-
spection of the religious instinct — it makes the cult warmer,
more ecstatic, more soulful. — Love is the state in which
humans most see things as they are *not*. There, the power of
illusion is at its height, likewise the power to sweeten and *transfigure*. One bears more in love than otherwise, one tolerates
everything. It was a question of inventing a religion in which
loving is possible: that way, one has transcended the worst
things in life — one no longer even sees it. — So much for the
three Christian virtues faith, love, hope:[88] I call them the three
Christian *ingenuities*. — Buddhism is too late, too positivistic,
to be ingenious in this way. —

24.[89]

Here I merely touch on the problem of the *emergence* of
Christianity. The *first* proposition for its solution is: Christianity can only be understood out of the ground from which it

grew — it is *not* a countermovement against Jewish instinct, it is itself its consequence, one inference further in its fear-inducing logic. In the Redeemer's formulation: "salvation is of the Jews."[90] The *second* proposition is: the psychological type of the Galilean is still recognizable, but only in its complete degeneration (which is simultaneously mutilation and overloading with foreign traits —) has it been able to serve as that for which it has been used, for the type of a *redeemer* of humanity. —

The Jews are the most remarkable people in world history because, when presented with the question of to be or not to be, they preferred to be, *at any cost* and with a completely uncanny mindfulness: this cost was the radical *falsification* of all nature, all naturalness, all reality of the whole inner world as well as the outer. They defined themselves *against* all conditions under which a people had hitherto been able to live, or been *allowed* to live, they created in themselves a counterconcept to *natural* conditions — one by one they irredeemably turned religion, cult worship, morality, history, psychology into the *contrary of their natural values*. We encounter the same phenomenon again and in vastly magnified proportions, albeit only as a copy: — the Christian Church, in contrast to the "holy people,"[91] is lacking any claim to originality. Precisely this makes the Jews the most *disastrous* people in world history: in their after-effect they have falsified humanity to such an extent that even today, the Christian can feel anti-Jewish without perceiving himself as the *ultimate Jewish consequence*.

In my *Genealogy of Morality*,[92] I gave a psychological presentation for the first time of the counterconcepts of a *noble* morality and a *ressentiment*-morality, the latter arising *from the No* of the former: but this is the Jewish-Christian morality through and through. In order to say No to everything that the *ascending* movement of life represents on earth, good breeding, power, beauty, self-affirmation, here the genius born from the instinct of *ressentiment* had to invent a *different* world from out of which that *life affirmation* appeared as evil, as reprehensibility as such. Speaking psychologically, the Jewish people is a

people of the toughest life force which, put in impossible conditions, freely chose the side of all *décadence*-instincts out of the
deepest shrewdness for self-preservation — *not* as if controlled
by them but because they divined in them a power with which
one could prevail *against* "the world." They are the opposite of all
décadents: they had to *portray* the latter to the point of illusion,
with *a non plus ultra* of thespian genius they managed to place
themselves at the forefront of all *decadence*-movements (— as
the Christianity of *Paul* —), in order to create something out of
them that is stronger than any *Yes-saying* party of life. For the
type of person craving power in Judaism and Christianity, a
priestly type, *décadence* is only a *means*: this type of human has a
life-interest in making humanity *sick* and in reversing the concepts "good" and "evil," "true" and "false" in a life-threatening
and world-slandering sense. —

25.

The history of Israel is invaluable as a typical history of all
denaturalization of natural values: I shall refer to five facts
accordingly. Originally, especially in the time of the Kingdom,
Israel too stood in the *correct*, that is, natural relationship to all
things. Their Yahweh was the expression of the consciousness
of power, of joy in itself, of hope for itself: in him, they expected
victory and salvation, with him they trusted nature to give
them what the people needed — above all rain. Yahweh is the
God of Israel and *consequently* the God of justice: the logic of
every people that is in power and has a good conscience about
it. In the festival cult, these two sides of a people's self-affirmation are expressed: it is grateful for the great destinies through
which it rose to the top, it is grateful in relation to the seasons of
the year and all good fortune in stock breeding and agriculture.
— This state of affair⟨s⟩ remained the ideal for a long time, even
when it was sadly done away with: anarchy within, the Assyrian
from without. But as their highest desirability, the people clung
to that vision of a king who is a good soldier and stern judge:
above all that typical prophet (that is, critic and satirist of the

moment), Isaiah. — But every hope remained unfulfilled. The old God *became incapable* of the things he was formerly capable of doing. They ought to have let him go. What happened? They *altered* his concept — they *denaturalized* his concept: at this price they kept him. — Yahweh the God of "justice," — *no longer* at one with Israel, an expression of the people's feeling of selfhood: now just a God subject to conditions . . . His concept becomes a tool in the hands of priestly agitators, who from now on interpret all fortune as reward, all misfortune as punishment for disobedience toward God, or "sin": that most mendacious manner of interpretation of an alleged "moral world order" with which, once and for all, the natural concept of "cause" and "effect" is stood on its head. Once natural causality is banished from the world through reward and punishment, an *anti-natural* causality is needed: the entire remainder of unnaturalness now follows. A God who *demands* — in place of a God who helps, gives advice, who is at bottom the word for every happy inspiration of courage and self-confidence . . . *Morality* no longer the expression of conditions for the life and growth of a people, no longer its most basic instinct for life, but instead turned abstract, turned into antithesis to life — morality as a fundamental degradation of the imagination, as the "evil eye" for all things. *What* is Jewish, *what* is Christian morality? Chance robbed of its innocence; misfortune besmirched with the concept of "sin"; well-being as danger, as "temptation"; physiological indisposition poisoned by the worm of conscience . . .

26.[93]

The concept of God falsified; the concept of morality falsified: — the Jewish priestly caste did not stop there. The entire *history* of Israel was of no use: away with it! — These priests brought about that miracle of forgery whose documentation is now available to us as a good portion of the Bible: with unmatched scorn for everything handed down, for every historical reality, they *translated* their people's past *into something religious*, that is, they made out of it a stupid salvation-mechanism of guilt toward

Yahweh and punishment, of piety toward Yahweh and reward. We would find this most disgraceful act of falsifying history much more painful if millennia of *ecclesiastical* interpretation of history had not made us nearly obtuse to demands for honesty *in historicis*. And the philosophers seconded the Church: the *lie* of a "moral world order" runs through the whole development of even the most recent philosophy. What does "moral world order" mean? That once and for all, there is a will of God directing what humans may and may not do; that the value of a people or individual is to be measured according to how much or how little the will of God is obeyed; that in the destinies of a people or individual, the will of God is shown as *sovereign*, that is, as punishing and rewarding according to the degree of obedience. Replacing this pitiful lie with *reality* means: a parasitic type of human who only thrives at the expense of all healthy forms of life, the *priest*, abuses the name of God: he calls a state of affairs in which the priest determines the value of things "the kingdom of God": he calls the means by which such a state is achieved or maintained "the will of God"; with cold-blooded cynicism, he takes the measure of peoples, ages, individuals according to whether they benefitted or resisted priestly predominance. Look at them at work: in the hands of Jewish priests, the *great* age in the history of Israel became an age of decline; the Exile, the prolonged misfortune was transformed into eternal *punishment* for the great age — an age in which priests were still nothing . . . According to their needs, they transformed the powerful, *very freely* successful figures in Jewish history into pathetic sneaks and bigots,[94] or the "Godless," they simplified the psychology of every great event into the idiotic formula "obedience *or* disobedience to God." — One step further: the "will of God," that is, the conditions for preserving the power of the priest, must be *known* — for which purpose a "revelation" is needed. In plain language: a great literary forgery becomes necessary, a "holy scripture" is discovered — it is made public amid all hieratic pomp, with days of atonement and lamentation about long-enduring "sin." The "will of God" had long been established: all harm lies in the fact that people had become estranged from "holy scripture" . . . Indeed "the will of God" had already been revealed to Moses . . . What happened? With severity, with pedantry, right down to the big and small taxes payable to him (not to forget the choicest cuts of meat: for the priest is a devourer of beefsteaks), the priest had formulated once and for all *what he wants to have*, "what is God's will" . . . From now on, everything in life is so ordained that the priest is *indispensable everywhere*; in all the natural occurrences of life, at birth, marriage, sickness, death, to say nothing at all of sacrifice ("Holy Communion"), the sacred parasite shows up to *denaturalize* them; in his words to "sanctify" them . . . For one must understand this: every natural custom, every natural institution (state, judicial order, marriage, care of the sick and the poor), every demand prompted by the instinct of life, in short, everything that has its value *in itself* is rendered fundamentally valueless, value-*averse* through the parasitism of the priest (or the "moral world order"): it requires a subsequent sanction — a value-*bestowing* power is needed to negate the nature in it, which thereby *creates* a value in the first place . . . The priest devalues, *profanes* nature: this is the price for him to exist at all. — Disobedience of God, that is, of the priest, of "the Law," now acquires the name "sin"; the means of "making atonement to God" are, as usual, means through which submission to the priest is ensured even more thoroughly: the priest alone "redeems" . . . Evaluated psychologically, "sins" are indispensable in every priestly-organized society: they are the real handles of power, the priest *lives* off sin, it is necessary to him that "sinning" occurs . . . Supreme principle: "God forgives those who repent" — in plain language: *who submit to the priest.* —

27.[95]

In a *false* soil of this sort, where every natural disposition, every natural value, every *reality* had the deepest instincts of the ruling class against it, *Christianity* grew, a form of deadly animosity toward reality that has yet to be surpassed. The "holy people," who had retained only priestly values and priestly words for all things, and who with fear-inducing consistency had isolated themselves against everything powerful that still existed on earth, shunning it as "unholy," as "world," as "sin" — this people produced a final formula for its instinct that was logical to the point of self-denial: as *Christianity*, it denied even the last remaining form of reality, the "holy people," the "chosen people," the *Jewish* reality itself. This case is first-class: the small, rebellious movement, baptized in the name of Jesus of Nazareth, is the Jewish instinct *once again* — or rather, the priestly instinct that can no longer tolerate the priest as reality, the invention of an even *more remote* form of existence, of an even more *unreal* vision of the world than the organization of a Church presupposes. Christianity *negates* the Church . . .

I cannot see what the revolt, understood or *misunderstood* as originated by Jesus, was directed against if it was not a revolt against the Jewish church, taking church in exactly the same sense as we take the word today. It was a revolt against the "good and the just," against "the saints of Israel," against the hierarchy of society — *not* against its corruption but against caste, privilege, order, formula; it was *disbelief* in the "superior humans," the *No* spoken against all that was priest and theologian. But the hierarchy, challenged in this way if only for a moment, was the pile dwelling, in the midst of the "waters," upon which the Jewish people continued to survive at all, the painstakingly achieved *last* chance for survival, the residue of its politically unique existence: an attack on it was an attack on the deepest instinct of the people, on the most tenacious people's will to life there has ever been on earth. This holy anarchist who incited the humble, the outcasts and "sinners," the *chandala* within Judaism, to protest against the ruling order — using language that even today would send him to Siberia, if the Gospels are to be believed, was a political criminal insofar as political criminals were possible in an *absurdly unpolitical* society. This put him on the cross: proof of which is the inscription on the cross. He died for *his* guilt — there are no grounds at all for saying, however often it's been claimed, that he died for the guilt of others. —

28.

It is quite another matter whether he was conscious of such a contrast at all — whether he was not just *perceived* to be this contrast. And here for the first time I touch on the problem of the *psychology of the Redeemer*. — I confess that I read few books with such difficulty as the Gospels. These difficulties are different from those in whose demonstration the scholarly curiosity of the German spirit celebrated one of its most unforgettable triumphs. The time is long past when I, like every young scholar, savored the work of the incomparable Strauss[96] with the prudent deliberateness of a refined philologist. I was twenty years old then: now I am too serious for that. What do I care about the contradictions of the "tradition"? How can one even call legends of saints "tradition"! The biographies of saints are the most ambiguous literature in existence: to apply scientific method to them *when no other documents are available* seems to me doomed from the start — mere scholarly idleness . . .

29.

What concerns *me* is the psychological type of the Redeemer. For the latter *could* still be included in the Gospels in spite of the Gospels, however mutilated or burdened with foreign traits they might be: as Francis of Assisi's is included in his legends in spite of the legends.[97] *Not* the truth about what he did, what he said, how he actually died: instead, the question *whether* his type can still be imagined at all, whether the tradition has "preserved" it? — The attempts I know to actually read out the *history* of a "soul" from the Gospels seem to me to be proof of a detestable psychological frivolity. Mister Renan, this clown *in psychologicis*, has brought together in his explication of Jesus as type the two *most irrelevant* concepts there can be for this: the concept of the *genius* and the concept of the *hero* ("*héros*"). But if anything is unevangelical, it is the concept of hero. Precisely the antithesis to all wrestling, to all feeling-oneself-in-struggle has become instinct here: the incapacity to resist becomes morality here ("resist not evil,"[98] the deepest word in the Gospels, their key in a certain sense), blessedness in peace, in gentleness, in not-*being-able*-to-be-enemy. What does "glad tidings" mean? True life, eternal life is found — it is not promised, it is here, it is *in you*: as living in love, love without subtraction and exclusion, without distance. Everyone is the child of God — Jesus claims nothing at all for himself alone — as a child of God, everyone is equal to everyone else . . . To make a *hero* out of Jesus! — And just what a misunderstanding that word "genius" is! Our whole concept, our whole cultural concept of "intellect," has no meaning at all in the world in which Jesus lives. A quite different word, spoken with the rigor of a physiologist, would sooner be appropriate: the word idiot.[99,100] We are familiar with a state of pathological irritability of the *sense of touch*, which then recoils from any contact or handling of a solid object. Translate a physiological *habitus*[101] like this into its ultimate logic — as instinctive hatred of *every* reality, as flight into the "inconceivable," the "incomprehensible," as aversion to every formula, to every concept of time and space, to everything that is solid, custom, institution, church, as being-at-home in a world no longer touched by any kind of reality, a merely "inner" world, a "true" world, an "eternal" world . . . "The kingdom of God is *within you*" . . . [102]

30.

The instinctive hatred of reality: result of an extreme capacity for suffering and irritability that no longer wants to be "touched" because it feels each touch too deeply.

The instinctive exclusion of all aversion, all hostility, all boundaries and distances of feeling: result of an extreme capacity for suffering and irritability that feels every resistance, every compulsion to resist, as an unbearable *displeasure* (that is, as *harmful*, as *advised against* by the instinct of self-preservation) and only knows bliss (pleasure) in no longer offering resistance, not to anyone, neither to misfortune nor evil — love as the single, as the *last* possibility of life . . .

These are the two *physiological realities* on which and out of which the doctrine of redemption has grown. I call it a sublime further development of hedonism on a thoroughly morbid foundation. Closely related to it is Epicureanism, paganism's doctrine of redemption, albeit with a large admixture of Greek vitality and strength of nerve. Epicurus, a *typical décadent*:[103] first recognized as such by me. — The fear of pain, of even the infinitesimal of pain — it *can*not end otherwise than in a *religion of love* . . .

31.[104]

I have given my answer to the problem in advance. Its presupposition is that the type of the savior has only been preserved for us in a strongly distorted form. On the face of it, this distortion has high probability: such a type could not, for a number of reasons, remain pure, whole, free of added ingredients. Both the milieu in which this strange figure moved, and even more its history, the *fate* of the first Christian community, must have left traces upon it: this retrospectively enriched the type with traits that are only intelligible in terms of war and for purposes of propaganda. That strange and sick world the Gospels introduce us to — a world like that of a Russian novel, where the scum of society, nervous disorders and "childish" idiocy seem to offer a rendezvous —[105] must have *coarsened* the type in any case: the first disciples in particular translated a state of being, awash with symbols and profundities, into their own crudity in order to understand anything of it at all — for them, the type only *existed* when it had been adapted into a more familiar form . . . The prophet, the Messiah, the future judge, the teacher of morality, the miracle worker, John the Baptist — just so many opportunities to mistake the type . . . Finally, we must not underestimate the *proprium*[106] of all

great, especially sectarian, veneration: it expunges the original, often embarrassingly strange traits and idiosyncrasies
from the revered being — *it does not even see them*. It is regrettable that no Dostoevsky lived in the vicinity of this interesting *décadent*, by which I mean someone who would know to
sense the thrilling charm of such a mixture of the sublime, the
sick and the childish. One last point: the type *could*, as *décadence*-type, actually be composed of an extraordinary diversity and contradictoriness: such a possibility is not to be completely ruled out. However, everything advises against it: for
such a case, the tradition would have to have been a remarkably faithful and objective one: which gives us reason to
assume the opposite. Meanwhile, there is a gaping contradiction between the sermonizer of the mount, lake and meadow,
whose arrival puts one in mind of Buddha on a soil with scant
little resemblance to India, and that fanatic of aggression, that
mortal enemy of theologian and priest whom Renan in his
malice has glorified as "*le grand maître en ironie*."[107] I myself
do not doubt that this great wealth of gall (even of *esprit*) first
flowed over to the type of the Master from the agitated state of
Christian propaganda; after all, we know full well how
unscrupulously all sectarians contrive their *apology* of themselves out of their master. When the first community needed a
judging, quarreling, scorning, wickedly caviling theologian,
against theologians, it *created* its "God" according to its requirements: just as it unhesitatingly put into his mouth those completely un-evangelistic concepts that they could no longer do
without, "Second Coming," "Last Judgment," every form of
temporal expectation and promise. —

32.[108]

To repeat, I resist the introduction of the fanatic into the
type of the Redeemer: Renan's use of the word *impérieux*[109] is
by itself already enough to *annul* the type. The "glad tidings"
means simply there are no opposites anymore; the kingdom of
Heaven belongs to *children*; the faith enunciated here is not a

faith gained by struggle — it is there, it is from the beginning,
a childishness, as it were, that has withdrawn into the spiritual. The case of puberty delayed or undeveloped in the organism is known at least to the physiologists as a manifestation of
degeneracy.[110] — Such a faith does not get angry, does not
blame, does not resist: it does not take up "the sword"[111] — it
has no idea at all to what extent it could ever be divisive. It
does not prove itself, neither through miracles or reward and
promise, nor even "by the scriptures": it is at every moment its
own miracle, its own reward, its own proof, its own "kingdom
of God." Nor does this belief formulate itself — it *lives*, it
resists formulas. Of course, chance determines the environment, language, initial shaping of a certain circle of concepts:
early Christianity applied *only* Jewish-Semitic concepts (—
eating and drinking at Holy Communion belongs here, this
concept so wretchedly misused by the Church, like everything
Jewish[112]). But one should beware of seeing more in this than
a sign language, a semiotic, an opportunity for parables. Precisely that no word of his can be taken literally is the prerequisite for this antirealist to be able to say anything at all. Among
Indians, he would have made use of the concepts of Sankhya,[113]
and among Chinese concepts those of Lao-Tse — and would
not have felt a difference between them. — One could, with a
degree of license, call Jesus a "free spirit" — he pays no regard
to anything solid: the word *kills*, everything that is solid *kills*.
In him, the concept, the *experience* of "life" as he alone knows it,
strains against every form of word, formula, law, belief, dogma.
He speaks only of what is innermost: "life" or "truth"[114] or
"light" are his words for what is innermost — all the rest, the
whole of reality, the whole of nature, language itself, possesses
for him merely the value of a sign, of a parable. — At this point,
one should not be deceived, however great the seduction might
be that is found in Christian, or rather *ecclesiastical* prejudice:
such a symbolism par excellence stands apart from all religion,
all concepts of cult, all history, all natural science, all experience
of the world, all knowledge, all politics, all psychology, all books,

all art — his "knowledge" is simply the *pure foolishness*[115] of the notion *that* these sorts of things exist. *Culture* is unknown to him even through hearsay, he has no need to fight it — he does not deny it . . . The same goes for the *state*, for the whole civic order and society, for *work*, for war — he never had reason to deny "the world," he never had an inkling of the ecclesiastical concept "world" . . . *Denial* is the one thing entirely impossible for him. — Likewise dialectics are lacking, the notion is lacking that a faith, a "truth," could be proved through reasons (— *his* proofs are inner "lights," inner feelings of pleasure and self-affirmations, nothing but "proofs of strength" —). Such a doctrine *can*not contradict either, it does not grasp that there are or *can* be other doctrines, it does not know in the least how to imagine a contradictory judgment . . . Where it encounters one, it will mourn about "blindness" with sincerest sympathy — for it sees the "light" — but will raise no objection . . .

33.[116]

   In the whole psychology of "the Gospel," the concept of guilt and punishment is lacking; likewise the concept of reward. "Sin," any kind of distancing effect between God and human, is abolished — *that is precisely what the "glad tidings" are.* Blessedness is not promised, nor is it tied to conditions: it is the *only* reality — the rest is signs for speaking about it . . .

   The *consequence* of such a state projects itself into a new *practice*, the genuinely evangelical practice. "Faith" does not distinguish the Christian: the Christian acts, he is distinguished by a *different* way of acting. By not resisting, neither in word nor in his heart, someone who has been evil to him. By not distinguishing between foreigner and native, between Jew and non-Jew ("the neighbor" being actually the comrade in faith, the Jew). By not being angry at anyone, by not despising anyone. By neither letting himself be seen in court nor induced to take part ("not swearing an oath"). By not divorcing his wife, under any circumstance⟨s⟩, not even in the case of proven infidelity of the wife. — All this at bottom one principle, all this the results of one instinct. —[117]

The life of the Redeemer was nothing other than *this* practice — nor was his death anything different . . . He had no need for formulas or rites for his dealings with God — not even prayer. He settled his account with the whole Jewish doctrine of repentance and reconciliation; he knows that it is only through the *practice* of living that one feels "godly," "blessed," "evangelical," at all times a "child of God." *Not* "repentance," *not* "prayer for forgiveness" are ways to God: *evangelical practice alone* leads to God, it *is* in fact "God" — What was *abolished* with the Gospel was the Judaism of the concepts "sin," "forgiveness of sin," "faith," "redemption through faith" — the whole of Jewish *ecclesiastical* doctrine was negated in the "glad tidings."

The deep instinct for how one should *live* in order to feel oneself "in heaven," in order to feel "eternal," whereas in every other behavior one absolutely does *not* "feel oneself in heaven": this alone is the psychological reality of "redemption." — A new mode of life, *not* a new faith . . .

34.[118]

If I understand anything at all about this great symbolist,[119] it is that he only took *inner* realities as realities, as "truths," — that he understood the rest, everything natural, temporal, spatial, historical, merely as signs, as an opportunity for parables. The concept of "the Son of Man"[120] is not a concrete person that belongs within history, something individual and unique, but an "eternal" factuality, a psychological symbol freed of the concept of time. The same is true again, and in the highest sense, of the *God* of this typical symbolist, of the "kingdom of God," of the "kingdom of Heaven," of the "filiation of God." Nothing is more unchristian than the *ecclesiastical crudities* of God as *person*, of a "kingdom of God" yet to *come*, of a "kingdom of Heaven" *beyond*, of a "son of God" as the *second person* of the Trinity. All this is — pardon the expression — a *fist* in the eye — oh, what an eye! — of the Gospel; a *world-historical cynicism* in the mockery of a symbol . . . But it is quite obvious what is touched on with the signs "father" and "son" — not obvious to everyone, I admit: with the word "son" is expressed *entry* into the overall-transfiguration-feeling of all things (blessedness), with the word "father" *this feeling itself,* the feeling of eternity, of perfection. — I am embarrassed to recall what the Church has made of this symbolism: did it not put an Amphitryon-story[121] at the threshold of the Christian "faith"? And on top of that, a dogma of the "immaculate conception"? . . . [122] *But with that, it has maculated conception* — —

The "kingdom of Heaven" is a state of the heart — not something that comes "above the earth" or "after death." The whole concept of natural death is *lacking* in the Gospel: death is not a bridge, not a transition, it is lacking because it belongs to a quite different, merely apparent world, one merely of use for symbols. The "hour of death" is *not* a Christian concept — the "hour," time, physical life and its crises do not exist at all for the teacher of the "glad tidings" . . . The "kingdom of God" is nothing that one expects; it has no yesterday and no tomorrow, it will not come in "a thousand years" —[123] it is an experience of the heart; it exists everywhere, it exists nowhere . . .

35.[124]

This "bringer of glad tidings" died as he lived, as he *taught* — *not* in order to "redeem humanity," but to show how one should live. It is his *practice* that he bequeathed to humanity: his conduct before the judges, before the bailiffs, before the accusers and all kinds of slander and scorn — his behavior on the *cross.* He does not resist, he does not defend his rights, he takes no step that would ward off the extreme, on the contrary, *he provokes it* . . . And he implores, he suffers, he loves *with* those, *in* those, who do him evil . . . The words to the *thief* on the cross contain the whole Gospel. "This is truly a *godly* man," a "child of God," says the thief. "If that is what you feel" — answers the Redeemer — "*you are in Paradise,* you too are a child of God . . ."[125] *No* self-defense, *no* anger, *no*

making-responsible . . . Instead, no resisting even the evil-doer
— *loving* him . . .

36.[126]

— Only we, we spirits who have *become free*, have the prerequisite for understanding something that nineteen centuries
have misunderstood — that righteousness turned into instinct
and passion that wages war on the "holy lie" even more than
any other lie . . . People were unspeakably far from our loving
and cautious neutrality, from that discipline of mind that alone
enables the figuring out of such strange and delicate things: the
whole time, with a shameful selfishness, they wanted only their
own advantage from it, they erected the *Church* out of the
opposite of the Gospel . . . [127]

Anyone who searched for signs that an ironic divinity was
secretly manipulating the great play of world would find no
small support in the *tremendous question mark* that is called
Christianity. The fact that humanity is on its knees before the
opposite of what was the origin, meaning, the *right* of the
Gospel; that it declared holy within the concept of "Church"
precisely what the "bringer of glad tidings" felt was *beneath*
him, *behind* him — we seek in vain for a greater form of
world-historical irony — —

37.

— Our age is proud of its historical sense: how has it been
able to make the nonsense credible that at the beginning of
Christianity stands the *crude fable of the miracle-worker and
redeemer* — and that everything spiritual and symbolic is only
a later development? On the contrary: the history of Christianity — and indeed from the death on the Cross on — is the
history of an ever-cruder, step-by-step misunderstanding of an
original symbolism. With every spreading of Christianity to
still broader, still coarser masses who increasingly lacked the
presuppositions from which it grew, it became more necessary
to *vulgarize*, to *barbarize* Christianity — it swallowed up the

teaching and rites of all the *underground* cults of the *imperium Romanum*,[128] the nonsense of all kinds of sick reason. The destiny of Christianity lies in the necessity that its own faith had to become as sick, low and vulgar as the sick, low and vulgar needs it was supposed to satisfy. This *sick barbarism* itself finally intensifies into power as Church — the Church, this form of mortal animosity toward everything righteous, toward every *loftiness* of the soul, toward all discipline of the mind, toward all frank and kindly humanity. — Christian values — *noble* values: only we, we spirits who have *become free*, have rehabilitated this greatest value-contrast that there is! — —

38.

— At this point, I do not suppress a sigh. There are days when I am afflicted by a feeling, blacker than the blackest melancholy — *contempt for humans*. And to leave no doubt about *what* I despise, *whom* I despise: it is the human of today, the human with whom I am fatefully contemporaneous. The human of today — his bad breath suffocates me . . . With regard to what has gone before, I, like every knower, have great tolerance, that is, *magnanimous* self-control: I pass through the world-madhouse of whole millennia, calling them "Christianity," "Christian faith," "Christian Church" with a gloomy precaution — I refrain from making humanity responsible for its mental illnesses. But my feelings change, break out, as soon as I enter more modern times, *our* times. Our time is *cognizant* . . . What was formerly merely sick is indecent today — it is indecent to be a Christian today. *And this is where my disgust begins.* — I look around: not a word remains of what used to be called "truth," we can no longer bear it[129] if a priest so much as breathes the word "truth." Even with the most modest claim to righteousness, one *must* know today that a theologian, a priest, a pope not only errs with every sentence he speaks, but *lies* — that he is no longer at liberty to lie from "innocence" or "ignorance." Even the priest knows as well as anyone that there is no longer a "God," a "sinner," a "Redeemer" — that "free will," "moral world order" are *lies*: — seriousness, the deep self-overcoming of the intellect[130] no longer *permits* anyone *not* to know about this . . . *All* church concepts are recognized for what they are, the most malicious counterfeiting there is, for the purpose of *devaluing* nature and natural values; the priest himself is recognized for what he is, the most dangerous sort of parasite, the veritable poison-spider[131] of life . . .[132] We know, our *conscience* knows today — precisely *what* those uncanny inventions of the priest and church are worth, *what purpose they served*, and by which a state of self-violation of humanity has been achieved that it is capable of making us nauseous at the sight of it — the concepts "beyond," "Last Judgment," "immortality of the soul," the "soul" itself; they are instruments of torture, systems of[133] cruelty by means of which the priest became master, remained master . . . Everyone knows that: *and yet everything stays the same*.[134] Where did that last feeling of decency, respect for oneself, come from if even our statesmen,[135] otherwise very candid types of humans and antichristians of action through and through, still call themselves Christians today and go to Holy Communion? . . . A young[136] prince at the head of his regiment, magnificent as an expression of the selfishness and arrogance of his people — yet, confessing himself a Christian *without* the least shame! . . . *Whom*, then, does Christianity deny? *What* does it call "world"? That a person is a soldier, a judge, a patriot; that they defend themselves; that they uphold their honor; that they seek advantage; that they are *proud* . . . Every practice at any moment, every instinct, every evaluation that brings forth a *deed*, is today antichristian: what an *abortion of falsity* the modern human must be, *not to be ashamed* of still being called a Christian! — — —

39.

— I shall continue, I shall relate the *genuine* history of Christianity. — Even the word "Christianity" is a misunderstanding

— at bottom there was only one Christian, and he died on the cross. The "evangel" *died* on the cross. Whatever is called "evangel" from this moment on was already the opposite of what *he* had lived: "*bad* tidings," a "*dysangel.*" It is false to the point of nonsense to see the mark of a Christian in a "faith," as perhaps in the faith in redemption through Christ: only Christian *practice*, a life like the one *lived* by him who died on the cross, is Christian . . . Even today, a life *such as this* is possible, even essential for *certain* humans: genuine, original Christianity is possible at all times . . . *Not* a faith, but a doing, above all a *not*-doing many things, a different *being* . . .[137] States of consciousness, random belief, a holding of something to be true, for example — as every psychologist knows — are of complete indifference and fifth-rate compared with the value of the instincts: put more strongly, the whole concept of our spiritual[138] causality is false. To reduce being a Christian, being Christ-like, to holding something to be true, to a mere phenomenality of consciousness, is to negate[139] Christianity. *In fact there have never been any Christians at all.* The "Christian," that which has been called Christian for two thousand years, is merely a psychological self-misunderstanding. On closer inspection, *in spite of* all "faith," *merely* the instincts ruled in him — and *what instincts*! — "Faith" was at all times, for example with Luther, just a cloak, a pretext, a *curtain*, behind which the instincts played their game — a clever *blindness* to the dominance of *certain* instincts . . . "Faith" — I have already dubbed this the genuine Christian *ingenuity* — one always spoke of "faith" but only ever *acted* on instinct . . . In the ideational world of the Christian, nothing happens that might even touch on reality: in contrast, we have recognized in the instinctive hatred *toward* all reality the one and only driving element in the root of Christianity. What is the result? That even *in psychologicis* the error here is radical, in other words, determinative of the essence, in other words, *substance.* Take away *one* concept, put one single reality in its place — and the whole of Christianity lurches into nothingness! — Seen from

on high, this strangest of all facts, a religion not only conditioned by errors, but inventive and even ingenious *only* in harmful, *only* in life-and-heart-poisoning errors, remains a *spectacle
for the gods* — for those divinities who are philosophers at the
same time and whom I, for example, encountered during those
famous dialogues on Naxos.[140,141] In the moment that *nausea*
recedes from them (— *and* from us!), they become grateful for
the spectacle of the Christian: the pathetically small star called
earth might deserve a divine glance, divine sympathy, solely on
account of *this* curious case . . . For we should not underestimate the Christian: false *to the point of innocence*, the Christian
is far above the ape — with regard to Christians, a famous theory of descent becomes a mere compliment . . .

40.[142]

— The doom of the evangel was determined by that death
— it hung on the "cross" . . . Only that death, that unexpected,
disgraceful death, only that cross, generally just reserved for
the *canaille*[143] — only this most horrific paradox made the disciples confront the actual riddle: "*who was that? what was that?*"
— The feeling of shock and being insulted to the core, the
suspicion that such a death might be the *refutation* of their
cause, the dreadful question mark: "why precisely like this?"
— this state is only too easily grasped. Everything about this
had to be necessary, had to have meaning, reason, supreme
reason; the love of a disciple does not acknowledge chance.
Only now did the chasm open up: "*who* killed him? *who* was
his natural enemy?" — This question shot forth like lightning.
Answer: *ruling* Judaism, its uppermost class. From this moment
on, one felt oneself in rebellion *against* order, one understood
Jesus in retrospect as being *in rebellion against order*. Up till
then, this militant, No-saying, No-doing trait in his image had
been *lacking*; even more, he was its antithesis. Obviously the
little community had *not* understood the most important
thing, the exemplary way of his dying, the freedom, the superiority *over* every feeling of *ressentiment*: — an indication of how

little they understood him at all! In fact, there was nothing
Jesus could want from his death besides publicly giving the
strongest test, the *proof* of his teaching . . . But his disciples were
very far from *forgiving* this death — which would have been
evangelical in the highest sense: or from *offering themselves up* to
a similar death in gentle and lovely peace of heart . . . Precisely
the most unevangelical feeling, *revenge*, came out on top again.
The matter could not possibly be at an end with this death:
they needed "retribution," "judgment" (— and yet what can
be even more unevangelical than "retribution," "punishment,"
"sitting in judgment"!). Once again, the popular expectation
of a Messiah came to the fore; a historic moment came into
focus: the "kingdom of God" comes to sit in judgment over its
enemies . . . But with that, everything is misconstrued: the
"kingdom of God" as a finale, as a promise! The evangel had
been precisely the existence, the fulfillment, the *reality* of this
"kingdom." Precisely such a death *was* this "kingdom of God"
. . . Only now were the whole contempt and bitterness toward
the Pharisees and theologians incorporated into the type of the
Master — this is how they *made* him into a Pharisee and theologian! On the other hand, the veneration gone wild of these
totally unhinged souls could no longer stand that evangelical
granting of equal rights to everyone to be a child of God, as
Jesus had taught: their revenge was to *raise* Jesus *aloft* in an
extravagant manner, and cut themselves off from him: just as
the Jews, out of revenge on their enemies, had formerly severed
themselves from their god and raised him aloft. The One God
and the One Son of God: both products of *ressentiment* . . .

41.[144]

— And from now on, an absurd problem came to the surface: "How *could* God allow that!" For which the disturbed
reasoning of the small community came up with an altogether
horribly absurd reply: God gave his son for the forgiveness of
sins, as a *sacrifice*. How the evangel came to an end all at once!
The *guilt sacrifice*, and indeed in its most abhorrent, most

barbaric[145] form, the sacrifice of the *innocent* for the sins of the guilty! What horrific heathenism! — Jesus himself had abolished the concept of "guilt," he disavowed any gulf between God and human, he *lived* this unity of God as human[146] as *his* "glad tidings" . . . And *not* as a prerogative! — From now on, step by step, new things enter into the type of the Redeemer: the doctrine of judgment and of the Second Coming, the doctrine of death as sacrificial death, the doctrine of the *resurrection*, with which the whole concept of "blessedness," the whole and single reality of the Gospel is conjured away — for the sake of a state *after* death! . . . Paul rationalized this interpretation, this *obscenity* of an interpretation, with the rabbinic presumption that characterizes him in all things: "*if* Christ was not resurrected from the dead, then our faith is in vain." —[147] And all at once the evangel was turned into the most despicable of all unfulfillable promises, the *disgraceful* doctrine of personal immortality . . . Paul himself continued to teach it as a *reward*! . . .

42.[148]

One can see *what* was ended with the death on the cross: a new, a completely original start to a Buddhistic peace movement, to an actual, *not* merely promised, *happiness on earth*. For this remains — as I have already stressed — the fundamental difference between both *décadence*-religions: Buddhism does not promise, but keeps; Christianity promises everything, but it *keeps nothing*. — On the heels of the "glad tidings" followed the *worst of all*: those of Paul. Paul embodies the antithetical type to the "bringer of glad tidings," the genius in hatred, in the vision of hatred, in the relentless logic of hatred. *What* didn't this dysangelist[149] sacrifice, all for hatred! Above all, the Redeemer: he nailed him to *his own* cross. The life, example, teaching, death, meaning and right of the whole evangel — nothing remained after this counterfeiter, motivated by hatred, comprehended what he alone could use. *Not* reality, *not* historical truth! . . . And once more the priestly

instinct of the Jew inflicted the same great crime on history
— he simply crossed out the yesterday, the day before yesterday of history, he *invented his own history of early Christianity*.
Even more: he once again falsified the history of Israel so as to
appear as the prehistory for *his* deed: all the prophets had spoken of *his* "Redeemer" . . . Later, the Church even falsified the
history of humanity into the prehistory of Christianity . . .
The type of the Redeemer, the teaching, the practice, the
death, the meaning of that death, even what came after that
death — nothing was left untouched, nothing remained even
remotely similar to reality. Paul simply transferred the main
emphasis of that whole existence *behind* this existence — into
the *lie* of Jesus "resurrected." At bottom, he had no use at all
for the life of the Redeemer — he needed the death on the
cross *and* something else as well . . . To regard as honest a
Paul, whose homeland was at the main seat of Stoic enlightenment,[150] when he contrives the *proof* of the *continuing*-life of
the Redeemer from a hallucination, or even to give credence to
his tale *that* he had had this hallucination, would be a true
niaiserie[151] on the part of a psychologist: Paul wanted the end,
consequently he also wanted the means . . . What he himself
did not believe was believed by the idiots among whom he
hurled *his* teaching. — *His* need was *power*; with Paul, the
priest wanted to regain power — he could only make use of
concepts, doctrines, symbols with which masses are tyran-
nized, herds are formed. — *What* was the only thing Mohammed borrowed later from Christianity? Paul's invention, his
means to priestly tyranny, to forming herds: the belief in
immortality — *that is, the doctrine of the "judgment"* . . . [152,153]

43.

If one shifts life's main emphasis *not* into life but into the
"beyond" — *into nothingness* — then one has altogether removed
life's main emphasis. The great lie of personal immortality destroys
all reason, all that is natural in the instinct — everything within
the instincts that is benevolent, life-promoting, vouching for

the future, now arouses mistrust. To live *in such a way* that there is no longer any *meaning* in living, *that* now becomes the "meaning" of life . . . Why communal spirit, why gratitude for descent and forebears anymore, why cooperate, trust, why promote and focus on any kind of common well-being? . . . Just so many "temptations," just so many diversions from the "right path" — "*One* thing is needful"[154] . . . That everyone, as an "immortal soul," has equal rank with everyone else, that in the totality of all beings, the "salvation" of *each* individual can lay claim to an eternal significance, that little bigots and the three-fourths-crazy are allowed to imagine that for their sake, the laws of nature can be continually *broken through* — such[155] an intensification of every form of selfishness[156] into infinity, into *obscenity*,[157,158] cannot be branded with enough contempt. And yet Christianity owes its *victory* to *this* pitiful flattery of personal vanity —[159] using it to coax to its side precisely all the malformed, revolt-minded, underprivileged, the whole scum and garbage of humanity. The "salvation of the soul" — in plain language, "the world revolves around *me*" . . . The poison of the doctrine "*equal* rights for all" — Christianity was most fundamental in sowing it; Christianity, from the most secretive corners of its bad instincts, has waged lethal war on every feeling of respect and distance between one human and another, that is, on the *prerequisite* for every elevation, every growth in culture — it forged from the *ressentiment* of the masses its *main weapon* against *us*, against all that is noble, cheerful, high-minded on earth, against our happiness on earth . . . [160] To concede "immortality" to every Peter and Paul has been the greatest, most malicious assassination attempt ever on *noble* humanity. — *And* let us not forget the disaster that has crawled out of Christianity even into politics! Today, nobody any longer has the courage for special rights, rights to rule, for a feeling of self-respect and respect for peers — for a *pathos of distance* . . . Our politics is *sick* from this lack of courage! The aristocratic mentality was undermined in the most subterranean manner by the lie of the equality of souls; and if faith in the "prerogative of the majority" makes revolutions and *will make* them, it is Christianity, there is no doubt about it, it is *Christian* value judgments that will transform every revolution into mere blood and crime![161] Christianity is a revolt of all things that creep along the ground against things that stand *tall*: the evangel of the "lowly" *makes* low . . . [162]

44.[163]

— The Gospels are invaluable as evidence for the already unstoppable corruption *within* the first community. What Paul later pursued to its end with the logical cynicism of a rabbi was nevertheless just a process of decline that began with the death of the Redeemer. — One cannot read these Gospels too cautiously; there are difficulties behind every word. I confess, if I may be so bold, that this is exactly what makes them a first-rate pleasure for the psychologist — as the *opposite* of all naïve corruption, as refinement par excellence, as artistry in psychological corruption. The Gospels stand on their own. The Bible in general admits of no comparison. One is among Jews: the *first* point of view, so as not to lose the thread completely here. Passing oneself off as "holy" has simply become genius here, and is otherwise never remotely achieved in books or among humans, this counterfeiting of word and gesture as an *art*, is not an accident of a random, unique talent or a random, exceptional nature. *Race* is required here. In Christianity, as the art of lying in a holy manner, the whole of Judaism achieves its ultimate mastery with its centuries-long Jewish and most serious possible training and technique. The Christian, this *ultima ratio*[164] of the lie, is the Jew once more — even *three* times more . . . — The fundamental will to employ only concepts, symbols, attitudes that are proven by priestly practice, the instinctual rejection of every *other* practice, any *other* kind of value- and utility-perspective — that is not just tradition, that is *heritage*: only as heritage does it work like nature. The whole of humanity, even the best of heads in the best ages — (except for one, who is perhaps a mere nonhuman)

— has let itself be deceived. People have read the Gospel as the *book of innocence* . . . : no small indication as to the virtuosity that has been playacted here. — Of course, if we were to *see* them, if only in passing, all these strange bigots and fake saints, that would put an end to it — and precisely for that reason, because *I* cannot read any words without seeing gestures, *I put an end to them* . . . I cannot stand a certain way they have of opening their eyes wide. — Fortunately, books are just *literature* for most people — — One must not let oneself be fooled: "judge not!"[165] they say, but they dispatch to hell everything that stands in their way. By letting God judge, they themselves judge; by glorifying God, they glorify themselves; by *demanding* precisely those virtues of which they themselves are capable — even more, which they need just to stay on top — they give themselves a grand appearance of struggling for virtue, of battling for mastery of virtue. "We live, we die, we sacrifice ourselves *for the good*" (— the "truth," "the light," the "kingdom of God"): in truth, they do what they have to do. By getting their way in the style of sneaks, sitting in corners and leading shady lives in the shadows, they make a *duty* out of it: as a duty,[166] their life is seen as humility, as humility it is one more proof of piety . . . Oh this humble, chaste, merciful form of mendacity! "Virtue itself vouches for us" . . . One should try reading the Gospels as books of seduction through *morality*: these petty people monopolize morality — they know what use morality can be put to! Morality is the best way to lead humanity *by the nose*! — The reality is that here, the most deliberate[167] *arrogance of the elect* pretends to humility: they positioned *themselves*, the "community," the "good and just," once and for all on one side, on that of the "truth" — and the rest, "the world," on the other . . . *That* was the most fateful sort of megalomania there has ever been on earth: tiny malformed bigots and liars began to appropriate the concepts "God," "truth," "light," "spirit," "wisdom," "life" for themselves, as though these words were synonymous with themselves, in order to delimit themselves in relation to "the world," little superlative-Jews, ripe for any kind of madhouse, rechanneled all values toward *themselves*, just as though only the Christian were the meaning, the salt, the measure, also the *Last Judgment* of all the rest . . . The whole calamity was only made possible because the world already had a related, racially related kind of megalomania, the *Jewish*: the moment the chasm broke open between Jews and Jewish Christians, the latter had no choice but to use *against* the Jews themselves the same procedures of self-preservation that Jewish instinct dictated, whereas the Jews had up till then only used them against everything *non*-Jewish. The Christian is just a Jew of a "freer" denomination.[168] —

45.[169]

— I shall provide a few examples of what these petty people have got into their heads and what they *have put into the mouth* of their master: strictly confessions of "beautiful souls." —

"And whosoever shall not receive you, and hear you,[170] when ye depart thence, shake off the dust under your feet for a testimony against them. Verily I say unto you: It shall be more tolerable for Sodom and Gomorrah in the day of judgment, than for that city" (Mark 6:11). — How *evangelical*! . . . [171]

"And whosoever shall offend one of these little ones that believe in me, it is better for him that a millstone were hanged about his neck, and he were cast into the sea" (Mark 9:42). — How *evangelical*! . . .

"And if thine eye offend thee, pluck it out. It is better for thee to enter into the kingdom of God with one eye, than having two eyes to be cast into hell fire; where their worm dieth not, and the fire is not quenched" (Mark 9:47{–48}). — It is not exactly the eye that is meant . . .

"Verily I say unto you, that there be some of them that stand here, which shall not taste of death, till they have seen the kingdom of God come with power" (Mark 9:1). — *Well-lied*, lion . . . [172]

"Whosoever will come after me, let him deny himself, and take up his cross, and follow me. *For* . . . " (*Footnote from a psychologist*: Christian morality is refuted by its "*fors*": its "reasons" refute — that makes it Christian.) Mark 8:34{–35}. —

"Judge not, *that* ye be not judged. For with what judgment ye judge, *ye* shall be judged" (Matthew, 7:1{–2}). — What a concept of justice, of a "just" judge! . . .

"For if ye love them which love you, *what reward have ye*? Do not even the publicans the same? And if ye salute your brethren only, *what do ye more than others*? Do not even the publicans so?" (Matthew 5:46{–47}) — Principle of "Christian love": it wants ultimately to be *paid* well . . .

"For if *ye*[173] forgive not men their trespasses, neither will your Father in heaven[174] forgive" (Matthew 6:15). — Very compromising for the said "Father" . . .

"But seek ye first the kingdom of God, and his righteousness; and all these things shall be added unto you" (⟨Matthew 6:33⟩). All these things: namely, food, clothing, all necessities of life. An *error*, to put it mildly . . . Whereupon[175] God appears as a tailor, at least in certain cases . . .

"Rejoice ye in that day, and leap for joy: *for* behold, your reward is great in heaven. For in the like manner did the fathers unto the prophets" (⟨Luke 6:23⟩). *Shameless* mob! It even likens itself to the prophets . . .

"Know ye not that ye are the temple of God, and that the Spirit of God dwelleth in you? If any man defile the temple of God, *him shall God destroy*: for the temple of God is holy, which temple *ye are*" (Paul, 1 Corinthians 3:16{–17}). One cannot sufficiently despise this sort of thing . . .

"Do ye not know that the saints shall judge the world? And if the world shall ⟨be⟩ judged by *you*: are ye unworthy to judge the smallest matters?" (Paul, 1 Corinthians 6:2). Unfortunately, not just the talk of a lunatic . . . This *terrible deceiver* continues word for word: "Know ye not that *we* shall judge angels? How much more things that pertain to this life?" . . .

"Hath not God made foolish the wisdom of this world? For after that in the wisdom of God the world by wisdom knew not God, it pleased God by the foolishness of preaching to save them that believe."[176] "Not many wise men after the flesh, not many mighty, not many noble, are called. But the foolish things of the world, *which God hath chosen*, to confound the wise; and the weak things of the world, which God hath chosen, to confound the things which are mighty; and base things of the world, and things which are despised, hath God chosen, yea, and things which are not, to bring to naught things that are. That no flesh should glory in his presence"[177] (Paul, 1 Corinthians 1:20ff.). — In order *to understand* this passage, a testament of the very first order for the psychology of chandala morality, one should read the first treatise of my *Genealogy of Morality*: in it I revealed, for the first time, the contrast between a *noble* morality and a chandala morality born of *ressentiment* and impotent revenge. Paul was the greatest of all apostles of revenge . . .

46.[178]

— *What follows from this?* That it is well to put gloves on when reading the New Testament. The proximity of so much uncleanliness practically forces us to it. We would be as unlikely to associate with "first Christians" as we would with Polish Jews: not that there would be a need to object to them . . . Neither of them smells good. — I have searched in vain in the New Testament for a single sympathetic trait; there is nothing there that is free, kind, open-hearted, honest. Here, humaneness has not yet made its earliest beginnings — the instincts for *cleanliness* are lacking . . . There are only *bad* instincts in the New Testament, there is not even the courage for these bad instincts. Everything is cowardice, everything in it amounts to turning a blind eye and self-deception in it. Every book becomes clean when one has just read the New Testament: to give an example, immediately after reading Paul, I read with delight that most charming, most exuberant scoffer Petronius, of whom one could say what Domenico Boccaccio wrote to the Duke of Parma about Cesare Borgia: "*è tutto festo*"[179,180] — immortally healthy, immortally cheerful and well-turned-out . . . Actually, these little bigots are mistaken as to the main point. They attack, but everything they attack is thereby *distinguished*. Anyone attacked by a "first Christian" is *not* sullied . . . on the contrary: it is an honor to be opposed by "first Christians." One does not read the New Testament without a preference for what is mistreated in it — to say nothing of the "wisdom of this world," which an impudent windbag vainly seeks to destroy "by the foolishness of preaching" . . . [181] But even the Pharisees and Scribes benefit from such opposition: they must have been worth something after all to have been hated in such an indecent fashion. Hypocrisy — that would be an accusation that "first Christians" would be *allowed* to make! — They were the *privileged*, after all: this suffices, chandala hatred needs no further reasons. The "first Christian" — and, I fear, the "last Christian," *whom I may possibly live to see* — is a rebel against all that is privileged out of deepest instinct — he lives, he fights always for "*equal* rights" . . . On closer inspection, he has no choice. If someone aspires personally to be one of "God's elect" — or a "temple of God" or a "judge of angels" — then every *other* principle of selection, for example, according to uprightness, to intelligence, to manliness and pride, to beauty and freedom of heart, is just "world" — *evil in itself* . . . Moral: every word in the mouth of a "first Christian" is a lie, every action he takes is an instinctive falseness — all his values, all his goals are harmful, but *whom* he hates, *what* he hates, *that has value* . . . The Christian, particularly the Christian priest, is a *criterion for values* — — Do I still need to say that in the whole of the New Testament there is only one *single* figure whom we should honor? Pilate, the Roman governor. To take a Jewish affair *seriously* — of that he cannot convince himself. One Jew more or less — what does it matter? . . . The noble scorn of a Roman, before whom a disgraceful misuse of the word "truth" was perpetrated, has enriched the New Testament with the only phrase *that has value* — that is its criticism, indeed its *annihilation*: "What is truth?" . . . [182]

47.[183]

— It is not this that sets *us* apart from finding God again, either in history, nature, or behind nature — but the fact that we perceive what was revered as God not as "godly," but pitiful, absurd, harmful, not just as an error but as a *crime against life* . . . We deny God as God . . . If the God of the Christians were *proved* to us, we would be even less able to believe in him. — In a formula: *deus, qualem Paulus creavit, dei negatio.*[184] — A religion like Christianity that has no point of contact with reality and collapses the minute reality asserts its rights at even a single point, must be, in fairness, a mortal enemy of the "wisdom of the world," in other words, *of science* — it will endorse all means by which training of the intellect, clarity and rigor in matters of intellectual conscience, and noble coolness and freedom of the mind can all be poisoned, slandered, *denounced.* "Faith" as an imperative is a *veto* against science — *in praxi*, the lie at any price . . . Paul *comprehended* that the lie — that "faith" was necessary; in turn, the Church understood Paul. — That "God" whom Paul invented for himself, a God who "ruins" the "wisdom of the world" (in the narrower sense, the two great opponents of all superstition, philology and medicine), is in truth only the resolute *decision* of Paul to do so: calling his own will "God," Torah, is ur-Jewish.[185,186] Paul *wants* to ruin the "wisdom of the world": his enemies are the *good* philologists and physicians of the Alexandrian school — on them he makes war. In fact, nobody can be a philologist or doctor without being an *anti-Christian* at the same time. For as a philologist, one looks *behind* the "Holy Books," and as a doctor one looks *behind* the physiological depravity of the typical Christian. The doctor says "incurable," the philologist says "swindle" . . .

48.[187]

— Has anyone actually understood the famous story placed at the beginning of the Bible — about God's hellish fear of *science*? . . . It has not been understood. This priestly-book par excellence begins, of course, with the priest's great inner difficulty: *he* faces only one great danger, *consequently*, "God" faces only one great danger. —

The old God, all "spirit," all High Priest, all perfection, takes a pleasant stroll[188] in his garden: however, he is bored. Against boredom even gods struggle in vain.[189] What does he do? He invents the human — the human is entertaining . . . But what do you know, the human is bored as well. God's pity for the only distress shared by all paradises knows no bounds: he immediately creates some more animals. God's *first* mistake: the human did not find the animals entertaining — he ruled over them, he did not even want to be an "animal." Consequently, God created woman. And in fact, that brought boredom to an end — but something else, too! Woman was God's *second* mistake. — "Woman is in her essence serpent, Eve"[190] — every priest knows that; "from woman comes *every* harm in the world" — again, every priest knows that. "*Consequently, science* comes from her as well" . . . Only through woman did man learn to eat from the tree of knowledge. — What had happened? A hellish fear had seized the old God. The human had turned out to be his *biggest* mistake, he had created a rival for himself, science makes people *godlike* — it is all over with priests and gods when the human becomes scientific! — *Moral*: science is what is forbidden as such — it alone is forbidden. Science is the *first* sin, the germ of all sins, the *original* sin. *This alone is morality*. — "Thou shalt *not* know": the rest follows from this. — God's hellish fear did not stop him from being clever. How does one *defend* oneself against science? that became his main problem for a long time. Answer: away with humans from Paradise! Happiness, idleness give rise to thoughts — all thoughts are bad thoughts . . . The human *shall* not think. — And the "priest as such" invents distress, death, the mortal danger of pregnancy, every kind of misery, old age, toil, above all, *sickness* — nothing but means in the battle against science! Distress does not *allow* the human to think . . . And yet! how dreadful! The work of knowledge piles up, storming heaven, twilighting the gods —[191] what is to be done! — The old God invents *war*, he divides the peoples, he causes them to annihilate one another (— the priests have always needed war . . .). War — among other things, a great disturber of science! — Unbelievable! Knowledge, *emancipation from the priests*, even increases in spite of wars. — And the old God arrives at a final decision: "humans became scientific — *it's no use, they will have to be drowned!*" . . .

<h2 style="text-align:center">49.</h2>

— I've been understood. The beginning of the Bible contains the *entire* psychology of the priest. — The priest knows only one single danger: that is science — the healthy grasp of cause and effect. But on the whole, science only flourishes under happy circumstances — one must have time, one must have intellect in *superabundance*, in order to "know" . . . "*Consequently*, humans must be made unhappy," — this was the priest's logic at all times. — One can already guess *what*, according to this logic, then entered the world for the first time: "*sin*" . . . The concept of guilt and punishment, the whole "moral world order," was invented to *counter* science — to *counter* the freeing of humanity from the priest . . . The human shall *not* look outside, he shall look into himself; he shall *not* look prudently and carefully *into* things, as a learner, he shall not look at all: he shall *suffer*. And he shall suffer in such a way that he needs the priest at all times. — Away with doctors! *A savior is needed.* — The concept of guilt and punishment, together with the doctrine of "grace," of "redemption," of "forgiveness" — *lies* through and through and devoid of any psychological reality — have been invented to destroy the human's *sense of causation*: they are an assassination attempt on the concept of cause and effect! — And *not* an assassination attempt with fist, with knife, with honesty in hatred and love! Instead, out of the most cowardly, cunning, base instincts! Assassination attempt by *priests*! Assassination attempt by *parasites*! A vampirism of

pale, underground bloodsuckers! . . . When the natural results
of a deed are no longer "natural," but are thought of as caused
by conceptual ghosts of superstition, by "God," by "spirits," by
"souls," as merely "moral" consequences, as reward, punishment, sign, means of education, then the precondition for
knowledge is destroyed — *then the greatest crime against humanity has been committed.* — [192,193] Sin, I say again, this human
form of self-defilement par excellence, was invented to make
science, culture, every enhancement and nobility of humanity
impossible: the priest *rules* through the invention of sin. —

50.

— At this point I shall not forgo a psychology[194] of "belief,"
of "believers," for the benefit, naturally, of precisely those
"believers." If there is still no lack today of those who do not
know how *indecent* it is to be a "believer" — *or* that it is a
badge of *décadence*,[195] of broken will to life — by tomorrow
they will surely know it. My voice reaches[196] even the hard of
hearing. — It appears, if I have not otherwise misheard, that
there is among Christians a sort of criterion of truth that is
called "demonstration of power." —[197] "Faith makes blessed:
therefore it is true." First it should be objected here that precisely the making blessed is not proved but merely *promised*:
blessedness conditional upon "faith"[198] — one *shall* be blessed
because one has faith . . . But *whether* what the priest promises
the believer actually occurs, for a "hereafter" that is impervious
to any verification, how can *that* be proved? — The ostensible
"demonstration of power" is therefore at bottom just one more
belief that the effect someone expects from faith will not fail to
materialize. In a formula: "I believe that faith makes blessed
— *consequently* it is true." — But with that, we have already
reached the end. This "consequently" would be absurdity itself
as the criterion for truth. — But let us posit, with a certain
indulgence, that making blessed through faith were proven —
not merely desired, *not* merely promised from the rather suspect mouth of the priest: would blessedness — speaking more

technically, *pleasure*, ever be a proof of truth? So little that it practically produces the counterproof, in any case the highest suspicion against "truth," when sensations of pleasure join the conversation over the question "what is true." The proof of "pleasure" is a proof *for* "pleasure" — nothing more; how on earth could it be established that precisely *true* judgments provide more enjoyment than false and, according to a preestablished harmony, necessarily bring pleasant feelings along with them? — The experience of all rigorous, all profoundly inclined intellects teaches *the reverse*. One has to wrestle for the truth every step of the way, one has to sacrifice almost everything to which our heart, our love, our trust in life are otherwise attached. Greatness of soul is required for that: the service of truth is the hardest service.[199] What then does it mean to be *honest* in intellectual matters? That one is strict toward one's heart, that one despises "beautiful feelings," that one's conscience is engaged in every Yes and No! — — — Faith[200] makes blessed: *consequently* it lies . . .

51.

The fact that faith makes blessed in certain circumstances, that blessedness does not make a fixed idea into a *true* idea, that faith does not move mountains but rather *places* them where there are none: a brief walk through a *madhouse* sufficiently clarifies this. *Not* the priest, of course: for he instinctively denies that sickness is sickness and madhouse is madhouse. Christianity *needs* sickness, roughly as Hellenism needed a superabundance of health — *making*-sick is actually the ulterior motive[201] of the Church's entire system of salvation procedures. And the Church itself — is it not the Catholic madhouse as ultimate ideal? Earth in general as a madhouse? — The religious human as the Church *wants* him is a typical *décadent*; the point in time when a religious crisis gains mastery over a people is characterized by nervous epidemics every time; the "inner world" of the religious human can easily be mistaken for the "inner world" of those who are overexcited and exhausted; the "highest" states that Christianity has dangled over humanity as the value of all values are forms of epilepsy —[202] the Church has sanctified only lunatics *or* great deceivers *in majorem dei honorem* . . . [203] I once took the liberty of designating the entire Christian penance- and redemption-training[204] (best studied today in England) as a methodically produced *folie circulaire*,[205] naturally on a ground already prepared for it, that is, a thoroughly morbid one.[206] Nobody is free to become a Christian: one is not "converted" to Christianity — one must be sick enough for it . . . we others who have the *courage* for health *and* also for contempt,[207] how *we* are permitted to despise a religion that taught people to misunderstand the body! that refuses to get rid of the superstition of the soul! that turns insufficient nourishment into an "achievement"! that fights health as a sort of enemy, devil, temptation! that persuaded itself that humans could carry around a "perfect soul" in a cadaver of a body, for which they needed to concoct a new notion of "perfection," a pale, sickly, idiotically fanatic entity, so-called "holiness" — holiness, itself merely a series of symptoms of the impoverished, enervated, incurably corrupted body! . . . The Christian movement, as a European movement, has from the start been nothing but a collective movement of all kinds of refuse- and garbage-elements: — the latter wants to come to power via Christianity. It does *not* express the decline of a race, it is an aggregation of forms of *décadence* from all over, clustering together and seeking each other out. It was *not*, as is believed, the corruption of antiquity itself, of *noble* antiquity, that made Christianity possible; the scholarly idiocy that still upholds something like that even today cannot be contradicted harshly enough. In the time when the sick, ruined chandala castes were becoming Christianized throughout the empire, the exactly *opposite type*, nobility, was present in its most beautiful and mature form. The greater number took control; the democratization of Christian instincts *triumphed* . . . Christianity was not "national," not conditional upon race — it turned toward the disinherited in life of every kind, it had its allies everywhere. Christianity has at its bottom the rancor of the sick, directing its instinct *against* the healthy, *against* health. Everything that has turned out well, proud, high-spirited, above all, beautiful, hurt its ears and eyes. Let us once again recall the invaluable word of Paul: "But God hath chosen the *foolish* things of the world and God hath chosen the *weak* things of the world and *base* things of the world, and things which are *despised*":[208] *that* was the formula, *in hoc signo*,[209] *décadence* triumphed. — *God on the cross* — do we still not understand the terrible ulterior motivation of this symbol? — Everything that suffers, everything that hangs on the cross, is divine . . . We all hang on the cross, consequently *we* are divine . . . We alone are divine . . . Christianity was a victory, a *nobler* mentality was destroyed by it — Christianity has up till now been the greatest calamity for humanity. — —

52.

Christianity also stands in opposition to everything *intellectual* that has turned out well — it *can* only use sick reasoning as Christian reasoning, it takes sides with everything idiotic,[210] it pronounces a curse on the "mind," against the *superbia*[211] of the healthy mind. Because sickness belongs to the essence of Christianity, the typical Christian state, "faith," *must* also be a form of sickness, while the Church *must* reject all upright, honest, scientific paths to knowledge as *forbidden* paths. Doubt is already a sin . . . The complete lack of psychological cleanliness in the priest — betrayed in his glance — is a *resultant* manifestation of *décadence* — one should observe in hysterical women, as well as children with a propensity to rickets, how regularly instinctive falseness, pleasure in lying for the sake of lying and an incapacity to look straight and walk straight, are the expression of *décadence*. "Faith" means not-*wanting*-to-know what is true. The Pietist, the priest of either sex, is false *because* of sickness: his instinct *demands* that truth should at no point come into its own. "Whatever makes us sick is *good*; whatever comes from abundance, from superabundance, from power, is *evil*":

that is what the believer feels. *The unfreedom to lie* — from that I can spot every predestined theologian. — Another sign of the theologian is his *ineptitude for philology*. By philology should be understood here, in a very general sense, the art of reading well — recognizing facts *without* falsifying them through interpretation, *without* losing caution, patience, finesse in the drive for comprehension. Philology as *ephexis*[212] in interpretation: whether concerning books, newspaper columns, destinies or weather events — to say nothing of the "salvation of the soul" . . . The way in which a theologian, regardless of whether in Berlin or Rome, interprets a "word of Scripture" or an experience, for example a victory of his country's army, under the higher illumination of the Psalms of David, is always so *audacious* that it drives a philologist up the wall. And what is he supposed to do when Pietists and other cows from Swabia[213] use the "finger of God"[214] to finagle the pitiful tedium and parlor smoke of their existence into a miracle of "grace," of "providence," of "experiences of salvation"! The most modest outlay of intelligence, not to mention *decency*, would certainly have to convince these interpreters of the complete childishness and unworthiness of such an abuse of divine dexterity. If we had even the smallest trace of piety deep down, we ought to view a God who cures a cold at the right time or has us climb into a carriage at the very moment of a cloudburst as so absurd that we would have to get rid of him, even if he existed. A God as a domestic servant, a postman, a calendar-maker — at bottom, a word for the most stupid sort of all accidents[215] . . . "Divine Providence," as believed today by roughly every third human being in "educated Germany," would be such an objection against God that a stronger one could not be conceived. And in any case, it is an objection against the Germans! . . . [216]

53.

— The idea that *martyrs* prove something about the truth of a cause is so little true that I would like to deny that a martyr ever had anything at all to do with the truth. The tone with which a martyr throws into the world's face what he holds to be true already expresses such a low degree of intellectual honesty, such *obtuseness* for the question of truth, that one need never refute a martyr. The truth is not something one might have and another might not: at best, only peasants or peasant-apostles in Luther's mode, can think like this about truth. You can be sure that, in keeping with the level of conscientiousness in matters of the intellect, modesty and *moderation* on this point will continually increase. To *know* about five things, and with gentle hands to refuse to know anything *else* . . . "Truth," as every prophet, every sectarian, every free-thinker, every socialist, every cleric understands the word, is proof positive that not so much as a start has been made to the discipline and self-overcoming of the intellect necessary for the discovery of the smallest, indeed minutest, truth. — By the way, the deaths of martyrs are a great historical misfortune: they *seduced* . . . The inference of all idiots, women and peoples included, that a cause for which someone goes to his death (or which even, as in early Christianity, produces suicidal epidemics) must have something to it — this inference has become an unspeakable stumbling block to verification, to the spirit of verification and caution. Martyrs have *damaged* truth . . . Even today, all we need is a crudity of persecution to create an *honorable* name for some otherwise indifferent sectarianism.[217] — What? Does it alter the value of a cause somewhat if somebody lays down his life for it? — An error that becomes honorable is an error that possesses one more seductive charm: do you think, dear theologians, that we would give you the opportunity to make martyrs of yourselves for your lie? — A matter can be refuted by respectfully putting it on ice — theologians can be refuted in like manner . . . That precisely was the world-historical stupidity of all persecutors, that they gave the opposing cause an honorable appearance — that they endowed it with the fascination of martyrdom . . . Woman still goes down on her knees before an error because she has been told that someone died for it on the cross. *So is the cross an argument?* — — But on all these matters, only one single person has said the word that has been necessary for millennia — *Zarathustra.*

> They wrote signs in blood on the path they traveled, and their folly taught that truth is proven by blood.
>
> But blood is the worst evidence of truth; blood poisons even the purest doctrine, turning hearts toward delusion and hatred.
>
> And if people walk[218] through fire for their[219] doctrine — what does this prove! In fact, it means more when our doctrine comes from the fire within us.[220]

54.[221]

We should not let ourselves be led astray: great intellects are skeptics. Zarathustra is a skeptic. Strength, *freedom* through force and superior force of the intellect *prove* themselves by skepticism. Humans of conviction do not at all come into consideration for anything fundamental to value and non-value. Convictions are prisons. They do not see far enough, they do not see *below* themselves: but in order to be allowed to join the conversation about value and nonvalue, one must see five hundred convictions *below* oneself — *behind* oneself . . . An intellect that desires greatness as well as the means for it is by necessity a skeptic. Freedom from any kind of conviction *belongs* to strength, the *ability* to gaze freely . . . Great passion, the ground and the power of his being, more enlightened, more despotic than he himself is, takes his entire intellect into service; it makes him dauntless; it even inspires the courage for unholy means; it even *grants* him convictions under certain circumstances. Conviction as a *means*: much is achieved only by means of conviction. Great passion uses and uses up convictions, it does not succumb to them — knowing itself sovereign. — Conversely: the need for faith, for some kind of unconditional Yes and No, Carlylism, if one will excuse my use of this term,[222] is a need out of *weakness*. The human of faith, the "believer" of any kind, is of necessity a dependent human — someone who cannot posit *himself* as an end, who for his own part cannot posit ends in general. The "believer" does not belong to *himself*, he can only be a means, he must be *used up*, he needs someone to use him up. His instinct awards the highest honor to a morality of unselfing: he is persuaded to it by everything, his cleverness, his experience, his vanity. Every kind of faith is itself an expression of unselfing, self-alienation . . . If one considers how necessary a regulating influence is to most people, that binds them externally and unites them, how compulsion, in a higher sense, *slavery*, is the only and final condition under which the weaker-willed human, especially woman, can thrive: then one also understands conviction, "faith." The human of conviction owes his backbone to it. *Not* to see many things, to be impartial at no point, to be partial through and through, to have a rigorous and necessary perspective in all values — this alone conditions whether such a human can exist at all. But it is therefore the opposite, the *antagonist*, of truthfulness — of truth . . . The "believer" is not free to even have a conscience for any question of "true" or "untrue": to have integrity at *this* point would immediately be his destruction. The pathological conditioning of his perspective makes a fanatic out of the man of conviction — Savonarola, Luther, Rousseau, Robespierre, Saint-Simon — the countertype to the strong spirit who has become *free*.[223] But the grand posing of these *sick* intellects, these conceptual epileptics, affects the great multitude — fanatics are picturesque, humankind would rather see gestures than hear *reasons* . . . [224]

55.[225]

— One step further into the psychology of conviction, of "faith." It has already been a long time since I floated for consideration whether convictions are not more dangerous enemies to truth than lies (*Human, All Too Human*).[226] This time I would like to put the decisive question: does any contrast at all exist between a lie and a conviction? The whole world believes this; but what doesn't the whole world believe! — Every conviction has its history, its early forms, its tentative stages and mistakes: it *becomes* a conviction after it has *not* been one for a long time, after it has *scarcely* been one for an even longer time. What? Could not the lie also be among these embryonic forms of conviction? — Now and then merely a change of person is needed: in the son, conviction becomes what was still a lie in the father. — I call it a lie *not* to want to see something that one sees, not to want to see something *as* one sees it: whether the lie takes place in front of witnesses or without witnesses is irrelevant. The most ordinary lie is the one with which one lies to oneself; lying to others is relatively an exception. —[227] Now this *not* wanting to see things that one sees, this not wanting to see something *as* one sees it, is practically the first condition for all who show *partiality* in any sense of the word: the party man becomes by necessity a liar. For example, German historiography is convinced that Rome was despotism, that the Teutonic tribes brought the spirit of freedom into the world: what is the difference between this conviction and a lie? Is it still any wonder if all parties, even the German historians, instinctively mouth grand words about morality — that morality virtually *survives* because the party man of any persuasion needs it every moment? — "This is *our* conviction: we confess it before the whole world, we live and die for it — respect for all who have convictions!" — I have even heard the like from the mouths of anti-Semites. On the contrary, gentlemen! An anti-Semite absolutely does not become more decent because he lies on principle . . .[228] The priests, who are subtler in such things[229] and understand well the objection that in the concept of a conviction lies a fundamental mendaciousness *because* it is expedient, have commandeered the Jews' ingenuity of inserting the concept "God," "will of God," "revelation of God" at this point. Kant as well, with his categorical imperative, was on the same path: his reason became *practical* in this matter.

— There are questions where it is *not* given to humans to decide between truth and untruth; all the supreme questions, all the supreme problems of value are beyond human reason . . . to understand the limits of reason — *that* alone is truly philosophy . . . Why did God reveal himself to humanity? Would God have done anything superfluous? Humans *can*not know of themselves what good and evil is, therefore God taught them his will . . . Moral: the priest does *not* lie — the question of "true" or "untrue" in such things spoken of by priests allows for no lying at all.[230] For in order to lie, a human must have been able to decide *what* is true here. But that is just what the human *can*not do; which makes the priest only the mouthpiece of God. — A priestly syllogism of this nature is absolutely not confined to Jews and Christians: the right to lie and the *ingenuity* of "revelation" belong to the priestly type, to *décadence*-priests as well as heathen priests (— all are heathens who say Yes to life, to whom "God" is the word for the great Yes to all things[231]). — The "law," the "will of God," the "holy book," "inspiration" — all just words for the conditions *under* which the priest comes to power, *with* which he upholds his power — these concepts are found at the foundation of all priestly organizations, all priestly or philosophically-priestly structures of ruling. The "holy lie" — common to Confucius, the code of Manu, Mohammed, the Christian Church: it is not lacking in Plato. "The truth is there": this means, wherever word gets out, *the priest is lying* . . .

56.

— Ultimately it depends on the *end* for which someone is lying. The fact that "holy" ends are lacking in Christianity is *my* objection to its means. Only *bad* ends: poisoning, slander, denial of life, contempt for the body, denigration and self-violation of the human through the concept of sin — *consequently* its means are bad as well. I read the code of *Manu* with the opposite feeling, an incomparably intelligent and superior work, such that even comparing it with the Bible in the same

breath would be a sin against the *spirit*. One discovers immediately: it has a real philosophy behind it, *in* it, not just a foul-
smelling Judaine[232] of rabbinism and superstition — it gives
even the most pampered psychologist something to bite on.
Not to forget the main thing, its fundamental difference from
any kind of Bible: with this book, the *noble* classes, philosophers and warriors provide protection to the multitudes;[233]
noble values everywhere, a feeling of perfection, a saying Yes
to life, a triumphant feeling of well-being in one's self and in
life — the *sun* shines on the whole book. — All things upon
which Christianity vents its unfathomable churlishness, procreation for example, woman, marriage, are handled here with
reverence, with love and trust. Really, how can one place a
book into the hands of children and women which contains
the vile passage: "to avoid fornication, let every man have his
own wife, and let every woman have her own husband: for it is
better to marry than to burn."[234] And is one *permitted* to be a
Christian as long as the concept of *immaculata conceptio*[235]
Christianizes the origin of humankind, that is, *sullies* it? . . . I
know of no book where so many tender and kind things are
said about women as they are in the code of Manu; these old
graybeards and saints have a way of being courteous toward
women that is perhaps unsurpassed. In one place it says: "The
mouth of a woman, the breast of a girl, the prayer of a child,
the smoke of sacrifice, are always pure."[236] Another passage:
"There is nothing purer than the light of the sun, the shadow
of a cow, air, water, fire and the breath of a young girl." One
final passage — perhaps another holy lie — : "all orifices of
the body above the navel are pure, all below are impure. Only
with the young girl is the whole body pure."

57.

One catches *in flagranti*[237] the *unholiness* of Christian means
when one compares the *Christian goal* with the goal of the
code of Manu — when one sheds strong light on this greatest
contrast of goals. The critic of Christianity cannot avoid making

Christianity *despicable*. — A code of law such as that of Manu
arises like every good book of law: it summarizes the experience, prudence and experimental morality of long centuries, it
concludes, it creates nothing more. The precondition for a
codification of this kind is the insight that the means of lend-
ing authority to a slowly and expensively won truth are fundamentally different from those with which it might be proved.
A code of law never tells the use, reasons, casuistry in the prehistory of a law: that is precisely what would forfeit the imperative tone, the "Thou shalt," the prerequisite for its being
obeyed. This is exactly where the problem lies. — At a certain
point in the development of a people, its most circumspect
class, that is, the one that gazes furthest back and furthest out,
declares the experience according to which they should live
— that is, *can* live — as finished. Their objective is to bring
home the richest and most complete possible harvest from the
times of experimentation and *bad* experience. Consequently,
what is to be avoided above all now is the continuance of experimentation, the perpetuation of a fluid state of values, the
testing, choosing, exercising of criticism of values *in infinitum*.
A double wall is erected against this: first, *revelation*, which is
the claim that the rationality of these laws is *not* of human
descent, *not* slowly sought and found amid blunders, but
merely communicated, of divine origin, whole, perfect, without a history, a gift, a miracle . . . Then *tradition*, which is the
claim that the law had already existed since time immemorial,
that it would be impiety, a crime against ancestors, to place it
in doubt. The authority of the law is founded on the propositions: God *gave* it, the ancestors *lived* it. — The higher reasoning of such a procedure is the aim of repressing step by step
the consciousness of a life judged to be appropriate (that is,
demonstrated by a tremendous and rigorously sifted experience): so that complete automatism of instinct is reached —
this precondition for every kind of mastery, for every kind of
perfection in the art of living. To draw up a law code such as
that of Manu means henceforth allowing a people to become

masters, to become perfect — to aspire to the highest art of living. *For that, it has to be made unconscious*: this is the purpose of every holy lie. — The *order of castes*, the supreme, dominating law, is merely the endorsement of a *natural order*, natural lawfulness of the first rank, over which no arbitrariness, no "modern idea" has power. In every healthy society, three mutually conditioning types emerge, gravitating differently in physiological terms, each with its own hygiene, its own sphere of labor, its own version of a feeling of perfection and mastery. Nature, *not* Manu, divides up those who are predominantly intellectual, those who are predominantly strong in muscle and temperament, and the third section, the mediocre, who do not excel in either group — the latter as the great majority, the former as the elite. The supreme caste — I call it *the fewest*, being perfect, also has the prerogatives of the fewest: which include representing happiness, beauty, goodness on earth. Only the most intelligent humans are entitled to beauty, *to* the beautiful: only with them is goodness not weakness. *Pulchrum est paucorum hominum*:[238] the good is a prerogative. Nothing on the other hand can be less conceded to them than ugly manners or a pessimistic mien, an eye that *renders ugly* — or even indignation at the overall aspect of things. Indignation is the prerogative of the chandala: pessimism likewise. "*The world is perfect*"[239] — thus speaks the instinct of the most intelligent, the Yes-saying instinct: "imperfection, anything that is *beneath* us, distance, the pathos of distance, even the chandala still belongs to this perfection." The most intelligent humans, as the *strongest*, find their happiness where others would find their destruction: in the labyrinth, in their severity toward themselves and others, in experimentation: their pleasure is self-mastery: in them, asceticism becomes nature, need, instinct. A difficult task is considered by them a privilege; playing with burdens that would crush others, a *recreation* . . . knowledge — a form of asceticism. — They are the most venerable kind of human: which does not exclude the fact that they are the most cheerful, the most charming. They rule, not because they want to, but because they *are*, they are not at liberty to be second. — The *second*: these are the guardians of the law, the keepers of order and safety, these are the noble warriors, above all, this is the *king*, as the highest formula of warrior, judge and upholder of the law. The second are the executives of the most intelligent, what is closest and belongs to them, the ones who remove everything *vulgar* from the task of ruling — their entourage, their right hand, their best pupils. — To say it again, there is nothing in all this that is arbitrary, nothing "contrived": what *differs* from this, is contrived, — then nature is ruined by this contrivance . . . The order of castes, the *order of rank*, only formulates the supreme law of life itself, the separation of the three types is necessary to maintain society, to make possible the superior and the supreme types — the *inequality* of rights is the first precondition for the existence of any rights at all. — A right is a prerogative. Everyone's mode of being is also their prerogative. We should not underestimate the prerogatives of the *mediocre*. A life striving for the *heights* becomes harder and harder — coldness increases, responsibility increases. A high culture is a pyramid: it can only stand on a broad base, its uppermost prerequisite is a strongly and robustly consolidated mediocrity. The crafts, trade, farming, *science*, the greatest part of art, in a word, the whole epitome of occupational activity, is really only compatible with a mediocre measure of ability and desire: such matters would be out of place among exceptional individuals, since the attendant instinct would contradict both aristocratism and anarchism. For someone to be a public boon, a cog, a function, there is a natural predisposition to this: *not* society but the sort of *happiness* of which the majority alone are capable makes intelligent machines out of them. For the mediocre one, being mediocre is his happiness; mastery of a single thing, specialization, a natural instinct. It would be completely unworthy of a profounder mind to object to mediocrity as such. It is even the *primary* necessity that makes exceptions possible: a high culture is dependent on it. When an exceptional human being handles those who are mediocre more gently than himself and his peers, this is not merely politeness of the heart[240] — it is simply his *duty* . . . Who do I hate most among today's rabble? The socialist rabble, the apostles of chandala who undermine the worker's instinct, pleasure, the feeling of contentment with his small existence — who arouse his envy, who teach him revenge . . . Injustice never resides in unequal rights, it resides in the claim to "*equal*" rights. What is *bad*? But I have said it already: everything that stems from weakness, from envy, from *revenge*. — The anarchist and the Christian share the same descent . . .

58.

Indeed, it makes a difference to what end someone lies: whether it is used to uphold or to *destroy*. One may posit a perfect equivalence between a *Christian* and an *anarchist*: their end, their instinct is bent on destruction alone. The proof of this premise need only be read in history: it is contained there, in appalling clarity. If we just now examined a religious legislation whose purpose was to "perpetuate" a grand organization of society as the supreme condition for life to *prosper*, Christianity found its mission in putting an end to precisely such an organization *because life prospered in it*. In the former, the rational fruit of long ages of experimentation and uncertainty was supposed to be laid out for the furthest possible use and the harvest brought home in the grandest, most abundant, most complete way possible: in the latter, by contrast, the harvest was *poisoned* overnight . . . What stood there as *aere perennius*,[241] the *imperium Romanum*,[242] the most magnificent form of organization under difficult circumstances yet achieved, in comparison to which everything before and after is patchwork, bungling, dilettantism — those holy anarchists made themselves a "piety" out of destroying "the world," *that is*, the *imperium Romanum*, until no stone was left on top of another — until even the Teutons and other louts were able to assume mastery over it . . . The Christian and the anarchist: both *décadents*, both incapable of having any effect besides disintegrating, poisoning, atrophying, *bloodsucking*, both the instinct of *lethal hatred* toward everything that stands, that stands there in greatness, that lasts long, that promises life a future . . . Christianity was the vampire of the *imperium Romanum* — overnight it undid the Romans' colossal deed of gaining ground for a great culture *that would have time.* — Is this still not understood? The *imperium Romanum* that we know, that the history of the Roman province teaches us to know better and better, this most awe-inspiring artwork in the grand style, was a beginning, its construction was calculated to *prove* itself over millennia — up till now, nobody has built like this, nor even so much as dreamed of building *sub specie aeterni*[243] on the same scale! — This organization was sufficiently secure to outlast bad emperors: the randomness of persons must have nothing to do with such matters — *first* principle of all great architecture. But it was not sufficiently secure against the *most corrupt* form of corruption, against the *Christian* . . . This stealthy worm slithered up to every single individual in night, fog and ambiguity, and sucked out of each individual the earnestness for *true* things, the very instinct for *realities*; this cowardly, effeminate and sugar-laden pack, alienated the "souls" from this colossal structure step by step — those valuable, those manly noble natures who felt that the cause of Rome was theirs too, their own earnestness, their own *pride.* The sneakiness of bigots, the secretiveness of the conventicle, obscure concepts like hell, the sacrifice of the innocent, like *unio mystica*[244] in drinking blood, above all the slowly fanned fire of revenge, of chandala-revenge — *that* became master over Rome, the same kind of religion on whose preexistent form Epicurus had already waged war. Read Lucretius to understand *what* Epicurus fought against, *not* paganism but "Christianity," or rather, corruption of souls through guilt, through the concept of punishment and immortality. — He fought against the *underground* cults, the entire latent Christianity — to deny immortality back then was already a true *redemption.* — And Epicurus would have triumphed, every respectable intellect in the Roman Empire was an Epicurean: *then came Paul* . . . Paul, the chandala-hatred against Rome, against "the world," turned flesh and genius, the Jew, the *wandering* Jew[245] par excellence . . . What he discovered was how a "world conflagration" could be kindled with the help of a small sectarian Christian movement set apart from Judaism, how, with the symbol of "God on the Cross," all losers, all who were secretly rebellious, the whole legacy of anarchistic instigations in the empire, could be consolidated into a tremendous power. "Salvation comes from the Jews."[246] — Christianity as a formula to outbid the underground cults of every kind, for example that of Osiris, the Great Mother, of Mithras — *and* sum them up: this insight constitutes the genius of Paul. His instinct for this was so sure that, with merciless violence to the truth, he put the ideas with which those chandala-religions fascinated into the mouth of the "Savior" he had invented, and not just into his mouth — so that he *made* something out of him that even a Mithras priest could understand . . . This was his Damascus moment: he realized that he *needed* the immortality-belief in order to devalue "the world," that the concept of "hell" would one day gain mastery over Rome itself — that with "the beyond," *life is killed* . . . Nihilist and Christ(ian): it rhymes, it doesn't just rhyme . . . [247]

59.

The whole labor of the ancient world *in vain*: I have no words to express my feelings about something so tremendous. — And considering that their labor was a preliminary, that the mere foundations for a labor of millennia had been laid with a granite self-assurance, the whole *meaning* of the ancient world in vain! Why the Greeks? Why the Romans? — All the preconditions for a learned culture, all scientific *methods* were already there; they had already established the great, incomparable art of reading well — this prerequisite for a tradition of culture, for unified science; natural science, in league with

mathematics and mechanics, was on the best track possible
— the *sense for facts*, the ultimate and most valuable of all the
senses, had its schools, its already centuries-old traditions! Is
that understood? Everything *essential* had been discovered for
work to commence: — the methods, one has to say it ten
times, *are* what is essential, also what is most difficult, also
what are opposed by habits and laziness for longest. What we
have reconquered now with unspeakable self-restraint — for in
some way we all still embody the bad instincts, the Christian
ones — the open view on reality, the cautious hand, patience
and earnestness in the smallest things, the whole *integrity* of
knowledge — it was already there! Already more than two
thousand years ago! *And*, added to that, good, refined tact and
taste! *Not* as brain-training! *Not* as "German" education with
loutish manners! Rather as body, gesture, instinct — as reality,
in a word . . . *All in vain!* Overnight, nothing but a memory!
— Greeks! Romans! Nobility of instinct, taste, methodical
research, the genius of organization and administration, the
belief in and *will* for a human-future, the great Yes to all things
manifesting as the *imperium Romanum*, manifesting for all the
senses, grand style no longer merely art but become reality,
truth, *life* . . . — And not buried overnight by a catastrophe of
nature! Not trampled underfoot by Teutons and other ponder-
ous beasts! Instead, ravished by cunning, secretive, invisible,
anemic vampires! Not conquered — just sucked dry! . . . Hidden lust for revenge, petty envy became *master*! Everything
pitiful, suffering from itself, afflicted-by-bad-feelings, the whole
ghetto-world of the psyche was *on top* all at once! — — Just
read any Christian agitator, Saint Augustine[248] for example, to
understand, to *smell*, what kind of insalubrious fellows came
out on top. One would be wholly deceived to presuppose any
sort of lack of intelligence among the leaders of the Christian
movement: — oh, they are shrewd, shrewd to the point of
sanctity,[249] these distinguished Church Fathers! What they lack
is something quite different. Nature has neglected them —
it forgot to endow them with a modest dowry of honorable, of

decent, of *clean* instincts . . . Spoken in confidence, they are not even men . . . If Islam despises Christianity, it is right to do so a thousand times over: Islam has men as a prerequisite . . .[250]

60.[251]

Christianity deprived us of the harvest of antique culture, later again it deprived us of the harvest of *Islamic* culture. The wonderful Moorish cultural world of Spain, at bottom more closely related to *us*, more conducive to our senses and taste than Rome and Greece, was *trampled underfoot* — I will not say by what kind of feet — and why? because it owed its emergence to noble, to manly instincts, because it said Yes to life even with the rare and refined treasures of Moorish life! . . . [252] Later, the Crusaders fought something before which they would have done better to prostrate themselves in the dust — a culture in comparison to which even our nineteenth century might appear very poor, very "late." — Of course, they wanted spoils: the Orient was rich . . . Let's be uninhibited after all! Crusades — a superior piracy, nothing more! — The German nobility, at bottom Viking nobility, was now in its element: the Church knew only too well what it takes to *own* the German nobility . . . The German nobility, ever the "Swiss" of the Church, ever in the service of all the bad instincts of the Church — but *well paid* . . . That the Church should have carried out its war of deadly hatred against everything noble on earth precisely with the aid of German swords, German blood and bravery! At this point there are a number of painful questions.[253] The German nobility is practically *absent* from the history of higher culture: one can guess the reason . . . Christianity, alcohol — the two *major* means of corruption . . . Really, there should be no choice when faced with Islam and Christianity, as little as between an Arab and a Jew. The decision has been given, nobody is free to make a choice here anymore. Either one *is* chandala or one is *not* . . . "War with Rome at knife point! Peace, friendship with Islam": that is what that great free-thinker, that genius among German emperors, Friedrich the Second, felt and *did*.[254] What? Must a German first be a genius, first be a freethinker, to have feelings of *decency*? I do not understand how a German could ever feel *Christian* . . .

61.

Here it is necessary to touch on a memory a hundredfold more painful for the Germans. The Germans deprived Europe of the last great harvest of culture that could still be brought home — that of the *Renaissance*. Does anyone finally understand, *want* to understand, *what* the Renaissance was? The *revaluation of Christian values*, the attempt, undertaken using every means, every instinct, every genius, to render victorious the *counter*values, the *noble* values . . . Up till now there has been only *this* great war, till now, there has never been a more decisive formulation of the question than that of the Renaissance — *my* question is its question — : nor has there ever been a more fundamental, a straighter, more rigorously executed form of complete frontal *attack* on the center! Attacking the decisive spot, at the very seat of Christianity itself, bringing *noble* values onto the throne, in other words, *inserting* them into the instincts, into the deepest needs and desires of those seated there . . . I see a *possibility* before me of a completely superterrestrial magic and colorful allure: — it seems to me that it glitters with every shudder of refined beauty, that there is at work in it an art so divine, so devilishly divine, that one could search for millennia in vain for a second possibility of its kind; I see a spectacle so ingenious, so wonderfully paradoxical at the same time, that all the deities of Olympus would have had occasion for immortal laughter — *Cesare Borgia as pope* . . . Do you understand me? . . . Well then, *that* would have been the only victory that *I* am craving today — : with that, Christianity was *abolished*![255] — What happened? A German monk, Luther, came to Rome. This monk, who embodied all the vindictive instincts of a hapless priest, was outraged in Rome *against* the Renaissance . . . Instead of gratefully acknowledging the tremendous thing that had happened, the conquest of Christianity in its own *seat*, only his hatred knew how to feed on this spectacle. A religious human thinks only of himself.

— Luther saw the *corruption* of the papacy, whereas precisely the opposite was palpable: the old corruption, *peccatum originale*, Christianity, was *no* longer seated on the papal[256] throne! But life! But the triumph of life! But the great Yes to all lofty, beautiful, audacious things! . . . And Luther *restored the Church*: he attacked it . . . The Renaissance — an event without meaning, a great *in vain*! — Oh, these Germans, how much they have cost us already! In vain — that was always the *work* of the Germans. — The Reformation; Leibniz; Kant and so-called German philosophy; the wars of liberation; the Reich — every time an "in vain" for something that had been there already, for something *irretrievable* . . .[257] I confess, these Germans are *my* enemies: I despise in them every manner of uncleanliness pertaining to concepts and values, of *cowardliness* toward every honest Yes and No. For almost a millennium they have tangled and confused everything that their fingers touched, they have on their conscience all the half-measures — three-eighths measures! — that have made Europe sick — they also have on their conscience the uncleanest form of Christianity there is, the most incurable, the most irrefutable, Protestantism . . . If we cannot have done with Christianity, it will be the *Germans'* fault . . .

62.

— With that, I have reached the end and I pronounce judgment. I *condemn* Christianity, I raise against the Christian Church the most terrible of all charges that an accuser has ever uttered. To me, it is the worst of all conceivable corruptions, it has had the will to the absolute ultimate possible corruption. The Christian Church allowed nothing to remain untouched by its corruption, it turned every value into an unvalue, every truth into a lie, every integrity into a vileness of the soul. Let anyone dare speak to me about its "humanitarian" blessings! *Doing away* with any kind of distress went against its deepest expediency — it lived on distress, it *created* distress in order to eternalize *itself* . . . The worm of sin, for example: it was only the Church that enriched humanity with this distress! — The "equality of souls before God," this falsehood, this *pretext* for the *rancunes*[258] of all the basest mentalities, this explosive of a concept that has ultimately become revolution, modern idea and the principle of decline of the entire social order — is *Christian* dynamite . . . "Humanitarian" blessings of Christianity! To breed out of *humanitas* a self-contradiction, an art of self-violation, a will to lie at any price, an aversion, a contempt for all good and righteous instincts! — To me these are the blessings of Christianity! — Parasitism as the *sole* practice of the Church; with its anemia and "holiness" ideal drinking up any blood, any love, any hope from life: the beyond as will to the denial of all reality; the cross as the distinguishing mark of the most subterranean conspiracy that ever existed — against health, beauty, turning out well, bravery, intelligence, *kindness* of soul, *against life itself* . . .

This eternal charge against Christianity I will write on all walls, wherever walls are found — I have letters that could make even the blind see . . . I name Christianity the one great curse, the one great innermost corruption, the one great instinct for revenge, for which no means is sufficiently poisonous, covert, subterranean, *petty* — I name it the one immortal stain on humanity . . .

And we calculate *time* based on the *dies nefastus*[259] with which this calamity began — based on the *first* day of Christianity! — *Why not based on its last day instead? — Based on today?*[260] Revaluation of all values! . . . [261]

       *   *   *   *

        *   *

        *   *

       *

Law Against Christianity.

Passed on the day of grace, the first day of Year One (— on the 30th of September 1888 of the false calculation of time)

War to the death against vice: vice is Christianity

First Proposition: — Every form of anti-nature is a vice. The most vicious kind of human is the priest: he *teaches* anti-nature. To counter the priest we do not have reasons, we have the penitentiary.

Second proposition: — Any participation in a church service is an assassination attempt on public morality. We should be harsher toward Protestants than Catholics, harsher toward liberal Protestants than toward those of strict faith. The criminality of being a Christian increases proportionate to one's proximity to knowledge.[1] The criminal of criminals therefore is the *philosopher.*

Third proposition: — The cursed site upon which Christianity hatched its basilisk eggs shall have its earth leveled and shall be the abomination of all posterity as a *heinous* place on earth. Poisonous snakes shall be bred there.

Fourth proposition: — The preaching of chastity is a public incitement to anti-nature. Every disparagement of sexuality, every defilement of the same by the concept "impure," is the very sin against the holy spirit of life.

Fifth proposition: — To share a dinner table with a priest is disqualifying: one thereby excommunicates oneself from honorable society. The priest is *our* chandala — he shall be defamed, starved, and driven into any kind of desert by us.

Sixth proposition: — We should call the "holy" story by the name it deserves, the *accursed* story; we should use the words "God," "savior," "Redeemer," "saint" as invectives, as terms to designate criminals.

Seventh proposition: — Everything else follows from this.

The Antichrist

Ecce Homo.[1,2]

How One Becomes What One Is.[3]

Foreword.

1.

Anticipating that I must shortly approach humanity with the heaviest demand that has ever been made on it, I find it imperative to say *who I am*. Basically, you ought to know: for I have not "left myself without a testimonial." But the mismatch between the greatness of my task and the *smallness* of my contemporaries found expression in that nobody either heard me or indeed saw me. I live on my own credit, perhaps it is just a preconception that I am alive? . . . I need only talk to any "cultured" person visiting the Upper Engadine in summer to[1] convince myself that I am *not* alive . . . Under these circumstances, I actually have the duty, against which my habit and, even more so, the pride of my instincts fundamentally revolts, to say: *Hear me! for I am so-and-so. Above all, don't mistake me for someone else!*

2.

For example, I am certainly no bogey or monster of morality — I even have the opposite nature to the type of human hitherto honored as virtuous. Between ourselves, I believe that very fact does me proud. I am a disciple of the philosopher Dionysus, I would prefer to be a satyr rather than a saint. But just read this work. Perhaps I have succeeded, perhaps this work had no other purpose than to articulate this antithesis in a cheerful and humane way. The last thing that *I* would promise would be to "improve" humanity. I shall set up no new idols; the old ones can learn what it is to have feet[2] of clay. *To topple idols* (my word for "ideals") — that is more consistent with my craft. Reality has been shorn of its value, its purpose, its veracity in proportion to how people have *invented* an ideal world . . . The "true world" and the "apparent world"[3] — in plain language, the *made-up* world and reality . . . The *lie* about the ideal has hitherto been a curse on reality, through it humanity itself became mendacious and false right down to its deepest instincts — to the point of worshipping the *reverse* values of those with which, alone, its prosperity and future, the lofty *right* to a future would be guaranteed.[4]

3.

— Anyone who knows how to breathe the air of my works knows that it is the air of the heights, *strong* air. You have to be born to it, otherwise there is no little danger you will catch cold in it. Ice is nearby, the solitude is immense — but how peacefully everything lies in the light! How freely you breathe! You feel how much there is *beneath* you![5,6] — Philosophy, as I have understood and lived it so far, is choosing to live in an area of ice and high mountains — the seeking out of all that is strange and dubious in existence, everything that morality had hitherto placed beyond the pale. From long experience provided[7] by such a journey *in the forbidden*, I learned to view the causes thus far of moralizing and idealizing in a very different way than might be wished: the *hidden* history of the philosophers, the psychology of their great names, came to light for me. — How much truth does a spirit *bear*, how much truth does it *dare*? That increasingly became for me the real measure of value. Error[8] (— the belief in the ideal —) is not blindness, error is *cowardice* . . . Every achievement, every forward step in knowledge *follows* from courage and severity toward oneself, from cleanliness toward oneself . . . I do not refute ideals, I just wear gloves in case . . . *Nitimur in vetitum*:[9] someday this sign will mark a victory for my philosophy, for people have hitherto always forbidden outright only what was the truth — .

4.[10]

— Among my works, my *Zarathustra* stands alone. With it, I presented humanity with the greatest gift it ever received.[11] This book, with a voice sounding down the millennia, is not only the loftiest book that there is, the real book for the air of the heights — the whole fact of the human lies an immense distance *beneath* it — it is also the *deepest*, born out of the innermost wealth of truth, an inexhaustible well where no bucket descends without coming back full of gold and goodness. No "prophet" speaks here, none of those ghastly crossbreeds of sickness and will to power that we call founders of religion. You must above all *hear* aright the tone that comes from this mouth, this halcyon tone, to avoid doing lamentable injustice to the meaning of its wisdom. "The stillest words are the ones that summon the storm, thoughts that arrive on doves' feet steer the world —"[12]

> The figs fall from the trees, they are good and sweet: and as they fall, their red skin splits. I am a north wind to ripe figs.
> Thus, like figs, these doctrines fall to you, my friends: now drink their juice and their sweet pulp! It is autumn all around and clear skies and afternoon —[13]

This is not the talk of a fanatic, no "preaching" is done here, no *faith* is demanded here: from an unending wealth of light and depth of happiness there falls drop for drop, word for word — a delicate slowness is the tempo of these discourses. The like of this reaches only the most select; it is an unparalleled privilege to listen here; nobody is at liberty to have ears for Zarathustra . . . Is Zarathustra with all that not a *seducer*? . . . But what does he himself say when he first returns to his solitude? Precisely the opposite to what any "sage," "saint," "redeemer of the world," and other *décadent* would say in a similar case . . . He does not just speak differently, he *is* different, too . . .

I am now departing alone, my disciples! Now you, too, are departing from here, alone! This is how I want it.

Go forth from me and guard yourselves against Zarathustra! And better still: be ashamed of him! Perhaps he has deceived you.

People of knowledge[14] must be able not only to love their enemies but also to hate their friends.

Always remaining only a pupil offers little reward for the teacher. And why don't you want to tear at my laurels?

You revere me: but what will happen when one day your reverence *falls away*? Be careful that a falling statue does not slay you!

You say you believe in Zarathustra? But what does Zarathustra matter! You are the ones who believe in me, but what do all believers matter!

You had not yet searched for yourselves: that is when you found me. All believers act in this way; that is why all believing means so little.

Now I call upon you to lose me and to find yourselves; and only *when you have all denied me*, will I want to return to you . . .[15]

FRIEDRICH NIETZSCHE.

Contents[1]

*

* *

On this perfect day, when everything is ripening and the grapevine is not the only thing getting brown, a ray of sunshine has just fallen on my life: I looked behind, I looked beyond, never did I see so many and such good things all at once. I did not bury my forty-fourth year in vain today, I was *sanctioned* to bury it — whatever life it possessed is saved, immortal. The *Revaluation of All Values*, the *Dionysus Dithyrambs*, and, for relaxation, the *Twilight of the Idols*[2] — all gifts of this year, in fact, of its last quarter! *How could I not be thankful to my whole life?* And so I tell myself my life.[3]

* *

*

Why I Am So Wise.

The good fortune of my existence, perhaps its uniqueness, lies in its fatefulness: I am, to put it in the form of a puzzle, as my father already dead, as my mother[1] still alive and growing old. This double descent, as it were from the highest and lowest rungs on the ladder of life, simultaneously *décadent* and *beginning* — this, if anything, explains that neutrality, that independence in relation to the whole problem of life that perhaps marks me out. I have a finer instinct for the signs of beginning and decline than any human has ever had, I am its teacher par excellence — I know both, I am both. — My father died aged thirty-six:[2] he was delicate, gentle and ailing, like a being destined to be merely transitory — more of a kindly recollection of life than life itself. At the same age as his life went downhill, mine went downhill too: in my thirty-sixth year I reached the lowest point of my vitality — I was still alive, but unable to see three steps ahead. At the time — it was 1879 — I gave up my professorship in Basel, lived through the summer in St. Moritz like a shadow and the next winter, the most sun-starved of my life, *as* a shadow in Naumburg.[3] This was my minimum: *The Wanderer and His Shadow* came into being during that time. Without a doubt, I knew all about shadows then . . . The following winter, my first in Genoa,[4] that sweetening and inspiration which is practically dependent on extreme lack of blood and muscle brought forth *Dawn*. The perfect brightness and

cheerfulness, indeed, exuberance of spirit mirrored by the said
work, is, with me, consistent not just with the deepest physiological weakness, but even with an excess of a feeling of pain.
In the midst of agonies that an uninterrupted three-day-long
migraine with painful vomiting of phlegm brings in its wake
— I possessed a dialectician's clarity par excellence and analyzed most cold-bloodedly things for which in healthier circumstances I was not enough of a climber, not honed, not *cold*
enough. My readers perhaps know the extent to which I regard
dialectics as a symptom of *décadence*, for example in the most
celebrated case of all: in the case of Socrates. — All pathological disturbances of the intellect, even that semi-numbness
which fever brings in its wake, have remained for me to this
day completely alien things, the nature and frequency of which
I first had to teach myself in a scholarly fashion. My blood
runs slowly. Nobody has ever been able to confirm I had a
fever. A doctor who treated me for some time as suffering from
anxiety, finally said: "No! It's nothing to do with your nerves,
the only one who is nervous is me." No local degeneration
could be detected whatsoever; no organic reason for stomach
pain, however much, as a result of complete exhaustion, the
gastric system {had a} severe weakness.[5] My eye pain as well, at
times perilously approaching temporary blindness, was just a
result, not cause: so that with every increase of vital strength
my vision has improved as well. — Recovery in my case means
a long, all-too-long procession of years — unfortunately it also
means at the same time relapse, decline, periods of a sort of
décadence. Need I say, after all that, that I am *experienced* in
questions of *décadence*? I have spelled it out forwards and backwards. Even that filigree art of grasping and comprehending,
those fingers for nuances, that psychology of "seeing round the
corner" and whatever else is characteristic of me was learned
only then, being a gift from that time when everything became
more rarified for me, observation itself as well as the organs of
observation. Looking from the perspective of the invalid toward
healthier concepts and values, and again, the other way round,

looking down from the wealth and self-certainty of *rich* life into
the secret work of the instinct of *décadence* — that was my longest apprenticeship, my actual experience, if I was going to be
master of anything it was of that. I now have it in hand, I am
handy[6] at *transposing perspectives*: the prime reason why, perhaps
for me alone, a "revaluation of all values" is at all possible. —

2.

Granted, then, that I am a *décadent*, I am also the opposite.
My proof for that is, among other things, that I always instinctively chose the *right* means of countering bad circumstances:
while the *décadent* as such always chooses means that are disadvantageous to him. As *summa summarum*[7] I was healthy, as a
niche, a specialty I was *décadent*. That zeal for absolute solitude
and release from habitual circumstances, the pressure upon me
not to allow myself to be cared for, served, *doctored* — that
reveals the absolute certainty of instinct as to *what* was needed
then above all else. I took myself in hand, I made myself healthy
again: the prerequisite for that — every physiologist will admit
— is *that one is healthy in principle.* A typically ailing being
cannot become healthy, still less make himself healthy; whereas
for a typically healthy being, to be ill can even be an active
stimulant to life, to more life. In fact, that is how I *now* perceive that long period of sickness: I discovered life anew, as it
were, myself included, I tasted all good and even small things
as others could not easily do — I made my will to health, to
life, into my philosophy . . . For let us note: the years of my
lowest vitality were the ones when I *stopped* being a pessimist:
the instinct to restore myself to health forbade me a philosophy of poverty and discouragement . . . And basically, how
can one recognize that someone has *turned out well*! By the
fact that someone who has turned out well does our senses
good: he is carved out of wood at once hard, choice, and fra-
grant. He savors only what is beneficial; his pleasure, his desire
ceases when the limit of what is beneficial has been passed. He
divines cures for injuries and uses bad circumstances to his

advantage; what does not kill him makes him stronger. He instinctively collects his *own* sum from everything he sees, hears, experiences: he is a principle of selection, rejecting a great deal. He is always in *his own* company, whether dealing with books, humans or landscapes: he honors by *choosing*, by *allowing*, by *placing trust*. He reacts to any kind of stimulus slowly, with that slowness inculcated by long circumspection and studied pride — he scrutinizes the approaching stimulus and has no intention of going to meet it.[8] He believes in neither "misfortune" nor "guilt": content with himself, with others, and knowing how to *forget* — he is strong enough that everything *must* redound to his best advantage. Well then, I am the *opposite* of a *décadent*: for I have just described *myself.*

3.[9]

I regard it as a great privilege to have had such a father: the farmers to whom he preached — for he was, after having lived some years at the Altenburg court, in the last years a preacher — said that was what an angel must look like. — And with that, I shall touch on the question of race.[10] I am a Polish nobleman *pur sang*,[11] with not a drop of bad blood mixed in, least of all German. When I search for the deepest antithesis to myself, the ineradicable meanness of the instincts, I always find my mother and sister — to believe myself related to such *canaille*[12] would be a profanation of my divinity. The treatment I have received at the hands of my mother and sister up to the present moment instills in me an unspeakable dread: a hellish machine is at work here, reliably accurate as to the moment when I can be bloodily wounded — in my most exalted moments . . . for at that point, you lack all strength to defend yourself against poisonous vermin . . . Physiological contiguity enables such a *disharmonia praestabilita*[13,14] . . . But I confess that the deepest objection against "eternal recurrence," my truly *abysmal* thought, always remains mother and sister.[15] — But even as a Pole I am a tremendous atavism. You would have to go back centuries to find, in this noblest of races there has been on earth, the same measure of pure instinct as I represent. Toward everything that calls itself *noblesse*[16] today I have a sovereign feeling of distinction — I would not allow the young German Kaiser[17] the honor of being my coachman. There is one single instance where I recognize my equal — I confess to it with deep gratitude. Frau Cosima Wagner is by far the noblest of natures; and so that I do not say a word too little, I declare that Richard Wagner was the man most closely related to me by far . . .[18] The rest is silence[19] . . . All prevailing concepts about degrees of relatedness are unmitigated physiological nonsense. Today the Pope[20] is still trading on this nonsense. One is *the least* related to one's parents: it would be the most extreme sign of coarseness to be related to one's parents. Higher natures have their origin vastly further back, the slowest process of collecting, heaping up, saving up for them was necessary.[21] The *great* individuals are the oldest: I do not understand how, but Julius Caesar could be my father — *or* Alexander, this incarnate Dionysus . . . At the moment of writing this, the post has brought me a Dionysus-head . . . [22]

4.

I have never understood the art of creating a prejudice against myself — that too I owe to my incomparable father — and even when it seemed to me to be of greatest value. In fact, I have never even been prejudiced toward myself, however unchristian that might seem. You can twist my life this way and that without finding a single trace in it, with that one exception,[23] of somebody harboring ill will toward me — but perhaps too many traces of *good* will . . . My experiences even with such people as everyone finds objectionable speak without exception in their favor; I tame every bear, I even make clowns behave. In my seven years of teaching Greek to the top class at Basel grammar school, I never had occasion to impose a punishment; the laziest were industrious with me. I am always a match for chance; I must be unprepared if I am to be master of myself. Whatever instrument you like, even if it is as out of tune as only the instrument "human being" can be — I would have to be ill not to succeed in coaxing something acoustically tolerable out of it. And how often have I not heard it from those "instruments" themselves that they had never heard themselves *like that* before . . . Perhaps the best example was Heinrich von Stein, who died unforgivably young, and who once, having painstakingly sought permission, turned up in Sils-Maria for three days, telling everyone that he had *not* come on account of the Engadine. This excellent human being who had waded into the Wagnerian swamp (— and into that of Dühring besides!) with the perfectly impetuous naïveté of the Prussian Junker, was during these three days as though transformed by a gust of freedom, like one who is suddenly raised to *his* height and takes wing. I always told him the good air up here does that, it is the same with everyone, not for nothing are we 6000 feet above Bayreuth — but he didn't want to believe me . . . If, nevertheless, many a small or large offence was committed against me, the reason was not "the will," still less *ill* will: rather, I would have — as already mentioned — more to complain about with goodwill, which caused no small mischief in my life. My experiences entitle me to complete mistrust with regard to so-called selfless drives, the whole of "loving thy neighbor," always ready in word and deed. I count it as weakness as such, as one example of the incapacity to resist stimuli — only with *décadents* is *compassion* a virtue. My reproach against those who are compassionate is that they easily lose all modesty, respect, sensitivity to distances, that compassion in the twinkling of an eye smells of the mob and looks identical to bad manners — that compassionate hands can intrude with destructive effect into a great destiny, into an isolation where there are wounds, into a *predilection* for heavy guilt. I count the overcoming of compassion among the *noble* virtues: I have written of one case, as "Zarathustra's temptation,"[24] where a great cry of distress[25] comes to him and where compassion threatens to ambush him like one last sin, to lure him away from *himself*. To remain master here, to keep the *peak* of his task pure of the much baser and more short-sighted impulses at work in so-called selfless actions, that is the test, perhaps the final test, a Zarathustra must undergo — his real *proof* of strength . . .

5.

And in another sense I am just my father yet again and as it were his continuation of life after an all too early death. Like anyone who never lived among his equals and for whom the concept "retaliation" is as inaccessible as, for instance, the concept of "equal rights," I forbid myself any countermeasure or protective measure in cases where a small or *very large* stupidity has been inflicted on me — any defense, any "justification" as well, as is fitting. My kind of retaliation consists of sending something clever in pursuit of foolishness as fast as possible: that way you might catch it up. To speak figuratively: I send a jar of confection to get rid of a *sour* story . . . A person just has to do one bad thing to me, and I "retaliate," you can be sure of that: I soon find an opportunity to express my thanks to the "wrongdoer" (occasionally even for the wrongdoing) — or to *ask* him for something, which can be more binding than to give something . . . Also, it seems to me that the rudest word, the rudest letter is better-natured even, more honest even, than silence. Those who keep silent nearly always lack delicacy and heartfelt politeness; silence is an excuse, choking back necessarily creates a bad character — it even ruins the stomach. All those who keep silent are dyspeptic. — As you see, I do not want to see rudeness undervalued, it is by far the most *humane* form of contradiction and, amid modern pampering, one of our prime virtues. If you are rich enough for it, it is even good fortune to be wrong. If a god came to earth, he could *do* nothing else but wrong — not to take upon himself punishment, but *guilt*, would alone be godly.

6.

Freedom from *ressentiment*, enlightenment about *ressentiment* — who knows, in the end, how much I have to thank my long sickness for that as well! The problem is not exactly simple: one has to have experienced it in strength and weakness. If anything at all must be raised against sickness, against weakness, it is that the actual healing instinct, that is the *instinct for defense and attack* in humans, becomes worn down. You don't know how to get rid of anything, you don't know how to cope with anything, you don't know how to fight anything off — everything hurts. Human and thing come obtrusively close, experiences hurt too deeply, memory is a festering wound. Being sick *is* a kind of *ressentiment* itself. — The patient has just one great cure — I call it *Russian fatalism*, that fatalism without revolt with which a Russian soldier, for whom the campaign is getting too hard, finally lies down in the snow. Taking nothing more, taking nothing more on, taking nothing more *in* — not reacting at all any more . . . The great good sense of this fatalism, which is not always simply the courage for death, as something that supports life in the most life-threatening circumstances, is the reduction of metabolism, its slowing down, a sort of will to hibernation. A few steps further with this logic and you have the fakir, who sleeps in a grave for weeks . . . You no longer react to anything because you would exhaust yourself too quickly, *if* you reacted at all: that is the logic. And nothing burns you up faster than *ressentiment*-affects. Anger, sickly vulnerability, powerlessness to take revenge, the desire, the thirst for revenge, mixing poison in every sense — that is surely the most inexpedient way of reacting for those who are exhausted: there is certain to be a rapid use of nervous energy, a sickly increase in harmful excretions, for example, bile in the stomach. *Ressentiment* is the forbidden *in itself* for the patient — *his* evil: unfortunately his most natural inclination, too. — That deep physiologist Buddha grasped this. His "religion," which one does better to designate as a *hygiene* so as not to confuse it with pitiable things like Christianity, made its effect dependent on victory over *ressentiment*: freeing the soul *from that* — first step toward recovery. "Not through animosity does animosity come to an end, it is through friendship that animosity comes

to an end":[26] that stands at the beginning of Buddha's teaching
— that is *not* what morality dictates, but physiology. — *Ressentiment*, born out of weakness, to none more harmful than to the
sick person himself — alternatively, where a rich nature is a
precondition, a feeling of *superfluity*, a feeling to remain master of which is almost the proof of wealth. Anyone who knows
the seriousness with which my philosophy took up the struggle against feelings of revenge and empathy right through to
the teaching of "free will" — the struggle with Christianity is
just an individual case of this — will understand why, precisely here, I bring to light my personal feelings, my *sureness of
instinct* in praxis. I *forbade* myself this as harmful in times of
décadence; as soon as life was rich and proud enough again for
it, I forbade myself this as *beneath* me. That "Russian fatalism"
of which I spoke entered my behavior in that for years I clung
fiercely to almost unbearable locations, places, lodgings, social
circles, once they had been established by chance — it was
better than changing them, than *feeling* them open to change
— than standing up against them . . . I took it as a deadly
offence at that time if I was disturbed in my fatalism or forci-
bly awoken: — in truth it really was a deadly peril every time.
— To take oneself for a destiny, not wanting one's self any
"different" — in such circumstances, that is *great reason* itself.

7.

War is another matter. By nature I am warlike. Attack is
one of my instincts. *To be able* to be a foe, to be a foe — that
perhaps demands a strong nature, at all events it is a prerequisite in every strong nature. It needs resistance, consequently it
seeks resistance: *aggressive* pathos belongs just as necessarily to
strength as does the feeling of revenge and rancor to weakness. For example, woman is vindictive: that is a prerequisite
of her weakness, just as much as is her sensitivity to a stranger's distress. — The strength of an attacker has a sort of *gauge*
in the opposition needed; all growth reveals itself by seeking
out a mightier opponent — or problem: for a philosopher who

is warlike also challenges problems to a duel. The task is *not* to become complete master over resistance, but over what every power, skill and prowess-in-arms must mobilize against — over *equal* opponents . . . equality before the foe — first requirement for an *honorable* duel. Where you despise, you *cannot* wage war; where you command, where you see something *beneath* you, you *have* no need to wage war. — My war praxis can be summed up in four sentences. First: I only attack things that are victorious — if necessary, I wait until they are victorious. Second: I only attack things where I would find no other accomplice, where I stand alone — where I compromise myself alone . . . I have never taken a step in public that was not compromising: that is *my* criterion of correct behavior. Third: I never make a personal attack — I just use the person as a strong magnifying glass to make visible a general if surreptitious and elusive crisis. That is how I attacked David Strauss, or rather, the *acclaim* of a superannuated book within German "culture," — I caught this culture out in the very act . . . Thus did I attack Wagner, or more precisely, the falsity, the instinctive mediocrity of our "culture," which mistakes the fine for the rich and the late for the great. Fourth: I attack only things where any kind of personal difference is excluded, where there is no background of bad experiences. On the contrary, for me to launch an attack is a token of goodwill, possibly even gratitude. By coupling my name with that of a thing or person, I thereby honor and bestow distinction: for or against — all the same to me. If I wage war on Christianity, that is my due, since I have never experienced fatalities or obstructions from that quarter — the most devout Christians have always been fond of me. I myself, an opponent of Christianity *de rigueur*, bear no hard feelings toward an individual for what is the calamity of millennia. —[27]

8.

May I venture to point out one final trait in my personality that causes me no small difficulty in my dealings with human beings? A completely uncanny sensitivity of the instinct for cleanliness is peculiar to me, so that the proximity, or — how shall I put it? — the viscera, the "entrails" of every soul is something I perceive physiologically — *smell* . . . This sensitivity provides me with the psychological feelers to pass my fingers over and pry out every secret: I recognize almost at first touch the amount of *hidden* dirt underlying many a nature, perhaps conditioned by bad blood, but whitewashed by good breeding. If I have observed correctly, natures inimical to my cleanliness are themselves sensible of how prudent is my disgust: it does not make them smell any better . . . As has always been my way — extreme cleanliness toward myself is a requirement for my existence, I perish in unhygienic conditions — I continually swim and bathe and splash as though in water, in any kind of perfectly transparent and sparkling element. This makes my relations with fellow humans no small test of patience; my humanity does *not* consist in sympathizing with the human but in *withstanding* the fact that I sympathize . . . My humanity is a continual self-overcoming. — But I need *solitude*, or rather, convalescence, a return to myself, the breath of a free, light, playful air . . . The whole of my *Zarathustra* is a dithyramb to solitude, or, if I have been understood, to *purity* . . . Fortunately not to *pure folly.*[28] — Anyone with an eye for color would call it diamond. — *Disgust* at the human, at the "rabble," was always my greatest danger . . . Do you want to hear the words Zarathustra uses to speak about *redemption* from disgust?

> But what happened to me? How did I deliver myself from disgust? Who rejuvenated my eyes? How did I fly up and reach the heights where no more rabble sits at the fountain?
>
> Did my disgust itself create wings for me and water-divining powers? Truly, I had to fly up to the pinnacle so that I could find the wellspring of delight once again! —
>
> Oh, I found it, my brothers! Here at the pinnacle the wellspring of delight gushes forth for me! And there is a life in which no rabble drinks beside me!

Almost too forcefully do you flow for me, fount of delight! And often you empty the cup again with your desire to fill it.

And still I must learn to approach you more humbly: my heart flows forth all too forcefully in response to you:

— my heart, in which my summer burns, the short, hot, melancholy, overly blissful summer: how my summer heart longs for your coolness!

Gone, the faltering sorrow of my spring! Past, the snow-flakes of my malice in June! I have become entirely summer and a summer's noon —

— a summer at the pinnacle with cold springs and blissful stillness: oh come, my friends, so that the stillness may become even more blissful!

For this is *our* pinnacle and our ancestral home: here, where we live, it is too high and too steep for all the unclean and their thirst.

You friends, just take a look with your pure eyes into the wellspring of my delight! How could looking at it make it murky? It will laugh back at you with *its* purity.

We are building our nest in the tree of the future; eagles will bring meals in their beaks to us solitary ones!

Truly, no meals that the unclean may share with us! They would imagine they were feeding on fire and would burn their maws!

Truly, we are not setting aside any homesteads here for the unclean! Our happiness would be an ice cave to their bodies and their minds!

And we wish to live above them like strong winds, neighbors of the eagles, neighbors of the snow, neighbors of the sun: this is how strong winds live.

And one day, like a wind, I want to blow among them and with my spirit to take away the breath of their spirit: my future wants it that way.

Truly, Zarathustra is a strong wind to all that lies below: and this is the advice he gives to his enemies and to all who spit and spew: be careful not to spit *into* the wind! . . . [29]

Why I Am So Clever.

1.

— Why do I happen to know rather *more*? Why am I so clever, anyway? I have never pondered over questions that don't exist — I have never been spendthrift with myself. — For example, I have not experienced actual *religious* difficulties as such. The extent to which I am supposed to be "sinful" has escaped me utterly. Likewise I lack a reliable criterion for what a pang of conscience is: considering what you *hear* about it, a pang of conscience seems to be something disreputable . . . I would not want to leave a deed in the lurch *afterwards*,[1] I would prefer to leave a bad outcome, the *consequences*, completely out of the evaluation. A bad outcome makes it all too easy for you to lose the *correct* eye for what you have done: I view a pang of conscience as a kind of "*evil* eye." To treasure something that has gone wrong all the more *because* it has gone wrong — that is more likely to fit into my morality. — "God," "immortality of the soul," "redemption," "the Beyond," nothing but concepts to which I never devoted either time or attention, not even as a child — perhaps I was never childlike enough for that? — I do not know atheism at all as a result, still less as an event: for me it is self-evident, a matter of instinct. I am too curious, too *equivocal*, too boisterous, to accept a ham-fisted answer. God is a ham-fisted answer, an indelicacy toward us thinkers — fundamentally even just a ham-fisted *prohibition* on us: thou shalt

not think! . . . Of quite different interest to me is a question on
which more "salvation of humanity" hangs than any theologian's novelty: the question of *nourishment*. A handy way of
formulating it is like so: "How exactly do *you* nourish yourself
in order to reach your maximum of strength, of *virtù* in the
Renaissance style, of moraline-free[2] virtue?" — My experiences
here have been as bad as possible; I am amazed at how late I
heard this question and how late I learned "reason" from my
experiences. Only the complete worthlessness of our German
education — its "idealism" — explains to me in some measure
why, precisely here, I was backward to the point of saintliness.
This "education," which from the start instructs one to lose
sight of *realities* in order to chase after so-called ideal goals, for
example, "classical education": — as though merging "classical" and "German" into one concept were not doomed from
the start! Moreover, it is entertaining — just imagine a "classically educated" person from Leipzig! — In fact, right up to
my ripest years I only ever ate *badly* — expressed morally, in
an "impersonal," "selfless," "altruistic" way for the sake of the
cooks and other fellow Christians. For example, when I was
first studying Schopenhauer (1865), I seriously denied my "will
to life" thanks to Leipzig cuisine. To wreck my stomach as well
through eating too little — I thought this problem would be
admirably resolved by said cuisine. (Apparently, 1866 brought
about a change here.[3]) But German cooking in general —
surely it has everything on its conscience! Soup *before* the meal
(still called *alla tedesca*[4] in sixteenth-century Venetian cook-
books); overcooked meats, vegetables cooked in fat and flour;
the degeneration of desserts to paperweights! If you just add
the practically bovine need of the older, and not just the *older*,
Germans to swill everything down, you understand the descent
of the *German spirit* — from upset bowels . . . The German
spirit is a form of indigestion — it cannot finish with anything.
— But the *English* diet, too, which compared to the German
or even the French is a kind of "return to nature," namely to
cannibalism, goes deeply against my own instincts; I think it

gives the spirit *heavy* feet — Englishwomen's feet . . . The best cuisine is that of *Piedmont.* — Alcoholic drinks affect me badly; a glass of wine or beer during the day is quite enough to make my life a "vale of tears," — my antipodes live in Munich. Granted that I grasped this rather late, I actually *sensed* it from childhood on. As a boy, I believed that drinking wine, like smoking tobacco, was at first just a *vanitas*[5] of young men, later a bad habit. Perhaps Naumburg wine is also responsible for this *harsh* verdict. To believe that wine would *cheer me up*, I would have to be Christian, in other words, believe something that, for me, is just an absurdity. Strangely enough, in view of this extreme intolerance with small, heavily diluted measures of alcohol, I am almost a seaman when it comes to *strong* measures. Already as a boy I was rather bold in this direction. Writing a long Latin essay late at night and then even copying it out, with the ambition in my pen to emulate my model Sallust in rigor and terseness and pouring the stiffest of grogs over my Latin, this did not, when I was a pupil of the prestigious Schulpforta, stand in opposition to my physiology in the least, nor indeed to that of Sallust — however much it might to the prestigious Schulpforta . . . Later, of course, approaching midlife, I was increasingly *against* each and every "spirituous" beverage: an opponent of vegetarianism from experience, just like Richard Wagner, who converted me,[6] I cannot recommend too strongly to all *more spiritual* natures the complete abstinence from alcohol. *Water* works . . . I prefer places (Nice, Turin, Sils) where there is everywhere the opportunity to drink from a water fountain; a little glass dogs my steps. *In vino veritas:*[7] apparently I am out of kilter yet again with the whole world regarding the concept "truth": — in my case, the spirit moves over the *water*[8] . . . A few more tips from my morality. A large meal is easier to digest than one that is too small. First prerequisite for a good digestion is that the stomach as a whole sets to work. You must *know* the size of your own stomach. For the same reason, those tedious meals that I call phased sacrificial feasts, those at the *table d'hôte*, are to be rejected.

— No snacks, no coffee: coffee makes you miserable. *Tea* beneficial only in the morning. Little, but strong; tea is very bad for you and impairs the whole day if it is the slightest bit too weak. In this respect, we all have our own measure, often within the narrowest and most delicate of bounds. In a climate that is very *agaçant*,[9] tea first thing is not to be recommended: start by ordering a cup of strong, fat-free cocoa one hour before. — *Sit* as little as possible; give no credence to any thought unless it is born in the fresh air when you are on the move — while your muscles are celebrating a festival as well. All prejudices proceed from the bowels. — Sitting tight[10] — as I have said before — the real *sin* against the Holy Ghost. —

2.

Most closely related to the question of nourishment is the question of *place* and *climate*. Nobody is free to live everywhere; and somebody who has great tasks to complete, demanding all his strength, actually has a very narrow choice. The influence of the climate on *metabolism*, slackening or accelerating it, is so great that a mistake in place or climate can not only alienate people from their task, but can completely rob them of it: they never set eyes on it. Their animal vigor has never become strong enough for that heady and overflowing freedom reached when somebody realizes: I alone can do *that* . . . A really trivial intestinal sluggishness that has become a bad habit is quite enough to render a genius something mediocre, something "German"; the German climate alone is sufficient to discourage strong and even heroically inclined bowels. The tempo of metabolism stands in direct relationship to the fleetness or lameness of the spirit's *feet*; for the "spirit" itself is just a form of this metabolism. If you list the places where there are or have been brilliant human beings, where happiness included wit, refinement and malice, where genius almost from necessity made its home, they all have excellent dry air. Paris, Provence, Florence, Jerusalem, Athens — these names prove something: that genius is *conditional* upon dry air, a clear sky — in other words,

on rapid metabolism and the possibility of repeatedly supply-
ing oneself with great and even massive amounts of strength. I
have in my mind's eye a case where an eminent mind disposed
to freedom became narrow, warped, a specialist full of sour
grapes, simply by lacking a fine instinct for things climatic.
And I myself could have become this case in the end, had
sickness not compelled me to see reason, to ponder about reason in reality. Now, when from long practice on myself as on a
very finely tuned and reliable instrument, I read the effects on
me of climatic or meteorological origin, and, on a short journey like Turin to Milan, physiologically check the change in
the level of humidity, I think with horror of the *uncanny* fact
that I only ever lived my life, right up to the last ten years, the
life-threatening years, in the wrong places and those practically *forbidden* to me. Naumburg, Schulpforta, the whole of
Thuringia, Leipzig, Basel — just so many scenes of disaster for
my physiology. If I have no pleasant memories at all of my
whole childhood and youth, it would be folly here to put this
down to so-called moral causes — such as the indisputable
lack of *sufficient* companionship: for this lack exists now as it
always has done, without preventing me from being cheerful
and intrepid. Instead, ignorance *in physiologicis*[11] — that cursed
"idealism" — is the real catastrophe in my life, the superfluous
and stupid thing about it, something from which nothing good
has grown and for which there is no compensation, no coun-
terbalance. I account for all my mistakes as a result of this
"idealism," all the great aberrations of instinct and "modesties"
deflecting from my life's *task*, for example, the fact that I became
a philologist — why not at least a physician or something else
eye-opening?[12] During my time in Basel, my whole spiritual
diet, including the daily schedule, was a completely senseless
misuse of extraordinary powers without any kind of supplemen-
tation to cover depleted powers, without even a consideration of
depletion and replenishment. There was none of that more refined
selfishness, that commanding instinct's *care*, it meant placing
oneself on a par with everyone else, "selflessness," forgetting one's

distance — something for which I shall never forgive myself. When I was almost finished, *because* I was almost finished, I began to wonder about this irrationality fundamental to my life — "idealism." Only *sickness* made me see reason. —

3.

Choice of nourishment; choice of climate and location; — the third category, where you must not make a mistake at any price, is choice of *your* mode of *recreation*. Here as well, depending on the degree to which a mind is sui generis,[13] the limits to what it is allowed, that is to say *useful*, become ever more restricted. In my case, all *reading* is among my recreations: consequently among what frees me from myself, what lets me stroll through sciences and souls foreign to me — what I no longer take seriously. Indeed, in reading I recover from *my* seriousness. At times when I am working hard, I have no books about me: I would take care not to let anyone near me speak or even think. For that is what reading would be . . . Has anyone actually noticed that in that state of deep suspense to which pregnancy condemns the mind and basically the whole organism, a chance occurrence or any kind of external stimulus works too vehemently and "strikes" too deep? One must avoid chance occurrence and any kind of external stimulus as much as possible; a form of self-immurement is one of the pregnant mind's first instinctive insights. Would I allow an alien thought to secretly climb over the wall? — For that is what reading would be . . . A period of recreation follows periods of work and fruitfulness: out you come, you pleasing, brilliant, cold-shouldered books! — Will they be German books? . . . I have to count back half a year to catch myself with a book in my hand. What was it now? — An excellent study by Victor Brochard, *les Sceptiques Grecs*,[14] where my Laertiana[15] are also put to good use. The Skeptics, the only *honorable* type among the ambito quintiguous[16] pack of philosophers! . . . Otherwise I nearly always take refuge in the same books, essentially just a few, the books that have actually *proved* themselves for me. Perhaps it is

not my way to read much and widely: a reading room makes
me ill. Nor is it my way to love much or widely. Caution, even
hostility toward new books is rather more akin to my instinct
than "tolerance," "*largeur du cœur*"[17] and other forms of "loving thy neighbor" . . .[18] Basically it is to a small number of
elderly Frenchmen that I return again and again: I believe in
French culture alone and consider anything else that calls
itself "culture" in Europe a misunderstanding, to say nothing
of German culture . . . The few cases of high culture that I
discovered in Germany were all of French descent, above all
Cosima Wagner, by far the foremost voice in questions of taste
that I have heard . . . That I *love* rather than read Pascal, as
Christianity's most instructive sacrifice, slowly murdered, first
physically then psychologically, the whole logic of this most
gruesome form of inhuman cruelty; that I perhaps have a trace
of Montaigne's archness in my mind, and perhaps, who knows?
in my body, too; that my artist's taste, not without fury,
upholds the names of Molière, Corneille and Racine against
the wild genius of Shakespeare: none of that, in the end, rules
out my finding the most recent Frenchmen charming company, too. I do not know in which century of history one
could fish out such inquisitive and at the same time sensitive
psychologists as in today's Paris: I name provisionally — for
their number is by no means small — Messieurs Paul Bourget,
Pierre Loti, Gyp,[19] Meilhac, Anatole France, Jules Lemaître,
or, to highlight someone from a strong race, a genuine Latin,
to whom I am particularly partial, Guy de Maupassant.
Between ourselves, I prefer *this* generation even to their great
teachers, who have all been ruined by German philosophy:
Taine, for instance, through Hegel, whom he has to thank for
his misunderstanding of great humans and great times. As far
as Germany extends, it *ruins* culture. Only war "redeemed"
the spirit in France . . . Stendhal, one of the most beautiful
chance occurrences of my life — for everything epoch-making
in it was driven my way by chance occurrence, never recom-
mendation — is absolutely invaluable with his anticipatory

psychologist's eye, with his grasp of the facts, which reminds us of the proximity of that greatest of facts (*ex ungue Napoleonem*[20] —); last and not least, as an *honest* atheist, a rare and almost undiscoverable species in France — all due respect to Prosper Mérimée . . . Perhaps I myself am envious of Stendhal? He robbed me of the best atheist joke I could have made: "God's only excuse is that he does not exist"[21] . . . I myself have said somewhere:[22] what has hitherto been the greatest objection to existence? *God . . .*[23]

4.

Heinrich Heine has provided me with the highest concept of a lyricist. I comb all the empires of millennia in vain for a similarly sweet and passionate music. He possessed that divine sense of mischief without which I cannot conceive of perfection — I estimate the value of humans and races by how necessary they find it to understand god and satyr as inseparable. — And how he handles the German language! One day, people will say that Heine and I were by far the leading lights of the German language — at an incalculable distance from everything mere Germans have done with it. — I must be a near relative of *Byron's* Manfred: I found all these chasms in myself — at thirteen I was ripe for this work. I have not a word, only a look, for those who dare to pronounce the word Faust in the presence of Manfred. The Germans are *incapable* of any conception of greatness: witness Schumann. Once, furious with this sugary Saxon, I composed a rival *Manfred* overture, eliciting Hans von Bülow's comment that he had never seen a score like it: it was a rape of Euterpe.[24] — When searching for my highest formula for *Shakespeare*, I only ever find this: that he conceived the type of Caesar.[25] You cannot guess a thing like that — you are it or you are not it. The great poets draw on their reality *alone* — to the point where they cannot stand the work afterwards . . . Whenever I have had a peep at my *Zarathustra*, I walk up and down the room for half an hour, unable to master an unbearable spasm of sobbing.[26] — I know no more heart-rending reading matter than Shakespeare: what must a person have suffered to have such a need to be a clown? — Does anyone *understand* Hamlet? It is not doubt but *certainty* that drives you mad . . . But to feel in such a manner, you must be deep, an abyss, a philosopher . . . All of us *fear* the truth . . . And here I confess: I am instinctively sure and certain of the fact that Lord Bacon[27] is the originator, the animal-self-tormentor of this uncanniest kind of literature: what do *I* care about the deplorable prattle of American muddle-heads and fatheads?[28] But the power to achieve the mightiest realization of a vision is not merely compatible with the mightiest power to do a deed, a monstrous deed, a crime — *it is its precondition* . . . We do not know nearly enough about Lord Bacon, that first realist in the grand sense of the word, to know *what* he actually did, *what* he wanted, *what* he experienced personally . . . And you critics, the devil take you, gentlemen! Even if I had christened *Zarathustra* with a different name, for example that of Richard Wagner, the quick-wittedness of two millennia would not have sufficed for you to guess that the author of *Human, All Too Human*[29] is the visionary of *Zarathustra* . . .

5.[30]

Here, while speaking about the recreations in my life, I need to say a word to express my gratitude for what has provided me with the deepest and most heartwarming relaxation by far. This was without a doubt my more intimate association with Richard Wagner. I hold the rest of my human relationships cheap; not for any price would I discard the days at Tribschen[31] from my life, days of trust, of cheerfulness, of sublime incidents — of *profound* moments . . . I do not know what others experienced with Wagner: no cloud ever passed over our sky. — And that brings me back to France again — I have no residual reasons, just a contemptuous smirk, for Wagnerians *et hoc genus omne*[32] who think they are paying homage to Wagner by finding him similar to *themselves* . . . The way I am, alien in my deepest instincts to everything German, so that even the proximity of a German delays my digestion, my first contact with Wagner was also the first sigh of relief in my life: I experienced, I honored him as *abroad*, as counterpart, as bodily protest against all "German virtues" — We who were children in the swampy air of the fifties are necessarily pessimists about the concept "German"; we cannot be anything but revolutionaries — we will not accept any state of affairs where *the bigot* is uppermost. I am entirely indifferent as to whether he toys with other colors today, whether he robes himself in scarlet or puts on a hussar's uniform . . . So be it! Wagner was a revolutionary — he ran away from the Germans . . . As an *artist* you have no home in Europe apart from Paris; only in Paris is found that *délicatesse* in all five of the artistic senses that Wagner's art demands, the fingers for *nuances*, that psychological morbidity. Nowhere else do you have this passion in questions of form, this seriousness toward mise en scène — which is Parisian seriousness par excellence. In Germany, one has no conception at all of the tremendous ambition that lives in a Parisian artist's soul. The German is good-natured — Wagner was not at all good-natured . . . But I have already said enough (in *Beyond Good and Evil*, p. 256f.[33]) as to where Wagner belongs and to whom he is most closely related: to late French Romanticism and that type of high-flying, highfalutin kind of artist like Delacroix, like Berlioz, with a stock of sickness, of incurability in their being, utter fanatics of *expression*, virtuosos through and through . . . Who was the first *intelligent* follower of Wagner, anyway? Charles Baudelaire,[34] the very same who first understood Delacroix, that typical *décadent* in whom a whole race of artists recognized themselves — he was perhaps the last as well . . . What have I never forgiven Wagner? The fact that he *condescended* to the Germans — that he became a German of the Reich . . . As far as Germany stretches, it *ruins* culture. —

6.[35]

Come to think about it, I would not have survived my youth without Wagnerian music. For I was *sentenced* to the Germans.

If you want to be released from an unbearable pressure, you need hashish. Well then, I needed Wagner. Wagner is the anti-poison par excellence to all things German — poison, I do not deny . . . From the moment there was a piano score of *Tristan*[36]— my compliments, Herr von Bülow! — I was a Wagnerian. I viewed Wagner's earlier works as beneath me — still too coarse, too "German" . . . But today I am still searching for a work that has the same dangerous fascination, the same terrible and sweet inconclusiveness as *Tristan* — I search in all the arts in vain. All Leonardo da Vinci's oddities lose their charm at the first note of *Tristan*. This work is without doubt Wagner's *non plus ultra*;[37] he recovered from it with *The Mastersingers* and *The Ring*. To get better — that is a *retrograde step* for a nature like Wagner . . . I take it to be a first-rate piece of luck to have lived at the right time and actually to have lived among Germans, so that I was *ripe* for this work: my psychologist's curiosity goes that far. The world is poor for anyone who has never been sick enough for this "rapture of hell": we are allowed and virtually required to make use of a mystic's formula here. — I think I know better than anybody what immense feats Wagner could achieve, the fifty worlds of strange delights for which no one but he had the wings; and in my present state, strong enough to turn to advantage even the most questionable and dangerous things and strengthen myself thereby, I name Wagner as the greatest benefactor of my life. What binds us to each other, the fact that we have suffered more deeply than humans of this century ought to suffer, at each other's hands as well, will always link our names together; and as certainly as Wagner is a complete misapprehension among the Germans, so too am I, and always will be. — Two hundred years of psychological and artistic discipline *first of all*, my dear Teutons! . . . But there's no catching up that. —

7.[38]

— I will say one more word for the most discerning of ears: what *I* actually[39] want of music. That it be bright and deep, like an afternoon in October. That it be individual, lively, tender, a

sweet little woman of guile and grace . . . I shall never allow
that a German *could* know what music is. Those who are called
German musicians, the greatest at the head, are *foreigners*,
Slavs, Croats, Italians, Dutch — or Jews; otherwise Germans
of the strong race, Germans who have *died out*, like Heinrich
Schütz, Bach and Handel. I myself am still Pole enough to give
up the rest of music for Chopin: for three reasons I make an
exception for Wagner's *Siegfried Idyll*, perhaps also for Liszt,[40]
whose noble orchestral accents outdo all other musicians;
finally, everything else that has sprung up beyond the Alps —
this side[41] . . . I would not know how to do without Rossini, still
less *my* South in music, the music of my Venetian maestro Pietro
Gasti.[42] And when I say beyond the Alps, I actually just mean
Venice. If I seek another word for music, I still only find the
word Venice. I do not know how to distinguish between tears
and music, I do not know how to think of happiness, the
South, without a shudder of trepidation.

> At the bridge I stood
> of late in browning night.
> In the distance song:
> golden droplets welling
> their way over the trembling surface.
> Gondolas, lanterns, music —
> swimming drunken into twilight . . .
>
> My soul, like string music
> invisibly touched, sang itself
> a secret gondola song to it,
> trembling with vibrant bliss.
> — Did anyone listen? . . .

8.

In all this — in the choice of nourishment, of place and
climate, of recreation — direction comes from an instinct for
self-preservation that expresses itself most unambiguously as

the instinct for *self-defense*. Not to see many things, not to hear them, not to let them approach — first stroke of cleverness, prime evidence that one is not an accident but a necessity. The accepted word for this instinct for self-preservation is *taste*. Its imperative not only orders you to say No where a Yes would be a "selfless act," but also to say *No as little as possible.* To separate yourself, to cut yourself off from anything that necessitates No again and again. The sense in this is that a defensive outlay, however trivial, will bring about an extraordinary and completely superfluous impoverishment as it turns into rule and habit. Our *greatest* expenditures are the most frequent small ones. Defending oneself, not letting anything near, is an outlay — make no mistake about it — a force *squandered* for negative purposes. Just through the continual need for defense you can become so weakened as to be unable to defend yourself. — Suppose I were to step outside my house and find, instead of peaceful, aristocratic Turin, a small German town: my instinct would have to put up barricades to press back anything that intrudes on it from this flattened and cowardly world. Or I might find the German city, this built-up depravity, where nothing grows, where every last thing, good or bad, is hauled in. Wouldn't I have to turn into a *hedgehog* at that point?[43] But having quills is an extravagance, indeed, a double luxury when you are free to have no quills, but *open* hands . . .

Another cleverness and self-defense consists of reacting *as seldom as possible* and withdrawing from locations and circumstances where you would be required to walk out, so to speak, on your "freedom," your initiative, and become a mere reagent. I take as example the handling of books. The scholar who basically just "pores over" books — the philologist with the massive need for about 200 a day — in the end completely loses the ability to think for himself. If he isn't poring he isn't thinking. He *responds* to a stimulus (— a thought he has read about) when he thinks — finally, all he does is just react. The scholar expends his whole strength in saying Yes and No, in

WHY I AM SO CLEVER

criticizing what has already been thought — he himself no longer thinks . . . With him, the instinct for self-preservation has become worn down; otherwise he would defend himself against books. The scholar — a *décadent*. — I have seen this with my own eyes: gifted, rich and liberally minded natures by the time they are thirty "read to ruin," just matches you have to rub to get a spark — a "thought." To read a *book* early in the morning at break of day, when you are fresh, at the dawn of your strength — I call that depraved! — —

9.

At this point I can no longer avoid giving the actual answer to the question as to *how you become what you are*. And with that I touch upon the masterstroke in the art of self-preservation — *selfishness* . . . Granted namely that the task, the definition, the *destiny* of the task lies significantly beyond the average measure, no danger would be greater than facing up to yourself *with* this task. That you become what you are presupposes that you do not have the slightest clue *what* you are. From this point of view, even life's *blunders* have their own meaning and value, the temporary side roads and wrong paths, the delays, the "modesties," the earnestness wasted on tasks that lie beyond *the* task. In this way, a great and even supreme cleverness can ⟨come⟩[44] to expression: where *nosce te ipsum*[45] would be the recipe for decline, then forgetting the self, *misunderstanding* the self, belittling, constricting, disparaging the self, becomes reason itself. Expressed morally: loving thy neighbor, living for other people and things, *can* be the protective measure for upholding the hardest self-centeredness. This is the exceptional case where, against my rules and conviction, I take the side of "selfless" drives: here, they are working in the service of *selfishness* and *self-discipline*. — The whole surface of consciousness — consciousness *is* a surface — must be kept clear of any great imperative. Even beware of each grand word and each grand posture! Nothing but threats that the instinct might "understand itself" too soon — — Meanwhile, the organizing

"idea," called forth to mastery, grows and grows in the depths
— it begins to command, it leads you *back* from side roads and
wrong paths, it prepares *individual* qualities and skills that one
day will prove indispensable means to the whole — it trains all
subordinate abilities one by one before it breathes a word about
the dominant task, the "aim," "purpose," "meaning." — Seen
from this angle, my life is simply wonderful. Perhaps more
powers were needed for the task of a *Revaluation of All Values*
than have ever yet cohabited in one individual, especially contradictory powers as well, without the latter having the sanction to be disruptive or destructive to one another. Hierarchy
of powers; distance; the art of separating without becoming
enemies; no mixing up, no "making up"; a huge plurality that
is nevertheless the opposite of chaos — this was the precondition, the long, secret work and artistry of my instinct. Its *higher
concern* manifested itself in such strong measure that at no
point did I even guess what was growing in me — that one day
all my powers would suddenly *burst forth*, ripe to sublime perfection. I have no recollection of ever having had to strive —
no hint of *struggle* can be traced in my life, I am the opposite of
a heroic nature. To "want" something, "strive" after something,
have an "aim," a "wish" in view — I don't know any of that
from experience. At this very moment I can spy out my future
— a *broad* future! — as though it were a calm sea: no craving
makes a ripple over it. I have not the slightest desire for anything to be any different than it is; I myself do not want to be
any different. But I have always lived like that. I never had a
wish. Someone who can say after his forty-fourth year that he
never bothered about *honor*, about *women*, about *money*! —
Not that there was any lack . . .[46] So, for example, one fine day
I was a university professor — I had never remotely thought of
the like, for I was barely 24 years old. In the same way, two
years previously I was a philologist: in the sense that my *first*
philological work,[47] my beginning in every sense, was requested
by my teacher Ritschl for publication in his *Rheinisches Museum*
(*Ritschl* — I say with respect — the one scholar of genius that I

have set eyes on up to today. He possessed that pleasant dissi-
pation which marks us Thuringians out and renders even a
German agreeable: — even to attain the truth, we still prefer
subterfuge. I do hope I have not underrated my close compa-
triot, the *clever* Leopold Ranke, with these words . . .)

10.

At this point there is need for a great reflection.[48] You will
ask why I have actually narrated all these petty and, according
to conventional opinion, inconsequential things; I harm myself
thereby, all the more so in that I am destined to take on great
tasks. Answer: these petty things — nourishment, place, climate, recreation, the whole casuistry of selfishness — are incon-
ceivably more important than anything people have found
important up till now. It is right here that people should start
to *change their ways*. The things humanity has hitherto considered serious are not even realities, just imaginings, to put it
more strongly, *lies* emanating from the bad instincts of natures
that are sick and in the deepest sense harmful — all the concepts "God," "soul," "virtue," "sin," "the Beyond," "truth," "eternal life" . . . But people have searched in them for the greatness
of human nature, its "divinity" . . . All questions of politics,
social order, upbringing are well and truly falsified because
people mistook the most harmful humans for the greatest —
because they taught themselves to despise "petty" things, by
which I mean the essential concerns of life . . . Our culture
today is ambiguous in the highest degree . . . The German
Kaiser making a pact with the Pope,[49] as though the Pope
were not the representative of deadly animosity against life! . . .
Buildings put up today will have collapsed after three years.
— If I measure myself against what I *can* do, not to speak of
what will come after me, unprecedented destruction and construction, I have more claim than any other mortal to the
word greatness.[50] If I compare myself now to humans honored
up till now as the *first* humans, the difference is tangible. I
don't even count these so-called firsts as humans at all — for

me, they are the dregs of humanity, monstrous products of sickness and vengeful instincts: they are nothing but malign, basically incorrigible monsters taking revenge on life . . . I want to be the opposite of that: my prerogative is having the finest discrimination for all signs of healthy instincts. I have no trace of disease in me; even in times of grave affliction I was not diseased; you will seek in vain for a trait of fanaticism in my nature. At no moment in my life could it be proved that I had a presumptuous or pathetic stance. Pathos of attitude does *not* belong to greatness; whoever needs attitudes at all is *false* . . . Beware of all picturesque humans! — Life has been easy for me, at its easiest when it made the heaviest demands on me. Nobody who saw me during the seventy days of autumn this year, when, with responsibility for all millennia after me, I ceaselessly created things of the first rank which no human will be able to copy — or has yet been able to do, will have detected any tension in me, rather a brimming freshness and cheerfulness. I have never eaten with greater feelings of pleasure, I have never slept better. — I know of no other way to go about great tasks than *play*: this is, as a sign of greatness, an essential precondition. If the slightest coercion, a dark look, a harsh tone in the throat are all objections against a human, how much more so against his work! . . . You must not have nerves . . . Even *suffering* from solitude is an objection — I have only ever suffered from "*manytude*" . . .[51] At an absurdly early age, seven years old, I already knew that no human word would touch me:[52] has anyone ever seen me in distress over this? — Today, I still have the same affability toward everyone, I am even full of concern for the lowliest: in all this, there is not a grain of pride or clandestine scorn. *Anyone* I scorn can *guess* that I scorn them: merely by my presence I offend all those with bad blood in their veins . . . My formula for greatness in humans is *amor fati*: that you wish for nothing different, neither in the future, nor the past, nor in all eternity. Not just bearing necessity, still less concealing it — all idealism is hypocrisy in the face of necessity — but *loving* it . . .

Why I Write Such Good Books.

I am one thing, my writings are another. — Here let the question as to the understanding or *non*-understanding of these writings be touched upon before I actually speak about them. I shall do it as casually as is decently possible: for it is still decidedly not the time for this question. It is still not the time for me: some are born posthumously.[2] — One day, institutions will be needed where people live and teach as I understand living and teaching; possibly professorships will be established specifically for interpreting *Zarathustra*. But it would be a complete self-contradiction if, right now, I were to expect ears *and hands* for *my* truths: that people today do not hear, that today they do not know how to take from me, is not only understandable, it even seems to me to be the right thing. I do not want people to muddle me up — and of course, I do not want to muddle myself up. — I repeat, there is little of "ill will" to be detected in my life; I would hardly be able to tell you of an instance even of literary "ill will." Instead, too much *pure folly*[3] . . . It strikes me as one of the rarest compliments people can pay themselves if they take a book of mine in their hand — I even assume they take off their shoes — to say nothing of boots . . . When Doctor Heinrich von Stein on one occasion complained in all honesty that he had not understood a word of my *Zarathustra*, I told him this was in order: to have understood, meaning to have *experienced*, six sentences of it would transport anyone to a higher level of mortals than "modern" humans could reach. How *could* I, with *this* feeling of distance, even want the "moderns" of my acquaintance — as my readers! My triumph is the exact reverse of that of Schopenhauer — I say "*non legor, non legar.*"[4] — Not that I want to underrate the pleasure that the *innocence* in saying No to my writings has often provided me. Even this summer, when with my weighty, too weighty literature I was perhaps capable of shaking all the rest of literature out of kilter, a well-intentioned professor at Berlin University gave me to understand that I really ought to use a different form: nobody was going to read things like that. — In the end it was not Germany but Switzerland that delivered the two most extreme instances. An essay on *Beyond Good and Evil* by Dr. V. Widmann in the *Bund* with the title "Nietzsche's Dangerous Book,"[5] and a review article on all my books by Herr Karl Spitteler,[6] likewise in the *Bund*, are a maximum in my life — of what, I shall refrain from saying . . . For example, the latter treated my *Zarathustra* as a "higher exercise in style," adding the wish that I might later care to pay attention to content; Dr. Widmann expressed to me his respect for the courage with which I diligently did away with all decent sentiments. — Through a little quirk of fate, with a logical consistency I had to admire, every sentence there was a truth stood on its head: basically, you had nothing to do but "revalue all values" to hit the nail on the head about me in a most remarkable fashion — instead of striking my head with a nail . . .[7] I shall try all the harder to explain. — In the end, your ears cannot extract more from things, books included, than you already know. You cannot have an ear for things for which you have no access from experience. Let us now imagine the most extreme case, where a book tells of nothing but experiences that lie wholly outside the possibility of being experienced either frequently or seldom — where it is the *first* utterance of a new series of experiences. In this case, simply nothing will be heard, with the acoustic deception that where nothing is heard, *nothing is there either* . . . In the final analysis this is my average

WIIY I WRITE SUCH GOOD BOOKS   249

experience and, if you prefer, the *originality* of my experience. Those who thought they had understood something by me fashioned something of me in their own image — not infrequently the opposite of me, for example an "idealist";[8] those who understood nothing of me denied that I came into consideration at all. — The word *"superhuman"* to designate the type that has turned out best, in contrast to "modern" humans, to "good" humans, to Christians and other nihilists — a word that becomes, in the mouth of a Zarathustra, that *destroyer* of morality, a most thought-provoking word, is almost invariably, and completely innocently, understood in the sense of those values whose opposite was manifested in the figure of Zarathustra, in other words, as the "idealistic" type of a superior kind of human, half "saint," half "genius" . . . This has caused other learned cattle to suspect me of Darwinism; they have even recognized in it the "hero cult," so wickedly rejected by me, of Carlyle, that great unconscious, unintentional counterfeiter. When I whispered in someone's ear that he should look around for a Cesare Borgia rather than a Parsifal, he could not believe his ears. — You must excuse me for the fact that I have not a trace of curiosity about reviews of my books, especially in newspapers. My friends and publishers know this and do not speak to me on matters like that. In a particular instance I once set eyes on all the wrongs committed against an individual book — it was *Beyond Good and Evil* — ; I could have told a nice tale about that. Would you believe it, the *Nationalzeitung*[9] — a Prussian newspaper, my foreign readers please note, I myself, by your leave, read only the *Journal des Débats*[10] — in all seriousness made the book out to be a "sign of the times," as the true, right-wing *Junker philosophy* for which the *Kreuzzeitung*[11] only wants the courage? . . .

2.[12]

That was said for Germans: for I have readers everywhere else — all of them of *rare* intelligence, distinguished characters raised in high posts and responsibilities; I even have true geniuses among my readership. In Vienna, in St. Petersburg, in Stockholm, in Copenhagen, in Paris and New York — I have been discovered everywhere: but *not* in Europe's flatland, Germany . . . [13] And let me confess, I am even better pleased by my nonreaders who have heard neither my name nor the word philosophy; yet everywhere I go, here in Turin, for example, every face is cheered and heartened to see me. What has flattered me most up to now is that old market-women[14] cannot rest until they have picked out their sweetest grapes for me. That is *how far* one must be a philosopher . . . Not for nothing are the Poles dubbed the French among the Slavs. No charming Russian woman would mistake where I belong for a moment. I am no good at standing on ceremony, the most I can manage is embarrassment . . . To think German, to feel German — I can do anything, but *that* is beyond my resources . . . My old teacher Ritschl once even claimed that I conceived my philological treatises like a Parisian *romancier*[15] — absurdly thrilling. In Paris itself, people are amazed at "*toutes mes audaces et finesses*"[16] — the expression is Monsieur Taine's[17] — ; I fear that even in the highest forms of the dithyramb you will find with me some addition of that salt, *esprit,*[18] that can never be crude — "German" — . . . I can do no other, God help me. Amen![19] — We all know, a few even know from experience, about asses' ears. Well then, I dare to declare that I have the smallest of ears. This is of no small interest to the little women — it seems to me, they feel I understand them better? . . . I am the *anti-ass* par excellence and thereby a world-historical ogre — I am, in Greek, and not just in Greek, the *Antichrist*[20] . . . [21]

3.[22]

I know my prerogatives as author to some extent; in individual cases I have even been convinced how much a familiarity with my writings "ruins" taste. You simply cannot stand other books anymore, least of all philosophical ones. It is an incomparable distinction to step into this noble and refined world — and of course, you must certainly not be a German;

ultimately, it is a distinction you have to have earned. However, those who are related to me by the *loftiness* of their desire
thereby experience true ecstasies of learning:[23] for I come from
heights where no bird has flown, I know chasms where no foot
has strayed.[24] Some have said to me that they cannot put a
book of mine down — I even disturb their night's rest . . .
There are absolutely no prouder and at the same time more
subtle books: — occasionally, they reach the summit of what
can be achieved on earth, cynicism; you must take possession
of them with the lightest of fingers as well as the boldest of
fists. Any feebleness of soul rules them out for you, once and
for all, as does the slightest dyspepsia: no nerves, you must
have joy in your belly. Not only does the poverty and stuffy air
of a soul form a barrier, much more so does all that is cowardly, unclean, and any clandestine gut feeling of vindictiveness: a word of mine drives all bad instincts into the open.
Among my acquaintances I have several guinea pigs and I treat
myself to their different, very instructively different reactions
to my writings. Those who want nothing to do with their content, my so-called friends, for example, become "impersonal":
they congratulate me at having once again "pulled it off," — and
tell me progress can also be detected in a slightly greater cheerfulness of tone . . . Completely vicious "spirits," "beautiful
souls," those who are mendacious through and through, have
no idea whatever what to do with these books — consequently,
they view them as *beneath* them, the beautiful logical consistency of all "beautiful souls." The cattle of my acquaintance,
mere Germans, by your leave, give me to understand that they
are not always, but sometimes, of my opinion, for example . . .
I have even heard this about *Zarathustra* . . . Likewise, any
"feminism" in a person, even a man, means closing time for
me: they will never enter this labyrinth of daring knowledge.
You need to have been unsparing toward yourself, you need
to have had *severity* in your habits, to be in good spirits and
cheerful among nothing but hard truths. If I conjure up an
image of the perfect reader, the result is always a monster of

courage and curiosity, as well as something pliable, crafty, cautious, a born adventurer and discoverer. Finally: if I were to divulge who are basically the only people I speak to, I could put it no better than Zarathustra has done: to *whom* does he want to relate his riddle exclusively?

> To you, the brave ones who quest and question, and those
> who have ever embarked with cunning sails on fearful oceans
> to you, who are drunk on riddles, who rejoice in twilight,
> whose souls are lured by flutes into every labyrinthian chasm:
> — because you do not want to feel around with a cowardly
> hand for a thread; and whenever you can *guess* something,
> you hate *figuring it out* . . . [25]

4.

At the same time, I shall say a general word about my *art of style*. To *communicate* a state, an inner tension of pathos, through signs, including the tempo of these signs — that is the meaning of every style; and considering that I have an extraordinary number of inner states, the possibilities of style with me are legion — the most manifold art of style a human has ever had at his disposal. Every style is *good* that really communicates an inner state — that does not mix up signs, the tempo of signs, *gestures* — all laws of rhetorical punctuation are the art of gesture. My instinct here is infallible. — Good style *in itself* — *pure folly*, mere "idealism," rather like the "beautiful *in itself*," the "good *in itself*," the "thing *in itself*" . . . Always assuming that there are ears — that such exist who are capable and worthy of a similar pathos, and that there is no lack of those with whom you are *sanctioned* to communicate. — Meanwhile, my Zarathustra, for example, is still searching for such as these — ah! he will have to search for much longer! — You must be *worthy* of hearing him . . . And till then, there will be nobody who understands the *art* lavished here: nobody ever had more of the new, original, truly tailor-made methods of art to lavish. That the likes of this was possible in the German language, of

all things, remained to be seen: I myself would have rejected it
most harshly earlier. Before me, nobody knew what could be
done with the German language — what could be done with
language *in general*. — I was the first to discover how to make
the art of *great* rhythm, the *great* style of rhetorical punctuation into the expression of an immense ebb and flow of sublime, superhuman passion; with a dithyramb like the last of the
third part of *Zarathustra*, entitled "The Seven Seals," I flew a
thousand miles beyond what had hitherto been called poesy.

5.

— That from my writings there speaks a peerless *psychologist*
is perhaps the first insight achieved by a good reader — a
reader such as I deserve, who reads me as good old philologists
read their Horace. The propositions on which all are fundamentally in agreement, not to mention the hackneyed philosophers, moralists and other hollow-pots, heads of cabbage[26] —
are treated by me as naïve blunders: for instance, the belief that
"unegoistic" and "egoistic" are opposites, whereas the ego itself
is just a "higher swindle," an "ideal" . . . There are *neither* egoistic *nor* unegoistic actions: both concepts are psychological nonsense. Or the proposition: "humans strive for happiness" . . . Or
the proposition "happiness is the reward of virtue" . . . Or the
proposition "pleasure and displeasure are opposites" . . . The
Circe of humanity, morality, has thoroughly falsified — *moral-
ized* — all *psychologica* right down to the dreadful nonsense
that love is supposed to be something "unegoistic" . . . You
must be certain of *yourself*, you must stand bravely on your own
two feet, otherwise you *cannot* love at all. Of course, the little
women know that only too well: they tell men who are selfless
and merely objective to go to the devil . . . May I assume, in
passing, that I *know* the little women? It is part of my Dionysian dowry. Who knows? perhaps I am the first psychologist of
the eternal-feminine. They all love me — an old story: except
for women *who are failures*, the "emancipated," who lack what
it takes to create a child. — Fortunately, I am not prepared to

let myself be torn apart: the perfect woman lacerates when she loves . . . I know these charming maenads . . . Oh, what a dangerous, sneaking, covert little predator! And so pleasant with it! . . . A little woman running after revenge would knock down fate itself. — Woman is unspeakably more wicked than man, cleverer too; goodness in a woman is already a form of *degeneration* . . . With all so-called beautiful souls there is a fundamental physiological malfunction — I shall not disclose everything, otherwise I would turn medicynical.[27,28] The struggle for *equal* rights is actually a symptom of disease: every doctor knows that. — Woman, the more she is a woman, completely resists rights hand and foot: the natural state, everlasting *war* between the sexes, of course gives her first rank by far. — Did you have ears for my definition of love?[29] it is the only one worthy of a philosopher. Love — in its methods, war, at its foundation, hatred of the sexes. — Have you heard my answer to how a woman can be *cured* — "redeemed"? Make her pregnant. Woman needs children, the man is always only[30] a means: thus spoke Zarathustra. — "Emancipation of woman" — that is the instinctive hatred of the woman who has *turned out badly*, in other words the barren woman, toward one who has turned out well — the struggle against the "man" is always just means, pretext, tactic. While they elevate *themselves*, as "woman as such," as "higher woman," as "woman idealist," they want to bring *down* woman's general level of rank; no surer way of doing that than high school education, trousers and political rights of voting-cattle. Basically, the emancipated are the *anarchists* in the world of the "eternal-feminine," the ones who have lost out, whose lowest instinct is revenge . . . A whole category of malicious "idealism" — which, by the way, occurs in men as well, Henrik Ibsen, for example, that typical old virgin — aims to *poison* good conscience and naturalness in sexual love . . . And to remove any doubt in this regard as to my opinion, forthright as it is strong, I shall impart yet another proposition from my moral code against *vice*: with the word vice I attack every kind of anti-nature, or, if you like nice words, "idealism." The proposition is: "the preaching of chastity is a public incitement to anti-nature. Every disparagement of sexual life, all defilement of the same by the concept 'unclean,' is the highest crime against life — it is the very sin against the holy spirit of life." —[31,32,33]

6.[34]

In order to give you an idea of myself as psychologist, I take a curious piece of psychology that is found in *Beyond Good and Evil* — by the way, I forbid all speculation as to whom I am describing at this juncture. "The genius of the heart, as possessed by that great hidden one, the tempter-god and born pied piper of consciences whose voice knows how to descend into the underworld of every soul, who does not say a word, does not glance a glance in which there is not a consideration and recess of temptation, whose mastery includes that he knows how to seem — and not what he is but whatever is one *more* compulsion for his followers to press ever closer to him, in order to follow him ever more inwardly and thoroughly . . . The genius of the heart, that causes everything loud and self-satisfied to fall silent and teaches it to listen, that smooths rough souls and gives them a taste of a new yearning — to lie still, as a mirror, so that the deep sky mirrors itself in them . . . The genius of the heart, that teaches the oafish and overhasty hand to pause and reach out more delicately; that guesses the hidden and forgotten treasure, the drop of kindness and sweet spirituality beneath dull, thick ice and is a divining rod for every grain of gold that has lain buried for a long time in a dungeon of much mud and sand . . . The genius of the heart, from whose contact everyone walks away richer, not graced and surprised, not as if blessed and oppressed by some external good, but instead richer in himself, newer than before, broken open, blown upon and sounded out by a thawing wind, less certain perhaps, more delicate, more fragile, more broken, but full of hopes that still have no name, full of new willing and currents, full of new unwillingness and countercurrents . . . "

THE BIRTH OF TRAGEDY.

I.

To do justice to *The Birth of Tragedy* (1872), you will have to forget a few things.[35] It made its *effect* and even fascinated by what was wrong with it — its utilization of *Wagnerism*, as though that were a symptom of *ascent*. That was what made this publication an event in the life of Wagner: only from that point were there great hopes for the name of Wagner.[36] Even today people remind me, if necessary right in the middle of *Parsifal*: of how *I* really have it on my conscience that such a high opinion of the *cultural value* of this movement should have arisen. — I found the work was cited several times as the "*Re*birth of Tragedy out of the Spirit of Music:"[37] people only had ears for a new formulation of *Wagner's* art, aim, **task** — which meant they were deaf to the fundamentally valuable things the publication hid . . . "Hellenism and Pessimism": that would have been a less ambiguous title: namely the first instruction on how the Greeks dealt with pessimism — what they did to *overcome* it . . . Tragedy is precisely the proof that the Greeks were *not* pessimists: Schopenhauer got it wrong here, as he got everything wrong. — If handled with some degree of neutrality, *The Birth of Tragedy* looks very unfashionable: nobody would ever dream that it was *begun* amidst the thunder of the Battle at Wörth.[38] I thought through these problems before the walls of Metz, in cold September nights, in the middle of my service as a medical orderly; the work could easily be taken for fifty years older. It is politically neutral — "un-German," one would say today — it smells offensively Hegelian, a few formulas only are tainted with Schopenhauer's ghoulishly bitter perfume. An "idea" — the antithesis of the Dionysian and Apollonian — translated into metaphysics; history itself as the development of this "idea"; in tragedy, this antithesis sublated into a unity; from this viewpoint, things that had never looked each other in the face before were suddenly juxtaposed, illuminated by each other and *understood* . . . For example, opera and revolution . . .[39] The two decisive *innovations* in the book are, first, the Greeks' understanding of the *Dionysian* phenomenon: it provides the first psychology of it, and sees therein the one and only root of the whole of Greek art. Next is the understanding of Socratism: Socrates recognized for the first time as the tool of Greek disintegration, as typical *décadent.* "Rationality" *against* instinct. Rationality at any price as dangerous, as a life-undermining power! — Deeply hostile silence on Christianity in the whole book. It is neither Apollonian nor Dionysian; it *negates* all *aesthetic* values — the only values that *The Birth of Tragedy* recognizes: it is nihilistic in the profoundest sense, whereas the furthest limit of *affirmation* is achieved in the Dionysian symbol. On one occasion, Christian priests are alluded to as "dwarfs of malicious bent," as "subterraneans" . . . [40]

2.

This beginning is incredibly unusual. I had *discovered* the only resemblance and parallel in history to my own innermost experience — and in doing that, I was the first to grasp the wonderful phenomenon of the Dionysian. Likewise, in recognizing Socrates as *décadent,* the unlikelihood that the sureness of my psychological grasp would run into danger from any moral idiosyncrasy was proved beyond doubt: — morality itself as a symptom of *décadence* is something new, a first-rate singularity in the history of knowledge. How high I soared with both of these above ninnies and their pitiful twaddle about optimism *versus* pessimism!

— I was the first to see the real antithesis: — the *degenerating* instinct that turns itself against life with subterranean vindictiveness (— Christianity, Schopenhauer's philosophy, in some sense already Plato's philosophy, all idealism, as typical forms) and a formula, engendered by abundance, superabundance, for *highest affirmation*, an unreserved "Yes-saying," even to suffering, even to guilt, to everything questionable and strange about existence itself . . . This last, most joyous, most effusively boisterous Yes to life, is not only the highest insight, it is also the *deepest*, the one that is most strictly confirmed and upheld by truth and science. Nothing that is, can be discounted, nothing is dispensable — indeed, the aspects of existence rejected by Christians and other nihilists are of an infinitely higher order in the hierarchy of values than what the *décadence*-instinct has been pleased to approve, *to call good.*[41] Understanding this requires *courage* and, as its precondition, a surplus of *strength*: for precisely as far as courage *dares* to venture forward, according to that very measure of strength we draw nearer to the truth. Knowledge, saying Yes to reality, is just as much a necessity for someone strong as is, for someone weak and imbued with weakness, cowardice and *flight* from reality — the "ideal" . . . They are not free to know: *décadents need* the lie, it is one of their preconditions for survival. — Whoever not only comprehends the word "Dionysian," but also comprehends *himself* in the word "Dionysian," has no need to refute Plato or Christianity or Schopenhauer — he *smells the decay* . . .

3.

The extent to which I had thereby discovered the concept "tragic," the final knowledge about what the psychology of tragedy is, I finally put into words in *Twilight of the Idols* page 139.[42] "Saying Yes to life even in its strangest and hardest problems; the will to life, rejoicing in its own inexhaustibility through the *sacrifice* of its highest types — *that* is what I called Dionysian, that is what I understood as the bridge to the psychology of the *tragic* poet. *Not* in order to break free from horror and compassion, not in order to be purged of a dangerous emotion by vehemently discharging it — as Aristotle misunderstood[43] it: but, beyond horror and compassion, *to be oneself* that eternal joy in becoming, this joy that also even incorporates the *joy in destruction . . .* " In this sense I have the right to see myself as the first *tragic philosopher* — meaning the exact antithesis and antipode of a pessimistic philosopher. Before me, this transposition of the Dionysian into a philosophical pathos did not exist: *tragic wisdom* was lacking — in vain have I searched for signs of it, even with the *great* Greeks of philosophy, those of the two centuries *before* Socrates. I still had a lingering doubt with *Heraclitus*, whose mere proximity is warmer to me and more pleasing than anything else. Affirmation of decline *and destruction*, the decisive thing in a Dionysian philosophy, saying Yes to opposition and war, *becoming*, with a radical rejection of the very idea of "being" — I must concede that these thoughts are closer kin to me than any hitherto, whatever the circumstances. The doctrine of "eternal recurrence," by which I mean the unconditional, endlessly repeated circulation of all things — this doctrine of Zarathustra's just *might* have already been taught by Heraclitus. At the very least the Stoics, who inherited nearly all their fundamental ideas from Heraclitus, have traces of it. —

4.

A terrific hope speaks out of this work. I have really no reason to repudiate my hope in a Dionysian future for music. Let us look a century into the future, and let us suppose my assault on two millennia of anti-nature and violation of humankind were to succeed. This new section of life that takes in hand the greatest of all tasks, the higher breeding of humanity, including the merciless destruction of everything degenerate and parasitical, will again make possible that *surplus of life* on earth out of which the Dionysian state, too, must continue to develop. I promise a *tragic* age: tragedy, the highest art in saying Yes to life, will be reborn when humanity has behind it an awareness of the most violent yet necessary wars *without suffering thereby . . .*

A psychologist might add that what I heard in Wagnerian music in younger years has nothing at all to do with Wagner; that when I described Dionysian music, I described what *I* had heard — that instinctively, I had to translate and transfigure everything into the new spirit that I carried within. The proof for that, *as strong as only a proof can be*, is my work *Wagner in Bayreuth*:[44] at any psychologically decisive passage I am only ever speaking of myself — you can substitute my name or the word "Zarathustra" without hesitation wherever the text gives the word Wagner. The whole image of the *dithyrambic* artist is the image of the preexisting poet of *Zarathustra*, delineated with infinitesimal depth and without touching on the Wagnerian reality for a moment. Wagner himself had an inkling of that; he did not recognize himself in the work. — Likewise, the "idea of Bayreuth" had turned into something that will not have been a riddle to those who know my *Zarathustra*: into the *great noon*, when the most select dedicate themselves to the greatest of all tasks — who knows? the vision of a festival I may yet experience . . . The pathos of the first pages is world-historical; the *look*, spoken about on page seven,[45] is Zarathustra's authentic look; Wagner, Bayreuth, the entire petty German ghastliness is a cloud in which an unending fata morgana of the future is reflected. Even psychologically, all the decisive traits of my nature are carried over into Wagner's — the juxtaposition of the brightest with the most doom-laden forces, the will to power such as no human has ever possessed, remorseless bravery in things of the mind, unlimited energy to learn without it crushing the will to act. Everything in this work is prophetic: the imminence of the return of the Greek spirit, the necessity of *anti-Alexanders* to re*tie* the Gordian knot of Greek culture after it had been cut[46] . . . You can hear the world-historical accent with which, on page 30,[47] the concept of "tragic outlook" is introduced: the accents in this work are exclusively world-historical. This is the most bizarre "objectivity" there can be: absolute certainty about what I *am* projected itself onto some random reality — the truth about myself spoke from a dreadful depth. On page 71,[48] Zarathustra's *style* is described and anticipated with penetrating certainty; and never will you find a more magnificent expression for the *event* of Zarathustra, for the act of an immense purification and sanctification of humanity, than that found on pages 43–46. —[49]

THE UNFASHIONABLES.

I.

The four *Unfashionables* are thoroughly warlike. They prove I was no "John-a-dreams,"[50] that I enjoy drawing my sword — perhaps, too, that I have a dangerously supple wrist. The *first* assault (1873) concerned German culture, which even then I looked down on with implacable contempt. Without meaning, without substance, without aim: a mere "public opinion." There is no more pernicious misunderstanding than to believe that the Germans' great success under arms proves anything at all in favor of this culture — still less *its* victory over France . . . The *second Unfashionable* (1874) brings to light what is dangerous, life-eroding and life-poisoning in the way we pursue science — : life *sickened* by this dehumanized machinery and apparatus, by the "*im*personality" of the worker, by the false economy of "division of labor." Gone is the *end*, culture: — the means, pursuing modern science, *barbarizes* . . . In this essay, the "historical sense" on which this century prides itself was diagnosed for the first time as a sickness, as a typical sign of decline. — Against this, in the *third* and *fourth Unfashionables*, as pointers toward a *higher* concept of culture, a restoration of the concept of "culture," two images were produced of the most stringent *selfishness*, *self-discipline*, unfashionable types par excellence, full of sovereign contempt for everything around them that went by the name of "Reich," "culture,"

"Christianity," "Bismarck," "success," — Schopenhauer and Wagner, *or*, in a word, Nietzsche . . . [51]

2.

Of these four assassination attempts, the first was an extraordinary success. The clamor it evoked was splendid in every sense. I had touched a victorious nation on the raw — the fact that its victory was *not* a cultural event, but perhaps, perhaps something quite different . . . The reply came from all directions and certainly not just from the friends of David Strauss, whom I had ridiculed as the typical German cultivated philistine, *satisfait*,[52] in short, as author of his taproom gospel of the "old and new faith"[53] (— the phrase "cultivated philistine" comes from my work and has remained in the language). These old friends, natives of Württemberg and Swabia, to whom I had dealt a body blow by finding their mascot, their Strauss, funny, answered in the most strait-laced and uncivil way I could have wished for; the Prussian ripostes were cleverer — they had more "Berlin blue"[54] in them. A Leipzig paper, the notorious *Grenzboten*,[55] managed to be the most indecent; I had trouble keeping the outraged inhabitants of Basel from acting as seconds. Only a few old men came down on my side without reserve, for diverse and partly unfathomable reasons. Among these was Ewald in Göttingen,[56] who hinted that my assassination attempt had proved fatal for Strauss. Likewise the old Hegelian Bruno Bauer,[57] in whom I found one of my most attentive readers from then on. In his last years he liked making reference to me, giving Herr von Treitschke, for example, the Prussian historiographer, a tip as to who could inform him about the concept of "culture," that having escaped him. The most thoughtful and lengthiest response to the work and its author came from a former student of the philosopher von Baader, one Professor Hoffmann[58] in Würzburg. From my work, he predicted a great vocation for me — bringing about a sort of crisis and highest adjudication on the problem of atheism, discerning in me its most instinctive and ruthless type. Atheism was what led me

to Schopenhauer. — By far the best heard and bitterest felt
was an extraordinarily strong and bold defense by the otherwise so temperate Karl Hillebrand,[59] the last of the *humane*
Germans to know how to wield the pen. His essay appeared in
the *Augsburger Zeitung*; today, it can be read in a somewhat
more guarded form in his collected works. Here, my work was
presented as an event, turning point, first self-reflection, sign
of promise, as a real *return* of German seriousness and German
passion for things of the mind. Hillebrand was full of high
esteem for the work's form, for its mature taste, for its perfect
tact in distinguishing person from thing: he honored it as the
best polemical piece written in German — in what was, precisely for the Germans, so dangerous and inadvisable an art as
polemics. Unconditionally saying Yes, even more penetrating
than me in what I had dared to say about language-demolition
in Germany (— today, they play the purists and cannot put a
sentence together any more —), with the same contempt
toward the "first writers" of this nation, he finished by expressing his admiration for my *courage* — that "supreme courage
that lands even the nation's favorites in court" . . . The after-
effect on my life of this publication has been simply inestimable.
Nobody has yet picked a quarrel with me. Silence reigns, in
Germany they treat me with subdued caution: for years I have
practiced an absolute freedom of speech for which nobody, least
of all in the "Reich," has enough of a free *hand*. My paradise is
"under the shadow of my sword" . . . Basically, I put into practice a maxim of Stendhal's:[60] he advises making one's entry
into society with a *duel*. And what an opponent I had picked!
The first German free spirit! . . . In the event, a quite *new* way
of freethinking thus came to expression: till this very day,
nothing is stranger and more unrelated to me than the entire
species of European and American "*libres penseurs*."[61] With
them, as with incorrigible ninnies and fools of "modern ideas,"
I even find myself in deeper disagreement than with any of
their opponents. They too, in their own way, want to "improve"
humanity after their image, they would make inexorable war

on what I am, what I *want*, assuming they understood it —
the whole pack of them still believe in the "ideal" . . . I am the
first *immoralist* —

3.

That the *Unfashionables* bearing the names of Schopenhauer
and Wagner might, in particular, serve an understanding or
even a psychological questioning of both cases is not something I want to assert, except for specific things, as is proper.[62]
Thus, for example, already in this work I portrayed with deep
sureness of instinct the fundamentals of Wagner's nature as an
actor's talent merely fulfilled by its means and purposes. Essentially, I wanted to proceed with something quite different from
psychology in these publications: — an unparalleled problem
of education, a new concept of *self-discipline*, *self-defense* to the
point of severity, a pathway to greatness and world-historical
tasks demanded its first expression. All in all, I grabbed two
famous and completely unestablished types by the scruff of
the neck, as you grab an opportunity by the scruff of the neck,
so as to say something, so that I had to hand a few more formulas, signs, linguistic devices. I finally point this out with
uncanny sapience on p. 93[63] of the third *Unfashionable*. Plato
similarly used Socrates as a semiotic for Plato. — Now, when
I review at a certain distance those circumstances to which these
works bear witness, I would not deny that they basically just
talk about me. The work *Wagner in Bayreuth* is a vision of my
future; on the other hand, in *Schopenhauer as Educator*, my innermost story, my *becoming*, is inscribed. Above all, my *oath*! . . .
What I am today, *where* I am today — at a height where I no
longer speak with words but with bolts of lightning — oh, how
far I was then from all that! — But I *saw* the land — not for
one moment did I deceive myself as to path, sea, danger —
and success! What great peace of mind in promising, what a
happy glimpse into a future that will not just remain a promise! — Here, every word was deeply, inwardly felt; no shortage
of the most painful things, some of the words are downright

bloodcurdling. But a blast of *great* freedom sweeps over everything; *no* exception made, even for the wound. — How I see the philosopher as a terrible explosive device putting everything in danger, how I set my concept of "philosopher" miles apart from a concept that includes even a Kant, to say nothing of academic "cud-chewers" and other professors of philosophy: on such topics, this work[64] provides invaluable instruction, even granted that really it is not "Schopenhauer as Educator" but his *opposite*, "Nietzsche as Educator" speaking here. — Considering that my craft was that of a scholar at that time, and also perhaps that I *understood* my craft, it is not insignificant that an astringent chunk on the psychology of the scholar suddenly appears in this work: it expresses the *feeling of distance*, the deep certainty about what my *task* may be and what the mere methods, intermissions and by-products may be. I have been astute enough to do much and travel much in order to become one thing — in order to be able to come to one thing. So I *had* to also be a scholar, for a while. —[65]

HUMAN, ALL TOO HUMAN.[66]

With Two Sequels.

I.

Human, All Too Human is the memorial to a crisis. It calls itself a book for *free* spirits: nearly every sentence in it marks a victory — I used it to free myself of anything *not belonging* to my nature. Idealism does not belong to me: the title says: "where *you* see ideal things, *I* see — what is human, sadly only all too human!" . . . I know the human *better* . . . The phrase "free spirit" should not be understood in any other sense here: a spirit *that has become* free, that has taken possession of itself again. The tone and timbre are completely different: people will find the book clever, cool, potentially strident and mocking. A highbrowed element of *noble* taste seems to be continually fending off a more passionate current at the bottom. In this connection, it is significant that it is actually the centenary of *Voltaire*'s death that provides an excuse, as it were, for publishing the book in 1878.[67] For Voltaire, in contrast to everyone who wrote after him, was above all a *grandseigneur* of the mind: exactly what I am, too. — The name Voltaire on a book of mine — that really was progress — *toward myself.* If you look more closely, you discover a merciless spirit that knows all the hideaways where the ideal is at home — where it has its dungeons and so to speak its final refuge. With torch in hand that lights with never a "flicker," I shine piercing brightness into this *underworld* of the ideal. It is war, but war without powder and

smoke, without warlike attitudes, without pathos and mangled limbs — all of which would still be "idealism." One error
after another is calmly put on ice, the ideal is not refuted — *it
freezes to death* . . . For example, here we have "the genius"
freezing to death; one *hideaway* further on, "the saint" freezes
to death; "the hero" freezes to death under a thick icicle; finally
"faith," so-called "conviction," freezes to death, "compassion"
is also cooling down considerably — nearly everywhere, "the
thing in itself" is freezing to death . . .

2.[68]

The beginnings of this book belong to the weeks of the first
Bayreuth festival;[69] one of its preconditions was a deep alienation from everything that surrounded me there. Anyone with
a notion of what kind of visions had already crossed my path
can imagine what I felt like when I woke up in Bayreuth one
day. It was just as if I were dreaming . . . So where was I? I did
not recognize a thing, I hardly recognized Wagner. In vain I
leafed through my memories. Tribschen — a far distant Blessed
Isle:[70] not a shadow of similarity. The incomparable days of
laying the foundation stone, the small circle who *belonged*, who
celebrated it and whose dexterous delicacy left nothing to be
desired: not a shadow of similarity. *What had happened?* Wagner
had been translated into German! The Wagnerian had become
master over Wagner! — *German* art! *German* master! *German*
beer! . . . The rest of us, who knew only too well the type of refined
artist and cosmopolitanism of taste to which Wagner's art exclusively appeals, were beside ourselves to rediscover Wagner bedecked
with German "virtues." — I think I know the Wagnerian, I have
"gone through" three generations, from the late Brendel,[71] who
confused Wagner with Hegel, to the "idealists" of the *Bayreuther
Blätter*,[72] who confuse Wagner with themselves — I have heard
"beautiful souls" make all sorts of confessions[73] about Wagner.
A kingdom for one sensible word![74] — Actually, a hair-raising
pack! Nohl, Pohl, *Kohl*[75] with *grazie*,[76] *in infinitum*! Not one
monstrosity is lacking, not even the anti-Semite. — Poor Wagner!

What had he let himself in for! — If only he had ended up among the swine![77] But among Germans! . . . In fact, for the instruction of posterity, a genuine Bayreuther should be stuffed, better still, preserved in spirits, for spirits is what we lack — with the inscription: the "spirit" on which the "Reich" was founded looked like this . . . Enough, in the midst of it all, I left for a few weeks, very suddenly, even though a charming Parisienne[78] tried to console me; I apologized to Wagner for my absence just with a fatalistic telegram. At Klingenbrunn, a town hidden deep in the Bohemian forest, I carried around my melancholy and contempt for Germans like a sickness — *and* wrote the odd proposition from time to time in my notebook under the collective title "The Plowshare," nothing but hard *psychologica* that can perhaps still be detected in *Human, All Too Human.*

3.[79]

What settled the matter for me then was not really a breach with Wagner — I experienced a total aberration of instinct, for which a particular blunder, be it Wagner or the Basel Professorship, was just a token. *Impatience* with myself overcame me; I perceived that it was high time to switch my thoughts back to *myself.* All at once it was horribly clear to me how much time had already been wasted — how useless, how arbitrary my whole philologist's existence looked, compared with my task. I was ashamed of this *false* modesty . . . Ten years behind me where my mental *nourishment* had actually come to a halt, where I had not learned anything new that was of use, where I had forgotten a ridiculous amount about the junk of dusty scholarship. Punctiliously worming my way through ancient metrists with my bad eyes — that was what I had come to! — I stared in pity at myself, so thin, so starved: *realities* were virtually absent from my inmost knowledge and "idealities" could go to the devil! — A truly raging thirst seized me: from then on, I have actually dealt with nothing but physiology, medicine, and the natural sciences — I only returned to real historical studies when the importunate *task* compelled me to. That was also the first time I realized the connection between choosing an activity abhorrent to one's instinct, what is termed a "calling," the *last* thing to which one is called — and that need to *deaden* the feeling of desolation and hunger through a narcotic art — for example, through Wagnerian art. With a more circumspect glance I discovered that a large number of young men were in the same state of distress: one action against nature positively *compels* a second. In Germany, in the "Reich," to be precise, simply too many are condemned to decide too soon and then, under a burden that can no longer be jettisoned, *to waste away* . . . They clamor for Wagner as for an *opiate* — they forget themselves, they lose themselves for a moment . . . What am I saying! for *five or six hours*! —

4.[80]

At that time my instinct had relentlessly decided against further giving in, going along, muddling myself up. Every type of life, the least favorable conditions, sickness, poverty — all seemed to me to be preferable to that unworthy "selflessness" into which I had first stumbled through ignorance, through *youth*, and where I had later got stuck through lethargy and "sense of duty." — Here, that *dreadful* legacy from my father's side — basically, a portent of his early death — came to my aid in a way that I can only marvel at, and just at the right moment. Sickness *slowly released me*: it spared me any break, any violent or offensive step. I did not sacrifice any good will at that time and gained a great deal. Sickness likewise gave me the right to completely alter my habits; it allowed, it *commanded* me to forget; it bestowed on me the *requirement* to lie still, to be at leisure, to wait and be patient . . . But of course, that means to think! . . . My eyes alone put an end to all bookworming, in plain language: philology: I was released from the "book," for years on end I read nothing — the *greatest* favor I have ever done myself! — That submerged self, as if buried alive, as if muted amid a continual *mandatory* hearkening to other selves (— and of course, that is what reading means!) slowly awoke, shy and doubting — but finally *it spoke again*. Never have I been so happy with myself as in the sickest and most painful times of my life: you only have to have a look at *Dawn* or maybe *The Wanderer and His Shadow* to grasp what this "return to *myself*" was: *recovery* itself in its supreme form! . . . The other just followed on from that. —

5.

Human, All Too Human, that memorial to a rigorous self-discipline with which I put a sudden end to all my baggage of "higher swindle," "idealism," "fine sentiment" and other womanly traits, was mainly written in Sorrento; I wrote the conclusion and put it into its final form during a winter in Basel under much less favorable circumstances than those in Sorrento. Basically Mister *Peter Gast*, then studying at Basel University and very attached to me, has this book on his conscience. I dictated, my head bound and painful, he wrote down and made corrections as well — essentially, he was the actual writer, while I was merely the author. When I finally had in my hands the finished book — to the great surprise of one so ill — I also sent two copies, among others, to Bayreuth. By some miracle of meaningful coincidence, at the same time a beautiful copy of the text of *Parsifal* arrived with Wagner's dedication to me: "to his dear friend Friedrich Nietzsche, Richard Wagner, Church Councillor." — This crossing of the two books — it seemed to me as if I heard an ominous sound. Didn't it sound as though two *swords* had crossed? . . . At least we both thought so: for we both remained silent. — Around this time, the first issues of *Bayreuther Blätter* appeared: I understood *for what* it had been high time. — Unbelievable! Wagner had become pious . . .

6.

How I thought about myself at that time (1876), the huge certainty with which I handled my task and what was world-historical about it, is evidenced by the whole book, but above all by a very expressive passage: except that with my instinctive guile, I once again avoided the little word "I" here, and this time shone world-historical radiance over, not Schopenhauer, not Wagner, but one of my friends, the distinguished Dr. Paul Rée[81] — fortunately, far too fine an animal to . . . *Others* were less fine: I have always recognized the hopeless cases among my readers, for example, the typical German professor, because they think, from this passage, that they have to regard the whole book as higher Réealism . . . In truth, it contradicted about five or six of my friend's propositions: you might like to consult the preface to the *Genealogy of Morality* about them. — The passage reads: "Yet what is the central proposition at which one of the boldest and coldest thinkers, the author of the book *On the Origin of Moral Sensations* (*lisez*:[82] Nietzsche, the first *immoralist*), arrives, thanks to his incisive and decisive analyses of human action? 'The moral person does not stand any nearer to the intelligible world than the physical person — *for* there is no intelligible world . . . ' This proposition, hardened and sharpened by the hammer blows of historical knowledge (*lisez*: *Revaluation of All Values*) can perhaps someday, at some future time — 1890! — serve as the axe that gets laid to the root of humanity's 'metaphysical need,' — whether more as blessing than as curse upon humanity, who could say? But in any case as a proposition with the most considerable consequences, fruitful and frightful at the same time and looking into the world with the *double vision* that all great realizations have"[83] . . .

DAWN.

Thoughts on Morality as Presumption.[84]

I.

With this book begins my campaign against *morality*. Not that it has the slightest whiff of gunpowder about it: — in it, you will make out quite different and more pleasing scents, assuming you have a modicum of sensitivity in your nostrils. Neither large guns nor even small ones: if the effect of the book is negative, its means are much less so, those means from which an effect follows like an inference, *not* like a cannon shot.[85] That you take leave of the book with a shy wariness of everything up till now honored and even worshipped under the name of morality does not contradict the fact that in the whole book there is not one negative word, no attack, no malice — rather, that it lies in the sun, round, happy, like a sea-creature sunning itself between the rocks. Ultimately, it was me, that sea-creature: nearly every proposition in the book is thought up, *caught up* in that tumble of rocks near Genoa, where I was alone and still shared secrets with the sea. Even now, if I accidentally have contact with the book, nearly every proposition becomes a handle with which I again haul something matchless from the depths: its whole skin trembling with tender quivers of memory. The art, by no means negligible, in which it is most skilled, that of capturing somewhat things that dart past lightly and silently, moments that I call divine lizards — unlike the cruelty of that young Greek god[86] who simply spiked

the poor little lizard — though to be sure, with something
pointed, with the pen . . . "There are so many dawns that have
not yet broken"[87] — this *Indian* inscription stands at the threshold of the book. *Where* does its originator *seek* that new morning, the as yet undetected delicate pink with which another day
— oh, a whole series, a whole world of new days — dawns? In a
revaluation of all values, in an escape from all moral values, in a
Yes-saying and placing of trust in everything that has hitherto
been forbidden, disparaged, damned. This *Yes-saying* book pours
out its light, its love, its tenderness upon nothing but bad things,
restoring their "soul," good conscience, supreme right and *prerogative* to exist. Morality is not attacked, it just no longer
comes into consideration . . . This book ends with an "Or?" —
it is the only book that ends with an "Or?" . . . [88]

2.

My task, to prepare for a moment of the highest self-reflection
for humanity, a *great noontime*, where they look back and look
around, where they step forth from the mastery of chance and
of priests, and pose for the first time *as a whole* the question of
why?, wherefore? — this task follows with necessity from the
insight that humanity is *not* by itself upon the right path, that
they are absolutely *not* divinely governed, that instead, precisely
beneath their most sacred value-concepts, the instinct of negation, of corruption, the *décadence*-instinct has seductively reigned.
The question about the descent of moral values is therefore a
question of the *first rank* for me, because it conditions the future
of humanity. The demand for everyone to *believe* that basically
everything is in the best hands, that a book, the Bible, gives the
ultimate reassurance about divine guidance and wisdom in the
fate of humanity is, translated back into reality, the will to suppress the truth about the deplorable contrary, to wit, that humanity up till now has been in the *worst possible* hands and is ruled
by those who have come off badly, by those who are cunningly
vengeful, by the so-called saints, those world-slanderers and
violators of the human. The decisive sign that establishes how

the priest (— including those *clandestine* priests, the philosophers) has gained mastery not just within a certain religious
community but overall, and how *décadence*-morality, the will
to the end, counts as morality *as such*, is the unconditional value
placed on what is unegoistic and the animosity shown everywhere toward what is egotistic. I regard anyone who is at odds
with me on this point as *infected* . . . But all the world is at odds
with me . . . For a physiologist, a juxtaposition of values like
this admits of no doubt. When within the organism the smallest
organ fails, be it ever so slightly, to perform its self-maintenance,
its energy renewal, its "egoism," with complete confidence, the
whole degenerates. The physiologist demands *excision* of the degenerating part, he eschews any solidarity with what degenerates,
he would be the last to show it compassion. Yet the priest *wants*
precisely the degeneration of the whole, of humanity: therefore
he *conserves* what is degenerating — at that price, he gains dominance . . . What significance do those lying concepts, those
auxiliary concepts of morality, "soul," "spirit," "free will," "God,"
all have if not the physiological ruination of humanity? . . . If you
deflect serious attention away from the importance of the body's
self-maintenance and energy increase, *in other words life*, if you
construct an ideal out of anemia, or "the sanctity of the soul" out
of contempt for the body, what else is that but a recipe for *décadence*? — Losing sight of what is important, resisting natural
instincts, in a word, "selflessness" — that has been called *morality*
up till now . . . With *Dawn*, I first took up the struggle against
the morality of unselfing. —

THE JOYFUL SCIENCE.

("la gaya scienza")

Dawn is a Yes-saying book, profound, but bright and kindly. The same goes for the *gaya scienza*, once again, and to the highest degree: in nearly every one of its sentences, deep thinking and ebullience tenderly hold hands. A verse expressing gratitude for the most wonderful month of January that I have ever experienced — the whole book is its gift — reveals well enough from what depth "science" has here become "joyful":

> You who with your lances burning
> Melt the ice sheets of my soul,
> Speed it toward the ocean yearning
> For its highest hope and goal:
> Ever healthier it rises,
> Free in fate most amorous: —
> Thus your miracle it prizes
> Fairest Januarius![89]

As to what I call "highest hope and goal" here, can anybody who has seen the diamantine beauty of the first words of *Zarathustra* illuminating the conclusion of the fourth book be in any doubt about that? —[90] Or who reads the granite words at the end of the third book[91] which first formulate a destiny *for all times*? The *Songs of Prince Vogelfrei*, mostly composed in Sicily,[92] are a quite explicit reminder of the Provençal concept of *gaya scienza*, that union of *singer*, *knight* and *free spirit* which raises that wonderful early Provençal culture above all ambivalent cultures; the final poem in particular, "To the Mistral,"[93] an ebullient dancing song, which, if you'll pardon the expression, dances above and beyond morality, is a complete Provençalism. —

THUS SPOKE ZARATHUSTRA.[94]

A Book for All and None.

I.

I shall now relate the story of *Zarathustra*. The basic conception of the work, the *thought of eternal recurrence*, this highest formula of affirmation that can be achieved at all — belongs to the August of 1881: it was jotted down on a piece of paper with the subheading: "6000 feet beyond people and time." That day, I walked along Lake Silvaplana through the woods; I came to a halt at a mighty boulder soaring into a pyramid not far from Surlei. That's where this thought came to me. — If I calculate a few months back from that day, I find as portent a sudden and deeply decisive alteration in my taste, above all for music. You can perhaps classify the whole of *Zarathustra* under music; — certainly, a rebirth in the art of *hearing* was a precondition for it. In Recoaro, a little mountain spa not far from Vicenza, where I spent the spring of 1881, I discovered, together with my maestro and friend Pietro Gast, who was likewise "reborn," that the phoenix of music had flown over us with the lightest and most brilliant plumage it had ever displayed. On the other hand, if I calculate forward from that day to the sudden onset of labor, under the unlikeliest of circumstances, in February 1883 — the *finale*, the very same from which I have cited a few sentences in the *foreword*,[95] was accomplished at precisely the hallowed hour when Richard Wagner died in Venice — that comes to eighteen months for the pregnancy. This number of precisely eighteen months might suggest the thought, at least to Buddhists, that I am a female elephant. —[96] The "*gaya scienza*," manifesting a hundred indications that something incomparable is near, belongs in the interval; in fact it even provides the beginning of *Zarathustra* itself,[97] tendering the basic thought of Zarathustra in the penultimate passage of the fourth book.[98] — Likewise belonging to that interval is the *Hymn to Life* (for mixed choir and orchestra), the score of which was published two years ago by E. W. Fritzsch in Leipzig: a perhaps not insignificant symptom of my condition in that year, when the *Yes-saying* pathos par excellence, which I call tragic pathos, dwelled in me with the highest intensity. Sometime in the future people will sing it in my memory. — The text, I say expressly, as there is currently a misunderstanding about it, is not by me: it is the astonishing inspiration of a young Russian woman with whom I was friendly at the time, Fräulein Lou von Salomé. Whoever is able to extract a meaning from the last words of the poem will realize why I singled it out for admiration: they are magnificent. Pain is *not* treated as an argument against life: "If you have no more happiness left to give me, well then! *still you have your pain* . . ." Perhaps my music is magnificent too at this point. (The last note of the oboe[99] is C sharp, not C natural, printing error.) — I spent the winter that followed in the charming, peaceful bay of Rapallo near Genoa, carved out between Chiavari[100] and the foothills of Porto Fino. My health was not the best; a cold winter and unseasonably wet; a small *albergo*, situated right by the sea, so that at night, the high sea made sleep impossible, offered more or less the opposite of what could be desired. Nevertheless, and almost as proof of my proposition that everything decisive comes about "nevertheless," it was in this winter and under these unfavorable circumstances that my *Zarathustra* emerged. — In the mornings, I set off for the heights in a southerly direction along the glorious road to Zoagli, past pines and looking down on the panorama of the sea; in the afternoons, as often as my health permitted, I walked round the whole bay from Santa Margherita right up to

Porto Fino. This place and its surroundings were dearer to my heart because of the great affection the unforgettable German[101] Kaiser Friedrich the Third had for them; in autumn of 1886, I happened to be on this coast again when he visited this forgotten little world of bliss for the last time. — On these two pathways, the whole of the first book of *Zarathustra* came to me, especially Zarathustra himself, as a type: more correctly, he *overcame me* . . .

2.

To understand this type, you must first be clear about his physiological precondition: which is what I call *great health*. I cannot elucidate the idea better or more *personally* than I have already done in one of the final passages of the fifth book of the "*gaya scienza*."[102] You read there: "We new, nameless, hard to understand ones, we premature births of a still unproven future — for a new end we also need a new means, namely a new health, a stronger, savvier, tougher, more daring, merrier one than all healths of the past. Someone whose soul thirsts to have experienced the entire scope of previous values and desiderata, to have circumnavigated all coasts of this ideal 'mediterranean sea,' who wants to know from the adventures of his most authentic experiences how a conqueror and discoverer of the ideal feels, likewise an artist, a saint, a legislator, a sage, a scholar, a pious man,[103] an old-fashioned divine loner: for this he needs one thing above all, the *great health* — of the kind that one does not merely have, but also continuously acquires and must acquire, because one gives it up again and again, must give it up[104] . . . And now, after we've been under way for a long time in this manner, we Argonauts[105] of the ideal, more courageously perhaps than is prudent, and often enough shipwrecked and damaged but, as mentioned, healthier than one would like to give us credit for, dangerously healthy, healthy again and again — now it seems to us as though, as a reward for this, we have a yet undiscovered land before us, whose boundaries no one has yet surveyed, something beyond all previous lands and corners of the ideal, a world so superabundant in what is beautiful, strange, questionable, terrible and divine, that our curiosity as well as our craving to possess are beside themselves — oh, that nothing is capable of sating us anymore! How could we, after such vistas and with such ravenousness in our conscience and science,[106] still be satisfied with the *current human being*? Bad enough: but it is inevitable that we look upon his worthiest goals and hopes with merely a poorly maintained seriousness and perhaps don't look upon them at all anymore. A different ideal runs ahead of us, an unusual, seductive, danger-ous ideal to which we want to persuade no one because we do not so easily concede anyone the *right to it*: the ideal of a spirit who plays naïvely, that is, involuntarily and from overflowing fullness and power, with everything that has so far passed for holy, good, untouchable, divine; for whom the supreme, which is justifiably the measure of value of the common people, would instead equate with danger, decline, debasement or, at least, with recuperation, blindness, temporary self-oblivion; the ideal of a human-superhuman well-being and benevolence, that will often enough appear *inhuman*, for instance, when it shows up next to all previous earthly seriousness, next to every kind of solemnity of gesture, word, tone, look, morality and task look-ing like their incarnate and involuntary parody — and perhaps only with it, in spite of everything, *the great seriousness* begins, the real question mark is posed for the first time, the destiny of the soul turns, the clock hand advances, the tragedy *begins* . . . "

3.

— Has anybody at the end of the nineteenth century a clear conception of what poets in strong ages called *inspiration*? In case not, I shall describe it. — With the merest trace of super-stition in you, you would in fact scarcely know how to ward off the impression of being a mere incarnation, mere mouthpiece, mere medium of overpowering forces. The notion of revelation in the sense that suddenly, with indescribable certainty and refinement, something becomes *visible*, audible, something that

profoundly unnerves and disconcerts you, simply describes a
state of fact.[107] You hear, you do not seek; you take, you do not
ask who gives; like lightning, a thought lights up, inescapable,
unhesitating as to its form — I never had a choice. A rapture
whose immense tension occasionally erupts in a flood of tears,
while your step involuntarily races then slackens; you feel completely outside yourself, with the most distinct consciousness of
countless faint shivers and tingles right down to your toes; you
have a feeling of deep bliss where what is most painful and upset-
ting does not have a contradictory effect but instead acts as conditioned, demanded, as a *necessary* color within such a superfluity
of light; an instinct for rhythmic connections that spans forms of
vast extent — the length, the requirement for a *wide-spanned*
rhythm is almost the measure for the power of inspiration, a sort
of compensation for its pressure and tension . . . All this takes
place completely involuntarily, but as though in a tumult of feeling free, of being unrestricted, of power and divinity . . . The
involuntariness of image, of metaphor, is the most striking thing;
you no longer have a notion of what is image, what metaphor,
everything offers itself as the closest, the most correct, the simplest expression. It really does seem, to recall a saying of Zarathustra's, as though the things approached all of themselves and vol-
unteered to be metaphors (— "here come all things adoring
your speech and flattering you: for they want to ride on your
back. Here you ride on every metaphor to every truth. Here all
words and word-shrines of being spring open for you; all being
wants to become word here, all becoming wants to learn from
you how to speak — "[108]). This is *my* experience of inspiration; I
do not doubt that you have to go back millennia to find someone
who can say to me "that's mine, too." —

4.

After that I lay sick for a couple of weeks in Genoa. There
followed a downcast spring in Rome,[109] where I took life as it
came — it was not easy. Basically, this most unpleasant place

on earth for the author of *Zarathustra*, which I had not chosen voluntarily, depressed me beyond measure; I tried to leave — I wanted to go to *Aquila*, the counterconcept to Rome, founded out of animosity toward Rome, just as I shall one day found a place in memory of an atheist and enemy of the church *comme il faut*,[110] my near relative the great Hohenstaufen Kaiser Friedrich II.[111] But there was inevitability in all of this: I had to return.[112] Finally I made do with the Piazza Barberini, after I had tired of my efforts to find an *anti-Christian* area. I fear that once, to get as far away as possible from the bad smells, I even enquired at the Palazzo del Quirinale[113] whether they had a quiet room for a philosopher. — On a *loggia* high over the said *piazza* from which one could survey Rome and hear the *fontana*[114] splashing down below, I penned that most solitary poem ever written, *Night Song*; around this time, a melody of unspeakable melancholy went round in my head constantly, the refrain of which I rediscovered in the words "dead of immortality . . . " That summer, returning to the hallowed spot where the first lightning bolt of the thought of *Zarathustra* had hit me, I found the second *Zarathustra*. Ten days sufficed; with none of the others did I need more, neither with the first, nor with the third and last. The following winter, under the halcyon sky of Nice that shone into my life for the first time, I found the third *Zarathustra* — and had finished. Hardly a year, counting the whole of it. Many hidden spots and heights in the landscape of Nice have become sacred to me by unforgettable moments; that decisive section bearing the title "On Old and New Tablets" was thought up as I climbed laboriously from the station to Eza,[115] that wonderful Moorish aerie — my muscular agility has always been at its greatest when my creative energy is in full flow. The *body* is eager: let's leave the "soul" out of it . . . You could have often seen me dancing; that was when I could walk in mountains for seven, eight hours with no notion of fatigue. I slept well, I laughed a lot — I was perfectly spry and patient.

5.[116]

Apart from these ten-day works, the years during and particularly *after Zarathustra* were distressing beyond belief. You pay dearly for being immortal: dying several times while still alive. — There is a thing I call the *rancune*[117] of the great: everything great, a work, a deed, immediately turns *against* its perpetrator the moment it is finished. Because he has done it, he is now *weak* — unable to stand his deed any longer, unable to look it in the face. To have something *behind* you that you were never sanctioned to will, something tied to the knot in the fate of humanity — and then to have it *on* you! . . . It almost crushes you . . . the *rancune* of the great! — Another thing is the dreadful silence you hear around you. Solitude has seven skins; nothing more can slip through. You mix with people, you greet friends: new wilderness, no more friendly looks. At best a sort of revolt. I experienced such a revolt, to a very different degree, from almost everyone who was close to me; apparently, nothing can insult more deeply than suddenly establishing the fact of distance — those with *noble* natures, who do not know how to live without paying respect, are rare. — A third thing is the absurd sensitivity of the skin to little bites, a sort of helplessness in the face of anything small. I think this is determined by the huge wastage of all defensive energies that every *creative* deed, every deed produced by one's ownmost, innermost, undermost presupposes. The *small* defensive capabilities are, so to speak, suspended; no energy flow replenishes them. — I even wager that you will have worse digestion, be unwilling to move, be only too exposed to frosty feelings and mistrust as well — mistrust that in many cases is just an etiological mistake. In such a situation, because my thoughts had turned milder and more cordial toward people, I once sensed a herd of cows even before I saw them: *that* has warmth in it . . . [118,119,120]

6.

This work stands completely by itself. Let us put poets to one side: perhaps nothing has ever been done at all from an equal surplus of energy. My concept of "the Dionysian" became here the *highest deed*; measured against that, all the rest of human endeavor seems poor and contingent. That a Goethe, a Shakespeare would not be able to breathe for a moment in this tremendous passion and height, that Dante held against Zarathustra is merely a believer and not someone who first *creates* the truth, a *world-governing* spirit,[121] a destiny — that the poets of the Veda[122] are priests and not even worthy to unloosen the straps of a Zarathustra's shoes,[123] all that is the least of it and gives no notion of the distance, the *azure* solitude where this work dwells. Zarathustra has an eternal right to say: "I draw circles around myself and holy boundaries; fewer and fewer people climb with me up higher and higher mountains, — I am building a mountain range out of holier and holier mountains."[124] Just add together the spirit and goodness of all great souls: the whole lot would not be in a position to produce a single one of Zarathustra's discourses. The ladder on which he ascends and descends is tremendous; he has seen further, willed further, had more *ability* than any other human. This most Yes-saying of all spirits contradicts with every word; in him, all opposites are bound into a new union. The highest and lowest forces of human nature, the sweetest, most frivolous and most dreadful, stream out from one fount with undying sureness. Until then, nobody knows what is high, what is deep; and still less what is the truth. Not a moment of this revelation of truth could have been anticipated or even suspected by a single one of the greatest. There was no wisdom, no study of the soul, no artistry of speech before Zarathustra; what is familiar, what is everyday speaks here of unprecedented things. The aphorism[125] a-shudder with passion; eloquence transformed into music; bolts of lightning hurled into the distance toward hitherto unsuspected futures. The mightiest power of analogy there has so far been is a poor plaything in contrast to this return of language to the nature of imagery. — And how Zarathustra descends to say a kind word to everyone! How he gently takes the hand of even his opponents, the

priests, and shares their suffering of themselves! — Here, at
every moment, the human being is overcome, here the concept
"superhuman" has become the highest reality — at an infinite
distance lies everything that was ever found great in the human
being, *beneath* him. Nobody ever dreamed that the halcyon
mien, the lightness of foot, the ever-present mischief and high
spirits and all else typical of the Zarathustra-type would be
essential to greatness. Right here, in this expanse of space, with
this access to what is contrary, Zarathustra sees himself as the
highest form of all beings; and if you hear how he defines this,
you will give up trying to make a comparison:

> — the soul which has the longest ladder and can reach
> down the deepest,
> the most extensive soul, which can run and stray and
> wander the furthest within itself,
> the most necessary one, which throws itself with delight
> into chance,
> the soul that is, that wills itself into becoming, the soul
> that has, that *wills* itself into wanting and demanding —
> the soul that flees from itself, the soul that catches up to
> itself within the widest circles,
> the wisest soul, which folly entreats most sweetly,
> the soul that loves itself the most, in which all things have
> their surging and resurging and ebb and flow — —[126]

But that is the concept of Dionysus himself. — A different consideration yields the same result. The psychological problem with
the Zarathustra-type is how someone who says No to everything to an inordinate degree, *does* No to everything to which
hitherto everyone said Yes, can nevertheless be the opposite of a
No-saying spirit; how this spirit bearing the weightiest of destinies, a fatality of a task, can nevertheless be the lightest and
most unworldly — Zarathustra is a dancer — ; how one who
has thought the "most abysmal thought"[127] nevertheless finds
in it no objection to existence, not even to its eternal recurrence
— but rather, yet another reason *to himself be* the eternal Yes to

all things, "the immense unlimited yes- and amen-saying" . . .
"I still carry my yes-saying blessings into all abysses"[128] . . . *But
that is the concept of Dionysus yet again.*

7.

— What language will such a spirit speak when speaking
with himself alone? The language of the *dithyramb*. I am the
inventor of the dithyramb. Just listen to how Zarathustra
speaks with himself in *Before Sunrise* (III, 18): before me, no
tongue ever held such emerald felicity, such divine gentleness.
Even the deepest melancholy of such a Dionysus still becomes
dithyrambic; I take as indicator the *Night Song*, his undying
lament at being condemned not to love through a surfeit of
light and power, his *sunny* nature.

> It is night: now all gushing fountains speak more loudly.
> And my soul, too, is a gushing fountain.
> It is night: all the songs of those who love just now awaken.
> And my soul, too, is the song of someone who loves.
> Something unquenched, unquenchable lies within me,
> wanting to be heard. A lust for love is within me which itself
> speaks the language of love.
> I am light: alas, if only I were night! But this is my
> solitude, that I am surrounded by light.
> Alas, that I were dark and like the night! How I would
> want to suckle at the breasts of light!
> And you yourselves are those whom I would still want to
> bless, you twinkling little stars and fireflies up above! — and
> to be blissful about your gifts of light.
> But I live in my own light, I drink back inside me the
> flames that flare out of me.
> I do not know the happiness of those who receive; and I
> have often dreamed of this, that it must be even more blessed
> to steal than to receive.[129]
> This is my poverty, that my hand never rests from giving;
> this is my envy, that I see expectant eyes and the glowing
> nights of yearning.

Oh wretchedness of all those who give! Oh dimming of my sun! Oh lusting after lust! Oh feeling ravenous in being satiated!

They receive from me: but am I still touching their souls? There is a gap between receiving and giving; and the smallest gap is the last to be bridged.

A hunger grows out of my beauty: I would like to hurt those whom I illuminate, I would like to rob those to whom I give — thus do I hunger for malice.

Withdrawing my hand when another hand is already extended; like a waterfall that hesitates in midcascade: thus do I hunger for malice.

My completeness is plotting this kind of revenge; spite like this spills forth from my solitude.

My delight in giving died as I was giving, my virtue grew weary of itself as it overflowed!

Those who are always giving run the danger of losing their sense of shame; those who are always dispensing grow callouses on their hands and hearts as a result of this alone.

My eyes no longer well up over the shame of those who beg; my hand has become too hard for the trembling of filled hands.

Where did the tear in my eye go and the soft down of my heart? Oh solitude of all those who give! Oh silence of all those who illuminate!

Many suns circle through desolate space: to all that is dark, they speak with their light — to me they are silent.

Oh this is the enmity of the light toward that which illuminates: mercilessly it moves in its orbits.

Unjust in its heart toward that which illuminates, cold toward suns — every sun moves in this way.

The suns move in their orbits like a storm, this is how they move, they follow their relentless will, this is their coldness.

Oh you of the dark, you of the night, there was no one before you who had created warmth out of that which illuminates! Oh, there was no one before you who had drunk milk and taken comfort from the udders of light!

Alas, ice surrounds me, the iciness burns my hand! Alas, there is a thirst within me that longs for your thirst!

It is night: alas that I have to be light! And a thirst for things of the night! And solitude!

It is night: now my craving gushes forth from me like a wellspring — I crave to speak.

It is night: now all gushing fountains speak more loudly. And my soul, too, is a gushing fountain.

It is night: all the songs of those who love do now awaken. And my soul, too, is the song of someone who loves. —[130]

8.

Never has the like been written, never felt and never *suffered*: thus does a god, a Dionysus, suffer. The reply to such a dithyramb on a sun's increasing loneliness in the light would be Ariadne . . .[131] Who knows, apart from me, what Ariadne is! . . . Nobody has yet had the solution to such riddles as these, I doubt whether anyone has ever even seen riddles here. — Zarathustra once rigorously specified his task — it is mine, too — so that no mistake as to *meaning* can be made: he is Yes-saying right up to the justification for and redemption of all that is past.

I walk among people as I do among fragments of the future: of that future that I see.

And this is the sum of my poetic compositions and endeavors, that I compose and bring together whatever is fragment and riddle and dreadful chance.

And how could I bear being human if humans were not also poets and riddle-solvers and redeemers of chance?

To redeem the people of the past and to reshape every "It was" into a "This is how I willed it!" — only then, in my view, would this be called redemption![132]

In another place, he defines as rigorously as possible what "the human" can be for him — *not* an object of love or even of compassion — Zarathustra has even mastered his *great disgust*[133] at the human being: the human, for him, is something unformed, some matter, an ugly stone needing a sculptor.

No more *willing* and no more *evaluating* and no more *creating*: oh, that this great weariness would stay away from me forever!

Even in the process of knowing I feel only the lust to procreate and the lust to become; and if there is innocence in the knowledge I have gained, this happens because the *will to procreate* is within the knowledge I have gained.

This will lures me away from God and gods: besides, what would be left to create if gods — were there!

But it drives me ever anew to human beings, my fervent will to create; thus the hammer is driven toward the stone.

Oh, you humans, a shape[134] is sleeping in the stone, the shape of all shapes! Alas, that it has to be sleeping in the hardest, ugliest stone of all!

Now my hammer rages cruelly against its prison. Pieces fly off the stone like dust: what do I care!

I want to finish it, for a shadow came to me — the stillest and lightest thing of all things once came to me!

The beauty of the superhumans came to me as a shadow: what do I care anymore — about gods! . . . [135]

I will stress one final point: the italicized verse occasioned this. For a Dionysian task, the hardness of the hammer, the *pleasure even in destroying* are a decisive part of its preconditions. The imperative "become hard!,"[136] the most deep-seated certainty *that all creators are hard*, is the real seal of a Dionysian nature. —

BEYOND GOOD AND EVIL.

Prelude
to a Philosophy of the Future.

1.

Now the task for the following years was mapped out as rigorously as possible. After the Yes-saying part of my task had been fulfilled came the turn of the No-saying, *"No-doing"* half: the revaluation of the former values themselves, the great war — the summoning up of a day of decision. This includes the slow look round for relatives, for those who, out of strength, would lend me a hand *in destroying.* — From then on, all my works are fishhooks: perhaps I know as much as anyone about angling? . . . If nothing was *caught,* the fault does not lie with me. *There were no fish . . .*

2.

This book (1886) is essentially a *critique of modernity,* not excluding the modern sciences, the modern arts, even modern politics, alongside pointers to an opposite type, the least modern it is possible to be, a noble, Yes-saying type. Ultimately, the book is a *school for the gentilhomme,*[137] that concept being taken more intellectually and *more radically* than ever before. You must have fire in your belly just to survive it, you must not have learned fear[138] . . . Everything of which the age is proud is construed as a contradiction of this type, almost as bad manners, that famous "objectivity," for example, "fellow feeling for all that suffers," the "historical sense" with its servility to foreign taste, its groveling to *petits faits*,[139] "scientificity." — When you consider that the book follows *after Zarathustra*, you can perhaps also guess the dietary regime to which it owes its emergence. The eye, indulged by a tremendous necessity to see *far* — Zarathustra is more far-sighted than the Czar[140] — is here forced to focus on what is nearest, our time, what is *"around us."* In all aspects, especially its form, you will find the same *deliberate* avoidance of the instincts that had made a *Zarathustra* possible. Refinement in form, in intent, in the art of remaining *silent*, is in the foreground, psychology is handled with avowed hardness and cruelty — the book eschews every good-natured word . . . All of this is recreational: who can speculate as to *which* kind of recreation such a lavishment of goodness — for that is what *Zarathustra* is — might necessitate? . . . Speaking theologically — now listen, as I don't often speak as a theologian — it was God himself, in the guise of the serpent, who laid himself down under the tree of knowledge at the end of his day's work: this was his recreation from being God . . . He had done everything too well . . . The devil is just God on that seventh day, having a rest . . . [141]

GENEALOGY OF MORALITY.

A Polemic.

The three essays comprising the *Genealogy* are possibly, with regard to their expression, purpose and art of surprise, the uncanniest ever written. Dionysus is, one knows, also the god of darkness. — Each one has a beginning *designed* to lead astray, cool, scientific, even ironic, intentionally to the fore, intentionally staving off. Gradually more restless; the odd flash of lightning; very unpleasant distant truths becoming audible with a muffled grumble — until at last they reach a *tempo feroce*[142] where everything surges ahead in great suspense. At the end of each, amid absolutely dreadful detonations, a *new* truth is sighted among thick clouds. — The truth of the *first* essay is the psychology of Christianity: the birth of Christianity out of the spirit of *ressentiment, not,* as one might think, out of the "spirit," — a reactionary movement in its very nature, the great uprising against the dominion of *noble* values. The *second* essay provides the psychology of *conscience*: which is *not,* as one might think, "the voice of God in the human being," — it is the instinct of cruelty turning back on itself when it can no longer discharge itself outwards. Cruelty brought to light here for the first time as one of the oldest and indispensable foundations of culture. The *third* essay provides an answer to the question of the provenance of the immense *power* of the ascetic ideal, the priestly ideal, even though this is the *damaging* ideal par excellence, a will to the end, a *décadence*-ideal. Answer: *not* because God is at work behind the priests, as is probably thought, but rather *faute de mieux*[143] — because it was the only ideal there had been hitherto, because it had no competition. "For the human would sooner will nothingness, than *not* will"[144] . . . Above all, a *counter-ideal* has been lacking — *until Zarathustra.* — I have been understood. Three decisive preliminary works by a psychologist for a revaluation of all values. — This book contains the first psychology of the priest.

TWILIGHT OF THE IDOLS.

How to Philosophize with a Hammer.

1.

This work, not even 150 pages long, both cheerful and fateful in tone, a demon that laughs —[145] the work of so few days that I forbear to state the number, is the complete exception among books: there is nothing richer in substance, more independent, more subversive — more wicked. Anyone wanting to gain a brief notion of how upside down everything was before me should start off with this book. The *idol* of the title page is quite simply what has been called truth until now. *Twilight of the Idols* — in plain language: the old truth is coming to an end . . .

2.

There is no reality, no "ideality," that this work does not touch upon (touch upon: what a cagey euphemism! . . .) Not just the *eternal* idols, also the most recent, inevitably the weakest because of their age. "Modern ideas," for example. A great wind is blowing through the trees, everywhere the fruits are falling — truths. The cause is the prodigality of an all-too-rich autumn: people are stumbling over truths, trampling one or two to death — there is a glut of them . . .[146] But what you have in your hands is no longer questionable, they are decisions. I am the first to have in my hand the gauge for "truths," the first who *can* decide. As though a *second consciousness* had grown within me, as though "the will" in me had lit a light

illuminating the *crooked* path it ran down until now . . .[147] The
crooked path — they used to call it the way to "truth" . . . All
"dark yearning" has come to an end, the *good* human had
precisely the least idea about which was the right path[148] . . .
And in all seriousness, nobody before me knew the right way,
the way *upwards*: only after me are there hopes, tasks, prescribed routes to culture[149] — *I bring glad tidings*[150] *of them* . . .
And that makes me also a destiny. — —[151]

3.

Directly after the completion of the above-mentioned work
and without losing a single day, I launched into the immense
task of the *Revaluation* in an incomparable sovereign mood of
pride, sure of my immortality at every moment and engraving
sign after sign onto bronze tablets with the sureness of a destiny. The foreword was written on 3 September 1888: when,
having written it, I stepped into the open air that morning, I
discovered it was the most beautiful day the Upper Engadine
had ever shown me — clear, aglow with colors, containing every
contrast, every median between ice and the South. — [152] Only
on 20 September did I leave Sils-Maria, delayed by floods until
finally I was by some margin the only visitor left in this wonderful place, to which I will show my gratitude by rendering
its name immortal. After a journey with incidents of even a
life-threatening nature in flooded Como, which I reached only
at dead of night, I arrived on the afternoon of 21 September in
Turin, my *established* place, my domicile from now on. I took
the same apartment again as I had lived in before, via Carlo
Alberto 6, III, opposite the mighty Palazzo Carignano, where
Vittore Emanuele was born, with a view to the Piazza Carlo
Alberto and the hilly terrain beyond. Without hesitation,
without giving myself a moment's respite, I went to work
again: only the last quarter of the work remained to do. Great
victory on 30 September; completion of the *Revaluation*;[153]
idle as a god on the river Po. And still that day I wrote the

Foreword to *Twilight of the Idols*, the proofs of which I had corrected in September, as a recreation. — I have never experienced an autumn like that, never even thought that something of that sort was an earthly possibility — a Claude Lorrain projected into infinity, each day of the same boundless perfection. —

THE CASE OF WAGNER.

A Musicians' Problem.

I.

To be fair to this work, you need to suffer from the fate of music as from an open wound. — *What* do I suffer from if I suffer from the fate of music? From the fact that music has been cheated out of its world-transfiguring, Yes-saying character — that it is *décadence*-music and no longer the flute of Dionysus . . . But assuming that you feel the same way about musical affairs as you would about your *own* affairs, your *own* story of suffering, you will find this work full of consideration and remarkably moderate. To be cheerful in such cases and mock oneself with a good grace — *ridendo dicere severum*,[154] where the *verum dicere*[155] would justify any amount of severity — is humanity itself. Who can really doubt that I, old artillerist that I am, did not have it in my grasp to turn my *heavy* guns on Wagner?[156] — I kept everything crucial in this matter to myself — I loved Wagner.[157] Finally there took place an attack on a craftier "unknown," whom nobody else would easily guess, in the sense and manner of my work — oh, I still have "unknowns" to reveal quite different from a Cagliostro of music[158] — and of course, even more an attack[159] on the German nation, growing ever more torpid and poorer in instinct, ever more *upright*, as far as spiritual matters are concerned, while it continues to feed itself, with enviable appetite, on opposites, and to gobble down "belief" as easily as things

THE CASE OF WAGNER

scientific, "Christian love" as easily as anti-Semitism, the will to power (to the "Reich") as easily as the *évangile des humbles*,[160] with no problems as to digestion . . . This lack of preference between opposites! This neutrality of stomach and "selfless-ness"! This sense of fair play of the German *palate* that awards equal rights to all — that finds everything to its taste . . . no doubt about it, the Germans are idealists . . . When I last vis-ited Germany, I found German taste exercised with granting equal rights to Wagner and the Trumpeter of Säckingen;[161] I myself witnessed *firsthand* how, in honor of Master *Heinrich Schütz*, one of the most genuine, most German of musicians, in the old sense of the word German, not just a German of the Reich, a Liszt Association was founded in Leipzig with the aim of promoting and furthering a *sly*[162] church music . . . No doubt about it, the Germans are idealists . . .

2.[163]

But here, nothing is going to stop me from being rude and telling the Germans a few truths: *who will do it otherwise?* — I am speaking here of their bad breeding *in historicis*. Not only have the German historians completely lost their *overall view* of the process, of the values of culture, not only are they fools, one and all, in politics (or the Church —): they have even *spurned* this overall view. First you have to be German, have "breeding," then you can decide about all values and nonval-ues *in historicis* — you establish them . . . "German" is an argument, "*Deutschland, Deutschland über alles*"[164] a principle, the Teutons are the "moral world order" in history; the bearers of freedom in regard to the *imperium romanum*, in relation to the eighteenth century the restorers of morality, of the "cate-gorical imperative" . . . There is a Reich-German way of writ-ing history, I fear there is even an anti-Semitic one — there is a *courtly* way of writing history, and Herr von Treitschke has no shame . . . Recently, an idiotic judgment *in historicis*, a proposi-tion by that aesthetic Swabian Vischer,[165] fortunately deceased, made the rounds of the German newspapers as a "truth" to which every German *had to say Yes*: "Only when together do both the Renaissance *and* the Reformation make a whole — aesthetic rebirth *and* ethical rebirth." — With a proposition like this, my patience runs out and I feel the desire, I even regard it as my duty, to tell the Germans once and for all *what* it is they have on their conscience. *They have all the great crimes of culture of the last four hundred years on their conscience!* . . . And always for the same reason, out of their innermost *cowardice* before reality, which is also cowardice in the face of the truth, out of untruthfulness that has become instinctive with them, out of "idealism" . . . [166] The Germans have cheated Europe out of the harvest, out of the meaning of the last *great* period, the Renaissance period, at a moment when a higher order of values, those noble, life-affirming values guaranteeing the future, had achieved victory at the seat of the opposing *values of decline — right down into the instincts of those already ensconced there!* Luther, that catastrophe of a monk, reestablished the Church as well as Christianity, which is a thousand times worse, at the moment *when it was defeated* . . . Christianity, this *denial of the will to life* turned into religion! . . . Luther, an impossible monk who attacked the Church because he was "impossible" and then — in consequence! — reestablished it . . . Catholics would have grounds for holding Luther festivals and writing Luther plays . . . Luther — and "ethical rebirth"! To the devil with all psychology! — Without doubt, the Germans are idealists. Twice the Germans, just when an upright, unambiguous, completely scientific way of thought had been achieved with immense courage and self-overcoming, have been able to find hidden paths to the old "ideal" and compromises between truth and the "ideal," essentially formulas for the right to deny science, for the right to *lies*. Leibniz and Kant — the two greatest stumbling blocks to Europe's intellectual integrity! — Finally, just when a force majeure of genius and will strong enough to create a union, a political *and economic* union targeted at world domination, was visible at the bridge between two centuries of *décadence*, the Germans with

their "Wars of Liberation"[167] cheated Europe out of the significance, the amazing significance of the existence of Napoleon
— in doing so, they have on their conscience everything that
resulted and is still in force today, this *most culturally antagonis-
tic* sickness and nonsense there is, nationalism, this *névrose
nationale*[168] infecting Europe, this perpetuation of Europe's
small kingdoms, *small* politics:[169] they have even robbed Europe
of its meaning, its *reason* — they have led it down a blind alley.
— Does anybody besides myself know a *way* out of this blind
alley? . . . A task large enough to *reunite* the peoples? . . .

3.

— And really, why shouldn't I put my misgivings into words?
Even in my case the Germans will once more try everything to
make a tremendous destiny give birth to a mouse.[170] They have
compromised themselves with me so far, I don't suppose they
will be any better in future. — Oh, in this instance, how I
would love to be *wrong* as prophet! . . . At the moment, my natural readers and listeners are Russian, Scandinavian and French
— will they always be so? — The Germans are inscribed into
the history of knowledge with a string of ambiguous names,
they have only ever brought forth "unconscious" counterfeiters
(— Fichte, Schelling, Schopenhauer, Hegel, Schleiermacher
all deserve this title as well as Kant and Leibniz, they are all
mere veilmakers[171] —): none will ever have the honor of seeing
the first *honest* spirit in the history of spirit, the spirit in which
truth will come to pass judgment on the counterfeiting of four
centuries, combined with the German spirit. The "German
spirit" is *my* bad air: I breathe with difficulty when close to this
filth *in psychologicis* that has become instinctive, that a German's every word, every look betrays. None of them have plod-
ded through a seventeenth century of severe self-examination
like the French, a La Rochefoucauld or a Descartes is a hundred times superior in honesty to the foremost Germans —
they have had no psychologist to this day. But psychology is
virtually a yardstick for the *cleanliness* or *uncleanliness* of a race

. . . And if you are not even cleanly, how can you be *deep*?
With the German, almost the same as with a woman, you
never get to the base, *he doesn't have one*: that's all. But that
means they are not even shallow.[172] — What is called "deep"
in Germany is exactly that filthy instinct toward the self which
I am just speaking about: people do not *want* to be clear about
themselves. Might I suggest the word "German" as an interna-
tional coinage for *this* particular psychological degeneration?
— At this moment, for example, the German Kaiser[173] is calling it his "Christian duty" to free the slaves in Africa: we *other*
Europeans would simply call that "German" . . . Have the
Germans ever produced a single book that had depth? Even
the concept of what constitutes depth in a book escapes them.
I have met scholars who held Kant to be deep; I fear that at the
Prussian court,[174] Herr von Treitschke[175] is held to be deep.
And when I occasionally praise Stendhal as a deep psycholo-
gist, I have encountered German university professors who
had me spell the name . . .[176]

4.[177]

— And why should I not carry on to the end? I like to make
a clean sweep. It is part of my ambition to be seen as a scourge
of the Germans par excellence. I already expressed my *mistrust*
toward the German character at the age of twenty-six[178] (third
Unfashionable p. 71[179]) — the Germans are for me impossible.
If I think up a type of human antithetical to all my instincts,
it always turns out to be a German. The first test when I "sound
out the kidney"[180] of a human being is whether that person
has an aura of physical distance and everywhere sees rank,
grade, order between one human and the next, whether he
distinguishes: this makes you into a *gentilhomme*; in every other
case you belong irretrievably among the big-hearted, oh!
so-good-humored category of *canaille*. But the Germans are
canaille — oh! they are ever so good-humored . . . You lower
yourself by associating with Germans: the German *puts* everything on the *same level* . . . If I leave out my dealings with a

few artists, above all Richard Wagner, I have not spent a single good hour with Germans . . .[181] Assuming that the deepest spirit of all millennia were to appear among the Germans, any sort of goose of the Capitol[182] would take it that her very unbeautiful soul would be at least as worthy of esteem . . . I cannot stand this race, with whom one is always in bad company, which has no fingers for nuances — woe is me! I am a nuance — with no *esprit* in its feet and not even able to walk . . . In fact, the Germans have no feet at all, just legs . . . Germans lack any concept of how vulgar they are, yet that is the supreme vulgarity — they are not even *ashamed* of themselves for being mere Germans . . . They chip in with a view about everything and even consider themselves decisive, I fear they have even decided about me[183] . . . — My whole life is proof de rigueur of these remarks. In vain do I search in it for a sign of tact, of *délicatesse* toward myself. From Jews, yes, never yet from Germans. It is my nature to be temperate and well-disposed toward everyone — I have a *right* not to make any distinction — : this does not stop me from having my eyes open. Nobody is excepted, least of all my friends — I hope that in the end, this has not detracted from my humanity toward them! There are five or six things I have always made into a point of honor. — However, it remains the case that I interpret nearly every letter I have been receiving for years as cynicism: there is more cynicism in being well-disposed toward me than in any sort of hatred . . . I tell all my friends to their face that they have never found it sufficiently worth the effort to *study* any of my works; I gather from the smallest sign that they do not even know what they are about. Even with regard to my *Zarathustra*, who of my friends will have seen more in it than an impermissible, fortunately entirely indifferent presumption? . . . Ten years: and nobody in Germany had a guilty conscience about not defending my name against the absurd silence under which it lay buried: it was a foreigner, a Dane, who first had enough instinctive decency and *courage* for that, indignant at my so-called friends . . . At which German university would lectures on my philosophy be possible today of the kind given last spring in Copenhagen by Dr. Georg Brandes, thereby proving himself even more of a psychologist?[184] — I myself never suffered from all this; what is *necessary* does not harm me; *amor fati* is my innermost nature. But this does not exclude the fact that I love irony, even world-historical irony. And so, about two years before the shattering lightning bolt of the *Revaluation*, which is destined to send the earth into convulsions, I sent *The Case of Wagner* into the world: once more, the Germans could make another immortal blunder about me — and be *immortalized*! there is still time for that! Has that happened? — To perfection, my dear Teutons! I send you my compliments . . . Just now, so that there is no lack of friends either, an old friend wrote that she was now *laughing* at me . . . And this at a time when an inexpressible responsibility rests upon me — when no word can be too tender, no look respectful enough toward me. For I bear the destiny of humanity on my shoulder. —[185]

Why I Am a Destiny.[1]

I.[2]

I know my fate. One day my name will be associated with the memory of something monstrous — a crisis such as the earth has never seen, the most profound collision of conscience, a decision conjured up *against* everything up till now believed, demanded, sanctified. I am no human, I am dynamite. — And for all that, I have nothing in me of a founder of religion — religions are affairs of the mob, I need to wash my hands after contact with religious humans . . . I do not *want* "believers," I think I am too spiteful to believe in myself, I never address the masses . . . I have a terrible fear that one day I shall be pronounced *holy*: you can guess why I have brought out this book *in advance*, it is to prevent people from causing mischief with me . . . I do not want to be a saint, a clown would be better . . . Perhaps I am a clown . . . And nevertheless, or rather, *not* nevertheless — for so far nothing has been more mendacious than saints — the truth speaks out of me. — But my truth is *dreadful*: for the *lie* has hitherto been called the truth. *Revaluation of all values*: that is my formula for humanity's act of supreme self-reflection made flesh and genius in me. My lot dictates that I must be the first *decent* human being, that I know myself to be opposed to the mendacity of millennia . . . I was the first to *discover* the truth, by perceiving the lie as a lie — *smelling* it . . . My genius is in my nostrils . . . I contradict in a way nobody has contradicted before and am nevertheless the opposite of a "No-saying" spirit. I am the bearer of *glad tidings* like no other: I know tasks so elevated that so far there has not been a concept for them; only after me will there be hope again.[3] With all that, I am also, of necessity, the man of destiny. For when truth steps up to fight the lie of millennia, we shall have eruptions, a convulsion of earthquakes, a moving of mountain and valley such as nobody has yet dreamed up. Then the concept of politics will have been completely taken up into a spiritual war, all the power arrangements of the old society will be detonated — all of them rest on the lie: there will be such wars as there have not yet been on earth. Only after me will the earth have *grand politics.* —[4]

2.[5]

Would you like a formula for a destiny such as this that *becomes human*? — It is found in my *Zarathustra*.

> *— and those who want be creators in the realm of good and evil, they must first be annihilators and must smash values into little pieces.*
> *Therefore the greatest evil is part of the greatest good: yet this good is the creative kind.*[6]

I am by far the most dreadful human there has ever been; this does not exclude the fact that I shall be the most beneficial. I know the pleasure of *destruction* at a pitch equal to my *strength* to destroy — in both cases I obey my Dionysian nature that does not know how to distinguish between doing No and saying Yes. I am the first *immoralist*: which makes me the *destroyer* par excellence. —

3.[7]

I have not been asked, I ought to have been asked, what exactly the name of *Zarathustra* means in my mouth, the mouth of the first immoralist: for what goes to make up the immense uniqueness of that Persian in history is the exact opposite.

Zarathustra is the first to see in the battle of good and evil the actual wheel that drives things — the translation of morality into the metaphysical, as force, cause, purpose in itself, is *his* work. But in reality, this question might already be the answer. Zarathustra *created* this most disastrous of errors, morality: consequently, he must also be the first to *acknowledge* it. Not only because he has longer and greater experience here than any other thinker — history in its entirety is just an experimental refutation of the proposition of so-called moral world order — : more important, Zarathustra is more truthful than any other thinker. His teaching and it alone has truthfulness as supreme virtue — in other words, the opposite to the *cowardice* of the "idealist" who takes flight before reality, Zarathustra bodies forth more courage than all thinkers put together. To speak the truth and *shoot well with arrows*, that is Persian virtue.[8] — Have I been understood? . . . The self-overcoming of morality through truthfulness, the self-overcoming of the moralist into his antithesis — into *myself* — that is what the name Zarathustra means in my mouth.

4.

There are two fundamental negations that my word *immoralist* incorporates. On the one hand, I negate the type of human who hitherto counted as the highest, the *good*, the *benevolent*, the *beneficent*; on the other hand, I negate a form of morality that has gained respect and predominance as morality as such — *decadence*-morality or, to speak about it more plainly, *Christian* morality. One could be forgiven for viewing the second antithesis as the more decisive, as the overvaluing of goodness and kindness already counts with me as a result of *décadence*, as a symptom of weakness, as incompatible with ascending Yes-saying life: within Yes-saying, negation *and destroying* are requirements. — For the time being, I shall stay with the psychology of the good human. To evaluate what a type of human is worth, the price of maintaining it must be calculated — the requirements for its existence must be known. The requirement for existence of those who are good is the *lie* — : to put it another way, not-*wanting*-to-see at any price what reality consists of at its core, namely *not* such as to stimulate kindly instincts all the time, still less such as to tolerate the intrusion of short-sighted, well-meant hands at any moment. To view all kinds of *distress* simply as an objection, as something to be *wiped out*, is *niaiserie*[9] par excellence, on the whole a true mischief in its results, a fatality of stupidity — almost as stupid as would be the will to wipe out bad weather — out of compassion for the poor, perhaps . . . In the great economy of the whole, real calamities (in their affects, desires, will to power) are incalculably more necessary than any kind of petty happiness, so-called goodness; you must even be indulgent to grant it a place at all, as its instinctive mendacity is preconditioned. I shall have a great occasion to demonstrate for the whole of history the incalculably strange consequences of *optimism*, that monstrosity of the *homines optimi*.[10] Zarathustra, the first to understand that the optimist is just as *décadent* as the pessimist, and perhaps even more harmful, says: *good people never speak the truth. Good people taught you the wrong coastlines and wrong safety measures;*[11] *you were born and sheltered in the lies of good people. Everything, from the ground up, falsified and fabricated by good people.*[12] Fortunately, the world is not built on instincts in such a manner that only the good-natured herd animal would find its narrow happiness within it; to demand that all become "good people," herd animals, blue-eyed, well-disposed, "beautiful souls" — or, as Herbert Spencer desires, altruistic, would be to deprive humanity of its *great* character, to castrate humanity and reduce it to a feeble Chineseness. — *And this has been tried!* . . . *This is exactly what people call morality* . . . In this sense, Zarathustra sometimes calls good people "the last humans," sometimes "the beginning of the end"; above all, he feels they are the *most harmful type of human* because they make their way in life at the cost of *truth* as much as of the *future*:

> Good people — they cannot *create*, they are always the beginning of the end —

— they crucify those who write *new* values on new tablets, they sacrifice the future for *themselves*, they crucify the future of all humankind!

Good people — have always been the beginning of the end . . .

And whatever damage world-deniers may do, *the damage done by good people is the most damaging damage of all.*[13]

5.

Zarathustra, the first psychologist of the good, is — therefore — a friend of evil. When a *décadence* kind of human has climbed to the rank of the most superior kind, this could only happen at the expense of their opposite kind, the strong kind of human confident about life. When the herd animal glows in the radiance of the purest virtue, the exceptional human must have been devalued into evil. When mendacity at any price appropriates the word "truth" for its perspective, a really truthful person must be relegated to the worst of names. Here, Zarathustra leaves no doubt: he says that his recognition of the good, the "best," was exactly the thing that aroused his horror at the human in general; through *this* dislike, his wings had grown ready "to float away into distant futures,"[14] — he does not conceal the fact that *his* type of human, a relatively superhuman type, is superhuman precisely in relation to the *good people*, and that the good and the just people would call his superhuman *devil* . . .

> You most superior humans who catch my eye, this is what I doubt about you and why I laugh in secret: I suspect you would call my superhumans — devils!
>
> Your souls are so[15] alienated from greatness that the superhumans would be terrifying to you in their excellence . . .[16,17]

At this point, and nowhere else, you must make an attempt to understand what Zarathustra *wants*: the type of human he conceives, conceives reality *as it is*: it is strong enough for it

— the type is neither alienated nor reserved toward it, it is *reality itself*, it contains all its dreadfulness and uncertainty in itself as well, *only in this way can the human have greatness* . . .

6.[18]

— But I have chosen the word *immoralist* for myself as a mark, a mark of honor, in yet another sense; I am proud to have this word that raises me above humanity in its entirety. Nobody has yet felt the *Christian* morality as *beneath* them: for that, a height, a long view, a hitherto unheard-of psychological depth and inscrutability were required. Christian morality was up till then the Circe of all thinkers — they were in her service. — Who before me has climbed into the caverns out of which the poisonous fumes of this type of ideal — *calumniation of the world!* — spew forth? Who has even dared to suspect *that* there are caverns at all? Who before me was a *psychologist* at all among philosophers and not, rather, its opposite, "higher swindler," "idealist"? Before me there was no psychology. — To be the first here can be a curse, but at any rate, it is a destiny: *for you are also the first to despise* . . . *Disgust* at the human is the danger for me . . .

7.

Have I been understood? — What defines me and sets me apart from the whole of the rest of humanity is my having *discovered* Christian morality. That was why I needed a word that contained the sense of a challenge to everybody. Not to have opened its eyes here sooner is what I judge to be the greatest uncleanness humanity has on its conscience, to be untruthfulness grown into instinct, a thoroughgoing will *not* to see every event, every cause, every reality, to be counterfeiting *in psychologicis* to the point of crime. Blindness toward Christianity is the *crime* par excellence — crime *against life* . . . The millennia, the peoples, the first and the last, the philosophers and the old wives — discounting five, six historical moments, myself as the seventh — in this respect they all deserve each other. The Christian was hitherto *the* "moral being," a curiosity beyond compare — and, *as* "moral being," more absurd, mendacious, vain, frivolous, *more disadvantageous to himself* than even the greatest despiser of humanity could dream up. Christian morality — the wickedest form of the will to the lie, the real Circe of humanity: that which has *ruined* it. It is *not* error as error that appalls me at this spectacle, *not* a millennia-long lack of "good will," breeding, decency, spiritual courage that betrays itself in its victory: — it is the lack of what is natural, it is the completely ghastly state of affairs whereby *anti-nature* itself received the highest honors as morality and as law, as categorical imperative remained suspended above humanity! . . . To be wrong to such an extent, *not* as an individual, *not* as a people, but as humanity! That people taught contempt for the very first instincts of life; that they *made up* a "soul," a "spirit," to bring shame upon the body; that they taught others to feel something impure in the precondition for life, sexuality; that in the deepest necessity for flourishing, in *strict* selfishness (— the very word is slanderous! —), they seek the evil principle; that they see, on the contrary, in the typical signs of decline and instinctual contradictoriness, in "selflessness," in loss of the center of gravity, in "depersonalization and in "loving thy neighbor" (— neighbor-*dependency*!), a *higher* value, what am I saying! *value as such*! . . . Well! is humanity itself in *décadence*? Has it always been? — What is certain is that only *décadence* values have been *taught* as supreme values. The morality of unselfing one's self is the morality of decline par excellence, the fact of "I am going to ruin" translated into the imperative: "you *shall* all go to ruin" — and *not just* into the imperative! . . . This, the only morality to have been taught up till now, the morality of unselfing the self, lays bare a will to the end, it *denies* life in its deepest foundation. — Here, the possibility remains open that humanity itself might not be degenerate, but just that parasitic type of human, the *priest*, who in the case of morality has lied his way up to being its arbiter of value — who detected in Christian morality the means to *power* . . . And in fact, that is *my* insight: the teachers, the leaders of humanity, theologians one and all, were also *décadents* one and all: *therefore* the revaluation of all values into hostility to life — *therefore* morality . . . *Definition of morality*: morality — the idiosyncrasy of *décadents* with the ulterior motive of taking *their* revenge *on life* — *and* succeeding. I place value on *this* definition. —

8.

— Have I been understood? — I have not said one word just now that I would not have said through the mouth of Zarathustra five years ago. — The *unmasking* of Christian morality is an event with no equal, a true catastrophe. Anyone who can explain it is a force majeure, a destiny — he breaks the history of humanity into two pieces. You live *before* him, you live *after* him . . . The lightning bolt of truth hit precisely what had stood highest until then: whoever understands *what* was destroyed there might care to see if anything at all remains in his hands. Everything that used to be called "truth" is acknowledged to be the most dangerous, malicious, subterranean form of the lie; the holy pretext of "improving" humanity to be the stunt of *sucking out* life itself and making it anemic. Morality as *vampirism* . . .[19] Whoever uncovers morality has uncovered at the same time the worthlessness of all values that people believe in or have believed in; he sees in the most exalted types of human, even those pronounced *holy*, nothing venerable anymore, he sees in them the most doom-laden form of monstrosities, doom-laden *because they were fascinating* . . . The concept "God" invented as counter-concept to life — everything harmful, poisonous, slanderous, the whole deadly animosity toward life, brought into a horrendous union! The concept "beyond," "true world," invented to devalue the *only* world there is — to leave no goal, no rationality, no task for our earthly reality! The concept "soul," "spirit," and ultimately even "immortal soul" invented to denigrate the body, to make it sick — "holy" — to produce a horrible superficiality toward all things in life worth taking seriously, the questions of nourishment, dwelling, spiritual diet, treatment of the sick, clean-

liness, weather! Instead of health, the "health of the soul" —
by which I mean a *folie circulaire*[20] between penitence-pangs
and salvation-hysteria! The concept "sin" invented together with
its attendant instrument of torture, the concept of "free will," to
confuse the instincts, to make it second nature to mistrust the
instincts! Within the concept of the "selfless," the "self-denying,"
the real insignia of *décadence*, being *seduced* by what is harmful,
"not *being able* to find a use for oneself anymore," self-destruction
made into the stamp of value in general, into "duty," "holiness,"
"godliness" in humans! Finally — what is worst of all — the
concept of the *good* human joining forces with everything weak,
sick, malformed, suffering from itself, everything *that ought to
perish* — the law of *selection* crossed through, an ideal constructed
from the opposite of the proud, well-formed, Yes-saying human,
certain of the future, guarantor of the future — who from now
on is called *the evil one* . . . And all that was believed in *as morality*!
— *Écrasez l'infâme!*[21] — —

9.

Have I been understood? — *Dionysus versus the Crucified* . . .

Dionysus Dithyrambs.

Contents

Nur Narr! Nur Dichter!

Bei abgehellter Luft,
wenn schon des Thau's Tröstung
zur Erde niederquillt,
unsichtbar, auch ungehört
— denn zartes Schuhwerk trägt
der Tröster Thau gleich allen Trostmilden —
gedenkst du da, gedenkst du, heisses Herz,
wie einst du durstetest,
nach himmlischen Thränen und Thaugeträufel
versengt und müde durstetest,
dieweil auf gelben Graspfaden
boshaft abendliche Sonnenblicke
durch schwarze Bäume um dich liefen
blendende Sonnen-Gluthblicke, schadenfrohe.

„Der *Wahrheit* Freier — du? so höhnten sie
nein! nur ein Dichter!
ein Thier, ein listiges, raubendes, schleichendes,
das lügen muss,
das wissentlich, willentlich lügen muss,
nach Beute lüstern,
bunt verlarvt,
sich selbst zur Larve,
sich selbst zur Beute
das — der Wahrheit Freier? . . .

Just a Fool! Just a Poet![1,2]

When the light grows dim,
when the dew's comfort
is already spilling down upon the earth,
unseen, unheard as well
— for, like all gentle comforters,
dew the comforter wears delicate footwear —
then do you think back, do you think back, heart aflame,
how you once thirsted
for tears from heaven and drops of dew,
thirsted, parched, and weary,
even as on yellow grassy paths
mischievous evening sunbreaks
ran around you through black trees,
blinding glowing rays, full of malice.

"A wooer *of truth* — you? that was how they mocked you
no! just a poet!
an animal, a tricky, thieving, slinking animal,
that has to lie,
that knowingly, willingly has to lie,
that has to lust for prey,
colorfully masked,
becoming a mask to itself,
becoming its own prey
this — is a wooer of truth? . . .

Nur Narr! Nur Dichter!
Nur Buntes redend,
aus Narrenlarven bunt herausredend,
herumsteigend auf lügnerischen Wortbrücken,
auf Lügen-Regenbogen
zwischen falschen Himmeln
herumschweifend, herumschleichend —
nur Narr! *nur* Dichter! . . .

Das — der Wahrheit Freier? . . .

Nicht still, starr, glatt, kalt,
zum Bilde worden,
zur Gottes-Säule,
nicht aufgestellt vor Tempeln,
eines Gottes Thürwart:
nein! feindselig solchen Tugend-Standbildern,
in jeder Wildniss heimischer als in Tempeln,
voll Katzen-Muthwillens
durch jedes Fenster springend
husch! in jeden Zufall,
jedem Urwalde zuschnüffelnd,
dass du in Urwäldern
unter buntzottigen Raubthieren
sündlich gesund und schön und bunt liefest,
mit lüsternen Lefzen,
selig-höhnisch, selig-höllisch, selig-blutgierig,
raubend, schleichend, *lügend* liefest . . .

Oder dem Adler gleich, der lange,
lange starr in Abgründe blickt,
in *seine* Abgründe . . .
— oh wie sie sich hier hinab,
hinunter, hinein,
in immer tiefere Tiefen ringeln! —
Dann,

Just a fool! Just a poet!
Just saying colorful things,
speaking colorfully out of fools' masks,
climbing around on lying bridges of words
on rainbows of lies
between false skies
roving around, slinking around —
just a fool! *just* a poet! . . .

This — is a wooer of truth? . . .

Not silent, stiff, smooth, cold,
not turned into a statue,
not turned into a pillar for a god,
not erected in front of temples,
gatekeeper of a god:
no! hostile to such monuments of virtue,
more at home in any wilderness than in temples,
full of kittenish playfulness
jumping through every window
whoosh! into every chance,
sniffing after every forest primeval,
so that you roamed around in primeval forests
among shaggy and colorful predators
sinfully healthy and beautiful and colorful,
roamed around licking your chops,
blissfully sneering, blissfully hellish, blissfully bloodthirsty,
preying, slinking, *lying* . . .

Or like an eagle who for a long,
long time stares unblinking into abysses,
into *its* abysses . . .
— oh how they circle lower,
down, into them,
into ever deeper depths! —
Then,

plötzlich,
geraden Flugs
gezückten Zugs
auf *Lämmer* stossen,
jach hinab, heisshungrig,
nach Lämmern lüstern,
gram allen Lamms-Seelen,
grimmig gram Allem, was blickt
tugendhaft, schafmässig, krauswollig,
dumm, mit Lammsmilch-Wohlwollen . . .

Also
adlerhaft, pantherhaft
sind des Dichters Sehnsüchte,
sind *deine* Sehnsüchte unter tausend Larven,
du Narr! du Dichter! . . .

Der du den Menschen schautest
so *Gott* als *Schaf* — ,
den Gott *zerreissen* im Menschen
wie das Schaf im Menschen
und zerreissend *lachen* —

das, das ist deine Seligkeit,
eines Panthers und Adlers Seligkeit,
eines Dichters und Narren Seligkeit! . . .

Bei abgehellter Luft,
wenn schon des Monds Sichel
grün zwischen Pupurröthen
und neidisch hinschleicht
— dem Tage feind,
mit jedem Schritte heimlich
an Rosen-Hängematten
hinsichelnd, bis sie sinken,
nachtabwärts blass hinabsinken:

suddenly,
straight in flight
sharp in turn
swoop down upon *lambs*,
down quickly, ravenous,
lusting for lambs,
a foe to all lamb souls,
a grim foe to whatever looks
virtuous, sheep-like, woolen-curly,
dumb, with lambs-milk benevolence . . .

And so
they are eagle-like, panther-like
the yearnings of the poet,
they are *your* yearnings under a thousand masks,
you fool! you poet! . . .

You who have viewed humans
as *gods* and *sheep* — ,
to tear apart the god in humans
as you would the sheep in humans
and *laughing* as you do it —

this, this is your bliss,
bliss of a panther and of an eagle,
bliss of a poet and of a fool! . . .

When the light grows dim,
when the sickle of the moon
is already creeping green
with envy between purple reds
— an enemy to the day,
secretly with every step
bringing its sickle down on hammocks of roses
until they fall sinking,
pale, downward into night:

so sank ich selber einstmals,
aus meinem Wahrheits-Wahnsinne,
aus meinem Tages-Sehnsüchten,
des Tages müde, krank vom Lichte,
— sank abwärts, abendwärts, schattenwärts,
von Einer Wahrheit
verbrannt und durstig
— gedenkst du noch, gedenkst du, heisses Herz,
wie da du durstetest? —
dass ich verbannt sei
von aller Wahrheit!
Nur Narr! *Nur* Dichter! . . .

thus I myself once sank,
out of my truth-inflamed madness
out of my daytime yearnings,
tired of the day, sick from the light,
— sank downward, into evening, into shadow,
burned by one truth
and thirsty
— do you still think back, do you think back, heart aflame,
how you thirsted then? —
that I be banned
from all truth!
Just a fool! *Just* a poet! . . .

Unter Töchtern der Wüste.

1.

„Gehe nicht davon! sagte da der Wanderer, der sich den Schatten Zarathustras nannte, bleibe bei uns — es möchte sonst uns die alte dumpfe Trübsal wieder anfallen.

Schon gab uns jener alte Zauberer von seinem Schlimmsten zum Besten, und siehe doch, der gute fromme Papst da hat Thränen in den Augen und sich ganz wieder aufs Meer der Schwermuth eingeschifft.

Diese Könige da mögen wohl vor uns noch gute Miene machen: hätten sie aber keine Zeugen, ich wette, auch bei ihnen fienge das böse Spiel wieder an,

— das böse Spiel der ziehenden Wolken, der feuchten Schwermuth, der verhängten Himmel, der gestohlenen Sonnen, der heulenden Herbstwinde,

— das böse Spiel unsres Heulens und Nothschreiens: bleibe bei uns, Zarathustra! Hier ist viel verborgenes Elend, das reden will, viel Abend, viel Wolke, viel dumpfe Luft!

Du nährtest uns mit starker Mannskost und kräftigen Sprüchen: lass es nicht zu, dass uns zum Nachtisch die weichlichen weiblichen Geister wieder anfallen!

Du allein machst die Luft um dich herum stark und klar! Fand ich je auf Erden so gute Luft als bei dir in deiner Höhle?

Among Daughters of the Desert.[1]

1.

"Don't leave! the wanderer who called himself Zarathustra's shadow then said, stay with us — otherwise our same old dull affliction might befall us again.

That old sorcerer has already done his worst for our own good, and look at that, the good pious pope over there has tears in his eyes and has again completely launched himself out on the ocean of melancholy.

These kings over there may well put on a good face in our presence: but if they didn't have witnesses, I bet that the vicious cycle would begin again even with them,

— the vicious cycle of gathering clouds, of sodden melancholy, of overcast skies, of stolen suns, of howling autumn winds,

— the vicious cycle of our wailing and cries of distress: stay with us, Zarathustra! Much hidden misery is here, misery that wants to speak, much evening, much cloudiness, much damp air!

You fed us with hearty fare fit for men and with powerful phrases: do not let the weak, womanly spirits attack us again after dinner!

You alone make the air around you bracing and clear! Did I ever find such fine air anywhere on earth like the air at your place in your cave?

Vielerlei Länder sah ich doch, meine Nase lernte vielerlei
Luft prüfen und abschätzen: aber bei dir schmecken meine
Nüstern ihre grösste Lust!

Es sei denn — , es sei denn — , oh vergieb eine alte
Erinnerung! Vergieb mir ein altes Nachtisch-Lied, das ich
einst unter Töchtern der Wüste dichtete.
Bei denen nämlich gab es gleich gute helle morgenlän-
dische Luft; dort war ich am fernsten vom wolkigen feuchten
schwermüthigen Alt-Europa!
Damals liebte ich solcherlei Morgenland-Mädchen und
andres blaues Himmelreich, über dem keine Wolken und
keine Gedanken hängen.
Ihr glaubt es nicht, wie artig sie dasassen, wenn sie nicht
tanzten, tief, aber ohne Gedanken, wie kleine Geheimnisse,
wie bebänderte Räthsel, wie Nachtisch-Nüsse —
bunt und fremd fürwahr! aber ohne Wolken: Räthsel, die
sich rathen lassen: solchen Mädchen zu Liebe erdachte ich
damals einen Nachtisch-Psalm."

Also sprach der Wanderer, der sich den Schatten Zarathustras
nannte; und ehe Jemand ihm antwortete, hatte er schon die
Harfe des alten Zauberers ergriffen, die Beine gekreuzt und
blickte gelassen und weise um sich: — mit den Nüstern aber
zog er langsam und fragend die Luft ein, wie Einer, der in
neuen Ländern eine neue Luft kostet. Endlich hob er mit
einer Art Gebrüll zu singen an.

2.

Die Wüste wächst: weh dem, der Wüsten birgt ...

3.

Ha!
Feierlich!
ein würdiger Anfang!
afrikanisch feierlich!

You know, I have seen many countries, I have learned to test and gauge many kinds of air with my nose: but my nostrils are experiencing their greatest pleasure at your place!

Unless — , unless — , oh forgive me an old memory! Forgive me an old after-dinner song which I once composed among daughters of the desert.

For there was oriental air around them that was just as clear and fine as here; there I was as far as I could be from cloudy sodden melancholy Old Europe!

Back then, I loved oriental girls like them and a different blue heavenly realm with no clouds and no thoughts hanging over it.

You would not believe how demurely they sat there when they were not dancing, profound but without thoughts, like little secrets, like beribboned riddles, like after-dinner nuts —

colorful and foreign, to be sure! but cloudless: riddles that can be solved: back then I made up an after-dinner psalm for the pleasure of girls like that."

Thus spoke the wanderer who called himself Zarathustra's shadow; and before anyone had answered him, he had already seized the old sorcerer's harp, crossed his legs, and looked around serenely and wisely: — yet he slowly and searchingly drew air in through his nostrils, like someone sampling new air in new countries. Finally, with a kind of roar, he began to sing.

2.

The desert grows: woe to those who harbor deserts . . .

3.

Ha!
Solemnly!
a worthy beginning!
solemnly African!

eines Löwen würdig
oder eines moralischen Brüllaffen . . .
— aber Nichts für euch,
ihr allerliebsten Freundinnen,
zu deren Füssen mir,
einem Europäer unter Palmen,
zu sitzen vergönnt ist. Sela.

Wunderbar wahrlich!
Da sitze ich nun,
der Wüste nahe und bereits
so ferne wieder der Wüste,
auch in Nichts noch verwüstet:
nämlich hinabgeschluckt
von dieser kleinsten Oasis
— sie sperrte gerade gähnend
ihr liebliches Maul auf,
das wohlriechendste aller Mäulchen:
da fiel ich hinein,
hinab, hindurch — unter euch,
ihr allerliebsten Freundinnen! Sela.

Heil, Heil jenem Walfische,
wenn er also es seinem Gaste
wohlsein liess! — ihr versteht
meine gelehrte Anspielung? . . .
Heil seinem Bauche,
wenn es also
ein so lieblicher Oasis-Bauch war,
gleich diesem: was ich aber in Zweifel ziehe.
Dafür komme ich aus Europa,
das zweifelsüchtiger ist als alle Eheweibchen.
Möge Gott es bessern!
Amen!

worthy of a lion
or of a moral howler monkey . . .
— but not something for you,
you dearest darlings,[2]
at whose feet I,
a European, have leave to sit
under the palm trees.[3] Selah.[4]

Truly wonderful!
Here I am sitting now,
near the desert and yet again
so far from the desert,
still desolate, even within nothingness:
swallowed up as I am
by this smallest of oases
— yawning, it just opened
its delightful muzzle,
this tiny muzzle that smells sweeter than all other tiny
    muzzles:
then I fell into it,
down, through it — fell among you,
you dearest darlings! Selah.

Hail, hail to that whale,[5]
if it indeed made its guest feel
so comfortable! — you understand
my scholarly allusion? . . .
Hail to its belly,
if it was indeed
such a delightful oasis-belly,
like this: which I doubt, however.
After all, I come from Europe,
which is more prone to doubt than all the silly old wives put
    together.
May God improve it!
Amen!

Da sitze ich nun,
in dieser kleinsten Oasis,
·einer Dattel gleich,
braun, durchsüsst, goldschwürig,
lüstern nach einem runden Mädchen-Maule,
mehr aber noch nach mädchenhaften
eiskalten schneeweissen schneidigen
Beisszähnen: nach denen nämlich
lechzt das Herz allen heissen Datteln. Sela.

Den genannten Südfrüchten
ähnlich, allzuähnlich
liege ich hier, von kleinen
Flügelkäfern
umtänzelt und umspielt,
insgleichen von noch kleineren
thörichteren boshafteren
Wunschen und Einfällen —
umlagert von euch,
ihr stummen, ihr ahnungsvollen
Mädchen-Katzen
Dudu und Suleika
— *umsphinxt*, dass ich in Ein Wort
viel Gefühle stopfe
(— vergebe mir Gott
diese Sprachsünde! . . .)
— sitze hier, die beste Luft schnüffelnd,
Paradieses-Luft wahrlich,
lichte leichte Luft, goldgestreifte,
so gute Luft nur je
vom Monde herabfiel,
sei es aus Zufall
oder geschah es aus Übermuthe?
wie die alten Dichter erzählen.
Ich Zweifler aber ziehe es in Zweifel,
dafür komme ich

Here I now sit,
in this smallest of all oases,
like a date,
brown, sweet through and through, heavy as gold,
lusting for a rounded girl-muzzle,
yet even more for
ice-cold snow-white ripping
girlish fangs: for the heart of all hot dates
is panting for those teeth. Selah.

Like the exotic fruits of which I spoke,
like them, too much like them,
I lie here, swarmed by little
winged bugs
that dance around and play around,
likewise by even smaller
more foolish, more naughty
wishes and fancies, —
surrounded by you,
you silent, you sinister
girl kittens
Dudu[6] and Suleika[7]
— *Sphinx-encircled*, so that I cram
many feelings into one word
(God forgive me
this sin of speech! . . .)
— sitting here, sniffing the finest air,
truly the air of paradise,
clear crisp air, tinged with gold,
air as fine as ever
fell down from the moon,
whether by chance
or did it happen out of pure exuberance?
as in the tales of poets of old.
A doubter, yet I begin to doubt it,
after all, I come

aus Europa,
das zweifelsüchtiger ist als alle Eheweibchen.
Möge Gott es bessern!
Amen.

Diese schönste Luft athmend,
mit Nüstern geschwellt gleich Bechern,
ohne Zukunft, ohne Erinnerungen,
so sitze ich hier, ihr
allerliebsten Freundinnen,
und sehe der Palme zu,
wie sie, einer Tänzerin gleich,
sich biegt und schmiegt und in der Hüfte wiegt
— man thut es mit, sieht man lange zu . . .
einer Tänzerin gleich, die, wie mir scheinen will,
zu lange schon, gefährlich lange
immer, immer nur auf *Einem* Beinchen stand?
— da vergass sie darob, wie mir scheinen will,
das *andre* Beinchen?
Vergebens wenigstens
suchte ich das vermisste
Zwillings-Kleinod
— nämlich das andre Beinchen —
in der heiligen Nähe
ihres allerliebsten, allerzierlichsten
Fächer- und Flatter- und Flitter-Röckchens.
Ja, wenn ihr mir, ihr schönen Freundinnen,
ganz glauben wollt,
sie hat es *verloren* . . .
Hu! Hu! Hu! Hu! Hu! . . .
Es ist dahin,
auf ewig dahin,
das andre Beinchen!
Oh schade um dies liebliche andre Beinchen!
Wo — mag es wohl weilen und verlassen trauern,

from Europe,
which is more prone to doubt than all the silly old wives put
    together.
May God improve it!
Amen.

So I sit here,
breathing this most lovely air,
with nostrils flaring like cups,
without a future, without memories, you
dearest darlings,
and watch the palm tree,
as it, just like a dancer,
bends and dips and sways its hips
— if you watch it long enough, you do it, too . . .
like a dancer who, it would seem to me,
for too long, for a dangerously long time,
has always, always been standing on only *one* little leg?
— and in doing that it forgot, it would seem to me,
the *other* little leg? [8]
Although in vain,
I sought the missing
twin-treasure
— namely the other little leg—
near the holy place
of the palm tree's most dear, most sheer
folded and fluttering and flitting little skirt.
Yes, believe it or not,
you beautiful darlings,
it had *lost* it . . .
Boo-hoo! Boo-hoo! Boo-hoo! . . .
It is gone,
gone forever,
the other little leg!
Oh what a shame about this other lovely little leg!
Where — can it be hiding and grieving, abandoned,

dieses einsame Beinchen?
In Furcht vielleicht vor einem
grimmen gelben blondgelockten
Löwen-Unthiere? oder gar schon
abgenagt, abgeknabbert —
erbärmlich wehe! wehe! abgeknabbert! Sela.

Oh weint mir nicht,
weiche Herzen!
Weint mir nicht, ihr
Dattel-Herzen! Milch-Busen!
Ihr Süssholz-Herz-
Beutelchen!
Sei ein Mann, Suleika! Muth! Muth!
Weine nicht mehr,
bleiche Dudu!
— Oder sollte vielleicht
etwas Stärkendes, Herz-Stärkendes
hier am Platze sein?
ein gesalbter Spruch?
ein feierlicher Zuspruch? . . .

Ha!
Herauf, Würde!
Blase, blase wieder,
Blasebalg der Tugend!
Ha!
Noch Ein Mal brüllen,
moralisch brüllen,
als moralischer Löwe vor den Töchtern der Wüste brüllen!
— Denn Tugend-Geheul,
ihr allerliebsten Mädchen,
ist mehr als Alles
Europäer-Inbrunst, Europäer-Heisshunger!
Und da stehe ich schon,

this lonesome little leg?
Perhaps in fear of a
fierce tawny blond-maned
lion-beast? or even
gnawed off, chomped off —
pity and woe! woe! chomped off! Selah.

Oh don't cry for me,
soft-hearted ones!
Don't cry for me, you
date-like hearts! Bosoms full of milk!
You little licorice
heart drops!
Be a man, Suleika! Courage! Courage!
Stop crying,
pale Dudu!
— Or perhaps
something invigorating, invigorating for the heart
would be fitting here?
an anointed saying?
a solemn affirmation? . . .

Ha!
Arise, dignity!
Blow, blow again,
blowhards of virtue!
Ha!
Roar once again,
roar morally
roar like a moral lion in front of the daughters of the
    desert!
— For, virtuous howling,
you dearest girls,
is greater than all
the ardor of Europeans, the burning hunger of Europeans!
And here I stand now,

als Europäer,
ich kann nicht anders, Gott helfe mir!
Amen!

*   *
*

Die Wüste wächst: weh dem, der Wüsten birgt!
Stein knirscht an Stein, die Wüste schlingt und würgt.
Der ungeheure Tod blickt glühend braun
und *kaut* — sein Leben ist sein Kaun . . .

Vergiss nicht, Mensch, den Wollust ausgeloht:
du — bist der Stein, die Wüste, bist der Tod . . .

*   *
*

as a European,
I can do no other, God help me!
Amen![9]

*   *

*

The desert grows: woe to those who harbor the desert!
Stone grinds on stone, the desert coils and strangles.
Monstrous death gazes,[10] glowing brown[11]
and *chews* — chewing is its life . . .

You human being, consumed by lust,[12] do not forget:
you — are the stone, the desert, you are[13] death . . .[14]

*   *

*

Letzter Wille.

So sterben,
wie ich ihn einst sterben sah — ,
den Freund, der Blitze und Blicke
göttlich in meine dunkle Jugend warf.
Muthwillig und tief,
in der Schlacht ein Tänzer — ,

unter Kriegern der Heiterste,
unter Siegern der Schwerste,
auf seinem Schicksal ein Schicksal stehend,
hart, nachdenklich, vordenklich — :

erzitternd darob, *dass* er siegte,
jauchzend darüber, dass er *sterbend* siegte — :

befehlend, indem er starb
— und er befahl, dass man *vernichte* . . .

So sterben,
wie ich ihn einst sterben sah:
siegend, *vernichtend* . . .

Last Will.[1]

To die like that,
as I once watched him die — ,
the friend who, like a god, hurled lightning bolts
and piercing glances[2] into my dark youth.
Playful and profound,
a dancer in battle — ,

the most cheerful of warriors,
most decisive of victors,
a destiny standing atop his destiny,
hardhearted, reflecting, anticipating — :

trembling *because* he was victorious,
jubilant that, *in dying*, he was victorious — :

commanding through dying
— and his command was to *annihilate* . . .

To die like that,
as I once watched him die:
victorious, *annihilating* . . .

Zwischen Raubvögeln.

Wer hier hinabwill,
wie schnell
schluckt den die Tiefe!
— Aber du, Zarathustra,
liebst den Abgrund noch,
thust der *Tanne* es gleich? —

Die schlägt Wurzeln, wo
der Fels selbst schaudernd
zur Tiefe blickt — ,
die zögert an Abgründen,
wo Alles rings
hinunter will:
zwischen der Ungeduld
wilden Gerölls, stürzenden Bachs
geduldig duldend, hart, schweigsam,
einsam . . .

Einsam!
Wer wagte es auch,
hier Gast zu sein,
dir Gast zu sein? . . .
Ein Raubvogel vielleicht:
der hängt sich wohl
dem standhaften Dulder

Among Birds of Prey.[1]

Those who want to descend here,
how quickly
the depths swallow them up!
— But you, Zarathustra,
still love the abyss,[2]
the way a *fir tree* does? —

It sinks its roots where
the cliff itself looks shuddering
into the depths — ,
the fir tree hesitates at the edge of abysses,
into which everything around it
wants to fall:
between impatient
wild roaring, cascading streams,
patiently enduring, unyielding, silent,
alone . . .

Alone!
Who[3] would dare,
to be a guest here, anyway,
to be *your* guest? . . .
Perhaps a bird of prey:
full of malice
it would probably attach itself

schadenfroh in's Haar,
mit irrem Gelächter,
einem Raubvogel-Gelächter . . .

Wozu so standhaft?
— höhnt er grausam:
man muss Flügel haben, wenn man den Abgrund liebt . . .
man muss nicht hängen bleiben,
wie du, Gehängter! —

Oh Zarathustra,
grausamster Nimrod!
Jüngst Jäger noch Gottes,
das Fangnetz aller Tugend,
der Pfeil des Bösen!
Jetzt —
von dir selber erjagt,
deine eigene Beute,
in dich selber eingebohrt . . .

Jetzt —
einsam mit dir,
zwiesam im eignen Wissen,
zwischen hundert Spiegeln
vor dir selber falsch,
zwischen hundert Erinnerungen
ungewiss,
an jeder Wunde müd,
an jedem Froste kalt,
in eignen Stricken gewürgt,
Selbstkenner!
Selbsthenker!

Was bandest du dich
mit dem Strick deiner Weisheit?
Was locktest du dich

to the hair of the one who resolutely endures,
with crazy laughter,
the laughter of a bird of prey . . .

Resolute *to what end*?
— the bird of prey cruelly mocks:
you must have wings if you love the abyss . . .
you don't need to hang around,
as you do, hanged man! —[4]

Oh, Zarathustra!
Nimrod[5] most cruel!
Not long ago, still a hunter of God,
a snare to all virtue,
the arrow of evil!
Now —
hunted to extinction by you yourself,
your own prey,
impaled by you yourself . . .

Now—
alone with yourself,
divided[6] in your own knowledge,
among the false reflections
of a hundred mirrors,
among a hundred memories,
uncertain,
wearied by every wound,
chilled by every frost,[7]
strangled in your own noose,
You who know yourself!
You who are hanging yourself![8]

What were you doing when you tied yourself up
with the rope of your wisdom?
What were you doing when you lured yourself

ins Paradies der alten Schlange?
Was schlichst du dich ein
in *dich* — in *dich*? . . .

Ein Kranker nun,
der an Schlangengift krank ist;
ein Gefangner nun,
der das härteste Loos zog:
im eignen Schachte
gebückt arbeitend,
in dich selber eingehöhlt,
dich selber angrabend,
unbehülflich,
steif,
ein Leichnam — ,
von hundert Lasten überthürmt,
von dir überlastet,
ein *Wissender*!
ein *Selbsterkenner*!
der *weise* Zarathustra! . . .

Du suchtest die schwerste Last:
da fandest du *dich* — ,
du wirfst dich nicht ab von dir . . .

Lauernd,
kauernd,
Einer, der schon nicht mehr aufrecht steht!
Du verwächst mir noch mit deinem Grabe,
verwachsener Geist! . . .
Und jüngst noch so stolz,
auf allen Stelzen deines Stolzes!
Jüngst noch der Einsiedler ohne Gott,
der Zweisiedler mit dem Teufel,
der scharlachne Prinz jedes Übermuths! . . .

into the paradise of the old serpent?
What were you doing when you crept
into *yourself* — into *yourself*? . . .

A sick man now,
sickened by the serpent's venom;[9]
a prisoner now,
who drew the shortest straw:
stooped over, working
in your own pit,[10,11]
having tunneled into yourself,
digging into yourself,
helpless,
stiff,
a corpse — ,[12]
piled high with a hundred burdens,
overburdened by yourself,
someone who knows!
someone who knows himself!
the *wise* Zarathustra! . . .

You sought the heaviest burden:
there you found *yourself* — ,
you cannot cast your self aside . . .

Lurking,
cowering,
someone who can no longer stand up straight!
To me, you are becoming deformed even with your gravedigging,
deformed mind! . . .[13]
And not long ago, still so proud,
on all the stilts of your pride!
Not long ago, still a hermit without God,
sharing quarters with the devil,[14]
the scarlet prince of all arrogance! . . . [15]

Jetzt —
zwischen zwei Nichtse
eingekrümmt,
ein Fragezeichen,
ein müdes Räthsel —
ein Räthsel für *Raubvögel* . . .

sie werden dich schon „lösen,“
sie hungern schon nach deiner „Lösung,“
sie flattern schon um dich, ihr Räthsel,
um dich, Gehenkter! . . .
Oh Zarathustra! . . .
Selbstkenner! . . .
Selbsthenker! . . .

Now —
wedged in
between two nothings,
a question mark,
a riddle posed too often —
a riddle for *birds of prey* . . .

they will soon "solve" you,
they are already hungering for your "solution,"
they are already fluttering around you, you riddle,
around you, hanged man! . . .
Oh Zarathustra! . . .
You who know yourself! . . .
You who are hanging yourself! . . .

Das Feuerzeichen.

Hier, wo zwischen Meeren die Insel wuchs,
ein Opferstein jäh hinaufgethürmt,
hier zündet sich unter schwarzem Himmel
Zarathustra seine Höhenfeuer an,
Feuerzeichen für verschlagne Schiffer,
Fragezeichen für Solche, die Antwort haben . . .

Diese Flamme mit weissgrauem Bauche
— in kalte Fernen züngelt ihre Gier,
nach immer reineren Höhn biegt sie den Hals —
eine Schlange gerad aufgerichtet vor Ungeduld:
dieses Zeichen stellte ich vor mich hin.

Meine Seele selber ist diese Flamme,
unersättlich nach neuen Fernen
lodert aufwärts, aufwärts ihre stille Gluth.
Was floh Zarathustra vor Thier und Menschen?
Was entlief er jäh allem festen Lande?
Sechs Einsamkeiten kennt er schon — ,
aber das Meer selbst war nicht genug ihm einsam,
die Insel liess ihn steigen, auf dem Berg wurde er zur
    Flamme,
nach einer *siebenten* Einsamkeit
wirft er suchend jetzt die Angel über sein Haupt.

The Beacon.

Here, where the island grew between oceans,
a sacrificial altar lifted high and sheer,
here, under black skies,
Zarathustra kindles his fire of the heights,
a beacon for sailors lost at sea,
a question mark for those who have the answer . . .

This flame with belly of lightest gray
— extends its tongue of lust into cold expanses,
it bends its neck up toward ever purer heights —
a serpent uncoiled, upright in its impatience:
this is the beacon I placed in front of myself.[1]

My soul itself is this flame,
its glow blazing upward, silently
upward, unquenchable in its lust for new expanses.
What made Zarathustra flee from animals and people?
What drove him to make his steep escape away from any
    mainland?
He already knows *six* solitudes — ,
but the ocean itself was not solitude enough for him,
the island allowed him to climb, on top of the mountain he
    became a flame,
fishing now for a *seventh* solitude
he aims his casts above his head.[2]

Verschlagne Schiffer! Trümmer alter Sterne!
Ihr Meere der Zukunft! Unausgeforschte Himmel!
nach allem Einsamen werfe ich jetzt die Angel:
gebt Antwort auf die Ungeduld der Flamme,
fangt mir, dem Fischer auf hohen Bergen,
meine siebente *letzte* Einsamkeit! — —

Sailors lost at sea! Ruins of old stars!
You oceans of the future! Heavens not yet completely
    explored!
now I aim my casts at everything solitary:
give an answer to the impatience of the flame,
catch for me, the angler on mountain heights,
my seventh *final* solitude! — —

Die Sonne sinkt.

1.

Nicht lange durstest du noch,
   verbranntes Herz!
Verheissung ist in der Luft,
aus unbekannten Mündern bläst mich's an
   — die grosse Kühle kommt . . .

Meine Sonne stand heiss über mir im Mittage:
seid mir gegrüsst, dass ihr kommt
   ihr plötzlichen Winde
ihr kühlen Geister des Nachmittags!

Die Luft geht fremd und rein.
Schielt nicht mit schiefem
   Verführerblick
die Nacht mich an? . . .
Bleib stark, mein tapfres Herz!
Frag nicht: warum? —

2.

Tag meines Lebens!
die Sonne sinkt.
Schon steht die glatte
   Fluth vergüldet.

The Sun Is Sinking.

1.

You will not be thirsty for long,
    heart burned to ashes!
The air is full of promise,
its gusts reach me from unknown mouths
    — a great coolness comes . . .

At noon my sun stood hot above me:
I welcome your coming
    you sudden winds[1]
you cool spirits of the afternoon!

The air moves strange and pure.
Does the night not leer at me
    with a twisted,
seductive look? . . .
Be strong, my brave heart!
Ask not: why? —[2]

2.

Day of my life!
the sun is sinking.
The smooth floodtide has
    already turned to gold.

Warm athmet der Fels:
  schlief wohl zu Mittag
das Glück auf ihm seinen Mittagsschlaf?
  In grünen Lichtern
spielt Glück noch der braune Abgrund herauf.

Tag meines Lebens!
gen Abend gehts!
Schon glüht dein Auge
  halbgebrochen,
schon quillt deines Thaus
    Thränengeträufel,
schon läuft still über weisse Meere
deiner Liebe Purpur,
deine letzte zögernde Seligkeit . . .

                    3.

Heiterkeit, güldene, komm!
  du des Todes
heimlichster süssester Vorgenuss!
— Lief ich zu rasch meines Wegs?
Jetzt erst, wo der Fuss müde ward,
  holt dein Blick mich noch ein,
  holt dein *Glück* mich noch ein.

Rings nur Welle und Spiel.
  Was je schwer war,
sank in blaue Vergessenheit,
müssig steht nun mein Kahn.
Sturm und Fahrt — wie verlernt er das!
  Wunsch und Hoffen ertrank,
  glatt liegt Seele und Meer.

Siebente Einsamkeit!
  Nie empfand ich

The cliff's breath is warm:
   did happiness take its noonday nap[3]
at noon, sleeping soundly up on the cliff?
   The brown abyss still[4] spews forth happiness
in hues of green.

Day of my life!
evening approaches!
Already your eyes are shining,
   half-dimmed,
already the teardrops of your dew
   are spilling forth,
already your purple love,
your last lingering bliss,
is running silently across white seas . . . [5]

3.

Come, golden good cheer!
you most secret sweetest foretaste
   of death!
— Did I run too fast on my way there?
Only now, when my feet have grown tired,
   does your look still overtake me,
   does your *happiness* still overtake me.

All around only the play of waves.
   Anything that had ever been heavy,
has sunk into blue oblivion,
my bark now sits there uselessly.
Storm and voyage[6] — how could my bark have forgotten this!
   Wishes and hopes have drowned,
   soul and sea lie there smoothly.

Seventh solitude!
   Never have I felt

näher mir süsse Sicherheit,
wärmer der Sonne Blick.
— Glüht nicht das Eis meiner Gipfel noch?
   Silbern, leicht, ein Fisch
   schwimmt nun mein Nachen hinaus . . .

sweet security this near,
the glance of the sun this warm.
— Isn't the ice of my peaks still glowing?
    Silver, light, a fish
    my boat now swims outward . . . [7]

Klage der Ariadne.

Wer wärmt mich, wer liebt mich noch?
   Gebt heisse Hände!
   gebt Herzens-Kohlenbecken!
Hingestreckt, schaudernd,
Halbtodtem gleich, dem man die Füsse wärmt,
geschüttelt ach! von unbekannten Fiebern,
zitternd vor spitzen eisigen Frostpfeilen,
   von dir gejagt, Gedanke!
Unnennbarer! Verhüllter! Entsetzlicher!
   Du Jäger hinter Wolken!
Darnieder geblitzt von dir,
du höhnisch Auge, das mich aus Dunklem anblickt!
   So liege ich,
biege mich, winde mich, gequält
von allen ewigen Martern,
   getroffen
von dir, grausamster Jäger,
du unbekannter — *Gott* . . .

Triff tiefer!
Triff Ein Mal noch!
Zerstich, zerbrich dies Herz!
Was soll dies Martern
mit zähnestumpfen Pfeilen?
Was blickst du wieder

Ariadne's Lament.[1,2]

Who keeps me warm, who still loves me?
 Give me hot hands!
 give me a heart of glowing coal!
Stretched out, shuddering,
Like a half-dead man whose feet are being warmed,
shaken, alas! by unknown fevers,
shivering from sharp, icy arrows of frost,
 hunted by you, my thought![3]
Unnameable! Shrouded! Horrifying!
 You hunter behind clouds!
Struck down by your lightning bolt,
you mocking eye, that gazes at me out of the darkness!
 I lie here,
turning, twisting, tormented
by all eternal tortures,
 struck
by you, most cruel hunter,
you unknown — *god* . . .

Strike deeper!
Strike yet again!
Sting this heart to ribbons, break this heart to pieces!
What's the point of this torture
with arrows like worn teeth?
Why are you looking at me again

der Menschen-Qual nicht müde,
mit schadenfrohen Götter-Blitz-Augen?
Nicht tödten willst du,
nur martern, martern?
Wozu — *mich* martern,
du schadenfroher unbekannter Gott?

Haha!
Du schleichst heran
bei solcher Mitternacht? . . .
Was willst du?
Sprich!
Du drängst mich, drückst mich,
Ha! schon viel zu nahe!
Du hörst mich athmen,
du behorchst mein Herz,
du Eifersüchtiger!
     — worauf doch eifersüchtig?
Weg! Weg!
wozu die Leiter?
willst du *hinein*,
ins Herz, einsteigen,
in meine heimlichsten
Gedanken einsteigen?
Schamloser! Unbekannter! Dieb!
Was willst du dir erstehlen?
Was willst du dir erhorchen?
was willst du dir erfoltern,
du Folterer!
du — Henker-Gott!
Oder soll ich, dem Hunde gleich,
vor dir mich wälzen?
Hingebend, begeistert ausser mir
dir Liebe — zuwedeln?
Umsonst!

with gods' lightning eyes that delight in suffering,
not yet tired of human torment?
So you don't want to kill,
only to torture, torture?
What's the point — of torturing *me*,
you unknown god who delights in suffering?

Haha!
You sneak toward me
at a midnight hour such as this? . . .
What do you want?
Speak!
You are pressuring me, pushing me,
Ha! already much too close!
You hear me breathe,
you are listening to my heart,
you jealous one!
     — but what are you jealous of?
Go away! Away!
what's the ladder for?
do you want to *go in*,
into my heart, to climb in,
to climb
into my most secret thoughts?
You shameless one! Unknown one! Thief!
What do you think you'll gain by stealing?
What do you think you'll gain by listening in?
what do you think you'll gain by torturing,
you torturer!
you — executioner-god!
Or should I roll around in front of you
like a dog?
Submitting, eager, out of my mind
with love for you — wagging my tail?
There's no point!

Stich weiter!
Grausamster Stachel!
Kein Hund — dein Wild nur bin ich,
grausamster Jäger!
deine stolzeste Gefangne,
du Räuber hinter Wolken . . .
Sprich endlich!
Du Blitz-Verhüllter! Unbekannter! sprich!
Was willst du, Wegelagerer, von — *mir*? . . .

Wie?
Lösegeld?
Was willst du Lösegelds?
Verlange Viel — das räth mein Stolz!
und rede kurz — das räth mein andrer Stolz!

Haha!
Mich — willst du? mich?
mich — ganz? . . .

Haha!
und marterst mich, Narr, der du bist,
zermarterst meinen Stolz?
Gieb *Liebe* mir — wer wärmt mich noch?
   wer liebt mich noch?
gieb heisse Hände,
gieb Herzens-Kohlenbecken,
gieb mir, der Einsamsten,
die Eis, ach! siebenfaches Eis
nach Feinden selber,
nach Feinden schmachten lehrt,
gieb, ja ergieb
grausamster Feind,
mir — *dich*! . . .

Davon!

Keep stinging me!
Most cruel stinger!
Not a dog — I am merely your prey,
most cruel hunter!
your proudest prisoner,
you robber behind clouds . . .
Say something!
You who are veiled in lightning! Unknown one! speak!
What do you want, you who lies in wait, from — *me?* . . .

What are you saying?
Ransom?
What kind of ransom do you want?
Demand a lot — that's what my pride advises!
and keep it short — that's what my other pride advises!

Haha!
Me — you want? me?
me — all of me? . . .

Haha!
and you torture me, fool that you are,
you stretch my pride out on the rack?
Give me *love* — who still keeps me warm?
    who still loves me?
give me hot hands,
give me a heart of glowing coal,
give to me, the loneliest one of all,
for whom ice, yes! ice sevenfold,
is a teacher of the longing for the enemy itself,
for the enemy,
give yourself to me, yes,
most cruel enemy,
— *surrender to me!* . . . [4]

Gone!

Da floh er selber,
mein einziger Genoss,
mein grosser Feind,
mein Unbekannter,
mein Henker-Gott! . . .
Nein!
komm zurück!
Mit allen deinen Martern!
All meine Thränen laufen
zu dir den Lauf
und meine letzte Herzensflamme
dir glüht sie auf.
Oh komm zurück,
mein unbekannter Gott! mein *Schmerz*!
  mein letztes Glück! . . .

Ein Blitz. Dionysos wird in smaragdener Schönheit sichtbar.

Dionysos:

Sei klug, Ariadne! . . .
Du hast kleine Ohren, du hast meine Ohren:
steck ein kluges Wort hinein! —
Muss man sich nicht erst hassen, wenn man sich lieben soll? . . .
Ich bin dein Labyrinth . . .

ARIADNE'S LAMENT 367

Then he fled, he himself,
my only companion,
my great enemy,
my unknown one,
my executioner-god! . . .
No!
come back!
With all your tortures!⁵
All my tears are tracing
a path to you
and the last ember of my heart
sets them aglow for you.
Oh come back,
my unknown god! my *pain*!
   my ultimate happiness! . . .

A bolt of lightning. Dionysus becomes visible in his emerald beauty.

Dionysus:

Be clever, Ariadne! . . .
You have little ears, you have my ears:
fill them with a clever phrase! —
Don't we have to hate ourselves before we can love
   ourselves? . . .
I am your labyrinth . . .

Ruhm und Ewigkeit.

1.

Wie lange sitzest du schon
   auf deinem Missgeschick?
Gieb Acht! du brütest mir noch
   ein Ei,
   ein Basilisken-Ei
aus deinem langen Jammer aus.

Was schleicht Zarathustra entlang dem Berge? —

Misstrauisch, geschwürig, düster,
ein langer Lauerer — ,
aber plötzlich, ein Blitz,
hell, furchtbar, ein Schlag
gen Himmel aus dem Abgrund:
— dem Berge selber schüttelt sich
das Eingeweide . . .

Wo Hass und Blitzstrahl
Eins ward, ein *Fluch* — ,
auf den Bergen haust jetzt Zarathustra's Zorn,
eine Wetterwolke schleicht er seines Wegs.
Verkrieche sich, wer eine letzte Decke hat!
Ins Bett mit euch, ihr Zärtlinge!
Nun rollen Donner über die Gewölbe,

Fame and Eternity.

How long have you been sitting
   on your misfortune?
Pay attention! for me, you will yet hatch
   an egg,
   a basilisk-egg
out of your prolonged misery.

Why is Zarathustra slinking around the mountain? —

Mistrustful, ulcerous, gloomy,
someone who lies in wait for a long time — ,[1]
but suddenly, a bolt of lightning,
bright, terrible, a blow
against heaven from out of the abyss:
— shaking the entrails
of the mountain itself . . . [2]

Wherever hatred and bolts of lightning
become one, a *curse* — ,
now Zarathustra's anger resides in the mountains,
a storm cloud, his anger slinks along its path.
Let anyone who still has a blanket crawl away and hide!
Hide under the covers, you weaklings![3]
Now thunder rolls across the vaulted ceiling,

nun zittert, was Gebälk und Mauer ist,
nun zucken Blitze und schwefelgelbe Wahrheiten —
    Zarathustra *flucht* . . .

                              2.

Diese Münze, mit der
alle Welt bezahlt,
Ruhm — ,
mit Handschuhen fasse ich diese Münze an,
mit Ekel trete ich sie *unter* mich.

Wer will bezahlt sein?
Die Käuflichen . . .
Wer *feil* steht, greift
mit fetten Händen
nach diesem Allerwelts-Blechklingklang Ruhm!

— *Willst* du sie kaufen?
sie sind Alle käuflich.
Aber biete Viel!
klingle mit vollem Beutel!
— du *stärkst* sie sonst,
du stärkst sonst ihre *Tugend* . . .

Sie sind Alle tugendhaft.
Ruhm und Tugend — das reimt sich.
So lange die Welt lebt,
zahlt sie Tugend-Geplapper
mit Ruhm-Geklapper — ,
die Welt *lebt* von diesem Lärm . . .

Vor allen Tugendhaften
    will ich schuldig sein,
schuldig heissen mit jeder grossen Schuld!
Vor allen Ruhms-Schalltrichtern
wird mein Ehrgeiz zum Wurm — ,

now whatever is post-and-beam and wall is trembling,
now lightning bolts and brimstone-colored truths are stirring—
   Zarathustra *curses* . . .

2.

This coin with which
all the world makes payments,
fame — ,
I put on gloves to take hold of this coin,
in disgust I trample it *under* my feet.

Who wants to be paid?
The ones who can be bought . . .
Those who are *for hire*,
with their slimy hands
they grab for this worldwide tinpot-ching-ching fame!

— Do you *want* to buy them?
they can all[4] be bought.
But offer plenty!
let your full purse jingle!
— otherwise you will *strengthen* them,
otherwise you will strengthen their *virtue* . . .

They are all virtuous.
Fame and virtue — belong together.
As long as the world keeps living,
it rewards virtue-blabbering
with fame-jabbering — ,
the world *thrives* on[5] this noise . . .

I want to be guilty
   in the eyes of all virtuous people,
I want to be judged guilty of every grave transgression![6]
My ambition turns into a worm
whenever I stand before all the noisemakers of fame — ,

unter Solchen gelüstet's mich,
der *Niedrigste* zu sein . . .

Diese Münze, mit der
alle Welt bezahlt,
Ruhm — ,
mit Handschuhen fasse ich diese Münze an,
mit Ekel trete ich sie *unter* mich.

3.

Still! —
Von grossen Dingen — ich *sehe* Grosses! —
soll man schweigen
oder gross reden:
rede gross, meine entzückte Weisheit!

Ich sehe hinauf —
dort rollen Lichtmeere:
— oh Nacht, oh Schweigen, oh todtenstiller Lärm! . . .

Ich sehe ein Zeichen — ,
aus fernsten Fernen
sinkt langsam funkelnd ein Sternbild gegen mich . . .

4.

Höchstes Gestirn des Seins!
Ewiger Bildwerke Tafel!
Du kommst zu mir? —
Was Keiner erschaut hat,
deine stumme Schönheit —
wie? sie flieht vor meinen Blicken nicht?

Schild der Nothwendigkeit!
Ewiger Bildwerke Tafel!
— aber du weisst es ja:
was Alle hassen,

when I am among them, I lust,
to be the *lowest of the low* . . .[7]

This coin with which
all the world makes payments,
fame — ,
I put on gloves to take hold of this coin,
in disgust I trample it *under* my feet.

3.

Quiet! —
Concerning great things — I *see* greatness! —
we must be silent
or else we must speak boastfully:
speak boastfully, my delighted wisdom!

I look upward —
oceans of light are rolling there:
— oh night, oh silence, oh the noise of deathly stillness! . . .

I see a sign — ,
coming from some untold distance
a twinkling constellation is slowly sinking toward me . . .

4.

Highest star of being!
Tablet of eternal figures!
You are coming to be with me? —
Your voiceless beauty,
which no one has ever seen —
what? this beauty does not flee from my gaze?

Signpost of necessity!
Tablet of eternal figures![8]
— but you know it, don't you:
what all people hate,

was allein *ich* liebe,
dass du *ewig* bist!
dass du *nothwendig* bist!
Meine Liebe entzündet
sich ewig nur an der Nothwendigkeit.

Schild der Nothwendigkeit!
Höchstes Gestirn des Seins!
— das kein Wunsch erreicht,
das kein Nein befleckt,
ewiges Ja des Sein's,
ewig bin ich dein Ja:
denn ich liebe dich, oh Ewigkeit! — —

what *I* alone love,
that you are *eternal*!
that you are *necessary*!
My love is kindled,
eternally, through necessity alone.

Emblem of necessity!
Highest star of being!
— that no wish attains,
that no "no" defiles,
eternal "yes" of being,
eternally, I am your "yes":
for I love you, oh eternity! — —[9]

Von der Armut des Reichsten.

Zehn Jahre dahin — ,
kein Tropfen erreichte mich,
kein feuchter Wind, kein Thau der Liebe
— ein *regenloses* Land . . .
Nun bitte ich meine Weisheit,
nicht geizig zu werden in dieser Dürre:
ströme selber über, träufle selber Thau
sei selber Regen der vergilbten Wildniss!

Einst hiess ich die Wolken
fortgehn von meinen Bergen —
einst sprach ich „mehr Licht, ihr Dunklen!"
Heut locke ich sie, dass sie kommen:
macht dunkel um mich mit euren Eutern!
— ich will euch melken,
ihr Kühe der Höhe!
Milchwarme Weisheit, süssen Thau der Liebe
ströme ich über das Land.

Fort, fort, ihr Wahrheiten,
die ihr düster blickt!
Nicht will ich auf meinen Bergen
herbe ungeduldige Wahrheiten sehn.
Vom Lächeln vergüldet
nahe mir heut die Wahrheit,

On the Poverty of the Richest Man.[1]

Ten years have passed — ,
no drop of rain has reached me,
no moist wind, no dew of love
— a land *without rain* . . .
Now I ask my wisdom,
not to become stingy during this drought:
let yourself stream over, let your own dew fall
let yourself be rain to the sun-bleached desert![2]

Once I told the clouds
to get away from my mountains —
once I said "more light,[3] you dark ones!"
Today I lure them so that they come:
make everything around me dark with your udders!
— I want to milk you,
you cows of the heights!
I pour out wisdom warm as milk,
sweet dew of love across the land.[4]

Be gone, be gone, you truths,
you who look so gloomily!
I do not want to see bitter impatient truths
in my mountains.
Let the truth approach me today,
gilded with smiles,

von der Sonne gesüsst, von der Liebe gebräunt —
eine *reife* Wahrheit breche ich allein vom Baum.

Heut strecke ich die Hand aus
nach den Locken des Zufalls,
klug genug, den Zufall
einem Kinde gleich zu führen, zu überlisten.
Heut will ich gastfreundlich sein
gegen Unwillkommnes,
gegen das Schicksal selbst will ich nicht stachlicht sein
— Zarathustra ist kein Igel.

Meine Seele,
unersättlich mit ihrer Zunge,
an alle guten und schlimmen Dinge hat sie schon geleckt,
in jede Tiefe tauchte sie hinab.
Aber immer gleich dem Korke,
immer schwimmt sie wieder obenauf,
sie gaukelt wie Öl über braune Meere:
dieser Seele halber heisst man mich den Glücklichen.

Wer sind mir Vater und Mutter?
Ist nicht mir Vater Prinz Überfluss
und Mutter das stille Lachen?
Erzeugte nicht dieser Beiden Ehebund
mich Räthselthier,
mich Lichtunhold,
mich Verschwender aller Weisheit Zarathustra?

Krank heute vor Zärtlichkeit,
ein Thauwind,
sitzt Zarathustra wartend, wartend auf seinen Bergen —
im eignen Safte
süss geworden und gekocht,
unterhalb seines Gipfels,
unterhalb seines Eises,

sweetened by the sun, browned by love —
I will pick only one *ripe* truth from the tree.

Today I stretch out my hand
toward the lion's mane[5] of chance,
clever enough to lead chance
like a child, to outwit it.
Today I want to be welcoming
to whatever is unwelcome,
I do not want to raise my quills against destiny itself
— Zarathustra is no hedgehog.[6]

My soul,
insatiable with its tongue,
it has already been licking all good and bad things,
it dives down into every depth.
But it always floats back to the surface,
just like a cork,
it dances like oil across brown seas:
this soul is the reason I have been called a happy man.[7]

Who are my father and mother?[8]
Is Prince Overflow not my father
and silent laughter[9] not my mother?[10]
Did not the nuptials of both of them beget
me, beast full of riddles,
me, demon of light,
me, squanderer of all wisdom, Zarathustra?

Today, sickened by tenderness,
a wind that thaws,
Zarathustra sits waiting, waiting in his mountains —[11]
sweetened and stewed
in his own juices,
below his peak,
below his ice,

müde und selig,
ein Schaffender an seinem siebenten Tag.

— Still!
Eine Wahrheit wandelt über mir
einer Wolke gleich —
mit unsichtbaren Blitzen trifft sie mich.
Auf breiten langsamen Treppen
steigt ihr Glück zu mir:
komm, komm, geliebte Wahrheit!

— Still!
Meine Wahrheit ists!
Aus zögernden Augen,
aus sammtenen Schaudern
trifft mich ihr Blick,
lieblich, bös, ein Mädchenblick . . .
Sie errieth meines Glückes *Grund*,
sie errieth *mich* — ha! was sinnt sie aus? —
Purpurn lauert ein Drache
im Abgrunde ihres Mädchenblicks.

— Still! Meine Wahrheit *redet*! —

Wehe dir, Zarathustra!
Du siehst aus, wie Einer,
der Gold verschluckt hat:
man wird dir noch den Bauch aufschlitzen! . . .

Zu reich bist du,
du Verderber Vieler!
Zu Viele machst du neidisch,
zu Viele machst du arm . . .
Mir selber wirft dein Licht Schatten — ,
es fröstelt mich: geh weg, du Reicher,
geh, Zarathustra, weg aus deiner Sonne! . . .

weary and blissful,
a creator on his seventh day.

— Quiet!
One truth wafts over me
like a cloud, —
it strikes me with invisible bolts of lightning.
Its happiness climbs
wide slow stairways up to me:[12,13]
come, come, beloved truth!

— Quiet!
It is *my* truth!
Its gaze finds me,
coming from lingering eyes,
from silken shuddering,
loving, evil, a girlish gaze . . .
She figured out the *reason* for my happiness,
she figured *me* out — ha! what is she plotting? —
A dragon lies in wait, purple
in the abyss of her girlish gaze.

— Quiet! My truth *is speaking*! —

Woe unto you, Zarathustra!
You look like someone
who has swallowed gold:
they will have to slit open your belly! . . .

You are too rich,
you corrupter of so many people!
You are making too many people envious,
you are making too many people poor . . .
Your light casts its shadows, even over me — ,
I am chilled: get away, you rich man,
get away, Zarathustra, from your sunlight! . . .

Du möchtest schenken, wegschenken deinen Überfluss,
aber du selber bist der Überflüssigste!
Sei klug, du Reicher!
Verschenke dich selber erst, oh Zarathustra!

Zehn Jahre dahin — ,
und kein Tropfen erreichte dich?
Kein feuchter Wind? kein Thau der Liebe?
Aber wer *sollte* dich auch lieben,
du Überreicher?
Dein Glück macht rings trocken,
macht arm an Liebe
— ein *regenloses* Land . . .

Niemand dankt dir mehr,
du aber dankst Jedem,
der von dir nimmt:
daran erkenne ich dich,
du Überreicher,
du *Ärmster* aller Reichen!

Du opferst dich, dich *quält* dein Reichthum — ,
du giebst dich ab,
du schonst dich nicht, du liebst dich nicht:
die grosse Qual zwingt dich allezeit,
die Qual *übervoller* Scheuern, *übervollen* Herzens —
aber Niemand dankt dir mehr . . .

Du musst *ärmer* werden,
weiser Unweiser!
willst du geliebt sein.
Man liebt nur die Leidenden,
man giebt Liebe nur dem Hungernden:
verschenke dich selber erst, oh Zarathustra!

— Ich bin deine Wahrheit . . .

You would like to give gifts, to give from your overflow,
but you yourself are the man who overflows the most!
Be clever, you rich man!
First give of yourself, oh Zarathustra!

Ten years have passed — ,
and no drop of rain has reached you?
No moist wind? no dew of love?
But who *should* really love you,
you superrich man?
Your happiness brings drought in every direction,
causes love to wane, creates
— a land *without rain* . . .

No one thanks you anymore,
yet you thank anyone,
who takes from you:
that's how I recognize you,
you superrich man,
among all of the rich, you are the *poorest*!

You sacrifice yourself, your wealth *torments* you — ,
you deliver yourself up,
you don't spare yourself, you don't love yourself:
a great agony compels you ever more,
the agony of goblets *filled to the brim*,[14] of a heart *filled to
    overflowing* —
but no one thanks you anymore . . .[15]

You must become *poorer*,
foolish sage!
if you want to be loved.
Only those who suffer are loved,
only those who hunger are given love:
first give of yourself, oh Zarathustra!

— I am your truth . . .

Nietzsche Contra Wagner.

Documents of a Psychologist.

Contents.

Foreword.[1]

The following chapters have been selected, not without due care, entirely from my earlier works — a few go back to 1877 — perhaps elucidated here and there, and above all, shortened. Read one after the other, they will leave no doubt as to Richard Wagner nor indeed myself: we are antipodes. People will also understand other things thereby: for example, that this is an essay for psychologists, but *not* for Germans . . . I have my readers everywhere, in Vienna, in St. Petersburg, in Copenhagen and Stockholm, in Paris, in New York — I do *not* have them in Europe's flat land, Germany[2] . . . And I would perhaps have a word to whisper into the ear of the Italian signors, whom I *love* as much as I . . . *Quousque tandem, Crispi . . .*[3] Triple Alliance:[4] with the "Reich" an intelligent people can only make a misalliance . . .

FRIEDRICH NIETZSCHE.

Turin, Christmas, 1888.

Where I Admire.[1]

I believe artists often do not know what they do best: they are too vain for that. Their minds are trained on something prouder than these little plants seem to be, that are new, rare and beautiful, capable of growing to real perfection in their soil. What is actually good in their own garden and vineyard is casually dismissed by them, and their love and their insight are not of equal rank. There is a musician who more than any other musician has his expertise in finding sounds from the realm of suffering, oppressed, tortured souls and giving voice even to dumb misery.[2] No one is his equal in the colorings of late autumn, the indescribably stirring happiness of a last, very last, very briefest enjoyment, he has a sound for those mysterious-uncanny[3] midnights of the soul, where cause and effect seem to have come unhinged and in any moment something can arise "out of nothing." He draws most successfully of all artists from the deepest bottom of human happiness and from its drained cup, so to speak, where the bitterest and most repulsive drops have mingled for better or worse with the sweetest. He knows that weariness of the soul that has to push itself, that can no longer leap and fly, indeed can no longer walk; he has the shy look of concealed pain, of understanding without comfort, of taking leave without confessing; indeed as the Orpheus of all secret misery he is greater than anyone, and only through him some things have been added to art generally that previously seemed inexpressible and even unworthy of art — the cynical rebellions, for instance, of which only the most suffering are capable, likewise[4] some very small and microscopic things of the soul, the scales as it were of its amphibian nature[5] — indeed he is the *master* of the miniature. But he does not *want* to be! His character instead loves great walls and daring frescoes! . . . It escapes him that his spirit has a different taste and inclination — an opposing optics[6] — and prefers to sit quietly in the nooks of collapsed buildings: here, hidden, hidden from himself, he paints his real masterpieces, which are all very brief, often only a single bar in length — only here does he become entirely good, great and perfect, perhaps here alone. — Wagner is someone who has suffered deeply — his *advantage* among other musicians. — I admire Wagner in everything in which he puts *himself* to music. —[7]

Where I Object.[8]

By this, I do not mean that I take this music to be healthy, least of all at the very point where it speaks of Wagner.[9] My objections to Wagner's music are physiological objections: why disguise them first with aesthetic formulas? Aesthetics is just applied physiology. — My "fact of the matter," my "*petit fait vrai*,"[10,11] is that I no longer breathe freely when this music starts to affect me; that suddenly my *foot* becomes angry at it and revolts: it has a need for rhythm, dance, march — even the young German kaiser cannot march to Wagner's "Kaiser March" —[12] it demands from music above all the delights found in *good* walking, striding, dancing.[13] But doesn't my stomach also protest? My heart? My blood pressure? Are my bowels not upset?[14] Doesn't all this unnoticeably make me hoarse . . . To listen to Wagner I need Géraudel pastilles . . . And[15] so I ask myself: what on earth does my whole body *want*

from music? *Since* there is no soul[16] . . . I believe, its own *relief*:
as if all animal functions could be accelerated by light, bold,
unbridled, self-assured rhythms; as if iron and leaden life
could lose its heaviness through golden, tender, unctuous melodies.[17] My melancholy wants to relax in the hiding places
and abysses of *perfection*: for this I need music. But Wagner
makes you ill.[18] — What do *I* care about theater?[19] About the
cramps of its moral ecstasies, from which the common people
— and who isn't "common people"![20] — derive their satisfaction? About the whole gesture-hocus pocus of an actor! —
One can see,[21] I am essentially antitheatrical by disposition,
deep down in my soul I have, like every artist today, the profoundest scorn for the theater, that *mass art* par excellence.
Success in the theater — in my estimation, that plunges a person into oblivion; *failure* — here I prick up my ears and start
to pay attention[22] . . . But Wagner, conversely, *next to* the
Wagner who made the loneliest music that exists,[23] was essentially still the man of the theater and the actor, the most
fanatic mimomaniac that ever existed, *even as a musician*[24] . . .
And, incidentally speaking, if it has been Wagner's theory
"that drama is the end, while music is always merely the
means" — his *practice* on the contrary was from start to finish
"the pose is the end, the drama, even the music, is always
merely its means." Music as the means to clarification, intensification, internalization of the dramatic gesture and the actor's
convincingness; and Wagnerian drama merely an opportunity
for many interesting[25] poses! — He possessed, along with all
other instincts, the *commanding instinct* of a great actor in all
and sundry: and, as mentioned, also as a musician. — I made
this clear once, not without *effort*, to a Wagnerian *pur sang*[26]
— clarity and Wagnerians! I shall say no more. —[27] I had[28]
reason to add "just be a bit more honest with yourself: we're
not in Bayreuth after all! In Bayreuth,[29] one is only honest as
one of the masses; as an individual one lies and lies to oneself.
One leaves oneself at home when one goes to Bayreuth,[30] one

dispenses with the right to one's own tongue and choice, to one's taste, even to one's courage as one possesses and practices it before God and world[31] within one's own four walls. No one brings into the theater the finest senses of his art, least of all[32] the artist who works for the theater — solitude is lacking, everything perfect tolerates no witness . . .[33] In the theater one becomes common people, herd, woman, Pharisee, voting cattle, subscriber, idiot — *Wagnerian*: there, even the most personal conscience succumbs to the leveling magic of the greatest number, the neighbor rules there, one *becomes* a neighbor there . . ."[34]

Intermezzo.[35]

— I will say one more word for the most discerning of ears: what *I* actually want of music. That it be bright and deep, like an afternoon in October. That it be individual, lively, tender, a sweet little woman of guile and grace . . . I shall never allow that a German *could* know what music is. Those who are called German musicians, the greatest at the head, are *foreigners*, Slavs, Croats, Italians, Dutch — or Jews; otherwise Germans of the strong race, Germans who have *died out*, like Heinrich Schütz, Bach and Handel. I myself am still Pole enough to give up the rest of music for Chopin: for three reasons I make an exception for Wagner's *Siegfried Idyll*, perhaps also for Liszt, whose noble orchestral accents outdo all other musicians; finally, everything else that has sprung up beyond the Alps — *this side*[36] . . . I would not know how to do without Rossini, still less *my* South in music, the music of my Venetian maestro Pietro Gasti. And when I say beyond the Alps, I actually just mean Venice. If I seek another word for music, I still only find the word Venice. I do not know how to distinguish between tears and music, I do not know how to think of happiness, the *South*, without a shudder of trepidation.

At the bridge I stood
of late in browning night.
In the distance song:
golden droplets welling
their way over the trembling surface.
Gondolas, lanterns, music —
swimming drunken into twilight . . .

My soul, like string music
invisibly touched, sang itself
a secret gondola song to it,
trembling with vibrant bliss.
— Did anyone listen? . . .

Wagner as Danger.

I.[37]

The aim pursued by modern music in what now gets described
in very strong but vague terms as "infinite melody" can be made
clear by going down into the sea, gradually losing our secure grip
upon the bottom, and finally surrendering ourselves unconditionally to the elements: we are supposed to be *swimming*.
In the older music, one had to do something quite different,
namely[38] *dance*, moving back and forth in a graceful or solemn or
fiery way, faster and slower. The measure required for maintaining a certain balanced pace of time and energy demanded continual *self-possession* from the soul of the listener — the spell of all
good music was based upon the opposition between this cooler
current of air, arising from self-possession, and the thoroughly
warmed breath of musical enthusiasm. — Richard Wagner wanted
a different sort of movement — he overturned the previous
physiological precondition of music. Swimming, floating — not
walking and dancing anymore . . . Perhaps that says what is crucial. "Infinite melody" *wants* to break all symmetry of tempo and

energy, sometimes even mocking them — its wealth of invention is precisely what sounds to older ears like rhythmical paradoxes and blasphemies. It is impossible to exaggerate the danger for music that might ensue from the imitation or hegemony of such a style — the complete degeneration of a feeling for rhythm, *chaos* in place of rhythm . . . The danger comes to a head when such music relies ever more closely upon a completely naturalistic art of acting and language of gesture, untrained and uncontrolled by any higher plastic art, that wants *effect* and nothing more . . . The *expressivo* at any price and music in service, in servitude to the theatrical pose — *that is the end result* . . . [39]

2.[40]

What? is it really the principal virtue of performance, as the artists performing music now seem to believe, to achieve as much high relief under any circumstances that cannot be surpassed?[41] Isn't this principle, if applied to Mozart, for example, not really a sin against his spirit, the cheerful, impassioned, tender, enamored spirit of Mozart, who fortunately was not a German and whose seriousness is a kindly, golden seriousness and *not* the seriousness of a German philistine . . . let alone the solemnity of the "stone guest"[42] . . . But you think *all* music is the music of the "stone guest" — *all* music should leap out of the wall and shake the listener to the core? . . . Music can only *work* like that! — Upon *whom* does it make an effect? Upon those on whom no *noble* musician should ever make an effect — on the mass! On the immature! On the blasé! On the ailing! On idiots! On *Wagnerians*! . . .[43]

─────────

A Music with No Future.[44]

Music, of all the arts that know how to flourish in a specific cultural soil, is the last of all the plants to appear, perhaps because it is the most inward and consequently arrives the latest — in the wilting autumn of each particular culture of which it is a part. It was in the art of the Dutch masters that the soul of the Christian Middle Ages first found its resonance — their tonal architecture is the late-born, but legitimate and equally highly born sister of the Gothic. It was in Handel's music that what was best in the souls of Luther and his kindred, the Judeo-heroic disposition that gave the Reformation a trait of greatness, first resounded — the Old Testament turned into music, *not* the New. It was Mozart who first delivered in *tones* of gold the age of Louis the Fourteenth and the art of Racine and Claude Lorrain; it was in the music of Beethoven and Rossini that the eighteenth century first sang forth, the century of visionary enthusiasm, of shattered ideals and of *fleeting* happiness. All true, all original music is a swan song. — It is possible that our most recent music, however much it now rules and yearns to rule, has merely a short span of time ahead of it: for it has sprung from a culture whose soil is rapidly subsiding — a culture that will soon have *sunk into oblivion*. Its preconditions are a certain catholicism of feeling and a pleasure in some kind of archaic-nativist so-called "national" character, or lack of it. Wagner's appropriation of old sagas and songs in which educated prejudice had taught people to see something Teutonic par excellence — we laugh about it today — the reanimation of these Scandinavian monstrosities with a thirst for enraptured sensuality and desensualization — Wagner's whole taking and giving with regard to subject matter, figures, passions and nerves, also clearly expresses the *spirit of his music*, provided that this itself, like every music, were not incapable of speaking of itself unambiguously: for music is a *woman* . . . We should not let ourselves be misled by the fact that at the moment, we are actually living in a reaction *within* a reaction. The age of national wars, of ultramontane martyrdom, the whole sense of *intermission* that is peculiar to the circumstances of Europe, may in fact help an art like that of Wagner's to attain a sudden glory, without thereby guaranteeing it a *future*. The Germans themselves have no future . . .

We Antipodes.[45]

One may perhaps recall, at least among my friends, that in the beginning I went at this modern world with a few errors[46] and overestimations and in any case as someone who was *hopeful*. I understood — who knows based on what personal experience? — the philosophical pessimism of the nineteenth century as a symptom of a superior force of thought, of a more triumphant fullness of life than had come to expression in the philosophy of Hume, Kant, and Hegel[47] —I took *tragic* insight as the most beautiful *luxury* of our culture, as its most precious, noble, dangerous kind of squandering, but nevertheless, based on its superabundance, as its *permitted* luxury.[48] Similarly, I made a point of construing Wagner's music[49] as the expression of a Dionysian mightiness of the soul,[50] in it I believed I heard the earthquake that was finally released by a primal force of life[51] dammed up since time immemorial, indifferent to whether everything that calls itself culture today had to start teetering.[52] One sees what I failed to recognize, one sees likewise what I *bestowed* on Wagner and Schopenhauer — by myself . . . [53,54] Every art, every philosophy may be regarded as a remedy and aid in the service of growing or declining[55] life: they always presuppose suffering and sufferers. But there are two kinds of sufferers; first those who suffer from the *superabundance* of life, who want a Dionysian art and likewise a tragic insight and view[56] into life — and then those who suffer from the *impoverishment* of life, who seek rest, quiet, smooth seas, *or* those who demand intoxication, spasms, numbness from art and philosophy. Revenge on life itself — the most voluptuous kind of intoxication for such paupers! . . . Wagner as well as Schopenhauer meet the latter's double need — they deny life, they slander it, which makes them my antipodes.[57] — The one richest in fullness of life, namely the Dionysian god and human being, can allow himself not only the sight of what is terrible and questionable, but the terrible deed itself and that luxury of destruction, disintegration, negation — in him, what is evil, absurd and ugly is permitted, as it were, as it seems to be permitted in nature,[58] as a result of a superabundance of begetting, restorative[59] energies that are still capable of turning any desert into a lush farmland. Conversely, the most suffering and poorest in life would mostly need mildness, peacefulness, goodness — what people nowadays call humanity —[60] in thought as well as in deed, if possible a god who is actually[61] a god for the sick, a *savior*; likewise logic as well, the conceptual comprehensibility of existence even for idiots — the typical "freethinkers," like the "idealists" and the "beautiful souls," are all *décadents* —[62] in sum, a certain warm, fear-repelling narrowness and enclosure in optimistic horizons that permits *dumbing down*[63] . . . This is how I gradually came to understand Epicurus, the opposite of a Dionysian Greek,[64] likewise the Christian, who in fact is merely a kind of Epicurean and with his "faith makes *blessed*" follows the principle of hedonism *as far as possible* — well beyond any intellectual integrity . . . If I have any advantage over all psychologists, then it is that my eye is better honed[65] for that most difficult and trickiest form of *backward inference* in which most mistakes are made — the backward inference from the work to the maker, from the deed to the doer, from the ideal to the one who *needs* it, from every manner of thinking and valuing to the commanding *need* behind it. — Regarding artists of any kind,[66] I now avail myself of this major distinction: has *hatred* against life or *superabundance* of life become creative here?[67] In Goethe, for example, superabundance became creative, in Flaubert, hatred: Flaubert, a new edition of Pascal, but an artist with instinctive judgment for this reason: "Flaubert est toujours *haïssable*, l'homme n'est rien, *l'oeuvre est tout*"[68] . . . He tortured himself when he wrote, just as Pascal tortured himself when he thought — both perceived things unegoistically . . . "selflessness" — the principle of *décadence*, the will to the end in art as well as in morality.[69] —

Where Wagner Belongs.[70]

Even now France is still the seat of the most spiritual and sophisticated culture in Europe and the *preeminent* school of taste: but one has to know where to find this "France of taste." The *Norddeutsche Zeitung*,[71] for example, or whoever finds his mouthpiece in it, sees "barbarians" in the French — I, for myself, seek the *black* continent, where "the slaves" ought to be liberated, near the North Germans . . . Whoever belongs to *that* France,[72] keeps himself well hidden: it may be a small number in whom it actually lives, and what's more, these are people who do not stand on the strongest of legs, some are fatalists, dark souls, the sick, some are pampered and affected, those who have the *ambition* to be artificial[73] — but they have in their possession all of the world's remaining loftiness and tenderness. Within this France of the spirit, which is also the[74] France of pessimism, Schopenhauer is more at home than he ever was in Germany; his main work already translated twice, the second time excellently, so that I now prefer to read Schopenhauer in French (— he was an *accident* among the Germans, just as I am such an accident — the Germans have no feel for us, they don't have any fingers at all, they just have paws). To say nothing of Heinrich Heine — *l'adorable Heine* they say in Paris — who long ago was adopted into the flesh and blood of the deeper and more soulful lyric poets of France.[75] What would German horned cattle make of the *délicatesses* of such a nature! — Finally, in what concerns Richard Wagner, one grasps with open hand, though perhaps not with closed fist, that Paris is the true *ground* for Wagner: the more French music conforms to the requirements of the "*âme moderne*,"[76] the more it will Wagnerize — it is already doing that quite enough. —[77] We should not allow ourselves to be led astray by Wagner himself — it was real malevolence on his part to deride Paris in its agony in 1871 . . . [78] Yet for all that, Wagner in Germany is no more than a misunderstanding: who,

for example, could be less capable of understanding Wagner
than the young kaiser?[79] — It remains, nevertheless, a well-
known fact for every connoisseur of the European cultural
movement that French Romanticism and Richard Wagner
belong inseparably together. All of them dominated up to
their eyes and ears by literature — the first artists of Europe
educated in *world* literature — most of them even themselves
writers, poets, mediators and mixers of the senses and the arts,
fanatics of *expression* one and all, all of them great discoverers
in the realm of the sublime, also of the hideous and horrific,
even greater discoverers in the realm of effects, in exhibition,
in the art of window displays, all of them talents far beyond
their genius — *virtuosos* through and through, with uncanny
passages to everything that seduces, lures, compels, overthrows,
born enemies of logic and the straight line, greedy for the foreign, the exotic, the monstrous, all the opiates of the senses
and of common sense. On the whole, an audaciously daring,
magnificently violent, high-flying and uplifting kind of artist,[80] who first had to teach *their* century — it is the century of
the *masses* — the concept of "artist."[81] Albeit *sick* . . . [82,83]

Wagner as Apostle of Chastity.

I.[84]

— Is this even German? —
From German hearts such steamy lamentation?
From German bodies this self-laceration? [85]
German these priestly outstretched arms,
These incense-reeking sensuous charms?
German this plunging, halting,[86] reeling,
This sugar-laden[87] ding-dong-pealing?
This nunnish ogling midst *Ave*-tinkling knells,
This heaven over-heavened by phony rapture spells? . . .

— Is this even German? —
Stop and think! You are still at the gate . . .
For what you hear is *Rome, — Rome's faith without words!*[88]

2.[89]

There is no necessary opposition between sensuality and chastity;[90] every good marriage, every genuine affair of the heart transcends this opposition. But even where there really is that opposition between chastity and sensuality, fortunately it need not by any means be a tragic opposition. This should at least apply for all better-constituted, better-tempered mortals who are far from blithely counting their labile equilibrium between angel and *petite bête*[91] among the arguments against existence — the subtlest, the brightest, like Hafiz, like Goethe,[92] have even seen in it one more stimulus to life . . . Just such contradictions seduce us to existence . . . On the other hand it is only too clear that once Circe's damaged animals[93] get to the point of worshipping chastity, they will only see and *worship* in it their opposite — and oh with what tragic grunting and zeal! we can imagine it — that embarrassing and completely superfluous opposition that Richard Wagner indisputably still wanted to set to music and bring to stage at the end of his life. *But why?* as is only fair to ask.

3.[94]

Here, of course, we cannot ignore that other question, namely: what did he care anyway about that manly (alas, so unmanly) "country bumpkin," that poor devil and nature boy Parsifal, whom he finally made over into a Catholic using his so insidious methods — what? was this Parsifal in any way meant *seriously*? For I would be the last to deny the fact that he has been *laughed* at, as would Gottfried Keller . . . [95] In particular, one might wish that Wagner's *Parsifal* was meant as a joke, as an epilogue and satyr play with which the tragedian Wagner wanted to take leave from us, also from himself, above all *from tragedy* in a manner precisely suited to and worthy of himself, namely with an excess of the highest and most mischievous parody of tragedy

itself, of the whole horrific earthly seriousness and earthly misery of former times, of the *silliest form* in the anti-nature of the
ascetic ideal. Yes, Parsifal is operetta material par excellence . . .[96]
Is Wagner's *Parsifal* his secret laugh of superiority at himself, the
triumph of his ultimate, highest artist's freedom, artist's transcendence — did Wagner know how to *laugh* at himself? . . .[97]
We would like to think so, as noted, for what would a *seriously
meant Parsifal* be? Do we really have to see in him (as someone
expressed it to me) "the spawn of an insane hatred of knowledge,
spirit and sensuality"? A curse on the senses and the spirit in a
single hatred and breath? An apostasy and return to Chris-
tian-pathological and obscurantist ideals? And in the end even
this self-denial and self-effacement on the part of an artist who
up till then had aimed with all the power of his will for the
opposite, namely for the highest spiritualization and sensualiza-
tion of his art? And not only his art, his life too? Recall how
enthusiastically Wagner followed in the footsteps of the philosopher Feuerbach in his day: Feuerbach's words about "healthy
sensuality" — in the thirties and forties that sounded to Wagner
as to many Germans (— they called themselves the *young* Germans) like the watchword of salvation. Did he *learn otherwise* in
the end? Because at least it appears that in the end he had the
will to *teach otherwise*? . . . Did the *hatred of life* become dominant in him, as it did in Flaubert? . . . For *Parsifal* is a work of
cunning, of vindictiveness, of a secret poisonous brew against
the presuppositions of life, a *bad* work. — The preaching of
chastity remains an incitement to anti-nature: I despise everyone
who does not find *Parsifal* an assault on decency. —[98,99]

How I Freed Myself from Wagner.

I.[100]

As early as the summer of 1876, during the first of the
Bayreuth festivals, I had taken my leave of Wagner. I cannot

stand ambiguities; ever since Wagner came to Germany he stooped down to everything I despise, step by step — even to anti-Semitism . . .[101] It was in fact high time then *to take leave*: I immediately received proof of this. Richard Wagner, seemingly the most triumphant, but in truth a decaying, despairing *décadent*,[102] suddenly sank down, helpless and shattered, before the Christian cross . . . Did no German have eyes in his head or sympathy in his conscience at that time for this terrifying spectacle? Was I the only one who — *suffered* from him? Enough, this unexpected event, like a flash of lightning, gave me clarity about the place that I had forsaken — and also the belated horror felt by everyone who has passed through a colossal danger unaware. As I alone went farther, I was trembling; not long afterward I was sick, more than sick, that is, *weary* — weary from the ceaseless disillusionment about everything that remained for the inspiration of us modern human beings, at the energy, labor, hope, youthfulness, love, everywhere being *wasted*, weary from disgust at all of the idealistic deceitfulness and softening up of conscience that had here, once again, carried off the victory over one of the most courageous ones; weary finally, and not least, from the sorrow of a relentless suspicion — that I was condemned to mistrust more deeply, to despise more deeply, to be more deeply *alone*, than ever before. For I had had nobody but Richard Wagner . . .[103] I was always *condemned* to Germans . . .[104]

2.[105]

Solitary henceforth and badly mistrustful of myself, I took sides at that time, not without anger, *against* myself and *for* everything that caused me pain and was difficult: — so I found the way once again to the courageous pessimism that is the opposite of all idealistic[106] deceitfulness and also, as it now seems to me, the way to *myself* — to *my* task . . . That concealed and dictatorial something for which for a long time we have no name, until it finally reveals itself as our task — this tyrant in us takes a terrible revenge for every attempt that we

make to evade or to escape it, for every premature determination, for every time we set ourselves equal to those to whom
we do not belong, for every activity, however estimable, if it
diverts us from our primary matter, indeed — even for every
virtue that would like to protect us against the harshness of
our most personal responsibility. Sickness, every time, is the
answer when we wish to doubt our right to *our* task, when we
begin to make things easier for ourselves in any way whatsoever. Strange and frightening at the same time! Our *allevia-
tions* are what we must pay for most harshly! And if we wish to
get back to health, there remains only one choice for us: we
must burden ourselves *more heavily* than we have ever been
burdened before . . .

The Psychologist Has His Say.

I.[107]

The more a psychologist — a born, inevitable psychologist
and diviner of souls — turns his attention to the more choice
cases and human beings, the greater his danger becomes of
choking on compassion. He *needs* hardness and cheerfulness
more than other people do. For corruption and destruction of
the superior human beings, of souls of a stranger type, is the
rule:[108] it is a terrible thing to constantly have this rule before
one's eyes. The manifold torments of the psychologist who discovered this destruction, who first discovers and then *almost*
always rediscovers throughout all history this whole inner "hope-
lessness" of the superior human being, this eternal "too late!" in
every sense — it could possibly lead him someday to turn bit-
terly against his fate and attempt his own self-destruction —
lead him to his own *corruption* . . . With nearly every psychologist we will perceive a telling predisposition and pleasure in
associating with ordinary and well-adjusted people: this reveals
that he always needs a cure, that he needs a kind of escape and

forgetting, away from what his insights and incisions, from what his craft has placed on his conscience. He is characterized by fear of his memory. He is easily silenced by the judgment of others, he listens with a stony face as others venerate, admire, love, transfigure where he has actually *seen* — or he conceals even his silence by expressly agreeing with some foreground opinion. Perhaps the paradox of his situation grows horrible to the extent that the "educated" develop their own great admiration precisely where he developed *great compassion* alongside *great contempt* . . . And who knows whether in all great cases so far it has not been the same — that a god was worshipped — and that the god was only a wretched sacrificial animal . . . *Success* has always been the biggest liar — and the *work*, the *deed* is a success . . . The great statesman, the conqueror, the discoverer are disguised in their creations to the point of unrecognizability; the work, that of the artist, of the philosopher, only invents the man who created it, who was *supposed* to have created it . . . The "great men" as they are venerated are small, paltry fictions after the fact — in the world of historical values counterfeiting is the *rule*.

2.[109]

— These great poets for instance, your Byron, Musset, Poe, Leopardi, Kleist, Gogol — I do not dare to name much greater names, but I mean them —[110] as they simply are and must be: human beings of the moment, sensual, absurd, fivefold,[111] frivolous and precipitous in their mistrust and trust; with souls harboring some breach that needs repairing; often taking revenge in their works for an inner contamination, often trying to find forgetfulness in their high-flying from an all-too-faithful memory, idealists who come from the vicinity of the *swamp* — what a *torment* these great artists and so-called superior human beings generally are for someone who has first figured them out . . . We are all advocates of the average . . .[112] It is understandable that *they* so readily enjoy those eruptions of boundless *compassion* from women, who are clairvoyant in

the world of suffering and unfortunately also addicted to helping and rescuing far beyond their own powers, eruptions on
which the masses, especially the *admiring* masses pile their
curious and self-complacent interpretations. This compassion
routinely deceives itself about its power: women want to
believe that love can do *anything* — it is their true *superstition*.[113] Oh, those who know hearts realize how poor, helpless,
presumptuous, mistake-prone is even the best profoundest
love — how it *destroys* rather than saves . . . [114]

3.[115]

— The spiritual nausea and arrogance of anyone who has
suffered deeply — *how* deeply people can suffer practically
determines rank order — his shuddering certainty, completely
permeating and coloring him, of *knowing more* than the cleverest and wisest could know by virtue of his suffering, of being
familiar with and once having been at home[116] in many remote,
appalling worlds of which "*you* know nothing!" . . . this spiritual, silent arrogance of the sufferer, this pride of the chosen
one of knowledge, of the "initiate," of the one who was almost
sacrificed finds it necessary to have all sorts[117] of disguise in
order to protect itself from contact with obtrusive and compassionate hands and generally from everything that is not its peer
in matters of pain. Deep suffering makes noble; it separates.
One of the most subtle forms of disguise is Epicureanism and a
certain openly displayed courageousness of taste that takes
suffering lightly and resists everything sad and profound.
There are "cheerful people" who use cheerfulness because on
its account they are misunderstood: — they *want* to be misunderstood. There are "scientific minds"[118] who use science
because it provides a cheerful appearance, and because scientific character lets others infer that someone is superficial —
they *want* to seduce others to a false conclusion . . . There are
free impudent spirits who would like to conceal and deny that
they essentially are shattered, incurable hearts — it is the case

of Hamlet: and then foolishness itself can be the mask for an ill-fated, all-too-certain knowledge. —[119]

Epilogue.

I.[120]

I have often asked myself whether I am not more deeply indebted to the most difficult years of my life than any of the others. As my innermost nature teaches me, everything necessary, seen from on high and in the sense of a *great* economy, is also what is useful in itself — one should not just bear it, one should *love* it . . . *Amor fati*: that is my innermost nature. —[121] And concerning my long invalidism, do I not have unspeakably more to thank it for than my health? I have it to thank for a *higher* health, one made stronger by all that does not kill it! — *I also have it to thank for my philosophy* . . .[122] Only great pain is the ultimate liberator of the spirit, as the school master of the *great suspicion* that makes an X out of every U,[123] a prim and proper X, that is, the *penultimate* letter before the final one . . . Only great pain, that long slow pain that takes its time, in which so to speak we are burned as if on green wood, compels us philosophers to descend into our ultimate depth and rid ourselves of all trust, all that is good natured, cloaking, mild, mediating where[124] perhaps we had formerly placed our humanity. I doubt whether such pain "improves" us: but I know that it *deepens* us . . . Now whether it is because we learn to counter it with our pride, our scorn, our will power, as does the American Indian who repays his torturer with the malice of his tongue, no matter how badly he is tortured; whether we withdraw from pain into that nothing,[125] into that mute, rigid, deaf self-surrender, self-forgetting, self-extinguishing: one emerges from such long dangerous exercises of mastery over oneself as a different human being, with a few *more* question marks — above all with the

will henceforth to question more, more deeply, more rigorously, more harshly, more evilly, more quietly than had ever
before been questioned on earth . . .[126] The trust in life is gone;
life itself became a *problem*. — But we should not believe for a
second that this necessarily turns one into a gloom monger,
into a barn owl![127] Even the love for life is still possible — only
one loves *differently* . . . It is the love for a woman who makes
us have doubts . . .[128]

<h2 style="text-align:center">2.[129]</h2>

One thing is strangest of all: afterwards, one has different
taste — a *second* taste. One returns from such abysses, even
from the abyss of *great suspicion*[130] as if newborn, having shed
one's skin, more ticklish, more malicious, with a more refined
taste for joy, with a tenderer tongue for all good things, with
keener senses, with a second more dangerous innocence in joy,
simultaneously more childlike and a hundred times more cunning than one had ever been. Moral: one does not go unpunished for being the deepest spirit of all millennia — nor does
one go *unrewarded* . . . I shall provide a sample right now.[131]

Oh how repulsed one is now by pleasure, crude, dull, brown
pleasure as it is otherwise understood by our pleasure seekers,
our "educated," our rich and rulers! How maliciously we now
listen to the great fairground boom-boom with which the "educated" person and metropolitan today let themselves be raped
by art, books and music for "spiritual pleasures," with the aid of
alcoholic spirits! How the theater-cry of passion now hurts in
our ears, how foreign to our taste has become the whole romantic uproar and sensual confusion loved by the educated rabble,
along with their aspirations for the sublime, elevated, deviated![132] No, if we convalescents still need an art,[133] then it is a
different art — a mocking, light, fleeting, divinely undisturbed,
divinely artificial art that blazes like a pure[134] flame into a
cloudless sky! Above all: an art for artists, *for artists only*! Afterwards we have a better understanding of what is chiefly necessary *for this*, cheerfulness, *all* cheerfulness, my friends! . . .[135]

We know some things too well, we knowers: oh how from now on we are learning to forget well, to *not* know well, as artists! . . . And as concerns our future: one will scarcely find us again on the paths of those Egyptian youths who make temples unsafe at night, embrace statues and want to unveil, uncover, shed bright light on absolutely everything that with good reason should remain concealed.[136] No, this bad taste, this will to truth, to "truth at any cost," this youth's insanity in the love for truth — are spoiled for us: for this we are too experienced, too earnest, too fun-loving, too burned, too *deep* . . . We no longer believe that truth still remains truth after one has lifted her *veil* — we've lived too much to believe this . . . Today we regard it as a matter of decency that one would not want to see everything naked, be present for everything, understand and "know" everything. *Tout comprendre — c'est tout mépriser* . . . [137] "Is it true that dear God is present everywhere?" a little girl asked her mother: "but I find that indecent" — a hint for philosophers! . . . One should better honor the *modesty* with which nature has hidden herself behind riddles and colorful uncertainties. Perhaps truth is a woman who has grounds *for not letting her grounds be seen*?[138] . . . Perhaps her name, to speak it in Greek, is *Baubo*?[139] . . . Oh these Greeks! They knew how to *live*: this requires stopping bravely at the surface, the fold, the skin, worshipping appearance, believing in forms, tones, words, in the entire *Olympus of appearance*![140] These Greeks were superficial — *out of profundity* . . . And are we not just now coming back to this, we daredevils of the spirit, we who have climbed the highest and most dangerous peak of present-day thought and have looked around from up there, we who have *looked down* from up there? Are we not in this point precisely — Greeks? Worshippers of forms, tones, words? And therefore — *artists*? . . .

On the Poverty of the Richest Man.[1]

Ten years have passed — ,
no drop of rain has reached me,
no moist wind, no dew of love
— a land *without rain . . .*
Now I ask my wisdom,
not to become stingy during this drought:
let yourself stream over, let your own dew fall
let yourself be rain to the sun-bleached desert!

Once I told the clouds
to get away from my mountains —
once I said "more light, you dark ones!"
Today I lure them so that they come:
make everything around me dark with your udders!
— I want to milk you,
you cows of the heights!
I pour out wisdom warm as milk,
sweet dew of love across the land.

Be gone, be gone, you truths,
you who look so gloomily!
I do not want to see bitter impatient truths
in my mountains.
Let the truth approach me today,
gilded with smiles,

sweetened by the sun, browned by love —
I will pick only one *ripe* truth from the tree.

Today I stretch out my hand
toward the lion's mane of chance,
clever enough to lead chance
like a child, to outwit it.
Today I want to be welcoming
to whatever is unwelcome,
I do not want to raise my quills against destiny itself
— Zarathustra is no hedgehog.

My soul,
insatiable with its tongue,
it has already been licking all good and bad things,
it dives down into every depth.
But it always floats back to the surface,
just like a cork,
it dances like oil across brown seas:
this soul is the reason I have been called a happy man.

Who are my father and mother?
Is Prince Overflow not my father
and silent laughter not my mother?
Did not the nuptials of both of them beget
me, beast full of riddles,
me, demon of light,
me, squanderer of all wisdom, Zarathustra?

Today, sickened by tenderness,
a wind that thaws,
Zarathustra sits waiting, waiting in his mountains —
sweetened and stewed
in his own juices,
below his peak,
below his ice,

weary and blissful,
a creator on his seventh day.

— Quiet!
One truth wafts over me
like a cloud, —
it strikes me with invisible bolts of lightning.
Its happiness climbs
wide slow stairways up to me:
come, come, beloved truth!

— Quiet!
It is *my* truth! —
Its gaze finds me,
coming from lingering eyes,
from silken shuddering,
loving, evil, a girlish gaze . . .
She figured out the *reason* for my happiness,
she figured *me* out — ha! what is she plotting? —
A dragon lies in wait, purple
in the abyss of her girlish gaze.

— Quiet! My truth *is speaking*! —

Woe unto you, Zarathustra!
You look like someone
who has swallowed gold:
they will have to slit open your belly! . . .

You are too rich,
you corrupter of so many people!
You are making too many people envious,
you are making too many people poor . . .
Your light casts its shadows, even over me — ,
I am chilled: get away, you rich man,
get away, Zarathustra, from your sunlight! . . .

You would like to give gifts, to give from your overflow,
but you yourself are the man who overflows the most!
Be clever, you rich man!
First give of yourself, oh Zarathustra!

Ten years have passed — ,
and no drop of rain has reached you?
no moist wind? no dew of love?
But who *should* really love you,
you superrich man?
Your happiness brings drought in every direction,
causes love to wane, creates
— a land *without rain* . . .

No one thanks you anymore.
Yet you thank anyone,
who takes from you:
that's how I recognize you,
you superrich man,
among all of the rich, you are the *poorest*!

You sacrifice yourself, your wealth *torments* you — ,
you deliver yourself up,
you don't spare yourself, you don't love yourself:
a great agony compels you ever more,
the agony of goblets *filled to the brim*, of a heart *filled to
    overflowing* —
but no one thanks you anymore . . .

You must become *poorer*,
foolish sage!
if you want to be loved.
Only those who suffer are loved,
only those who hunger are given love:
first give of yourself, oh Zarathustra!

— I am your truth . . .

Nietzsche's Unpublished Writings 1885–1888 and the "Will to Power"

Mazzino Montinari

The decades-long controversy concerning Nietzsche's so-called magnum opus {*Hauptwerk*}, *The Will to Power*,[1] is rendered pointless by the opening up and philological exploration of Nietzsche's unpublished writings (*Nachlaß*) of 1885–1888, made possible by the publication of the complete manuscripts in their authentic form and chronological order (see *CW* 16–18). The works *Twilight of the Idols* and *The Antichrist* in volume 9 are the consequence of Nietzsche's altered plans for *The Will to Power*. Accordingly, what follows here may serve as an introductory piece to volume 9, a synoptic description of the set of issues that surround *The Will to Power*. It will show the development of Nietzsche's plans and attempt to finally clear away the erroneous and still widely held views concerning Nietzsche's "magnum opus" promulgated by Elisabeth Förster-Nietzsche and Peter Gast.

The "will to power" is initially a philosophical proposition, then a literary project of Nietzsche's, but finally also the compilation from the unpublished writings known by this title, edited

1. {Montinari is not always consistent in how he punctuates "will to power." In the translation of this essay, we consistently punctuate the three referents of "will to power" as follows: (1) the will to power = a concept, a "philosophical proposition," in Nietzsche's philosophy; (2) the "Will to Power" = a book, a "literary project," Nietzsche planned but never completed; (3) *The Will to Power* = the book, "the compilation from the unpublished writings known by this title," that Nietzsche's sister Elisabeth Förster-Nietzsche and his friend Peter Gast edited and published.}

by Heinrich Köselitz (alias Peter Gast) and Elisabeth Förster-Nietzsche (Nietzsche's sister), appearing in 1906 in its final, and to some degree, even today, its canonical form. The conceptual parameters for the "will to power" were readied from 1880 forward by reflections on the "feeling of power" that found their expression in *Dawn* (spring 1881) and in the unpublished fragments of summer/autumn 1880. The first lengthy description of the "will to power" is found in the second part of *Thus Spoke Zarathustra*, in the chapter "On Self-Overcoming," written in summer 1883:

> Wherever I found living things, there I found will to power; and even in the will of those serving I found the will to be master [. . .] And life itself told me this secret. "Behold," it spoke, "I am that *which must always overcome itself* [. . .] And even you, the ones who know, are merely a path and a footprint of my will: truly, my will to power steps on the toes even of your will to truth! He who shot at the truth with the phrase 'will to exist' certainly did not hit it: this will — does not exist! For: that which is not, cannot will; yet what is in existence, how could this still will to exist! Only, where there is life, there is also will: but not will to live, rather [. . .] will to power! There is much that the living value more highly than life itself; nevertheless, out of valuation speaks — the will to power!"

A book of aphorisms from autumn 1882 has as its first maxim: "Will to live? I have always found only will to power in its place" (*CW* 14, 5[1]1, 166).

The will to power is thus the "insatiable, proliferating will to live {*Lebens-Wille*}," it is the "will to be master," it is what Nietzsche "has to say about life and about the nature of all living things," it is life itself and for Nietzsche this remains valid to the end. This will to power is not a metaphysical principle like Schopenhauer's will to existence or to life; it does not "appear" but instead is quite simply another way to articulate life, to designate life. Life is in this sense "that which must always overcome itself," a tension between the stronger and the weaker: the lesser submit to the greater "in order that they may take pleasure in and have power over the least"; even the greatest submit and "for the sake of power — wager life itself" {*Z* II "On Self-Overcoming"}. And even the will to truth — that which at the time of *Dawn* Nietzsche calls the "passion of knowing" — as "mirror and reflection" of the mind {*des Geistes*}, as the "will to make all existing things conceivable," which should "pay deference and submit" to the "greatest sages," is: will to power. Whatever "the people believe to be good and evil" reveals the "ancient will to power" of the creators of values {*Z* II "On Self-Overcoming"}.

The title "The Will to Power" appears for the first time in Nietzsche's manuscripts from late summer 1885, preparations for which were seemingly made in a series of notes from spring of the same year. One finds, of course, the theme of the will to power in earlier manuscripts (from 1882); in the same way it is one theme among others in the manuscripts of 1885 already mentioned. The historical sense, knowledge as falsification to make life possible, the critique of modern moral tartuffery, the philosopher as lawgiver and experimenter in new possibilities, so-called grand politics and the characterization of the "good European": all these themes and others are elaborated in the notebooks of this period. In this case as well, Nietzsche's unpublished writings reveal themselves for what they essentially are: a supremely complex intellectual diary in which were recorded all the attempted theoretical elaborations of intuitions and concepts, notes on Nietzsche's readings (often in the form of excerpts), letter drafts, plans and titles for projected works.

In a notebook of summer/autumn 1884, immediately before the composition of *Z* IV, the following title is found:

> *Philosophy of Eternal Recurrence.*
> Attempt at the Revaluation of All Values.
> (*CW* 15, 26[259])

The preface to a "*Philosophy of Eternal Recurrence*," under the title "*The New Order of Rank*" {*CW* 15, 26[243]}, or alternatively

"*On the Order of Rank of Intellect {des Geistes}*" {*CW* 15, 26[258]},
is sketched "in opposition to the morality of equality" {*CW* 15,
26[243]}. Nietzsche speaks here of the "order of rank of those
who create values (with regard to the setting of values)" —
who are: artists, philosophers, lawgivers, founders of religions,
"superior humans" (as "rulers of the earth" and "creators of the
future" who finally "destroy" themselves). All are conceived as
having "lost out" (unmistakably prefiguring the leitmotiv of *Z*
IV). This preface culminates in a description of "Dionysian
wisdom":

> The supreme power, *to feel* as necessary (*worthy of eternal
> repetition*), everything that is imperfect, everything that
> suffers, and this out of an excess of creative power, which
> must founder again and again and which chooses the most
> audacious, most difficult paths (principle of the greatest
> possible stupidity, God as devil and symbol of arrogance)
>
>   Humans up to now as *embryos*, into which all configuring
> powers *penetrate* — basis of humans' profound *restlessness* {. . .}
> (*CW* 15, 26[243])

A few pages later, Nietzsche develops a set of problems having to
do with the will to power: the will to power in the functions of
the organic, in its relation to pleasure and displeasure, in so-called
altruism (motherly love and sexual love) {*CW* 15, 26[273]}, as present even in inorganic matter {*CW* 15, 26[274]}. There follows the
sketch for the authentic philosophy of eternal recurrence, where
the doctrines of "eternal recurrence of the same," "revaluation of
all values," and "will to power" follow one after another. The
thought of eternal recurrence is the "weightiest thought": for it to
be borne, there must be a "revaluation of all values"; but of what
does this consist? That we no longer take pleasure in certainty
but rather in uncertainty, that we no longer see "cause and
effect" but rather that which is "continuously creative," that
the "will to power" replaces the will to survive, that we no longer modestly say: "everything is *merely* subjective," but rather
"'this is *our* work, too!', let's be proud of it!" {*CW* 15, 26[284]}.

The preface to a "Philosophy of Eternal Recurrence" is found again beneath various headings (the most important are "*The New Enlightenment*" {*CW* 15, 26[293] (underlined once) and [298] (underlined twice)}, and "**Beyond Good and Evil**" (*CW* 15, 26[325]), until it becomes itself a subtitle with a new main title: "**Noon and Eternity.** / *A Philosophy of Eternal Recurrence*" (*CW* 15, 26[465]). For a long while, there is no further mention of "Revaluation of All Values" in Nietzsche's projected book titles. "New Enlightenment" and "Beyond Good and Evil" soon afterwards become central parts of a new plan titled "*Eternal Recurrence.* / A Prophecy" {*CW* 15, 27[80]; cf. also 27[58]}. At the end of this plan stands the culminating piece vis-à-vis the recurrence, {where it is described as a "*hammer* in the hands of the most *powerful* human beings."}[2]

The completion of *Zarathustra* by the publication of *Z* IV (in early 1885) at Nietzsche's own expense was an event that took place wholly outside of the public eye. Only forty copies of this last part were printed, a small number of which were sent to close friends and acquaintances; it was becoming ever quieter around Nietzsche. Since 1884, he had been embroiled in a protracted battle with Ernst Schmeitzner over his books and a portion of his scanty royalties. That autumn he still nurtured plans of having a public presence as a writer. The years 1885 and 1886 were marked by repeated attempts to find a publisher prepared to buy the stock of his earlier works that Schmeitzner still possessed as well as to publish his new writings. Not until the summer of 1886 was the solution found: Ernst Wilhelm Fritsch, his very first publisher, purchased the earlier works from Schmeitzner, from *The Birth of Tragedy* through the third part of *Thus Spoke Zarathustra*, and Nietzsche decided to publish, at his own expense, his new works with Leipzig printer Constantin Georg Naumann. How these publication problems weighed on Nietzsche should not be forgotten when assessing his plans,

2. {Montinari mistakenly cites the title "The Hammer and the Great Noon" from 27[82].}

but neither should they be exaggerated. Nietzsche's broadly conceived attempt at reworking *Human, All Too Human*, undertaken in spring and summer 1885, should be understood from the perspective of his return to a public presence. The same motivation is evident in slightly earlier drafts, now continued in parallel, in which Nietzsche addresses himself to the Germans, or alternatively, the "good Europeans." We should not overlook the continued plans for a new Zarathustra work (mostly under the title "**Noon and Eternity**" *CW* 16, 34[145]). Apart from evident revisions to the aphorisms in *Human, All Too Human*, the bulk of Nietzsche's notes are nevertheless not amenable to being apportioned among and subsumed within these respective plans. In the course of his reflections, Nietzsche arrives at certain titles and drafts that are, in each case, equally justified from an alternative literary (as well as philosophical) standpoint. The plans alternate with each other, replace one another, and in each case illuminate the totality of the notes from a particular Nietzschean view. The homogeneity of Nietzsche's venture — though not systematic in a traditional sense — throws light on the entirety of the unpublished writings, which thus for this reason alone should be published only in their actual, unsystematic form.

When the fragments are read sequentially in their apparent chaos, as Nietzsche put them down, they give illuminating insights into the movement of his thought, into his "labyrinthine circling" (E{ckhard} Heftrich[3]). The notes from this time are undergirded by the thought of "eternal recurrence," while the frequency of plans for *Zarathustra* (none of them realized) points to the centrality of that thought, which Zarathustra had already proclaimed (in *Z* III, early 1884). We read in a notebook from the summer of 1885: "Zarathustra can only *succeed* after the order of rank has been established. At first this will be

3. {Eckhard Heftrich, *Nietzsches Philosophie: Identität Von Welt und Nichts* ("Nietzsche's philosophy: Identity of world and nothingness") (Frankfurt am Main: Klostermann, 1962).}

taught" (*CW* 16, 35[73], 107). Accordingly, the thought of the eternal recurrence can only succeed once the order of rank has been established; this sheds light on why the "Philosophy of Eternal Recurrence," the previously discussed draft of summer 1884, is introduced as an attempt at a revaluation of all values through a preface on the new order of rank, the order of rank of spirit {*die Rangordnung des Geistes*}. What's more, among notes for the revision of *Human, All Too Human* we find the phrase "Philosophy of Dionysus" as a further cipher for eternal recurrence. Nietzsche's attempt to write a book for free spirits failed: numerous aphorisms later found in *Beyond Good and Evil* emerged from that summer's diligent work, particularly those where the tempter-god Dionysus speaks. (And for that matter, it is from the same material that aphorism 1067 is drawn in the compilation by Elisabeth Förster-Nietzsche and Heinrich Köselitz {cf. *CW* 16, 38[12], 168–69}.) Nonetheless, it was not from the perspective of a revaluation of all values and eternal recurrence that we encounter the draft where "The Will to Power" first appears as a title for a work planned by Nietzsche. This title, in a notebook dated August 1885, reads:

The Will to Power.

Attempt
at a New Interpretation
of All Events.

By
Friedrich Nietzsche. (*CW* 16, 39[1], 176)

This deals with a shift in accent; in the notes that follow, Nietzsche traces nourishment, procreation, adaptation, inheritance, and division of labor back to the will to power {cf. *CW* 16, 19[12], 179}. The will to truth is a form of the will to power, as are the will to justice, the will to beauty, the will to help {cf. *CW* 16, 19[13], 181}. This draft has a preface and an introduction. In the preface, a new interpretation is sketched out:

How naïvely we carry our moral valuations into things, e.g., when we speak of *laws of nature*! It might be useful once to conduct an experiment of a *completely different* manner of interpretation: so that through an embittered contradiction we come to understand how very unconsciously *our moral canon* (preference for truth, law, rationality etc.) *reigns* in our *entire so-c⟨alled⟩ science.*

Put popularly: God has been refuted, but not the devil: and all divine functions are also part of his nature: the opposite did not work! (*CW* 16, 39[14], 181–82)

And the introduction anticipates the whole complex of problems that Nietzsche later referred to as nihilism:

The great danger is not pessimism (a form of hedonism), the calculating of pleasure and pain, and whether perhaps human life includes an excess of painful feelings. Instead, the *meaninglessness* of all events! The moral interpretation has become invalid at the same time as the religious interpretation: this they do not know of course, the superficial! The more impious they are, the more instinctively they cling with their teeth to moral valuations. Schopenhauer as atheist uttered a curse upon anyone who divests the world of its moral significance. In England they strive to associate morality with physics, Mister von Hartmann morality and the irrationality of existence. But the actual great fear is: *the world no longer has a meaning*

To what extent the previous morality has also fallen away with "God": they mutually supported one another.

Now I bring a new interpretation, an "immoral" one, in relation to which our previous morality appears as a special case. Put popularly: God has been refuted, but not the devil. — (*CW* 16, 39[15], 182; neither 39[14] or [15] was included in the compilation!)

In the following notebook, we find a proposal where the motif of meaninglessness is indeed addressed; it has a systematic, very general character of a type never adopted by Nietzsche in his books:

The Will to Power.
Attempt at a New Interpretation of all Events.
(Preface on the threatening "meaninglessness."
Problem of pessimism.)
Logic.
Physics.
Morality.
Art.
Politics. (*CW* 16, 40[2], 185)

Noteworthy is the deliberate opposition to Schopenhauer's pessimistic metaphysics, present already in the passage quoted above from *Zarathustra* as Nietzsche juxtaposes the will to power and the will to life. Now it is a question of interpretation, which according to Nietzsche is not explanation. The dispute with Gustav Teichmüller (*Die wirkliche und die scheinbare Welt* {"The real and the apparent world"}, 1882) and Afrikan Spir (*Denken und Wirklichkeit* {"Thought and reality"}, 1877) is a component part of Nietzsche's epistemological meditations, which all point to contempt for the so-called world of appearance as the root of pessimism. "[T]he world of thought only a second degree of the world of appearance —" (*CW* 16, 1[36], 269), Nietzsche noted again in an identically formulated draft for the will to power as "new interpretation of all events," taking up his own stance against the word "appearance":

against the word "*appearances.*"[4]

NB. *Appearance* as I understand it is the actual and single reality of things — that which first merits all existing predicates and which relatively speaking is best described with all, therefore even the most opposing predicates. But with this word nothing more can be expressed than its *inaccessibility* for logical procedures and distinctions: therefore "appearance" as

4. {Montinari includes this line, which subsequent revision of the *KGW* has revealed to belong at the conclusion of the preceding fragment 40[52]. Fragment 40[53] begins with "NB."}

opposed to "logical truth" — but which itself is only possible in an imaginary world. Thus I do not posit "appearance" in opposition to "reality" but conversely take appearance as the reality that resists transformation into an imaginary "truth-world." A specific name for this reality would be "the will to power," namely described from the inside and not from the standpoint of its incomprehensible fluid protean nature. (*CW* 16, 40[53], 208; not included in the compilation!)

For a time, the title "The Will to Power" as a new interpretation of all events stands with equal merit alongside other titles, of which the most important remains "Noon and Eternity" (as *Zarathustra*-work). Nor is there at this time any lack of drafts for a prelude to a philosophy of the future (summer 1885–summer 1886). The most common title is "Beyond Good and Evil," for which Nietzsche completed the printer's manuscript in the winter of 1885/86. "Beyond Good and Evil" was conceived as a plan running parallel to other works ("The Will to Power" and "Noon and Eternity"). In an important manuscript that contains what is for the most part a second draft of *Beyond Good and Evil* is a plan with the heading: "**The titles of 10 new books**" dated "Spring 1886": these ten are: 1. "*Thoughts concerning the Ancient Greeks.*"; 2. "*The Will to Power.* Attempt at a New World-Interpretation."; 3. "*The Artists.* Ulterior Motives of a Psychologist"; 4. "*We Godless Ones*"; 5. "*Noon and Eternity.*"; 6. "*Beyond Good and Evil.* Prelude to a Philosophy of the Future."; 7. "*Gai Saber.* Songs of Prince Vogelfrei."; 8. "*Music.*"; 9. "*Experiences of a Literary Scribe.*"; 10. "*On the History of Modern Dimming.*" (*CW* 16, 2[73], 337–38). For each of these titles there is a specific set of notes in the manuscripts, and each of these titles sets earlier notes in a specific light. Furthermore, the titles themselves provide the starting point for further elaborations. Indeed, one title even alludes to an already completed printer's manuscript (*Beyond Good and Evil*), while the later "Songs of Prince Vogelfrei" were drafted in 1884 (in part since 1882). Whoever castigates Nietzsche, as Podach did in 1963 after an examination of the notebooks, for not having stayed true to plan but having "wasted his efforts in a struggle with a systematic magnum opus"[5] loses any insight as to the real significance of Nietzsche's drafts, proposals, plans, and titles. One must regard these as entirely provisional, not as a binding summary of material at hand or overviews of further projects, especially as they themselves are mostly fragments that clarify a specific declaration by Nietzsche and are ultimately only intelligible within the overall growing mass of the notes. Furthermore, a struggle with a magnum opus never took place: taken as a whole, Nietzsche's unpublished writings portray an experiment broken off by illness. To declare for this reason that Nietzsche's life's work remained unfinished borders on naïveté.

A few weeks later — by which time *Beyond Good and Evil* had appeared — Nietzsche composed a new draft dated "Sils-Maria, Summer 1886":

The Will to Power.
Attempt
at a Revaluation of All Values.

In four Books.

First Book:	the danger of dangers (description of nihilism) (as the *necessary consequence of previous valuations*)
Second Book:	critique of values (of logic etc.
Third Book:	the problem of the lawgiver (including the history of solitude) *How* must human beings be constituted who make inverse valuations? — Human beings who have *all* the properties of the modern soul but are strong enough to transform them into sheer health.

5. {Cf. Erich Podach, *Ein Blick in Notizbücher Nietzsches* ("A look into Nietzsche's notebooks") (Heidelberg: Rothe, 1963), 84.}

Fourth Book: the hammer
                their means to their task. — (*CW* 16,
                2[100], 350)

Nihilism, critique of values, revaluation of values in the sense of the will to power, eternal recurrence:[6] Nietzsche varies these four elements in numerous later versions. Once again, we find motifs with which we are familiar from earlier notes. (Nietzsche also refers back to the subtitle "Philosophy of the Eternal Recurrence" from the year 1884.)[7] To be sure, they are now clarified by the division of the work into four books, which in turn determines the direction of the reflections that follow.

From the time of this draft onwards, one is justified in speaking of a work planned in four books that Nietzsche wanted to publish under the title "The Will to Power: Attempt at a Revaluation of All Values." He announces it on the back of the dust jacket of *Beyond Good and Evil* (summer 1886), and a year later he hints at it in the text of *On the Genealogy of Morality* (summer 1887).[8] *Beyond Good and Evil* cannot be separated in any way (as the compilers of *The Will to Power* claimed) from "The Will to Power," but it is no more than a collection of everything that Nietzsche considered worth making public from the material of the *Zarathustra* period (1881–85) and the subsequent attempt at a revising of *Human, All Too Human* as a prelude to a philosophy of the future. This prelude was prepared for print in winter 1885/86. The prefaces and various supplements to the new editions of *The Birth of Tragedy, Human, All Too Human, Dawn,* and *The Joyful Science* (written between summer 1886 and spring 1887) also originate from notes Nietzsche had written specifically for these new editions. They likewise cannot be separated from a collection of notes ostensibly designated for "The Will to Power." Naturally, interrelationships between this material and the draft for "The Will to Power" can be found; yet one must

6. {Cf. *CW* 15, 27[80], where Nietzsche explicitly links "the hammer" with "eternal recurrence."}

7. {Cf. *CW* 15, 26[259].}

8. {See *GM* III, 27; *CW* 8, 346.}

know how to distinguish the specific aspects of literary intention, as we have seen in the draft of summer 1886, from all previous notes or parallel expositions of other kinds. What Nietzsche did not wish to forget of his earlier material he made note of in a rubric with fifty-three numbers that he set up in spring 1887 {cf. CW 17, 5[50]}. This rubric is neither plan nor draft but merely a list of possibly usable notes. Quite remarkable is the fact that the famous final aphorism of the Köselitz–Förster-Nietzsche compilation (no. 1067) did *not* appear in the rubric. If Nietzsche's literary intentions are deemed to have any value at all, we are bound to conclude that this aphorism had, in Nietzsche's view, fulfilled its purpose when he published a different version of it in *Beyond Good and Evil* (aph. 36). It goes without saying that it keeps its philosophical value within the unpublished writings, but it did not belong among the notes that Nietzsche wished to save in spring 1887.

Another plan for "The Will to Power" is found from this period, this time with a section cut away at the top border, so that its relevance to "The Will to Power," though highly likely, remains speculative:

[+++] *of all Values*

First Book.
European Nihilism.

Second Book.
Critique of the Highest Values.

Third Book.
Principle of a New Determination of Value.

Fourth Book.
Breed and Breeding.[9]

drafted 17 March 1887, Nice.
(*CW* 17, 7[64])

9. {*Zucht* and *Züchtung* can be translated in several different ways, here as "Breed and Breeding," in *CW* 16 by Adrian Del Caro as "Discipline and Cultivation."}

This plan is important insofar as Förster-Nietzsche and Köselitz reckoned it to be the most suitable for their shoddy compilation. It hardly differs from the plan for summer 1886. Here as well are nihilism, critique of values, revaluation of values, and eternal recurrence (as hammer and thus as a principle of breed and breeding, as we know from the plan of summer 1886) as four motifs for the four books.

Following the work on the new editions of his earlier writings, Nietzsche dedicated himself with particular intensity to a central problem from his drafts of summer 1886 and spring 1887: the problem of nihilism. These meditations culminated in an impressive fragment titled "*European Nihilism*," dated "Lenzer Heide, the 10th of June, 1887," a short essay of sixteen sections (*CW* 17, 5[71]). The text was incomprehensibly dismembered in Förster-Nietzsche and Köselitz's canonical compilation (whereas in the first *Will to Power* of 1901 it was published as an integral whole). Only the readers of the critical apparatus written by Otto Weiss for vol. XVI of the *Großoktav-Ausgabe* (1911) came to learn that the so-called aphorisms 4, 5, 114, and 55 (read in this order) constituted an organic essay.

After publication of *On the Genealogy of Morality*, Nietzsche concentrated his efforts in autumn 1887 on "The Will to Power." This work peaked around the middle of February 1888 in a categorization of 372 notes he had until then written in two quarto and one folio notebooks. For this categorization Nietzsche used a further notebook in which he entered a key word or short phrase for all 372 fragments (actually 374, since the same number {46 and 71} was used on two occasions). The first three hundred key words and phrases were divided into four books, Nietzsche having written beside each entry the Roman numeral I, II, III, or IV in pencil.[10] These numerals refer to an untitled plan found in the notebook containing the categorization.[11] The plan is divided into four books, but the titles of the four books are also lacking:

10. {See *CW* 18, 12[1].}
11. {*CW* 18, 12[2].}

⟨for the first book⟩[12]

1. *Nihilism, completely thought through to the end.*
2. *Culture, civilization*, the ambiguity of what is "modern."

⟨for the second book⟩

3. *The Origin {Herkunft} of Ideals.*
4. *Critique of Christian Ideals.*
5. *How Virtue becomes Victorious.*
6. *The Herd Instinct.*

⟨for the third book⟩

7. *The "Will to Truth."*
8. *Morality as Circe for Philosophers*
9. *Psychology of the "Will to Power"* (pleasure, will, concept etc.

⟨for the fourth book⟩

10. *The "Eternal Recurrence"*
11. *Grand Politics.*
12. *Our Life Recipes.*

(*CW* 18, 12[2])

Again, the primary motifs — nihilism, critique of values, revaluation of values, and eternal recurrence — are retained. The four books are divided into chapters, each of which offers a particular modulation of the primary motifs.

A closer inspection of the indexed and partially categorized fragments provides valuable insight into the editorial practice employed by Förster-Nietzsche and Köselitz in their compilation. The four books of the plan according to which Nietzsche catalogued the fragments correspond exactly to the four books of the plan of 17 March 1887 {*CW* 17, 7[64]} chosen by the editors of the compilation. One might have expected that Nietzsche's instructions would have been followed — at least in this specific instance in which he left explicit instructions. To the contrary, Köselitz fancied himself at times a better philosopher and writer

---

12. {This is not how note 12[2] appears on the page of Nietzsche's notebook; Montinari has rearranged the order to follow Nietzsche's directions for the four books.}

than Nietzsche, and Nietzsche's sister had gone so far as to have taken lessons in philosophy from Rudolf Steiner. {Here is what we find:}

1. Of the 374 fragments Nietzsche had numbered prospectively for use in "The Will to Power," 104 were not included in the compilation; of those, 84 were never published in any form, and 20 were banished to vols. XIII and XIV as well as to Otto Weiss's annotations in vol. XVI of the *Großoktav-Ausgabe*. Yet Frau Förster-Nietzsche wrote in her foreword to vol. XIII of the *Großoktav-Ausgabe*: "Vols. XIII and XIV contain the unpublished writings . . . with the exception of anything the author himself expressly designated for the Will to Power."

2. Of the remaining 270 fragments, 137 are incomplete or have arbitrary alterations to the text (omission of titles, often of whole sentences, dismemberment of texts that belong together, etc.) Of these 137, one should note that:

   (a) 49 are corrected by Otto Weiss in the annotations of vol. XVI; the ordinary user of *The Will to Power*, that is, for example, the reader of later editions published by Kröner (edited by Alfred Bäumler), would never learn of these corrections;

   (b) 36 of the corrections found in Weiss's annotations are flawed, in part as Weiss makes inaccurate statements about the text, often erring when deciphering passages that had been omitted;

   (c) last, 52 fragments lack any annotation, although they contain mistakes like those in other fragments where Otto Weiss thought a note necessary.

3. Nietzsche himself divided the first 300 fragments between the four books of his plan. In at least 64 instances, Förster-Nietzsche and Köselitz did not bother to abide by this division.

Nietzsche was by no means happy with the results of his work. "I have finished the first draft of my 'Attempt at a Revaluation':

all in all, it was torture, and beyond that, I absolutely do not yet have the courage for it. In ten years I'll want to do it better" (N to Heinrich Köselitz, 13 February 1888 {KGB III:5, 252}). And thirteen days later: "And you must not believe that I just wrote more 'literature': I wrote this down for *myself*; every winter from now on I want to draft, *for myself,* one piece after another like this — the thought of 'making this public' is wholly out of the question" {KGB III:5, 264}. In the same letter, Nietzsche gave an account of his reading of Baudelaire's *Œuvres posthumes*, which had recently been published. And we do in fact find in this folio notebook, immediately after the last numbered fragment (372) {CW 18, 11[138]}, twenty pages of excerpts from Baudelaire[13] — now and then interrupted by his own meditations — followed by other wide-ranging excerpts from Tolstoy's *Ma religion*; the Goncourt Brothers' *Journal* (vol. I); Benjamin Constant's introduction to his own translation of Schiller's *Wallenstein*; Dostoevsky's *The Possessed* (in French translation); Julius Wellhausen's *Prolegomena zur Geschichte des Volkes Israel*;[14] and Renan's *Vie de Jésus* {The Life of Jesus}. Traces of these readings, important but partially hidden, can be identified in Nietzsche's writings of the year 1888. While Nietzsche, until that point, had mainly pursued his encounter with nihilism, especially with Christianity, on a historical and psychological basis, at the outset of the immediately following folio notebook {CW 18, 14 = W II 5}, whose first note is dated "Nice, 25 March 1888,"[15] a metaphysical aspect steps into the foreground and indeed — significantly — in the form of a wide-ranging, albeit fragmentary, essay on

13. {The excerpts from Baudelaire begin with CW 18, 11[160] and run nearly continuously through 11[234]. For full annotation of these and the following excerpts, see the associated notes in CW 18.}

14. {The title of Wellhausen's book is actually *Prolegomena zur Geschichte Israels*, translated into English by J. Sutherland Black and Allan Menzies as *Prolegomena to the History of Israel* (Edinburgh: Adam and Charles Black, 1885).}

15. {Montinari mistakenly writes: 26 March.}

art and truth in *The Birth of Tragedy*.[16] This essay was mangled in the compilation; nonetheless, within it the important problem of the "true" and the "apparent" world is taken up once again, becoming in the notes that follow a focal point for "The Will to Power." Belief in a true world, counterpoised against an apparent world, is, according to Nietzsche, what characterizes the nexus of phenomena that he successively designates with the names pessimism, nihilism, and from this juncture onwards, *décadence* as well. In fact, we find the key phrase "The True and the Apparent World" as the first chapter title in the plan for "The Will to Power," Nietzsche having classified most of the notes in this important folio according to the chapter titles {in *CW* 18, 14[169]}.[17] At this point, the plans take on a rather different shape than those previously mentioned.

It is noteworthy that hardly any other kinds of draft titles than those for the "The Will to Power" appear in the manuscripts from autumn 1887 to summer 1888. This further shows that during this period, Nietzsche dedicated himself to "The Will to Power" more intensively than he had done before (apart from the time spent writing *The Case of Wagner*, begun in spring 1888). Some plans do show certain compositional variations, with Nietzsche appearing to prefer the use of eight to twelve chapters rather than a division into four books. Particularly important is the following plan in eleven chapters:

1. The True and the Apparent World.
2. The Philosopher as Type of *décadence*.
3. The Religious Human as Type of *décadence*.

16. {While *The Birth of Tragedy* is not mentioned by name in the fragment *CW* 18, 14[1], Nietzsche makes the connection between art and tragedy later in the same folio; see 14[14, 35, 47, 117, 119, 169]. With respect to Montinari's claim that 14[1] opens an "essay on art and truth in *The Birth of Tragedy*," cf. Montinari's note to *CW* 18, 14[14]: "With this fragment Nietzsche begins a series of observations on *BT* which culminate in the second draft found at *CW* 18, 17[3]."}

17. {The folio Montinari refers to is W II 5 (in which *CW* 18, 14[169] is found). See his discussion in the following paragraph.}

4. The Good Human as Type of *décadence*.
5. The Countermovement: *Art*.
   Problem of the Tragic.
6. Heathenism in Religion.
7. Science versus Philosophy.
8. *Politica*.
9. Critique of the Present.
10. Nihilism and its Counterpart: What Will Recur {*die Wiederkünftigen*}.
11. The Will to Power. (*CW* 18, 14[169])[18]

It was according to these chapter headings that Nietzsche classified the notes found in the wide-ranging folio mentioned above, beginning with the date 25 March 1888. Working within this plan, and in terms commensurate with the content of the preceding notes, Nietzsche illustrates the relationship between belief in a "true" world and *décadence* as well as the countermovement, that is, the movement away from that belief. Apropos of this, Nietzsche furnishes the fragmentary essay mentioned above on *The Birth of Tragedy* with the heading "The Countermovement: *Art*" for chapter 5 in this plan and another similar one.[19] Nietzsche's attempt to make these fragments fit the plan is just as important as the attempt of February 1888; it is also just as fragmentary, since it is limited to the notes of one, albeit very wide-ranging, notebook, and it was likewise abandoned at a later stage. (It goes without saying that the editors of the compilation ignored Nietzsche's attempt.) In Turin, Nietzsche used two more large folio books.[20]

18. {Cf. *CW* 18, 16[51], where N divides this final chapter title into two discrete titles: "11. The Will to Power as Life: Highpoint of Historical *Self-Consciousness* (the latter conditions the *sick* form of the modern world . . .) / 12. The Will to Power: as Discipline."

19. {*CW* 18, 16[51]. See Montinari's note to 16[51]: "*CW* 18, 14 = W II 5 is, in part, categorized according to this plan." Cf. also 14[14, 169].}

20. {Nietzsche was in Turin from April 5 to June 5, 1888. The notebooks under discussion are *CW* 18, 15 = W II 6a and *CW* 18, 16 = W II 7a. See the Chronicle of Nietzsche's Life in *CW* 19, and *Nachbericht, Beschreibung der Manuskripte, KGW* IX 9, 48, 54.}

By this time, his notes had become indecipherable through countless additions and corrections. At times Nietzsche wrote them down on lined loose sheets. Some constituted short, self-contained essays, or else Nietzsche simply transcribed notes into a second draft without any particular organization. This activity took place in Turin during the last weeks of spring 1888. Nietzsche brought the notes with him to Sils-Maria, where his first task was to prepare *The Case of Wagner* for print.[21]

Meanwhile, Nietzsche had made a second draft of a section of his philosophical notes. Unsatisfied with the result, he wrote to Meta von Salis on 22 August 1888 {*KGB* III:5, 397}: "Compared to last summer . . . *this* summer has been a 'complete flop.' I am really sorry about that: the stay this spring {in Nice} did me good for once and I brought *more* energy up here {to Sils} than last year. And everything was ready for a *great* and *highly specific* task." Nietzsche had requested from von Salis a copy of his *On the Genealogy of Morality* (at the same time making mention of this work, in particular, in his epilogue to *The Case of Wagner*): the renewed reading of his own work was not without consequences. He wrote in the same letter: "I was met with surprise at the first glance: I discovered a long *foreword* to the "Genealogy" that I had *forgotten* even existed . . . Basically, I only remembered the titles of the three essays: the rest, i.e., the *content*, escaped me. This was the result of extreme mental exertion that took up the winter and spring and that had, as it were, placed a *barrier* in between. Now the book is alive to me — and so too the conditions of last summer out of which it arose. Extremely difficult problems for which there was no language or terminology: but I must have been in a state of almost uninterrupted inspiration at that time for the writing to flow like the most natural thing in the world. There is no trace of effort in it — The style is vigorous and vibrant, yet full of subtleties; and pliant and colorful too, prose written in a way I had never really managed before." This

21. {Nietzsche was in Sils-Maria from June 6 to September 20, 1888. See Chronicle of Nietzsche's Life in *CW* 19.}

straightforward assessment perfectly reflects the last stage of Nietzsche's work; however, its full importance emerges if one compares the date of the letter — 22 August — with two other dates: that of the last plan for "The Will to Power" {26 August 1888} and that of a plan for a foreword to a new book: "*The Revaluation of All Values*" {3 September 1888}.

Concerning the last plan for "The Will to Power," Erich Podach (in *Friedrich Nietzsches Werke des Zusammenbruchs* {"The works of Friedrich Nietzsche's collapse"}, 196{1}, p. 63) gave only the date, but not the plan itself; Otto Weiss (*Le* XIV, p. 432) published the plan without the date. Podach later published the plan in his *Ein Blick in Notizbücher Nietzsches* {"A look into Nietzsche's notebooks"}, 1963, pp. 149–60), but without connecting it with its date. This occurred because the plan itself and the date are on different sheets; nevertheless, there can be no doubt that the two sheets belong together (the paper, format, ink, and handwriting are identical on both sheets; the edges of both sheets show they were stored together for a long period). The plan runs:

Draft of
plan for:
the Will to Power.
Attempt
at a Revaluation of All Values

— Sils-Maria
on the last Sunday of the
month of August 1888

We Hyperboreans. — *Laying the Foundation Stone of the Problem.*

First Book: *"what is Truth?"*
First Chapter. Psychology of Error.
Second Chapter. Value of Truth and Error.
Third Chapter. The Will to Truth (first justified in the Yes-value of life

Second Book: *Origin {Herkunft} of Values*
First Chapter. The Metaphysicians.
Second Chapter. The *homines religiosi.*[22]
Third Chapter. The Good and the Improvers.

Third Book: *Struggle of Values*
First Chapter. Thoughts about Christianity.
Second Chapter. The Physiology of Art.
Third Chapter. On the History of European Nihilism.

Psychologist's Diversion.

Fourth Book: *The Great Noon.*
First Chapter. The Principle of Life "Order of Rank."
Second Chapter. The Two Paths.
Third Chapter. The Eternal Recurrence.

(*CW* 18, 18[17])

The problem of truth has gradually developed as the theme of the first book. The second book remains reserved for a critique of values as in the earlier four-part plans, but in the sense of a history of the values themselves and of those who uphold them. In the third book, Nietzsche intends to deal with the struggle of values, and his chapter headings exactly correspond to the content of his notes on Christianity, the physiology of art, and the history of European nihilism. After an "Intermezzo" (probably containing maxims, of which Nietzsche had set down a large collection) comes the fourth book, dedicated to eternal recurrence, as in all the other plans.

The last plan for "The Will to Power" was written, as Nietzsche says, on "the last Sunday of the month of August 1888," that is, 26 August, four days after his complaint that the summer in Sils-Maria had been a "flop." Nietzsche fit a number of earlier notes to this plan, but he remained with the original approach. He repeated his complaint in a letter to his mother dated 30 August {*KGB* III:5, 406}: "I am once again fully engaged — I hope it

22. *homines religiosi]* "religious humans" {Cf. *JS* 350, 358; *BGE* 45, 59.}

will last a while, as work on a project, well- and long-prepared
for and scheduled for completion this summer, was literally 'a
flop.'" Yet these lines express a hope for eventual success. In
fact, the completion of the "well- and long-"prepared for project
took on a completely different form than had been sketched out
in all the earlier plans. From the middle of August, Nietzsche
had begun again to transcribe his notes, a portion of which
were already in second draft, as self-contained, finished pieces,
always with a view to the planned "Will to Power." He then
decided to publish everything that was currently ready. A loose
sheet, on the front side bearing merely the title "Revaluation of
All Values," bears on the reverse a series of titles suggesting an
"abstract" of Nietzsche's philosophy:

Thoughts for the Day after Tomorrow.
Abstract of My Philosophy

Wisdom for the Day after Tomorrow
My Philosophy
in Abstract.

Magnum in Parvo.[23]
A Philosophy
in Abstract.

(CW 18, 19[3])

These are the provisional titles for the planned abstract.
Even more important is the list of attendant chapters (all on
the same sheet):

1. *We Hyperboreans.*
2. *The Problem of Socrates.*
3. *Reason in Philosophy.*
4. *How the True World Finally Became a Fable.*
5. *Morality as Anti-nature.*

23. *Magnum in Parvo]* "Great in Little"

> 6. *The Four Great Errors.*
> 7. *For Us — Against Us.*
> 8. *Concept of a Décadence-Religion.*
> 9. *Buddhism and Christianity.*
> 10. *From My Aesthetics.*
> 11. *Among Artists and Writers.*
> 12. *Sayings and Arrows.*

(CW 18, 19[4])

Numbers 2, 3, 4, 5, 6, and 12 are now the titles of chapters of the same name, and 11 is the original title of the chapter "Forays of an Untimely One" in *Twilight of the Idols*; on the other hand, numbers 1, 7, 8, and 9 are the titles — crossed out — that can still be read in the printer's manuscript for *The Antichrist*, viz.: "We Hyperboreans" for the current sections 1–7; "For Us — Against Us" for sections 8–14; "Concept of a *Décadence*-Religion" for 15–19; "Buddhism and Christianity" for 20–23. Since Nietzsche dated as "beginning of September" a preliminary draft for his foreword to "A Psychologist at Leisure" (later = *Twilight of the Idols*), and since on 3 September he composed a foreword to the "Revaluation of All Values" according to the four-book plan, of which the first was to have been *The Antichrist*, we can conclude that in the days between 26 August and 3 September the following took place:

1. Nietzsche abandoned the until then planned "Will to Power."
2. He may have briefly considered publishing the material already in a second draft under the title "Revaluation of All Values."
3. He nonetheless chose instead to publish an "abstract" of his philosophy.
4. He gave this abstract the name "A Psychologist at Leisure" (later *Twilight of the Idols*).
5. Immediately thereafter he extracted from the "abstract" the chapters "We Hyperboreans," "For Us — Against Us," "Concept of a *Décadence*-Religion," and "Buddhism

and Christianity," which together yielded twenty-three[24] paragraphs on Christianity plus an introduction ("We Hyperboreans").

6. The magnum opus now and going forward had the title "Revaluation of All Values," which had originated as the subtitle of what had been to that point the projected "Will to Power." It was planned as four books; of these four the first, *The Antichrist*, was at least one-third complete (the twenty-three paragraphs mentioned immediately above).

7. On 3 September, Nietzsche wrote a foreword for the "Revaluation." The "A Psychologist at Leisure" was for him a synopsis of his "most essential philosophical heterodoxies," as he put it in letters (to Gast, 12 September {*KGB* III:5, 417}, and Overbeck, 14 September {*KGB* III:5, 434; Montinari mistakenly writes: 16 September}), and was the result of his last year's philosophizing, ripe for communication. It consisted purely of notes drafted with an eye toward "The Will to Power." The "Revaluation of All Values" in four books was nonetheless his new work project. A good half of its first book, *The Antichrist*, originates from previous meditations — such an origin {*Herkunft*} understood in the sole sense appropriate here, that of *literary* origin, a descent {*Herkunft*} from earlier notes, "preliminary drafts" — in fact the book had "detached" itself from the "abstract" of his philosophy that Nietzsche had already set down, and hence from the earlier material for "The Will to Power"; yet, in terms of its *literary* intention, it was a *new* departure: in *The Antichrist*, sections 1–7 play the role of a kind of introduction (just as the chapter "We Hyperboreans" had been the introduction to the "abstract"), while sections 8–23 represent a general treatise on Christianity that Nietzsche wanted to develop in an integrated fashion —

24. {In *KSA*, Montinari wrote "24"; in *Nietzsche Lesen*, he corrected this to "23."}

particularly with regard to style. With this, he had found the "form" for communicating his "magnum opus." And we believe that his fresh reading of *On the Genealogy of Morality*, the work whose style so closely resembles *The Antichrist*, aided him in this discovery.

Consequently, Nietzsche wrote to his friend Meta von Salis on 7 September 1888 {*KGB* III:5, 410}: "In the meantime I was very diligent — to the degree that I have reason to retract the sigh about the 'summer being a complete flop' in my last letter. Indeed, I have been *more* than successful, something I dared not expect . . . Admittedly the result has been that over the last few weeks my life has been somewhat chaotic. Multiple times I've been up at two in the morning, driven by my thoughts to write down what had just been going through my head. At that point I heard my landlord, Herr Durisch, carefully opening the door to slip out to hunt chamois {*Gemsenjagd*}. Who knows! perhaps I too was hunting chamois . . . The *third* of September was a most remarkable day. Early I wrote the foreword to my *Revaluation of All Values*, the most impressive[25] foreword that has perhaps ever been written.[26] Afterwards I went out — and behold! the most beautiful day I had ever seen in the Engadine — a luminosity of all colors, a blue of lake and sky, a purity of air, utterly incredible . . . " And he continues: "I am leaving for *Turin* on 15 September; regarding winter, because of the deep concentration I'll need, the attempt at Corsica is a bit risky . . . But who knows — Next year I'll make the decision to bring to press my *Revaluation of All Values*, the most independent book there is . . . *Not* without great trepidation! The first book is, for example, called the *Antichrist*."

We know of six versions of plans for the new literary project, that is, the "Revaluation of All Values" in four books. The titles of the books clarify Nietzsche's intentions (the numbers denote chronological order):

25. *most impressive]* {Montinari mistakenly wrote "most beautiful."}
26. {See *CW* 18, 19[1, 7]}

[1][27]

First Book.
The Antichrist. Attempt at a Critique of Christianity.

Second Book.
The Free Spirit. Critique of Philosophy as a Nihilistic
Movement.

Third Book.
The Immoralist. Critique of the Most Fateful Kind of
Ignorance, Morality.

Fourth Book.
Dionysus. Philosophy of Eternal Recurrence.
                              (*CW* 18, 19[8] {September 1888})

[2]

Book 1: *The Antichrist.*
Book 2: *The Misosoph.*[28]
Book 3: *The Immoralist.*
Book 4: *Dionysus.*[29]
                    (*CW* 18, 11[416] {November 1887–March 1888[30]})

[3]
The Antichrist. Attempt at a Critique of Christianity.
The Immoralist. Critique of the Most Fateful Kind of
                    Ignorance, Morality.
We Yes-sayers. Critique of Philosophy as a Nihilistic
                    Movement.

27. {In versions 1, 2, and 3, Nietzsche's fragment is preceded by "**Revaluation of All Values.**" followed by a blank line.}

28. *Misosoph]* "Hater of Wisdom"

29. {"Dionysus." is followed in the notebook by a blank line and then:
"*Revaluation of All Values.*"}

30. {Although notebook 11 (= W II 3) is dated "November 1887–March
1888," a note to fragment 11[416] in *CW* 18 indicates that this fragment was
"Inserted in late summer 1888," thereby preserving Montinari's chronology.}

Dionysus. Philosophy of Eternal Recurrence.
                    (*CW* 18, 22[14] {September–October 1888})

[4]
I.   The Redemption from *Christianity*: the Antichrist
II.   from *Morality*: the Immoralist
III.   from the "*Truth*": the Free Spirit.
IV.   from *Nihilism*:
                    (*CW* 18, 22[24] {September–October 1888})

[5]
IV. Dionysus
    The Lawgiver Type
                    (*CW* 18, 23[8] {October 1888})

[6]
            The Free Spirit
        Critique of Philosophy
        as Nihilistic Movement

            The Immoralist
        Critique of Morality
    as the Most Dangerous Kind of Ignorance

            Dionysus philosophos
                    (*CW* 18, 23[13] {October 1888})

Apparently, the last plan was written after the completion of *The Antichrist*. One notices a variation in the order of the second and third books: in the first, second, and sixth plans, the critique of philosophy comes in second position, that of morality in the third position; in the third and fourth plans, the critique of morality comes first, then the critique of philosophy. The overall conception remains the same: after the critique of Christianity, morality, and philosophy, Nietzsche intends to announce his own philosophy. This is the philosophy of Dionysus, the philosophy of the eternal recurrence of the same.

With respect to *content*, the "Revaluation of All Values" was in a certain sense the same as "The Will to Power," but for this very reason it was its *literary* negation. Or then again: from the notes for "The Will to Power," *Twilight of the Idols* and *The Antichrist* emerged; the rest is — *Nachlaß*.[31]

Translated by George H. Leiner

31. {A revised version of this essay appears as "Nietzsches Nachlaß von 1885 bis 1888 oder Textkritik und Wille zur Macht," in Mazzino Montinari, *Nietzsche Lesen* (Berlin: Walter de Gruyter, 1982), 92–119. English translation: "Nietzsche's Unpublished Writings from 1885 to 1888; or, Textual Criticism and the Will to Power," in *Reading Nietzsche*, trans. Greg Whitlock (Urbana: University of Illinois Press, 2003), 80–102.}

Notes

The following symbols are used throughout the text and notes:

[ ]	Deletion by Nietzsche
| |	Addition by Nietzsche
{ }	Addition by the translator
⟨ ⟩	Addition by the editors (Colli and Montinari)
— — —	Unfinished or incomplete sentence or thought
Italics	Underlined once by Nietzsche
Bold	Underlined twice or more by Nietzsche
NL	Books in Nietzsche's personal library

Variants and editions of Nietzsche's works are referred to by the following abbreviations:

CW	*The Complete Works of Friedrich Nietzsche*
KGB	*Briefwechsel: Kritische Gesamtausgabe*
KGW	*Werke: Kritische Gesamtausgabe*
KSA	*Werke: Kritische Studienausgabe*
Cp	Correction in the proofs
Le	Twenty-volume 1894 Leipzig edition of Nietzsche's works (*Großoktav-Ausgabe*)
Pd	Preliminary draft
Pm	Printer's manuscript (clean final copy of handwritten MS)

Pp	Page proofs
Sd	Second draft
Se	Subsequent emendation
Up	Uncorrected proofs
WP²	*The Will to Power* (= *Le* XV and XVI, 1911)

Titles of Nietzsche's works are referred to by the following abbreviations:

AC	*The Antichrist*
BGE	*Beyond Good and Evil*
BT	*The Birth of Tragedy*
D	*Dawn*
DD	*Dionysus Dithyrambs*
DS	*David Strauss the Confessor and the Writer*
EH	*Ecce Homo*
GM	*On the Genealogy of Morality*
HAH	*Human, All Too Human*
HL	*On the Utility and Liability of History for Life*
JS	*The Joyful Science*
MM	*Mixed Opinions and Maxims*
NCW	*Nietzsche Contra Wagner*
SE	*Schopenhauer as Educator*
TI	*Twilight of the Idols*
UO	*Unfashionable Observations*
WA	*The Case of Wagner*
WB	*Richard Wagner in Bayreuth*
WP	*The Will to Power*
WS	*The Wanderer and His Shadow*
Z	*Thus Spoke Zarathustra*

The editorial apparatus has been supplemented with information drawn from Andreas Urs Sommer's two-volume Commentary to Nietzsche's texts in *KSA* 6:

Kommentar zu Nietzsches *Der Fall Wagner, Götzen-Dämmerung*. In: Editions of the Heidelberger Akademie der Wissenschaften: *Historischer und kritischer Kommentar zu Friedrich Nietzsches Werken*. Bd. 6.1. Berlin/Boston: de Gruyter, 2012.

Kommentar zu Nietzsches *Der Antichrist, Ecce homo, Dionysos-Dithyramben, Nietzsche contra Wagner*. In: Editions of the Heidelberger Akademie der Wissenschaften: *Historischer und kritischer Kommentar zu Friedrich Nietzsches Werken*. Bd. 6.2. Berlin/Boston: de Gruyter, 2013.

References to Sommer's commentaries are cited as "Sommer," followed by volume and page numbers.

Citations from Schopenhauer's works use the following abbreviated titles and translations:

Parerga 1	*Parerga and Paralipomena: Short Philosophical Essays*. Volume 1. Translated and edited by Sabine Roehr and Christopher Janaway. Cambridge: Cambridge University Press, 2014.
Parerga 2	*Parerga and Paralipomena: Short Philosophical Essays*. Volume 2. Translated and edited by Adrian Del Caro and Christopher Janaway. Cambridge: Cambridge University Press, 2015.
World 1	*The World as Will and Representation*. Volume 1. Translated by Judith Norman, Alistair Welchman, and Christopher Janaway. Cambridge: Cambridge University Press, 2010.
World 2	*The World as Will and Representation*. Volume 2. Translated and edited by Judith Norman, Alistair Welchman, and Christopher Janaway. Cambridge: Cambridge University Press, 2017.

Editorial Note to Volume 9

The editorial apparatus from *KSA* 14 for *CW* 9 is extensive. In order to distinguish the Colli-Montinari editorial apparatus from Nietzsche's variants and letters and from the translators' and editors' notes, this volume follows the *KSA* convention of italicizing Colli's and Monti-nari's editors' notes.

The Case of Wagner

A major problem exercising N in spring 1888 was the problem of *décadence*, which he illustrated by means of this little Turin pamphlet dedicated to an exemplary case, *The Case of Wagner*. The relevant notes are in Notebooks W II 6 and W II 7; they reveal how *The Case of Wagner* emerged from surrounding problems but do not indicate that N took material from *The Will to Power* for *The Case of Wagner*. The work was conceived as a "Letter from Turin": the first notes (in W II 6) make that clear. A first version was the lengthy fragment in eight sections; this differs greatly from the final version and is therefore published as Fragment 15[6] in *CW* 18. A few insights on Wagner from earlier notebooks dating back to autumn 1887 are used as well.

On 20 April 1888, N wrote to Peter Gast {*KGB* III:5, 298}: "I am in a good mood, working from early till late — fingers busy with a little pamphlet on music . . ." On 26 June, from Sils-Maria, N sent the manuscript to his publisher C. G. Naumann in Leipzig {*KGB* III:5, 342–43}: "Here's something to print. If convenient for you, please press right ahead with this little matter at once. It is only a brochure, but its presentation should be as *aesthetic as possible*. It concerns questions of art: therefore, we mustn't compromise ourselves with our taste . . . so I strongly recommend that we have a try with German letters {Fraktur type}, just for once . . . I think I have remarked already that Germans are completely indifferent to questions of style and its beauty the minute they read Roman type. Their receptiveness to a style's aesthetic only emerges with *German* type. (Possibly because they are used to reading their classics in this type? — —) In sum, my *Roman* typeface has up till now done me a great deal of harm. Particularly with *Zarathustra* . . . " However, immediately after this, N dropped the experiment with "German letters" and by 28 June was writing {*KGB* III:5, 344}: "Taking everything into consideration, there is no point with *German* letters. I cannot disavow all of my preceding writings. With time one can compel others to one's own taste. And

I at least find the Roman letters incomparably nicer!" Between 28 June and 1 July, N fired off numerous additions that he wanted to have inserted into the Printer's Manuscript; as a result, the typesetter became confused and Naumann sent the whole Printer's Manuscript back to Sils-Maria. N undertook a new revision and wrote a new copy. To his publisher on 12 July {KGB III:5, 350}: " . . . I was glad you sent the ms back. I had written it when I was in such a state of weakness that even I found it unreadable. I have been ill for more than five weeks; a very unwelcome return of my old complaint; deep nervous exhaustion with continual migraine and vomiting. I shall not mention the *abominable* weather into which my evil star has cast me this time. As soon as my strength allows, I shall set about transcribing the whole of the manuscript as legibly as possible. I cannot possibly give you a more exact deadline . . . I examined the *samples of lettering* with interest. The one with the familiar type used in my earlier works, and now with a line around it, has my complete approval." And yet he wrote four days later, " . . . I am getting better: and here is the *proof*! —The manuscript I am sending you is completely *finished*: will you please begin work on it at once" (16 July 1888 {KGB III:5, 351}). On 17 July {KGB III:5, 355}, N announced the printing of *The Case of Wagner* to Peter Gast and asked him to help with the corrections. At the end of July he sent a telegram asking for the "Concluding Remark" back, and replaced this (to Naumann, 2 August 1888 {KGB III:5, 380}) with two "Postscripts" and finally an "Epilogue," dispatched to Naumann on 24 August {mentioned in a postcard to Gast, cf. KGB III:5, 398}. In mid-September, N received his first copy of the work, *The Case of Wagner: A Musicians' Problem*, Leipzig 1888, C. G. Naumann Press.

Neither of the Printer's Manuscripts has survived, nor have the proofs. One single page with two additions to the "Epilogue" is now to be found in the Basel University Library. This page was part of the literary remains of Paul Lauterbach, editor of Max Stirner's *Der Einzige und sein Eigenthum* {*The Ego and Its Own*}. (Lauterbach belonged to the circle of friends around Peter Gast and Gustav Naumann, the publisher's nephew; Gast had given the page to him as a gift in 1892.)

Foreword

1. *Turning . . . story!] Notes in W II 7, 70:* Saying farewell to Wagner — crippled with Wagnerism / dark, ambiguous, full of forebodings. *Cf. CW 18, 16[74] for references of a similar abbreviated nature on style.*

2. *I am . . . a décadent] Cf. EH "Why I Am So Wise" 2 (beginning). {décadent is here underlined by N.}*

3. *He must be . . . times] Cf. BGE 212.*

Letter from Turin of May 1888

MOTTO

1. *ridendo dicere severum]* "through what is laughable, say what is *somber*" *{severum is underlined by N.} Cf. Horace, Satires I, 1, 24: Quamquam ridentem dicere verum quid vetat? {*"What forbids telling the truth while laughing?"}

I

2. *Yesterday . . . weather.] W II 6, 38:* I shall cite those impressions that I experienced often enough in succession and could compare: the impression Bizet's masterpiece *Carmen* makes on me and that made by an opera by Wagner. I sit through the former with tranquil devotion, fleeing from the latter . . . *Cf. CW 18, 15[111]; variants to Postscript [pp. 32–33]. N first heard Bizet's Carmen in Genoa on 27 November 1881 (cf. his letter to Gast, 28 November 1881 {KGB III:1, 144}); he attended several more performances of this work, the last in spring 1888 in Turin, at the time he was writing The Case of Wagner; cf. e.g., his letter to Gast of 20 April 1888 on the performances at the Teatro Carignano {KGB III:5, 299}:* "Successo piramidale, tutto Torino carmenizzato!" {"Magnificent success, all Turin Carmenized!"}

3. *"unending melody"] Wagner's phrase.*

2

4. *Wagner . . . "redeemer."] Cf. N to Gast, 11 August 1888 {KGB III:5, 390}:* The "leitmotif" of my bad jokes about "Wagner as Redeemer" naturally refers to the inscription in the crest of the Munich Wagner Society: "Redemption to the Redeemer" . . . *cf.*

pp. 30–31 to the Postscript and the associated notes below {p. 461, notes 7–9}.

5. *limpidezza]* "limpidity" {Underlined by N.}

6. *I envy Bizet . . . satisfied for once!] Cf. CW 17, 10[36]; CW 18, 11[49].*

7. *Senta-sentimentality] Senta is the heroine of Wagner's The Flying Dutchman* {1843}.

8. *"What has . . . love you?"] Cf. Goethe, Wilhelm Meisters Lehrjahre, IV, 9; and Dichtung und Wahrheit, III, 14.* {Respectively, Goethe, *The Collected Works,* vol. 9: *Wilhelm Meister's Apprenticeship,* ed. and trans. Eric A. Blackall (Princeton, NJ: Princeton University Press, 1989), 139; and *The Collected Works,* vol. 4: *From My Life: Poetry and Truth: Parts 1–3,* trans. Robert R. Heitner (New York: Suhrkamp, 1987), 459. {Cf. Baruch Spinoza, *Ethics,* V, P19.}

9. *"L'amour" . . . généreux." (B. Constant.)]* "Love is of all the affections the most egoistic and, in consequence, when it is hurt, the least generous." {The quotation is from chapter 6 of Benjamin Constant's best-known work, the novel *Adolphe* (1816).}

3

10. *"Il faut . . . musique:"]* "Music must be Mediterraneanized:"

11. *(Beyond Good and Evil, p. 220).] Cf. the end of BGE 255.*

12. *Tannhäuser]* {Early opera by Wagner (1845).}

13. *Kundry]* {Character in *Parsifal,* Wagner's last opera (1882).}

14. *Mastersingers]* {Refers to Walther von Stolzing, the hero of Wagner's opera *The Mastersingers of Nuremberg* (1868).}

15. *Isolde]* {Female protagonist in Wagner's opera *Tristan and Isolde* (1865).}

16. *Ring]* {Wagner's *Der Ring des Nibelungen* (*The Ring of the Nibelung;* 1869–76) consists of four operas, I: *Das Rheingold* (*The Rhinegold*); II: *Die Walküre* (*The Valkyrie*), where Brünnhilde leads the Valkyries; III: *Siegfried,* where Siegfried and Brünnhilde fall in love; and IV: *Götterdämmerung* (*Twilight of the Gods*), where Valhalla collapses and even Wotan perishes.}

17. *I — guard . . . it . . .] W II 7, 107:* Not a riddle for your teeth. An *eternal* riddle! Even the Bayreuthers have not cracked it.

18. *Lohengrin]* {Eponymous hero of Wagner's opera *Lohengrin* (1850).}

19. *Tristan]* {Tragic hero of *Tristan and Isolde*.}

20. *"I cannot . . . out."]* Cf. *CW 4, 30[110] from summer 1878.*

21. *"wandering Jew"]* {N uses the standard German phrase *ewigen Juden* ("eternal Jew"), which has no resonance in English. In the following sentence, this Jew "stops wandering" (or as N writes, "stops being eternal").}

22. *Translated . . . to the woman.]* *This passage relates to Wagner's wife Cosima; cf. the notes in CW 18, 11[27, 28] dated Nice, 25 November 1887. Cosima plays an ambivalent role in the whole of the final period before N's collapse, as does Wagner himself; cf. EH "Why I Am So Wise" 3. A puzzling draft letter from N to Cosima should be mentioned at this point; it is contained in the notebook that also contains the last sketches for The Case of Wagner; there, N defends himself against a public attack on him made by "Wagner's widow" — though this cannot yet have taken place, the draft having been written in Sils-Maria around the middle of September 1888 {KGB III:5, 586–87}: Reply to a letter by Wagner's widow distinguished by its civility /* You do me the honor of publicly attacking me on account of my publication, *the first* to provide *revelations about Wagner* — You yourself make an attempt to reveal something about me. I confess why I am at a disadvantage: I have too much right on my side, too much reason, too much *sun* to *allow* a fight in such circumstances. Who knows me? — Frau Cosima the very least. Who knows Wagner? Nobody besides me, not even Frau Cosima, who knows I *am right* . . . she knows her opponent is ⟨right⟩ — I bow to you in everything but this one position: in such circumstances, woman loses her charm, her *reason* almost . . . It is not wrong to remain silent: when one is wrong, of course . . . *Si tacuisses, Cosima mansisses* {"If you had been silent, you would have remained Cosima," humorously reworking a remark on the philosopher attributed to Boethius} . . . You know very well how thoroughly I realize what influence you had over Wagner — you know even better how much I *despise* this influence . . . At the very moment the *swindle* started, I turned my back on you and Wagner . . . If the *daughter* of Liszt wants to have a say in German culture or even religion, I have no pity . . . My compliments as appropriate under the circumstances.

23. *eternal-feminine . . . know that.] W II 3, 161:* Oh, how she knows how to use that to her advantage, the cunning female "eternal feminine"! *Cf. Goethe, Faust II, end.* {N frequently plays with Goethe's coinage of the "Ewig-Weibliche" (from the end of *Faust* II, penultimate line).}

24. *moraline-sour] moralinsauren* {N coined the word "Moralin" by analogy with chemical substances such as nicotine. Difficult to translate, it has a negative quality and is close to "hypocrisy." Goethe married a young woman from the lower classes and was not welcome in Weimar society unless he left her at home.}

25. *he had . . . Jewesses.] In spring 1888, N had read Viktor Hehn's Gedanken über Goethe* {"Thoughts on Goethe"} *(Berlin*{: Gebrüder Borntraeger,} *1887); cf. especially the chapter "Goethe und das Publikum"* {"Goethe and the Public"}, *49–185. Excerpts from this work appear in CW 18, 16[36]; cf. Hehn, 139: "Only Jewish women . . . were less severe and were able to discern not just Goethe's poetic but also his ethical greatness: which means they had more common sense than the good, nice but conventionally restricted . . . blonde female residents of Lower Saxony."*

26. *Schiller . . . hearts.] Cf. Hehn, Gedanken über Goethe, 107.*

27. *Venetian Epigrams]* {Collection of sexually explicit poems written in Venice, 1790.} *Gast wrote to N on 15 August 1888* {*KGB* III:6, 269}: "When I was looking earlier on at the proof sheets of your new work, my gaze fell on the words 'Venetian Epigrams.' I am afraid I did not notice while I was correcting that you *really* meant *Roman Elegies* {another collection of erotic verse by Goethe} . . . Shall I make a note of this error on the last page?" *On 18 August* {*KGB* III:5, 393} *N replied:* "I did, in fact, mean the *Venetian Epigrams* (and not the *Roman Elegies*). *Historically* (I have learned from Hehn's book), they had the greater effect."

28. *Klopstock sermonized him early on;] Cf. Hehn, Gedanken über Goethe, 60ff.*

29. *Herder . . . Goethe.] Cf. Hehn, Gedanken über Goethe, 96.*

30. *Wilhelm Meister]* {Eponymous hero of Goethe's *Wilhelm Meisters Lehrjahre* ("Wilhelm Meister's Apprenticeship") (1795–96).}

31. *Biterolf]* {Character in Wagner's opera *Tannhäuser.*}

32. *"menagerie . . . things"]* Cf. Hehn, *Gedanken über Goethe,* *100–101.*

33. *"Wartburg"]* {Setting of Wagner's opera *Tannhäuser.*}

34. *"unclean spirit"]* Friedrich Jacobi's phrase in a letter of 18 February 1795, cited in Hehn, *Gedanken über Goethe,* 110.

35. *Everyone . . . aloft . . .]* Cf. the whole passage with Hehn's chapter "Goethe and the Public" (49–185) in *Gedanken über Goethe; excerpts are found in CW 18, 16[36].* {In the final line of *Faust* II, Gretchen draws Faust aloft; here, a "higher virgin" draws Goethe aloft.}

36. *"suffocation . . . absurdities."]* Cf. Goethe to the composer K. F. {Carl Friedrich} Zelter, 20 October 1831 (on the subject of Friedrich Schlegel), cited by Hehn, *Gedanken über Goethe,* 110.

37. *Parsifal]* {Eponymous hero and legendary "pure fool" of Wagner's *Parsifal.*}

38. *Sanctity — . . . by nature myopic.]* W II 3, 8: Sanctity is a misunderstanding; a philosopher denies the saints as he denies miracle workers. But the rabble and women all have a right to this misunderstanding: for them, it is a level of truth, of wisdom, still growing visible.

39. *la philosophie . . . sainteté. —]* "philosophy is not enough for a large crowd. It needs sanctity. —" *Citation from Ernest Renan, Vie de Jésus (Paris* {: Michel Lévy Frères,} *1863, 451–52. Cf. CW 18, 11[402].*

4

40. *wicked optimism]* Cf. Schopenhauer, *Welt* 1, 384–85, §59 {*World* 1, 352: "Still, I cannot hold back from declaring here that *optimism,* where it is not just the thoughtless talk of someone with only words in his flat head, strikes me as not only an absurd, but even a truly *wicked* way of thinking, a bitter mockery of the unspeakable sufferings of humanity."}

41. *Beni . . . feci]* "I had a good voyage, even though I was shipwrecked" *Saying of Zeno the Stoic (cf. Diogenes Laërtius,* {*Lives of the Famous Philosophers,*} *VII, 4) familiar to N through Schopenhauer's Latin translation; cf. Schopenhauer, Parerga 1, 216* {*Parerga 1,* 178}; *N uses the same quotation in CW 10, 3[19] (March 1875) and CW 18, 16[44].*

42. *Circe]* {Sorceress in Homer's *Odyssey*.}

43. *The World as Will and Representation]* {Book 4 of Schopenhauer's main work is devoted to ethics.}

5

44. *A typical . . . fulfillment.]* Cf. *CW 18, 15[88]*.

45. *spirit]* {Cf. Matthew 5:3.}

46. *More air!]* {Goethe's dying words were: "more light!"}

47. *St. Petersburg]* Reference to Dostoevsky.

48. *Oh, the . . . unto him!]* Cf. *Matthew 19:14*{; Mark 10:14; Luke 18:18}.

49. *Wagner est une névrose.]* "Wagner is a neurosis." {Playing with the phrase *"Le génie est une névrose"* ("Genius is a neurosis") attributed to French psychiatrist Jacques-Joseph Moreau (1804–84).}

50. *degenerescence]* {Allusion to *Dégénérescence et criminalité* ("Degenerescence and criminality") by Charles Féré (Paris: Alcan, 1888), *NL*, which N had studied intensively on its publication.}

51. *Cagliostro]* {Alias of the Sicilian occultist Giuseppe Balsamo (1743–95). The German writer} *Karl Gutzkow* {(1811–78)} *was the first to compare Wagner to Cagliostro; N first called Wagner "Cagliostro" in JS 99; cf. N's letters to Gast on 25* {and 30} *July 1882* {*KGB* III:1, 231, 233} *and draft letter to Malwida von Meysenbug* {13 July 1882; *KGB* III:1, 224}.

52. *(idiotic)]* {Reference to Dostoevsky's *The Idiot* (1868–69).} Here, N uses the word "idiotic" in the way Dostoevsky intended it; cf. *CW 18, 11[314]*.

6

53. *My friends . . . Wagnerian?]* Before this, as a title in W II 6, 116: *On the Influence of Wagner on Composers: A Farce.*

54. *Pulchrum est paucorum hominum.]* "Beauty is for few men." Cf. Horace, Satires, I, 9, 44.

55. *horned Siegfrieds]* {In *The Ring*, Brünnhilde is tricked into cuckolding Siegfried, whom she loves.}

56. *Second]* Preceded in W II 6, 116 by: Second, with regard to profundity: it is sufficient to roll out personally in front of oneself the mud of the thickest and brownest harmony. Immediately the

listener reaches pessimistically into his own breast — and becomes profound . . . *cf. p. 18:* Undaunted, . . . natural . . .

57. *(they open . . . would say)]* {Probable allusion to the chorus "Lift up your heads, O ye gates" (a setting of Psalms 24:7) in part 2 of Handel's most famous oratorio, *Messiah* (1741–42).}

58. *Sursum]* {Short for *Sursum corda,* "Lift up your hearts," a phrase in the Eucharist liturgy. With the next word, in German *bumbum,* N ridicules the liturgy.}

59. *So let us improve humanity]* Cf. *TI* "The 'Improvers' of Humanity."

60. *sit venia verbo]* "if you will pardon the expression"

61. *"Religion and Art"]* *Wagner wrote Religion und Kunst while working on Parsifal; it was first published in 1880 in the Bayreuther Blätter, and again in a further collection along with other writings: Richard Wagner: "Parsifal": Ein Bühnenweihfestspiel und andere Schriften und Dichtungen* {"'Parsifal': A stage-consecrating festival play and other writings and compositions"} (Leipzig, n.d.). *NL. Wagner writes:* "'Do you perhaps want to found a religion?' the writer of this piece might be asked" ({*Gesammelte Schriften und Dichtungen* ("Complete writings and poetry"), vol. 10 (Leipzig: Fritzsch, 1883),} 322), *and on the previous page:* " . . . we suspect, indeed we feel and see that even this seemingly inescapable world of the will is just a transitory condition in the face of the one: 'I know that my Redeemer liveth!'" *On p. 289, Wagner alludes to N in speaking of the "free spirits" who refuse to believe in the original sin of humanity.*

7

62. *Cf. CW 18, 11[321], where one also finds the name Paul Bourget, whose thought influenced N's remarks on décadence style.*

63. *"On the Physiology of Art"]* {Cf. *CW* 18, 17[9].} *At the beginning of spring 1888 in Turin, N began to fill Notebook W II 9 with jottings under this heading, some of which ended up later in TI "Forays of an Untimely One" (§§8–11), while others on the same theme can be found in notebooks and on loose paper from this period.*

64. *What characterizes . . . décadence:]* Cf. *Paul Bourget, Essais de psychologie contemporaine (Paris*{: Lemerre,} *1883), I, 25: "Une*

même loi gouverne le développement et la décadence de cet autre organisme qui est le langage. Un style de décadence est celui où l'unité du livre se décompose pour laisser la place à l'indépendance de la page, où la page se décompose pour laisser la place à l'indépendance de la phrase, et la phrase pour laisser la place à l'indépendance du mot." {"The same law governs the development and *décadence* of that other organism, language. A decadent style is one where the unity of the book dissolves to give way to the independence of the page, the page dissolves to give way to the independence of the sentence, and the sentence to the independence of the word.}
Wilhelm Weigand was the first to rightly point out this borrowing in his book F. Nietzsche: Ein psychologischer Versuch ("F. Nietzsche: A psychological essay") (Munich{: H. Lukaschik,} *1893), 67–68. Others followed: Ernst Bertram (1918), J. Hofmiller (1931); C. von Westernhagen (1938 and 1956). N had jotted the Bourget passage down in the winter of 1883–84, already linking it to Wagner. Cf. CW 10, 24[6] end.*

65. *In the beginning] im Anfang* {N's use of *im Anfang*, not the more usual *am Anfang* ("at the beginning") points to his deliberate copying of John 1:1: "In the beginning was the Word . . ."}

66. *How pathetic . . . distress.] W II 7, 42:* How brazenly and clumsily he stumbles about! How torturous his false counterpoint sounds! His manners meanwhile — polish instead of inspiration — are reminiscent of the *frères de Goncourt*: so much distress arouses a kind of pity.

67. *(— in this . . . humans . . .)] Cf. BGE 11.*

68. *I repeat: . . . smallest space.] Cf. CW 4, 30[50], written ten years earlier in summer 1878:* Wagner's art for myopics — need to be far too close (miniature) but longsighted at the same time. No normal vision.

69. *Believe me . . . fresco.] W II 7, 77:* The whole of the rest is playacting, counterfeiting or whatever you want to take it for: music for ["idiots"] the "masses."

70. *agaçant]* "provocative"

71. *bourgeois respectability] Biedermännerei* {With the addition of the pejorative suffix *-erei*, the word "Biedermann" here denotes a petty bourgeois and cultivated philistine.}

72. *"an ado about nothing"*] {The German *ein Lärm um Nichts* recalls the standard German title for Shakespeare's *Much Ado About Nothing*: *Viel Lärm um Nichts*.}

73. *how music . . . hypnotize*] Cf. *CW 18, 11[323]*.

74. *magnétiseur*] {Reference to Franz Anton Mesmer (1734–1815), German quack who used "animal magnetism" and hypnotism to treat his patients.}

75. *But apart . . . happiness*] Cf. e.g., N to Gast, *21 January 1887* {*KGB* III:5, 13} *regarding the Parsifal Prelude:* Has a painter ever portrayed such a doleful glance of love as Wagner did with the last notes of his prelude?

76. *What do we care . . . compassion — — —*] Cf. *the following note in W II 6, 110–11, with the title: "Personal Views on the Taste for Wagnerian Music":* Everything by Wagner that is popularly acclaimed even away from the theater is music of questionable taste and *ruins* your taste. I put myself on my guard against the *agaçante* {"provocative"} brutality of the Overture to *Tannhäuser*, just as I did as a small boy: that turns me into an aesthetic hedgehog [I stick out all my prickles], I mean prickly / I have not been able to find a way into all these older works of Wagner's: something warned me against condescending to a taste like that. "That is theatrical music, it does not concern you" — I was only thirteen and already I said that. Wagner only became a possibility with me through *Tristan*; and [first] *established* through the *Mastersingers*. I think a lot of others have had the same experience . . . // In my youth, the great culture of Mendelssohn was uppermost: from it we learned extreme caution toward vulgarity and arrogance *in rebus musicis et musicantibus* {"in things musical and to do with musicians"} . . . // We gave in to Wagner in proportion to how much he aroused our trust through his methods, how much he appeared to be less of an actor: — he had overcome our instinctual prejudice against his theatrical pathology and sensibility. To declare the opposite, namely that Wagnerian sensibility was indeed specific and [— — —] German was something reserved for the most devoted of his [admirers] followers . . . // But we Germans then still had no idea that music can have its actors as

well: I am afraid we defended ourselves with hand and foot, what am I saying? with reasons . . . If we gradually — oh so gradually! — gave in to Wagner, this happened according to how much trust in his methods he inspired in us — how much *less of an actor* he appeared to be. That again was naiveté; something [—] and [—] at the same time: in truth, Wagner had just *improved as an actor*! . . . He had merely been better at *deceiving* us!

8

77. *just bend down, you can do no other.]* {Cf. Luther's alleged declaration at the Diet of Worms, 1521: "Here I stand, I can do no other."}

78. *histrio]* "actor"

79. *music as language.]* Cf. this deleted variant in W II 6, 127: Wagner did something similar for music as language to what Victor Hugo did for language as music. Since then, the whole sensuousness of music has been virtually rediscovered [developed into the unending]: nobody before Wagner so much as dreamed of all that sound can *say*.

80. *ancilla dramaturgica]* "the handmaiden of dramaturgy"

81. *Talma]* {François-Joseph Talma (1763–1826), French actor.}

82. *Wagner . . . teeth into.]* Cf. TI "Forays of an Untimely One" 13, Carlyle on Emerson.

83. *"alla genovese"]* "in the Genoese style"

84. *I have christened . . . recitativo secco.]* Cf. W II 7, 83: Wagnerian *recitativo*, now *troppo secco* {too dry}, now *troppo bagnato* {too soaked}. {*Recitativo secco* is a technical term in music for the kind of operatic recitative (sung speech) accompanied by only one or two instruments and not a full orchestra.}

85. *As for the Wagnerian "leitmotif" . . . of it.]* Cf. W II 7, 82: For me, the "leitmotif" is a totally *indigestible* dish; I haven't a clue how to translate it into culinary terms.

9

86. *Note]* The same distinction is made in CW 12, 23[74], winter 1876–77.

87. *"the one thing needful"]* Cf. Luke 10:42.

88. *rather . . . misunderstanding.]* Cf. AC 29.

89. *Erda]* {Earth goddess (and mother of Brünnhilde by Wotan) in *Siegfried.*}

90. *He . . . sings] Reference to Wotan's conjuring up of Erda at the beginning of Siegfried, Act 3.*

91. *Madame Bovary]* {Eponymous heroine of Flaubert's novel *Madame Bovary* (1857).}

92. *Wagnerus . . . auctoritas.]* "Spoken by the foremost authority on chastity, Wagner." *Cf. W II 7, 86:* Wagner teaches that, see his *Collected Works. Indeed N had first intended to cite a passage from Wagner in which he wrote:* "even *in italics . . .* that 'chastity works *wonders*' . . . " *(N to Gast, 17 July 1888* {*KGB* III:5, 355}, *citing "Religion and Art," 280–81; cf. note 61 above).*

10

93. *It is perhaps worth noting that even in WB (1876), paragraph 10 was devoted to Wagner's writings.*

94. *whoever . . . hear.]* {Cf. Matthew 11:15.}

95. *"Music . . . means"]* {Cf. Richard Wagner, the introduction to *Oper und Drama* ("Opera and drama") in *Gesammelte Schriften und Dichtungen* (Leipzig: Fritzsch, 1872), 3:282. *NL.*}

96. *Elsa . . . revolutionary"]* Cf. Richard Wagner, "Eine Mittheilung an meine Freunde" {"A message to my friends"}, *in Wagner, ibid., 4:368–69. NL:* "Elsa is the unconsciousness, the involuntariness, in which the conscious, deliberate being of Lohengrin yearns to redeem itself . . . Elsa, the woman — the woman I did not understand but now do — this most vital expression of the purest, sensual involuntariness — made me into a complete revolutionary. She was the spirit of the people for whom I, as an artistic human being, also yearned, to be my salvation."

97. *And how . . . perfection . . .] Cf. CW 18, 15[6] 6.*

11

98. *Riemann's] Hugo Riemann* {1849–1919}, *German music theorist; cf. N to Carl Fuchs, 26 August 1888* {*KGB* III:5, 400–402}.

99. *people demand . . . rule] N says the same about a "good school" in a fragment from W II 5 (Spring 1888); cf. CW 18, 14[170].*

100. *Espressivo]* "Expressively" {musical term}

101. *obedience] substitutes for W II 7, 64:* morality.

102. *Alfieri]* {Count Vittorio Alfieri (1749–1803), Italian dramatist and poet.}

Postscript

1. *Postscript] Cf. CW 18, 15[11] for the thoughts expressed here.*

2. *The seriousness . . . costs us.] Cf. W II 7, 57: Note.* The seriousness of the last words permits me to add a few sentences from an unpublished essay ("Richard Wagner Refuted Physiologically").

3. *The Germans . . . youngest.] Cf. AC 61; EH "Books" WA §4; WB 3.*

4. *vulture]* Geyer

5. *eagle]* Adler. "Adler" is a very common Jewish surname. However, Ludwig Geyer was not Jewish, nor is it certain that Wagner was his son. N's mischief-making becomes obvious in the light of Wagner's anti-Semitism (shared by almost all his circle). *Cf. N to Gast, 11 and 18 August 1888 {KGB III:5, 388–89, 393}, and Gast to N, 11 August 1888 {KGB III:6, 251}.*

6. *fable convenue]* "accepted legend"

7. *"Redemption to the Redeemer!"] The final words of Wagner's Parsifal. (Cf. the comment by Gast in his letter to N, 11 August 1888 {KGB III:6, 262–63}).*

8. *in rebus . . . musicantibus]* "in things to do with music and musicians"

9. *theatrocracy]* {Plato introduced the term in *Laws*, III, 700a–d, but in the rather different sense of "government by the people assembled in their theater."}

10. *demolatry]* "worship of the masses"

11. *all the . . . beyond] Cf. W II 7, 53, substituting for:* Buddhist nothingness [*Nirvâna*].

12. *I admire . . . understand it] Cf. N to Gast, 25 July 1882 {KGB III:1, 231}:* On Sunday I was in Naumburg to prepare my sister somewhat for *Parsifal.* I felt really strange! Finally I said: "My dear sister, I made *music exactly like this* as a boy when I composed my Oratorio" — and off I went to fetch the old papers and play them again after a long interval: *mood* and *expression* were marvelously *identical*! In fact, a few passages, e.g., "The Death of the Kings," appeared to both of us to be more gripping than

anything we had performed from *Parsifal*, and yet quite Parsifa-lesque! I confess: I was truly shocked to realize once again *how* closely related to Wagner I *actually* am.

13. *femininisms] Femininismen* {At the time, both "*Feminis-men*" and "*Femininismen*" were in use, although the former was more common.}

14. *idiotikon]:* "private dictionary" {Greek *idiōtēs* = private individual}

15. *Klingsor]* {Evil sorcerer in *Parsifal.*}

16. *magic maidens]* {Reference to the flower maidens in the magic garden in Act II of *Parsifal.*}

17. *cave canem]* "beware of the dog" {The name "Cynic" derives from ancient Greek *kynikos*, meaning "dog-like."}

18. *⟨debasement of⟩] Added in line with W II 7, 57.*

19. *Bayreuther Blätter]* {Monthly newsletter for visitors to the Bayreuth Festival where Wagner's operas were performed. Wagner and many in his circle published their articles in its pages.}

20. *Bayreuth rhymes with cold-water clinic.] Bayreuth reimt sich auf Kaltwasserheilanstalt.* {It does not in fact rhyme; N is being facetious: hydrotherapy, using either "hot wet" or "cold wet" compresses, the latter to reduce swellings and pain, was fashionable at the time.}

21. *betimes bemoaned.] bereits bereut. Cf. N's letter (from Bayreuth) to his sister Elisabeth, 25 July 1876* {KGB II, 5, 178}: . . . I almost *regretted* it! For it has been wretched up till now. Headache from Sunday noon to Monday night, relaxing today, I can hardly hold my pen.

22. *Walk through . . . the other.] W II 7, 57:* You do not stroll to Bayreuth unpunished. — Wagner's effect on woman is an even more fateful [problem] question. You cannot, from the stand-point of young women, be too serious in presenting this alternative: one thing or the other. *Aut liberi aut* [Wagner] [Bayreuth] *lyrici* {"Either children or [Wagner] [Bayreuth] lyrics"} . . . A performance of *Tristan*, experienced and felt as Wagner himself understands the two words, [ranks with the worst debauches] signifies debauchery. *Cf. also CW 18, 16[78], and Goethe's well-known saying from Elective Affinities* {1809}: "One does not stroll beneath palms unpunished."

23. *No one can serve two masters]* {Matthew 6:24.}

24. *Off to Crete!"] Chorus from La belle Hélène (1864) by Jacques Offenbach. Cf. N to Gast, 24 August 1888* {KGB III:5, 398}. {The legend of the Minotaur takes place in Crete.}

Second Postscript

1. *Rhinoxera]* N's neologism, possibly combining "rhinoceros" and "phylloxera" (vine louse). Cf. his letters to J. V. Widmann, 15 September 1887 {KGB III:5, 156}, and his mother, {10} October 1887 {KGB III:5, 164}: The rhinoceros for to see / In Germany I must be. {Grape phylloxera spread from eastern North America into Europe in the mid-nineteenth century, devastating much of the European wine-growing industry.}

2. *Kreuzzeitung]* Nickname of the *Neue Preussische Zeitung*, a right-wing daily newspaper, Berlin 1848–1938.

3. *Literarisches Zentralblatt]* Scholarly review published weekly in Leipzig by F. Zarncke, in which N and his friend Erwin Rohde published reviews.

4. *Bernini]* N endorses the opinions of Stendhal and Burckhardt on Bernini; cf. e.g., Jacob Burckhardt, *Der Cicerone*{, vol. 2} (Leipzig {: E. A. Seemann,} 1869), 690–91 and 696. NL. Stendhal provides a noteworthy use of the term "Berninism" in the world of music: ". . . le célèbre Mayer habite Bergame ainsi que le vieux David. Marchesi et lui furent, à ce qu'il me semble, les Bernin de la musique vocale, des grands talents destinés à amener le règne du mauvais goût"{" . . . the celebrated Mayer lived in Bergamo as did old David. He and Marchesi were, it seems to me, the Berninis of vocal music, great talents destined to inaugurate the reign of bad taste"}. Cf. Stendhal, *Rome, Naples, et Florence* (Paris{: Michel Lévy Frères,} 1854), 404. NL. For N's views on the baroque in music, cf. HAH 219; MM 171; see also N to Carl Fuchs, end July 1877 {KGB II, 5, 261–62}, and 26 August and 9 September 1888 {KGB III:5, 401, 415} (in the latter, N explicitly likens Wagner to Bernini).

5. *one musician]* {N is referring to his friend Heinrich Köselitz, whom he dubbed} *Peter Gast*; cf. N to Gast, 9 August 1888 {KGB III:5, 382}.

6. *If you discount . . . stylistic forms]* Cf. *Gast to N, 11 August 1888 {KGB* III:6, 262}.

7. *"poor in spirit"]* Cf. *Matthew 5:3.*

8. *Goldmark]* {Karl Goldmark (1830–1915), Hungarian composer whose opera *The Queen of Sheba* premiered in Vienna in 1875.} *But cf. N's letter to Gast dated 2 December 1888 {KGB* III:5, 499} *(on the Sakuntala Overture* {1860}).

9. *Rossini]* Cf. *EH* "Why I Am So Clever" §7 *and the almost identical NCW* "Intermezzo."

Epilogue

1. *(— the gospels . . . portray)]* Cf. *AC 31.*

2. *"gospel of the humble"]* After Renan's *"évangile des humbles";* cf. *TI* "Forays of an Untimely One" 2.

3. *feminini generis]* "of the feminine gender" (grammatical term); "effeminate"

4. *Le moi . . . haïssable.]* "The self is always *detestable.*" Cf. *Blaise Pascal, Pensées, fragments et lettres,* ed. Prosper Faugère {(Paris: Andrieux, 1844)}, I, 197; cf. also *MM 385 and D 79.*

5. *"because . . . full."]* Cf. *Matthew 12:34.*

6. *foeda superstitio]* "a *disgusting* superstition" {N underlines *foeda*} Perhaps following *"exitiabilis superstitio"* {"pernicious superstition"} *in Tacitus, Annals XV 44* {cf. *CW* 17, 10[181]}.

7. *I remind . . . the cross.]* Cf. *Venetian Epigrams* {66}: "There is much that I can bear. Most things people find bothersome / I bear with silent fortitude, as a god bids me do. / A few, though, are, like snakes and poison, vile to me; / Four in number: tobacco smoke, bedbugs, garlic and †." {† = the Cross}.

8. *If Wagner . . . opposites . . .)] This passage is on the only surviving sheet of the Pm (in Basel), inserted by N during the proof corrections along with the asterisked note, for which the original is lost. However, the concluding passage* {A diagnosis . . . you can hear . . . } *survives, as it was written on the same Pm sheet as that now in Basel.*

9. *That Wagner . . . us."]* N is parodying a passage from John 1:14: "And the Word was made flesh, and dwelt among us . . . "

10. *Cagliostro]* Cf. "Letter" note 51 above {p. 455}.

11. *A diagnosis . . . you can hear]* Cf. note 8 above.

Twilight of the Idols

N changed the title from *A Psychologist at Leisure* (*Müßiggang eines Psychologen*) on 27 September 1888 {cf. *CW* 13, 12[225]}. On receipt of the first proofs from the Leipzig printers, Peter Gast had written to N on 20 September {*KGB* III:6, 309–10}: "The title 'A Psychologist at Leisure' sounds too modest when I picture how colleagues will react to it. You have taken the artillery up the highest mountains, big guns like no other, and all you need do to create terror in the surroundings is to fire off blindly. If the mountains shudder at the passage of a giant, you cannot call it leisure anymore. Besides, leisure today only comes after work, and is usually coupled with fatigue. Incompetent as I am, I beg for a more splendid and glorious title!" N answered on 27 September {*KGB* III:5, 443}: "Concerning the *title*, your *very kind* objection to it anticipated my own; at length, I found a formula in a passage of the *Foreword* that will perhaps meet your requirements as well. I can do no more than accept what you say about the 'big guns,' midway through finishing the first book of the 'Revaluation' as I am. There are some truly horrible detonations going on . . . " N wrote in the same letter that the new title was "another practical joke on Wagner," the latter having composed *Twilight of the Gods* {the fourth and final opera of the *Ring* cycle}. The emergence of the new title can be accurately traced in *CW* 18, 22[6]. In sequence, N tried the titles "Hammer of the Idols. / A Psychologist at Leisure." then: "Hammer of the Idols. / Or: / How a Psychologist asks Questions." At the end came the final title. These draft titles were in fact jotted down between the preliminary stages of *AC* 47 and 48. As indicated already, *TI* should be viewed as a sort of "twin work" with *AC*. The *Pm* and proofs for *TI* are extant. The printing of *TI* was finished in early November, and sales were to begin in 1889. Around 25 November 1888, N received four copies of *Götzen-Dämmerung oder Wie man mit dem Hammer philosophirt*, Leipzig 1889, published by C. G. Naumann (= *TI*). Some sheets from the second draft of *TI* are kept in the Bodmer Library in Geneva.

Foreword

1. *Two longish fragments of a similar "Foreword" are found in the loose sheets of Mp XVI 4. The first to be written is dated* Sils-Maria, beginning of September 1888, *out of which emerged another version dated* Sils-Maria, 3 September. *Judging by his letter to Meta von Salis dated 7 September {KGB III:5, 410}, N initially wanted to use this "3 September version" as the foreword for the Revaluation of All Values. Between 7 and 11 September he changed his mind, choosing it for the foreword to the Psychologist at Leisure. Of its three paragraphs, the third was deleted on N's instruction and replaced with a new text in the Pm (N to Naumann, 13 September {KGB III:5, 422}). In a letter to Naumann on 18 September {KGB III:5, 442}, N had this to say of the previous foreword:* Enclosed is the relevant Foreword. The Foreword I already sent you (aside from the third paragraph, of course *[i.e., the third paragraph that had been replaced by a different text on 11 September]*), has been somewhat extended by me so that {it} can be included in the book — specifically as the *penultimate* chapter (— the *final one* will be "Forays of an Untimely One"). Let's give it the title *What the Germans Lack.* With the extension that I am sending you today, it now has 7 short sections in all. Correspondingly, this title must be added to the Contents page. The Foreword is now much shorter — *and* more germane to the task. *The preliminary drafts of the new foreword are found in Notebook W II 6, 144–45 (where the preliminary drafts of the "extended" previous foreword are also found). Once N had finally settled on the title of his book, he made a few relevant changes to the final foreword of 18 September, among others including the date:* Turin, 30 September 1888, on the day when the first book of the *Revaluation of All Values* was completed. *And in fact, in Notebook W II 8 the preliminary drafts of the final part of AC are found alongside the changes to the TI Foreword. The deleted text of §3 of the original foreword (i.e., the foreword dated "3 September," which was now the chapter "What the Germans Lack") went to make up the short foreword to The Antichrist.*

2. *case of luck]* {As N had just finished *The Case of Wagner*, he takes the opportunity to make a pun with the word *Glücksfall* — "stroke of luck." Cf. *WA* Epilogue, p. 39 above.

3. *increscunt . . . virtus.]* "by wounding, the spirit grows, strength is restored." {From the ancient Roman poet} *Furius Antias, quoted in Aulus Gellius, Noctes Atticae ("Attic nights"), 18, 11, 4.* {German translation: *Die attischen Nächte*, 2 vols. (Leipzig: Fues, 1875–76). NL.}

4. *someone with ears . . . audible]* W II 8, 134: a psychologist, particularly when he is basically [no more than an] old musician

5. *as the title betrays]* W II 8, 134: like *The Case of Wagner*

6. *new idols being sounded out? . . .]* W II 8, 134: gods being overthrown again?

Sayings and Arrows

1. *For this whole section, cf. CW 18, 15[118], "Sayings of a Hyperborean."*

2. *Cf. CW 13, 12[7, 121]; CW 18, 11[107].*

3. *Aristotle]* Cf. *Politics 1253a29.*

4. *"All truth is simple."]* Cf. Schopenhauer, "Simplex sigillum veri" {*Parerga 2*, 218: "Simplicity is the seal of the true"}

5. *Cf. CW 18, 11[296], excerpt from the Journal des Goncourt (Paris*{: Charpentier,} *1887), I, {3}92.*

6. *human's? —]* Cf. W II 3, 184: human's? — You have to decide. Cf. also W II 7, 154, and CW 17, 9[72].

7. *What . . . stronger.]* Cf. EH "Why I Am So Wise" 2.

8. *The principle . . . neighbor.]* {Cf. Mark 12:31.}

9. *pang of conscience]* Gewissensbiss {English speakers feel pangs of conscience, Germans "bites" of conscience.}

10. *of the philosopher]* Mp XVI 4: of Carlyle

11. *Cf. W II 3, 9 at the beginning:* Woman, the "eternal-feminine": just an imaginary value believed in only by man. *Cf. CW 18, 11[296]:* Man has made woman by imbuing her with all his poetic fancies . . . Gavarni. *Also cf. this excerpt from the Journal des Goncourt, I, 283: "De là, la causerie saute à la femme. Selon lui, c'est l'homme qui a fait la femme en lui donnant toutes ses poésies."* {"From there, the chat shifts to woman. According to him {Gavarni}, it was man who made woman and gave her all his poetic fancies." The quotation from the *Journal des Goncourt* in KSA 14, 412 is inaccurate; it has been corrected here.}

12. *Cf. W II 3, 85:* You know what you need to multiply your strength: zeros. *On the page adjacent (W II 3, 84), there is an excerpt from the Journal des Goncourt:* — they seek a *zero* to increase their value tenfold. *Cf. CW 18, 11[296].* {Section [296] relates to vol. I of the Goncourts' *Journal*; [297] to vol. II.}

13. *authority . . .] W II 3, 184:* authority! (For *comprendre c'est égaler . . .*) {"to understand is to match . . . "}

14. *pudeurs]* "modesty" "shame"

15. *panem et Circen]* "bread and Circe" {"*Circen*" is underlined by N. The Latin *panem et circenses* ("bread and circuses": Juvenal, *Satires*, X, 81) was a government panacea to quell civil discontent. By cutting the last word short, and emphasizing it, N raises the specter of the sorceress Circe in Homer's *Odyssey*.}

16. *The perfect . . . notices . . .] Cf. CW 18, 11[59]; Mp XVI, 4 at end:* she knows how well a [small] brown stain of decomposition [brown putrefaction] suits the perfect woman —

17. *N extracted this from a longer fragment found in Notebook W II 6 under the title "Asceticism of the Strong"; cf. CW 18, 15[117].*

18. *"Evil . . . songs."] Adage from the poem "Die Gesänge"* {"The Songs"} *by Johann Gottfried Seume; N also extracted this adage from a longer fragment (in Mp XVI, 4)* {written July/August 1888}; *cf. CW 18, 18[9].*

19. *"German intellect"]* "Deutscher Geist" {*Geist* could also be translated as "spirit."}

20. *contradictio in adjecto]* "contradiction in terms"

21. *eighteen years]* That is, since the founding of the {second} Reich in {January} 1871.

22. *get to the bottom of her. Woman] Mp XVI, 4; W II 3, 70:* get to the bottom of her. But woman has no foundation: she is the Danaides' jar. Woman {All but one of Danaus's fifty daughters murdered their husbands, and as punishment, Hades made them perpetually fill bottomless jars with water.}. *Cf. also Gavarni's saying in the Journal des Goncourt I, 325: "Nous lui demandons s'il a jamais compris une femme? 'Une femme, mais c'est impénétrable, non pas parce que c'est profond, mais parce que c'est creux!'"* {"We ask him if he had ever understood a woman? 'A woman, but she's

impenetrable, not because she's deep, but because she's hollow!'"
The quotation from the *Journal des Goncourt* in *KSA* 14, 412 is
inaccurate; it has been corrected here.}

23. *How . . . happiness!] Cf. Z IV "At Noon."*

24. *Without . . . error.] Cf. N's letter to Peter Gast, 15 January
1888 {KGB III:5, 232}.*

25. *God singing songs.] Cf. Ernst Moritz Arndt, Des Deutschen
Vaterland (1813): "Soweit die deutsche Zunge klingt / Und Gott im
Himmel Lieder singt."* {"As far as speech is heard in German / Songs
are sung to God in heaven." Like many of his countrymen, N chose
to ignore the implied dative in the second line ("to God"), and pretends here that God sings songs.} *Peter Gast, in a letter of 20 September 1888 {KGB III:6, 309}, correctly noted:* "I think that the 'God' . . .
actually is dative, and not nominative." *N replied (27 September 1888
{KGB III:5, 443–44}):* "Old friend, you are not at all on my wave-
length {literally, "at my level"} with your distinction between dative
and nominative in the concept of God. The nominative makes the
passage *funny,* it is its sufficient reason for existing . . ."

26. *On ne peut penser et écrire qu'assis]* "Only if you are seated
can you think and write." *Cf. Guy de Maupassant, foreword to
Lettres de Gustave Flaubert à Georges Sand (Paris{:* Charpentier,}
1884), iii. NL.

27. *To be steadfast] Das Sitzfleisch* {"perseverance," "steadfast-
ness"; literally "sitting flesh"}

28. *The psychologist . . . at all.] Mp XVI 4:* Then you have to
ride into and *against* the sun.

29. *Cf. CW 17, 10[107].*

30. *we] Pm:* the

31. *For aphorisms 37, 38, and 40, cf. CW 17, 10[145]; CW 18, 11[1].*

32. *Cf. CW 18, 11[1].*

33. *Cf. AC 1, at end.*

The Problem of Socrates

1. *The Problem of Socrates] Mp XVI 4:* Socrates as Problem*;
according to one plan for "The Will to Power," N intended to open
his chapter on Philosophy as Décadence with a similar discussion. Cf.
CW 18, 15[5].*

1

2. *Living . . . cock.*"] Cf. Plato's *Phaedo, 118a.* {In ancient Greece, a cock was sacrificed to the god of medicine, Asclepius, in gratitude for recovery from an illness.}

3. *consensus sapientium]* "consensus of the wise"

4. *those wisest of all times]* Cf. Goethe's "Coptic Song"; also cited in *HAH 110.*

5. *What does this . . . excite? . . .] W II 5, 50:* What does this *prove?* — Formerly people would have said — (and people did say it! [a thousand times!] finally Schopenhauer as well and most [strongly] innocently! —) "Something here must be true!" We, we lately come [we Hyperboreans to whom life has denied the gift of innocence], all of us say [to that]: Something here must be sick! Those wisest of all times — one must take a [good] close look at them! Were they all perhaps unsteady on their [feet] legs? Late? Shaky? *décadents?* Autumnless? Would wisdom perhaps manifest itself on earth as a raven that already scents the proximity of cadavers? *W II 5, 51:* What does that *prove?* . . . what does that *indicate?*? Formerly people would have said — [and even Schopenhauer himself belongs to former times] and people have said it a thousand times! Schopenhauer last and the strongest — "something here must be true!" We, we lately come, we [immoralists] Hyperboreans say: something here must be *sick*! Those wisest of all times — [let's have a closer look!] one must [take a close look?] take a close look at them! Are they perhaps [it is not impossible, wise from tiredness, from *décadence*, from racial decline?] all sick, tired, humans in decline, ruined types? . . . [Does wisdom perhaps appear as symptom of the end? . . . [Is its value judgment *against* life] [is a value judgment] does a value judgment on declining life prove an instinct for destruction a [premonition of] *need* for the end . . .] Would wisdom perhaps manifest itself as a raven that [scents] already scents the stench of [death itself — — —] putrefaction? . . .

2

6. *Judgments . . . stupidities.] W II 5, 51:* We count judgments about life, for or against, as symptoms; they have no other interest for us than insofar as they are symptoms. [Actually, to hold court

over life indicates folly on the part of someone alive: and on the part of someone dead, a [an unsolvable] trick that would be difficult to solve] In themselves such value judgments are stupidities.

3

7. *monstrum . . . animo]* "monster in face, monster in soul"

8. *At the . . . me, dear sir!"] Cf. Cicero, Tusculanae Disputationes, IV 37, 80; cited by Georg Christoph Lichtenberg, Über Physiognomik, Vermischte Schriften (Gottingen{: Dieterich,} 1867), 4, 31. NL.*

4

9. *"Socrates' daimon"]* "Socrates' guiding spirit" *Cf. Plato's Apology, 31d.*

10. *buffo]* {Comic part (usually bass) in eighteenth-century Italian opera.}

11. *it.] Mp XVI 4:* it. (The older equation was: virtue = instinct = fundamental unconsciousness)

5, 6, 7

12. *In Notebook W II 5 there are two more versions for these sections — the later one (W II 5, 109) has no major alterations differing from the printed text of this paragraph, the earlier on p. 109 is as follows*: Socrates — Plato — dialecticians / This reversal of taste in favor of dialectics is a cardinal fact. The plebeian {*Roturier*} Socrates, who forced it through, thereby had a victory over noble taste, the taste of the nobles. The rise of dialectics meant the rise of the rabble. The display of reasons opposes all that is aristocrat and instinct: — they are in authority. Authority commands . . . Nor do people believe in dialectics. All good things avoid keeping their reasons to hand. What allows itself to be true is not worth much. Dialectics is indecent . . . That dialectics arouses mistrust, that it does little to convince, is known to the shrewdness of every speaker of every party. Dialectics can only be a *defense*: you must *be* in distress to *enforce* your right, otherwise no one makes use of dialectics . . . The Jew is a dialectician: and so was Socrates: you have a dreadful tool in your hand: you refute by laying bare your opponent's understanding — you put him on trial while rendering him helpless — you provide your victim with proof that you are not an idiot . . . oh, — — —

6

13. *Reynard the Fox]* {Hero of several European cycles of animal tales from medieval times down to Goethe's *Reinecke Fuchs* (1794).}

8

14. *agon]* "contest" {*agon* is underlined by N.}

"Reason" in Philosophy

1. *"Reason" in Philosophy] Mp XVI 4:* Philosophy as Idiosyncrasy. *W II 5, 72:* The true and the apparent world

1

2. *sub specie aeterni]* "from the viewpoint of eternity"

2

3. *duration] Cf. W II 5, 73, crossed out:* We think about that today as thoroughgoing Heracliteans.

4. *With great . . . unity.]* {Cf. Victor Brochard, *Les sceptiques grecs* ("The Greek skeptics") (Paris: Imprimerie Nationale, 1887), 7: "L'un des premiers, sinon le premier, Héraclite a montré que la sensation suppose un double facteur, le mouvement de l'objet et celui du sujet. Parménide récusait le témoignage des sens, parce qu'ils nous montrent la multiplicité et le changement; Héraclite, parce qu'ils nous représentent les choses comme ayant de l'unité et de la durée." ("One of the first, if not the first, Heraclitus showed that sensation supposes a double factor, the movement of the object and that of the subject. Parmenides rejected the testimony of the senses, because they show us multiplicity and change; Heraclitus, because they represent things to us as having unity and duration.")}

5. *Eleatics]* {Pre-Socratic school of philosophy founded in the 5th century BCE, whose chief exponents, Parmenides and Zeno, lived in Elea, a Greek city in what is now southern Italy. In addition to denying the validity of sense-experience, their doctrine held that only a single, unchanging being existed and that becoming and change were illusions.}

4

6. *the "highest . . . reality] Mp XVI 4:* any one of those superfluous and obstructive diluted and vaporized concepts like the concept "good," the concept "true"

7. *causa sui]* "cause of itself"

8. *ens realissimum]* "the most real being"

5

9. *projects belief . . . grammar . . .] W II 5, 68 (first version):* carries over the subject-appearance on to all the remainder, everywhere sanctifying being and setting up being as cause. If these old sages, like the Eleatics among the Greeks, had such a great persuasive power for everyone, even for materialist physicists (— Democritus submitted to the Eleatics' fixing of the concept "being" when he discovered his atom), we must not forget who they had on their side, the instinct within language, that so-called reason. The latter believes in a world of being, its categories would not be provable in a world of absolute becoming . . . — in fact, today we are in the difficult position of no longer having a formula for our conception {corrected in *KGW* IX, 8} at hand and have to drag in the old categories everywhere: so we still make use of the word "cause" today, but have *emptied* it of its content — and I fear all our formulas make use of old words in a sense that is completely arbitrary.

How the "True World" Finally Became a Fable

1. *This brief chapter — according to a plan from spring 1888 — was originally destined to be the first chapter in "The Will to Power"; the Pd in W II 5, 64–65, therefore begins with the heading "First Chapter." Cf. CW 18, 14[156].*

2. *clever . . . Plato] W II 5, 64:* reasonable, simple, factual, *sub specie Spinozae* Paraphrase of the proposition "I, Spinoza

3. *"I, . . . truth."]* {Cf. John 14:6.}

4. *unproved . . . Königsbergian.] W II 5, 64–65:* for now, perhaps also impossible to promise, but already as a belief a consolation, a repose, a redemption (the idea become sublime, phantasmal; Sphinx light of former time, a midnight for metaphysicians and other Hyperboreans but the object of great veneration and hope) {Kant lived and died in Königsberg.}

5. *The true world . . . Königsbergian.]* {In W II 5, 64–65, the following variant also appears: "The true world, unattainable for now, perhaps also impossible to promise, but already as a belief a consolation, a repose, a redemption (the idea become sublime, phantasmal;

reflex light of former time, a midnight for metaphysicians and other Hyperboreans) [. . .] The true world; eternally unattainable, but the object of great veneration and hope." (*KGW* IX 8; W II 5, 64, 22–28; 65, 48–50.) The same passage in N's unrevised version reads: "The true world, unattainable, unproved, unpromised, but the mere thought of it a consolation, a⟨n⟩ obligation, an imperative, a repose, a redemption (the idea become sublime; pale, northern, Königsbergian; basically the same old sun⟨,⟩ [. . .] but through fog and skepticism) [. . .] The true world: unattainable, perhaps also not promised, but already as a belief a consolation, redemption, rest." (*KGW* IX 8; W II 5, 64, 22–28; 65, 48–51).}

6. *of positivism.*] *W II 5, 64:* of reason.

7. *bon sens*] "good sense"

8. *Plato's*] *W II 5, 64:* reason's

9. *INCIPIT ZARATHUSTRA*] "ZARATHUSTRA BEGINS" {Cf. *JS* 342}; *W II 5, 64:* INCIPIT PHILOSOPHIA {"PHILOS-OPHY BEGINS"}

Morality as Anti-Nature

1. *According to the relevant plan of spring 1888, this chapter consists of two parts, of which the second was the first to be written (§§4–6 in Notebook W II 5, 47–49) under the heading "Morality as a Type of Décadence." Sections 1–3 are found in W II 6, 43–44. In Mp XVI 4 there is a copy of §§1–2 under the heading "Schopenhauer and Sensuality." A copy of §§4–6 is also found there, but in a different context. The two parts were merged when N made a second draft in August 1888, from which — after abandoning plans to publish "The Will to Power" — Twilight of the Idols and The Antichrist emerged. The first version of §§1–3 in W II 6, 43–44 reads:* The victory over stupidity about passion seems to me to be the greatest victory that has ever been won: to wit, passion itself in a stranglehold but so thoroughly soured with spirit, nuance, caution, that it becomes a *joy of existence.* Formerly because of the stupidity of passion and the resultant bad consequences, people just wanted to *destroy* it, which is just a second stupidity. The formula for that is in the New Testament in that famous Sermon on the Mount where, however, things are absolutely not viewed *from on high.* It is obvi-

ous that the spiritualization of passion was not even imaginable as a tendency for such chandala: the word "spirit" itself in the New Testament is merely a misunderstanding. Yes, they fight with all their strength *against* the "intelligent": can one expect an intelligent war against passion from them? . . . Therefore, in every sense the battle of the Church against passion is *excision*, castratism . . . The considerations of church⟨ly⟩ discipline always turn around this point: how can desire, pride, mastery, greed be *destroyed*? . . . It is just as obvious that the same means, cutting and excision, will be chosen by those who are too *weak-willed* to inflict *measured* discipline: — the natures who need *la Trappe*, any drastic and final declaration of hostility between themselves and a passion . . . And in that, a very common type of degeneration finds expression. It is frequent in so-called pessimists: it is, e.g., the Sch⟨openhauer⟩ type in regard to his attitude toward sexuality. A person⟨al⟩ inability to be master over himself in this, tried and attested a hundred times, finally produces a habitual *rancune* {rancor} against *what* becomes master here — which is understandable, albeit hardly philosophical yet . . . The hatred peaks when such natures lack the strength of will for that extreme measure, renunciation of the "devil"; the most poisonous enmity against the senses in the whole history of phil⟨osophy⟩ |and art| comes neither from the "impotents" nor indeed from the ascetics, but from the *failed* ascetics who really needed to be ascetics . . . The Christian August⟨ine⟩ is nothing but [a revenge on his defeated "devil" —] the unbridled triumph of the revenge of a failed ascetic . . . The spiritualization of enmity consists of making people deeply aware of what value there is in having enemies: briefly, that they must act and decide in the opposite way to how they formerly acted and decided when enmity was still stupid — formerly, people wanted the destruction of the enemy: nowadays you have an interest in maintaining your enemies — There are creations like the new German Reich, that see themselves as necessary only through a sort of brooding hatred — so that the *artificium* {artifice} in regard to its emergence is gradually forgotten. The same applies to inner antagonism: whoever buys peace of soul at the price of *simply* annulling (starving out, wiping out, *abolishing* . . .) his soul, belongs to the "old game"

— and has no understanding of his own highest interest. All strong natures know that they have contradictions in their body — and that their fertility and inexhaustibility depends on the eternal struggle, on account of which the celebrated "peace of soul" ⟨is⟩ set aside. This applies to statesmen and artists alike . . . You are a proven *décadent* if you treasure peace of soul higher than war, than *life*, than fertility . . . Or to put it another way: because you feel infertile, you opt for peace . . .

I

2. *"il faut tuer les passions"]* "the passions must be killed"
3. *"If . . . out"]* Cf. *Matthew 5:29.*
4. *"poor in spirit"]* Cf. *Matthew 5:3.*

2

5. *those natures . . . la Trappe]* Cf. *SE 3; CW 2, p. 191.* {La Trappe was an abbey in Soligny, France, famed for its austere regime.}

3

6. *Twilight . . . soul" . . .]* Pm: [Revaluation of All Values] "Psychologist at Leisure": also a kind of "peace of the soul" . . . *Variation of this change in proofs Pp: Idol-Hammer:* who knows? perhaps also a sort — — — "How a Psychologist Asks Questions": — This work is also, like the "Case of Wagner," above all — — —

4, 5, 6

7. *Mp XVI 4 and W II 5 contain parts of §§4–6 within a different context; the complete first draft of this configuration is found in W II 5, 47–49; it consists of four sections numbered 1–4 by N; 2, 3, and 4 correspond to what are now 4, 5, and 6; §1 remained unused, and reads as follows:* Morality as type of *décadence.* / If [a community, for quite definite and transparent conditions of existence, decrees that "we shall act in this and this way among ourselves, among ourselves we shall *not* act in this and this way," command and veto given thus] from a communal instinct, we issue instructions and forbid certain actions, we forbid ourselves not a kind of "being," not an "attitude," but only, as is sensible, a certain direction and application of this "being," this "attitude." But along comes the [morality] insane ideologue of virtue, the *moralist,* and says: "God examines the heart! What is the use of refraining from

certain actions: it does not make you any better!" Answer: my dear [ass] long-eared and virtuous Sir, we have absolutely no desire to be better, we are quite satisfied with ourselves, the only thing we want to avoid is *harming* each other — which is why we forbid certain actions in consideration of certain people, namely ourselves, while we cannot praise enough the same actions on condition that they apply to opponents of the community only — you, for example — [honor and promote, propagate by means of training and education. Were we to be of that senseless radicalism that they recommend to us, in forbidding attitudes {at this point, the version cited in *KSA* 14 becomes garbled; we translate here the version that appears in *KGW* IX 8, cited in Sommer 1, 324–25} (i.e., a kind of being and fate), we would destroy the manipulation of our power, of our self-preservation — precisely the attitude we honor most . . . from whose inexpedient outbreaks and outlets we merely seek to protect ourselves]. With these in mind, we raise our children, train them up . . . Were we to be of that "God-pleasing" radicalism [as you are], which your saintly insanity recommends, were we to be mooncalves enough [like you], were we to judge your source, the "heart," the "attitude" by those actions, that would mean judging our existence and with it, [deny] [of it] its main preconditions — an attitude, a heart, a passion that we honor with the highest respect. Through our decrees, we prevent this attitude from breaking out and seeking outlets in an inappropriate fashion — how clever we are to give ourselves such laws, how *ethical*, too . . . Do you not suspect, at least at a distance, what sacrifices we have made, how much taming, self-overcoming, harshness toward ourselves that required? We are vehement in our desires, there are moments when we would like to gobble ourselves up . . . But communal reason becomes master over us: take note, that is practically a definition of ethics . . . *The version of this paragraph in Mp XVI 4 connects to the rest of the text (§§4–6) by means of the words:* This, the speech of a moral naturalist *cf. WP² 281; CW 18, 18[8].*

4

8. *"God . . . heart"]* Cf. Luke 16:1{5}.
9. *castrate]* Castrat

5

10. *value of life]* Cf. N's preparatory studies for HAH, in particular the excerpt from a book of this title by Eugen Dühring, found in CW 10, 9[1].

11. *décadence-instinct]* {N here underlines both *décadence* and *instinct*.}

6

12. *"ecce homo!"]* "behold the man!" *Pilate's words in John 19:5. N used it for the title of a poem in JS in 1882 and for his autobiography in this volume.*

The Four Great Errors

1. *The four great errors were originally three, as §§1–2 were late insertions into the Pm. The first version of §3 is found in W II 6, 104–5, under the rubric Philosophy and as a free-standing text; likewise the copy in Mp XVI 4 where, however, the section also acquired a title at the time this published version of TI was written. The first version of §§4–6 is found in W II 7, 38, 39, 36; here, they form the draft of one of the books of "The Will to Power" and in fact correspond to the plan on p. 34 of the same manuscript (see CW 18, 16[86]), which was one of the last plans before the emergence of Twilight of the Idols (and indeed before N finally gave up his plan to publish a "Will to Power.") The contrast "error-truth" is crucial for this plan; the titles for the four books are:* I. Psychology of Error . . . / II. False Values . . . / III. The Criterion of Truth . . . / IV. The Struggle of False and True Values . . . *Here we also find a connection to scheme 16[85] on p. 37 of W II 7: Psychology of Error. /* 1) Confusion of Cause and Effect / 2) Confusion of Truth with What Is Believed True / 3) Confusion of Consciousness with Causality. *Point 1 of this scheme is developed in §§1–2 of this chapter of TI; point 2 in §6; point 3 in §§3–5. In the division of the first book of 16[86], we find, after three chapter titles that are identical with the three titles from the scheme in 16[85], the title for a fourth chapter:* 4) Confusion of Logic with the Principle of the Real. *This chapter in the abandoned plan does not correspond to any other material here; instead, N extracted the current §§7 and 8 from a different context,*

a larger text in Notebook W II 6 (CW 18, 15[30]). He copied what he needed for "Error of Free Will" onto a blank page of the earlier Notebook W II 3 from winter 1887–88 (p. 129). WP² 765 comes from a crossed-out preliminary draft (in W II 3).

1

2. *Cornaro]* Cf. *Ludwig Cornaro* {1475–1566}, *Die Kunst, ein hohes und gesundes Alter zu erreichen* ("The art of reaching an advanced and healthy age") *(Berlin*{: Mode, 1881}, *NL; German translation by Paul Sembach of Lodovico* {Luigi} *Cornaro, Discorsi della vita sobria* (1558). *Cf. N to Franz Overbeck, 27 October 1883* {*KGB* III:1, 449–50} *and* {28} *March 1884* {*KGB* III:1, 488}.

3. *Crede experto.]* "Believe the expert." *Cf. N to Overbeck,* {28} *March 1884* {*KGB* III:1, 488}: I hold on to Nice: it is climatically my "Promised Land." But one must eat properly here and not live à la Cornaro.

2

4. *light feet . . . divinity).]* Cf. *WA 1*, p. 5 above: "What is good is light, everything divine moves on delicate feet."

3

5. *Error of a false causality.]* Mp XVI, 4: {earlier section titles} Theory of Spirit as Cause; of the Error [of the Cause of Will] of the Spiritual Cause; A False Kind of Cause

6. *antecedentia]* "antecedents"

7. *being]* Sein

8. *being]* seiend

9. *horrendum pudendum]* "terrible shameful thing" {Traditional euphemism for genitalia.}

10. *with reality]* Mp XVI, 4: posited as being {*Sein*}, with being {*Sein*}

11. *measure of reality!]* Mp XVI, 4: judge of the world.

12. *And calling it God! —]* Mp XVI, 4; W II 6, 105: And calling it God! — [Let us delete the concept of spiritual "cause"! In one's experience there is no such cause. — Must I demonstrate that it is of no use anymore? That in actual fact it is not used in science anymore? All that remains is the word, but empty, puffed-up yet without content: we think about it quite differently. For example, *equivalences*

between "cause" and "effect" — — "*causa aequat effectum.*" {"cause corresponds to effect"} —]

4

13. *Error] W II 7, 38:* Theory; *for the completion of this paragraph, cf. HAH 13.*

14. *biding its time . . . as its cause. —] W II 7, 38:* but finally it is experienced as *understood*, as *explained* — — : it is presented as causality and that makes it count as having been explained . . .

15. *nervus sympathicus]* "sympathetic nervous system"

6

16. *For §6, N rewrote almost word for word a scheme from W II 7, 36.*

17. *666)] Die Welt als Wille und Vorstellung,* vol. II, chap. 46, bk. 4 (1859); *World 2,* p. 596.

18. *faith, love, hope] Cf. 1 Corinthians 13:13.*

19. *Morality . . . state.] W II 7, 37:* The happy outcome of a venture does not make the melancholic happy; and a great loss cannot cloud the bubbling cheerfulness of a Benvenuto Cellini.

7

20. *invented . . . to do that . . .] W II 3, 129:* a theory of the right to revenge. "God will punish": that means the ruling priesthood of former social entities wants to have the right.

21. *in psychologicis]* "in psychological matters"

22. *a metaphysics . . . hangman . . .] Pm:* the metaphysics of revenge.

8

23. *causa prima]* "first cause"

24. *responsibility in God] Verantwortlichkeit in Gott; Cp:* responsibility as God [*als Gott*]; *Pm, Up:* responsibility of God [*Gottes*].

The "Improvers" of Humanity

1. *This chapter also arose from the material for the abandoned "Will to Power," especially that intended for the third chapter, "The Good and the Improvers," of the second book, "Descent of Values," in the last plan (dated 26 August 1888). The same thoughts are found*

in the jottings of winter 1887–88 under the title "How Virtue Comes to Victory"; *that is again the title of the second chapter of the second book in the plan from the start of 1888 (cf. CW 18, 12[2]). In spring 1888, N's thoughts on this subject were supplemented by his reading of the laws of Manu.*

2. *The "Improvers" of Humanity.*] *Mp XVI 4:* "Improving" People! [The Background of Morality]

I

3. *first . . . myself*] *Cf. GM* {Preface 3}.

2

4. *In W II 6, 72 Pd:* In order to have a fair opinion of morality, we have to replace the term with two *zoological* concepts, *taming* of the beast and *breeding of a specific species*. In every age, the priests pretended that they wanted to be "*improvers*" . . . But the rest of us laughed whenever a tamer wanted to talk about his "improved" animals. The taming of the beast is achieved in most cases by harming the beast; just as the moral human is no better a human, merely a weakened one. But he is less harmful. *Cf. WP² 397.*

5. *"blond beast"*] *Cf. GM I, 11.*

3

6. *law of Manu*] {In Indian mythology, the first man, Manu, inaugurated a Sanskrit code of law.} *N read details of this in Les législateurs religieux: Manou – Moïse – Mahomet ("Religious legislators: Manu – Moses – Mohammed") (Paris*{: Lacroix,} *1876) by the Indologist Louis Jacolliot* {1837–90; cf. *AC* note 236}. *NL. N wrote to Gast on this reading matter on 31 May 1888* {*KGB* III:5, 325}: I am grateful to these last weeks for immense *enlightenment*: I found a French translation of the Lawbook of *Manu* which was produced in India under the tight supervision of the highest-placed priests and scholars. This completely *Aryan* product, a priestly code of morality based on the Vedanta, the conception of castes and age-old usage — *not* pessimistic, however much it was priestly — supplements my perception of religion in the most remarkable manner. I confess to the impression that everything else we have in terms of great moral laws seems like an imitation and indeed caricature of it: Egyptianism in first place; but even Plato seems

to me in all main points to be nothing other than *well-taught* by a Brahmin. In comparison, the Jews looked like a chandala race which learned from their *masters* the principle of how a *body of priests* becomes master and how a people is organized . . . The Chinese, too, appear to have produced their Confucius and Lao Tzu under the impression of this *age-old, classical lawbook.* Medieval organization resembles a strange groping to recoup all the perceptions on which ancient Indo-Aryan society stood — but with *pessimistic* values, which take their descent from the soil of *décadence*-races. — The *Jews* seem to be simply "go-betweens" even here — they invent nothing.

7. *chandala.]* {Class of people in India looked down upon as outcasts and untouchables.}

8. *The third edict . . . each other . . .] Cf. Jacolliot, 105–6.*

9. *"The chandalas . . . pedigree."] Cf. Jacolliot, 102–3.*

4

10. *For N's view of "Aryan," cf. his letter to the anti-Semite Theodor Fritsch* {29 March 1887, *KGB* III:5, 51}. *Fritsch was editor of the journal "Anti-Semitic Correspondence," friend of N's sister and her husband Bernhard Förster, the author of a Handbuch der Judenfrage* {"Handbook of the Jewish question"} *(1907)* {an updated and expanded version of his *Antisemiten-Catechismus* ("Anti-Semitic catechism") (Langensalza: Verlag Hermann Beyer, 1887)}, *and fellow-traveler of National Socialism. N writes:* . . . Believe me, this abominable desire of *noioso* {tedious} dilettantes to speak about the *value* of humans and races, this submission to "authorities" which are rejected with cool contempt by every more considered mind (e.g., E. Dühring, R. Wagner, Ebrard, Wahrmund, P. de Lagarde — who among them is the most unjust, the most unfair in questions of morality and history?), these constant absurd falsifications and clarifications of the vague concepts "Germanic," "Semitic," "Aryan," "Christian," "German" — all these in the long run could make me truly incensed and propel me from the ironic benevolence with which I have up till now contemplated the velleities and Pharisaisms of present-day Germans. — And finally, what do you think I feel when the name *Zarathustra* is uttered by anti-Semites? . . .

11. *the Book of Enoch]* N *had noted down in Notebook W II 3 the following from* Vie de Jésus *(1863, 181) by Ernst Renan:* Le livre d'Hénoch contient des malédictions plus violents encore que celles de l'Évangile contre le monde, les riches, les puissants. {"The Book of Enoch contains even more violent curses than the Gospels on the world, the rich, the powerful."} *Cf. CW 18, 11[405].*

5

12. *pia fraus]* "pious fraud"
13. *Neither Manu . . . immoral. —] Cf. AC 55, ending.*

What the Germans Lack
   1. *On the development of this chapter, see the notes to the Foreword.*

I

   2. *liberties with it . . .] Cf. W II 3, 184; W II 7, 154: liberties* with it. Among the French you must have courage to be German.
   3. *the race of thinkers] The first to speak of "the race of thinkers and poets" was — according to Georg Büchmann,* Geflügelte Worte {"Winged words"} {(Berlin: Haude & Spener, 1864)} — Karl Musäus *in the preliminary note to his Volksmärchen ("Folktales") (1782.)*
   4. *"Germany, Germany above all"] "Deutschland, Deutschland über Alles"* {First line of German national anthem composed in 1841 by Hoffmann von Fallersleben. Nowadays, only the politically neutral third verse is sung.}
   5. *— Would I . . . mediocrity! —] Cf. CW 18, 19[1], 3:* Should I confess which books people read now? — Dahn? Ebers? Ferdinand Meyer? I have heard university professors praise these Bieder-Meyers to the detriment of Gottfried Keller. Confounded instinct of mediocrity! {The "Biedermeier" cultural period in Germany in the mid-nineteenth century was cozy, if complacent; N weaves this into a pun, using Meyer's surname. The fictitious Gottlieb Biedermaier was invented by the writer Ludwig Eichrodt (1827–92) and the physician Adolf Kussmaul (1822–1902).}

2

   6. *lounging around] Schlafrock* {"dressing gown"}

7. *once*] I.e., in DS, the essay attacking D. F. Strauss, *Der alte und der neue Glaube* {(Leipzig: S. Hirzel, 1872).} NL; {*The Old Faith and the New*, trans. Mathilde Blind (London: Asher and Co., 1873).}

8. *Not for . . . verse*] Cf. D. F. Strauss, *Gesammelte Schriften* ("Complete works"), ed. E. Zeller, vol. 12: *Gedichte aus dem Nachlaß* {("Posthumous poems")} (Bonn: Verlag Emil Strauß, 1877)}.

3

9. *Germany . . . flatland. —*] Cf. EH "Why I Write Such Good Books" 2; NCW Foreword.

4

10. *"Wars of Liberation"*] {Successful campaign by the Prussian armies against the forces of Napoleon (1813–15).}

11. *Culture and the state . . . consideration.*] Cf. W II 6, *139, 141*: Culture and the state are antagonists: [today the state claims to participate in questions of culture and make decisions — as though the state were not a means to culture, and a very inferior means to culture! How many "German Reichs" would you give for just one Goethe!] — all great periods of culture were politically times of decline. [Actually there is no question] Today, when [the state] the Reich claims to participate in questions of culture and make decisions, it is well to ask a little question in return: how many "German Reichs" would one give for a Goethe? Meanwhile, the "Reich" is a disaster for the history of culture: Europe has grown poorer since the German mind {*Geist*} finally renounced the "intellect" {"*Geist*"}. — People abroad know something about this: let the Germans not deceive themselves!

12. *That there . . . at that. —*] Cf. W II 6, *141*: That there is no German philosopher is a first-rank finale. Nobody is so unfair as to hold it against the Germans if prattling nobodies, like the unconscious Mister Eduard von Hartmann or a rabid bilious pack animal like the Berlin anti-Semite Mister E. Dühring, misuse the word philosopher — the latter does not have a single decent human in his entourage, the former has no decent "understanding."

5

13. *Educators . . . educated*] Cf. CW 13, 5[25] (1875).
14. *"higher wet-nurses"*] Cf. CW 17, 10[12].

15. *Burckhardt]* Cf. *N's letter to Overbeck, 22 December 1888* {*KGB* III:5, 547–48}: Jakob Burckhardt, cited twice [in *TI*] with greatest respect, received the very first copy that Naumann sent to *me*.

16. *pulchrum est paucorum hominum]* "beauty is for few men"; cf. Horace, Satires I, 9, 44 *(also cited in WA 6 {and AC 57}.)*

17. *the democratism . . . commonplace . . .] der Demokratismus der "allgemeinen," der gemein gewordnen "Bildung"* . . . {N puns on *gemein* and *allgemein*, which are sometimes interchangeable, meaning "general"; *"allgemeine Bildung"* is "a (good) general education"; but *gemein* by itself means "nasty," "mean," or as here, "common."}

18. *young man]* {In the new Reich, state education for girls ceased at age sixteen, and they therefore could not obtain the qualification — *Abitur* — for university. Some women of N's acquaintance received private tuition to pass the *Abitur* and then studied at Swiss universities.}

6

19. *All . . . impulse.]* Cf. *TI* "Morality as Anti-Nature" 2.

7

20. *light feet]* Cf. *TI* "The Four Great Errors" 2 and *WA 1*.
21. *charm]* Anmut {N is being sarcastic.}

Forays of an Untimely One
   1. *This whole chapter also emerged from material N drafted between autumn 1887 and summer 1888 with a view to "The Will to Power," and is further proof that TI is a product of his resolution to abandon that work. In the first Pm of summer 1888 — i.e., where TI and AC were still a coherent whole — the current §§1–18 of this chapter came under the heading "Among Artists and Writers," §§19–31 and 45–51 under the heading "From My Aesthetics"; N added §§32–44 between 4 and 13 October during his corrections: they too had originally been intended for "The Will to Power."*

I

   2. *Cf. CW 18, 11[409].*
   3. *in impuris naturalibus]* "in natural filth"

4. *morality-trumpeter of Säckingen]* Cf. *the popular epic poem by Joseph Victor von Scheffel* {(1826–86)}, *Der Trompeter von Säckingen: Ein Sang vom Oberrhein* {"The trumpeter of Säckingen: A song from the upper Rhein"} *(Stuttgart*{: Metzler,} *1854).*

5. *School of Velocity — after women.]* {A pun on *The School of Velocity,* piano exercises by Carl Czerny (1791–1857), and Liszt's reputation for chasing after women.}

6. *lactea ubertas]* "milk in abundance"; *Journal des Goncourt, II, 25, NL: "Dans son attitude, il y a une gravité, une placidité, quelque chose du demi-endormement d'un ruminant"* {"In her attitude, there is a gravity, placidity and something of the semi-somnolence of a ruminant"}; and *"Mme Sand, un sphinx ruminant une vache Apis"* {"Mme Sand, a ruminating Sphinx an Apis cow"} {In Egyptian mythology, Apis was a sacred bull. Sommer 1, 397, suggests that more likely sources for N's remark on Sand are Émile Faguet, *Dix-neuvième siècle. Études littéraires. Chateaubriand, Lamartine, Alfred de Vigny, Victor Hugo, A. de Musset, Th. Gautier, P. Mérimée, Michelet, George Sand, Balzac* (Paris: Boivin & Cie., 1887), 408; and Jules Lemaître, *Les contemporains. Études et portraits littéraires. Troisième série. Octave Feuillet – Edmond et Jules de Goncourt – Pierre Loti – H. Rabusson – J. de Glouvet – J. Soulary – Le duc d'Aumale – Gaston Paris – Les femmes de France – Chroniqueurs Parisiens – Henry Fouquier – Henri Rochefort – Jean Richepin – Paul Bourget,* 2nd ed. (Paris: Lecène et Oudin, 1887), 255–56, each of whom mentions "*lactea ubertas.*"}

7. *Les frères de Goncourt]* "The Goncourt brothers" {Edmond (1822–96) and Jules de Goncourt (1830–70).}

8. *Ajaxes]* {Ajax the Greater and Ajax the Lesser are two very different heroes in the *Iliad.*}

9. *contest]* {An ironic allusion to the ancient Athenian drama contest from which only Aeschylus's *Oresteia* (458 BCE) has survived intact.} Cf. *Journal des Goncourt, III, 80: "je pris la voix plus douce pour affirmer que j'avais plus de plaisir à lire Hugo qu'Homère"* {" . . . I said as softly as possible that I had more pleasure in reading Hugo than Homer."}

10. *Zola: . . . stinking."—]* {Cf. Louis Desprez, *L'évolution naturaliste* ("Naturalistic evolution") (Paris: Tresse, 1884), 238. *NL.* This is the only place in N's published works where he mentions Zola.}

2

11. *For this section, cf. CW 17, 9[22, 20] (autumn 1887).*

12. *Renan. — . . . regularity.] Cf. W II 3, 9:* How does it come about that such a refined and [flexible] applied mind as Renan goes wrong every time he trusts his instincts? In an absurd way, becomes a theologian and feminine?

13. *an aristocracy of the mind] W II 3, 9:* a St. Francis aristocracy of the mind. *For Renan's concept of aristocracy of the mind, cf. the Goncourts' descriptions of the conversations at the famous "dinners at Magny's" and — above all — Renan's Dialogues philosophiques, which N had read in German translation (Ernst Renan, Philosophische Dialoge und Fragmente, trans. Konrad von Zdekauer (Leipzig{: Koschny,} 1877). NL. Cf. esp. 60–61, 73, 76–77, 83ff.; the pages show traces of N's reading). Another participant of the dinners, G. Flaubert, shared Renan's theory that France (and the whole world) should be governed by an oligarchy of scholars; this is evident from his letters to Sand, which N also read.*

14. *évangile des humbles]* "gospel of the Humble"

15. *a Christian . . . adoration . . .] W II 3, 9. 11:* a Catholic and feminine! His ruses are all female priest ruses — they almost give a man the creeps. Renan's hatred is not firsthand and ⟨he is⟩ innocent and at any rate harmless: but he knows how to adore in a lethal fashion.

3

16. *For this section, see CW 18, 11[9]. It is even more patently clear from this fragment that N used the Journal des Goncourt for this description of Saint-Beuve; cf. e.g., Journal, II, 66: "La petite touche — c'est le charme et la petitesse de la causerie de Sainte-Beuve. Point de hautes idées, point de grandes expressions, point de ces images qui détachent en bloc une figure. Cela est aiguisé, menu, pointu, c'est une pluie de petites phrases qui peignent, à la longue, et par la superposition et l'amoncellement. Une conversation ingénieuse, spirituelle mais mince; une conversation où il y a de la grâce, de l'épigramme, du gentil ronron, de la griffe et de la patte de velours. Conversation, au fond,* qui n'est pas la conversation d'un **mâle** supérieur." {"The light touch — that is the charm and pettiness of Sainte-Beuve's conversation. *No elevated ideas, no grand expressions,* none of the images

that delineate a figure en bloc. It is honed, petty, pointed, it is a shower of little phrases that elaborate, in the long run, by both superimposition and accumulation. An ingenious discourse, witty but *trivial*; a discourse wherein there is grace, wit, gentle purring and a taloned *velvet paw*. A discourse that ultimately *does not belong to a superior* **male.**"} *(The words emphasized here are underlined by N in his copy, where the whole passage is marked in the margin, complete with an NB.) On p. 90 of the same work: "* . . . *Dans ces quelques paroles, jaillies* du plus secret *et* du plus sincère de son âme, *on sent, dans Sainte-Beuve, le* célibataire révolutionnaire, *et il nous apparaît presque avec la tête d'un conventionnel* niveleur, *d'un homme laissant percer contre la société du XIXe siècle* des haines à la Rousseau, ce Jean-Jacques auquel il ressemble un peu physiologiquement." {" . . . In these few words, springing *from what is most secret* and *most sincere in his soul*, one feels in Sainte-Beuve the *revolutionary celibate*, and he appears to us as almost having the head of a conventional *leveler*, a man unleashing on 19th-century society *the hates of Rousseau, that very Jean-Jacques whom he physiologically resembles somewhat.*"} *(Here, too, the words emphasized designate N's underlining, at the end of which N has written one of his familiar notes in the margin:* e⟨cce⟩ h⟨omo⟩.*) Again on p. 103: "* . . . *Voltaire amène chez Sainte-Beuve un éloge de Rousseau, dont il parle* comme *un esprit de sa famille,* comme *un homme de sa* **race**" {" . . . Voltaire leads Sainte-Beuve to a eulogy on Rousseau, of whom he speaks as though he were *a witty family member*, as though he were a *man of his* **race**"} *(The words emphasized denote N's underlining, as above, while "race" is underlined twice.)*

17. *médisance]* "slander"

18. *Port-Royal]* {Port-Royal-des-Champs was a Cistercian religious community famed for advancing Jansenism in the seventeenth century. Sainte-Beuve's three-volume *Port-Royal* (1840–48) chronicles the history of the movement.}

19. *hunched . . . foot]* Cf. *"Sayings and Arrows"* 31.

20. *In some . . . Baudelaire.]* Cf. *CW 18, 11 [231]: Sainte-Beuve to Baudelaire: "Vous dites vrai, ma poésie se rattache à la vôtre. J'avais goûté du même fruit amer, plein de cendres, au fond."* {"You are right to say my poetry links up with yours. In the main, I tasted the same bitter fruit, full of ashes."} *(Excerpt from Baudelaire's*

Œuvres posthumes {"Posthumous works"}*). In addition, N was familiar with Sainte-Beuve's connection to Baudelaire from reading* Les cahiers de Sainte-Beuve {"Sainte-Beuve's notebooks"} *(Paris*{: Lemerre,} *1876), NL; here we also find the designation "âne de génie"* {"ass of genius"} *which Baudelaire — "mon petit ami libertin"* {"my little libertine friend"}*, says Sainte-Beuve on p. 36 — coined for Victor Hugo and N adopted; cf. CW 16, 34[5]; 38[6].*

4

21. *Imitatio Christi]* {Underlined by N. Seminal devotional work reputedly written by the theologian Thomas à Kempis (1379/80–1471). Cf. Thomas à Kempis, *Vier Bücher von der Nachfolge Christi* {"Four books of the imitation of Christ"} (Hildburghausen and Leipzig: F. Kesselring, 1858). *NL.*}

22. *the eternal-feminine]* {Phrase that can be traced back to the Greeks, which Goethe used at the end of *Faust* II.}

5

23. *For this section, cf. CW 17, 10[163].*

24. *They have got . . . fanatics.]* {Cf. Arvède Barine (pseudonym of Louise-Cécile Vincens), "George Eliot, d'après sa correspondence," in *Revue des Deux Mondes* 68 (1 July 1885): 118.}

6

25. *For this section, cf. CW 18, 11[24]. On 10 February 1876 N had purchased Sand's Complete Works in German translation (Leipzig*{: Wigand,} *1844–47), with an introduction by Arnold Ruge. NL.*

26. *Lettres d'un Voyageur] Published in 1837.*

27. *She wound . . . wrote] Cf. T. Gautier's account in the* Journal des Goncourt, *II, p. 146: "Enfin vous savez ce qui lui est arrivé. Quelque chose de monstrueux! Un jour elle finit un roman à une heure du matin . . . et elle en recommence un autre, dans la nuit . . . La copie est une fonction chez Mme Sand . . . "* {"Finally, you know what happened to her. Something pretty terrible! She finishes a novel at one in the morning . . . and starts another the same night. Replicating is how Mme Sand works . . . "}

28. *writing-cow] Cf. TI "Forays" 1 and note 6 above.*

29. *Renan admires her] Cf. Journal des Goncourt, II, 112: " . . . je trouve beaucoup plus vraie Mme Sand que Balzac . . . chez elle les*

passions sont générales . . . dans trois cents ans on lira Mme Sand . . . "
{"I find Mme Sand much more authentic than Balzac . . . with
her, passions are general . . . people will read Mme Sand three
hundred years from now . . . "} *N in his own copy underlined these
comments by Renan during a "dinner at Magny's," likewise this
comment on p. 122: "Renan: — Mme Sand la plus grande artiste de
ce temps-ci, et le talent le plus vrai!"* {"Renan: — Mme Sand, the
greatest artist of our time and the most authentic talent!"}

7

30. *For this section, cf. CW 17, 9[64].*

31. *"from nature"] N writes "nach der Natur," the German translation of the French expression "d'après nature" as found for example
in Edmond de Goncourt's introduction to the Journal des Goncourt
(p. viii of the edition N reads): " . . . nous n'étions pas encore maîtres
de notre instrument, où nous n'étions que {d'}assez imparfaits rédac-
teurs de la note d'après nature"* {" . . . we were not yet masters of our
craft, in which we were rather poor redactors of the *note according
to nature*} *(E. de Goncourt's italics).*

32. *petits faits]* "small or insignificant facts"

8

33. *Sections 8–11 were to have formed the opening of the chapter
"On the Physiology of Art" that N had announced in WA 7:* in a
chapter of my chief work bearing the title "On the Physiology of
Art." *In the plan for "The Will to Power" of May 1888, the period
when N was at work on WA, Chapter 3 of Book III was indeed to be
entitled* "On the Physiology of Art." *At the same time (May 1888),
N began to make a second draft of his notes on that subject, now
found in the Turin notebook W II 9 under the heading* "On the
Physiology of Art". *When he gave up his plans for "The Will to
Power," N incorporated these four paragraphs from W II 9 into TI
virtually unaltered. In W II 5 there is a variant entitled* "On the
Genesis of Art" *which has a number of changes: W II 5, 164* {equiv-
alent to sections *TI* "Forays" 8 and 9; the translations of these
variants follow the corrected texts that appear in *KGW* IX, and
not the texts that appear in *KSA* 14}: "*On the Genesis of Art. //* All
art is traced back to circumstances where *intoxication {der Rausch}*

has increased the excitability of the whole machine: then it can make an assault on things and values / this can be the intoxication of sexual excitement / or the intoxication of cruelty / or the intoxication of narcotics / or the intoxication of spring / : of anger / : of great desires / : of feats of bravery / : of the contest / or the intoxication of the eye: a vision // Physiologically speaking, the precondition [. . .] for all art, all aesthetic doing and seeing is *intoxication*. / the extreme arousal of one *sense* in the condition of intoxication⟨,⟩ the power enabling related *spheres of intoxication* to be aroused . . . // in lyric poetry and music it is a delicate kind of sensuality above all else⟨,⟩ in tragedy cruelty // The *essential thing about intoxication* is the feeling of an increase in strength and fullness / out of this fullness we hand over to things, i.e., we idealize them / *idealizing* does *not* consist of subtracting lower and less important traits, rather of a tremendous *driving out* of the main traits, so that the others just disappear / you *enrich* everything out of your own abundance: you see it full, urgent, swollen with force, i.e., you transform things into a state where they represent a sort of *reflection of ourselves* // One can precisely imagine an *anti-artistic activity* that renders everything poorer, more attenuated, faded: who are these *anti-artists*, these starvelings who appropriate from things and make them more *meagre* — They are specifically pessimists: an artist who is a pessimist is a *contradiction*⟨;⟩ / Problem: *and yet there are pessimistic artists*! . . . "

In the version reworked by N at W II 5, 164–65 the same passage reads: "On the Genesis of Art. // Intoxication* must first have increased (the) excitability of the whole machine: or there can be no 'art.' [sic] All the very differently determined kinds of intoxication have the energy for this: I mention / [. . .] (the) intoxication of sexual excitement / the intoxication that accompanies great desires, great affects / the intoxication of cruelty / the intoxication of the contest, of victory, of the feat of bravery, of the celebration / or the intoxication after the use or abuse of narcotics / or the intoxication that arises under certain meteorological conditions: e.g., the [. . .] intoxication of spring / [. . .] lastly the intoxication of the power of will, of the accumulated and swollen will — or the intoxication of the eye: vision / Physiologically speaking, the precondition [. . .] for all

art, all aesthetic doing and seeing is *intoxication*. / the extreme
arousal of one *sense* in the condition of intoxication⟨,⟩ the power
enabling related *spheres of intoxication* to be aroused . . . // in lyric
poetry and music it is a delicate kind of sensuality above all
else⟨,⟩ [. . .] in tragedy cruelty // The *essential thing [. . .] about
intoxication* is the feeling of an increase in strength and full-
ness⟨,⟩ Out of this fullness we hand over to things, i.e., we idealize them⟨,⟩ / *idealizing* does *not* consist of subtracting and
discounting [. . .] lower and less important traits: rather of a tremendous *driving out* of the main traits, so that the others just
disappear / In this condition you *enrich* everything out of your
own abundance: what you see it wants [*sic?*], you see urgent,
swollen with force / The aesthetic human transforms things till
they reflect him [*sic*], till they are a *reflection* of his condition [. . .]:
this *having* to transform is art. Every departure from himself
becomes a [. . .] *pleasure in himself* . . . ; in art intoxication itself
enjoys itself. // One could imagine a specific anti-artistic activity, a
way of being that rendered everything poorer, more attenuated,
faded. And indeed, history is rich in such *anti-artists*, and such
starvelings of life, speaking figuratively: who of necessity have to
appropriate from things, devour them and make them more *meagre*
. . . The genuine Christians, for example, would be like this: a Christian who is an artist at the same time never happens. — Do not be
so childish as to cite Raphael to me: — R⟨aphael⟩ said Yes, and R⟨a-
phael⟩ *did* Yes — therefore he was not a Christian.

10

34. *W II 5, 165* {corresponding to *TI* "Forays" 10 and 11}: What
does the antithesis *"Dionysian"* and *"Apollonian"* mean, both understood as forms of *intoxication*? / The latter above all has the *eye*
aroused: so that it receives the power of vision. The former arouses
the whole *system of affects*: so that it unleashes the power of transfiguration, representation, transformation, play-acting and dancing . . . / the essential thing is the ease of metamorphosis: so that
the affect, once lightly expressed, immediately goes forth into
reality . . . / Music is, as it were, just an *abstraction* of that much
fuller expression of the release of affect . . . a residuum of histrionics / : we have (relatively at least) immobilized a number of

senses, above all our muscle sense: so that the human no longer
imitates and acts out everything he feels . . . Even so, the former is
the actual Dionysian total state: music is an *intensification* slowly
acquired at the cost of other Dionysian arts / ⟨T⟩he actor and the
musician are *fundamentally related* and are really one entity: but
so separated by specialization as to cause misunderstanding⟨;⟩
again, the lyricist has attached himself to the musician: really they
are one entity. / ⟨T⟩he architect represents a great [usefulness] act
of willing in its most convincing and proudest form [. . .]: in the
edifice power, the will to power should be made visible. The soul's
loquacity writ large . . . / Dionysian intoxication includes sexuality and lust, not lacking in the Apollonian, either. There must still
be a difference in pace between the two conditions . . . *The extreme
peace of certain experiences of intoxication* likes to be reflected in the
vision of the most peaceful gestures and acts of the soul. In the
main, the classical style represents this peace, simplification,
abridgement and concentration / *Intoxication in nature*: the *highest feeling of power* is concentrated in the classical type. Hardly
reacting: great awareness: no feeling of struggle:

The version of this passage reworked by N reads: What does the
antithesis *"Dionysian"* and *"Apollonian"* mean, both understood as
forms of *intoxication*? / The latter above all holds the *eye* aroused:
so that it receives the power of vision. The painter, the sculptor, the
epic poet are visionaries par excellence. The former moves and
heightens the entire *system of the affects* so that it discharges all the
means of expression of the affects⟨,⟩ so that it unleashes the power
of transfiguration, representation, transformation, play-acting and
dances . . . / the essential thing is the ease of metamorphosis: so
that the affect, once lightly expressed, immediately goes forth into
reality . . . / Music is, as it were, just an *abstraction* of that much
fuller expression of the release of affect . . . a residuum of original
histrionics / : we have (relatively at least) immobilized a number of
senses, above all our muscle sense: so that the human no longer
imitates and acts out everything he feels . . . Even so, the former is
the actual Dionysian total state: music is a *strengthening* of the
individual slowly acquired at the cost of other Dionysian arts / the
actor (i.e., dancer and mimic)⟨,⟩ the musician and the lyricist are

fundamentally related and are really one entity: but gradually so separated by specialization as to cause misunderstanding and contradiction⟨;⟩ the lyric poet remained united with the musician the longest ⟨:⟩ ⟨really⟩ they are one entity. / ⟨T⟩he architect represents a great act of will, the intoxication [. . .] of a great will in its most convincing and proudest form [. . .]: in the edifice power, will [. . .] to power should be made visible. Architecture is eloquence of the will in spatial forms . . . / Dionysian intoxication includes sexuality and lust, not lacking in the Apollonian, either. There must still be a difference in pace between the two conditions . . . The *extreme peace of certain experiences of intoxication* (more precisely, a deceleration of the feeling for time and space⟨)⟩) likes to be reflected in the vision of the most peaceful gestures and acts of the soul. In the main, the classical style represents this peace, simplification, abridgement, and concentration / *Intoxication in nature*: the *highest feeling of power* is concentrated in the classical type. Hardly reacting: great awareness: no feeling of struggle:

35. *What . . . Dionysian]* *Cf. BT (1872); just before the above drafts from W II 5 (March/April 1888), N had made copious notes on BT; cf. CW 18, 14[14–26].*

12

36. *Cf. CW 18, 11[45].*

37. {Most probably James Anthony Froude, *Thomas Carlyle*, 2 vols. (London: Longman, Green, and Co., 1882/1884), translated into German by Thomas Alfred Fischer as *Das Leben Thomas Carlyles* (Gotha: Perthes, 1887).}

38. *fortissimo]* musical term, meaning "very loud"

39. *cant]* {In English in the original.}

13

40. *"yo . . . mismo."]* "I shall succeed myself." {The source of this remark is most likely Émile Bérard-Varagnac, *Portraits littéraires* ("Literary portraits") (Paris: Calmann Lévy, 1887), 328. NL.}

41. *tamquam . . . gesta]* "acting as though things had gone well"

42. *Ut . . . voluptas."]* "Though the power be lacking, the lust is laudable." *The original phrase from Ovid, Ex Ponto, III, 4, 79, ends "the will [voluntas] is laudable."*

14

43. *"the Reich . . . us"]* *Reference to Luther's hymn "Ein' feste Burg ist unser Gott"* {"A mighty fortress is our God"}, {where N cites the last lines and puns on God's *Reich* and Bismarck's *Reich*}.

44. *mimicry]* {In English in the original.}

15

45. *Cf. CW 17, 9[99, 101].*

16

46. *I have . . . Hartmann"]* *Cf. CW 18, 11[101].*

18

47. *Cf. W II 6, 36, under the headings* "Towards Modernity" *and* "décadence."

48. *five meanings] fünfdeutig* {N's neologism, playing off the German word for "ambiguous" — *zweideutig* — literally "having two meanings."}

19

49. *Cf. Mp XVII under the heading: Aesthetica.* / Postulate: what is beautiful and ugly?

50. *"Oh Dionysus, . . . longer?"]* *Cf. BGE 295 and CW 17, 9[115]: Mix in:* short conversations between Theseus Dionysus and Ariadne. {Cf. also *DD* "Ariadne's Lament," later in this volume.}

20

51. *hatred] Hass* {The German words for "ugly" (*hässlich*) and "hatred" (*Hass*) are etymologically related.}

52. *in this . . . deep . . .] W II 7, 134:* In this hatred lies the whole philosophy of art.

22

53. *divine Plato] Cf. Plato's Symposium, 206b–d.*

54. {Schopenhauer refers to "the divine Plato" in the preface to the first edition of *The World as Will and Representation*. Cf. *World 1*, p. 8.}

23

55. *Plato . . . terrain.] Cf. Phaedrus 249c–256e.*

56. *amor intellectualis dei]* "intellectual love of God"

24

57. *Cf. CW 17, 9[119].*

58. *L'art pour l'art.]* "Art for art's sake." *The phrase was coined by Victor Cousin (1792–1867) in his lectures on philosophy of 1818, published in Paris in 1836 {Cours de philosophie sur le fondement des idées absolues du Vrai, du Beau et du Bien* ("Philosophy course based on the absolute ideas of the true, the beautiful and the good"), ed. Adolphe Garnier (Paris: L. Hachette, 1836), 224: *"Il faut de la religion pour la religion, de la morale pour la morale, {comme} de l'art pour l'art."* {"We must have religion for religion's sake, morality for morality's sake, like art for art's sake."}

59. *worm] Pm:* serpent

25

60. *Cf. CW 18, 11[2].*

27

61. *Cf. CW 18, 11[59].*

62. *"This picture is enchantingly beautiful!"]* Tamino's words {opening aria in Act I, Scene 4} *in Mozart's The Magic Flute* {1791}.

63. *"aut liberi aut libri"]* "either children or books"

64. *"je . . . d'esprit?"]* "I shall see myself, I shall read myself, I shall be ecstatic about myself, and I shall say: Is it possible that I have been so clever?" *Cf. Ferdinando Galiani (1728–87) to Mme d'Épinay (1726–83), 18 September 1769.*

28

65. *Cf. CW 17, 10[143].*

29

66. *machine] Mp XVI 4:* state-machine

30

67. *"dormant . . . Faust]* Cf. Goethe, Faust I, 1179–1185.*

68. *pure folly]* {A play on the description of Parsifal as a "pure fool" in Wagner's last opera.}

31

69. *Cf. CW 18, 11[79]; Plutarch, Caesar 17; and N to Gast, 13 February 1888* {KGB III:5, 251}.

32–35

70. *Sections 32–44 were added by N during his corrections to TI. He took §§32–35 from a more comprehensive Sd he had begun in Notebook W II 6 at the beginning of April 1888. This consisted of six paragraphs; the sixth is incomplete because someone, perhaps N, tore out the next page. The first two paragraphs in the second draft were later to become* {with only minor changes} *§§2 and 3 of The Antichrist and the following four became "Forays" 32–35. Immediately following these in Notebook W II 6, N wrote an aphorism with the title* "The Rehabilitation of Suicide, of 'voluntary death,'" *destined to become "Forays" 36. (There followed two jottings, one on a prohibition against procreation for the chronically ill (WP² 734); the other on the rehabilitation of prostitution was suppressed in WP².) "Forays" 37 was taken from fragmentary jottings N had written originally for the second book (according to the plan of September 1888) or third book (according to the plan of October 1888) of Revaluation of All Values:* "The Immoralist." *The title of §32 of "Forays,"* "The Immoralist Speaks," *suggests that N had for some time intended to use the current §§32–35 for* "The Immoralist," *and only gave this up during the proof corrections to TI in October 1888. Sections 38–39 stem from a different Sd in Notebook W II 6, which consisted of six smaller paragraphs under the title* "Modernity. / Vademecum of a Futurist." *Sections 40–44 were composed from earlier, disparate material.*

The already mentioned second draft in Notebook W II 6, 142–136, from which N derived §§32–35, reads: What is good? — Everything that increases the feeling of power, the will to power, power itself in humans. / What is bad? — All that stems from weakness. / What is happiness? — The feeling that power is growing, that resistance is being overcome. / Not contentment but more power; not peace at all, but more war; not virtue but proficiency (virtue in Renaissance style, *virtù*, moraline-free virtue). / The weak and deformed should perish: first principle of society. And we should even help them. / What is more harmful than any vice? — The act of compassion with everything deformed and weak — *Christianity* . . . // The problem that is posed by me here is not what should succeed humanity in the sequence of life forms; but — which type of human we should *breed*, should *will*, as being of higher value, worthier of life, more certain of a future. / This higher-valued type has existed often enough before: but as a stroke of luck, as an exception — never as *willed*. Instead, he was precisely the thing most feared, up till this point he was practically *the* fearful: and out of fear, the opposite type was willed, bred, *achieved*, the household pet, the herd animal, the animal with "equal rights," the *weak* human animal — the *Christian* . . . //

["Forays" 32]: Nothing offends the taste of a philosopher more than the human, *in so far as it desires* . . . If he merely sees the human in action, if he sees this bravest, toughest, shrewdest of animals in a struggle with labyrinthine difficulties, how admirable the human appears to him! But the philosopher despises the desiring human, as well as the desirable human — and all his desirable things, to boot, all the human's "ideals." If a philosopher could be a nihilist, it would be because he finds nothingness behind all the human's ideals: or indeed, not even nothingness — but just the good-for-nothing, the absurd, the short, the wretched, the sweet, the cowardly, the tired, dregs of all kinds from the *drained* chalice of his life . . . How does it come about that the human, so venerable as a reality, inspires so little respect when he desires? Is it that the huge exertions of brain and will demanded in all his doings must be paid for by an even greater mindless, will-less stretching into the imaginary? The story of the humans' desirable things is the *partie honteuse* {"shameful part"} of the human story; visualizing his ideals for too long might even end in disgust at the human. But his reality justifies him and will eternally justify him; for the actual human is infinitely more valuable than a human hitherto desired, dreamed up, tidied up, lied about — than any *ideal* human. / And only the "ideal human" offends the philosopher's taste.

["Forays" 33]: Egoism is worth as much as the physiological value of the one who possesses it. — Every individual is not just what morality makes him out to be, a certain something that begins with birth: he is the whole line of development right up to himself. If he represents the ascending human line, his value is in fact extremely high. The worry about supporting him and furthering his growth may well be extreme. (It is the worry about the promise of the future of the human within him that gives the privileged

individual such an extraordinary *right* to egoism.) If he represents *descending* development, decay, chronic disease (— diseases are, on the whole, just the results of decay, *not* its cause), little value is attached to him; and in all fairness, he should take as little space, strength and sunshine as possible from the privileged. In such a case, an animal will creep back into its lair. Here, the task of society is to *hold down egoism* (occasionally manifesting itself as absurd, sickly, rebellious), whether in regard to an individual or to whole degenerate strata of a people. A teaching and religion of "love," of humility and self-denial, of patience, forbearance, assistance, the reversal of word and deed, can be of the highest value within such strata, even when gauged by the eye of the rulers: for it holds down the feelings of rivalry, envy, *ressentiment* — feelings all too natural with the underprivileged! It even deifies these by naming them virtue and the sanctity of being lowly, being poor, being sick, being underneath. It is not just the shrewdness of the ruling caste, it is actually their wisdom to uphold the cult of self-lessness, the gospel of the lowly, of "God on the Cross" in those strata of the people: with these methods they fight against the perverse instinct of those who are suffering, against their *impermissible* egoism. A sick person, a figure of *décadence*, has no right to egoism.

["Forays" 34]: If the socialist, the mouthpiece for strata of the people in decline, demands with fetching indignation "law," "justice," "equal rights," he succumbs to the pressure of the inadequacy of his culture, which has no idea how to grasp why he is actually suffering, and what from. On the other hand, he derives some pleasure from it: all this poor devil can do is shout. If he were better physiologically, he would have no reason to shout: then he would certainly seek his pleasure elsewhere. Making a complaint never gets anywhere: it stems from weakness. Whether a person imputes his discomfort to others or himself — the socialist does the former, the Christian the latter — essentially makes no difference: somebody must be *blamed* if a sufferer suffers . . . Finally, even the Christian himself is no longer the cause: the concept of "blameworthiness," inserted as *causa et ratio* {"cause and reason"} when he feels unwell, does not suffice to vent his

ressentiment. He condemns the "world," slanders and curses it from the same mentality as that of the socialist when cursing society, the ruling order and the distance in rank between human and human. The Christian does not exclude himself: that is better taste than socialist taste, which never tires of shouting "we alone are the good and just!" In both cases, however, one does well not to take such shouting too seriously. Instead, it is better to think that it is physiological *décadence* (and not some sort of injustice) that is screaming to high heaven: the Christian's "guilt-iness" and socialist dissatisfaction are misunderstandings of those who suffer, and who unfortunately cannot be helped. Or rather: they *could* be helped — but this sort of human is just too cow-ardly for it . . .

["Forays" 35]: Wherever we find the *altruistic* method of evalua-tion predominant, the instinct of being generally underprivileged betrays itself. At its most fundamental, the value judgment means nothing more than "*I* am not worth much": thus speak exhaustion, a swoon, a lack of strongly toned "Yes-saying" feeling in the muscles, nerves, motor areas of the brain. This physiological value judgment is translated into a moral or religious value judgment. In general, the predominance of moral and religious values is an indication of *lower* culture. There, nothing further happens than that a physiological feeling of value seeks to establish itself from spheres whence the concept of value in general is accessible to such degenerates. The interpretation the Christian "sinner" uses to understand *himself* is not an attempt to *justify* a lack of power and self-certainty: he would rather feel guilty than feel bad in vain (— the human beast, with its hunger for reasons, gobbles down good and bad reasons indiscrimi-nately). Actually, it is a sign of decline to *need* interpretations of a Christian kind at all. — In other cases, as we have seen, someone who has lost out does not seek the reason for that in *his* guilt, but in that of society: the socialist, the anarchist, the nihilist, is therefore always the nearest relative to the Christian, they always interpret their existence as something for which somebody should take the blame (— I shall speak elsewhere about the innermost instinctual association between Christian, plebeian, invalid, pauper, idiot). Peo-ple think they can bear feeling unwell and being a failure better

(more clearly: the predominance of depressive states over the tonic) if somebody — — — *[The next page has been ripped out.]*

71. *partie honteuse]* "shameful part"

72. *"law," "justice," "equal rights"]* "Recht", "Gerechtigkeit", "gleiche Rechte"

73. *canaille]* "riff-raff" "rabble"

36

74. *Cf. W II 6, 134, where the original section (later fashioned into "Forays" 36) reads as follows: The Rehabilitation of Suicide, of "voluntary death"* / The invalid is a parasite on society. In a certain state, it is bad form to continue to live any longer, as an invalid . . . / To cowardly vegetate away in absurd dependence on doctors and procedures ought to produce contempt in public opinion. The doctors should have the courage to give their patients a daily taste of this contempt. / To create a new accountability: that of the doctor, for all questions where the collective interest of society demands the most ruthless observation of the individual — for example, with regard to marriage. / To die in a proud manner when it is no longer possible to live in a proud manner. / Death with a will, with brightness and joy, among witnesses and friends: so there can be a genuine farewell, likewise a genuine reckoning of what has been achieved and desired, in brief, a *summa vitae* {"sum of a life" or "life span"}| — and not that| pitiable and horrifying misuse of physiological dissolution, making judgments on the value of human and life with which the Christian Church has secured a scurrilous reputation for itself for all time. / The proper, that is physiological consideration of death: which indeed is nothing other than a suicide (— you never come to grief through anything else but yourself —) only in the most contemptible conditions an unfree death, a death at the *wrong time*, a slave death. One should *out of love for life* want death bravely, consciously, arising from strength . . . / We are not at liberty to avoid being born: but we can rectify this mistake. If you *do away* with yourself, you do the most admirable thing possible — society gains a greater advantage through this than any life of denial, *misère* {"misery"}, and self-contempt, like the life of Pascal. (The only means against pessimism: abolition of the gentlemen pessimists.

Everyone can contribute to this. I think Pascal would have been
of more use with a self-refutation of Pascal than with his apology
for Christianity, "*Pascalisme*" . . .) / Pessimism is contagious: like
cholera, it infects morbid natures — the very ones who are |already|
condemned in any case . . .

75. *pur, vert]* "pure and simple"

76. *I recall . . . deaths.]* {Cf. Charles Féré, *Sensation et mouvement: Études expérimentales de psycho-mécanique* ("Sensation and
movement: Experimental studies in psycho-mechanics") (Paris:
Alcan, 1887), 127.}

37

77. *Der Bund]* Daily newspaper printed in Berne; the "Swiss
editor" was Josef Viktor Widmann, who discussed BGE in 1886.

78. *As was . . . Much obliged!]* Cf. CW 18, 19[7]: {"Much obliged!"
is in German "*Sehr verbunden!*" — a pun on *Der Bund.*}

79. *l'impressionisme morale]* "moral impressionism" {N misspells
the French term *impressionnisme* with one "n", after the German
"*Impressionismus.*"}

38–39

80. *The first drafts of §§38 and 39, the second draft of which is
found in W II 6, 34–35, 32–33, 30, read as follows before their reworking for TI: Modernity. Vademecum of a Futurist. / ["Forays" 38]:* 1. /
The value of a thing does not lie in what we achieve with it but in
all the things we have to do to achieve it — what it *costs* us. I shall
give an example. / 2. / Liberal institutions, as soon as they have
been introduced, are detrimental to freedom in the worst and most
thoroughgoing way: — they undermine the will, they are institu-
tionalized slackness and leveling mania; they make everything
cowardly, tired, pleasurable; with them begins the rule of the herd
animals. On the other hand, as long as people campaign for liberal
institutions, in other words, as long as the rule of liberal instincts
lasts which accompanies every war, it can greatly promote freedom, and indeed among its enemies as well as its supporters. Freedom, by which I mean the will to self-accountability, maintenance
of distance, indifference toward exertions, deprivations, severities,
life and death, and the hegemony of manly, aggressive instincts
joyous in war and victory, over those that envision an absurd com-

NOTES TO PAGE III

placency of the kind found with shopkeepers, women, cows and

placency of the kind found with shopkeepers, women, cows and Christians: so-called "happiness." / 3. / What level of resistance must be continually overcome to remain *on top*, that is the gauge of freedom, whether for individuals or societies: freedom as a positive power, in the form of the will to power. In accordance with that, the highest form of sovereignty would most probably grow up in close proximity to its opposite, wherever the danger of slavery is at its most pressing. We can verify this in history: the times when the "individual" matures to perfection, in other words becomes free, when the classical type of *sovereign human* is achieved, have been the hardest, most unjust, illiberal times in history. 4. / You must not have a choice: either on top — or |down below, like a worm,| despised, destroyed, trampled. You must have tyranny against you, tyranny of every kind — that of circumstances, institutions, rivals, your own instincts: only in this way can you come to your maximum of "freedom," in other words, boldness, certainty, splendor and spirituality. The same goes for the aristocratic communities after the fashion of Rome and Venice, these greatest of all *hothouses* for the breeding of strong humans: — none of them knew how to express freedom otherwise than as something one had continually to conquer. /

["*Forays*" *39]*: 5. / What is most strongly attacked today is the instinct and will of *tradition*. All institutions that have this instinct to thank for their provenance go against the taste of the modern spirit. Basically, people do nothing that would in any way pursue the purpose of pulling out *this* sense of tradition by the roots. People take tradition as fatality; they study it, they recognize it (as "inheritance" {*Erblichkeit*} for example) — but they do not *want* it. The expansion of a will over long stretches of time, the selection of conditions and evaluations that make it |possible| for us to determine the future over centuries, precisely that, if anything at all, is *anti-modern*. The result is that our age receives its character from *disorganized* principles. — It is an age of *décadence* {underlined by N}. — / 6. / If our institutions are no longer any good, that lies not with them, but with us, we who have lost all instincts from which institutions grow: the will to tradition, to authority, to great responsibility, to the solidarity of long chains of generations. And because we no longer have the instincts that create institutions, we no longer feel that what we have, and could have, in the existing institutions is to our advantage: instead, it is an obstacle, nonsense, waste, tyranny. For example, all rationale has been driven out of modern marriage: however, that does not provide an argument against marriage, but against modernity . . . the rationale for marriage — legally, this lay in the sole responsibility of the husband (— only through that did the family acquire stability, whereas today it is lame in both legs —). The rationale for marriage: — that lay in its principle of indissolubility. With the growing indulgence toward the *love match*, the actual basis of marriage, that which makes it into an institution, has been eliminated: such a thing can never, ever, be founded on idiosyncrasies! Rather, on general drives, average needs, normal instincts! . . . As I said, marriage is *not* founded on "love," ⟨it⟩ is founded on the sexual drive; it is founded on the drive for property (wife and child as property); it is founded on the drive for control, which constantly organizes the smallest structure of control, the family, in order to thereby exercise influence within the greater structure of power; it is founded on the drive for control that needs children and heirs in order to retain an achieved amount of power, property and influence over and beyond the vagaries in the life of an individual, who therefore needs state guarantees and in addition, a *guaranteed state*. Marriage, as a normal form of the will to power, already encompasses within itself the affirmation of the state. —

40

81. *For this section, cf. CW 18, 11[60].*

41

82. *Freedom . . . mean . . . "]* Cf. the first verse of Max von Schenkendorf's song "Freiheit, die ich meine" (1813) {"Freedom that I mean"}.

83. *laisser aller]* "letting go"

84. *décadence]* {Underlined by N.}

43

85. *Procrustes]* {Bandit in Greek legend who mutilated his victims to fit his iron bed; the phrase is now a byword for forcing a person or thing to fit into an arbitrary pattern.}

86. *Crabwalk] Krebsgang* {In Germany, a well-known metaphor for not progressing or going forward.}

44

87. *their precondition . . . explosion.]* Cf. EH "Why I Am So Wise" 3.

88. *theory of milieu]* {Theory associated with Auguste Comte and Hippolyte Taine that held that one's environment ("milieu") plays a larger role in the formation of one's character than heredity.}

89. *will mind that.] After these words, we find in Mp XVI 4 the following deleted passage: will mind that*: there, it is democratic prejudice which can only conceive of the great man as a tool and puppet of the state: or Carlyle's prejudice [religious explanation] that represents England's Christianity and creates religious concepts out of the genius and hero.

45

90. *For this section, cf. CW 17, 10[50], first version, after which there are three more: W II 5, 171; W II 6, 132–130 (after the fragment on prostitution); Mp XVI 4. The W II 6 version reads as follows:* The criminal type: that is the type of the strong human in unfavorable circumstances, so that all his drives in the grip of suspicion, fear, dishonor, habitually intermingle with the *oppressive* affects and consequently, *degenerate* physiologically. The criminal is the sick type of strong human who prefers to do what he is best at secretly, with prolonged tension, caution, cunning, who must once and for all publicly renounce taking the credit for anything; who increasingly perceives what is disadvantageous and dangerous in his instincts, until he finally retains the instinct of the tyrant alone, having abandoned his self-respect . . . He no longer reaps the joy that freedom of will and action bring . . . He turns fatalistic . . . Society is, our tame, anxious, mediocre society, in which the strong human [necessarily] [degenerates] must degenerate to a criminal. Just think of those Siberian prisoners whom Dostoevsky portrays: he sees them as the strongest and most industrious natures[?] in the soul of Russia. Such natures lack the approval and conviction of being seen as useful and beneficial, as *equal*; they lack a pleasant visibility, public law, daylight on their deeds. The criminal has the

color of the subterranean in his thoughts and deeds: everything about him is pale. Public recognition and endorsement of our existence is sunshine, too. — I observe that almost unintentionally, every deviation, every lengthy, all too lengthy *submergence*, every unusual, unfathomable, opaque form of existence drives out the criminal type, whether with the so-called genius or the virtue-agitator . . . Viewed with a "kidney-tester's" eye, all great *innovators*, at the time when they were only beginning to innovate, when they were "unproved" as yet by success — look identical to hardened criminals. Nearly every genius, as part of its cocoon stage, experiences a sort of "Catilinarian existence," if only in the mind: happy beings, not that the non-geniuses would ever be able to get a whiff of them. There is much that keeps silent by nature. A history of the emergence of the exception ought never to be written. —

91. *Dostoevsky]* Cf. *N to Gast, 13 February 1887* {*KGB* III:5, 24}: Are you acquainted with Dostoevsky? No one apart from Stendhal has given me so much pleasure and surprise: a psychologist with whom I "am on good terms."

92. *Catilinarian existence]* {Phrase first used by Bismarck, in a pejorative sense, referring to Lucius Sergius Catilina (108–62 BCE), a Roman politician best known for the Catilinarian conspiracy, a failed attempt to challenge the power of the Roman Senate and overthrow the Roman Republic.}

46

93. *Here . . . free."]* Quotation from final scene of Goethe's *Faust II*, line 11989.

94. *il est . . . ressentent]* "it is unworthy of great hearts to disseminate the vexation that is making them angry" {Cf. Barine, "George Eliot, d'après sa correspondance," 121.}

47

95. *For this section, cf. CW 17, 9[116].*

48

96. *in rebus tacticis]* "in tactical matters"

97. *"Equality . . . equal."]* Cf. *Z II* "On the Tarantulas."

49

98. *For this and the following section, cf. CW 17, 9[179].*

99. *bore . . . himself:] Mp XVI 4:* unleashed its strongest drives and drove one against the other to a conclusion: thus he became master over them, achieving a higher type most closely related to the Renaissance. But what he achieved personally, that was clearly not for Europe — it is *not* our nineteenth century. Goethe found his whole century within himself.

100. *ens realissimum]* "the most real being"

50

101. *décadence]* {Underlined by N.}

51

102. *Cf. CW 18, 19[7].*

103. *we also . . . "Cross"] Cf. WA "Epilogue."*

104. *Zarathustra]* {Underlined by N.}

What I Owe the Ancients

1. *For the development of this chapter, see the preliminary remarks to the commentary on Ecce Homo.*

1

2. *aere perennius]* "more lasting than bronze" {Horace, *Odes* III, 30.}

2

3. *satura Menippea]* "Menippean satire" {The philosophy of the unconventional Greek Cynics, foremost among them Diogenes of Sinope, flourished from the fourth century BCE into Christian times; the "satires of Menippus," a third-century BCE Cynic, are lost.}

4. *Machiavelli's principe]* "Machiavelli's prince" {Machiavelli's chief work *Il Principe* (*The Prince*) was written in 1513 but not published until 1532.}

5. *culture of sophists]* {Wisdom propounded by teachers or sages in the fifth and fourth centuries BCE; Plato and Aristotle changed the meaning of the word "sophist" to "misleading teacher."}

6. *décadence]* {Underlined by N.}

3

ul souls"] {In Goethe's novel of 1795/6, *Wilhelm*
_ehrjahre (*Wilhelm Meister's Apprenticeship*), book VI is
_d "The Confessions of a Beautiful Soul."}

8. *composure in greatness . . . high simplicity]* {N is here para-
phrasing the influential characterization of Greek art by Johann
Joachim Winckelmann (1717–68).}

9. *"niaiserie allemande"]* "German foolishness" {Prosper Mérimée,
Lettres à une inconnue ("Letters to an unknown woman") (Paris:
Michel Lévy Frères, 1874), 1:328: "[Goethe's *Wilhelm Meister*] est un
étrange livre, où les plus belles choses du monde alternent avec les
enfantillages les plus ridicules. Dans tout ce qu'a fait Goethe, il y a
un mélange de génie et de niaiserie allemande des plus singuliers: se
moquait-il de lui-même ou des autres?" ("[Goethe's *Wilhelm Meister*]
is a strange book, where the most beautiful things in the world
alternate with the most ridiculous childish behavior. In everything
Goethe produces, there is the most remarkable mixture of genius
and German inanity: was he poking fun at himself or others?)"}

10. *philistinism]* *Biedermännerei* {The "Biedermann" is the
epitome of the narrow-minded, complacent petty bourgeois
character. The originally positive connotations of the term — as
in the title of Johann Christoph Gottsched's moralistic weekly
Der Biedermann (1727–29) — turned negative from the later
eighteenth century under the pressure of Romanticism.}

4

11. *Jakob Burckhardt]* *Cf. Burckhardt's letters to Verlag See-*
mann of 29 Nov. 1889 and 8 Dec. 1894, plus the foreword by Felix
Stähelin to Burkhardt's Griechische Kulturgeschichte {"History of
Greek culture"} *(Stuttgart{: Kröner,} 1930, XXIII–XXIX*{; see also
note below}.

12. *Culture of the Greeks]* {N knew Burckhardt was writing a
work on Greek culture, but it did not come out until after his
mental collapse. When Burckhardt died in 1897, the work was
still unfinished. Finally, Burckhardt's friends edited the work for
publication (1898–1902).}

13. {Lobeck's *Aglaophamus* (1829), written in Latin, was his most
important work. N cites this passage as it appeared in German translation, which he marked with three marginal lines, in Arnobius der

Afrikaner (d. ca. 330), *Sieben Bücher wider die Heiden* ("Seven books against the heathens"), trans. from the Latin by Franz Anton von Besnard (Landshut: Vogel, 1842), 564. *NL.*}

5

14. *I, . . . Dionysus]* Cf. *BGE* 295.

The Hammer Speaks
    1. *Thus Spoke Zarathustra, III.]* Cf. *Z* III "On Old and New Tablets" §29. {In the original, a page number (90) from the German edition of Part III was cited; cf. p. 537 below.} *Cf. the footnote to "Law Against Christianity" below, pp. 535–37, which demonstrates that this text was originally intended as the conclusion of AC.*

The Antichrist.
The *Pm* to *The Antichrist* is extant. It is in N's handwriting with occasional insertions by Gast primarily with regard to grammar and punctuation. From 20 November 1888 at the latest (letter to Georg Brandes {*KGB* III:5, 482}), N no longer viewed *The Antichrist* as the first book of the *Revaluation of All Values* but as the entire *Revaluation*, so that now the main title (*Revaluation of All Values*) became the subtitle, as he expressly pointed out to Paul Deussen in a letter of 26 November 1888 {*KGB* III:5, 492}: "My Revaluation of All Values, with the main title '**The Antichrist**,' is finished." In line with this "upgrading" of *The Antichrist* to the entire *Revaluation of All Values*, there are two title pages in the *Pm*; the first, earlier one reads: "*The Antichrist.* / Attempt at a Critique of Christianity. / *First Book* / of the *Revaluation of All Values.*"; the later one reads: "*The Antichrist.* / [Revaluation of All Values] / Curse upon Christianity.", where N ultimately crossed out the subtitle *Revaluation of All Values*. The final title of this text must therefore be: *The Antichrist. / Curse upon Christianity* (= *AC*). Karl Schlechta was the first to use this correct title in his edition (cf. II:1159; III:1388).
    The Antichrist was first published in 1895 in the *Großoktav-Ausgabe* begun under the editorship of Fritz Koegel, where it formed volume VIII; the title was printed inaccurately, and four passages in the text were suppressed. *The Antichrist* was republished in 1899 in the new *Großoktav-Ausgabe* now edited by Arthur

Seidl, still as volume VIII; the title remained inaccurate. In Koegel it was called: "The Antichrist. / Attempt at a Critique of Christianity"; now it was called: "The Will to Power. / Attempt at a Revaluation of All Values. / By / Friedrich Nietzsche. / Foreword and First Book: The Antichrist." In 1905, after the first edition of the randomly compiled notes from the *Nachlaß* appeared as the work *The Will to Power*, the title — still in volume VIII of the *Großoktav-Ausgabe* — was changed as follows: "Revaluation of All Values. / Foreword and First Book: The Antichrist." By this time, the Nietzsche-Archiv was the nominal editor of the new, henceforth definitive edition of the *Großoktav-Ausgabe*; however, Peter Gast, who had been working in the archive since 1900, was now the controlling authority in all matters relating to this edition of N's writings (albeit under the supervision of Elisabeth Förster-Nietzsche). In 1906, *The Antichrist* also appeared as volume 10 of the "pocket edition." Here the title read: "Revaluation of All Values. / (Fragment.) / By / Friedrich Nietzsche. / Foreword and First Book: The Antichrist." Elisabeth Förster-Nietzsche wrote the afterword herself, which included the well-known lies about the "lost" manuscripts of the "Revaluation," to which we shall return in the commentary on *Ecce Homo*. {See pp. 548–53 below.} The four suppressed passages in Koegel's edition of the *Le* were:

(a) section 29, {p. 161}, the three words: "the word idiot."

(b) section 35, {p. 167}: "The words to the *thief* on the cross contain the whole Gospel. This is truly a *godly* man, a 'child of God,' says the thief. 'If that is what you feel' — answers the Redeemer — *'you are in Paradise*, you too are a child of God . . . '" Presumably the reason for suppression was N's faulty citation from the Gospels; see the notes to section 35 below.

(c) section 38, {p. 170}: the word "young." This word was removed to mask the allusion to Wilhelm II.

(d) section 62, {p. 207}: the whole last paragraph.

After the 1899 edition, (d) was reinstated in all editions; (a) and (b) were suppressed in all the editions authorized by the Nietzsche-Archiv. Deletion (c) — that is, the word "young" — was, remarkably enough, only restored in the pocket edition of 1906; otherwise, it was lacking in all editions authorized by the Nietzsche-Archiv. Only in Arthur Seidl's postscripts (to the *Großoktav-Ausgabe* and *Kleinoktav-Ausgabe* of 1899) was any allusion made to the deletions; otherwise no hint as to the deletions was given in all remaining editions of *The Antichrist* authorized by the Nietzsche-Archiv. Josef Hofmiller in his article "Nietzsche" (*Süddeutsche Monatshefte*, November 1931), was the first to mention (a), (b), and (c). In 1956, Karl Schlechta's edition published *The Antichrist* under the correct title and with the deletions reinstated.

For the reasons for publishing the "Law Against Christianity" in *KGW* and *KSA*, see the notes to the end of this work {pp. 535–40}.

The edition of *The Antichrist* posed further problems, especially in regard to spelling and punctuation: what was necessary here was the removal of Peter Gast's interventions in N's *Pm*. It is not always possible to recognize these interventions with certainty; for this purpose, Overbeck's copy of *The Antichrist*, which is preserved in the Basel University Library, was consulted. Franz Overbeck finished his copy in February/March 1890, immediately after N's collapse, before he handed over the *Pm* of *The Antichrist* to Peter Gast. He made a few errors in deciphering but was otherwise a more faithful transcriber than Gast, since he did not have the latter's "compulsion to improve."

1. {N's title for this work, *Der Antichrist*, could justifiably be translated either as *The Anti-Christian* or *The Antichrist*. In German, *der Antichrist* does parallel *der Antisemit* — the anti-Semite — and titling this text *The Anti-Christian* would highlight N's view that Christian anti-Semitism is one of the great dangers facing Europe. Like previous translations, however, we have opted for *The Antichrist* in order to note that while N's text is not singularly opposed to Jesus, its fundamental target is the fiction of the Christ as an invention of Paul and the Church, and it wants to make clear that Jesus of Nazareth is *not* the Christ.}

Foreword

2. *Foreword.]* This text arose from section 3 of the original "Foreword" to *TI* which in itself first belonged to the "Foreword" of

"Revaluation": 3. / — But why should I bother with the Germans! I write, I *live* for the very few. They are everywhere — they are nowhere. In order to have ears for me, one must first be a *good European* — and a bit more besides! . . . The presuppositions under which my writings — the most serious literature that exists — can be understood and then understood *with necessity* — I know them only too well. An integrity turned into instinct and passion that blushes at what today is called moral. A perfect indifference, even malice, for whether truth becomes useful or unpleasant or fateful for the one who seeks it. A predilection for strength with problems nobody today has the courage to tackle; courage for the *forbidden*: predisposition for the labyrinth. A lesson of health for the brave, with the motto: *increscunt animi virescit volnere virtus* {"by wounding, the spirit grows, strength is restored"}. Experience out of seven solitudes; new ears for new music; new eyes for the most distant; a new conscience for truths that have remained mute hitherto. The will to economy of grand style: keeping its strength, its enthusiasm together . . . Respect toward oneself; love toward oneself; unconditional freedom toward oneself . . . The cheerfulness of someone accustomed to war and victory — of someone *who also knows death*! . . . / Well then! Those are my readers, my true readers, my necessary readers: what do the *rest* matter? — The rest is mere humanity. — One must be superior to humanity through strength, through *loftiness* of soul — through contempt . . . / *Sils-Maria*, Oberengadin / on 3 September 1888. *Cf. the notes to the "Foreword" of TI.*

3. *Some . . . posthu⟨mously⟩]* {N uses the identical wording in *EH* "Books" 1; cf. p. 247 above.}

4. *labyrinth.] Pm*: labyrinth. [A lesson of health for war, with the motto *increscunt animi virescit volnere virtus* {"*volnere*" ("wounding") is underlined by N}.] *N probably deleted this while writing the final version of the "Foreword" to TI. There, he used the "motto" from Aulus Gellius; cf. p. 43.*

I

1. *Sections 1–7 came under the title* We Hyperboreans, *the foreword to the "Will to Power" according to the plan dated 26 August 1888.*

2. *Hyperboreans]* {In Greek mythology, the Hyperboreans lived in a sunny land beyond the North Wind (*boreas*).}

3. *Pindar]* Cf. Pindar, *Pythian X, 29–30.*

4. *"I am . . . end;]* {Cf. Sommer 2, 29–30: "The formulation 'I am at my wit's end' is found already in Goethe's early work *Die Mitschuldigen* ("Partners in Guilt") (Act I, Scene 7): 'O das verfluchte Spiel! o wär' der Kerl gehangen! / Bei'm Abzug war's nicht just; doch muß ich stille sein, / Er haut und schießt sich gleich! / Ich weiss nicht aus noch ein.'" ("Oh this cursed gambling! oh I wish the churl were hanged! / It wasn't just the draw; yet I must bite my tongue, / Soon he'll want to fight and duel! / I am at my wit's end.") (Johann Wolfgang Goethe, *Sämmtliche Werke in vierzig Bänden: Vollständige, neugeordnete Ausgabe*, Bd. 7 [Stuttgart: J. G. Cotta, 1853], 58). *NL.*}

5. *largeur]* "largeness"

6. *that "pardons" . . . all]* Pm: that still calls all children to come to it

7. *Formula . . . goal . . .]* Cf. TI "Sayings" 44.

2

8. *Cf. CW 18, 11[414]; 15[120].*

9. *feeling of power]* {Sommer 2, 33–34, notes that N's concept of the "feeling of power" was influenced by his readings of Charles Féré, *Sensation et mouvement: Études expérimentales de psycho-mécanique* ("Sensation and movement: Experimental studies of psycho-mechanics") (Paris: Alcan, 1887); and Harald Høffding (see note 11 below).}

10. {Cf. *AC* 57, p. 200.}

11. *The feeling . . . overcome.]* {Cf. Harald Høffding, *Psychologie in Umrissen auf Grundlage der Erfahrung* ("Psychology in outlines on the basis of experience"), trans. from the Danish by F. Bendixen (Leipzig: Fues's [Reisland], 1887), 307. *NL.*}

12. *moraline-free virtue]* Moralinfrei Tugend {See *WA* 3 and *EH* "Why I Am So Clever" 1.}

13. *love of humanity]* From: society

3

14. *Cf. CW 18, 11[414]; 15[120].*

4

15. *Cf. CW 18, 11[413].*
16. *remains] Pm:* is
17. *deeply] Pm:* by far
18. *where] Pm:* wherein

5

19. *Cf. CW 18, 11[408].*
20. {Sommer 2, 46, suggests that the source of this remark on Pascal is probably Ferdinand Brunetière, *Études critiques sur l'histoire de la littérature française. Troisième série: Descartes – Pascal – Le Sage – Marivaux – Prévost – Voltaire et Rousseau – Classiques et Romantiques* ("Critical studies of the history of French literature. Third series: Descartes – Pascal – Le Sage – Marivaux – Prévost – Voltaire and Rousseau – Classiques and Romantiques") (Paris: Hachette, 1887), 54–55. *NL.*}

7

21. *Cf. CW 18, 11[361].*
22. *Christianity . . . compassion. —] Mp XVI 4: Pd was entitled "Compassion."*
23. *that heighten] Mp XVI 4:* that, like bravery or anger, heighten
24. *Through compassion] Mp XVI 4:* In such a way
25. *br⟨ings⟩] Mp XVI 4:* inflicts
26. *through compassion; under] Mp XVI 4:* through contagious compassion, nothing is more infectious than compassion. Under . . .
27. *(— the . . . point.)] Lacking in Mp XVI 4.*
28. *(— in . . . weakness —)] Lacking in Mp XVI 4.*
29. *⟨wr⟩ote denial of life on its shiel⟨d⟩] Mp XVI 4:* set as goal
30. *instinct] Mp XVI 4:* affect
31. *major instrument] Mp XVI 4:* principal means
32. *décadence] Mp XVI 4:* degeneracy
33. *not] In the Pm, N incorrectly wrote "nichts" instead of "nicht," which Gast corrected.*
34. *Aristotle] Cf. Aristotle, Poetics 1449b, 27–28, and 1453b, 1ff.*
35. *now and then] Mp XVI 4:* from time to time
36. *that] Pm:* the one
37. *Tolstoy] Cf. the many excerpts from Tolstoy's "Ma religion" in W II 3 {CW 18, 11}.*

38. *Christian] Mp XVI 4:* modern

39. *that is . . . humanity,] Addition in Pm.*

40. *philosophers,] Pm*: philosophers, [*we* philanthropists]

8

41. *Sections 8–14 were originally grouped under the heading: For Us — Against Us.*

42. *lineage] Pm*: lineage [and disposition]

43. *This poisoning . . . glance . . .] W II 7, 13:* I speak from experience

44. *answer . . . truth] W II 7, 14: cleanliness* in things of the spirit

9

45. *necessarily] Pm*: always

10

46. *peccatum originale]* "original sin"

47. *German philosophy . . . reason . . .] Pm*: even science is still continually poisoned by their efforts

48. *Tübingen Seminary]* {A famous Protestant seminary in Swabia} *where Hegel, Schelling, and Hölderlin studied.*

49. *two . . . errors] Pm*: two most worthless teachings; *W II 7, 15:* two most worthless lies

50. *craftily clever] Pm*: insidious

51. *Kant was . . . integrity — —] W II 7, 15:* Our whole culture *stinks* of theology . . .

52. *like . . . integrity] Pm*: the greatest obstacle to intellectual *integrity*

11

53. *Chineseness] Chinesenthum*

54. *idiocy] Idiotismus* {A nineteenth-century medical term referring to the state of mental weakening.}

55. *anti-nature] Pm*: disaster

56. *Did Kant not . . . Kant! —] Cf. Kant's essay* "The Conflict of the Faculties."

12

57. *Cf. CW 18, 15[28].*

58. *his "German"] Mp XVI 4:* all his

59. *tried] Mp XVI 4:* sought

60. *no longer] Mp XVI 4:* not

61. *stands] Mp XVI 4:* is

62. *outside] Mp XVI 4:* beyond

63. *And the priest . . . "untrue"!] Mp XVI 4:* The opposite of the origin of philosophy is sufficiently interesting, namely the origin of science. When a family dwells on a single kind of activity for a long time and achieves mastery in it, then it can happen that all of the stored excellence, the familiarity with consequence, with subtlety, with caution, with tenacity, finally gains sovereignty and spreads into the intelligence. The formal pre-schooling of the intellect detaches itself, as it were, from the previous purpose of this pre-schooling and becomes a need in itself, a hunger for problems — the means itself becomes end. — Scientificity is the expression of anciently inherited [solidity], *virtù* and subtlety in *thinking* and acting. Therefore, one finds the geniuses of science almost exclusively among the descendants of artisans, traders, merchants, doctors, lawyers; the son of a Jew has no small probability of becoming an excellent scholar. Conversely, the sons of ministers become — philosophers.

13

64. *Mp XVI 4:* The most valuable insights are discovered last; but the most valuable insights are *methods*. All methods, all prerequisites of our present-day scientism, have been for millennia subjected to the deepest contempt, on their account, people were excluded from honest society — branded as the "enemy of God," a despiser of truth, as one "possessed." Whoever had a scientific character was chandala . . . We have had the whole pathos of humanity against us — their *concept* of what truth ought to be, what the service of truth ought to be: our aims, our practices, our quiet, careful, mistrustful manner — to them it all seemed completely unworthy and contemptible. — It seems as though an opposition had been reached somewhere, a leap had been made. But this is only *appearance* talking. In truth, that schooling through hyperboles has itself prepared, step by step, that pathos of a milder kind that today becomes embodied and honored as scientific character. Conscientiousness in small things, the rigorous self-control of the religious human, was a preparatory exercise

and, as it were, an *early form* of the scientific character: above all, that attitude which takes problems seriously, even disregarding what results from it personally. Ultimately, one could ponder whether it was not *really* an aesthetic need that kept humanity in blindness for so long: they demanded of truth a *picturesque* effect, likewise they demanded that the connoisseur's knowledge should have a strong effect on the imagination. Our *modesty* was what offended their taste for longest . . . —

Earlier Pd (= *WP² 469*) *in W II 6, 66:* The most valuable insights are discovered last: but the most valuable insights are *methods*. All methods, all prerequisites of our present-day scientism, have been for millennia subjected to the deepest contempt, on their account, people were excluded from *honest* society — branded as the "*enemy of God*," as despiser of the highest ideal, as one "possessed." We have had the whole *pathos* of humanity against us, their *[= WP² 469 in error: our] concept* of what truth ought to be, what the service of truth ought to be. — Our objectivity, our method, our quiet, careful, mistrustful manner were completely *contemptible* . . . |Fundamentally it was an aesthetic [prejudice] *[the crossed-out word* {i.e., "prejudice"} *was not replaced by a different one in the manuscript; WP² 469: taste according to AC 13]* that has hindered humanity for the longest time: it believed in the picturesque effect of truth, it demanded of the connoisseur that he should make a strong impression on the imagination|It seems as though an *opposition*, a *leap* had been made somewhere: in truth, that schooling through moral [ideal] hyperboles has itself prepared, step by *step, that pathos* of a milder kind that [now occupying itself scientifically] became embodied as scientific character . . . The *conscientiousness in small things*, the se⟨l⟩f-control of the religious human, was a preparatory school for the scientific [instinct] character: above all, the attitude which *takes problems seriously*, even disregarding what results from it personally . . .

14

65. *learned different . . . respect.] Mp XVI 4, first version:* replaced the human among the animals, we have grown more modest.

66. *an] Mp XVI 4:* the

67. *machina]* "machine"; *Mp XVI 4:* mechanism

68. *is]* Mp XVI 4: will be

69. *better]* Mp XVI 4: differently

70. *discount . . . miscount]* {N here puns on *rechnen* ("discount") and *sich verrechnen* ("miscount").}

15

71. *Sections 15–19 were originally gathered under the heading: Concept of a Décadence-Religion.*

16

72. *In spring 1888, under the title* On the History of the Concept of God, *N wrote a small treatise in five sections that can be found in notebook W II 8. Sections 1–4 correspond to The Antichrist 16–19, while the fifth section was not used. The latter is now aphorism 1038 of WP² (torn from its context). The entire treatise is in CW 18, 17[4]; cf. CW 18, 11[346] and Z I "On the New Idol."*

73. *ardeurs]* "ardors" "passions"

17

74. *At the end of this section, cf. CW 18, 16[55, 56, 58].*

75. {Cf. Sommer, 2, 102–3: See Ernest Renan, *Vie de Jésus* (Paris: Michel Lévy Frères, 1863), 78: "Le Dieu de Jésus n'est pas le despote partial qui a choisi Israël pour son peuple et le protége envers et contre tous. C'est le Dieu de l'humanité. Jésus ne sera pas un patriote comme les Macchabées, un théocrate comme Juda le Gaulonite. S'élevant hardiment au-dessus des préjugées de sa nation, il établira l'universelle paternité de Dieu." (*The Life of Jesus*, trans. Charles Edwin Wilbour [New York: Carleton, 1864], 106: "The God of Jesus is not the partial despot who has chosen Israel for his people and protects it in the face of all and against all. He is the God of humanity. Jesus will not be a patriot, like the Maccabees, or a theocrat, like Juda the Gaulonite. Rising boldly above the prejudices of his nation, he will establish the universal fatherhood of God.")}

76. *sub specie Spinozae]* "from the viewpoint of Spinoza"

18

77. *sanctified! . . .] Cf. conclusion to CW 18, 17[4]3:* This is how far we've gone! . . . Don't people know yet? Christianity is a *nihilistic* religion — for its God's sake . . .

19

78. *ultimatum and maximum]* {N's Latin: "ultimate and maximum"}

20

79. *Sections 20–23 were originally gathered under the heading: Buddhism and Christianity.*

80. *décadence-religions] Pm*: final-religions

81. *spirituosa]* "spirits" {in the sense of alcoholic spirits}

82. *"animosity will not end animosity"] Cf. H*{ermann} *Oldenberg, Buddha*{: *Sein Leben, Seine Lehre, Seine Gemeinde*} *(Berlin*{: Wilhelm Hertz}, *1897), 337.* {1st ed., 1881, 299–302. *NL*. Cf. *Buddha: His Life, his Doctrine, His Order,* trans. William Hoey (London: Williams and Norgate, 1882), 293–96.}

83. *"one . . . needful"]* Luke 10:42.

84. *who raised . . . problems).] Pm*: who understood *egoism* as *the* morality.

21

85. *Christian is . . . cruelty,] Cf. HAH 142 (Novalis quotation).*

23

86. *esoteric wisdom] Pm*: of the Orient

87. *barrel of evils.)]* {In ancient Greek legend, Pandora opened the barrel that contained all manner of misery, whereupon all the evils except hope flew out to earth.}

88. *faith, love, hope]* Cf. 1 Corinthians 13:13.

24

89. *Originally under the heading, crossed out in Pm:* The Roots of Christianity

90. *"salvation is of the Jews"] John 4:22; cf. CW 17, 10[182].*

91. *"holy people"]* {Cf. Daniel 7:27.}

92. *Genealogy of Morality] Cf. GM First Treatise.*

26

93. *N's source for this paragraph and the following one as well as all his observations generally on the history of the Jews, was Julius Wellhausen, Prolegomena zur Geschichte Israels* {*Prolegomena to the History of Israel,* trans. J. Sutherland Black and Allan Menzies

(Edinburgh: Adam and Charles Black, 1885)} *(Berlin{: Georg Reimer,} 1883). NL. N's copy is replete with very many marginal notes, underlinings, markings, etc; see his excerpts in CW 18, 11[377].*

94. *sneaks and bigots]* Ducker und Mucker {N may draw this from *der Duckmäuser* ("sneak") and uses *Ducker* to produce the pun on *der Mucker*, the standard German word for "bigot."}

27

95. *Cf. CW 18, 11[280]. Sections 27–47 contain N's interpretation of early Christianity as being at first a peaceful uprising against the Jewish "church"; however, in terms of an uprising, it was already at odds with its founder. The posthumous fragments in CW 18 show for the first time which sources N used for his interpretation: in particular, besides the work of Ernest Renan, which he criticized many times, the writings of Leo Tolstoy and Fyodor Dostoevsky. The fragments on Tolstoy, hitherto denied publication, would have rendered completely superfluous the tedious arguments (J. Hofmiller, E. Hirsch, E. Benz, lastly also W. Kaufmann) about the question whether N had known Tolstoy's "Ma religion." The former Nietzsche-Archiv remained silent on the matter although N's excerpts from Tolstoy's work were well known to them; a few of these excerpts were even published as N's own fragments in the "Will to Power." Franz Overbeck's letter to Peter Gast of 13 March, 1889, offered the following judgment of N's interpretation of Christianity in AC:* "You might think that Nietzsche treats *Christianity* as Apollo treated Marsyas. Not, of course, the founder but everything that followed — inasmuch as all earlier attempts to make him into a human figure look silly, abstract, and merely like an illustration of rationalistic dogmatics next to Nietzsche's achievement and the way the original dimensions of the person, as well as his human element, leap to the fore. And yet I cannot help concluding that many things are treated excessively violently and with tyrannical injustice. In particular, I find Nietzsche's conception of Christianity rather too political and the equation Christ = anarchist is based on a historically very questionable evaluation of what *Christianity* in 'reality' amounted to in the Roman Empire. The 'Buddhist peace movement' that, according to Nietzsche, Jesus originally initiated, seems to me to have remained to a higher degree in the *Christianity* after him, however greatly it distorted

what had been initiated, than Nietzsche assumes. For all that, this 'Antichrist' remains a unique monument, even illuminating in an essential way Nietzsche's own hitherto rather scattered explicit opinions on the subject."

28

96. *Strauss] N had read David Strauss's Das Leben Jesu {The Life of Jesus*, trans. George Eliot (aka Mary Ann Evans) (New York: Calvin Blanchard, 1860)} {(Tübingen: Osiander, 1835)} *in Bonn in 1864.*

29

97. {Cf. Sommer, 2, 151: The source of the Francis analogy is Renan, *Vie de Jésus*, xv; cf. also 449. *Life of Jesus*, 17–18, cf. 368.}

98. *"resist not evil"] Cf. Matthew 5:39; cf. also CW 18, 11[246–47]. Tolstoy writes in "Ma Religion":* "The passage which became, for me, the key to everything is the one contained in the verses 38 and 39 of Matthew 5: 'Ye have heard that it hath been said, an eye for an eye and a tooth for a tooth: but I say unto you, that ye resist not evil.'"

99. *the word idiot] Cf. above, the lines* "Everyone is the child of God . . . word 'genius' is!" {For Jesus and the opposition between genius and idiot, cf. *CW* 18, 14[38].}

100. {Regarding the deletion of these three words in early editions of *AC*, see above (a), in introductory remarks on *The Antichrist*, p. 510.}

101. *habitus]* "condition"

102. *"The . . . within you"] Cf. Luke 17:21.*

30

103. *décadent]* {Underlined by N.}

31

104. *Cf. CW 18, 11[378].*

105. *Russian novel . . . rendezvous —] Cf. CW 18, 15[9], where the allusion to Dostoevsky becomes clear.*

106. *proprium]* "distinctive characteristic"

107. *"le grand . . . ironie."]* "the great master of irony." *Cf. Renan, Vie de Jésus, 334* {KSA 14 cites the first edition, but provides the wrong page; *Life of Jesus*, 285}; *cf. CW 18, 11[385].*

32

108. *Cf. CW 18, 11[368–69].*

109. *impérieux]* "imperious, assuming power without author-ity or justification" {Cf. Renan, *Vie de Jésus,* 59; *Life of Jesus,* 93.}

110. *degeneracy] Degenerescenz* {Cf. Sommer 2, 168. N takes this concept from the title of Charles Samson Féré's *Dégénéres-cence et criminalité: Essai physiologique* ("Degeneracy and crimi-nality: Physiological essay") (Paris: Alcan, 1888). *NL.*}

111. *"the sword"] Cf. Matthew 10:34.*

112. *eating and . . . Jewish.)]* N's source was *Julius Wellhausen, Reste des arabischen Heidentums* {"Remnants of Arabic heathen-ism"} *(Berlin*{: Georg Reimer,} *1887). NL; this work also was stud-ied and excerpted by N; cf. CW 18, 11[287–93].*

113. *Sankhya]* {Sankhya is one of the six schools of Hindu philosophy. It teaches eternal interaction between spirit and matter.}

114. *"life" or "truth"] Cf. e.g., John 14:6.*

115. *pure foolishness] Pm*: complete and utter ignorance. *N made the change for the sake of an allusion to Wagner's Parsifal.* {Wagner changed the spelling from "Parzival" to "Parsifal" because Persian "Fal Parsi" means "pure fool."}

33

116. *Cf. CW 18, 11[357].*

117. *The consequence . . . instinct. —] Cf. especially "The Ser-mon on the Mount," Matthew 5–7.*

34

118. *Cf. CW 18, 11[354–55].*

119. *symbolist] Symbolisten* {In the *Pm,* N has *Symbolikers,* which would also be translated by "symbolist."}

120. *"the Son of Man"] Cf. Renan, Vie de Jésus, 245* {*Life of Jesus,* 222} *and CW 18, 11[389].*

121. *Amphitryon-story]* {Theban general and husband of Alc-mene. While Amphitryon was away at war, Zeus seduced Alcmene, pretending to be her husband. After Amphitryon returned, Alc-mene gave birth to twin sons: Iphicles, whose father was Amphi-tryon, and Heracles, whose father was Zeus.}

122. *"immaculate conception"] The dogma of the "immaculate conception," 8 December 1854* {made dogma on this date by Pope Pius IX in his *Ineffabilis Deus*}, *did not refer to Christ (as N appeared to believe), but to Mary's birth, i.e., Mary was conceived by her mother without "original sin."*

123. *"a thousand years"] Cf. Revelations 20:4.*

35

124. *Cf. CW 18, 11[354, 378].*

125. *"The words . . . child of God . . . "] Cf. introductory note to AC. N refers to the conversion of one of the two thieves crucified with Jesus, a passage referred to only in the gospel of Luke (23:39–43; compare Matthew 27:44; Mark 15:31–32). The words N puts into the mouth of the thief are actually spoken by the Centurion* {who refers to a "righteous man"} *after Christ's death; cf. Luke 23:47; Matthew 27:54; and Mark 15:39. Perhaps the Nietzsche-Archiv wanted to avoid any doubt as to N being well-versed in the Bible, thus the passage was suppressed; cf. J. Hofmiller,* {"Nietzsche" *Süddeutsche Mornatshefte* (November 1931)}, *94ff.*

36

126. *Cf. CW 18, 11[358].*

127. *they erected . . . Gospel] Cf. CW 18, 11[257, 276]; and Tolstoy, "Ma religion," 220: "And I became convinced that Church doctrine, even though it had taken the name 'Christian,' singularly resembles those forces of darkness that Jesus fought against and exhorted his disciples to fight against."*

37

128. *imperium Romanum]* "Roman empire"

38

129. *we can . . . it] Pm:* I myself am completely incapable of bearing it

130. *intellect] Pm:* from the strictest, highest-minded intellects {*Geister*} of two millennia

131. *poison-spider] Pm:* bloodsucker

132. *priest himself. . . of life] W II 8, 151:* priest — this parasite, this [poison-mixer] vampire of life by instinct — this parasite and poisonous mushroom of life

133. *systems of]* Pm: psychological

134. *we can no longer . . . the same.]* W II 8, 147–48: Everyone knows, everyone *could* know, that there is neither a God, nor sin, nor a redeemer, nor "free will," nor a moral world order; that the priest is the most disgusting form of all parasites, that Christianity is the will to nothing, the will to decline, the will to humanity's self-violation — that the beyond, immortality of the soul, the soul itself have become pitiful *lies.* Yet everything stays the same: and precisely because everything has become new, has become modern, staying with the old arouses *contempt*

135. *statesmen]* Allusion to Bismarck.

136. *young]* Cf. introductory note to AC{, p. 510 above}.

39

137. *Even today . . . being]* W II 8, 146: Faith is what is absolutely wrong in the Christian "gospel."

138. *spiritual]* Pm: conscious-spiritual

139. *negate]* Pm: annul

140. *who are philosophers . . . Naxos.]* W II 8, 145: to whose number I also count psychologists.

141. *encountered . . . Naxos.]* Cf. TI "Forays" 19 and associated notes.

40

142. *Cf. CW 18, 11[378].*

143. *canaille]* "riff-raff" "rabble"

41

144. *Cf. CW 18, 11[378].*

145. *barbaric]* Pm: barbarous

146. *of God as human]* Le: of God and human *(corrected in Pm by Peter Gast)*

147. *"if . . . vain." —]* Cf. I Corinthians 15:14.

42

148. *Cf. CW 18, 11[378, 383].*

149. *dysangelist]* W II 8, 43; Le: dysangelist; Pm: dysevangelist

150. *at the main . . . enlightenment]* Pm: at the main university of ancient stoicism

151. *niasierie]* "piece of folly"

152. *that is . . . "judgment"]* W II 8, 143: With that, even a priest can arouse fear

153. *What was . . . "judgment"]* {Sommer 2, 201, points out that N's source here is Wellhausen, *Reste des arabischen Heidentums,* 209–10.}

43

154. *"One . . . needful"]* Luke 10:42.

155. *such]* Pm: such an obscene reestablishment and

156. *selfishness]* Pm: selfishness of the loafer

157. *into infinity, into obscenity]* Pm: under the pretense of "higher purpose"

158. *everyone, as an . . . obscenity]* W II 8, 141: in the totality of all beings the salvation of each individual has an eternal significance — that little bigots and pretend-saints dare to consider themselves a sort of central point of interest for God — this most obscene reestablishment of the selfishness of the loafer under the pretense of "higher tasks"

159. *personal vanity]* Followed, but then crossed out in Pm, by: the lowest

160. *The poison . . . on earth . . .]* W II 8, 142: With the soul-atomism of *"equal* rights for all," Christianity sowed at all times the poison of a rebellious uprising, *ressentiment* against all that was noble, beautiful, content — democracy, which causes revolutions, is merely one *more* practice of that Christian — — —

161. *and if . . . crime!]* W II 8, 141: The revolution-instigating faith in the prerogative of the majority is merely a transfer of Christian value judgments into the *muscles . . .*

162. *Christianity is . . . makes low]* Pm: Christianity is the mass uprising against everything *that has value* — the gospel of the "lowly"

44

163. *Cf. CW 17, 10[72, 73]. Pd in WII 8, 144 reads:* 43. / The gospels are invaluable as evidence for the [complete] already unstoppable corruption [in] within the first community: — what Paul later pursued to its end with the splendid [instinct-certainty]

cynicism of a rabbi was nevertheless just a process of decline that already began with the death of the Redeemer. [At this point, a word that is valid for the whole of the New Testament will not be unwelcome] One cannot read these gospels too cautiously: this kind of book comes with the greatest of difficulty. What is put into words here is the opposite of all naïve depravity, the gospels are the refinement [of depravity] par excellence in corruption. *Additional to this is W II 6, 13:* 43. / [For a psychologist, |assuming one is not a false one| reading in the New Testament becomes no small task. The impression of so much [—] corruption is too strong; he has almost heroic means to restore himself (a few pages of Petronius for example: [— — —]) This book goes its own way |— also has its way for itself|: it is the *opposite* of a |every| naïve corruption, it is the refinement |par excellence| in corruption] *This opening passage, crossed out by N, was replaced by the above-quoted version in W II 8 144; Pd continues in W II 6, 13:* One is among Jews: the first point of view, so as not to lose the thread completely here. This passing oneself off as "holy," has almost become genius here, this psychological counterfeiting as *art* is *not* the result [of an individual talent] [of an individual species] of a random talent, of a random exceptional nature: *race* is required here — in Christianity as the art of lying in a holy manner, the whole of Judaism [culminates] again [Jewish instinct] achieves [reaches its culmination] its ultimate mastery, a centuries-long Jewish training and technique. The fundamental [decision] |will to use only| [the] concepts, [the] words, | gestures| [One cannot believe a word: the words in the priestly — — —] [that which a priest alone can use,] that are useful in the priest's practice, the [closing of eyes] instinctive resistance against any possibility other than priestly [to talk, to behave, to allow other than priestly psychology] to allow values and attitudes, this is not only tradition, it is *heritage*: only as heritage [could it find expression with this perfection] [does it become genius here] does it work like nature here. *The |whole of| humanity has let itself be deceived*: no small indication |for| how [great art is here] well, how astonishingly they have play-acted here. — If one were *to see* them, if [only for a *moment*] only in passing, |all| these little bigots and saints, that would of course put an end to it: one would not [be able to digest] tolerate [swallow] |a| certain [way of opening their eyes] way of opening their eyes. Fortunately it is just *literature*: — the possibility of Christianity rests in the fact that it could not measure its "holy books" by the holy caricatures which in them [make "words" of themselves] [manipulate the art,] practiced their art ["to lie in a holy manner"] the art "of lying in a holy manner" . . . / Little devils, tethered to all malicious and narrow feelings, but perfectly certain of their task of how to represent the "saints" on earth: with every instinct for cloaked pride in gestures, in colors, in furrowed brows; psychologists in the art of satisfying all vain and self-seeking needs under the pretense of the contrary. Let us see them at work for a *moment*: — — —

164. *ultima ratio]* "final argument"

165. *"judge not!"]* Cf. *Matthew 7:1* {where there is no exclamation mark}.

166. *as a duty]* Le: out of duty *(correction by Peter Gast in the Pm)*

167. *deliberate]* Pm: nonsensical

168. *denomination]* Bekenntnisses {Usually translated as "confession," but in this context, modern English usage would be "denomination."}

45

169. *Cf. CW 17, 10 [179, 200].*

170. *and hear you]* Le: nor hear you *(Corrected as per Mark 6:11.)*

171. {Cf. *CW* 18, 11 [360].}

172. *Well-lied, lion]* From Shakespeare's *A Midsummer Night's Dream* {Act V, Scene 1: "well roar'd, Lion!"}

173. *For if ye]* Le: But if ye . . . *(Corrected as per Matthew 6:15.)*

174. *in heaven]* Le: your trespasses. *(Corrected as per Matthew 6:15.)*

175. *Whereupon]* Le: shortly before *(because the passage N meant, Matthew 6:{30} comes before Matthew 6:33).* {KSA 14 mistakenly identifies Matthew 6:29; the passage referred to ("will He not much more clothe you") is found in Matthew 6:30, which

comes before the exhortation "But seek ye first the Kingdom of God" in Matthew 6:33.}

176. *"Hath not . . . believe."*] {Paul, 1 Corinthians 1:20–21.}

177. *"Not many . . . presence"*] {Paul, 1 Corinthians 1:26–29.}

46

178. *Cf. CW 15, 25[338]; CW 17, 9[88]; CW 17, 10[69, 183]; Z IV "The Ugliest Human."*

179. *"è tutto festo"*] "completely festive"

180. {Cf. Sommer 2, 217: N here refers to Giovanni Boccaccio; the source behind N's mistaken reference to "Domenico" Boccaccio is most likely an essay by Albert Gagnière, "Le journal des médecins de Lucrèce Borgia, Duchesse de Ferrare" ("The diary of the doctors of Lucretia Borgia, Duchess of Ferrara"), *La Nouvelle Revue* 54 (September 1888): 304: " . . . César avait particulière- ment l'humeur sereine: *e tutto festo*, écrivait Domenico Boccaccio à son maître le duc de Ferrare." (" . . . Cesare was in a particularly serene mood: *e tutto festo*, wrote Domenico Boccacio to his mas- ter the Duke of Ferrara."}

181. *by . . . preaching"*] {Cf. 1 Corinthians 1:21.}

182. *"What is truth?"*] Cf. *John 18:38.*

47

183. *Cf. CW 18, 11[122].*

184. *deus . . . negatio*] "the God whom Paul created negates God"

185. *of the "wisdom . . . ur-Jewish.*] *W II 8, 132:* lead to a war of attrition to the death against every straight path that leads to knowledge, against all rigor of the mind, against all integrity and clarity in things of the mind. Paul *understood* the need for this; the church understood Paul . . . The God that Paul invented for himself, who ruins the "wisdom of the world" (our science, if I may say so —), is in truth just a ["pious wish"] resolute decision of Paul to do so: we, Paul, want to ruin science — "God" is the word for everything that Paul wants . . .

186. *That "God" . . . ur-Jewish.*] *W II 3, 145:* A God who "ruins the wisdom of the world" is, psychologically speaking, a God who has an appalling fear of knowledge. *Cf. 1 Corinthians 1:27.*

48

187. *Cf. CW 17, 9[72]; J. Wellhausen, Prolegomena, 310–36 (N's copy had numerous marginal notes, underlining, markings etc.).*

188. *takes a pleasant stroll]* Wellhausen, *Prolegomena, 321:* "Here, Jehovah does not descend from heaven, but takes a pleasant stroll in the garden in the evening as though he were at home there." *The word "lustwandelt"* {"takes a pleasant stroll"} *is underlined by N.*

189. *Against . . . in vain:]* {N paraphrases a line from Schiller's *The Maid of Orleans* (1801), Act III, Scene VI: "Against stupidity even gods struggle in vain."}

190. *"Woman is . . . Eve"]* {Cf.} *Wellhausen, 324, note.*

191. *twilighting the gods]* götter-andämmernd {The allusion is to Wagner's opera *Götter-Dämmerung* (*Twilight of the Gods*), the fourth and final opera of *The Ring.*}

49

192. *— have been invented . . . committed. —]* W II 8, 130: the human's *sense of cause* is destroyed once and for all. When the natural results of a deed are *no* longer "natural," when, instead, reward or punishment conceals a ruling power in the other world, then the *precondition* for knowledge has been destroyed. The concept of "reward and punishment" *does away* with science. *Cf. CW 18, 16[84].*

193. *against . . . committed. —]* Pm: brought into the world, the invention of sin

50

194. *psychology]* W II 8, 125: critique

195. *badge of décadence,]* W II 8, 126: sign of illness

196. *reaches]* Pm: heals

197. *"demonstration of power."]* {N is quoting from 1 Corinthians 2:4: "And my speech and my preaching *was* not with enticing words of man's wisdom, but in demonstration of the Spirit and of power [. . .]."}

198. *blessedness . . . "faith"]* W II 8, 126: as effect of faith

199. *for that: . . . service]* Pm: just to bear the sight of truth

200. *all rigorous, . . . Faith]* W II 8, 125–26: any rigorous, any profoundly inclined intellect is the reverse: it has to wrestle for

the truth every step of the way, it has had to sacrifice everything, repose, certainty, tranquility, trust — its *conscience* consists of not allowing itself to be persuaded by "pleasant thoughts" . . . Desire flatters, desire cheats — faith

51

201. *the ulterior motive]* W II 8, *121:* the surest way

202. *forms of epilepsy]* W II 8, *121:* known to every psychiatrist

203. *in . . . honorem]* "to the greater glory of God"

204. *training]* {In English in the original.}

205. *folie circulaire]* "circular madness" {Underlined by N. Now considered a bipolar disorder.}

206. *I once . . . morbid one.]* Cf. GM III; N took the idea of the "folie circulaire" from Féré, *Dégénérescence et criminalité, cf. note 110 above; cf. excerpts of this work found in CW 18, 14[172, 180].* {Cf. also Féré, *Sensation et mouvement,* 122–23; cf. note 9 above.}

207. *and also for contempt]* Pm: and for happiness

208. *"But God . . . despised"]* Cf. *1 Corinthians 1:27–28.*

209. *in hoc signo]* "in *this* sign" {N underlines *hoc,* "this."}

52

210. *everything idiotic]* Pm: all idiots

211. *superbia]* "pride" "arrogance"

212. *ephexis]* "indecision" {Underlined by N.}

213. *Pietists . . . Swabia]* Like *Jung-Stilling, whose autobiography N had read (and praised:* WS *109).* {Johann Heinrich Jung-Stilling (1740–1817) was a German author.}

214. *"finger of God"]* {Cf. Exodus 8:19 and 31:18; Deuteronomy 9:10; Luke 11:20.}

215. *the most . . . accidents]* W II 8, *119:* every fortunate accident

216. *Another sign . . . Germans!]* Cf. CW 18, 22[7, 8].

53

217. *Even today . . . sectarianism.]* W II 8, *117:* Still in this century, Carlyle's example provides evidence as to how that vulgar crudeness of maltreatment, execution arouses sympathy for certain things, a kind of advantage in favor — — —

218. *walk]* {In Z: *geht* (indicative); *gienge* (subjunctive) in *AC.*} N excerpted this passage from *Z* II "On Priests."

219. *people . . . their] Einer . . . seine* {Pluralized for the sake of gender neutrality. See the Translators' Afterword in *CW* 14, 730–32, for how the translators of *Thus Spoke Zarathustra* render singular universals.}

220. *within us.]* {"within us!" in *Z*.}

54

221. *Cf. CW 18, 11[48].*

222. *if one . . . term] Cf. TI "Forays" 12.*

223. *become free] W II 8, 101 (subsequently crossed out):* Nearest relative to conviction is the lie

224. *of these sick . . . reasons] W II 8, 101:* of the fanatic has so far been the most dangerous obstacle to knowledge

55

225. *Cf. CW 18, 14[159].*

226. *Human, All Too Human)]* {Cf. *HAH* 483.}

227. *The most . . . exception.] W II 8, 104:* whether one lies to *oneself* or others is immaterial. On closer examination, every interaction with oneself, that is to say, every phenomenality of consciousness presupposes a sort of duality, in short a *witness*. If one lies to oneself, one lies to something in oneself to oneself [*sic*] . . .

228. *An anti-Semite . . . principle . . .] Pm*: Nothing is more contemptible than convictions, even if that applies to you! . . .

229. *such things] Crossed out in Pm:* than anti-Semites

230. *the question . . . all] Le (having been corrected by Gast in Pm):* there is no question of "true" and "untrue" in such things spoken of by priests; these things allow for no lying at all

231. *to all things] Pm, subsequently crossed out:* to the Brahmins, for example

56

232. *Judaine] Judain* {Sommer 2, 267, suggests that N takes this word from the anti-Semitic rhetoric of Paul de Lagarde, with whose work N was familiar. The word appears only one other time in N's writings; cf. *CW* 18, 11[384].}

233. *warriors provide . . . multitudes] die Krieger halten mit ihm ihre Hand über die Menge* {*die Hand über jemanden halten* is idiomatic for protecting someone.}

234. *"to avoid . . . to burn."]* Cf. 1 Corinthians 7:2 and 7:9.

235. *immaculata conceptio]* "immaculate conception" {N underlines *immaculata*.}

236. *"The mouth . . . always pure."]* Cf. Jacolliot, *Les législateurs religieux: Manou-Moïse-Mahomet* {"Religious legislators: Manu, Moses, Mohammed" (Paris: Lacroix, 1876)}, *225ff. NL.* {Louis Jacolliot (1837–90) was a French lawyer and writer. See p. 481, note 6. His work on the *Laws of Manu* has been discredited, as have the translations N cites here. Annemarie Etter, in "Nietzsche und das Gesetzbuch des Manu," *Nietzsche-Studien* 16 (Berlin: Walter de Gruyter, 1987): 343–44, provides the following corrections to Jacolliot's translations from the *Laws of Manu*:

> "The mouth . . . pure.": "The mouth of women is always pure, pure is the bird that causes fruit to fall. Pure is the calf when spilling (milk from its mouth), pure is the dog when mauling a wild animal."

> "There is nothing . . . girl.": "The fly, the water drop, the shadow, the cow, the horse, sunbeams, dust, the earth, the wind and fire — let (these) be declared as pure to the touch."

> "all orifices . . . pure.": "Those orifices which are above the navel are completely pure. Impure are those which are below, and likewise the filth that falls from the body."}

57

237. *in flagranti]* "in the act of doing something wrong"

238. *Pulchrum est paucorum hominum]* "beauty is for few men"; cf. Horace, Satires I, 9, 44.

239. *"The world is perfect"]* Cf. *Z* IV *"At Noon."*

240. *politeness of the heart]* {A phrase from Goethe's *Die Wahlverwandtschaften* (1809); see *Elective Affinities*, trans. David Constantine (Oxford: Oxford University Press, 1994), 151: "There is no outward sign of politeness that does not have a basis deep in morality . . . There is a politeness of the heart, akin to love. From it derives the easiest politeness of outward behavior."}

58

241. *aere perennius]* "more lasting than bronze"; cf. Horace, Odes III, 30, 1.

242. *imperium Romanum]* {Underlined by N.}

243. *sub specie aeterni]* "from the viewpoint of eternity"

244. *unio mystica]* "mystical union"

245. *wandering Jew] ewige Jude* {Literally: "eternal Jew."}

246. *"Salvation comes from the Jews."] Cf. John 4:2.*

247. *This was . . . rhyme] Cf. CW 18, 11[281] (written after N had read Tolstoy).* {In the final line, "Nihilist" and "Christ" rhyme in German.}

59

248. *Augustine] Cf. N's letter to Overbeck, 31 March 1885* {KGB III:3, 34}*:* I have just read S⟨t⟩. Augustine's *Confessions* for relaxation, greatly regretting that you were not here with me. Oh this old rhetorician! What eye-rolling mendacity! How I laughed! (e.g., over the "theft" of his youth, basically a student's yarn.) What psychological falsity! (e.g., when he speaks about the death of his best friend, with whose soul he was at *one*, "he decided to stay alive so that in this way, his friend would *not quite* die." Something like that is disgustingly untrue.) Philosophical value nil. *Rabble Platonism*, in other words, a way of thought that was invented for the highest, most spiritual aristocracy, but contrived for slave natures. Besides, you see into the entrails of Christianity with this book: I look on with the curiosity of a radical physician and physiologist. —

249. *shrewd . . . sanctity] W II 8, 94:* shrewd, poisonously shrewd

250. *prerequisite . . .] W II 8, 93:* prerequisite — not semi-eunuchs and cowards . . . [what we praise and esteem with every beat of the heart]

60

251. *N read about Islam in Wellhausen's works; in addition, in a notebook from this period a work by August Müller is found, Der Islam in Morgen- und Abendland ("Islam in the East and West")* ({Berlin: Grote,} *1885–87), 2 vols.; cf. CW 18, 21[1].*

252. *The wonderful . . . Moorish life!] W II 8, 92:* the wonderful Moorish culture that was destroyed in Spain by Christian culture with the aid of that race of eunuchs par excellence, the Teutons; that noble spirit stemming from noble instincts, had yet again

aroused the deadly chandala-wrath of the Christians, the priests;
W II 8, 92: The fact that the [perfect Spanish] wonderful Moorish
culture of Spain had to be trampled down by Teutonic eunuchs!
— This culture that again owed its emergence to the noblest of
instincts, that again said Yes to life, to all rare and refined treasures of life

253. *The German nobility, ever the "Swiss" . . . painful questions.]* W II 8, 92: — and that the church, precisely with the Teutonic *nobility*, led the war on earth's "noble values" in favor of
chandala values, belongs, for a German, to the most painful of
questions — — — The Teutons, this servant-race of all the bad
instincts of the church!

254. *Really, there . . . felt and did.]* W II 8, 91: Really it would
be a sin against the intellect even to ask the question as to which
has more value, Christianity *or* Islam! For they are antithetical
values. One cannot choose otherwise, if one embodies noble
instincts, than the Hohenstaufen Friedrich the Second: fight
against Rome, peace, friendship with Islam! . . . *W II, 8, 92:* How
could anyone even put the question as to whom to choose when
it is a matter of Christianity or Islam! The antithesis of values is
pronounced in both religions! One is either chandala or one *is*
noble . . . A noble German cannot feel otherwise than did the
Hohenstaufen Friedrich the Second . . . war against Rome — — —

61

255. *I see a spectacle . . . abolished!] Cf. Jacob Burckhardt, Die
Cultur der Renaissance in Italien (Leipzig{: E. A. Seemann,} 1869),
91–95 {The Civilization of the Renaissance in Italy, trans. S. G. C.
Middlemore (London: Penguin Books, 1990), 88–90}, NL, in
particular this passage:* "In fact, there can be no doubt whatever
that Cesare, whether chosen Pope or not after the death of Alexander, meant to keep possession of the pontifical State at any
cost, and that this, after all the enormities he had committed, he
could not as Pope have succeeded in doing permanently. He, if
anybody, could have secularized the States of the Church, and he
would have been forced to do so in order to keep them. Unless we
are much deceived, this is the real reason of the secret sympathy
with which Machiavelli treats the great criminal; . . . And what

might not Cesare have achieved if, at the moment when his father died, he had not himself been laid upon a sickbed! What a conclave would that have been, in which, armed with all his weapons, he had extorted his election from a college whose numbers he had judiciously reduced by poison — and this at a time when there was no French army at hand! In pursuing such a hypothesis the imagination loses itself in an abyss."

256. *the papal*] *W II 8, 115:* Peter's

257. *he attacked it . . . irretrievable*] Cf. *CW 18, 22[9].*

62

258. *rancunes*] "rancor"

259. *dies nefastus*] "wicked day"

260. *today*] I.e., *30 September 1888.*

261. *There follows an instruction to the typesetter, crossed out by N, as follows:* After this, a blank page on which the only words are: *Law Against Christianity.*

Law Against Christianity

The fact that the sheet on which was written the "Law Against Christianity" lay in the box containing the *EH* manuscripts when Hans-Joachim Mette undertook the description and numbering of N's manuscripts in the former Nietzsche-Archiv does not necessarily mean in the least that the page belonged to *EH*. When making his initial inventory, Mette had to restrict himself to a provisional ordering and cataloguing of the material. At that time (1932), the actual work on publishing *EH* was by no means up-to-date. We should also remember that by that time, the *Pm* of that work had passed through several hands: 1. until mid-January 1889 it was with the printer C. G. Naumann in Leipzig; 2. Peter Gast safeguarded it until 17 November 1893; 3. it ended up in the possession of N's mother and sister in Naumburg until 1897, and then lay in Weimar in the Nietzsche-Archiv until 1908; 4. in the first half of the year 1908, Raoul Richter, professor of philosophy in Leipzig, used it for the first publication of *EH*; 5. it was returned to Weimar after Richter had finished his edition.

Mette's description connects the sheet with "Law Against Christianity" to another sheet also found in the *EH* box and containing

Z III "On Old and New Tablets" §30. Mette wrote: "There follows, in connection with p. 44, a sheet numbered 47: 'Passed on the day of grace, on the first day of Year One (— 30 September 1888 of the wrong calculation of time)' etc., as well as a page numbered 48/49 containing the section *Z* III "On Old and New Tablets" §30, earmarked as Epilogue at the time: but N in any case did not include pages 45–49 for the printers; pages 47–49 will have been found in his *Nachlaß*." The page numbers given by Mette originate from N himself; according to this, pages 45 and 46 of the *Pm* for *EH* are missing.

Erich F. Podach and Pierre Champromis {Champromis was the author of a brief article, "Podach: Nietzsches Werke des Zusammenbruchs oder Zusammenbruch der editorischen Werke Podachs?" ("Podach: Nietzsche's works of his collapse or the collapse of Podach's editorial works"), in *Philosophische Rundschau* 12, nos. 3–4 (January 1965): 250–54} are of the opinion that sheets 47 ("Law Against Christianity") and 48/49 (*Z* III "On Old and New Tablets" §30) belong together. Based on the instruction (crossed out by N) for the printer on the final sheet of the *Pm* of *AC* and the page number 46 on this same sheet, originating from N, Podach published both pages 47 as well as 48/49 (the latter numbered on both sides) as the conclusion to *AC*. Champromis has nothing against an *original* affiliation of both sheets to *AC*; in addition, he tries to prove that the "Law Against Christianity" is identical to the "Declaration of War" inscribed in N's original "Contents" list for *EH*. N wrote the "Contents" for *EH* at the beginning of December and enclosed it with the revised *Pm* {cf. p. 560 below}. At the end of the "Contents" list for *EH* are found: " . . . / Declaration of War. / The Hammer Speaks." {see p. 216} Champromis believes that "The Hammer Speaks" was the designation planned for sheet 47/48. Furthermore, at the close of the "Law Against Christianity" (sheet 46) is found the following instruction from N to the typesetter: "After that / an empty page / on which only the / words are written: / *The Hammer Speaks* / Zarathustra 3, 90." According to Champromis (p. 254), "sheets 47 and 48/49 followed in sequence thus: 1. Conclusion to *AC*; 2. Con-

NOTES TO PAGES 208–209

clusion to *EH*; 3. A text that N ultimately abandoned." In contrast, according to Podach, the text designated as "The Hammer Speaks" in the "Contents" for *EH* would have come at the end of *TI*.

In fact we do find the title "The Hammer Speaks" at the conclusion of *TI* with the reference "Zarathustra 3, 90." {See p. 132.} N refers to the pagination in the first edition of *Z* III §29 in the chapter "On Old and New Tablets," the *whole* of which is found on p. 90 of the first edition of *Z* III and forms the conclusion to *TI*. Regarding §30 of the same chapter (i.e., the text of sheet 47/48), only the first two paragraphs are found on p. 90 of the first edition of *Z* III.

Let us consolidate the following facts: the title "The Hammer Speaks" appears three times — as the conclusion for *TI*, *AC*, and *EH* — while the reference to "Zarathustra 3, 90" occurs twice: in *TI* and *AC*.

In the following, we shall test, 1: whether the "Law Against Christianity" is identical to the "Declaration of War" referred to in the "Contents" list for *EH*; and 2: whether the page numbered 47/48 in the *Pm* belongs to *AC* or *EH* (entitled in both "The Hammer Speaks").

The "Law Against Christianity" and "Declaration of War." In a draft letter to Georg Brandes at the beginning of December 1888 {*KGB* III:5, 500–502}, the original of which has not survived, N referred to the "Law" as the conclusion to *AC*: "When you finally read the *Law Against Christianity*, signed the 'Antichrist,' which forms the conclusion, who knows, I fear perhaps even you will tremble in every limb," N wrote, and cited a few propositions from the "Law." The letter to Brandes was intended to persuade him to translate *AC* into Danish: "I thought of you for the Danish and Herr Strindberg for the Swedish edition." Although there is doubt as to whether N actually posted this letter to Brandes, it is certain on the other hand that another letter sent at the same time, containing the suggestion for a Swedish translation, reached Strindberg; one can conclude this from the first letter Strindberg wrote to N, who received it on 7 December. Strindberg replied {in French} to N's suggestion thus: "And you want to be translated into our

Greenlandic language: why not into French, into English?" How-ever, no letter from N to Strindberg containing such a suggestion has survived. As the letter to Brandes was somewhat offensive and that to Strindberg was doubtless no less so, it seems probable that both letters were destroyed at some later time.

Strindberg's letter arrived in Turin on 7 December; N answered next day, taking up Strindberg's proposal for a French transla-tion, this time not of *AC* but of *EH* (cf. the Chronicle of N's Life in *CW* 19). In N's letter to Strindberg dated 8 December {*KGB* III:5, 509}, a sentence is included from *EH* that has been deleted from all editions hitherto. For insofar as N designates *EH* as "*anti-German* to the point of annihilation," he adds: "I name the young Kaiser a scarlet bigot" (this is the deleted sentence). Now in the current *Pm* of *EH* there is no passage with such words about the "young Kaiser" (Wilhelm II). It will be demonstrated in the *EH* commentary that the *Pm* of *EH* has not survived in the form in which N completed it on 2 January 1889. Yet here already we must anticipate a great deal of what is connected with the complicated textual history of *EH*.

Among the published fragments that date from December 1888 and possibly represent preliminary drafts for more or less compre-hensive lost second drafts composed by N during his work on *EH*, there are several that refer to a "Declaration of War": *CW* 18, 25[1, 6, 11, 13, 14]. They give us a rough idea of the content of the "Dec-laration of War." Among these, in turn, the most deserving of our attention is 25[6]. The fragment consists of two sections: the first corresponds (with variants) to the first section of the chapter "Why I Am a Destiny" in its final form; the second, however, does not correspond to anything in that chapter nor in the whole of (the surviving) *EH*. {Cf. *CW* 18: the ending of 25[6], section 2, reads: "There is more dynamite between ⟨heav⟩en and earth than these purpled idiots can dream up . . . "} With regard to the words "these purpled idiots" (compare the "scarlet bigot" in the letter to Strindberg), there is the following remark of Elisabeth Förster-Nietzsche: "an expression that appeared on the page, that our mother burned because of its *lèse majesté*." So this burned page belonged to *EH*, and it was the "Declaration of War," directed against the House of Hohenzollern and "its tool, Prince Bismarck" that N had designated in the "Contents" and sent off to Leipzig.

But why did Overbeck not copy down the "Law Against Christianity" when he completed his copy of the *AC* based on the *Pm* that remained in Turin? For it is a fact that the "Law" is missing from the copy still held today at the University Library in Basel. The only possible answer has been suggested by Podach (*Nietzsches Werke des Zusammenbruchs*, 400): The sheet containing the "Law" was "earlier glued together or had a sheet glued onto it . . . Indeed, the sheet escaped Overbeck's notice." We must have another look into the so-called *EH* box. Here we find not just sheets 47 ("Law") and 48/49 ("The Hammer Speaks"), but sheet 46 of the *Pm* of *AC* as well. This sheet contains the conclusion to §62 on the page N numbers 46; on the other side, there is nothing written but it shows traces of glue. Sheet 47 for its part also contains writing on its other side — not numbered — namely, a preliminary draft of §4 and notes for §5 of the *EH* chapter about "The Case of Wagner." Both sides of sheet 47 likewise reveal traces of glue. Now, the traces of glue on the side with the jottings to *EH* (the reverse side of sheet 47, with writing on it) match exactly the traces of glue on the (unwritten) reverse side of sheet 46. But what is the meaning of the traces of glue on the front side of sheet 47? The answer lies in a remark made by Peter Gast referring to a preliminary draft of the "Law" (W II 10, 135), which Podach was first to cite (*Nietzsches Werke des Zusammenbruchs*, 400). The remark is as follows: "hold the final glued-up sheet of *AC* up to the light to read, and compare *Z* I, p. 26." (W II 10, 135 refers to fragment 25[1] {in *CW* 18} and *Z* I 26 = *Z* II 1, 26, according to today's classification, hence to a genuine preliminary draft of the "Law.") So the "Law Against Christianity" was still glued over with a blank page during the period Peter Gast worked at the Nietzsche-Archiv (1900–1909), and moreover, still had the reverse side of the final sheet of *AC* glued to it. Since Overbeck transcribed the ending of *AC*, but not the "Law," he must have found the ending of the *Pm* in Turin in the state described. Which means that N himself had glued on and glued over sheet 47. The gluing together of the reverse side of sheet 47 and the reverse side of sheet 46 can be explained quite simply: on the reverse side of sheet 47, there were preliminary stages of *EH* which N had to block out so as not to cause confusion later at the printer. He went about other productions of his *Pm*s in like manner, as, for example, when he completed the chapter "What I Owe the Ancients" from *TI* for print; here, the reverse sides of sheets are glued together because — as we were able to ascertain — they contained preliminary drafts for the later work *EH*, namely fragment 24[10] (*CW* 18), among others. But what was his purpose in gluing over a blank sheet? Keeping the "Law" a secret, abandoning its publication? A definitive answer is not possible. What is certain is that the "Law Against Christianity" is in no case identical with the "Declaration of War," and that it forms a component of the *Pm* of *AC*.

Finally, we should remark that in *EH* "Why I Write Such Good Books" §5, N cites a passage from the "Law": "And to remove any doubt in this regard as to my attitude, forthright as it is strong, I shall impart yet another proposition from my Moral Code against *Vice*: with the word vice I attack every kind of anti-nature, or, if you like nice words, idealism. The proposition is: 'the preaching of chastity is a public incitement to anti-nature. Every disparagement of sexuality, every defilement of the same by the concept "impure," is crime itself against life — it is the very sin against the holy spirit of life.'—"

N wrote this conclusion to §5 in the chapter "Why I Write Such Good Books" during his revision at the beginning of December, when he added the "Declaration of War" to the printer's manuscript of *EH*. But how could he cite a passage from his "Moral Code Against Vice" in a section of the work whose conclusion was supposed to contain precisely that moral code (assuming that "Law" and "Declaration of War" were one and the same)? Was this not, on the contrary, an anticipation of the world-shattering — at least in N's eyes — "Revaluation of All Values," i.e., *The Antichrist*?

For all these reasons we publish the "Law" at the end of *AC* (with Podach, against Champromis). The smaller font should indicate to the reader that N glued over the "Law" and that no more definite conclusions can be drawn as to his intentions.

"The Hammer Speaks"— two times or three times? Podach believes that "The Hammer Speaks" at the end of the "Contents" to *EH* ended up in *TI*; that is, as Champromis correctly saw, chronologically wrong: *TI* was already published by the time N composed the "Contents" to *EH* (beginning of December 1888) and in fact it concluded with "The Hammer Speaks" (identical to *Z* III "On Old and New Tablets" §29).

Champromis thinks that by placing the "Law" at the end of *AC*, one should also add sheets 48–49 to the ending. However, "The Hammer Speaks" as conclusion to *EH* actually was not located in Turin (with the *Pm* for *AC*) but in Leipzig (with the *Pm* for *EH*), when N sent his dithyramb "Fame and Eternity" to C. G. Naumann on 29 December with the instruction: "The *Declaration of War* section is missing [*sic!* instead of "omitted"] — likewise 'The Hammer Speaks.'" {Montinari adds this parenthetical *sic* because N wrote *fehlt weg* instead of *fällt weg*. The word *fehlt* by itself means "is missing," but the words *fällt weg* mean "is omitted." Montinari points out N's error by drawing attention to the fact that N should not have added *weg*, implying his own preference for "is missing." Cf. the immediate paragraph below in which Montinari uses "missing."}

Against Champromis, there is our proof that the "Law" is not identical to the "Declaration of War," and the latter is in fact missing from the *Pm* of *EH*. The last preserved page we have of the *Pm* of *EH* was numbered by N himself as 44; the missing pages 45–47 must then have contained the "Declaration of War," which was destroyed (by N's relatives). The section "The Hammer Speaks," to which the "Contents" and the above-mentioned instruction by N allude, is sheet 48/49 (with *Z* III "On Old and New Tables" §30).

But which was the text that N alluded to at the end of the (now glued-over) "Law"? We have already remarked that the reference on p. 90 of the first edition of *Z* III is much more closely related to §29 than to §30 in the chapter "On Old and New Tablets." The "Law" was composed on 30 September, according to N himself; that same day, he wrote the foreword to *TI*. Chronologically it is justifiable to suggest that N at the last moment withdrew §29 from the *Pm* of *AC*, where it had originally belonged, redirecting it for the ending of *TI*. In addition, the paper constituting the sheet that contains "The Hammer Speaks" in the *Pm* of *TI* is identical to that used for the *Pm* of *AC* (including the "Law").

In summary: the title "The Hammer Speaks" alludes twice to §29 of the chapter "On Old and New Tablets" (*Z* III) and became successively the ending, first of *AC*, then of *TI*; it alludes a third time to §30 of the same chapter, which formed the conclusion to *EH* on 29 December 1888.

1. *knowledge]* *Wissenschaft* {In this context, *Wissenschaft* could also be translated as "science" or "wisdom."}

Ecce Homo

The Manuscripts: The printer's manuscript (*Pm*) for *Ecce Homo* is extant. The folder where it is found was put together after publication of the first edition (1908). The pages can be classified in the following manner:

(a) Sheets paginated (numbered) by N himself; written on one side or both sides of the page, some of which consist of various pieces glued together: the numbering is roman for the title page, foreword, and contents (I–V); the rest of the sheets are numbered 1–44 and 48–49. With N's own numbering, the following should be noted: instead of 6, it is numbered 6a–b, and instead of 12, 12a–b. The page number 27 appears twice: once at the top of the lower half of p. 26, apparently to separate the chapter on "Joyful Science" from the end of the chapter on "Dawn" so that it would be typeset on a new page; the other time on the first page of the immediately following chapter on "Thus Spoke Zarathustra." After page 30 there is a double sheet; all four of its sides are written on and all were headed 31 until a later hand added the letters a–d. In similar fashion, instead of 32 we find 32a–b; instead of 35, 35a–b. After p. 44 (end of the chapter "Why I Am a Destiny"), at the time when N was paginating in Turin (early December–6 December 1888), a "Declaration of War" was supposed to come

— and was even included in the table of contents drawn up at the same time. As the sheet which includes what the "Contents" calls the final text of *EH* ("The Hammer Speaks," i.e., *Z* III §30 of the chapter "On Old and New Tablets") is given the page numbers 48–49, the "Declaration of War" must have been on pp. 45–47. The "Declaration of War" was destroyed by N's relatives {i.e., mother and sister} (see the notes to *AC* above, pp. 537–39).

(b) Sheets not paginated by N, but which nevertheless N clearly indicated as destined to be included in the text of *EH*; these were later paginated using letters:

6c: the reverse of the sheet numbered 6b by N; 10a–h: the first page number is in N's hand, only the letter *a* was added; 14b–c follow the page numbered 14 by N; with 16a–b, N numbered 16, only the letter *a* was added; 19a–b follow the page numbered 19 by N; 24a is glued onto the bottom edge of the page numbered 24 by N; the sheets 10b, 10e, 14c, 16a–b, and 19a–b were inserted into the *Pm* by N himself while he undertook the pagination in Turin; he sent the rest of the sheets from Turin to the printing shop in Leipzig after 6 December 1888.

(c) Three pieces of paper which — following N's instructions on them — were pasted onto the relevant pages by the typesetter in Leipzig, as follows: 1 onto p. 13, the section "Through a little quirk . . . explain." (p. 248; cf. note 7 below to "Why I Write Such Good Books" §1); 2 onto p. 14b, the section "That was said . . . Europe's flatland, Germany." (pp. 249–50; cf. note 13 below to "Why I Write Such Good Books" §2); 3 onto p. 31b, the section "A third . . . warmth in it." (p. 284; cf. note 118 below to "Thus Spoke Zarathustra" §5).

(d) Sheets that ended up in the folder for *EH* after 1908 that do *not* belong in the text of *EH*. (1) A slip of paper with one of N's rejected draft titles "*Ecce Homo. / A Gift / to my Friends.*" and with a draft letter (on the reverse side: a version without alteration of the short introduction "On This Perfect Day . . . "). (2) A preliminary draft of §2 of the chapter "Why I Write Such Good Books" (cf. the associated note below, pp. 580–82); on the reverse side: preliminary drafts of the foreword to *NCW* and of an alteration to that text, together with a draft letter to Giosuè Carducci. (3) A slip of paper written by Elisabeth Förster-Nietzsche, apparently regarding p. 38 of the *Pm*, the so-called Paraguay Note (cf. note 181 below to §4 of the chapter "The Case of Wagner," pp. 615–16). (4) Pages 46 and 47 of the *Pm* for *AC* (numbered by N); p. 46 contains §62 from *AC* (i.e., the concluding section); p. 47 the "Law Against Christianity" (on the reverse of the page, there is a preliminary draft of §4 of the chapter "The Case of Wagner"; cf. the note to this section below, pp. 611–13). On the "Law," cf. the notes above, pp. 535–40. (5) A slip of paper bearing the title "Final Deliberation" and notes for the Leipzig typesetter that nevertheless stayed with N in Turin; he used the other side of the page for a draft of a dedication of *DD* to Catulle Mendès and for fragment 25[20] in *CW* 18.

The following deletions to the *Pm* of *EH* are of significance:

1. *Pm* p. 6a: cf. "Wise" note 27.
2. *Pm* p. 10a: cf. "Clever" note 23.
3. *Pm* p. 11: end of second deletion and earlier version of §5 in the chapter "Why I Am So Clever"; cf. "Clever" note 30.
4. *Pm* p. 12b, the first sentence of §10 in the chapter "Why I Am So Clever": "At this point there is need for a great reflection."
5. *Pm* p. 12b: "Our culture today . . . greatness" {cf. "Clever" note 50}.
6. *Pm* p. 13: the passage replaced by the first slip of pasted-on paper (see [c] above); {cf. "Books" note 7}.
7. *Pm* p. 14: earlier version (beginning of December) of §2 of "Why I Write Such Good Books," replaced by N in Turin {cf. "Books" note 12}.
8. *Pm* p. 14b: the version of the start of §2 (final version) of "Why I Write Such Good Books," replaced by the second slip of paper (see [c] above); {cf. "Books" note 13}.
9. *Pm* pp. 14–15: earlier version of §3 of "Why I Write Such Good Books"; cf. "Books" note 22.

10. *Pm* p. 15, crossed-out reverse side; replaced by "May I . . . spirit of life" (§5 of "Why I Write Such Good Books"); cf. "Books" note 31.

11. *Pm* p. 17, crossed-out reverse side: earlier version of §1 of "Why I Write Such Good Books"; cf. "Books" note 1.

12. *Pm* p. 20, pasted to the reverse side: crossed-out fragments of earlier version of the chapter on "The Unfashionables"; cf. "Books" note 64.

13. *Pm* pp. 22–23: half pasted-on earlier version of §2 of the chapter on "Human, All Too Human"; cf. "Books" note 68.

14. *Pm* p. 31b: the section of §5 of the chapter on "Thus Spoke Zarathustra" replaced by the third slip of paper (see [c] above) {cf. "Books" note 116}.

15. *Pm* p. 32a, reverse side: crossed-out fragment of an earlier version of §§5 and 6 of the chapter on "Thus Spoke Zarathustra"; cf. "Books" note 118.

16. *Pm* p. 35a, reverse side: crossed-out fragment of an earlier version of §2 of the chapter on "The Case of Wagner"; cf. "Books" note 163.

17. *Pm* p. 38, at the bottom of page 38, the end of §4 of the chapter on "The Case of Wagner": "Just now . . . shoulder" {cf. "Books" note 185}.

18. *Pm* p. 40, reverse side: crossed-out earlier version of §§1 and 2 of the chapter on "Twilight of the Idols"; cf. "Books" notes 145, 146, 151.

19. *Pm* p. 43, reverse side: crossed-out fragment of earlier version of the Foreword.

All these deletions — with the exceptions of 4, 5, and 17 — can be traced back to N, either to his revision from early December 1888 or to his subsequent indications from Turin (in which case, the deletions were made in the Leipzig printing shop). With regard to deletions 4, 5, and 17, N neither made these alterations nor, apparently, gave any instruction about them from Turin.

On deletion 4 {*Pm* p. 12b}: During a renewed check (in August 1972), the editors {Colli and Montinari} were obliged to acknowledge that these deletions were the work of Peter Gast. The sentence "At this point there is need for a great reflection" is actually deleted with an unbroken, very thin horizontal line, whereas deletions by N nearly always consisted of close vertical strokes or slim vertical zigzags (in a few rare cases, strong thick horizontal lines). In its ink and its execution, deletion 4 corresponds to other small deletions by Peter Gast in N's *Pm* which can easily be recognized as such. The deleted sentence must therefore be reinstated in the text; the beginning of §10 in the chapter "Why I Am So Clever" must be altered accordingly to: "10. / At this point there is need for a great reflection. You will ask [etc.]" (and not "10. / — You will ask [etc.]"; Gast even inserted the dash).

On deletion 5 {*Pm* p. 12b}: middle of the page, the passage "Our culture today . . . greatness" was crossed out in thick pencil; in no way does this correspond to the characteristics of N's midtext deletions. Besides, as Erich F. Podach already pointed out, this passage was present when Gast made his copy of *EH*: "It was therefore, in spring 1889, not yet deleted in the manuscript" (Podach{, *Nietzsches Werke des Zusammenbruchs* [Heidelberg: Rothe, 1961], 198}).

On deletion 17 {*Pm* p. 38}: the deleted passage is from the end of §4 of the chapter "The Case of Wagner" {"Just now . . . shoulder"}; here, too, the strokes indicate a person unknown. Cf. "Books" note 185.

Deletions 5 and 6 in the *Pm* were reinstated by Raoul Richter (1908 first edition) and Otto Weiss (1911 *Groß- and Kleinoktav-Ausgabe* XV), describing them as "only probably" N's deletions in their notes.*

If one compares the reverse of sheets 1, 2, 4, 5 of group (d) with those of sheets from groups (a) and (b), it is apparent that the preliminary drafts and other notes on the reverse pages of (d) have no

---

*Another deletion of this kind is on *Pm* p. 27, where N says of his composition *Hymn to Life:* "The text, I say expressly . . . is not by me: it is the astonishing inspiration of a young Russian with whom I was friendly at the time, Fräulein Lou von Salomé" (cf. *EH* III Z §1, p. 279). The words "with whom I was friendly at the time, Fräulein Lou von Salomé" are, as in deletion 5, similarly crossed through with thick pencil; however, they had not yet been deleted in the manuscript in spring 1889, since Gast incorporated them into his transcription. The deleted text was, as Podach remarks, "silently" accepted by Raoul Richter in his edition of *Ecce Homo* and hence in all other later editions.

deletions; it can therefore be stated with certainty that no sheet whose reverse contains early drafts and the like that have not been deleted ever belonged within the final version of the *Pm*.

Of course, the *Pm* contains, like all others by N, more or less extensive deletions in the unfolding text that are recognizable as N's own. Peter Gast's interventions can usually be easily recognized as such and were all removed from {the Colli-Montinari edition}; he assisted in some cases where N had not written a word clearly enough and in many cases corrected N's grammar and punctuation; he sometimes rearranged N's syntax and corrected the citations from *Z*, etc.

In the *Pm* for *EH*, the sections within each chapter are numbered continuously by N himself; whenever he inserted new sections into the text during his revision at the beginning of December, he altered the numbering himself. After that, any new sections he sent from Turin to Leipzig were accompanied by exact instructions as to the resulting alterations in the numbering. Accordingly, deletions and alterations at the head of sections, whether by N or somebody else (the typesetter or Gast), can be accounted for comprehensively and consistently. Only in the chapter "Why I Am a Destiny" does it appear that N, during the revision of the beginning of December 1888, did not correct the numbering of the sections himself; after sections 1, 2, and 3 of *Pm* p. 39, 2 was corrected to 4 by someone else (Gast?) (p. 40), 3 became 5 (p. 41), 4 and 5 became 6 and 7 (p. 42), 6 became 8 (p. 43) and 7 became 9 (p. 44). As a result, though, on account of N's numbering of the pages, the sequence for the sections of this chapter can be clearly determined.

Regardless of all the deletions, insertions and other changes, the *Pm* of *EH* can be read effortlessly as a continuous text; however, one cannot definitively exclude the possibility that: (1) some pages with instructions but no pagination inserted by N himself — during the revision at the beginning of December — might have gone missing; (2) notes or sheets sent later — from Turin — went missing, too. We thus find, for example, traces of glue on *Pm* p. 19, clearly indicating that a largish piece of paper, now lost, was stuck here. It pertains to the conclusion of §3 in the chapter on the "Birth of Tragedy."

Two proof sheets of *EH*, sent by Naumann from Leipzig to Turin on 15 or 19 December 1888, have been preserved. They contain the text from the brief preamble "On This Perfect Day" up to the middle of §3 in the chapter "Why I Am So Clever" ("loving thy neighbor . . . "). On the first page of the sheets is found the comment: "ready for print / N." N himself dated the first sheet: "*Turin*, 18 December 1888," so this was the date on which it was returned to Leipzig; the second was sent shortly before 27 December (N's letter to the printer C. G. Naumann in Leipzig bears this date). {Colli and Montinari} took account of these proof sheets in so far as they contain alterations in N's hand or those made by Gast which N had accepted. (As we know, Peter Gast went over the corrections at the same time as N and then sent them to him; N wrote his own corrections into Gast's copy of the corrections and sent it to the printing shop with the comment "ready for print.")

The main manuscripts containing drafts of *EH* are, in roughly chronological sequence: notebook W II 9 and notebook N VII 4 (both October/November 1888) and notebooks Z II 1 and W II 10 (both the second half of November–December 1888). Notebooks W II 6 and W II 8 contain a few jottings for *EH* from October 1888.

Extensive preparatory drafts of *EH* are found in Mp XVI 5. This folder consists of thirty-three loose sheets of varied format and origin. These are longer fragments of earlier versions of the *Pm*, preliminary drafts and sketches that are developed in *EH*, but also notes and longer writings, mainly from December 1888, to which no finished text in *EH* corresponds; of the latter kind are a few pages in the folders Mp VII 8 and Mp VIII 1b, as well as jottings in N VII 4, Z II 1, and W II 10.

Peter Gast, Elisabeth Förster-Nietzsche and the organization of the text of Ecce Homo: After N's mental collapse, Peter Gast — at that time in close collaboration with Franz Overbeck — took on the inspection of the printer's manuscripts and proof sheets (of *EH* and *NCW*), which were now with the Leipzig printing shop of C. G. Naumann. He completed a copy of *EH* in February/March 1889. Regarding this, Peter Gast wrote to Overbeck on 27 February 1889: "I just wanted that you, dear Professor, should learn about this writing first based on my copy, that is *without* those passages that give even me the impression of too great self-intoxication or of going too far in their contempt and injustice — thus so as to provide you with *the* impression that I am not really capable of having myself, as I bring to mind the eccentric passages too easily" {Franz Overbeck and Heinrich Köselitz, *Briefwechsel*, ed. David Marc Hoffmann, Niklaus Peter, and Theo Salfinger (Berlin: de Gruyter, 1998), 241.}. This passage in the letter is invaluable for the textual history of *EH*. The copy made by Peter Gast is — apart from insignificant differences of no material substance — identical to the *Pm* described above. The latter, then, no longer contains the "eccentricities," that is, the passages which gave even Gast "the impression of too great self-intoxication" and "going too far in their contempt and injustice." It is not a question of the few deletions described above, but rather of texts that were later destroyed, and not by Peter Gast but by N's mother and sister when they took charge of the manuscript in November 1893. In her so-called great biography {*Das Leben Friedrich Nietzsches* (Leipzig: C. G. Naumann) in three volumes: I: 1895, IIi: 1897, IIii: 1904}, N's sister wrote in 1904 (IIii, 921): "At that time, he also wrote a few sheets with strange fantasies in which the myth of Dionysus-Zagreus merged with the Passion of the Gospels and personalities closest to him from the present: torn apart by his enemies, the god wanders newly resurrected along the banks of the Po and now sees everything that he has ever loved, his ideals, the ideals of the present day in general, far below him. His friends and those closest to him have turned into enemies who have torn him apart. These pages attack Richard Wagner, Schopenhauer, Bismarck, his closest friends: Professor Overbeck, Peter Gast, Frau Cosima, my husband, my mother, myself . . . Even in these pages there still are passages of captivating beauty, but on the whole they can be characterized as pathological febrile delirium *[this description almost gives the impression that the pages were then — 1904 — still to hand!]*. In the first years after my brother's illness, when we were still clinging to the false hope that he might recover, these sheets were mostly destroyed. It would have hurt my brother's loving heart and his good taste most deeply if he had ever caught sight of such writings afterwards."

Through a discovery in July 1969 among the literary remains
of Peter Gast — now incorporated into the Nietzsche holdings at
the Goethe-Schiller Archive in Weimar — one of these destroyed
pages came to light again in Gast's copy. Mazzino Montinari
reported on the discovery and the questions associated with it in
the first volume of *Nietzsche-Studien* (Berlin{: Walter de Gruyter,} 1972). In this way, the editors of *KSA* 6 {*CW* 9} were able to
restore the authentic text of §3 in the chapter "Why I Am So
Wise," as well as making further amendments according to N's
instructions as transcribed by Gast.

The page arrived in Leipzig with N's instructions: "On proof
sheet 1 of *Ecce Homo* instead of the former section 3." According
to Naumann's testimony, it arrived on "one of the last two days
in December," so on 30 or 31 December 1888. It was part of the
extensive dispatch of additions and alterations that N posted
from Turin on 29 December. N sent the first proof sheet of *EH*
back to Leipzig on 18 December having declared it "ready for
print" (see above). N now wanted to replace the former §3 (of the
first chapter "Why I Am So Wise") on this sheet with a new text
that delivered the most scathing account of his mother and sister.
C. G. Naumann, alerted by his manager to the "highly offensive
form" of this text, did not, for the moment, add it to the sheets
approved by N as ready for printing, intending to check the matter with N. According to his subsequent, very detailed statement,
"the manuscript page (strong deckle-edged paper about 17–23 cm
in size — rough border on the right — with about 35–38 *very
cramped* lines of text) was written with perfectly clean calligra-
phy" and bore "the clear traces" of N's hand; in describing the
page, Naumann added: " . . . large letters and other marks to
distinguish it from earlier manuscripts were completely absent."

Immediately afterward came the news of N's mental collapse.
The page remained in Naumann's writing desk until Peter Gast
collected it on behalf of N's sister in early February 1892. He sent
it to Naumburg on 9 February 1892 with the following comments: "I went to Naumann first thing early on Monday. His
nephew *[Gustav Naumann]* was also called, by telephone. Next,
with Naumann's consent, I took possession of the enclosed page

of *Ecce Homo*. I do not believe that Naumann has a copy; it still lay in the box and in the same place as it had been when he showed it to me previously. Let's be thankful that we have it! But now it also *really* must be *destroyed*. Even though it is clear that it was written in complete madness, there will always be people who say: *that is why* it is significant, for his instincts spoke with complete truthfulness, without reserve." Probably Gast took this opportunity to make his copy of the page, which {Colli and Montinari} rediscovered among his literary remains. The title Gast placed at the head of his copy ran: "Copy of a page that Nietzsche, already in complete madness, sent to Naumann during the printing of *Ecce Homo* (at the end of December from Turin)." Afterwards, Gast deleted the words "already in complete madness," which in 1892 he had used out of consideration for N's relatives and included in his accompanying letter to Elisabeth Förster-Nietzsche, albeit against his better knowledge of the textual history of *EH*. After his final breach with Förster-Nietzsche in the summer of 1909, Gast no longer needed to hold back his true opinion on the matter. The fifth volume of the *Complete Letters* had just appeared; it contained N's letters to his mother and sister, and was — as we now know from Karl Schlechta {Schlechta discusses Elisabeth Förster-Nietzsche's forgery of her brother's letters in his edition of *Friedrich Nietzsche: Werke in drei Bänden* (Munich: Carl Hanser Verlag, 1954–56), 3:1408–23.} — a masterpiece of forgery. At this opportunity, Peter Gast wrote to Ernst Holzer (23 June 1909): "In your last card, you mentioned: '[T]he letters ({vol.} V) showed Nietzsche's *close* relationship to his sister beyond any doubt. Yes yes yes yes yes! But the close relationship required a lot of effort! Just how restricting this effort was for Nietzsche only became visible shortly before the outbreak of madness: namely, when he sent Naumann the large *Ecce* additional folio sheet on his mother and sister. There, finally disgusted by the charade, Nietzsche spoke frankly and freely, and nothing more devastating than what was said on that page has ever been said about anyone."

Two barely legible preliminary drafts in N's hand (see "Wise" note 9 below), which before the discovery of the sheet passed for the two final posthumous fragments in the edition, leave no doubt as to the authenticity of the new text. Certainly, the extreme psychic tension, the uncanny euphoria, cannot be ignored as harbingers of the imminent catastrophe: on this point, however, the new text of §3 in the chapter "Why I Am So Wise" is no different from many other passages in *EH*. As there can be no doubt about its authenticity, and as it can be inserted seamlessly into the text, it appears in *KGW* and *KSA* instead of the section known hitherto.

The rediscovered definitive text of §3 of "Why I Am So Wise" gives us an approximate idea of the contents of the "eccentricities" Gast omitted in his transcription, or rather those sheets which "still are passages of captivating beauty" and were nevertheless destroyed in Naumburg (or later in Weimar at the Nietzsche-Archiv). A few sparse fragments, mostly preserved for us in the folders in handwriting that is difficult to decipher, and which do not correspond to any final version of *EH*, suggest the possible content of those removed passages. These are the following fragments published in *CW* 18: 21[7] against the anti-Semites; 21[8] presumably about Paul Rée; 23[9] again, against the anti-Semites; 25[7] probably §5 of the chapter on "The Case of Wagner"; 25[8] on Stendhal; 25[9] on contemporary French writers (perhaps also the brief outline 25[4]); 25[11] on "officers and Jewish bankers" as N's "natural associates"; and 25[12] on Peter Gast. They have as little right to be incorporated into the text of *EH*, however, as the preliminary drafts that N worked on and as such are made available in the critical apparatus. Apart from §3 of "Why I Am So Wise" and other smaller changes referred to in the following pages, *EH* has to remain as we have come to know it.

The page transcribed by Peter Gast actually contains two further small alterations connected to the first sheets approved for printing. The first concerns §4 of the chapter "Why I Am So Wise" and was made necessary by the new text of §3 (cf. below, "Wise" note 23). The second concerns a passage in the short prologue ("On This Perfect Day") that follows the Foreword and introduces N's self-presentation. It is the passage where N makes a tally of his last works. The print-ready proof sheet (p. 1) reads: "The first book of the *Revaluation of All Values*, the *Songs of Zarathustra*, the *Twilight of the Idols*, my attempt to philosophize with a hammer" — now, according to N's instructions transcribed by Gast, it should read: "The *Revaluation of All Values*, the *Dionysus Dithyrambs* and, for relaxation, the *Twilight of the Idols*." Gast did actually make this alteration to the surviving print-ready proof sheet of *EH* with the remark: "Alteration in accordance with a note to Naumann." However, he did *not* correct "The first book of the *Revaluation of All Values*" to "The Revaluation of All Values." The latter correction did indeed correspond to the equation of "Antichrist = the whole Revaluation of All Values," which we know about through N's letter to Paul Deussen of 26 November 1888 {*KGB* III:5, 491–93}, but Gast ignored this at first because N had not informed him about the matter (cf. "Books" note 153 below).

Finally, one more important remark: the whole contemptible campaign in 1907/8 about allegedly lost manuscripts, which Elisabeth Förster-Nietzsche unleashed against Franz Overbeck, the one man of higher rank among those friends who remained loyal to her brother, was based on the assumption that N had always conceived the "Revaluation of All Values" in four books. The reasoning was: since N wrote about a "finished" "Revaluation of All Values" in his letter to Georg Brandes of 20 November {*KGB* III:5, 482}, when N fell ill, besides *The Antichrist* the three remaining "finished" books must also have been in Turin; Overbeck must have failed to secure them. However, the corrections N arranged for the text of *Ecce Homo* and N's letter to Paul Deussen of 26 November 1888 conclusively prove that: 1. When N spoke about a finished "Revaluation of All Values," he was referring to *The Antichrist*. 2. Both Elisabeth Förster-Nietzsche, who was aware of the letter to Deussen and had it in her possession — but *never* published it, unlike N's other letters to Deussen — and Peter Gast, who thoroughly acquainted himself with the textual history of *Ecce Homo* and *The Antichrist* at the Nietzsche-Archiv and yet (until 1909) joined in the campaign as a submissive puppet, acted against their better knowledge, in other words, lied.

The emergence of "Ecce Homo": During the proofreading of *Twilight of the Idols*, N wrote a brief self-presentation that would be the kernel of *EH*. This "Ur-Ecce Homo" is found in the Turin notebook W II 9, 130–106 and published in *CW* 18 as fragment 24[1].

The fragment is divided into eleven sections, the contents of which correspond to the following series of familiar texts in sequence: *EH*, chapter "Why I Am So Clever" §1; "Why I Am So Wise" §§6, 4, 5; *TI*, the whole chapter of "What I Owe the Ancients"; *EH* §§1 and 2 in the chapter "Why I Am So Wise." This original version displays numerous variations and omitted passages as against the corresponding final versions, concluding with the words "Well then, I am the opposite of a *décadent*, for I have just described myself." When, on 15 October 1888 — his 44th birthday — N took the decision to "tell himself the story of his life," he selected, after some hesitation (cf. *CW* 18, 24[2] and 24[9]), the sections on his relationship to "the ancients" and had them printed as the last chapter of *TI*. A second draft of the manuscript of W II 9 had just been completed; in fact, while doing this, N had added a little about his relationship to French literature and to Goethe. This second draft as such has not survived, as N used it to dispatch the chapter "What I Owe the Ancients" in *TI* to Leipzig; he cut out the paragraphs he needed from the second draft and glued them together or glued them over rejected passages (one of these being *CW* 18, 24[10] on Goethe and Adalbert Stifter).

On 24 October 1888, the Leipzig printing shop sent N the proofs of the new *TI* chapter (with "The Hammer Speaks"). We can thus presume the date when N began his self-presentation was his birthday — 15 October — as confirmed in his letters. The *TI* proof corrections were finished by the end of October, with N announcing his self-presentation to his publisher Naumann in Leipzig on 6 November {*KGB* III:5, 463–64} with the following words: " . . . don't be surprised now at anything I do! For example, once *Twilight of the Idols* has been finalized in every sense, we need to begin a new publication at once. I have completely convinced myself that I need another work, a *preparatory* work in the highest degree, in order to stride forth after a year or so with the first book of the *Revaluation*. There needs to be some real *suspense* — otherwise it will drag on, like *Zarathustra*. Now during these last weeks I have been most fortunately inspired, thanks to an incomparable feeling of well-being for once in my life, thanks also to a wonderful autumn and to the kindest consideration I have met with in Turin. In this way, I have *completed* an *extremely heavy* task — that of narrating myself, my books, my opinions and, piecemeal where necessary, *my life* — between 15 October and 4 November. I think *that* will be heard, perhaps too well . . . In which case all would be well."

An incomplete version we will call the "October Version," consisting of twenty-four continuously numbered subdivisions, falls within the period "15 October to 4 November."* This version can be accurately reconstructed by taking account of N's deletions and changes in subdivision numbers in the final printer's manuscript (when N merely altered the numbering later and left the text unchanged), or by referring to those subdivisions deleted from the text but preserved in Mp XVI 5 along with their original number. Immediately afterwards, in a phase we will name the "Intermediate Draft," N wrote a Foreword in seven sections; the second half of §3 as well as the subsequent §§4, 5, 6, 7, which were an elaboration of the last three sections of the October Version in this order: 24, 22, 23. N also wrote three short chapters without any subdivision on *BGE*, *WA*, and *TI*. From this fusion of the October Version with the Intermediate Draft, the printer's manuscript emerged which N sent to the Leipzig printing shop of C. G. Naumann shortly before mid-November; this meant that as early as 15 November, Naumann was able to give N an estimated length for the work.

By this time, the printer's manuscript of *EH* had taken on its basic structure. However, N embarked on further changes and additions in three phases: (1) between the middle and end of November *from* Turin; (2) between 1 and 6 December *in* Turin; (3) between 6 December 1888 and 2 January 1889, again *from* Turin. The following concordance represents the development of the *EH* text in six stages, starting with the October Version:

*The title of the new work was already fixed by 30 October, when N wrote to his friend Peter Gast {*KGB* III:5, 462}: "I began something new again on my birthday, which seems to be turning out well and is already considerably advanced. It is called **Ecce homo**. Or *How One Becomes What One Is*." Two rejected titles formed the immediate preliminary draft to that chosen: "ECCE HOMO / A Gift to my Friends" and "ECCE HOMO / Or / [A Psychologist's Problem] / why I know a thing or two more." Other earlier title drafts are found in W II 9, cf. *CW* 18, 24[2, 3, 4, 5, 8, 9].

October Version	Intermediate Draft	Mid-November	End November	6 December	End December
	Foreword				Foreword
	1	1*			1
	2	2*			2
20	[3]	3*			3
24	[4]	4**			4
				Contents ...	Contents
1	(—)	On this Perfect Day* Why I Am So Wise			On this Perfect Day* Why I Am So Wise
2	(—)	1			1
3	(—)	2			2
4	(—)	3			[3]
5	(—)	4			4*
6	(—)	5			5
7	(—)	6			6
8	(—)	7	7**		7
			8		8
		Why I Am So Clever			Why I Am So Clever
9	(—)	1			1
10	(—)	2			2
11	(—)	3	3**		3
					4
12	(—)	4	[4]		5
					6
					7
13	(—)	5			8
14	(—)	6			9
				7	10
		Why I Write Such Good Books		Why I Write Such Good Books	Why I Write Such Good Books

October Version	Intermediate Draft	Mid-November	End November	6 December	End December
15	(—)	1*..			1*
			2		[2]*
		2	3	3**...........	3
		3	4		4
		4	5	5**...........	5
				6	6
		BT			BT
16	(—)	1			1
		2			2
		3			3
				4	4
		UO			UO
17	(—)	1*..			1
18	(—)	2*..			2
19	(—)	3			3
		HAH			HAH
20	(—)	[1]			1
20	(—)	[2]			2
20	(—)	[3]			3
		4			4
20	(—)	[5]			5
					6
		D			D
21	(—)	[1]			1
		2			2
		JS			JS
		Z			Z
24	(—)	[?]		[1]	1
		[?]		2	2
		[?]		3	3
		[?]		4	4

October Version	Intermediate Draft	Mid-November	End November	6 December	End December
		Fragment		[5]	5**
		5 and Fragment		[6]	6
		6		7	7
		7		8	8
	BGE				BGE
		1			1
	One section.	2			2
	GM				GM
	WA				
	TI				TI
	One section	1**			1
	One section	2**			2
			3		3*
		WA			WA
	One section	1*			1
	One section	2**			2
		3			3
		4	[4]	4*	4
	Why I Am a Destiny				Why I Am a Destiny
				1	1
				2	2
24	[Foreword 4]→[1]	1		3	3
		2		4	4
		3		5	5
22	[Foreword 5]→[2]	4		6	6
22	[Foreword 6]→[3]	5		7	7

October Version	Intermediate Draft	Mid-November	End November	6 December	End December
23	[Foreword 7]→[4]	6		8	8
	5	7		9	9
			Declaration of War		Dropped
			The Hammer Speaks		Dropped
					Fame and Eternity (dropped on 2 January 1889)

The concordance above, when read from left to right, describes the developments of the various parts of the text. Through this it is possible to determine (1) whether a section simply was given a different number or not; (2) whether it displays any textual alterations when compared with the immediately preceding draft (in which case, the number will be followed by *); (3) or whether the textual changes are of a more extensive kind with altered contents (in which case, the number will be followed by **); and (4) whether the section has been radically altered or even replaced by a quite different text (in which case, the number will be within a square bracket). The sign (—) means that the intermediate draft displays no correspondence with the October Version (and was directly transferred into the Mid-November *Pm*).

When read from top to bottom, the concordance shows when the sections were first written and when they were altered.

Between mid-November and the end of that month (column "*End November*"), N added the following from Turin: §8 of "Why I Am So Wise" and §3 of "Twilight of the Idols"; and §4 of "The Case of Wagner" was replaced with an entirely new text.

As N wished to undertake extensive alterations, in particular to the chapter on "Thus Spoke Zarathustra," he first had the second half of the *Pm* sent from Leipzig back to him in Turin {cf. N's postcard to Naumann of 27 November 1888 (*KGB* III:5, 494)}, but then (to avoid confusion) he asked for the first half as well {cf. N's postcard to Naumann of 1 December 1888 (*KGB* III:5, 498)}; he proceeded to make a thorough revision which was finished by 6 December. During this phase (concordance column *"6 December"*), N added the "Contents" (after the "Foreword"), a §7 (destined to become §10) in the chapter "Why I Am So Clever," §6 in the chapter "Why I Write Such Good Books," §4 in "The Birth of Tragedy," §§1 and 2 in "Why I Am a Destiny," besides the "Declaration of War" and "The Hammer Speaks." Significant changes were made to the chapter on *Z*. The immediately preceding draft of this chapter (column *"Mid-November"*) is preserved in only fragmentary fashion; apparently it consisted of seven sections (the question marks in square brackets indicate this assumption). §1 in the chapter "Thus Spoke Zarathustra" stands in square brackets — in the column *"6 December"* — to indicate a complete reworking in comparison with §24 of the October Version. During the revision of the beginning of December, the following were rewritten to a greater or lesser extent: §7 in "Why I Am So Wise," §3 in "Why I Am So Clever," §§3 and 5 in "Why I Write Such Good Books," and §4 in the chapter "The Case of Wagner" (namely, the text which N sent to Leipzig from Turin toward the end of November). Finally, §4 (destined to become §5) of the chapter "Why I Am So Clever" was replaced with an entirely new text.

On 6 December 1888, N sent the revised *Pm* back to Leipzig {cf. N's letter to Naumann, *KGB* III:5, 505}. He did not want to make any more changes. Yet roughly from the middle of December to 29/30 December he sent important changes and additions from Turin to Leipzig (column *"End December"*): §§4, 6, and 7 of the chapter "Why I Am So Clever" were new texts; §2 of the chapter "Why I Write Such Good Books" had a completely new replacement text; §6 was added to the chapter "Human, All Too Human"; and the conclusion of §5 of the chapter "Thus Spoke Zarathustra" was altered. A minor alteration — concerning Spitteler and Widmann — was carried out in §1 of the chapter "Why I Write Such Good Books." The alterations to the already typeset work that were discovered by {Colli and Montinari} belong to the same period: the new §3 and the related alteration to §4 of "Why I Am So Wise," as well as the altered sentence in the little prologue

"On this Perfect Day." Connected to the latter is the alteration to §3 of the chapter "Twilight of the Idols" (relating to the "Revaluation of All Values"). N did not undertake all these alterations at the same time: even before 20 December, for example, he had sent the present §7 of the chapter "Why I Am So Clever" to Leipzig, whereas §6 of the same chapter arrived at the printing shop later, although it arrived before §4 of that chapter (cf. the note to the chapter "Why I Am So Clever"). On 29 December, after he had already sent a number of addenda, N announced to his publisher: "[T]he remainder of the manuscript, its entire contents being matters of the most extreme importance, including the poem with which *Ecce Homo* is supposed to close" {*KGB* III:5, 558}. The very last alteration took place on 2 January 1889 {*KGB* III:5, 555}, when N asked for the return of his concluding poems "Fame and Eternity" (in *EH*) and "On the Poverty of the Richest Man" (in *NCW*), reclaiming them for his final work, *Dionysus Dithyrambs*. It is impossible to establish with certainty what sort of material N had dispatched on 29 December; to judge by the foregoing remarks about the *Pm* and the comments made by Peter Gast and Elisabeth Förster-Nietzsche, also cited above, it must be assumed that much of it — like earlier and perhaps also later consignments — has not been preserved.

In the last alterations of 29 December 1888 and 2 January 1889, the ending of *EH* reverted to the ending of the first *Pm* version (column "*Mid-November*"). The alterations of 29 December concerned the "Declaration of War," no longer extant, and following on from that, the section "The Hammer Speaks" (= *Z* III "On Old and New Tablets" §30 {cf. the note concerning the "Declaration of War" above, pp. 537–42}). The "Declaration of War" had belonged to *EH* since the revision at the beginning of December; the so-called "grand politics" increasingly exercised N until 29 December 1888, when, as is evident from a draft letter to Peter Gast {*KGB* III:5, 565–66} that contains clear signs of the outbreak of madness, he composed a "Promemoria" against the House of Hohenzollern and sent it to the French writer, J{ean} Bourdeau {(1848–1928) in hopes it would be published in the *Journal des Débats*}. The latter replied on 4 January 1889 {*KGB* III:6, 418–19}: "J'ai reçu également votre manuscrit de Turin, qui témoigne de vos sentiments anti-prussiens

. . . Il ne me semble pas de nature à pouvoir être publié" {"I have also received your manuscript from Turin testifying to your anti-Prussian sentiments . . . It does not seem to me to be publishable."}. Fragments 25[13, 14, 15, 16, 18], found in *CW* 18, as well as some letters and drafts from the period, allow us to guess at the contents of the "Promemoria." While revising his "grand political" proclamations, N returned to the "Declaration of War"; he considered following the "Declaration of War" with a "Final Consideration" that he had already jotted down after fragments 25[13–14]. He made a fair copy of this "Final Consideration" and gave the instruction to the printer: "At the end, after the *Declaration of War*" and — at the margin to the lower right of the note, he added — "After this, a page that is empty apart from the words: *Fame and Eternity*." However, the note containing the "Final Consideration" stayed in Turin (N later made use of the reverse: see above), and N for that reason sent "Fame and Eternity" on 29 December with the stipulation: "The section *Declaration of War* canceled — likewise *The Hammer Speaks*." The removal from *EH* of the "Declaration of War" makes absolute sense from a literary point of view: after writing the "Promemoria," N found the "Declaration of War" "superseded." Finally, he demanded the return of "Fame and Eternity" for *DD* with a postcard on 1 January 1889 and a telegram the next day {*KGB* III:5, 571}, so §9 of "Why I Am a Destiny" again formed the conclusion to *EH* — as in the first *Pm*.

Title Page

1. {The title of this work plays on Pontius Pilate's remark to the mob prior to the crucifixion of Jesus (cf. John 19:5).}

2. *N's title page in Pm: Ecce homo.* / How one becomes what one is. / By / Friedrich Nietzsche / Leipzig, / Published by C. G. Naumann / 1889. *Mp XVI 5, 6 (October Version) has the half-title: How one becomes what one is.* / Planer au dessus et avoir / des griffes, voilà le lot des grands genies. {"Floating above and in possession / of claws, that is the lot of great geniuses."} / Galiani / Begun on 15 October, finished on 4 November 1888, in *Turin. (The citation from* {Italian economist Ferdinando} *Galiani is from a letter to Madame d'Épinay dated 24 November 1770.) A further instruction for the printer*

is found at the end of the Foreword in the Intermediate Draft: Followed by a page with nothing on it but the words: / *How one becomes what one is.* / Turin, 15 October 1888.

3. *How One Becomes What One Is.]* {Cf. Pindar, *Pythian Odes* II, 72.}

Foreword

1.

1. *in summer to]* Mp XVI 5 *(intermediate draft):* in summer — to say nothing of my friends, to spare them — to

2.

2. *feet]* Beinen {Literally "legs"; N is alluding to Daniel 2:33, 34, 42.}

3. *"true world" . . ."apparent world"]* Cf. *TI* "How the 'True World' Finally Became a Fable."

4. *guaranteed.]* After this in Mp XVI 5 *(deleted from intermediate draft):* Idealist — in my mouth, the word for the most dangerous counterfeiter . . . Revaluation of All Values! . . .

3.

5. *heights, . . . beneath you!]* Mp XVI 5, 7 *(intermediate draft) first deleted version: heights*: light, wafting, mild — *and so pure! so pure!* As all things lie free in the light! You think with pity of the air *below*, the malarial air of the "ideal" . . . Where can you find a stronger formula against all idealism than my proposition [(in *Human, All Too Human*, page — — —) {cf. *HAH* §483, *CW* 3, 264}]: *convictions are more dangerous enemies of truth than are lies*? — Do you know my definition of conviction, of "belief" in general? *an instinct turned into untruthfulness? . . .*

6. *beneath you!]* After this in Mp XVXI 5, 7 *(intermediate draft):* For example, you feel morality beneath you. *(Subsequently crossed out.)*

7. *provided]* Mp XVXI 5, 7 *(intermediate draft):* provided me

8. *Error]* After this in Mp XVXI 5, 7 *(intermediate draft):* (— Idealism —) *(subsequently crossed out).*

9. *Nitimur in vetitum]* "We strive for what is forbidden"; cf. Ovid, *Amores III, 4, 17.* {"*Vetitum*" is underlined by N.}

4.

10. *Intermediate draft of this section:* I have presented humanity with the greatest gift it ever received, I gave it my *Zarathustra*. This book, the *loftiest* there is — the whole fact of the human lies an immense distance *beneath* it — is also the deepest, an inexhaustible fount where no bucket descends without coming back full of gold and goodness. — Why is it called "Thus Spoke *Zarathustra*"? What exactly does the name of that ancient Persian mean here? — But of course you know what Zarathustra was the first to do and how he made a beginning: he saw in the struggle between good and evil the actual wheel that drives things, he translated morality into metaphysics, as force, cause, purpose in itself. Zarathustra *created* this greatest of errors: consequently he must be the first to *acknowledge* it. He has not just had longer and greater experience than any other thinker — he has had in his hand the experimental refutation of the proposition that the world is "arranged morally" for longest: and what is more important, he is more *truthful* than any other thinker. His teaching and it alone has truthfulness as *supreme* virtue: to speak the truth and shoot well with arrows is Persian virtue. The self-overcoming *of morality through* truthfulness, | the self-overcoming of the moralist into his antithesis — into *myself* — | that is what the name Zarathustra means in my mouth. *Cf. EH "Why I Am A Destiny" §§3, 6, 7, 8, and the note to §1 of the chapter on Thus Spoke Zarathustra.*

11. *With it . . . received.] Cf. TI "Forays" §51, final sentence; also CW 18, 11[417].*

12. *"The stillest . . . world —"] Cf. Z II "The Stillest Hour."*

13. *The figs . . . afternoon —] Cf. Z II "Upon the Blessed Isles."*

14. *People of knowledge] Der Mensch der Erkenntnis*

15. *I am now . . . return to you . . .] Cf. Z I "On the Virtue of Gift-Giving" §3.*

Contents

1. {The "Contents" here follows the "Contents" as it appears in the extant *Pm*; the titles of some of N's books differ slightly from the titles as they actually appear in the text of *EH*.}

On this Perfect Day . . .

2. *The Revaluation . . . Idols]* Cf. above, pp. 552–53.

3. *On this . . . life.] In the October Version §1, this passage is placed below the date:* Turin, 15 October 1888; *cf. CW 18, 23[14] for Pd to this section.*

Why I Am So Wise

1

1. *father . . . mother] Karl Ludwig Nietzsche, 1813–49; Franziska Nietzsche née Oehler, 1825–97.*

2. *My father . . . thirty-six] In 1849, N's father died of an illness of the brain; some letters of N's mother to friends reveal the untenability of the "fable convenue"* {"agreed-upon story"} *whereby the cause of N's father's illness was imputed to a fall down stairs; the letters were written while her husband lay ill.* {Montinari suggests these letters will appear in *KGB*; as of the publication of this volume, they have not yet appeared.}

3. *At the time . . . Naumburg.] See Chronicle of N's life* {in *CW* 19}.

4. *in Genoa]* {N arrived in Genoa for the winter in early November 1880.} *See Chronicle of N's life* {in *CW* 19}.

5. *{had a} severe weakness.]* {There is an implied verb in N's German.}

6. *I now . . . handy] Ich habe es jetzt in der Hand, ich habe die Hand dafür* {N's punning with the "hand" points back to the grasping (*Greifens*) and comprehending (*Begreifens*) earlier in this section.}

2

7. *summa summarum]* "sum of sums" {"totality"}

8. *He reacts . . . meet it.] Cf. TI* "What the Germans Lack" *§6.*

3

9. {In the light of the 1969 discovery of a page transcribed by Peter Gast (cf. above, pp. 550–52), the current version of §3 in the main text now replaces} *the former version, which reads as follows:* This *double* series of experiences, this access to apparently separate worlds, repeats itself in every respect in my character — I am a Doppelgänger, I have "second" sight besides the first. *And* perhaps

the third as well . . . By dint of lineage alone, I am permitted to glance beyond perspectives conditioned by what is merely local, merely national, it costs me no effort to be a "good European." On the other hand, perhaps I am more German than today's Germans, mere Germans of the Reich, are able to be — I, the last *anti-political* German. And yet my forebears were Polish nobility: from them, I embody a good deal of racial instinct: who knows, perhaps even the *liberum veto* {= Polish parliamentarian's power to halt legislation though use of veto}? If I consider how often I have been addressed as a Pole while en route, and by Poles themselves, and how seldom I have been taken for a German, it could seem that I belong among the *sprinkled-on* Germans. But my mother, Franziska Oehler, is at all events something very German; likewise my paternal grandmother, Erdmuthe Krause. The latter lived her whole youth at the center of good old Weimar, not without connection to the Goethe circle. Her brother, Krause the professor of theology at Königsberg, was appointed as Weimar's senior civil servant after Herder's death. It is not impossible that her mother, my great-grandmother, is mentioned in the young Goethe's diary under the name of "Muthgen." She married for the second time Superintendent Nietzsche in Eilenburg; she gave birth on 10 October of the great war year, 1813, on the day Napoleon marched into Eilenburg. As a Saxon, she was a great admirer of Napoleon; it could be that I still am as well. My father, born 1813, died 1849. Before he entered service as the pastor of Röcken, near Lützen, he lived at the Altenburg Castle for a few years and taught the four princesses who were there. His pupils are the Queen of Hanover, the Crown Princess Constantine, the Grand Duchess of Oldenburg and Princess Therese of Saxe-Altenburg. He had the profoundest respect for the Prussian King Friedrich Wilhelm the Fourth, from whom he also received his parish office; the events of 1848 depressed him beyond measure. I myself, born on the birthday of the said king, 15 October, received the Hohenzollern names *Friedrich* Wilhelm, as was fitting. The choice of this day had one advantage, anyway: throughout my whole childhood, my birthday was a public holiday. — I consider it a great privilege to have had such a father: I even believe that this explains all the other privileges that I have — *not* including life, the great Yes to life. Above all, the fact that I do not need to deliberately enter into a world of higher and finer things, I simply have to bide my time: I am at home there, only there can my innermost passion be free. The fact that I nearly paid with my life for such a privilege is certainly a good bargain. — To understand anything at all of my *Zarathustra*, perhaps you have to be in a similar condition to me — with one foot *beyond* life . . . *In connection with this major alteration, N had to make a number of additional changes to the Pm, which had not yet been set; see the notes to "Why I Am So Wise" §4, "Why I Write Such Good Books" §2, and "Thus Spoke Zarathustra" §5.*

Mp XVIII has two further preliminary drafts to the final text, as follows: I shall touch here on the question of race. I am a Polish noble⟨man⟩ *pur sang*, with not a drop of bad blood mixed in, least of all German. When I search for the deepest antithesis to myself, the ineradicable meanness of the instincts, I always find my mother and sister: — to believe myself related to such German *canaille* {"riff-raff" "rabble"} would be a profanation of my divinity. The treatment I have received at the hands of my mother and sister up to the present moment instills in me an immense dread — I confess that the deepest objection to my thought of eternal recurrence, which I call an abysmal thought, was always the thought of my mother and sister . . . But even as a Pole I am a tremendous atavism: you would have to go back centuries to find, in this noblest of races there has been on earth, the same measure of pure instinct as I represent. Toward everything that calls itself nobility I have a sovereign feeling of distinction — I would not tolerate the young German Kaiser in my carriage as my coachman. There is one single instance where I have found my equal — I confess to it with gratitude. Frau Cosima Wagner is by far the noblest of natures; and in relation to me, I have always only interpreted her marriage to Wagner as adultery . . . the case of Tristan

All prevailing concepts about degrees of kinship are a physiological contradiction, one that cannot be surpassed. One is least related to one's parents; sibling marriage, as was the rule, e.g., in the Egyptian r⟨oya⟩l family, is so little contrary to nature that in connection to it, every marriage is practically incest . . . To resemble your parents is the purest sign of coarseness; higher natures have their origin vastly further back, the slowest process of collecting, saving up for them was necessary — the great individual is the oldest individual — an atavism.

10. *And with that . . . of race] Cf. the variant at the beginning of "Why I Write Such Good Books" §2.*

11. *pur sang]* "pure-blooded"

12. *canaille]* "riff-raff" "rabble"

13. *disharmonia praestabilita]* "preestablished disharmony" {A pun on Leibniz's "preestablished harmony."}

14. *Physiological . . . praestabilita] Cf. the variant at the end of "Thus Spoke Zarathustra" §5.*

15. *But I confess . . . sister. —] Cf. Z III "The Convalescent" §2:* "alas, humans return eternally! Puny humans return eternally!"

16. *noblesse]* "nobility"

17. *Kaiser]* Wilhelm II

18. *Frau Cosima . . . by far . . .] Cf. N's draft letter to Cosima Wagner of the same period* {25 December 1888; *KGB* III:5, 551; the angled brackets do not appear in *KGB*; they were added in the revised paperback edition}: Honored Lady, basically the only lady I ever honored — be so good as to accept this, the first copy of *Ecce Homo.* In it the whole world is essentially treated badly, with the exception of Richard W⟨agner⟩ — and Turin, too. Malwida also appears as Kundry . . . The Antichrist.

19. *The rest is silence] Hamlet's last words in Shakespeare's Hamlet* {*Prince of Denmark* (Act V Scene 2)}.

20. *Pope]* {Leo XIII.}

21. *Higher natures . . . necessary.] Cf. TI "Forays of an Untimely One" §44.*

22. {Cf. Mazzino Montinari, *Reading Nietzsche*, trans. Greg Whitlock (Urbana: University of Illinois Press, 2003), 120n3: "We have still not been able to determine what Nietzsche could have meant concerning this postal parcel. A hallucination cannot be ruled out. Among Nietzsche's acquaintances was numbered,

from the Basel period, the 'Dionysian' personality of Frau Rosa-
lie Nielsen. Kurt Hezel reports: 'Even today I myself recall, from
among my student days, a photograph of a remarkable Dionysus
head (a photographed sculpture) dedicated to me from Frau Nielsen . . . If I recall correctly, Frau Nielsen had wanted Friedrich
Nietzsche himself to own the photograph of the Dionysus head.'"
See C. A. Bernoulli, *Franz Overbeck und Friedrich Nietzsche:
Eine Freundschaft* (Jena: E. Diederichs, 1908), 1:117.}

4

23. *in it, with that one exception]* *The original Pm, already typeset, read:* in it but seldom, basically just once; *N's correction, transcribed by Gast, was sent to Leipzig along with the alteration for §3*
{discussed above pp. 550–52}.

24. *"Zarathustra's temptation"]* *N intended to publish Z IV —
privately published in 1885 — under this title in Fall 1888; cf. CW
18, 22[13, 15, 16].*

25. *cry of distress]* Cf. *Z* IV "The Cry of Distress."

6.

26. *"Not . . . end"]* *Cf. also AC §20.* {Cf. Hermann Oldenberg,
Buddha: Sein Leben, Seine Lehre, Seine Gemeinde (Berlin: Wil-
helm Hertz, 1881), 299–302. *NL.* N alters Oldenberg's text, which
has "non-animosity" (*Nichtfeindschaft*) where N has "friendship."
Cf. *Buddha: His Life, his Doctrine, His Order,* trans. William
Hoey (London: Williams and Norgate, 1882), 293–96.}

7.

27. *millennia. —]* *In the Pm there follows a passage deleted by N
himself during his reworking at the beginning of December:* And
even in Wagner's case: how could I deny that from [my intima-
cies] my friendship with Wagner and Frau Wagner, the most
delightful and elevated memories |and only such memories|
remain behind — that there was never a shadow between us?
That and only that *allows* me the neutrality [|that impersonality|]
of view to see the problem of Wagner as a cultural problem in
general — *and* perhaps to solve it . . . Fifth and last proposition:
I only attack things that I fundamentally know — that I have
myself experienced, that I have to a certain extent myself *been*.

— The Christianity of my forebears |for example| reaches its con-
clusion in me — a severity [and clarity in things concerning
truth] of intellectual conscience, solar in its purity, brought up
[and trained to greatness] by Christianity itself turns its back on
Christianity: in me, Christianity judges [itself] and *overcomes*
itself. *At the time he made this deletion, N was devoting the whole of
"Why I Am So Clever" §5 to his relationship with Wagner.*

28. *pure folly]* {A reference to the title character of Wagner's
last opera, *Parsifal*, who is designated a "pure fool." Cf. *WA* §9,
p. 23 above, and *TI* "Forays" §30.}

29. *But what . . . wind! . . .]* Cf. *Z II* "On the Rabble."

Why I Am So Clever.
The genesis of this chapter is complicated by the later additions N
sent to Leipzig on 6 December 1888 from Turin. On 15 December
he sent to his Leipzig printers a page for *NCW* with the title
"Intermezzo." On the back of the pages was also the direction:
"*insert* at page *3* of the *Ms before* the chapter 'Wagner as Danger.'"
A few days later, on 20 December {*KGB* III:5, 541}, N asked Naumann to insert this text into *EH* "as was originally intended . . .
to be exact, in the second chapter (Why I Am So Clever) as *section* 5. After that, alter the numbers in sequence, and of course,
take out the title 'Intermezzo.'" In the proofs for *NCW* that
arrived soon afterwards with the stamp of the publisher C. G.
Naumann and dated 22 December 1888, the chapter "Intermezzo" had nevertheless also been typeset; N — as Podach correctly remarks — raised no objection, and indeed he gave
permission to print at Christmas, sending two postcards (29 and
30 December {*KGB* III:5, 563}) requesting the insertion of two
corrections into the "Intermezzo." When N subsequently decided
not to publish *NCW* (2 January 1889), the matter of where to put
the "Intermezzo" was settled: it belonged within *EH*. (If *NCW* is
published nonetheless, it should be in the last version authorized
by N.) It is the case that N originally planned to insert the "Intermezzo" into the chapter "Why I Am So Clever," as is revealed in
the following, deleted instruction to the printer (of 15 December),
which stood at the head of the page "Intermezzo": "To be inserted

into the second chapter: Why I Am So Clever." Sometime later, N sent another extract to Leipzig ("Come to think about it, I would not have survived my youth" etc.) with the direction: "To be inserted into the *second* chapter, 'Why I Am So Clever,' *before* the section which was originally headed 'Intermezzo.'" To prevent confusion, he designated this passage as number 5, and wrote at the end of the passage: "6. / — I shall say another word for the most discerning of ears: what I *now* want of music. / Continuation in the manuscript." Finally — judging from the early versions: on 29 December — N sent the last addition to Leipzig (on Heine, {now §4}) with the instruction (at the head of the page): "To be inserted into the *second* chapter: 'Why I Am So Clever' as §4"; at the end of the new passage he wrote: "NB. Now come the two passages dealing with Richard Wagner." These were the section numbered 4 in "Why I Am So Clever" inserted by N at the beginning of December and beginning with the words "Here, while speaking about the recreations of my life . . ." etc. {now §5}, and the section discussed above, beginning with the words "Come to think about it, I would not have survived my youth" etc. {now §6}. All alterations in the chapter "Why I Am So Clever" can be reliably reconstructed as one can see in the following concordance:

6 December	20 December	Later	End December
1			1
2			2
3			3
			4
4			5
		5	6
	5	6	7
5	6	7	8
6	7	8	9
7	8	9	10

I

1. *I would not . . . afterwards]* Cf. *TI* "Sayings" §10.
2. *moraline-free]* moralinfreier; cf. *AC* 2.

3. *Apparently . . . here.]* {Reference to the Austro-Prussian War in 1866, as well as the great cholera epidemic of that same year.}

4. *alla tedesca]* "in the German fashion"

5. *vanitas]* "vanity" "affectation"

6. *I was . . . converted me]* Cf. *Chronicle of N's life, CW 19.*

7. *in vino veritas]* "in wine there is truth" {N underlines "*veritas.*"}

8. *in my case . . . water]* Cf. *Genesis 1:2.*

9. *agaçant]* "irritating"

10. *Sitting tight] Das Sitzfleisch* {Literally "sitting flesh" or "posterior," usually denotes a person with perseverance; cf. N's attack on Gustave Flaubert in *TI* "Sayings" §34 (who preferred to sit when thinking).}

2

11. *in physiologicis]* "in physiological matters"

12. *eye-opening?] Pm, N deleted the following: —* so that I, instead of perceiving my antagonists in Wagner and Schopenhauer, could treat myself to them, oh! what a treat . . .

3

13. *sui generis]* "unique"

14. *Victor . . . Grecs]* {*Les sceptiques grecs,*} *Paris*{: Imprimerie Nationale,} *1887. NL.*

15. *Laertiana]* {N refers here to several philological essays he wrote on Diogenes Laërtius during his first two years in Basel:} "De Laertii Diogenis fontibus," *Rheinisches Museum* 23 (1868): 632–53; 24 (1869): 181–228 {*KGW* II:1, 75–167}; "Analecta Laertiana," *Rheinisches Museum* 25 (1870): 217–31 {*KGW* II:1, 169–90}; *Beiträge zur Quellenkunde und Kritik des Laertius Diogenes* {"Contributions on the sources and critiques of Diogenes Laertius"} (Basel{: Carl Schultze,} 1870) {*KGW* II:1, 191–245}.

16. *the ambi- to quintiguous] zwei- bis fünfdeutig* {"having two to five senses"; *zweideutig* = "ambiguous," "having two senses."}

17. *"largeur du cœur"]* "big-heartedness"

18. *"loving thy neighbor" . . .] The Pp ends here.*

19. *Gyp]* {N apparently did not realize that Gyp was the pen name for a woman: Sibylle Riqueti de Mirabeau, Comtesse de Martel de Janville.}

20. *ex ungue Napoleonem]* "we may judge Napoleon from his claw" {Cf. *ex ungue leonem*: "we may judge the lion from its claw"; i.e., "from the part you can judge the whole."}

21. *"God . . . not exist"]* {Cf. Paul Albert, *La littérature française au dix-neuvième siècle* (Paris: Hachette, 1885), 2:236. *NL.* Cf. also Paul Bourget, *Essais de psychologie contemporaine* (Paris: Lemerre, 1883), 260.}

22. *I . . . somewhere]* Cf. TI "The Four Great Errors" 8, conclusion.

23. *Basically, it is . . . God . . .]* *Before the corrections at the beginning of December, this passage ran as follows:* Of the French, I have always found *Montaigne* refreshing, perhaps through some affinity of temperament: he and I both have plenty of archness in spirit, who knows? perhaps in body, too. — A good disciple of Dionysus must also be a good satyr. — For ten years I have enjoyed *Stendhal*, one of my most pleasant acquaintanceships in the chance encounters of books: his psychological curiosity for adventure, his *hard* sense of reality, where a hint of Napoleon's paw still is stamped (*ex ungue Napoleonem*), finally, his *honest* atheism, well-nigh invaluable among the French, gives him a right to my *sympathie.* Stendhal made the best atheistic joke: "the only excuse for God is that he does not exist." — *Emerson*, with his *Essays*, has been a good friend and comfort to me, even in black times: he has so much skepticism, so many "possibilities" within him, that with him, even virtue becomes witty . . . A unique case: . . . Already as a boy I liked listening to him. Likewise *Tristram Shandy* is one of the earliest books to my taste; what I thought of *Sterne* is revealed at a very emphatic place in *Human, All Too Human* (II:113). Perhaps for related reasons I preferred *Lichtenberg* among German books, whereas even at only 13, the "idealist" Schiller placed arrows on my tongue . . . I do not want to forget *Abbé Galiani*, the most profound clown who ever lived. — Among *old* books, my strongest impressions derive from that boisterous Provençal *Petronius*, who penned the last *Satura Menippea.* This sovereign freedom in the face of "morality," "seriousness," or his own sublime taste, this *raffinement* {"refinement"} in mixing vulgar and "educated" Latin, this unbounded good humor, which graciously and mischievously skips off and away over all the animalities of the ancient "soul" — I cannot think of a book that made any similarly

liberating impression on me: its effect is *Dionysian*. In cases where I need to recuperate quickly from an unpleasant impression — as in the case of when, for the purpose of my critique of Christianity, I had to breathe the fetid air of the Apostle Paul for too long — a few pages of Petronius are a *heroic* cure: I am better again at once.

4

24. *Euterpe]* Cf. *Hans von Bülow's letter to N, 24 July 1872* {*KGB* II:4, 51–54}. {In ancient Greek religion, Euterpe was the Muse of music and lyric poetry.}

25. *Caesar]* {Cf. Shakespeare's *Julius Caesar*.}

26. *"Whenever . . . sobbing.]* Cf. *variant of EH "Thus Spoke Zarathustra"* §5.

27. *Lord Bacon]* {N subscribed to the then-current suspicion that Francis Bacon might have been the author of Shakespeare's plays.}

28. *American muddle-heads and fatheads]* {Americans Delia Bacon and Ignatius Donnelly were in the forefront of efforts to prove Bacon's authorship of the Shakespeare plays by means of far-fetched cryptographic analysis.}

29. *Human, All Too Human]* {N had toyed with the idea of publishing *HAH* under the pseudonym of Bernhard Cron.}

5

30. *Before the revision at the beginning of December, the whole section read thus:* Music — for heaven's sake! Let us hold on to it as *recreation* and nothing else! . . . Not for any price must it be to *us* what it has turned into today through the most almighty misuse — a *stimulant*, one more crack of the whip for exhausted nerves, a mere Wagnerism! — Nothing is more unhealthy — *crede experto!* {"believe the expert!"} — than the Wagnerian misuse of music, it is the worst kind of "idealism" out of all the possible idealistic hocus-pocus. I criticize myself for few things as much as I criticize my acting against my own instinct in having succumbed to the vice of Wagner while still a young man. Wagner and youth — but that is like saying *poison* and youth . . . Only for the last six years have I known *what* music is, thanks to a profound reflection on what was, in fact, my almost forgotten instinct in this respect, above

all thanks to the priceless good fortune of finding my nearest relative in instinct, my friend Peter Gast, who today still knows what
music is, and *can* still do it! — What do I *want* from music in
general? That it be bright and deep, like an afternoon in October.
Balmy, pleasant — *not* hot . . . That it lie in the sun, that everything about it be sweet, extraordinary, subtle and spiritual . . .
That it have *mischievous pranks* in its feet . . . Every attempt these
last six years to "engage" with Wagner went wrong. I hastily retreated
after every first act, deadly bored. How poorly, sparsely, shrewdly
this "genius" is disposed by nature! what patience you have to have
until something enters his head again! How many *stomachs* must
he himself have had to always chew the cud one more time, having just done it, without mercy, right in front of us . . . I call him
Re-cud Wagner . . . {N makes the pun *"Magner,"* an amalgamation
of *Magen* ("stomach") and Wagner.}

31. *Tribschen]* {The Wagner residence beside Lake Lucerne where
N first met the Wagners.}

32. *et hoc genus omne]* "and all of this kind"

33. *Evil, p. 256f.]* N *mistakenly cites the page number of the first edition of BGE* {he meant to cite §256, the concluding section in pt. 8}.

34. *Baudelaire]* Cf. N *to Peter Gast, 26 February 1888* {KGB
III:5, 262–65}.

6

35. *Cf.* N *to Peter Gast, 31 December 1888* {KGB III:5, 567}*:* "You
will find a marvelous page on *Tristan* in my *Ecce Homo*, on my
relationship to Wagner in general."

36. *Tristan]* I.e., *in 1861, when* N, *through his friend Gustav Krug,
became acquainted with the piano reduction of Tristan.*

37. *non plus ultra]* "highest point"

7

38. *Cf. the introductory note to the section "Why I Am So Clever."*

39. *actually]* In *the note for the printer,* N *wrote:* now. *But in the
corrections (to NCW), he left this:* actually; *therefore it stands as the
final version.*

40. *for Liszt]* Le *and in Podach (Nietzsches Werke des Zusammenbruchs):* for something by Liszt, *following the first edition of NCW in*

1889, edited by Gast; however, we {i.e., Colli-Montinari} *print this passage according to N's instructions; cf. N to C. G. Naumann, 30 December 1888* {*KGB* III:5, 563}*: At the end of p. 6, the text is to be expanded as follows: for three reasons I make an exception for Wagner's* Siegfried Idyll, *perhaps also for Liszt, whose noble orchestral accents outdo all other musicians; finally, everything else that has sprung up beyond the Alps —* this side *. . . I would not know how to do without Rossini etc. etc.*

41. *this side] diesseits* {Pun on *jenseits*, or "the Beyond," "the other side," and *diesseits*, "this world," "this side"; in this case N refers to the Turin side of the Alps, i.e., "cisalpine" music.}

42. *Pietro Gasti] Pm*: Peter Gast

8

43. *Wouldn't . . . point?] Cf. DD, "On the Poverty of the Richest Man":* "Zarathustra is not a hedgehog."

9

44. ⟨*come*⟩*] Addition according to Podach (Nietzsches Werke des Zusammenbruchs).*

45. *nosce te ipsum]* "know thyself"

46. *At this very moment . . . any lack . . .] Cf. CW 18, 16[44]; also N to Brandes, 23 May 1888* {*KGB* III:5, 317–19}.

47. *my first philological work] I.e.,* "Zur Geschichte der Theognideischen Spruchsammlung" ("On the history of the collected sayings of Theognis"), *Rheinisches Museum 22 (March 1867): 161–200.* {Friedrich Ritschl was then co-editor of the *Rheinisches Museum*; N's essay on Theognis is published in *KGW* II:1, 1–58.}

10

48. *At this point . . . reflection.]* {See discussion of "*On deletion 4*" pp. 545–46 above.}

49. *the Pope] In September 1888 Kaiser Wilhelm II visited Pope Leo XIII in Rome.*

50. *Our culture today . . . greatness.] Deleted in Pm by unknown hand; Peter Gast included the passage in his second draft (proof that the deletion is not by N); Raoul Richter (1908) and Otto Weiss (1911) printed it in their commentaries, but Karl Schlechta (1956) overlooked it, so that it was only published in its proper place in Erich*

Podach's Nietzsches Werke des Zusammenbruchs (1961). {Correcting an error in *KSA* 14, which has this deletion beginning with "The German Kaiser"; see discussion of "*On deletion 5*" p. 546 above.}

51. *solitude . . . "manytude"]* {N's terms are "Einsamkeit" and the neologism "Vielsamkeit," respectively.}

52. *At an . . . touch me] Cf. CW 4, 28[8], 314.*

Why I Write Such Good Books

I

1. *Cf. CW 18, 19[1, 7] and associated note. This chapter was origi-nally §15 of the "October Version." The following deleted reworking by N is found on the reverse side of page 17 of the* Pm: [15.] 1 / |I am one thing, my writings are another.| [I touch upon] Here let there be touched upon, before I actually speak about [my | the individual| writings] them, as casually as is decently possible, the question as to the understanding or non-understanding |of these writings| [it:]. It is decidedly not yet timely |. Later, they will need to build insti-tutions where people live and teach in my spirit; even before then, professorships for the interpretation of my *Zarathustra*. But| it would be a complete self-contradiction if, right now, [there were] I were to expect ears *and hands* for *my* truths [me]: that people |today| do not hear, that |today| they do not *take*, is [|for|] not only understandable, it [is] even seems to me to be the right [*right*] thing. I repeat, nothing is less visible in my life than "ill will"; I would hardly be able to tell you of an instance even of literary "ill will." |But certainly, *pure folly*! . . . | It strikes me as one of the rarest compliments people can pay themselves if they take a book of mine in their hand [; I]. Once I told Dr. Heinrich von Stein, who complained in all honesty that he had not understood a word of my *Zarathustra*, [this] that was in order: to have understood, meaning to have *experienced*, six sentences of it would transport anyone aloft to a higher level of [souls] mortals. How could I |, with *this* feeling of distance, even| [also] want [these] the "mod-erns" of my acquaintance — as my readers! My triumph is the |exact| reverse of that of Schopenhauer — I say *non legor, non legar* {N underlines "*non*" twice here} . . . — Not that I want to [deny]

underrate the pleasure that the *innocence* of saying no to my writings has often provided me. Even this summer, when with my weighty, too-weighty literature I was perhaps capable of shaking all the rest of literature out of kilter, a well-intentioned professor at Berlin University gave me to understand that I really ought to use a different form: nobody was going to read things like that. — In the end it was not Germany but Switzerland that delivered the two most *extreme* instances. An essay on *Beyond Good and Evil* by Dr. V. Widmann in the *Bund* with the title "Nietzsche's Dangerous Book," and a review article on all my [literature] books by Herr Karl Spitteler, |likewise in the *Bund*,| are [the] a maximum in my life — of what, I shall refrain from saying. |For example, the latter treated my *Zarathustra* as a *higher exercise in style*, adding the wish that |I might| later care to pay attention to content [. . .]| [*Not*] Not that there was a lack of good will in either case, still less of intelligence. Herr Spitteler strikes me as being one of the most welcome and subtlest of those who today practice criticism |: his — *not* yet publish⟨ed⟩ — work on French drama is first rate.| I shall try all the harder to explain. — In the end, your *ears* cannot extract |more| from things, books included, than you already know. You cannot have an ear for things for which you have no access from experience. Let us now imagine the most extreme case, where a book tells of nothing but experiences that lie wholly outside the possibility of being experienced either frequently or *seldom* — where it is the *first* utterance of a new series of experiences. In this case, simply nothing will be heard, with the acoustic deception that where nothing is heard, *nothing is there either* . . . In the final analysis, this is my average [|life|] experience[,] and if you prefer, the *originality* of my experience. Those who thought they had understood something by me have fashioned something of me in their own "image," — not infrequently the opposite of me, for example an "idealist"; those who understood nothing of me denied that I come into consideration at all. — The word "superhuman" |to designate the type that has turned out best — a word| that becomes [a] very clear [word] in the mouth of a Zarathustra, is almost invariably, and in complete innocence, understood in the sense of the values whose destroyer, whose *deadly enemy* Zarathustra [+ + +] This has caused other learned cattle to suspect me of Darwinism; they have even recognized in it the hero cult of Carlyle. [+ + +]

2. *some are born posthumously.]* Cf. *TI* "Sayings" §15; *AC* Foreword.

3. *pure folly]* {Cf. "Wise" note 28 above.}

4. *"non legor, non legar."]* "I am *not* read, I shall *not* be read." {N underlines "*non*" twice here.} *Reworking of Schopenhauer's "legor et legar" (I am read and shall be read) in the foreword to "On the Will in Nature," 2nd ed., dated "August 1854" (Werke, Frauenstädt-Ausgabe, IV:xiii, NL)* {already quoted by N in *SE* §3, *CW* 2, 186}.

5. *"Nietzsche's Dangerous Book,"]* Title of article by Josef Victor Widmann published in the Bernese daily newspaper Der Bund {"The Union"}, 16–17 September 1886; cf. N's letters from that period. Widmann was a friend of Carl Spitteler; he corresponded with N during 1887–88.

6. *review article . . . Spitteler]* The article by the poet Carl Spitteler (1845–1924), "Friedrich Nietzsche aus seinen Werken" {"Friedrich Nietzsche from his works"} had appeared in Der Bund, 1 January 1888. Cf. Spitteler, Meine Beziehungen {zu} Nietzsche {"My connections to Nietzsche"}, Munich{: Süddeutsche Monatshefte,} 1908.

7. *Through a little . . . nail . . .] Replaces:* Not that there was a lack of "good will" in either case, still less of intelligence. Herr Spitteler strikes me as being one of the most welcome and subtlest of those who today practice criticism: his work on French drama — not yet published — is perhaps first rate. *N made this substitution in Turin in the second half of December 1888; he sent the final version to Leipzig together with this — very precise — instruction to the printer:* In the *first* section of the *third* chapter "Why I Write Such Good Books" there is a short passage roughly in the middle that begins with the words {"}Not that there was a lack of intelligence, still less of good will{,"} for this, substitute what follows. *Cf. also N's letter to Overbeck of 17 September 1887 {KGB III:5, 158}.*

8. *Those who . . . "idealist"]* For this (and the following), cf. letter N wrote to his friend, the "idealist" Malwida von Meysenbug on 20 October 1888 {KGB III:5, 457–59}: For years, I have sent you my

works so that you can declare, once and for all, honestly and naively, "I abhor every word." And you would have had the right. For you are an "idealist" — and *I* treat idealism as something untruthful turned into an instinct, as a not-*wanting*-to-see reality at any price: *every* sentence in my works contains *contempt* for idealism . . . You yourself have — something I can never forgive — altered my concept "superhuman" to yet another "higher swindle." Something from the neighborhood of sibyls and prophets: while every *serious* reader of my works *must* know that a human type that is not to disgust me is precisely the opposite type to the bygone ideal-idols, a hundredfold more similar to a Cesare Borgia type than to a Christ. *Cf. Chronicle of N's life, CW 19.*

9. *Nationalzeitung]* {Liberal daily founded in Berlin in 1848.}

10. *Journal des Débats]* {Right-wing weekly newspaper founded in Paris in 1789.}

11. *Kreuzzeitung]* {Nickname for the *Neue Preussische Zeitung,* a right-wing daily founded in Berlin in 1848.}

2

12. *N sent the whole text of this section from Turin to Leipzig after the revision of the beginning of December 1888, with the instruction:* In the chapter "Why I Write Such Good Books," in place of the whole of the former paragraph 2. *The earlier section went as follows:* The Germans have never understood anything by me, let alone me myself. — Did anyone ever understand a thing by me — understand *me?* — One person, nobody else: Richard Wagner, one more reason for my doubt as to whether or not he actually was a German . . . Who of my German "friends" (— in my life, the concept of "friend" has to be in inverted commas) would have remotely let his glance plumb the *intensity* whereby Wagner, *sixteen years ago,* became a prophet for me. In a letter to the *Norddeutsche Zeitung* he introduced me to the Germans with these immortal words: "What we expect of you can only be a lifelong task, indeed, the life of a man we urgently need, and as such you announce yourself to all those who, from the noblest source of German spirit, from the deepest gravity in all it undertakes, demand enlightenment and direction as to what kind of German education there must be *if* it is to assist the resurrected

nation to its noblest aims." Wagner was simply right, he *is* right today. I am the only force majeure strong enough to redeem the Germans, and not just the Germans . . . He forgot, perhaps, that if I am destined to show culture the ropes, wouldn't I have to show them to Richard Wagner as well? Culture *and* Parsifal — impossible . . . *The Wagner quotation is found in the "open letter" Wagner wrote on 12 June 1872 on the occasion of Wilamowitz-Möllendorff's pamphlet against The Birth of Tragedy.*

In the Pm there is a preliminary draft (of the final version of this section) that N retained in Turin, as witnessed by his use of its reverse side for the foreword to NCW and for a draft letter. This preliminary draft reads as follows: Finally, this also touches on a racial question. The Germans are not sufficiently closely related to me — I express myself with caution: they are not at liberty to read me . . . |Whoever reads me in Germany has thoroughly *de-Germanized* himself prior to that, as I did: you know my slogan "being a good German means de-Germanizing oneself" {cf. *MM* §323}, or you are — no mean feat among Germans — of Jewish descent. — The Jews among mere Germans always the superior race — more refined, intellectual, kind . . . *L'adorable* {The adorable} Heine, they say in Paris —| I am proud that I am loved and singled out everywhere, *except* in Europe's flatland, Germany. In Vienna, in St. Petersburg, in Stockholm and Copenhagen, in London, in Paris, in New York — I have readers everywhere, of *rare* intelligence, distinguished characters raised in high posts and responsibilities. I have true geniuses in my readership. And let me confess, I am even better pleased by my nonreaders, who have no knowledge of either my name or the word philosophy; yet everywhere I go, here in Turin, for example, every face is cheered |to see me. My old market-woman does not rest until she has selected her sweetest grapes for me. — | Not for nothing are the Poles dubbed the French among the Slavs. No charming Russian woman would mistake where I belong for a moment. I was put down as Polish on the list of aliens in Nice. |You find my head in nearly every picture by Matejos — Strange!| I have never yet *thought* a proposition in German, |to say nothing of felt,| — but perhaps that is even beyond my resources? . . . My old teacher Ritschl once even claimed that I |still| conceived my philological treatises like a Parisian *romancier* — one *must* move on. In Paris itself, people are amazed at *toutes mes audaces et finesses* |— an expression of Monsieur Taine —|; and concerning *esprit*, which is such a disgusting concept for the Germans, you will find this "salt" added into almost every sentence in the highest forms of my dithyrambs. — I can do no other, God help me. Amen! — We all know |a few even from experience| about asses' ears: I dare to declare [having the smallest ears] that I have the smallest of ears, |absurdly small|. This is of [especial] no little interest to the little women — |it seems to me| they feel I understand them better? . . . I am the *anti-ass* par excellence |and thereby a world-historical ogre, I am| in Greek, the Antichrist . . . *A parte*, something to sing, but only for the excellent ears of Prince Bismarck: / Poland is not yet lost — / for Nie[t]zky still lives . . . *Champromis believes this was the final version because of N's instruction to the publisher:* "In the chapter 'Why I Write Such Good Books,' in place of the whole of the former paragraph 2." *But immediately afterwards he transferred the corrections and additions indicated above into the text, writing out a new fair version; the sheet with the new, final version of this section is blank on the reverse. The passage about Heine —* "L'adorable *Heine, they say in Paris*" *— was used in NCW in the section "Where Wagner Belongs." The new paragraph was sent off to Leipzig after 16 December, the day N received Taine's letter, which he cites above.*

13. *That was . . . Germany . . .*] Replaces: Finally, this also touches on a racial question. The Germans are not sufficiently closely related to me — I express myself with caution: they are not at liberty to read me . . . I am proud that I am loved and singled out everywhere but *not* in Europe's flatland, Germany. In Vienna, in St. Petersburg, in Stockholm and Copenhagen, in London, in Paris, in New York — I have readers everywhere, of *rare* intelligence, distinguished characters raised in high posts and responsibilities. I have true geniuses in my readership. *N made this further change at the end of December 1888 in conjunction with the new text of "Why I Am So Wise" §3, where he treats the race question more extensively and in quite different words. Cf. TI "What the Germans*

Lack" §3, N's letter to his mother, 21 December 1888 {KGB III:5, *542–44}, and the foreword to NCW.*

14. *old market-women]* Cf. *N to his mother, 21 December 1888* {*KGB* III:5, 542–44}.

15. *romancier]* "writer of novels"

16. *"toutes mes audaces et finesses"]* "all my bold and polished nuances"

17. *Taine's]* {The French historian Hippolyte Taine} *in a letter to N on 14 December 1888* {*KGB* III:6, 386–87}; *N received the letter in Turin on 16 December.*

18. *esprit]* "wit"

19. *I can . . . Amen!]* {Luther's concluding remark at the Diet of Worms, 1521.}

20. *Antichrist]* {With this reference to the Greek language, N indicates that the Greeks understood, as he does, the Antichrist to refer to the antithesis of Christ and did not identify this name with the devil.}

21. *Antichrist . . .]* Mp XVI 5 *includes a torn-off strip of paper containing the two verses that conclude the draft; no doubt the fragment was torn from the final version of this section. Since it is impossible to say with any certainty who did this (N himself or — more probably — Peter Gast or N's sister), the strip of paper was excluded from the published version. At all events, the fragment had the instruction "in italics" for the publisher. Otherwise its contents are identical with the draft. The "Polish Song" "Finis Poloniae"* {"End of Poland"} *was composed by Ernst Ortlepp; the opening verses (paraphrased by N) were a German version of the "Dombrowski March." Cf. N on Ortlepp to Wilhelm Pinder, 4 July 1864* {*KGB* I:1, 288}.

3

22. *This section in its present form was conceived while N revised the manuscript in early December; the earlier version (in the first Pm: mid-November version) had read as follows:* I know my prerogatives as author to some extent; and in individual cases I have been convinced how much the study of my writings "ruins taste." You simply cannot stand books anymore, at least of all *[sic!]* philosophical ones — I come from a different *depth*, I come likewise from a different *height*; without me, nobody knows what is high

or deep. [Finally] Fortunately, I |also| lack any philistinism, I aspire to integrity by being a master in [all] every art of seduction — [I scarcely think about it,] my ultimate ambition would be to cajole the Swabians and other bovines to my cause. What [however] above all *spoils* the readers used to my works is my courage: it always courts danger, |not for nothing is one friendly with the beautiful Ariadne| there is a particular interest in the labyrinth — acquaintanceship with Mister Minotaur is not ruled out by any means . . . Plato, not to mention the "back door" philosopher Kant, is a toady compared to me. — My writings are difficult — |— that is hopefully not an objection to them? —| To understand the *tersest* language ever spoken by a philosopher — in addition, the one with fewest formulae, the one most vibrant and artistic — you must use a procedure that is the *reverse* of that necessary for other philosophical literature. You must *condense* the latter, otherwise you will ruin your stomach — I have to be thinned, made fluid, diluted: otherwise you will likewise ruin your stomach. — Silence is, with me, just as much an instinct as prattle is with Messrs. Philosophers. I am *short*: my readers themselves must |be long| have broad range in order to draw together everything I have thought and have had in the back of my mind. — On the other hand, in order to "understand," there are preconditions to which |only| the rarest are equal|: you must know how to put the problem in the right place, by which I mean within the context of *related* problems — and for that, you must have topographically to hand the hiding places, the difficult areas of whole fields of knowledge and above all of philosophy itself. — Finally, I speak only of what I have experienced, not just "thought"; with me, there is no contrast between thought and life. My "theory" grows out of my "praxis" — oh, out of a praxis that is neither harmless nor indeed safe! . . . Listen to what Zarathustra has to say on this, the very man who upholds the proposition "good people never tell the truth!" — : / — boldly risking things, ever mistrusting things, cruelly saying / no, cutting into living flesh — how rarely all this comes together! / but truth is inseminated in just this way! / Everything that good people call evil must come together so that a single truth may be born . . . *(Z III "On Old and New Tablets" §7).*

23. *experience . . . learning*] Cf. *Peter Gast to N, 25 October 1888* {*KGB* III:6, 337}: "What 'revelations,' what ecstasies of learning I owe to your world-governing spirit!"

24. *for I . . . strayed*] Cf. *N to his publisher, 27 November 1888* {*KGB* III:5, 494–95}.

25. *To you . . . it out . . .*] *Z* III *"On the Vision and Riddle"* §1.

5

26. *hollow- . . . cabbage*] *Hohltöpfen, Kohlköpfen* {In *GM* III 8, N makes the pun *Hohlkopf, Hohltopf* — "hollow head, hollow pot" — to denote the vacuous agitator; here he compares hollow pots (*Hohltöpfen*) to heads of cabbages (*Kohlköpfen*), this time insulting vacuous philosophers, moralists and the like.}

27. *medicynical*] *medizynisch* {N conflates "medicine" and "cynical."}

28. *Woman is . . . medicynical*] *Variant in Mp XVI 5, Pd of final version:* Woman never thinks of feeling herself to be related to the male or even "equal": only an *unfortunate* little woman "emancipates herself" . . . A woman is a failure if she has no children. For example, virtue in woman, the so-called "beautiful soul" [in woman] is just a physiological *lack* — I shall not say everything, otherwise I would turn [have to speak] medicynical.

29. *definition of love?*] Cf. *WA* §2.

30. *always only*] *Pd:* for her just

31. *May I assume . . . spirit of life."* —] *Pm:* Please allow me to presume that I *know* the little women: it is part of my Dionysian dowry. But the verdict on the "eternal-womanly" is the standard, more or less the plumb line for the depth of a psychologist. To judge objectively about this, I find even Nietzsche's verdict on woman deeper, more radical, more *impartial* than a psychologist's verdict — for example, he dared to say: "Beneath her personal vanity, woman always retains her contempt for woman in general." {Cf. *BGE* 86} Unpleasant perhaps, but the unpleasant is, after all, the *sigillum veri* {"sign of truth"} . . . Here one must not judge from a remote corner, as do French gentlemen, who construe woman as *sickness*, meaning that they exploit their contingent presence in nineteenth-century Paris as a solution to the problem of "woman" in general — one has to know a little of the

history of woman. That woman is supposed to be the "weaker" sex is, for example, neither historically nor ethnologically true: nearly everywhere, there are or have been cultural structures where *mastery* was with women. It was an event, even, if you like, a sort of *decision* in the destiny of humanity, that woman finally succumbed — that all instincts of subordination came to the fore in her and *created* woman as a type . . . There really is no doubt about the fact that only from then on was woman something enchanting, interesting, versatile, cunning — a filigree of inscrutable psychology: with that, she ceased *to be boring* . . . Power is boring — just take a look at the "Reich"! Would not life on earth be positively insupportable if woman had not become a genius of entertainment and grace, if she had not become *woman*? — But to do that, you must be weak, . . . as well as a genius of malice! . . . even a little like the Maenads! . . . Gentlemen philosophers, let us not underestimate malice: — my *primary* objection against the Christian heaven is the fact that the angels there are not malicious . . .

32. *"Emancipation of woman" . . . spirit of life."* — *] Pd*: — In order not to leave any doubt as to my opinion, honest in every regard, I shall communicate a further proposition against *vice* from my moral codex ([its first proposition runs: *War to the death against vice! Anything that is anti-nature is depraved*] [its leitmotif runs thus] with the word vice I declare war on anything that is anti-nature —): the preaching of chastity is depraved as a public incitement to anti-nature. [an assault on public morals.] Every disparagement of sexuality, all defilement of the same by the concept "unclean," shall be punished as an assault on public morality. [is the very sin against the holy spirit of life. After the crime of *Parsifal*, Wagner should not have died in Venice but in prison. (— [To put forward] Not without value as an inscription for the Bayreuth Opera House.)] You can imagine how I received *Parsifal*. In the summer of 1882, when I was pregnant with Zarathustra, whom I [— — —]

33. *"the preaching . . . life."* —*] N is citing here clause 4 of his "Law Against Christianity," found at the end of AC. Cf. notes to this "Law" above.*

6

34. *For this section N cites BGE §295. At the end of the section, N noted for the printer: End of the* Chapter *"Why I Write Such Good Books"*

THE BIRTH OF TRAGEDY

1

35. *To do . . . things.]* Pm: To be fair toward *The Birth of Tragedy* is not easy for me today. Its harmful influence is still too fresh in my memory.

36. *were there . . . Wagner.]* Pm: were there *intelligent* adherents to Wagner's cause.

37. *I found . . . Music."]* Cf. *Heinrich Hart to N, 4 January 1877* {*KGB* II:6/1, 477}: "In the last couple of days (: or rather, nights) — should I say I have twice 'read through' or 'fevered through' your little work, *Die Wiedergeburt der Tragödie aus dem Geiste der Musik* {*The Rebirth of Tragedy out of the Spirit of Music*}, and found that probably no one has penetrated as deeply into the essential nature of art and artistic creation as yourself."

38. *Wörth]* {This early battle in the Franco-Prussian War was fought on 6 August 1870.}

39. *opera and revolution]* {In 1849, Wagner published the pamphlet *Kunst und Revolution* ("Art and revolution").}

40. *On one occasion . . . "subterraneans" . . .]* {Cf. ending of *BT* §24.}

2

41.   *to approve, to call good]* gutheissen = "to approve"; *gut heissen* = "to call good"

3

42. *I finally . . . 139.]* Cf. *TI* "What I Owe the Ancients" §5 {which N has altered only slightly}.

43. *misunderstood]* {In *TI*, N has "understood."}

4

44. *Wagner in Bayreuth]* Cf. *WB* §§7, 1, 4, 9, 6.

45. *page seven]* {N is citing the first edition of *Richard Wagner in Bayreuth*; cf. *WB* §1; *CW* 2, 262.}

46. *cut]* {In Greek legend, in 333 BCE, Alexander the Great cut the Gordian knot tied by King Gordius of Phrygia.}

47. *page 30]* {Cf. *WB* §4; *CW* 2, 279.}

48. *page 71]* {Cf. *WB* §9; *CW* 2, 310–11.}

49. *pages 43–46]* {Cf. *WB* §6; *CW* 2, 288–91.}

THE UNFASHIONABLES

I

50. *"John-a-dreams"]* {Hamlet likens himself to John-a-dreams in Shakespeare's *Hamlet, Prince of Denmark*, Act II, Scene 2, translated by August Wilhelm Schlegel as "Hans der Träumer."}

51. *or, in a word, Nietzsche . . .] Pm*: But the day came when Wagner climbed down — *descended*; when he stretched out his hands to everything that wanted to be reconciled with him, [on condition that everyone would read something into it] when he reconciled himself with the "Reich," with subscription "culture" and even with dear God — when he went to Communion! . . . Wagner compromised me. —

2

52. *satisfait]* "complacent"

53. *the "old and new faith"]* {In 1872, the theologian David Strauss (1808–74) published his controversial *Der alte und der neue Glaube*.}

54. *"Berlin blue"]* {Prussian blue pigment containing ferrocyanide.}

55. *Grenzboten] Article signed B.F. and printed under the title "Herr Friedrich Nietzsche und die deutsche Kultur," 42 (17 October 1873), 104–10.* {*Die Grenzboten* was a liberal newspaper for German émigrés founded in Brussels in 1841.}

56. *Ewald in Göttingen]* {Heinrich Ewald (1803–75) was a Protestant theologian and professor of theology and Oriental languages at the University of Göttingen. He published a review of N's *DS* in the *Göttingische Gelehrte Anzeigen* (1875): 1:119–21. Sommer notes that while Ewald does not make reference to N's assassination attempt, this metaphor does appear in an essay on N's work by Carl Spitteler in *Der Bund* of 1 January 1888 (Sommer 2, 497).}

57. *Bruno Bauer]* Cf. *Bruno Bauer, Zur Orientierung über die Bismarck'sche Ära* {"Guidance on the Bismarck era"} *(Chemnitz: Schmeitzner, 1880), §25: "Treitschke und Victor Hugo"; cf. also N to Gast, 20 March 1881 {KGB III:1, 72–73}; and the "Chronicle" in CW 19.*

58. *Hoffmann]* Cf. *Franz Hoffmann's review "Besprechung von David Strauss"* {"Review of David Strauss"} *in Allgemeiner litterarischer Anzeiger für das evangelische Deutschland 12 (November 1873): 321–36; (December 1873): 401–8; printed also in Philosophische Schriften 5 (Erlangen*{: Deiche}*, 1878), 410–47. Details are from Richard Frank Krummel, Nietzsche und der deutsche Geist, 2 vols. (Berlin: de Gruyter, 1974).*

59. *Hillebrand]* Cf. *Hillebrand's review, "Nietzsche gegen Strauss," which appeared in the Augsburger Allgemeine Zeitung, nos. 265 and 266, 22 and 23 September 1873; also reprinted in Zeiten, Völker und Menschen* {"Times, nations, and people"}*, vol. 2, "Wälsches und Deutsches"* {"Foreign and German"} *(Berlin*{: Oppenheim,}*) 1875), 291–310, NL.*

60. *Stendhal's]* Cf. *Prosper Mérimée's introduction to Stendhal's Correspondance inédite (Paris*{: Michel Lévy Frères,} *1855), 1:ix, NL.*

61. "*libres penseurs"]* "freethinkers"

3

62. *except for . . . proper.]* Pm: however grateful the intelligent [the most intelligent] individual admirers of both luminaries professed themselves to be — among them A. Bilharz, the most scientific, even [I should say]. *The physician and philosopher Alfons Bilharz {1836–1925} corresponded with N in August 1879; see the "Chronicle" in CW 19.*

63. *page 93]* Cf. *SE* §7; *CW* 2, 239–40.

64. *this work]* Cf. *SE* §8; *CW* 2, 254–55. *Fragments of the October Version of this chapter, crossed out by N, are found pasted to the reverse of loose sheet 20 in the Pm:* [19] Conclusion of section 18 / The aftereffect of this work has been absolutely inestimable in my life. I had, without knowing it, translated a maxim of Stendhal's into praxis: entering society with a *duel*. And I had chosen for myself an opponent who could guess who I was — I had challenged the

first German freethinker and *laughed at him* — With that, a new freethinking came to expression, no longer just an anti-theological one, [for the] something strange, for which the Germans |, ultimately not just the Germans| [have] lacked the ear, the understanding and even the word. Today they have the word, I gave it to them — *immoralist* . . . Integrity, intellectual conscience, which declares itself *against* morality . . . / 19. / That the *Unfashionables* bearing the names of Schopenhauer and Wagner might, in particular, serve toward an understanding or even a psychological questioning of both cases is not something I want to assert, however grateful intelligent individual admirers of both luminaries professed themselves to me to be in this respect — among them A. Bilharz, the most scientific, even [+ + +] / [+ + +] unreserved courage blows a wind of freedom over all suffering, *no* exception made for the wound. What a philosopher should be, which I was not at that time, I wrote on the wall with impatient hardness *toward* myself. — Would you like verification of how I felt in myself at that time — degenerate almost to a scholar, one more bookworm that crawled round [through] the ancient metrists with extreme precision and bad eyes [turning round and round] boring [harnessed] into a handiwork that did not just use up three-quarters of my strength but took away the very time I might have to think of a substitute [of the] for strength? I cite [that abysmal] that astringent piece of psychology of the scholar which suddenly jumps into one's face in the said piece as though [catapulted by an unspeakable something] out of an unspeakable experience beyond words.

Underneath this, scarcely legible, is the following preliminary draft of the October Version (§22; cf. the variants of §§6, 7, 8 of "Why I Am a Destiny"): I [— — —]. What distinguishes me is having first *discovered* morality and — consequently — [a merciless declaration of war to it] *against* it, [having chosen a word] being in need of a word that has the meaning of a merciless declaration of war. Morality seems to me to be the greatest uncleanness humanity ⟨has⟩ on its conscience, untruthfulness become instinct, counterfeiting *in psychologicis* to the point of crime . . .

65. *How I see . . . while.* —] Pm: What a philosopher *should* be, which I was not at that time, I wrote on the wall with impa-

tient hardness toward myself. — Would you like verification of how I felt in myself at that time, degenerate almost to a scholar, one more bookworm that crawled its way through the ancient metrists with extreme precision and bad eyes [turning round and round] boring [locked] into a handiwork that did not just use up three-quarters of my strength but took away the very time I might have to think of a substitute [of the] for strength? I cite [that abysmal] that astringent piece of psychology of the scholar which suddenly jumps into one's face in the said piece as though out of an unspeakable experience beyond words. *Cf. SE §3, HAH §252, EH III HAH §3.*

HUMAN, ALL TOO HUMAN

66. *Section 20 of the October Version provides a single variant for the whole of the chapter on Human, All Too Human; it reads:* Separated from the *Unfashionables* by two years, *Human, All Too Human* (1878) is a psychologically curious case. It calls itself a book "for *free* spirits": once again it is not a book for Germans. Anyone who leafs through it in the daylight robbery manner of educated or scholarly people [cultivated philistines not even coming into consideration] will find it clever, composed, occasionally witty and at all events, full of realities. Almost all problems are aired, however briefly, including political ones, which are discussed in anti-liberal fashion bordering on cynicism. You only understand the book when you can hear at full volume what is rejected by every proposition: for nearly every proposition expresses a *victory* [a victory over myself . . .] This book is the memorial to a catharsis. — And the composed, intellectual, almost neutral attitude is a victory as well. It is the contradiction that no longer contradicts, that has learned to say Yes [— the sense of well-being after the catharsis. —] The provenance of this book dates back to the time of the first Bayreuth festival; one of its determining features was a violent crisis against everything that surrounded me there. Not only the fact that at that time, the complete apathy and illusoriness of the Wagnerian "ideal" was palpably clear to me, I saw above all how even to those most closely involved, [the "matter"] the "ideal" was not the main thing — that quite different things were being taken more

seriously, more enthusiastically. In addition, the pitiful society of subscribing gentlemen and subscribing little women, all very much in love, very bored and unmusical to the point of a hangover. Typical was the old Kaiser applauding with his hands while shouting [loudly] to his adjutant, Count Lehndorf: "dreadful! dreadful!" — You had the whole leisured riff-raff [folk] of Europe together, and any old person [any old prince] went in and out of Wagner's house, as though in Bayreuth it was just a matter of one more sport. And basically it was nothing more than that. People had discovered a cultural excuse to add to the old excuses for leisure, a "grand opera" with hurdles; they found in Wagner's music, persuasive in its secret sexuality, a way of binding together a society in which everyone pursued their *plaisirs*. The rest and, if you like, the *innocence* in the "affair" were the idiots Nohl, Pohl, and Kohl — the latter the genius loci of Bayreuth — real pedigree Wagnerians, a godless and mindless set with strong stomachs who gobbled up everything the Maestro "left" to them. Wagner's music, as you well know, *consists* of leftovers . . . The performance itself had little value; I was [deadly] bored to ashen gray by this music, which had turned completely "mystical" and which, because of the absurd lower positioning of the orchestra, penetrated one's consciousness through harmonious (— as well as occasionally unharmonious) mist. Whatever is "return to nature" here, in other words, the complete transparency of the contrapuntal fabric, the use of every single instrument in its specific color, in its most natural and beneficial language, in sum, the most *sparing* use of the instruments, *delicacy* in place of dull subterranean instinctual stimulations — I later learned to appreciate through Bizet's orchestration. Enough, in the midst of it all I left for a few weeks, very suddenly, apologizing to Wagner merely with a telegram expressed in somewhat fatalistic terms. At Klingenbrunn, a little town hidden deep in the woods of the Bohemian Forest, I carried my melancholy around like a sickness — *and* wrote the odd proposition from time to time in my notebook under the collective title "The Plowshare," nothing but *hard psychologica* that can perhaps still be detected in *Human, All Too Human*. It was not just a breach with Wagnerism that was being decided for me then — I experienced [a radical compulsion to rid myself, by means of a *reality cure*, of the large amount of "idealism" I had, through bad company, brought into myself] a total aberration of my instinct, for which [my friendship with Wagner] my blunder with Bayreuth and Wagner was just a token, I perceived that it was high time to switch my thoughts back to *myself.* This retuning of my whole nature down to its essentials, the ever deepening feeling of how much time had already been wasted, how useless, arbitrary and worn out my thirty-two years, my life looked compared to my task, the doubting of myself, the doubting of my right to my task, the prospect of complete desolation and isolation — all of that also brought a shock to my health. *Impatience* with myself overcame me. You are healthy in so far as you are patient [in tune] with yourself. — At that time, my instinct's power of resistance was on the wane, and step for step the degeneration inherited from my father preponderated over the healthier and livelier dowry in my nature. What remained *strong* was that rigorous self-discipline *against* all "higher swindle," "idealism," "fine sentiment" and other [feminisms] womanly traits. A winter in Sorrento in which the greater part of *Human, All Too Human* was written down, despite the [near] proximity of Richard Wagner and family for a time; the result was proof that, however much I had been physiologically laid low, I had at least spiritually engineered my *will* to recovery, to life, to strong and unrelenting affirmation of reality, into victory. — The book was finished in Basel under considerably worse circumstances. Mr. [Heinrich Köselitz] Peter Gast himself, then studying at the university and very attached to me, basically has this book on his conscience. I dictated [from old manuscripts], my head bound — he wrote down and made corrections as well —he was the actual writer, while I was merely the author. When I finally had in my hands the finished book from the printers — to the great surprise of one so ill! — I sent two copies, among others, to Bayreuth. By some miracle of meaningful coincidence, at the same time a beautiful copy of the text of *Parsifal* arrived with Wagner's dedication to me: "to his dear friend Friedrich Nietzsche, Richard Wagner, Church Councillor." — This crossing of the two books — it seemed to me as if I heard an ominous sound: didn't it sound as though two swords had crossed? . . . At least we both thought so: *for we both remained silent*. Since then there has no longer been any contact, either direct or in letters, between Wagner and myself. Today I think about *this* breach with Wagner with deep gratitude. It took place without any hurtful word having been spoken, any welling up of coarse affects being involved — as though of necessity, stern, gloomy, deep: the parting company of two ships that meet up, were able to misunderstand and love one another for a short period — until their *task* drove them apart to opposite seas. For Wagner is my opposite. — And how I now sighed with relief: how great was my joy! With this "book for *free* spirits," everything promised in the *third Unfashionable* had already been fulfilled. Here, a height has been reached where truly an air of freedom blows: a light, wafting, mild air — and *so pure! so pure!* How all things [now] lie in the light! — You think with pity of the air *below*, the malarial air of the "ideal" . . . From now on, I no longer used reasons to defend myself against the realm of fibs and falsities of the "beyond," of ["morality"] "redemption," of ["truth"] "unselfing": a feeling of cleanliness, a sixth sense, was quite sufficient — I washed my hands after every contact with Christianity. — Is there a stronger formula *against* all "idealism" than my proposition where the quintessence of the whole book is formulated into the maxim: *convictions are more dangerous enemies to truth than lies?* . . . [War on convictions! . . .] Do you know my definition of conviction, of "belief"? *Untruthfulness that has become an instinct* . . . Philosophy, as I have understood and lived it since then, is the voluntary search for all that is strange and dubious in existence, everything that moraline had hitherto placed beyond the pale, that had been rejected by idealists as *beneath* them. After long experience provided by such a wandering through *forbidden terrain*, I learned to view the causes thus far of "idealizing" and "moralizing" in a very different way than [can be desirable to idealists and moralists] might be wished — the *hidden* history of philosophy, the psychology of their great names, came to light for me. — "How much truth does a spirit *bear*, how much truth does it *dare*?" — that became for me the

real measure of value. Error (— the "ideal" —) is *cowardice* . . .
Every achievement in knowledge *follows* from courage and severity toward oneself, from cleanliness toward oneself. "*Nitimur in
vetitum*" {N underlines "*vetitum*"} — in this sign the truth *is
victorious*, because people have hitherto forbidden outright only
what was the truth . . . *Cf. EH Foreword §3 and its variants (from
the intermediate draft).*

I

67. *In this . . . 1878.] Cf. the title page of the first edition of HAH
(1878):* "Dedicated to the memory of Voltaire, in commemoration
of his death, 30 May 1778."

2

68. *The revision of this section written at the beginning of December 1888 but then deleted by N on pp. 22–23 of the Pm reads as follows:* The provenance of this book dates back to the time of the
first Bayreuth festival. One of its determining features was a violent crisis against everything that surrounded me there. Not only
the fact that at that time, the complete apathy and illusoriness of
the Wagnerian "ideal" was palpably clear to me, I saw above all
how even to those most closely involved, the "ideal" was not the
main thing — that quite different things were being taken more
seriously, more enthusiastically. In addition, the pitiful society of
subscribing gentlemen and subscribing little women — I know
what I am speaking about, as I myself was a ["gentleman subscriber"] gentleman subscriber — all very much in love, very
bored and unmusical to the point of a hangover. Typical was the
old Kaiser applauding with his hands while shouting to his adjutant, Count Lehndorf: "dreadful! dreadful!" — you had the
whole leisured riff-raff |of Europe| together, and any old prince
went in and out of Wagner's house, as though it was just a matter
of one more sport. And basically it was nothing more than that.
People had discovered a cultural excuse to add to the old excuses
for leisure, a grand opera *with hurdles*; they found in Wagner's
music, persuasive in its secret sexuality, a way of binding together
a society in which everyone pursued their *plaisirs*. The rest and, if
you like, the *innocence* in the affair, its "idealists," were the idiots

Nohl, Pohl, Kohl — the latter, as is well known, the genius loci of Bayreuth — real pedigree Wagnerians, a godless and mindless set who credulously gobbled up everything the Maestro "left" to them. [Wagner's music, as you well know, consists of "leftovers" —] And what a lot Wagner "leaves over"! . . . The performance itself had little value; I was bored to ashen gray by this music, which had turned completely "mystical" and which, because of the absurd lower positioning of the orchestra, penetrated one's consciousness through harmonious (— as well as occasionally unharmonious) mist. Whatever is "return to nature" here, in other words the ability to see through and *hear through* the contrapuntal fabric, the use of every single instrument in its specific [language] color, in its most natural and beneficial language (Wagner commits indecent assault on all the instruments —), in sum, the most *sparing* use of the instruments, *delicacy* in place of dull, subterranean instinctual stimulations — I later learned to appreciate through Bizet's orchestration. Enough, in the midst of it all, I left for a few weeks, very suddenly, apologizing to Wagner merely with a telegram expressed in somewhat fatalistic terms. At Klingenbrunn, a little town hidden deep in the woods of the Bohemian Forest, I carried my melancholy around like a sickness — *and* wrote the odd proposition from time to time in my notebook under the collective title "The Plowshare," nothing but *hard psychologica* that can perhaps still be detected in *Human, All Too Human.*

69. *Bayreuth festival]* {summer 1876.}

70. *Blessed Isle]* {In Greek mythology, the sanctuary at the end of the earth for dead heroes.}

71. *Brendel]* *Karl Franz Brendel, cofounder of the "Allgemeiner Musikverein"* {"General Music Society"}.

72. *Bayreuther Blätter]* {Bayreuth-based journal founded in 1878 and dedicated to the discussion of Wagner's work.}

73. *"beautiful souls"* . . . *confessions]* {"Confessions of a Beautiful Soul" [*Bekenntnisse einer schönen Seele*] is the title of bk. 6 of Goethe's novel *Wilhelm Meister's Apprenticeship* (1795–96). In other words, N makes reference to Goethe and Shakespeare in successive sentences.}

74. *A kingdom . . . word!] From the well-known line of Shake-speare's Richard III{, Act V, Scene 4:* "A horse! A horse! My kingdom for a horse!"}

75. *Nohl, Pohl, Kohl] N read Karl Friedrich Ludwig Nohl's biography of Wagner (1883) in 1888; Richard Pohl attacked The Case of Wagner in the Musikalisches Wochenblatt {*"Musical Weekly"}; {N puns Johann Georg Kohl's name with *Kohl,* the word for "cabbage," but also used figuratively for rubbish, nonsense, probably because} *in 1873, Kohl had published a piece entitled: "Über Klangmalerei in der deutschen Sprache"* {"On tonal painting in the German language"} {where he supported Wagner's alliterative technique}; *cf. Curt Paul Janz, Friedrich Nietzsche: Biographie (Munich*{: Hanser,} *1978), 2:361.*

76. *grazie]* "grace" {a musical direction}

77. *swine]* Cf. Matthew 8:32. {Reference to Jesus casting out devils into the Gadarene swine; cf. also Mark 5:13; Luke 8:33.}

78. *Parisienne] Louise Ott née Einbrod; they corresponded in 1876/77 and 1882.*

3

79. *Compare this section with CW 17, 9[42].*

4

80. *N sent this paragraph to Leipzig in the second half of December with the following instruction for the typesetter:* To be inserted into the chapter on *Human, All Too Human* as the *final* paragraph. *Cf. the variant to NCW:* "We Antipodes."

6

81. *Dr. Paul Rée]* {Paul Rée (1849–1901), German philosopher and physician, was the third party in the triangular friendship involving N and Lou Salomé in the course of 1872. Rée's book *Der Ursprung der moralischen Empfindungen* (*The Origin of Moral Sensations*) appeared in 1877.}

82. *lisez]* "read"

83. *"Yet what . . . have"]* {N here quotes freely from *HAH* §37; cf. *CW* 3, p. 46.}

DAWN

84. {The subtitle of *Dawn* is in fact "Thoughts on the Presumptions of Morality."}

I

85. *With . . . cannon shot.*] *October Version:* In certain cases it is not cowardice that brings forth great scarecrows of morality and other saints but a *subterranean revenge* on the part of those who have lost out, who want to rob those who are lucky and have turned out well of their equanimity and confuse their instincts by means of morality. It would be a triumph for them to become master with their values and, as parasites under the sacred pretext of "improving" humans, to *suck out* life itself and make it anemic . . . Morality as vampirism. — I have reasons to make a pause right here in this presentation, for in the sequence of my works, my first campaign against morality, *Dawn: Thoughts on Morality as Prejudice* (1881), is next in line. Not that this book has the slightest whiff of gunpowder about it: this time, old artilleryman that I am, I have no gun, either large or small. You must use your discretion to make a distinction between the effect of this book and the means it deploys — from which the effect follows like a psychological inference, *not* like a cannon shot.

86. *Greek god*] {The Greek sculptor Praxiteles (370–330 BCE) portrayed Apollo as a lizard slayer.}

87. *"There . . . broken."*] {From the Hindu sacred text, the Rig Veda. Cf. *CW* 5, xi.}

88. *Morality . . . "Or?" . . . *] *October Version:* Morality is not attacked, it is simply no longer heard . . . *Beyond Good and Evil*! — *Dawn*, the *gaya scienza* (1882), my *Zarathustra* (1883) are above all pure *Yes-saying deeds* — the immoralist has his say in every proposition. Any negation there is merely a *conclusion*, it follows, it does not run ahead.

THE JOYFUL SCIENCE

89. *You who . . . Januarius!*] The motto of "Sanctus Januarius," bk. 4 of *JS*.

90. *who has seen . . . that? — *] Cf. *JS* §342.

91. *who reads . . . third book*] Cf. *JS* §§268–275.

92. *Sicily*] Cf. *Idylls from Messina* in *CW* 6.

93. *"To the Mistral"*] Composed in autumn 1884; cf. *N* to Gast, 22 November 1884 {*KGB* III:1, 558–61}.

THUS SPOKE ZARATHUSTRA

I

94. *Section 24 of the October Version corresponds in part to this section; it followed paragraphs 22 and 23, which N later used for the chapter "Why I Am a Destiny" (§§6, 7, and 8). It reads as follows:* At this turning point, where everything is decided and everything is put in question, for the undying memory of an unsurpassed event I wrote my *Zarathustra* as the *loftiest* book there is — the whole fact of "the human" lies an immense distance *beneath* it — also the *most profound* book there is: it is a completely inexhaustible fount which no bucket can plumb without coming up filled with gold and [kindly wisdom] goodness. The [first] basic conception of Zarathustra — in other words, the thought of *eternal recurrence*, this final and most extreme formula of affirmation that can be achieved — belongs to the August of 1881. I was walking along Lake Silvaplana through the woods; I came to a halt at a mighty boulder soaring into a pyramid. That's where the thought came to me. — If I calculate from that day to the sudden onset of labor, under the most unfavorable circumstances, in February 1883, it comes to eighteen months for the actual pregnancy (— which, it goes without saying, did not enter my consciousness as such: I did not think of related things in the slightest). The sum of these 18 months ought finally to suggest the thought that I might be essentially a female elephant. — First, what does the name of that ancient Persian mean here? — We know in what respect Zarathustra was first and how he made a beginning: — he saw in the battle of good and evil the actual wheel that drives things, he translated morality into metaphysics, as force, as cause, as purpose in itself. Zarathustra *created* this greatest of errors: consequently, he must also be the first to *acknowledge* it. He has here not just longer and more experience than [anyone else] any other thinker — [he has] the [longest] experimental refutation of the proposition that the world is "ethically" arranged and ethical in its [purposes] intentions comes to its *strongest* conclusion in him: Zarathustra is above all more truthful than [anyone else] any other thinker. His [religion] teaching and it alone was the one that taught truthfulness as

supreme virtue. The *self-overcoming of morality, through truthful-ness* — that is what in my [case the choice of the name] mouth the name Zarathustra means. *Cf. the variant to §4 of the Foreword.*

95. *foreword]* {At the close of the foreword to *Ecce Homo* (§4).}

96. *female elephant]* The same imagery is used for the emergence of *HAH* in *CW 12, 22[80].*

97. *in fact . . . itself]* Cf. *JS §342.*

98. *fourth book]* Cf. *JS §341.*

99. *oboe] Should be:* clarinet *(Gast).*

100. *Chiavari] Pm*: Cagliari *lapsus calami* {"slip of the pen"}.

101. *the unforgettable German] Gast deleted these three words in the Pm.* {In 1888, Friedrich III was Kaiser for ninety-nine days until his death.}

2

102. *"gaya scienza"]* {The Provençal words for poetry.} *Cf. JS §382.*

103. {N has deleted here "a soothsayer," which appears in *JS* §382.}

104. {N has here deleted the exclamation point that appears in *JS* §382.}

105. *Argonauts]* {In Greek legend, around fifty heroes who sailed with Jason in quest of the golden fleece. The "undiscovered land" mentioned later in the section echoes "the land" N sees in *EH* III UO 2.}

106. *conscience and science] Gewissen und Wissen* {Literally, "conscience and knowing."}

3

107. *The notion . . . of fact.]* Cf. *WB 7.*

108. *"here come . . . to speak — "]* Cf. *Z* III "The Return Home" {where N wrote "for me . . . from me" *(mir)* instead of *EH* version *(dir)*}.

4

109. *in Rome] N was in Rome 4 May–16 June, 1883.*

110. *comme il faut]* "in a suitable manner"

111. *Friedrich II]* {Kaiser Friedrich II (1194–1250) was Holy Roman Emperor from 1220 until his death.}

112. *return.]* *The following sentence was deleted in the Pm:* In Rome I had the experience of hearing *Parsifal* praised to my face — after which I had two fits of laughter. —

113. *Palazzo del Quirinale]* {The Quirinal Palace had been the official residence of the kings of Italy since 1871.}

114. *fontana]* "fountain"

115. *Eza]* {Eza is a Moorish chateau, located at the top of a steep path leading from the village of Èze, about eight miles east of Nice on the French Riviera.}

5

116. *The following earlier version (before the revision at the beginning of December) is found in Mp XVI 5:* The problem of how to get over the four years during and after *Zarathustra* was immense. It is by far the period of my life richest in wounds and poorest in solace. Do not overlook this fact: all great things, works or facts, are terrible the moment they are completed — they immediately *turn against* their perpetrator. And precisely because he was the perpetrator, he is *weaker* than he has ever been! . . . He has to go about with the feeling of having done something that was completely beyond human capacity, that nobody was sanctioned to desire, something in which [perhaps] the knot of destiny for humanity is bound — and feeling *weak* . . . He looks around. Everywhere wasteland, deadly silence — no ears . . . A form of revolt at best. — I experienced just such a revolt, to very varying degrees, from nearly everyone close to me. Humans hate nothing more than the sudden sighting of distance where they presumed there were equal rights. Those further off who by chance [came] were brought into contact with *Zarathustra* immediately spat poison at me in rage. I flatter them by calling it *poison*, it was something else, something that stank . . . And as though to put my "*Yes to life*" to the test, it was then that precisely *puniness* and human misery pounced upon me to the point of seasickness toward life. Weigh it up, seriously: human *puniness* remains the very worst objection to the human, a thing for which there is no cure — you can cope with all that is dreadful in the human because [it] the dreadful has greatness. — Around that time, I had my richest experience with so-called *good* people. It is

impossible to calculate all the bad, vengeful, totally ruthless instincts that lurk beneath the appearance of a battle against evil. Even filthy anti-Semites like Eugen Dühring claim to uphold the cause of the good . . . A second aspect — but no less fateful. Many of these "good people" [easily] arouse trust, it helps to have soft blue eyes — it is a seduction. Looked at afterwards [namely], this inhumaneness become instinct among the virtuous, called "idealism," this not-wanting-to-see reality at any price, this seizing of human and animal with the rosy fingers of the "beautiful soul," created nothing but mischief. Nearly all the "idealists" have substantial *malheurs* {"misfortunes"} on their conscience. — It was then, in the midst of Zarathustra's becoming, that I suddenly began to be horrified at my own thought. What! the *eternal recurrence* that would also eternally resurrect again and again everything puny, miserable, virtuously mendacious, the old "ideal"! . . . You will recall the catastrophe in Zarathustra's hermit-bliss, his seven-day sickness after he had summoned up the "most abysmal thought." Do people really know which thought that is? / — He will return again eternally, the human you are tired of, the *puny* human . . . / — Finally, reckoning the whole and taking a long view, even these experiences were completely invaluable. For me, pain in itself is not an objection; and since it opens the door to what I experience, and consequently to my knowledge, I regard it as virtually holy. There are cases where an Ariadne-thread *into* the labyrinth is needed . . . For the one who shoulders the task of summoning up the *great* war, the war against the virtuous (— Zarathustra calls them the good and just, also the "last humans," as well as "the beginning of the end" —), one must purchase a few experiences at almost any price: the price could even be the danger of losing *one's self*. A victory here is a double victory. What did not kill me has always made me stronger. Since then, I have been unremitting in my battle against virtue. — One day, I was *finished* with everything, I had learned to forget — the highest sign of convalescence, I even forgot my *Zarathustra* at the time. The "other," the will to the "other," even to the opposite, came first. An alienation, a complete not-understanding-myself-any-more threw itself over me out of the most profound and curative instinct, like

a veil. At that moment you could have proved to me that I was
Zarathustra's father: who knows whether I would have believed it?
— At all events, I did not want to catch sight of the book, I did
not possess a copy for two years. And in fact, there was inherent
danger in awakening this aspect of me. In one particular case
when, surrounded by the silence of Upper Engadine, I came upon
a couple of pages of its proofs, the feeling bearing down on me
was so strong that I collapsed and lay sick for a few days. —

117. *rancune]* "grudge" "rancor"

118. — *A third . . . warmth in it . . .] The following was sent to
Naumann at the end of December with the instruction:* In the 5th
section of the chapter *Thus Spoke Zarathustra this* is to replace the
ending, starting with the words *What is most profoundly unrelated
to me. The passage replaced reads:* What is most profoundly unrelated to me stepped into my path with merciless animosity at that
moment. No respect for my solitude any longer. Poison flung into
my face in rage in the midst of the ecstasies over Zarathustra | — I
flatter them by calling it poison, it was something else, something
that stank . . . | I touch on the uncanniest experience of my life,
[something that] my single *bad* experience that [affected it] unpre-
dictably and destructively intruded into it [: at]. At every moment
where I suffered from the immensity of my destiny, something
indecent in the extreme pounced upon me as well. In fact, this
experience lasted seven years; when I had finished the *Revaluation
of Values,* I knew it would not stay away. — The psychologist adds
that there are no circumstances where there is a greater lack of
defense and protection. Whenever there are any means at all to
slay humans *who are destinies,* the instinct of poisonous flies discovers these means. For the one who has greatness, there can be
no battle with puniness: consequently, what is puny becomes
master. — *There was also this instruction for Naumann from N:
New section in the text. Overleaf (page 32a in Pm) is found the following fragment which N deleted during the revision at the beginning of December:* [+ + +] held you on top. One has [+ + +] *that one
forgets them.* — And that happened. One day, I was finished with
everything. {NB. The text has no indication of where the fol-
lowing insertion by N concludes.} |I was saved. An alienation, a

complete not-understanding-myself-any-more threw itself over me out of the most profound curative instinct of life, like a veil. At that moment you could have proved to me that I was Zarathustra's father: who knows whether I would have believed it! At all events, I did not want to catch sight of the book I did not possess a copy for two years. And in fact, there was danger for me in awakening this aspect of me. In one careless moment when, surrounded by the silence of Upper Engadine, I came upon a couple of pages of its proofs again, the power of the feeling bearing down on me was so strong that I broke down in tears and lay sick for two days. — *There follows a direction for the typesetter that apparently refers to a passage in the upper border of the page, cut out by N:* insert! / It is not at all difficult to kill a hermit by [systematically plying him with] a shrewd dose of poisoned letters. — *Compare the above-mentioned variant from Mp XVI 5. On the same reverse page of 32a there is an earlier version of §6 (numbered 5), which does not, however, contain any variation (cf. Podach, Nietzsches Werke des Zusammenbruchs, 297). There are two other versions of this passage in W II 10, as follows. W II 10, 176:* [By far the most] I touch on the most absurd experience of my life, which has done incalculable damage to my health: at any moment when I suffer from the immensity of my destiny, something indecent in the extreme springs into my face. In fact, this experience has lasted seven years; when I had finished *Re⟨valuation⟩ of V⟨alues⟩*, I knew it would not stay away. — The psychologist should also think that in no circumstances is the defenselessness, the lack of protection of a *great* life, any greater; that whenever there are any means at all to slay humans who are destinies, [slyness] the instinct of poisonous flies [knows] gives away [precisely] [that] these means. There can be no battle with the puny when one has greatness . . . consequently, what is puny becomes master. — *W II 177:* I touch here on [the uncanniest experience of my] what is most uncanny in my life, something that has had incalculable consequences for my health. At all moments when I suffer from the immensity of my destiny, something indecent in the extreme *sprang* into my face. In fact, this experience lasted seven years; when I had finished the *Revaluation of Values*, I knew it would not stay away.

119. *Cf. N to Meta von Salis* {29 December 1888, *KGB* III:5, 561}: . . . my sister declared on my birthday with the utmost scorn that I might start to become "famous" . . . what a nice rabble might they be who believed in me . . . this has gone on for *seven* years now . . . *N's alteration in this passage is explained by the connection to the new version of §3 in the chapter "Why I am So Wise."*

120. *In such a . . . warmth in it . . .] Cf. CW 18, 19[7].*

6

121. *world-governing spirit] Cf. Gast to N, {25} October 1888* {*KGB* III:6, 337}.

122. *Veda]* {Series of ancient Hindu sacred writings.}

123. *straps . . . shoes] Cf. John 1:27.*

124. *"I draw . . . mountains."] Z III "On Old and New Tablets"* §19.

125. *aphorism] Sentenz*

126. *— the soul . . . and flow — —] Z III "On Old and New Tablets"* §19.

127. *"most abysmal thought"] Cf. Z III "The Convalescent."*

128. *"the immense . . . abysses"] Cf. Z III "Before Sunrise."*

7

129. *receive] nehmen* {A playful allusion to the words of Jesus that Luke reports in Acts 20:35: "It is more blessed to give than to receive."}.

130. *It is night . . . loves. ––] The whole of Z II "Night Song"* {with slight alterations}.

8

131. *would be Ariadne . . .] Pm:* would be [the invention of] Ariadne.

132. *I walk . . . redemption!] Z II "On Redemption."* {There are no italics for the phrase "To redeem the people of the past" in *Zarathustra.*}

133. *great disgust]* {*Z* II "On the Rabble."}

134. *shape] Bild*

135. *No more willing . . . gods! . . .] Z II "Upon the Blessed Isles."*

136. *"become hard!"] Cf. Z III "On Old and New Tablets"* §29.

BEYOND GOOD AND EVIL

2

137. *gentilhomme]* "gentleman" {Underlined by N.}

138. *learned fear]* {Allusion to one of *Grimms' Fairy Tales*, "The Story of the Youth Who Went Forth to Learn What Fear Was."}

139. *petits faits]* "petty facts"

140. *Zarathustra . . . Czar]* {A word game, *Zar*- and *Czar* sounding identical in German.}

141. *At the end of this passage, deleted:* And what does my great teacher *Dionysus* himself say, among other pleasant ambiguities, at the end of this hard and all too earnest book? *Cf. BGE §295, then, again deleted:* And what, behind a little psychology of my great teacher *Dionysus* that constitutes the ending of the book, does he himself say? What he says is almost the same as that famous serpent . . . *Cf. again BGE §§295 and 129.*

GENEALOGY OF MORALITY

142. *tempo feroce]* "furious pace" {in music}

143. *faute de mieux]* "for want of better"

144. *"For the human . . . than not will"]* Cf. *GM III §28, the final sentence* {slightly altered}.

TWILIGHT OF THE IDOLS

I

145. *that laughs —] earlier version:* like everything I write

2

146. *"Modern . . . them . . .] earlier version:* All political "modern ideas," including Reich ideas, the labor question, crime, suicide, marriage, the whole literary superstition of the day before yesterday, educational directives [false ones and my own], the ultimate aesthetic values — all is expressed [and overturned] in five words. A great wind is blowing through the trees, and everywhere fruits are falling — truths.

147. *As though . . . until now . . .] Cf. Gast to N, 25 October 1888* {*KGB* III:6, 337}: "I read your thoughts there as though I were drunk. It really is as though a *second consciousness* had grown

within you, as though everything up till now had been dark yearning, as though only now in your spirit the 'will' had lit its light to negate the *crooked* path down which it is running."

148. *"dark yearning" . . . right path]* Cf. Goethe, *Faust I, lines 328–29:* "A person good, in his dark drive, / Is well aware of the right path."

149. *only after . . . to culture]* Cf. Gast to N, 25 October 1888 {*KGB* III:6, 337}: "Only from you are there hopes, tasks, prescribed routes to culture again . . . "

150. *glad tidings]* {Cf. Luke 1:19; 2:10; 8:1.}

151. *And that . . . destiny. — —] earlier version:* Is it any wonder if I am sometimes afraid of myself and look at my hand with mistrust? . . . Does it not seem that I have the destiny of humanity in my hand? . . . *Cf. CW 18, 25[5] and "Why I Am a Destiny" §8, as well as N to Gast, 30 October 1888* {*KGB* III:5, 460}: You gave me great pleasure with your letter. Basically I have never even remotely had the experience of hearing from someone what a *strong* effect my thoughts have. The novelty, the courage for innovation, is truly first rank: — with regard to the *consequences*, now and then I look at my *hand* with some mistrust, because it seems to me I have the destiny of humanity "in my hand."

3

152. *The foreword . . . and the South. —] Cf. N to Meta von Salis, 7 September 1888* {*KGB* III:5, 410}.

153. *completion of the Revaluation]* Pm: seventh day. *Cf. Peter Gast to Elisabeth Förster-Nietzsche, 17 November 1893: "The transcription of Ecce Homo [which he had prepared in 1889 and had now sent to Naumburg] is verbatim. Only . . . I have permitted myself . . . to insert on p. 104 the words 'of the first book.'" Since Gast writes of "inserting," we must assume that the words* completion of the Revaluation *come from N. In N's Pm the traces of three words are visible even today, added in pencil and later erased, above the two words* seventh day, *which in turn bear the trace of an erased deletion in pencil. The first letter of the first of the substitute words placed above can still be recognized as a "B" in Gast's hand. The whole procedure can be reconstructed thus: 1.* completion of the Revaluation *instead of* seventh day *was a correction by N which he had sent*

to Leipzig belatedly, i.e., after the revision of the beginning of December; 2. the page or the strip of paper on which N gave the instruction for this correction has, like so much else, been lost or destroyed; 3. because the correction was on a separate sheet or strip of paper, it was immediately noticed by Gast when he fetched the Pm of EH from the printers together with the numerous amendments to it, hence the excited letter to Overbeck of 18 January 1889 ("If this work were finished — as I believe — Nietzsche went mad over celebrating the triumphs of human reason in it, over the completion of the work . . . ") and in the letter of 25 January (likewise to Overbeck) the remark: "In Ecce Homo the 'Revaluation of All Values' is referred to as completed" (in saying this, Gast was still thinking of a "Revaluation" in four books); 4. initially Gast replaced the words seventh day *with* completion of the Revaluation *(i.e., following an instruction from N); 5. but later, when he was making his copy, he wrote what seemed to him at that stage to be more correct:* completion of the first book of the Revaluation; *6. the first editor of EH, Raoul Richter, had no reason to alter the first version of the Pm — since he knew nothing of this — and left* seventh day. *Cf. the preliminary note to EH.*

THE CASE OF WAGNER

I

154. *ridendo dicere severum]* "through what is laughable say what is somber." {This motto for *The Case of Wagner* is adapted from Horace, *Satires*, I, 1, 24.}

155. *verum dicere]* "saying what is true"

156. *that I, old . . . on Wagner?]* Cf. Gast to N, 20 September 1888 {*KGB* III:6, 309}: "The title 'A Psychologist at Leisure' sounds . . . too modest to me: you have taken your artillery up the highest mountains, you have guns as never before . . . "

157. *I loved Wagner.]* Pm: "I can wait."

158. *Cagliostro of music]* Cf. *WA* §5 {, p. 14, and Epilogue, p. 39}.

159. *an attack]* Mp XVI 5: an attack on the German nation, in every respect grown lacking in instinct and dull [which can no longer even count to three] — which [today] gobbles [wolfs] down all contradictions with a good [conscience] appetite — anti-Semitism *and* compassion-morality, Christianity [for example] *and* science,

the will to power, to the "Reich" *and* the *évangile des humbles*, [Mozart *and* Wagner.] Goethe *and* [Kant] Scheffel Bismarck and Treitschke, Beethoven and Wagner [anti-Semitism and loving thy neighbor]. Among Germans you do *not* turn anti-Semitic, [oh what a boon a Jew is for me! . . .] I know that from experience. — And here, nothing is going to stop me saying a few hard things. *Who else is going to say them to the Germans?* — I shall not conceal it, they get in my way, I [have] a few too many reasons not to confuse my task with any old "Reichs-task." — Oh, these Germans! They already have such a lot on their conscience. Today Goethe and Scheffel, Bismarck and Treitschke, Beethoven and Wagner . . . *Cf. §2.*

160. *évangile des humbles]* "Gospel of the humble" {as described by Renan}.

161. *Trumpeter of Säckingen] by J. V. Scheffel; cf. TI "Forays" §1.*

162. *sly]* {N puns Liszt with the German *List*: "sly," "cunning," "wily."}

2

163. *N deleted the following fragmentary version of this section which is found on the reverse side of page 35 in the Pm:* [+ + +] they {are} the ruin of music — they themselves think they are thereby "of service to the ideal" . . . but that is their old game. For four centuries they have had all great cultural *malheurs* on their conscience, and always for the same reason — from their innermost *cowardice* before reality, which is also cowardice in the face of truth, from their untruthfulness that has become instinctive with them, from "idealism." — The Germans have cheated Europe out of the harvest, out of the *meaning* of the last great period, the Renaissance period: at a moment when a higher order of values, those *noble*, life-affirming values guaranteeing the future, had achieved victory even at the seat of the opposing values of *decline* — *and right down into the instincts of those already ensconced* — that catastrophe of a monk, Luther, reestablished the Church and, what is a thousand times worse, Christianity — Christianity, this [world calumny and rape of humanity] denial of the will to life turned into religion! — And at the end of the nineteenth century they are still holding Luther celebrations in Germany! — Twice the Germans, just when an upright, unambiguous and completely scientific way of thought

had been achieved with immense self-overcoming and courage, have known how to find hidden paths to the old "ideal," compromises between truth and the "ideal," in fact, formulas for the right to deny science, |for the right *to lies*|. Leibniz and Kant [are the two greatest stumbling blocks there have been until now on the path to |Europe's| intellectual integrity — they are subterranean counterfeiters and seducers] — these two greatest stumbling blocks there have ever been for intellectual integrity . . . |And finally| The Germans, [|even in this century|,] |at last| when [there was] [through an immense gift [of nature] of chance] a force majeure of genius and will became visible |at the bridge between two centuries of *décadence*|, strong enough to create a union out of Europe, a political and *economic* union, cheated Europe out of the meaning |out of the amazing meaning| of Napoleon's existence with their "Wars of Liberation," — in doing so, they have on their conscience everything that resulted and is still in force today, this *most culturally antagonistic* sickness and nonsense [of nationalism] called nationalism, this *névrose nationale*, this perpetuation of mini-states, of *small* politics [!] — they have |even| cheated Europe of its meaning, |of| its *reason* . . .

164. *Deutschland . . . Alles]* "Germany, Germany above all" {First line (and subsequent refrain) of the "Lied der Deutschen" ("Song of the Germans"), finally adopted as their national anthem in 1922.}

165. *Vischer] Friedrich Theodor Vischer* {(1807–87) was a German novelist and author of a three-volume work on aesthetics: *Aesthetik oder Wissenschaft des Schönen* {"Aesthetics or science of the beautiful"} (Leipzig: Mäcken, 1846). N might have in mind the following remark from Vischer's best known novel, *Auch Einer: Eine Reisebekanntschaft* ("Another one: A traveling acquaintance") (Stuttgart: Hallberger, 1879), 2:254: "Es ist wahr, die Renaissance war nur die eine Hälfte der Wiedergeburt, die andre die Reformation" ("It is true, the Renaissance was only one half of the rebirth, the other was the Reformation").}

166. *. . . And always . . . "idealism" . . .] Cf. N to Malwida von Meysenbug, 20 October 1888 {KGB III:5, 457–58}, cited in note 8 to "Why I Write Such Good Books" §1.*

167. *"Wars of Liberation"]* {The campaign fought by Prussian and Russian troops against Napoleon, 1813–15.}

168. *névrose nationale]* "national neurosis" {Underlined by N.}

169. *small politics]* {From 1815, when Germany emerged from the Congress of Vienna as a confederation (*Bund*) of thirty-nine states, to 1866, when the Prussians defeated Austria at the battle of Königgrätz, German politics had revolved round the question of *großdeutsch* or *kleindeutsch* politics, the former including and the latter excluding the Austrian portion of the *Bund*. After 1866, the Prussian *kleindeutsch* preference came into effect.}

3

170. *a mouse]* {Allusion to Horace, *Ars poetica* I, 139.}

171. *they are . . . veilmakers]* es sind Alles blosse Schleiermacher {N puns on the name of the German theologian Friedrich Schleiermacher: *Schleier* = "veil," *macher* = "maker."}

172. *With the . . . shallow.]* Cf. TI "Sayings" §27.

173. *German Kaiser]* Wilhelm II, cf. CW 18, 25[13].

174. *Prussian court]* Pm: in Bayreuth

175. *Herr von Treitschke]* Pm: Wagner

176. *Even . . . name . . .]* Mp XVI 3: But I will enumerate thirty French. — The German himself does not even know what depth is: I have met scholars who considered *Kant* deep . . . In Bayreuth, they consider Wagner deep . . . What people call deep in Germany is precisely that uncleanness toward oneself that I perceive at the core of every German. "Uncleanness" is itself a cautious expression for it . . . a euphemism . . . they think the French are shallow — — —

4

177. *N rewrote this section during his revision at the beginning of December. The earlier version of the Pm of mid-November still exists, as does a Pd. The latter is found on the reverse side of the page where the "Law Against Christianity" is written and reads as follows:* — And from which side did all the *major* obstacles, all [disorders of my |life's| powers] the fatalities in my life, originate up till now? Always from the German side |alone|. The German does me no good. |I have experienced signs of *délicatesse* from

Jews — never [not] yet from |a| Germans! —| The absurd lack of respect which is peculiar [to him] [to them] to the German |— [except before counterfeiters and the "Reich"] [except before the "Reich" and perhaps before certain counterfeiters] —| [his] [their] his complete lack of tact, of discretion for [*loftiness*] [loftiness] *loftiness* of the soul, for distance, in a word, [his] [their] his importunity with airs and graces, [his] [their] his step lacking *esprit* — the German has no feet at all, just legs — [his] [their] his psychological [*meanness*] meanness which has no finger for any |kind of| nuance, all this belongs to the most crippling and damaging things that blocked my path through life. You lower yourself by consorting with Germans: the German *puts* everything on the *same level* . . . I immediately climb up the wall when somebody with "trustworthy" eyes approaches me [. Indeed, at a time of great tension]; in times of great tension, a letter [to] for me from Germany is [like] sirocco [: it was one of my Genoese habits to take a warm bath afterwards. |[After every trip to G⟨ermany⟩ I brought a deep disgust] back with me, always somehow as though leaving my honor in the lurch.| Nearly all my winters in Nice were wasted, not through the proximity of Monte Carlo, [but] |always just| through [the |obstructive| proximity] proximity of German bovines [|and other anti-Semites|] [: that slows down my bowels — now I know that you can refute Germans with rhubarb]. Now I know how to refute Germans — [with rhubarb] *not* with reasons, with rhubarb . . .] — in Genoa I immediately took a bath afterwards . . . Does this happen to others? But it seems to me that consorting with Germans even ruins your character? I lose all mistrust, I feel the spore of loving thy neighbor mushrooming inside me — it has happened that to my deepest shame I have become *good-natured*. *Can* one sink any lower? . . . For me, you see, mischievousness is part of being happy |— I am no use when I am not being mischievous —| I find no little justification for existence in provoking tremendous stupidities against me. [|Hoohoohoohoohoo! —| You can guess who my victims are: the "beautiful souls," the "idealists"] |Oh, if I wanted to tell all! —| Finally you guess who my particular victims will be, the inflated geese |of both sexes|, the so-called "beautiful souls," in a word,

[all] the idealists, my fear and dread, toward whom I have not a penny's respect, [the only kind of human] [that whole kind of human calling themselves "idealist" —] this, the only kind of human that needs the *lie* as a precondition for existence, |and is even proud of the fact as well| . . . I am unrelenting with ["beautiful souls"] "idealists," they are my dancing bears, in half an hour I can make them "enthusiastic" about two opposite things, I egg them on to discover a "savior," a "martyr" in me, a [morality-monster] virtuous monster. — Another piece of mischief [another justification for existence] something else that makes my existence fortunate: I understand the art of writing |well-timed| *rude* letters to so-called ["]friends["], with purgative success: the complete falsity of [this] a so-called friendship — *or* "kinship" — [the words — or "kinship" — are first erased and then crossed out, and not by N; very probably by his sister Elisabeth] |suddenly| comes out [suddenly] at a completely unexpected point. Just now I am basking in the pleasure of just such a hoax |(there are three every year —)|: a so-called lady friend wrote to me that she would "nevertheless" continue to hold me in respect in view of the ["]heroic way["] I had borne my woes . . . So nothing, nothing, nothing had been understood! For eighteen years she had understood nothing about me! |[My "nearest" have always been furthest away from me! —] Is it part of the *curse* on me that my "nearest" must always be those furthest away? . . . | And this at a moment |when an unspeakable responsibility lies upon me,| when no word can be kind enough, no glance can be [kinder] respectful enough [to] for me . . . when I |have| [not a small] no small fear [that I have] for I have the fate of humanity [in my *hand*] on my shoulders . . . / [At least, I often sit around mischievously enough and just stare at my hands |to see| . . . |The Germans up till now have been the cup of hemlock in my life — nor would I deny| that they will kill me one day . . .]

On the same page there follow later fragmentary notes in connection with §5 of "Why I Write Such Good Books": Nor will you easily find such a juxtaposition of an inherently opaque problem, a [freer] [lighter hand] surer grasp, a more convincing clarity [before me, there had never been a |any| psychology of musicians. —] I

receive from all sides |for *The Case of Wagner*| genuine written
tributes [for a psychological masterpiece to which nobody [—]
apart from me is equal] as though for an excess of psychological
sagacity to which nobody apart from me [may be] is equal. / — I
know the elation of the young tiger, [which unites cunning with
power.] [which knows power only in conjunction with cunning]
which is unable to separate power from cunning. / The child is
necessary: the man is only ever means. [Without child, marriage
is merely concubinage] [Woman degenerates thereby —] |a woman
without child [is a] becomes a hermaphrodite| / Without child,
[there is] [every marriage becomes mere concubinage! —] there is
no marriage — just concubinage! — — / The child is necessary:
love is always only means. Without child, woman becomes a hermaphrodite. — / The child is necessary: the man is always only
means. / They all love me [:] [— a] familiar story. / Woman does
not redeem love, a child does that: the man is always mere means.
/ A woman without — — — She is a hermaphrodite / The [— —
—]: do the daughters of good society — — —

Mp XVI 5 Pm version of mid-November reads as follows: And
from which side did all the *major* obstacles, all the fatalities in my
life, originate? Always from the German side alone. The accursed
German anti-Semitism, this poisonous ulcer of *névrose nationale*,
intervened in my existence almost destructively at that decisive
juncture when not my fate, but the fate of humanity, was in question; I have to be grateful to the same element that my *Zarathustra* made its entry into the world as *indecent* literature — it had
an anti-Semite as publisher. In vain do I look around for a sign of
tact, *délicatesse* toward me: from Jews, yes, never yet from Germans. It is from long experience that I say that I paid for every
trip to Germany with a deep despondency. The absurd lack of
respect of this race — except when faced with power *and* [a few]
great ["Germans"] *[crossed out in pencil (by N?)]* counterfeiters —
their psychological meanness, which has no fingers for any kind
of nuances, their complete lack of discretion for *loftiness* of the
soul, for distance, in a word, their step lacking *esprit* — the German has no feet at all, just legs — their awkward importunity
with airs and graces, all this belongs to the most crippling and

damaging things that blocked my path through life. You lower yourself by consorting with Germans: the German *puts* everything on the *same level* . . . The Germans are by far the worst experience of my life; I have been left in the lurch for the past sixteen years, not just in terms of my philosophy but in terms of my acclaim. What respect can I have for the Germans when even my friends cannot distinguish between me and a liar like Richard Wagner? At its worst, people dance on the tightrope between me and the anti-Semitic *canaille* . . . And this at a time when an unspeakable responsibility lies upon me — when no word can be too kind, no look can be too full of respect toward me. For I carry the fate of humanity on my shoulder. — *Over this there is a later, penciled note:* Faced with a German book, you wash your hands [— — —]

178. *twenty-six]* {Actually, N was twenty-nine when he wrote *SE* in 1874.}

179. *(Third Unfashionable p. 71] Cf. SE §6; CW* 2, p. 219.

180. *"sound out the kidney"] nierenprüfe* {N sees himself as a "kidney-tester," an expression he coins from the phrase *auf Herz und Nieren prüfen*, meaning "to put something to the test," which in turn stems from Jeremiah 17:10: "I the Lord search the heart, I try the reins" (King James Bible), which in Luther's Bible is: "Ich der Herr kann das Herz ergründen und die Nieren prüfen." "Reins," archaic for the kidneys, was, according to the OED, associated following biblical use with "the seat of the feelings or affections." N first uses the metaphor of kidney-tester/*Nieren-prüfer* in *HL* §5; cf. *CW* 2, 119, line 21, where *der die Nieren prüft* is translated as "examines their innards." Cf. also *MM* §35; *JS* §§308 and 335; *Z* II "On the Land of Culture"; *CW* 14, 23[109]; and *CW* 17, 10[197].}

181. *with Germans . . .] At this point, according to Elisabeth Förster-Nietzsche, the so-called Paraguay Note should be inserted. This note is extant only in a copy by N's sister and runs as follows: [Instruction for the typesetter in Leipzig:]* to be inserted into the chapter *The Case of Wagner* Paragraph 4, after the words: "If I leave out my dealings with a few artists, above all Richard Wagner, I have not spent a single good hour with Germans . . . " /

Shall I spill the beans about my "German" [|so contradictory|] experiences? — Förster: long legs, blue eyes, blond (numbskull!) "German to the core," running with poison and gall up against anything that promises to have spirit and a future: Jewishness, vivisection etc. — but on his account, my sister left her "nearest" and plunged herself into a world full of dangers and mishaps. — Köselitz: smooth-tongued Saxon, occasionally a bungler, not to be moved from the spot, the embodiment of the law of gravity — but his music is first rank and runs along on light feet. — Overbeck: desiccated, embittered, defers to his wife, hands me the poisoned chalice of doubt and mistrust of myself as though he were Mime — but he turns out to be obligingly concerned about me and calls himself my "caring friend." Look at them all, three German types! *Canaille*! . . . Just think, if the most profound spirit of all the millennia were to appear among the Germans — — —

On the so-called "Paraguay Note": Podach in his edition (*Nietzsches Werke des Zusammenbruchs*, 314) renders the Paraguay Note in smaller letters. Champromis criticizes the procedure: "Seriously, one cannot publish a text as purportedly written by N when, apart from his sister, possibly no one has ever had sight of the original" (260). However, Podach correctly claims (199): "What is written on the note could by all means be the product of N's increased irritability toward his family and friends during certain periods of writing *Ecce Homo*." The Paraguay Note is unmistakably written in N's style; Förster-Nietzsche would never have managed to invent such sentences. Even so, the note can*not* be inserted into the *EH* text: 1. because there is no handwritten original to confirm its completeness and authenticity; 2. because it can be assumed with great certainty that N himself refused to insert the passage.

Regarding 1: In contrast to §3 of the chapter "Why I Am So Wise" (see above), we possess no drafts for the Paraguay Note which could give us some proof of its authenticity and integrity. Assuming that Förster-Nietzsche did have a genuine text, she could still have suppressed, modified, or inserted words or sentences according to her falsifying method (well known through

Schlechta's report on her edition of N's letters). The description of her whole — thoroughly irresponsible — procedure (see below, letter to Richter {22} June 1908) makes this supposition a virtual certainty.

Regarding 2: Elisabeth Förster-Nietzsche wrote to Raoul Richter, the first editor of *EH*, on 22 June 1908: " . . . after the death of my husband, I found an unspeakably sad and defamatory letter of my brother's that had been addressed to my husband, and a further 5 pages or so . . . which pained me considerably because they were directed against my husband and the Wagners; I still remember a few particulars which I shall relate to you. Two of the pages bore the instruction that they were to be integrated into a chapter, and my philological conscience did not allow me to destroy them, even though the content of one page was in part very painful to me . . . I brought these two pages of additions back to Germany in the original, and handed them to my mother, who as legal guardian at that stage had sole rights over the papers, and as I remember, the two pages still existed when I went back to Paraguay . . . My mother and I were entirely of one mind that we wanted to destroy the pages with defamatory contents which my brother had written at the onset of his illness . . . And yet the two pages I had brought back from Paraguay were completely clear and so I made a copy of both before I went to Paraguay, in fact I wrote out one of them on the other half of the original page and I copied everything exactly from the original half sheet written by my brother himself." Apparently N's mother later destroyed all "pages with defamatory content," among them the Paraguay Note; the other Paraguay page, belonging to *NCW* ("We Antipodes"), was not burned by his mother (in fact it is still extant). In this case, as in many others, it is not worth going into detail to prove the lack of credibility and contradictions in Elisabeth Förster-Nietzsche's account. The other Paraguay page is *now* in Mp XVI 5; N wrote preliminaries to *EH* "Why I Am So Clever" §6 on its reverse side as well as the already cited draft letter to Cosima Wagner, end of December 1888. Since N did *not* cross out the writing (on the reverse side), we can state with certainty that the whole page, in spite of its directive for the printer on the front side, was *not* destined for publication (as in other similar instances). Regarding the text itself (on the front side), we should note that N used this for *EH* III HAH §6, and duly dispatched it to Leipzig. From this we can conclude that the first side of the page in Mp XVI 5 was nothing more than one of N's rejected (and elsewhere recycled) textual drafts, in other words a variant of *NCW*. If N really did send the page to Paraguay, he did not do it by mistake. It is more likely that in the first few days of his mental collapse — when he was "scribbling away" in a manner which "left nothing to be desired" (letter to Burckhardt on 5 or 6 January 1889 {*KGB* III:5, 577–79}; it continues: "the post office is five paces away, I post the letters myself") — he also wrote the "unspeakably sad and defamatory letter" to his anti-Semitic brother-in-law, Bernhard Förster, and — as a kind of accompaniment — sent along other pieces of his writing such as the discarded variant to *NCW*. If that were so, then the note to *EH* "The Case of Wagner" §4 on Förster, Peter Gast, and Overbeck would be another text N had kept in Turin, discarded, and finally sent to Paraguay.

182. *goose of the Capitol]* {The cackling of geese alerted the Romans to the planned attack by Gauls on the Capitol in Rome in 390 BCE.}

183. *decided about me]* N wrote "canaille" after this phrase, then deleted it.

184. *Ten years . . . psychologist?]* written around 20 November 1888; cf. N to Brandes on this date {*KGB* III:5, 482–83}. A variant of notebook Z II 1, 26 reads: Who then has had the initial courage, delicacy of instinct, discrimination for the extraordinary and unusual, in order to deem it *proper* to talk about me in public? The excellent Dane Georg Brandes who gave a lecture series last winter on "the German philosopher Nietzsche." Which of my friends has had the courage for that . . . ?

185. *Just now . . . shoulder. —]* Deleted in the Pm by unidentified hand; probably another passage (now lost) was to be placed here, which N mentions as already published in a draft letter to Cosima Wagner {dated around 25 December 1888 (*KGB* III:5, 551)}: Malwida also turns up as Kundry . . . ; cf. N to Gast, {25} November 1888 {*KGB*

III:5, 489}: Recently it occurred to me to introduce Malwida as a *Kundry* who *laughs* at a decisive point in *Ecce Homo* . . . ; *according to legend, Kundry laughed at Christ on his way to Calvary (cf. Wagner, Parsifal, Act II).*

At the end of this section there was a further passage, deleted by N: See you, my fellow Germans! *for we will see each other again* . . . Long live the Triple Alliance . . . Otherwise — oh, I would willingly give my life for this |other| wise! . . . — One word of truth — and [the] all past is *expiated* . . .

A text left behind in Turin, found in Mp XVI 5, 32 and bearing the section number 5 was probably intended as the conclusion for the chapter on The Case of Wagner. This sheet incidentally has all kinds of preliminary jottings and notes to EH on both sides of the page, which N did not delete. This provides proof that N did not send the sheet to Leipzig; it remained with him in Turin. However, it is not impossible that N might have sent a copy to Leipzig. In that case, either Gast or one of N's relatives must have destroyed it. The sheet, which reveals traces of having been burned, is published in CW 18, 25[7].

Why I Am a Destiny

    1. *See the introductory remarks to EH on the emergence of this chapter, particularly the ending of EH. The fragments on* grand politics *show a close affinity with this chapter: cf. CW 18, 25[1, 6, 14, 19]; the preliminary draft is found in Z II, 1, 17: Why I Am a Destiny. / 1. / To my displeasure I am not at liberty to say what follows in a tone that is friendly to humans — I even fear that I shall have to be serious. Still, the apple is sour. Not that there is no compensation for its sourness and even more than a compensation. But to grasp that you would have to have already learned how to look* round the corner, *as I can — precisely so that your glance can anticipate the illustrious country to which at first a* crooked *path leads, a path through "fields of misfortune," as my friend Empedocles has just whispered to me {cf. Empedocles, fragment 121} . . . So for a moment let us at least make the attempt to be* serious: *in the last resort it is only a sin against good taste,* not *against virtue . . . 2. / I sometimes wonder why people do not ask me. Basically, there are a few too many reasons to ask*

me what the name of Zarathustra actually means when I, the first *immoralist*, speak it: for what makes up the prodigious unique-ness of that ancient Persian in history is — everybody knows — the exact opposite. — — —

I

2. *Cf. CW 18, 25[6] §1.*

3. *only after . . . again.]* Cf. *Gast to N, 25 October 1888* {*KGB* III:6, 337}: "Only from you are there hopes again . . . "

4. *grand politics]* {Cf. *CW* 18, 25[6] §2.}

2

5. *Cf. CW 18, 25[6] §2.*

6. *— and . . . creative kind.]* Cf. *Z II "On Self-Overcoming."*

3

7. *Cf. the notes to "Foreword" §4 and "Thus Spoke Zarathustra"* §1.

8. *Persian virtue]* {Herodotus in his *History* describes the Persian-Greek Wars from 499 to 479 BCE. One reason he gives in the first book for the Persians' dominance was their education for boys, who between the ages of five and twenty learned only to be truth-ful, good archers, and good horsemen.}

4

9. *niaiserie]* "foolishness"

10. *homines optimi]* "best of men"

11. *wrong coastlines . . . measures]* {The analogy here is to coastal navigation.}

12. *Good people taught . . . good people."]* Cf. *Z III "On Old and New Tablets"* §28.

13. *Good people — they . . . all.]* Cf. *Z III "On Old and New Tablets"* §26.

5

14. *"to float . . . futures"]* Cf. *Z II "On Human Prudence."*

15. *Your souls are so . . .] mit eurer Seele* {The use of the instru-mental preposition *mit* indicates that greatness is being encoun-tered rather than being located within.}

16. *excellence] Güte* {N means *Güte* in its principal sense of quality or excellence, not in the sense of kindness or benevolence; cf. Christoph Fr. Grieb, *Englisch-Deutsches und Deutsch-Englisches Wörterbuch* (Stuttgart: Neff, 1885), 2:404.}

17. *You most superior . . . excellence . . .] Cf. Z II "On Human Prudence."*

6, 7, 8

18. *Sections 22–23 of the October Version make up one single variant to these three sections of "Why I Am a Destiny." Printed below, because it has more variants, is the complete text and not the text of the first foreword (which constituted sections 5, 6, and 7 of the intermediate draft). It should not be forgotten that §21 of the October Version provides the variants to the chapter on Dawn (see relevant notes to that chapter):* 22 / This will not prevent me from drawing the following conclusion *here.* I invented the word *immoralist* for myself, I believe that I have shown a *height,* a breadth of vision, a hitherto completely monstrous psychological inscrutability, by feeling morality to be *beneath* me. Who before me has climbed into the *caverns* out of which the poisonous fumes of the "ideal" spew forth! Who even dared to suspect *that* there are caverns? Who before me was a *psychologist* at all among philosophers and not, rather, their opposite, "higher swindler," "idealist"? It can be a curse, at any rate it is a destiny, to be the first here — *for you are also the first to despise . . . Disgust* is my danger . . . I invented the name *immoralist* for myself. I am not sufficiently aware of whether anyone one at all has had thoughts on the matter. Such things pop into the thoughtless ears of my contemporaries — and pop out again. I would love to *nail back* these ears a little, until the pain made clear what I want — *to be heard* . . . What makes me stand out is my having *discovered* morality for the first time and, consequently, being in need of a word *against* it that would have the sense of a declaration of war. Morality appears to me to be the greatest uncleanness humanity has on its conscience, a depravity become instinct, a counterfeiting *in psychologicis* to the point of crime. Morality appears to me to be *crime itself against life.* Millennia, peoples, the first and the last, philosophers and old

women — in this respect they deserve each other. The human was hitherto the "moral being," a curiosity beyond compare — and, as a "moral being," more absurd, mendacious, vain, frivolous, *more disadvantageous to himself* than even the greatest despiser of humanity could dream up. Morality — the wickedest form of the will to the lie, the real Circe of humanity: that which has *ruined* it. It is *not* error as error that appalls me at this spectacle, *not* the millennia-long lack of "good will," breeding, decency, cleanliness in the spiritual: it is the lack of what is natural, it is the ghastly fact that *anti-nature* itself received the highest honors as morality and stayed posted up as *law* over humanity! . . . To be wrong to such an extent, *not* as an individual, *not* as a people or race, but as humanity — what does that point to? That people teach contempt for the nethermost instincts of life, that they teach others to feel something impure in the precondition for life, sexuality, that they see the principle of evil in the deepest necessity for the *flourishing* of life, selfishness — the very word is slanderous — that they see in the typical sign of decline, instinctive contradictoriness, in "selflessness," in loss of the center of gravity, in "depersonalization" and in "loving thy neighbor," essentially a *higher* value, what am I saying! *value in itself* ! . . . Well? might humanity itself be in *décadence*? Was it always? . . . What is certain is that only *décadence* values have been *taught* to it as the supreme value⟨s⟩. The morality of unselfing is the morality of decline p{a}r excellence — it lays bare a will to the end, it *denies* life at its deepest foundation . . . Here, the possibility would remain open that humanity itself is not in decline, but just a parasitic form of human who has lied his way up to being its arbiter of values . . . And in fact, that is *my* insight: the teachers, the *leaders*[, the religions] of humanity, were *décadents* one and all — *therefore* the revaluation of all values into hostility to life — *therefore* morality! . . . . *Écrasez l'infâme!* . . . Definition of morality. Morality — the idiosyncrasy of *décadents* with the ulterior motive of taking their revenge on life. I prize this definition. — *Qui chante son mal l'enchante*: {He who chants ("sings") his pain, enchants it}: a Provençal said that. [*Dixi.* {I said.}] *Id quod feci* {Which I did}. — / 23 / Have I been understood? The *unmasking* of morality is an event with no equal, a true catastrophe: you either live *before* it or *after* it. The light-ning bolt of truth hit what had stood highest up until then: who-ever understands *what* was destroyed there might care to see if anything at all remains in his hands afterwards. Whoever uncov-ers morality has uncovered at the same time the whole worthless-ness of all values that people believe in: he sees in the most exalted types of human, those pronounced holy, nothing venera-ble any more — he sees in them the most doom-laden form of monstrosities, doom-laden because they *were fascinating* . . . He sees in the concept "God" everything harmful, slanderous, poison-ous, covertly blood-sucking, the actual *deadly animosity* toward life brought into a horrendous union. The concept "*beyond*" invented to devalue this world, so as to recognize no goal, no final ratio-nality in the real world. The concept "*soul*," "*spirit*," and ulti-mately even "*immortal soul*" invented to shame the body. The concept "*sin*" invented to undermine trust in the fundamental instincts of life. In the value of what is "*selfless*," what is actually a sign of sickness is made into a stamp of value, into "duty," into "virtue," into the norm of godliness itself. — *Have I been under-stood*? . . . Anyone who can explain these things is a force majeure, like destiny, he *is* destiny itself, he breaks [in his hand] the history of humanity into two halves — into a *before* and an *after* . . . *This was followed by §24 of the October Version: cf. the notes to §1 of the chapter on Thus Spoke Zarathustra. The conclusion of §7 of the first foreword has a few variations: 7. /* — Have I been understood? Anyone who explain morality is a force majeure, a destiny — he breaks the history of humanity into two pieces. — This should not hinder me from being the most cheerful, halcyon human, I even have a right to this: who has ever done humanity a greater service? — *I bring it the gladdest possible tidings* . . . / *Friedrich Nietzsche. Followed by an instruction for the printer:* Then a page with just these words: / *How one becomes what one is* / Turin, 15 October, 1888

8

19. *vampirism]* {Cf. *JS* §372.}

20. *folie circulaire]* "circular madness" {Now considered a bipo-lar disorder.}

21. *Écrasez l'infâme!]* "Crush the infamous thing!" {Voltaire's slogan against the Christian Church.}

Dionysus Dithyrambs

In the summer of 1886, N compiled an index of works that he described as being "in preparation." He added this index to a compilation of works that were listed "by year of publication" on the fourth page of the cover of *BGE*. These were:

The Will to Power. Attempt at a Revaluation of All Values. In
   Four Books.
Eternal Recurrence. Sacred Dances and Processionals.
Songs of Prince Vogelfrei.

Only the last title made it into print, one year later, as an addendum to the second edition of *The Joyful Science.*

In the summer of 1888, when N gave up the publication of a work entitled *The Will to Power,* he collected his hitherto unused poetic fragments, especially from his Zarathustra notebooks, into a new notebook, W II 10, which he then used for his last poems, composed through the end of 1888: "The Sun Is Sinking," "Among Birds of Prey," "On the Poverty of the Richest Man," "Fame and Eternity," and "The Beacon."

N added "Last Will" (which originated in 1883) to the five poems discussed above and then transcribed a clean copy of them all on large sheets of folio paper (Mp X VIII 1). A number of prospective titles for this collection of poems can be found in Notebook W II 10 (cf. *CW* 18, 20[162–68]; for 20[167], cf. the advance notification on the *BGE* cover page cited above).

When the first draft of *EH* was completed, no later than mid-November 1888, the title of the poems, "The Songs of Zarathustra," which N mentioned in his prologue to *EH*, had also been determined. In a draft letter to an unknown publisher {*KGB* III:5, 495}, originating from this period, N offers *six* "Songs of Zarathustra" for publication. N himself dated the draft letter "Turin, 27 November 1888." From this point forward, specifically from mid-December 1888 to the beginning of January 1889, the fate of the "Songs of Zarathustra" was closely linked to the history of the origins of *EH* and *NCW*.

N sent the printed manuscript of *NCW* to Leipzig on 15 December; he wrote to Peter Gast (16 December {*KGB* III:5, 527}): " . . . Something appears at the conclusion, of which even friend Köselitz has no inkling: a song of Zarathustra's (or whatever you want to call it . . .), with the title *On the Poverty of the Richest Man* — you know, a little seventh beatitude and an eighth as well . . . *music* . . . " Yet by 22 December, N no longer wanted to have *NCW* published; he wrote to Gast {*KGB* III:5, 545–46}: "We do not want to publish the work N. contra W. The 'Ecce' contains all that is important even regarding this relationship . . . Perhaps I shall also incorporate the Song of Zarathustra as well — it is called *On the Poverty of the Richest Man* — . As an interlude between 2 main sections . . . " Three days later, when N gave his approval of the first twenty-four pages of his publication, he appeared to want to accept the prospect that this work would be published.

On 29 December a further song of Zarathustra, "Fame and Eternity," was sent from Turin to Leipzig. In the draft letter to Peter Gast that was dated 30 December 1888 {*KGB* III:5, 566}, N mentions this poem: "Yesterday I sent my *non plus ultra*, entitled *Fame and Eternity*, composed beyond all seven heavens, to the printer. It forms the conclusion of *Ecce Homo*. — It will kill anyone who reads it unprepared."

Between the end of the year 1888 and 2 January 1889, N again changed his instructions concerning how the two "Songs of Zarathustra" should be handled and demanded their return from Leipzig. In these final days, when the signs of N's mental collapse were increasing, what became known as the *Dionysus Dithyrambs* emerged. N prepared the printer's manuscript (D 24) during this brief period of time. The first page bears the title *Dionysus Dithyrambs*, and the last page contains an index composed by N himself in which *nine* poems are listed, i.e., the above-mentioned *six* "Songs of Zarathustra" and three additional dithyrambs, which are none other than a slightly revised version of three poems from *Z* IV, namely: "The Song of Melancholy," now with the title "Just a Fool! Just a Poet!"; "Among Daughters of the Desert" (this title remained unchanged); and, under the title of "Ariadne's Lament," the "Lament" from §1 in the chapter "The Sorcerer."

The fact that the final copying of *DD* took place between 1 and 3 January can be documented by a kind of preliminary draft that N wrote for the final dedication of *DD* to the French poet and novelist Catulle Mendès: "Eight Inedita and inaudita presented to my friend and satyr, the composer of Isoline: may he present my gift to humanity / N Dionysus / Turin, on 1 January, 1889."

Podach makes an attempt to decipher this draft, where all N's deletions are reproduced, but — working from preconceived assumptions regarding N's unreliability at the time, even as a writer — he proposes the absurd reading "Iinedita und inauditia"; in the case of "Iinedita" it has to do with N correcting the original "inedita" to "Inedita" (without deleting the small "i" after the initial capital letter "I"); in the case of "inauditia," Podach appears not to have known that the offset dot on the "i" in N's handwriting was something quite normal (one could offer countless examples from earlier manuscripts written by the "healthy" N where a similar shift has taken place); so in this case N places the dot on the "i" after the letter "t" of the word "inaudita," and because the cross on the "t" sinks a bit downwards, Podach reads the words as "inauditia."

Nevertheless, Podach is quite justified in his comments: "In Turin, Nietzsche was not bound to a particular view of Catulle Mendès. He addressed him as the 'composer of Isoline.' Mendès had only been called that since 26 December, 1888. *Isoline* had its premiere in the Renaissance-Theatre in Paris: *Isoline, conte des fées, en 10 tableaux* {"Isoline, a fairy tale in ten tableaus"}, by Catulle Mendès, music by André Messager. Without question, N learned of this through his favorite newspaper. The review appeared in the 31 December edition of the *Journal des Débats*, which was printed in Paris on the afternoon of 30 December. The paper could be bought in Turin a day later" (*Nietzsches Werke des Zusammenbruchs*, 372–73). Yet the dedication to Mendès takes up only the upper half of the small page. The lower part of the page is covered with N's almost illegible lettering: it concerns the most important change in the dithyramb "Among Daughters of the

Desert," e.g., the last inserted verse, which is not preserved in *Z* IV. That proves not only — as Podach says — that "the Dionysus Dithyrambs were not yet ready at that time [*on 1 January 1889*]," but also that N had only just started his transcription, since "Among Daughters of the Desert" is the *second* dithyramb, and the dithyrambs in *Pm* follow in order (the *Pm* is not made up of loose sheets of paper). Now, the fact that N speaks of "Eight Inedita and inaudita" (he had also first written "seven" and not "six," as opposed to Podach's deciphering of N's deletions) is consistent with the postcard that N sent to Leipzig on the same day (1 Jan. 1889 {*KGB* III:5, 570}), where he demanded the return of "Fame and Eternity" from the publishers. On 2 January {*KGB* III:5, 571}, he sent a telegram, also demanding the return of "On the Poverty of the Richest Man": "Manuscripts of the two concluding poems." For the first time, there were *nine* dithyrambs. In fact, "Fame and Eternity" was quickly returned by the publishers in Leipzig, and N placed it in the *DD* manuscript where Overbeck then subsequently found it. However, C. G. Naumann held back "On the Poverty of the Richest Man," since he apparently still hoped to persuade N to publish *NCW*, this in the face of N's unmistakeable missive of 2 January which read: "Circumstances have completely overtaken the little work Nietzsche contra W: send me the concluding poem at once, as well as the last poem I sent to you, '*Fame and Eternity*.'"

Franz Overbeck found the page with the final dedication to Catulle Mendès among Nietzsche's Turin papers, not, however, in the manuscript of the *Dithyrambs*. It reads: "In wanting to do something that will be of unending benefit to humanity, I give it the gift of my dithyrambs. I place them in the hands of the composer of Isoline, the greatest and foremost satyr alive today — and not just today . . . / Dionysus."

The *DD* must have been ready for printing on 3 January 1889. N communicated the event to Cosima Wagner in one of the "mad notes" that are still preserved in Bayreuth and that were made famous by Curt von Westernhagen in his Wagner-Biography (1956). The address "Madame Cosima feu Wagner / Bayreuth / Germany" is on the envelope of the dithyramb note. The postmark is: "Torino/

Ferrovia/3. 1. 89." The text reads: "I have been told that, a few days ago, a certain holy clown finished the Dionysus Dithyrambs . . . "

Just a Fool! Just a Poet!

1. *Cf. Z IV "The Song of Melancholy" and the accompanying notes.*
2. *Just a fool! Just a poet!] Pm*: From the Seventh Solitude

Among Daughters of the Desert

1. *Cf. the same-named chapter in Z IV {CW 7} and the accompanying notes.*
2. *darlings] Freundinnen* {He is here addressing the women.}
3. *European . . . under the palm trees.]* {Parodic quote after Ferdinand Freiligrath's (1810–76) poem "Europäer unter Palmen" ("Europeans under the palm trees") (Sommer 2, 669.)}
4. *Selah.]* {Thought to be a musical direction in the Old Testament Psalms.}
5. *whale,]* {Jonah 2:1 (also Matthew 12:40).}
6. *Dudu]* {Odalisque in Byron's *Don Juan* (1819).}
7. *Suleika]* {Allusion to the main female character in Goethe's collection of poems *West-östlicher Divan* (*West-Eastern Divan*) (1819).}
8. {We use the pronoun "it" in this stanza instead of "she" to reflect N's use of an extended simile.}
9. *Amen!]* {Apart from the words "as a European," the last four lines ("And here I stand . . . Amen") are identical to Martin Luther's pronouncement at the Diet of Worms in 1521.}
10. *gazes] Pd*: sits
11. *brown] Pd*: *followed by* and [is insatiable] its
12. *lust:] Pd*: desert:
13. *desert, you are] Pd*: desert and
14. *The desert grows . . . death . . .]* Cf. CW *15, 28[4].*

Last Will.

1. *Cf.* CW *14, 20[11].*
2. *piercing glances] Blicke* {We added the attributive adjective "piercing" to mark "glances" as a noun.}

Among Birds of Prey.

1. *Among Birds of Prey.]* Sd: At the [Hillside] Abyss

2. *still love the abyss,]* Sd: wish to befriend the abyss,

3. *Who]* Pd: Woe! And who

4. *hanged man! —]* Gehängter; Pd: hanged man (*Gehenkter*) {an older spelling}

5. *Nimrod]* Cf. Genesis 10:8–10.

6. *divided]* Zweisam {N is playing with the word "alone," *einsam*.}

7. *among a hundred . . . every frost]* Pd: [Locked up in] harnessed to a hundred memories, bleeding from every wound / trembling at every breath

8. *You who are hanging yourself!]* Selbsthenker! {In the eighteenth century, this was a word used for people who committed suicide by hanging themselves.}

9. *Nimrod most cruel! . . . sickened by the serpent's venom;]* Pd: you murderer of God / you seducer of the purest woman / you friend of evil / alone now! / divided in knowledge! / Among a hundred memories / harnessed / wearied by every wound / chilled by every frost / strangled in your own noose — / *The man who knows himself! The man who hangs himself!* / What were you doing when you tied yourself / to heartless knowledge! / What were you doing when you lured yourself / with the snake of [the] your own knowledge?

10. *a prisoner . . . pit]* {Cf. CW 14, 10[16].}

11. *A sick man . . . pit]* Pd: A prisoner who drew the shortest straw: / stooped over, working / In damp, dark pits: / a scholar

12. *stiff . . . corpse — ,]* Crossed out in Sd: Like a corpse / devoured while still alive / infested with worms while still alive /

13. *Lurking . . . mind! . . .]* Pd: He cowers, he lurks: / he can no longer stand straight. / He became deformed in his grave / [A] this deformed mind: / How could he ever *rise again*?

14. *a hermit without God, sharing quarters with the devil]* {N plays on the word *Einsiedler* (hermit, someone who lives alone) with the neologism *Zweisiedler* (someone sharing quarters). We have not been able to capture this pun in English. Cf. N's play with *einsam/zweisam* in Z I "On the New Idol."}

15. *And not long . . . arrogance! . . .] Pd*: Is this not Zarathustra's seducer? / The hermit with no god? / Sharing quarters with the devil, / The scarlet prince of darkness?

The Beacon

1. *This flame . . . in front of myself.] Pd*: This flame with belly of lightest gray / which bends its neck up toward ever purer heights, / my snake upright in its impatience: / this is the beacon I placed [for myself on high mountains] before myself.

2. *My soul itself . . . above his head.] Pd*: What made [me] Zarathustra flee from people — / What drove [me] him to make [my] his steep escape from any mainland? / Seeking for new solitudes, [I] he aimed his casts above his head / no ocean [was itself enough] was solitude enough for him: / the island itself drove me up the mountain / I was a flame on top of the mountain / Here [I blaze] Zarathustra as a quiet glow

The Sun Is Sinking.

1. *I welcome . . . sudden winds,] Pd*: I laud your coming, / you sudden winds, bringing comfort

2. *The air . . . why? —] Pd*: the air moves cool and pure; / already the night leers / at me with a twisted /seductive look: / already, too, the brave heart despairs / and asks: why?

3. *The cliff's breath . . . nap] Pd*: the cliff's breath is warm: / the sun slept on it by day

4. *The brown abyss still] Sd*: The abyss itself still

5. *Already your eyes . . . white seas . . .] Pd*: Already the tear-drops of dew are spilling forth / Already [streams] runs from half-dimmed eye / [Dying day] Across white seas, last of your [last] love, / purple lingering bliss / [Silently across white seas.]

6. *Storm and voyage —] Pd*: Voyage and goal

7. *outward . . .] Sd*: out into nothingness.

Ariadne's Lament.

1. *Ariadne's Lament.] Cf. Z IV "The Magician" §1 and the accompanying notes.*

2. *Ariadne's Lament.] Pm*: Unloved . . . (Ariadne's Song.)

3. *my thought] Gedanke* {The word "my" is not in the German, but we have added it to remove ambiguity between the nominal and participial forms in English.}

4. *give yourself . . . surrender to me! . . .]* {N's wordplay is between giving yourself (*sich geben*) and surrendering or surrendering yourself (*sich ergeben*).}

5. *tortures!] Crossed out in Pm following "tortures!": For the last of all lonely people . . .*

Fame and Eternity.

1. *someone who lies in wait for a long time — ,] Pd*: someone who lies in wait — , / a cave

2. *— shaking the entrails of the mountain itself . . .] Pd*: shaking the entrails / of the mountain itself [itself] / out of fear . . .

3. *weaklings] Pd: fearful ones*

4. *all] Alle* {N capitalizes the pronoun here and in the first verse of the next stanza.}

5. *thrives on] lebt von*

6. *I want to . . . transgression] Cf. CW 18, 20[112].*

7. *My ambition . . . of the low . . .] Pd*: With throttled ambition / when I am among them / I lust to be among the last of them

8. *Signpost of necessity . . . figures!] Pd*: Signpost of necessity! / Tablet of eternal figures! my burning heart cools itself / on your voiceless beauty

9. *For I love . . . eternity! — —] Cf. Z III "The Seven Seals (Or: The Yes- and Amen-Song)."*

On the Poverty of the Richest Man.

1. *On the Poverty of the Richest Man.] Pd*: Zarathustra Milks the Cows.

2. *Ten years . . . desert!] Pd*: This has lasted for ten years: / no drop of rain reaches me anymore, / no moist [breath] wind, no breath of love / — a land without rain / [I ask my soul] Now I ask my wisdom, / not to dry out in this drought: / to stream over, [dampen even the land] be a spring within yourself / let yourself be rain in the yellow [desert] wilderness

3. "more light] {*"mehr Licht"* ("More light") were reputed to be Goethe's last words.}

4. *Once I told . . . land.]* Pd: back then I said, "let there be light!" / Now I lure them so that they come: / come, you clouds! let there be night, / make everything around me dark / with your wings / hide me, you beautiful night wings!

5. *lion's mane]* Locken {*Deutsches Wörterbuch von Jacob und Wilhelm Grimm* (Leipzig, 1854–1961), 12:1104: *Locken* can mean the mane or the thick hair on the neck of an animal. N's word-play also extends to *Locken* in the sense of a "lure" or "bait."}

6. *Today . . . hedgehog.]* Pd: Today stretch out your hand to small coincidences, / be nice to whatever is unwelcome: / You shouldn't raise your quills against your fate, / unless you are a hedgehog.

7. *But it . . . happy man.]* Pd: you are like a cork, / made for the light / bobbing on the surface of all seas: / they call you a happy man

8. *Who are my father and mother?] Wer sind mir Vater und Mutter?* {"*Wer ist mir Vater und Mutter?*" is Siegfried's question to Mime in the opening scene of Wagner's *Siegfried.*}

9. *silent laughter] Pd from:* loving laughter{;} *from:* laughter, what is nice

10. *Is Prince . . . mother?]* Pd: is it not cruel fate/ and loving laughter?

11. *a wind . . . mountains —] Note in Pd:* moist with tenderness / a wind that thaws

12. *Its happiness . . . to me:] Note in Pd:* on the widest slowest stairway / to his happiness

13. *to me:] after which was crossed out:* its gaze moves upward

14. *goblets filled to the brim]* übervoller Scheuern {The more usual rendering is "barns," as in "barns too full" but the Grimms' *Deutsches Wörterbuch* 14:2619 identifies an alternative meaning of "cup" or "goblet," which works better with the liquid metaphors of the poem.}

15. *You sacrifice . . . anymore . . .] Note in Pd:* he sacrifices himself, this makes him rich: / he gives, gives of himself: / he neither spares nor loves himself — / great agony / compels him, the agony of goblets filled to the brim {or barns too full}

Nietzsche Contra Wagner

The germ of this work is contained in the letter that N wrote to Ferdinand Avenarius on 10 December 1888 {*KGB* III:5, 517–18}. In this letter, N cites the passages in his works after 1876 that are supposed to verify his opposition to Wagner: "The contrast of a *décadent* and someone who creates out of a surplus of strength, that is, a *Dionysian* nature, . . . is indeed palpable between us (a contrast expressed in about 50 passages in my books, e.g., in *Joyful Science* pp. 312ff. *[= JS 370, then the section* "We Antipodes" *in NCW]*) . . . A small handful of passages: *Human, All Too Human* (— written more than 10 years ago) vol. 2, p. 62: *décadence* and Berninism in Wagner's style *[= MM 144 {CW 4, 61–62}]; HAH* II, p. 51: his nervous sensuality *[= MM 116 {CW 4, 52–53}]; HAH* II, p. 60: degeneration in rhythm *[= MM 134 {CW 4, 58–59}, then §1 of NCW* "Wagner as Danger"]; *HAH* II, p. 76: Catholicism of feeling, his "heroes" physiologically impossible *[= MM 171 {CW 4, 72–74}, then the section of NCW* "A Music with No Future"]. *The Wanderer and His Shadow*, p. 93: against *espressivo* at any price *[WS 165 {CW 4, 220–21}, then §2 of NCW* "Wagner as Danger"]. *Dawn*, p. 225: Wagner's skill in deceiving the laity *[= D 255 {CW 5, 174–76}]. Joyful Science* p. 309: Wagner the actor through and through, even as musician *[= JS 368, then NCW* "Where I Object"]. *JS*, p. 110: Wagner admirable at refining sensual pain *[= JS 87, then NCW* "Where I Admire"]. *Beyond Good and Evil*, p. 221: Wagner belonging to *sick* Paris, actually a late French Romantic, like Delacroix, like Berlioz, all fundamentally possessing a *fond* {"core"} of incurability and, consequently, fanatics of expression {*= BGE 256, CW 8, 163–66*}."

The next day, 11 December 1888 {*KGB* III:5, 523–24}, N wrote a letter to Carl Spitteler, proposing he serve as the editor of a work "equal in composition and scope to the 'Case of Wagner' [. . .], consisting of only 8 fairly long but very select extracts from my writings, entitled: / Nietzsche *Contra* Wagner / Documents / from Nietzsche's Writings." The following passages were specified as sections for such a work in the letter to Spitteler:

1. *Two Antipodes* (*JS* pp. 312–16) *[= JS 370, then the section* "We Antipodes" *in NCW]*

2. *An Art with No Future* (*HAH* II pp. 76–78) *[= MM 171 {CW* 4, 72–74}, *then the section "A Music with No Future" in NCW]*

3. *Barocco* (*HAH* II pp. 62–64) *[= MM 144 {CW* 4, 61–62}]*

4. *Espressivo at any price* (*WS* p. 93; *HAH* II, last half) *[= WS 165 {CW* 4, 220–21}, *then the section 'Wagner as Danger" 2 in NCW]*

5. *Actor Wagner, Nothing More* (*JS* pp. 309–11) *[= JS 368, then the section "Where I Object" in NCW]*

6. *Wagner Belongs to France* (*BGE* pp. 220–24) *[= BGE 256 {CW* 8, 166}, *then just that section's final poem as the section "Wagner as Apostle of Chastity" 1 in NCW]*

7. *Wagner as Apostle of Chastity* (*GM* pp. 99–105) *[= GM III, §§2–3 {CW* 8, 286–89}, *then the section "Wagner as Apostle of Chastity" 2, 3 in NCW]*

8. *Nietzsche's Break with Wagner* (*HAH* II Preface VII–VIII) *[= HAH II Preface §§3–4 {CW* 4, 5–7}, *then the section "How I Freed Myself from Wagner" 1, 2 in NCW]*

On 12 December, however, N decided to edit the writing himself, making Spitteler's intended refusal of the original plan superfluous. N now wrote another plan for it (W 11 10, 98):

Nietzsche *Contra* Wagner / Documents / of a Psychologist.

f. W 1. *Astral-friendship [= JS 279]*

f W. 2. Where I Admire *[= JS 87, then in NCW with the same title]*

f W 3. Where I Object *[= JS 368, then in NCW with the same title]*

M. 4. Wagner as *Danger*
   for rhythm 59 *[= MM 134, then the section "Wagner as Danger" 1 in NCW]*
   in performance W. 93 *[= WS 165, then the section "Wagner as Danger" 2 in NCW]*

M. 5. A Music with No Future *[= MM 171, then with the same title in NCW]*

f W. 6. Why Wagner Said Stupid Things About Himself *[= JS 99]*

f W. 7 [We] Two Antipodes *[= JS 370, then the section "We Antipodes" in NCW]*

J. 8. Why Wagner Belongs to France *[N was perhaps already thinking about the section "Where Wagner Belongs," i.e., = BGE 254, 256 (without the latter's final poem?)]*

M. 9. How I Freed Myself from Wagner *[= HAH II Preface §§3–4, then the two sections with the same title in NCW]*

f W. 10. Why My Taste Changed *[= JS Preface §§3–4, then the "Epilogue" in NCW]*

While writing his "Documents," N made the following additional changes:

a) he left out the sections "1. Astral-friendship" *[= JS 279]* and "6. Why Wagner Said Stupid Things About Himself" *[= JS 99]*;

b) between "8: Why Wagner Belongs to France" and "9: How I Freed Myself from Wagner" N inserted the section "Wagner as Apostle of Chastity," which he had already included in his letter to Spitteler, although he also made the first section start with the poem found at the end of *BGE 256*;

c) he placed the section "The Psychologist Has His Say *[= BGE 269–70 {CW 8, 182–85}]* before the penultimate section "10. Why My Taste Changed";

d) he added a final poem: "On the Poverty of the Richest Man."

Of the passages from his works that N had mentioned in letters to Avenarius and Spitteler, *MM* 116 and 144 and *D* 255 remained unused in the final version of *NCW*.

Some of the final headings for the sections came into being during the second draft, at which point N altered a few expressions in his aphorisms, inserted a few additions, often modified the syntax, and made cuts. The manuscript he prepared in this manner he sent to his publisher Naumann in Leipzig on 15 December 1888 {*KGB* III:5, 525–26}, with a few accompanying remarks: "[. . .] here you have another lovely manuscript of which I am proud, rather short but well-wrought. After I wrote a little farce in the 'Case of Wagner,' I turn to *gravity* here: for we — Wagner and I — basically experienced a tragedy together. — It seems to me opportune indeed, having reawakened the question of our relationship in the 'Case of Wagner,' to tell, for once, an

extraordinarily remarkable story here. — Please would you calculate how many pages it will come to in the same format as
'Case of Wagner'? I estimate two to three sheets. — I would prefer that we attend to this little matter *at once.* That way I gain
time to readdress the translator-question with regard to *Ecce
Homo*, which so far has had little *Chance* {"luck"} [. . .]"

Around 17 December 1888, N sent off another page entitled
"Intermezzo" with the instruction: "To be *inserted* at page 3 of the
manuscript before the chapter Wagner as Danger." In the letter of
the same date that N probably sent together with the additional
page, we read {*KGB* III:5, 530}: "— In order for the title to tally as
closely as possible with the 'Case of Wagner,' we should write /
Nietzsche Contra Wagner / A Psychologist's Problem." But N himself canceled the alteration of the title when a bit later he sent the
publisher his final part of the "Epilogue" [= the conclusion of §4
of the preface to *JS*]. At the end of this belated addition he wrote:
"Retain as the title for this work: / *Nietzsche Contra Wagner* /
Documents / of a Psychologist."

Mention has already been made, in the notes to *EH* "Why I
Am So Clever," of yet another alteration that N added regarding
the page on which the "Intermezzo" was written. According to
this alteration, that text belongs in the above-mentioned chapter
of *EH* as §7. However, it has to appear in *NCW* as well. We must
here trace the apparently contradictory, yet from a writer's point
of view perfectly logical, development of N's intentions, based on
his letters beginning with 20 December 1888.

That same day (20 December 1888), N sent a telegram to
Leipzig: "Ecce Forwards — Nietzsche." Still that same day he
wrote an explanatory note {*KGB* III:5, 541}: "A new consideration
convinces me that we absolutely must first finish printing *Ecce
Homo* and only then N. c. W. [. . .]" Two days later, on 22 December 1888 {*KGB* III:5, 545–46}, N wrote to Peter Gast: "We do not
want to print the work N⟨ietzsche⟩ Contra W⟨agner⟩. The 'Ecce'
also contains everything decisive about this relationship. The section that, among others, also honors the maestro Pietro Gasti is
already included in 'Ecce.' I might still also include Zarathustra's
Song — it is called 'On the Poverty of the Richest Man.' — As an
interlude between two main sections."

Even so, N did not drop the title "Nietzsche Contra Wagner"; he again suggested to Avenarius on 22 December {*KGB* III:5, 544} that he might be interested in printing "[. . .] Herr Heinrich Köselitz's essay *[on The Case of Wagner]* separately as a brochure of a few pages [. . .] title: *Nietzsche Contra Wagner*." {NB. In the letter that appears in *KGB*, the words "title: *Nietzsche Contra Wagner*." do not appear.} N also wrote to Naumann to suspend the printing of *NCW*. Meanwhile, however, the page proofs (24 pages) that we still have of this text arrived in Turin. They had been ready on 22 December, as the Naumann firm's date stamp shows. The proofs of *NCW* were now as good as finalized. The arrival of the proofs made N change his mind; he revised them and gave them his imprimatur on Christmas. In his covering letter to Naumann of 27 December {*KGB* III:5, 552–53}, N wrote: "[. . .] most obliged to you for the energy with which publication has proceeded. I have returned the two printer-ready sheets of *Ecce* as well as the two sheets of N. Contra W." N's ideas about the publication sequence of his works had also changed in the following manner: "On balance, we should publish *Twilight of the Idols* and *Nietzsche Contra Wagner* in 1889: the latter perhaps *first*, since people on every side are writing to me to say that my 'Case of Wagner' has actually created true public awareness of me at last. *Ecce Homo*, which, as soon as it is published is to be handed over to the translators, cannot possibly be ready before 1890, in order for it to appear in three languages simultaneously. I do not yet have a deadline for the *Revaluation of All Values*. The success of *Ecce Homo* will need to have preceded it. — I have already written you that the work *[i.e., The Antichrist]* is ready for print."

N had abandoned his decision not to print *NCW*. Not only that: he gave his imprimatur to the corrected proofs of this work, which — consistent with his instruction of 20 December — contained the section "Intermezzo." In addition, on 28 and 30 December, he initiated by postcard a few alterations to this very section, which he thus — for whatever reason — considered integral to *NCW*.

However, immediately before his mental breakdown, N's plans took a new turn. On 2 January 1889 {*KGB* III:5, 571}, he sent a telegram to Leipzig saying: "manuscript of the two closing poems." This is explained in the following note, likewise directed to Naumann:

"Events have completely overtaken the little writing Nietzsche Contra W.: send me at once the poem that closes the work as well as the recently sent poem 'Fame and Eternity.' Onwards with *Ecce*!"

As this is the final extant manifestation of N's will "as a writer," it *has* to be regarded as the one that has final validity. According to this, N had, in the context of completing *Dionysus Dithyrambs* and other "events," given up on the publication of *NCW*. This means that *NCW* occupies a subordinate position among N's final writings. (For this reason, this writing is published in our edition *after Dionysus Dithyrambs*.)

One consequence of N's decision not to publish *NCW* is that we included the "Intermezzo" (naturally without title, according to N's instruction) in *EH* (with Champromis, against Podach). However, as we let *NCW* appear in our edition (with the above-mentioned restriction concerning the authorization of this work by N), we have to publish it as it was authorized by him — before his decision not to publish: thus with "Intermezzo" and closing poem (with Podach, against Champromis). Our edition of *NCW* is based on: the corrected script sanctioned by N; the printed manuscript; and the later changes contained in the postcards to Naumann of 28 and 30 December {*KGB* III:5, 555–56, 563}. Some earlier drafts of *NCW* can be found in the folders Mp XVI 6 and Mp XVI 5. In 1889, *NCW* appeared in a limited edition, moreover with "Intermezzo" and closing poem; in 1895, it was included in the *Großoktav-Ausgabe*, vol. VIII, without the "Intermezzo" and closing poem, likewise in all later editions of the *Großoktav-Ausgabe* (from 1899, also in vol. VIII); the Schlechta edition also reproduces the text of *NCW* in the same way. Only Podach (*Nietzsches Werke des Zusammenbruchs*) reverted to the edition of 1889, publishing in his notes the variants and manuscript material.

Foreword

1. *N sent the "Foreword" to Leipzig together with the corrected proofs. Mp XVI 6 contains an earlier discarded version that N wrote:* I consider it necessary to confront the complete lack of *délicatesse* with which my work *The Case of Wagner* has been received in Germany with some carefully selected quotes from my earlier writings.

Once more the Germans have compromised themselves with regard to myself — I have no reason why I should change my judgment concerning this race which is not of sound mind in questions of good manners. They have even failed to notice to whom alone I spoke, to musicians, to musicians' consciousness — as a musician . . . / Nietzsche / Turin, 10 December 1888.

2. *I . . . Germany.]* Cf. *EH "Why I Write Such Good Books"* 2.

3. *Quousque . . . Crispi . . .]* "How long, Crispi . . . " {Corruption of a phrase from Cicero. Francesco Crispi (1818–1901) was one of the leading figures in the unification of Italy in 1860 and served as prime minister of Italy from 1887 to 1891 and again from 1893 to 1896.}

4. *Triple Alliance]* {Military alliance between Germany, Austro-Hungary, and Italy that began in 1882 and lasted until the start of World War I in 1914.}

Where I Admire.

1. Cf. *JS* 87: "*On the vanity of artists.*"

2. *misery]* {*JS*: animals}

3. *mysterious-uncanny] heimlich-unheimlichen*

4. *— the cynical . . . likewise]* {Cf. *JS*: things for instance that could only be scared off by words, not grasped by them}

5. *the scales . . . nature]* {Missing in *JS*.}

6. *an opposing optics]* {Missing in *JS*.}

7. *Wagner is someone . . . to music. —]* Cf. *JS*: — But he doesn't know it! He is too vain to know it. {Wagner is not mentioned by name in *JS*.}

Where I Object.

8. Cf. *JS* 368: "*The cynic speaks.*"

9. *By this . . . Wagner.] Missing in JS.*

10. *Aesthetics is . . . vrai"] JS:* My fact

11. *petit fait vrai]* "true little fact"

12. *even the . . . March" —]* Missing in *JS*. {Wagner wrote the *Kaiser March* to celebrate German victory in the Franco-Prussian War, 1870–71.}

13. *striding, dancing.]* {*JS*: striding, leaping and dancing.}

14. *Are my . . . upset?] JS*: My bowels

15. *hoarse . . . To listen . . . And] JS*: hoarse? — And {Géraudel's pastilles were cough drops invented by French pharmacist Auguste Géraudel (1841–1906).}

16. *Since . . . soul]* {Missing in *JS*.}

17. *could lose . . . melodies.]* { *JS*: could be gilded by golden, good and tender harmonies.}

18. *But Wagner . . . ill.]* {Missing in *JS*.}

19. *theater?]* { *JS*: drama!}

20. *and who . . . people"!]* {Missing in *JS*.}

21. *see]* { *JS*: guess}

22. *deep down . . . attention]* {Missing in *JS*.}

23. *next to . . . exists]* {Missing in *JS*.}

24. *even . . . musician]* {Not underlined in *JS*.}

25. *interesting]* { *JS*: dramatic}

26. *pur sang]* "thoroughbred" { *JS*: righteous}

27. *— clarity . . . more. —]* {Missing in *JS*.}

28. *once, not . . . I had] JS*: I once made this clear to a righteous Wagnerian, with considerable effort; and I had

29. *Bayreuth . . . In Bayreuth,] JS*: the theater after all! In the theater,

30. *to Bayreuth,] JS*: to the theater,

31. *God and world] JS*: God and human {i.e., anybody}.

32. *least of all]* { *JS*: not even}

33. *solitude . . . witness . . .]* {Missing in *JS*.}

34. *works for the theater . . . there . . ."] JS*: works for the theater: there, one is common people, the public, herd, woman, Pharisee, voting cattle, democrat, neighbor, fellow man; there, even the most personal conscience succumbs to the leveling magic of 'the greatest number'; there, stupidity acts as lechery and contagion; there, the 'neighbor' rules; there, one *becomes* neighbor . . . " (I forgot to tell you what my enlightened Wagnerian replied to my physiological objections: "So you're really not healthy enough for our music?"—)

Intermezzo.

35. *Cf. EH "Why I Am So Clever"* 7.

36. *this side . . .]* {Pun on *jenseits*, or "the Beyond," "the other side," and *diesseits*, "this world," "this side"; in this case N refers to the Turin side of the Alps, i.e., "cisalpine" music.}

Wagner as Danger.

I

37. *Cf. MM 134:* "How the soul should be moved, according to modern music."

38. *do something . . . namely]* Missing in MM 134.

39. *Wagner wanted . . . result . . .] MM 134 {CW 4,* 59}: Wagner wanted a different sort of *movement of the soul,* one that is, as noted, related to swimming and floating. This is perhaps the most essential of all his innovations. His celebrated artistic technique, arising from and adapted to this desire — the "infinite melody" — strives to break and sometimes even to mock all mathematical symmetry of tempo and energy, and he is overly rich in inventing these effects, which sound to older ears like rhythmical paradoxes and blasphemies. He fears petrification, crystallization, the transition of music into something architectonic — and so he sets a three-beat rhythm against the two-beat one, frequently introduces the five- and seven-beat, repeats the same phrase immediately, but extending it so that it lasts two or three times as long. From complacent imitators of such art, a great danger for music can emerge: the degeneration, the decay of rhythmics has always lurked alongside an overripeness of rhythmical feeling. This danger becomes particularly great when such music relies ever more closely upon a completely naturalistic art of acting and language of gesture, untrained and uncontrolled by any higher plastic art, for this art and language have no measure in themselves and cannot impart any measure to the element that adheres to them, the *all-too-feminine* nature of music. *Addition to the end of this section of the Pm, subsequently crossed out by N:* But such a contrary nature to aesthetic taste is the proof of *décadence*

2

40. *Cf. WS 165:* "Concerning the principle of performance in music."

41. *What? is it . . . surpassed?"]* WS *165* {CW 4, 220–21}: Do the contemporary artists of musical performance really believe, then, that the highest commandment of their art is to give every piece as much *high relief* as possible and to make it speak a *dramatic* language at any price?

42. *"stone guest"]* {Alexander Pushkin's tragic drama *The Stone Guest* was written in 1830 after he had seen the premiere of the Russian-language version of Mozart's *Don Giovanni.*}

43. *really a sin . . . Wagnerians! . . .]* WS *165* {CW 4, 221}: really a sin against his spirit, the cheerful, sunny, tender, frivolous spirit of Mozart, whose seriousness is a kindly and not a terrible seriousness, whose images do not want to leap forth from the wall in order to chase the spectators away in terror and in flight. Or do you think that Mozartian music means the same thing as the "music of the stone guest"? And not only Mozartian, but all music? — But you reply, the greater *effect* speaks in favor of your principle — and you would be right insofar as the opposite question did not still remain, *upon whom* is it supposed to be having an effect, and upon whom *ought* an eminent artist really *to want* to be having an effect! Never upon the people! Never upon the immature! Never upon the sensitive! Never upon the sickly! But above all: never upon the dullards! *Addition to the end of this section of the* Pm*, subsequently crossed out by N:* But the *espressivo* at any cost is the proof of *décadence . . .*

A Music with No Future.

44. *Cf. MM 171* {Cf. CW 4, 72}: *"Music as the late fruit of every culture." The title is a pun on the common description of Wagner's music as the "music of the future." The whole passage represents a thorough revision of the original aphorism.*

We Antipodes.

45. *Cf. JS 370: "What Is Romanticism?" In Pm, the original title is "Two Antipodes." Compared with JS, certain passages are altered and shortened.*

46. *errors]* {JS: hefty errors}

47. *Hegel]* JS: Condillac

48. *as a symptom . . . permitted luxury.]* {*JS:* as if it were the symptom of a superior force of thought, of a more daring courage, of a more triumphant *fullness* of life than had characterized the eighteenth century, the age of Hume, Kant, Condillac and the sensualists: so that tragic insight appeared to me as the genuine *luxury* of our culture, as its most precious, noble and dangerous kind of squandering, but nevertheless, based on its superabundance, as its *permitted* luxury.}

49. *Wagner's music]* *JS:* German music

50. *soul,]* *JS:* German soul:

51. *of life]* {Missing in *JS.*}

52. *teetering]* {*JS:* trembling}

53. *One sees . . . myself . . .]* *JS:* One sees that back then, I failed to recognize both in philosophical pessimism and in German music what constitutes their actual character — their *romanticism.* What is romanticism?

54. *by myself . . .]* *N* planned to insert the following, found in *Mp XVI 5 (cf. Podach, Nietzsches Werke des Zusammenbruchs, p. 57), but immediately changed his mind. He wrote to the typesetter: insert* the following in the chapter *Two Antipodes* after the words "— by myself . . . ": My writings have a wealth of such 'gifts'; be on your guard if I name names. I have said all the decisive things about myself in such a way that anyone affected practically swooned with pleasure. The third *Unfashionable* is called, for example, "Schopenhauer as Educator"; admirers of Schopenhauer nearly fell on their knees with gratitude. *Lisez* {"Read"}: Nietzsche as Educator and, perhaps, *as something more . . .* The book ends with this thought: whenever a great thinker appears on earth, everything is in danger. It is as though a conflagration has taken hold in a [big] city where nobody knows what is still safe or where it will end. Love of truth is something dreadful and mighty, it *is* a conflagration: the humans that are called to seek *power* should know the source of what is heroic that flows in them. — The fourth *Unfashionable* is called: Richard Wagner in Bayreuth. Oh, those Wagnerian acolytes! how grateful to me they were! Finally, even the venerable Levi {Hermann Levi (1839–1900) was a German Jewish orchestral conductor who had a long friendship with

Wagner and who, among other things, conducted the first performance of *Parsifal* at Bayreuth in 1882. N corresponded with him
on several occasions.}, when I met him again a few years ago.
Lisez: Nietzsche-Zarathustra and the festival of the future, the
great noon. Nothing but world-historical accents; the first psychology of the first writer of dithyrambs, of the poet of Zarathustra.
— On page 45 of *Human, All Too Human [= HAH 37 {CW 3, 46}]*
it says: yet what is the central proposition, at which one of the
boldest and coldest thinkers, the author of the book "on the Origin of Moral Sensations" {Paul Rée's work *Der Ursprung der moralischen Empfindungen* was published in 1877} (— *lisez*: Nietzsche,
the first *immoralist* —) arrives, thanks to his incisive and decisive
analyses of human action? "The moral person does not stand any
nearer to the intelligible world than the physical person: *for* there
is no intelligible world." This proposition, hardened and sharpened by the hammer blows of historical knowledge (— *lisez*: first
book of the *Revaluation of Values* —) can perhaps, someday, at
some future time (— 1890! —) serve as the axe that gets laid to
the root of the "metaphysical need" of human beings — whether
more as blessing than as curse upon humanity, who could say?
but in any case as a proposition of considerable consequence,
fruitful and frightful at the same time and looking into the world
with the double vision that all great intuitions have. — Finally,
in the last pages of "Beyond Good and Evil," I present a nugget
of psychology about myself — I shall refrain from saying under
which name and circumstance . . . *[there follows the instruction to
the typesetter:]* What in the manuscript comes *after* the words "by
myself . . . " is to be inserted as section 2 of this chapter. It follows
that the beginning of the chapter receives the number 1. *N did
not send this note to Leipzig; instead, he wrote a new text based on
HAH 37, among others, as one of his last additions to EH, §6 of the
chapter on Human, All Too Human. According to Elisabeth Förster-
Nietzsche, the rejected note was sent to Paraguay; cf. the note {pp.
615–18 above} to EH III "The Case of Wagner" §4 on the Paraguay
Note. In the polemic surrounding N's putative "lost manuscripts of
the Revaluation," the phrase on this sheet: "lisez: first book of the*

Revaluation of Values," was used by those at the Nietzsche-Archiv as proof that N had still, around the middle of December, regarded The Antichrist as the first book of the Revaluation of All Values. But this very proof can be turned against the Nietzsche-Archiv, since N modified that same phrase in the final version, i.e., EH §6 of the chapter on Human, All Too Human, where it says: "lisez: Revaluation of All Values."

55. *growing or declining]* {*JS*: growing, struggling}

56. *insight and view]* {*JS*: view and insight}

57. *or those . . . antipodes.]* {*JS*: redemption from themselves through art and knowledge, or intoxication, spasms, numbness, madness. All romanticism in art and knowledge corresponds to the dual needs of the *latter type*; it corresponded (and still does) likewise to Schopenhauer and Richard Wagner, to mention those most famous and explicit romantics who were *misunderstood* by me at the time — incidentally *not* to their disadvantage, as should be conceded to me in all fairness.}

58. *as it seems . . . nature,]* {Missing in *JS*.}

59. *restorative]* {*JS*: fertilizing}

60. *[— what . . . humanity —] Missing in JS.*

61. *is actually] JS*: would actually be

62. *even for idiots — . . . décadents —] JS*: for logic calms, inspires confidence

63. *that permits . . . down]* Missing in *JS*.

64. *Greek] JS*: pessimist

65. *with his "faith . . . honed] JS*: like him, essentially a romantic — and my eye grew ever sharper

66. *artists of any kind,] JS*: all aesthetic values

67. *has hatred . . . here?]* {*JS*: I ask, in each individual case, "is it hunger or superabundance that has become creative here?" At this point N ceases to quote or paraphrase from *JS* 370, which continues for another page and a half.}

68. *"Flaubert . . . tout"]* "Flaubert is always *hateful,* man is nothing, *the work is everything*" {Cf. Paul Bourget, *Essais de psychologie contemporaine* ("Essays on contemporary psychology") (Paris: Lemerre, 1883), 114.}

69. *In Goethe . . . morality.]* {Missing in *JS*.}

Where Wagner Belongs.

   70. Heavily reworked version of the first part of *BGE* 254.

   71. *Norddeutsche Zeitung]* {Founded in Stettin in 1857.}

   72. *that France]* {*BGE*: it}

   73. *to be artificial]* {*BGE*: to hide}

   74. *the]* {*BGE*: a}

   75. *the deeper . . . France]* {*BGE*: the subtler and more demanding lyric poets of Paris}

   76. *"âme moderne"]* "modern soul"

   77. *— it is . . . enough. —]* {*BGE*: this is predictable — it is already doing that quite enough!}

   78. *— it was . . . in 1871 . . .] Up*: from 1870 on, Wagner thought it was clever to be rude to the French . . . *Here, N refers to the comedy "The Capitulation" written by Wagner after the fall of Paris.*

   79. *the young kaiser?] Up*: the blockheads of the *Bayreuther Blätter*

   80. *artist]* {*BGE*: higher human being}

   81. *"artist"]* {*BGE*: "higher human being"}

   82. *Albeit sick . . .] Missing in BGE.*

   83. *We should not . . . sick . . .]* Heavily reworked version of a part of *BGE* 256.

Wagner as Apostle of Chastity.

                                        I

   84. *Cf. final verse of BGE 256.*

   85. *self-laceration?] Sich-selbst-Zerfleischen?*; *BGE*: *Sich-selbst-entfleischen* {"self-flagellation"}

   86. *plunging, halting,] BGE*: halting, plunging,

   87. *sugar-laden] Zuckersüss*; *BGE*: *ungewisse* {"uncertain"}

   88.   — Ist das noch deutsch?
Aus deutschem Herzen kam dies schwüle Kreischen?
Und deutschen Leibs ist dies Sich-selbst-Zerfleischen?
Deutsch ist dies Priester-Hände-Spreizen,
Dies weihrauchdüftelnde Sinne-Reizen?
Und deutsch dies Stürzen, Stocken, Taumeln,

Dies zuckersüsse Bimbambaumeln?
Dies Nonnen-Äugeln, Ave-Glockenbimmeln,
Dies ganze falsch verzückte Himmel-Überhimmeln? . . .

   — Ist das noch deutsch?
Erwägt! Noch steht ihr an der Pforte . . .
Denn was ihr hört, ist *Rom, — Roms Glaube ohne Worte*!

2

89. *Partial reworking of GM III 2.*

90. *between . . . chastity]* {*GM*: between chastity and sensuality}

91. *petite bête]* "little beast" {*GM*: "animal and angel"}

92. *like Hafiz, like Goethe]* {*GM*: like Goethe, like Hafiz}

93. *damaged animals]* {"swine" in *GM* III 2. In the *Odyssey*, Circe changes the followers of Odysseus into swine.}

3

94. *Reworked version of GM III 3.*

95. *For . . . Keller . . .] Missing in GM.*

96. *Yes, Parsifal . . . excellence . . .]* GM III 3: That, as noted, would have been worthy of precisely a great tragedian: who, like any artist, only comes to the pinnacle of his greatness when he knows how to see himself and his art *beneath* him — when he knows how to *laugh* at himself.

97. *— did . . . himself? . . .]* {Missing in *GM*.}

98. *Did the hatred . . . decency. —]* GM III 3: And not only from the stage with his *Parsifal* trombones: — in the murky writings of his last years, as unfree as they are clueless, there are a hundred passages betraying a secret desire and will, a despondent, uncertain, unacknowledged will quite literally to preach reversal, conversion, negation, Christianity, medievalism and to tell his disciples "it's no good! Seek salvation somewhere else!" Even the "blood of the Redeemer" is invoked at one point . . .

99. *The preaching . . . decency. —]* Here *N cites again, as in EH "Why I Write Such Good Books" §5* {cf. p. 255} *from the fourth proposition of the "Law Against Christianity"* {found at the end of *The Antichrist,* pp. 208–9}. *N later inserted the hidden quote into the Pm of NCW.*

How I Freed Myself from Wagner.

1

100. *Partial reworking of HAH II Preface §3.*

101. *As early as . . . anti-Semitism . . .] Missing in HAH II Preface §3.*

102. *décadent,] HAH II Preface §3:* Romantic

103. *For I . . . Wagner . . .] Addition in Pm.*

104. *I was . . . Germans . . .] Added in Pp: cf. EH "Why I Am So Clever" §6.*

2

105. *Cf. HAH II Preface §4, with negligible alteration.*

106. *idealistic] HAH II Preface §4:* Romantic

The Psychologist Has His Say.

1

107. *Scarcely altered version of the first part of BGE 269.*

108. *rule] Here the text of Pp concludes.*

2

109. *Revised continuation of BGE 269, with a few changes and cuts.*

110. *— I do . . . mean them —] Missing in BGE; however, cf. Se of BGE.*

111. *sensual, absurd, fivefold] {BGE:* inspired, sensual, childish}

112. *We . . . average . . .] {Missing in BGE.}*

113. *superstition.] {BGE:* faith}

114. *how . . . saves . . .] {Missing in BGE.}*

3

115. *Scarcely altered version of BGE 270.*

116. *at home] {BGE:* "at home"}

117. *sorts] {BGE:* forms}

118. *minds] {BGE:* people}

119. *hearts — . . . knowledge. —] BGE 270:* hearts; and sometimes foolishness itself is the mask for an ill-fated, all-too-certain knowledge. From which it follows that part of a more refined humanity is having respect "for the mask" and not practicing psychology and curiosity in the wrong place.

Epilogue.

1

120. *Reworking, with some alteration and abridgement at the close, of JS Preface §3.*

121. *I have . . . nature. —] Outline plan for this, with insignificant variations, is found in Mp XVI 6.*

122. *And concerning . . . my philosophy . . .] JS Preface §3:* And as concerns illness: are we not almost tempted to ask whether we could even dispense with it?

123. *an X out of every U]* {To try to convince someone that a U is an X is an idiom for hoodwinking or duping someone.}

124. *where]* {*JS:* in which}

125. *into that nothing]* {*JS:* into that oriental nothing — we call it Nirvana —}

126. *than had . . . earth . . .]* {*JS:* than one had questioned before.}

127. *, into a barn owl]* {Missing in *JS.*}

128. *doubts.]* {*JS* Preface §3 has seven more lines of text not included here.}

2

129. *Little changed from JS Preface §4.*

130. *One thing . . . suspicion]* {*JS:* Finally, to ensure that the most essential point does not go unsaid: one returns from such abysses, from such severe infirmity, even from the infirmity of severe suspicion}

131. *Moral: . . . right now.] Missing in JS Preface §4. With this sentence the Pm that N sent off to Leipzig on 15 December 1888 concluded. He subsequently copied the rest of JS Preface §4 and sent the page to his publisher with the note:* "At the end of the book, before the poem, continuation of the text." *At the bottom of the page he wrote:* {leave} a *blank* page except for the words: *On the Poverty of the Richest Man* NB. set the poem with the same *spaces* as the Preface! As title of the work be sure to put: *Nietzsche Contra Wagner* / Documents / of a Psychologist. *The 1889 edition included this continuation but did not include that very sentence* {"Moral . . . right now."}, *which all subsequent editions left out. Podach does, however, (Nietzsches Werke des Zusammenbruchs) include it in his notes. Since there was no instruction to delete the sentence,* {Colli and Montinari} *have restored it to the text.*

132. *elevated, deviated]* Gehobenen, Verschrobenen {elevated, perverse; "deviated" to preserve rhyme}

133. *art,]* {*JS*: art at all,}

134. *pure]* {*JS*: bright}

135. *friends! . . .]* {*JS*: friends! Also as artists — : I would like to prove it.}

136. *remain concealed]* {Cf. Friedrich Schiller's poem "Das verschleierte Bild zu Sais" ("The veiled image at Sais") and Novalis's fragmentary novel "Die Lehrlinge zu Sais" ("The Apprentices at Sais"); both romantic texts allude to the goddess Isis and the Egyptian myths as handed down to Plutarch.}

137. *Tout comprendre . . . mépriser . . .]* "To understand *everything* is to despise everything . . . " {N underlines "Tout"} *The usual phrase, believed to be derived from Mme de Staël, is: "Tout comprendre, c'est tout pardoner."* {"To understand everything is to forgive everything."} *The sentence is missing in JS Preface §4.*

138. *grounds . . . grounds be seen?]* das Gründe hat, ihre Gründe nicht sehn zu lassen?

139. *Baubo]* {Also known as Iambe, daughter of Echo and Pan, servant in Demeter's house who cured Demeter's depression by exposing her genitalia to her.}

140. *appearance . . . appearance!]* {*Pd* to *JS* Preface §4: to worship appearance, to deify forms, sounds, words, the moment}

On the Poverty of the Richest Man.

1. This poem is excerpted from *DD*, translated by Paul S. Loeb and David F. Tinsley, pp. 376–83 above; cf. the notes for this poem, pp. 631–33.

Afterword[1]

Giorgio Colli

The Writings of 1888

The writings of the year 1888 resound like a stormy finale: they
follow one another in rapid succession that breaks off suddenly
into a final silence. The contrast between forward-looking, broad-
based plans and their fragmentary, hasty realization — whereby
the considered preparation necessary in the objective interest of
the work is overtaken by a restless compulsion to act at once —
for the first time indicates an uncontrollable mental involution.
Given the tight time frame (in less than a year, Nietzsche considers five or six works to be finished and ready for publication),
it is only natural that these works lose their scope in comparison
to the earlier works, which even in their external construction
received long reflection. Impatience to publish blunts architectonic sensitivity. Parallel to this, there is a deterioration in the
theoretical, and to a certain degree even systematic, tendency
that — as we see from the wealth of notes, fragments, and drafts
— had prepared a new development in the period following
Beyond Good and Evil and *On the Genealogy of Morality*.

In 1888, Nietzsche is plunged into a hopeless situation — less
in a physical sense than hopeless for his existence as a thinker,
that is, with regard to the relationship between his thought
and his literary activity. The paradoxical nexus of his existence,

1. Giorgio Colli's "Afterword" was written for the Italian edition of
Nietzsche's *Complete Works* and translated into German for the *KGW*.

what he himself had designated as "untimeliness," now proceeds to destroy him. For it is the doubly anomalous nature of this untimeliness that allows an initial rift to increase until it precipitates complete destruction. Therein lies Nietzsche's pathological disposition, already discernible in a more moderate form from *The Birth of Tragedy* onwards. All values propagated by the present are contemptible: such is the formula of his "untimeliness," more or less the leitmotif of his thinking. If it is difficult to live with such a conviction, then it becomes virtually impossible if you stubbornly try to force this conviction onto your own present day and so make "untimeliness" timely. That is absurd — but that is precisely what constitutes Nietzsche's pathological aberrance. All of us can make fun of the present day as much as we like, and many have done it with complete peace of mind as well — but you cannot expect to convince the present age by that, to the point where it despises itself in everything.

All Nietzsche's works reveal themselves as stages of development to mark out the limits of his untimeliness — either positively, by conjuring an experience that is completely contrary to the present (with the help of the Dionysian vision of tragedy and more generally the "human"[2] conception of antiquity), or negatively, by the progressive demolition of the "idols" on which the concepts of value and content of beliefs of the modern world are based: morality, Christianity, metaphysics, art, democracy, and progress. Everything Nietzsche writes, from the Basel years to the *Genealogy of Morality*, is an illustration of his "untimeliness," but his tone only seldom achieves the balance, distance, and calm that is appropriate to such an undertaking. It often seems that the knowing protest against the present is targeted at the actual removal of this present. The youthful enthusiasm for Wagner and the prophetic tone of *Zarathustra* betray a secret desire for direct involvement. That is why Nietzsche's untimeliness is so "timely." In rejecting the modern world, he takes it terribly seriously, throwing his whole self at the problem of today and

2. [M.M.] Cf. Giorgio Colli's afterword to *Richard Wagner in Bayreuth* in *KSA* I:908–12.

aspiring to be a problem for today at any price. And curiously enough, it is just this position of Nietzsche's that has provoked an almost morbid interest in him in the twentieth century.

This irresolvable inner conflict, with its destructive blend of impulses, ultimately shatters the unity of Nietzsche's organ of thought. The works of 1888 are an eloquent testimony to this final agony. Here, untimeliness and timeliness are no longer reconciled in a controlled expression, but rather break apart into two opposed poles. The demon "untimeliness" rages and expresses itself in an absolutely personal, aggressive, and vehement manner. The theoretical illusion of the will to power shows itself to be too objective (far too detached from the present!); in *Twilight of the Idols* and *The Antichrist*, its very base, the theoretical credibility of the concept of the "will," crumbles away; every theoretical construct seems to be abandoned, and even what was earlier viewed as a sort of goal, the ideal of sovereign skepticism, no longer offers sufficient satisfaction. Nietzsche does not *explain* his contempt for the modern world: he shouts it in your face. He does not stop at the relatively measured statement "What is the first and last thing a philosopher demands of himself? To inwardly overcome his times, to become 'timeless'" (*WA* Foreword, p. 3) but has to blurt out shortly afterwards: "And to leave no doubt about *what* I despise, *whom* I despise: it is the human of today, the human with whom I am fatefully contemporaneous. The human of today — his bad breath suffocates me [. . .] my feelings change, break out, as soon as I enter more modern times, *our* times" (*AC* 38, p. 169). All theoretical arguments are quite obviously founded on disgust, a loathing of the present, and this loathing is modified, led back to its core problem: the problem of *décadence*. The key to this is Christianity, that force which brought forth our present day and represents (albeit under various guises) its inner motivation. Nietzsche finds it necessary to delineate his foe exactly, to simplify it, to reduce his polemic to a single target of attack against which he can off-load his hatred of the present. In all that arouses his indignation, he sees Christianity as the common root: it has corrupted art, the instincts of which are in decline today as well as being mendacious and nihilistic; it is the same root from which the ascetic ideals of metaphysics are derived and which shaped our morality and worldview, a morality and worldview founded on the denial of life, on revenge, hypocrisy, and the repression of all affirmative drives. Last but not least, it was Christianity that triggered the great slaves' revolt and thereby paved the way to democratic leveling.

In this passionate upsurge, the planned *Will to Power* loses all interest in Nietzsche's eyes and is replaced, surpassed, and encapsulated in *The Antichrist*. The problem of *décadence* is solved by the attack on Christianity. And by means of pathological transference, Nietzsche himself becomes the Antichrist. On the whole, the old themes are handled in a purely personal way, as Nietzsche's thought identifies itself with Nietzsche's person. This is why Richard Wagner also surfaces again in 1888 as a target for polemics. Nietzsche's intolerance for modern art is physiologically conditioned by his palpable discomfort in the Wagnerian milieu, and he now returns to this experience with marked vehemence. In the same way, his attack on the moral and political slant of the modern world is nothing more than the conceptual off-loading of many painful memories — now become obsessive — of his experiences with friends and relatives, above all with his sister. Hence, generalized in literary fashion, insults against the Germans and their vices, against the Reich and the anti-Semites, come to the fore in these last works. This mutual interpenetration of thought and person also explains the sudden decision to write an autobiography, *Ecce Homo*. The problems are now inherent to Nietzsche's own person and his concerns: they dwell within.

That is the point where Nietzsche loses contact with reality. It is patently clear that someone who lays stress on his untimeliness in so fanatical and angry a manner (and acts as a man of letters, not as a conqueror of peoples), ruptures his connection with the present and remains marginalized, alone, and rejected.

Here, where for Nietzsche untimeliness and the present have turned into two irreconcilable positions and where he has even increased the gap between the two into infinity, he experiences the hallucination of a wonderful convergence. He fantasizes that from now on, for his thought and for his person, timeliness has arrived — and yet he is already no longer of sound mind. And this mental disturbance does not just relate to the last days immediately before his collapse, but to the whole autumn in Turin. At the end of September 1888, Nietzsche — having completed *The Antichrist* — speaks of a "Law against Christianity" and designates the moment this law comes into force as the beginning of a new era of world history. It is a matter of political euphoria: in Nietzsche's naïve imagination, the political indicates the genuine realm of timeliness, that which is realized and is recognized by everyone. In like manner, Nietzsche treats every word of approval in letters from friends and acquaintances as recognition of the sign of his breaking fame, even of a great historical upheaval.

All that is well known. But the fact that Nietzsche, in his delusion, interwove untimeliness with an illusory timeliness leads us astray. In the works before 1888, Nietzsche's gaze (however critical it might be), directed at the present, and the connection between Nietzsche's thought and our problems are what still elicit interest in him today. On the other hand, Nietzsche's untimeliness, which offers the key to an understanding of his instinctive, original way of observing the present, has been ignored or else misunderstood as damning one thing in favor of something else, which for Nietzsche would always belong to the negativity of the present. That can be gleaned from the various Nietzsche interpretations, which either attempt to make demands on him, that is, to win over his thought for a worldview that in one way or another proceeds from and is attached to the present, or else to justify him, to differentiate between his positive and negative sides, to engage with him at the level of historical interpretation and take issue with distortions made by adherents and opponents. The essential point, however, does not lie in all this, but in the fact that we recognize Nietzsche's untimeliness in all its radicalism and see in it not a distancing from one theoretical position or historical interpretation in favor of another, but rather a distancing from everything that is modern — with a dizzying extension of the scope of modernity whereby the relation to the past serves to clarify its conditions. It is not a matter of seeing what Nietzsche's thinking brings to us today, where it captures, enriches, and excites modern problems. In reality, his thought serves only one single thing: to distance us from all our problems, to allow us to look beyond all our problems. For the problems of Nietzsche's time are still those of our time.

In the writings of 1888, the difficulty of distinguishing between Nietzsche's untimely and timely faces increases owing to the visionary intermingling already mentioned. At the same time, however, the fissure that only the madness could heal with the help of the hallucinatory vision of a modern world destroyed by the Antichrist Nietzsche, has preserved that untimely face for us in a particularly unambiguous and emphatic way: the very face that "must" not interest the modern world, for it is its most radical refutation, conveyed in a marvellously expressive performance in which studied stylistic brilliance triumphs over the disintegration of the individual. This two-faced herm is its creator's final riddle: it stares at us with the eyes of madness, but on its other face, two more eyes look backwards into the darkness, away from us.

The *Dionysus Dithyrambs*

The poet Nietzsche is none other than the philosopher Nietzsche and not one bit more exoteric. Indeed, the lack of any conceptual support makes access more difficult. Yet whoever loves the revelation of intuitive single moments, of blazing intensity, will dare to venture onto this path of lyrical utterance. If it is possible to comprise the *whole* in one single expression, if one can apprehend a verbal mosaic synoptically as a cipher to open up an inaccessible inwardness, then certainly many images in Nietzsche's

lyrics, some rhythmic passages, and numerous ironic, bitter, painful, absurd, or dreamlike moments will provide impressive material in this regard. Nevertheless, one will have to content oneself
with an unverifiable experience; to make judgments concerning
this lyrical form of expression — for instance regarding its aesthetic level — is already presumptuous owing to the unrepeat-
able nature of these inner states. Moreover, it is hardly justified,
precisely because this lyric poetry is internally connected to
Nietzsche's entire prose and to numerous elements that underlie
it; hence it lacks authentic expression per se.

This should not sound like an undervaluation, for it is quite
natural that anyone who dares to give a definite interpretation
accepts the possibility of expressive defeat. Plato expressed
that well when, to lend a statement a certain solemnity, he
quoted Homer: "[. . .] whenever you see works written by anyone at all [. . .], you can assume that they were not the deepest
thing for that person, if he really is deep, and that the deepest
thing belongs to the noblest part of his person; but whenever
he truly writes down the fruits of his depth, 'then it is certain
that' not gods but mortals 'have robbed him of his reason.'"[3]

Incidentally, apart from the episodic *Idylls from Messina*,
Nietzsche did not publish poems unless for an "architectonic"
reason, to emphasize playfulness and lightness within sophisticated prose works, or else to ease a certain tension in a pleasant
manner. Lyric poetry takes up a minor role, a complementary
position, in his work. Of course, Nietzsche did occasionally
contemplate the publication of a volume entirely of poetry,
only to reject each plan in turn. Only at the end, in the *Dionysus Dithyrambs*, did he give up the stance of apparent resistance
to the lure of poesy. The *Dionysus Dithyrambs* are the last work
that he himself saw through to print, and while he was making
a clean second draft of the manuscript with pedantic attentive-
ness, he was already — strangely split within himself — sending letters and messages dictated by madness.

3. {Cf. Plato's *Seventh Epistle*, 344c–d.}

Yet it remains true that Nietzsche did not compose the *Dionysus Dithyrambs* during these last days of his conscious life (they date from the epoch of *Thus Spoke Zarathustra* and the last autumn in Turin), but merely collected them and copied them with a few additions and changes. So one must take care not to speak of a final transfiguration through lyricism. If Nietzsche's literary life ends in emblematic poesy, this can be interpreted mainly by means of the indications he himself gives to the concept of "poesy." In addition, we should remember that the *Dionysus Dithyrambs*, as a manuscript destined for publication, are closely linked to the completion of *Ecce Homo*, a work, then, in which interest in objective problems of thought changes into an overwrought consideration of his own person that becomes a truncated and visible concentration of these problems. A half-mystical, half-pathological event lies at the bottom of this final, retrogressive process. It is as though the theoretical knots were suddenly loosened, if not fully untied; the agonizing onslaught of problems that Nietzsche had vainly tried to quell, to overcome, in the final years suddenly stopped; the grand plan to work out a systematic philosophy was suddenly dropped, without any noticeable manifestation of inner disturbance, sign of indecision, or crisis. Perhaps a weariness toward the difficulties and enticements of reason has set in, the need to lay bare the roots of human behavior is extinguished; perhaps even the truth imperceptibly ceases to be worth striving for. Or perhaps it was a question of helplessness — the helplessness of the hunter who has shot all his arrows. What is remarkable is that this defeat — for the abandonment of a long-held plan must be viewed as such — was not accompanied by swoons or a state of depression, but on the contrary, expresses itself in a feeling of relief, in exuberance even, in irreversible euphoria, as though a heavy burden had been lifted. Here, the pathological comes into play, for a visionary impetus allows frustration to appear as conquest, and with the aid of an anomalous transposition even strives, without inhibitions, for quick literary results. The mystical aspect of the problem is that

Nietzsche's own person practically becomes the subject matter rather than its problems: in hallucinatory fashion, Nietzsche sees himself released from himself. "And so I tell myself my life," we read at the beginning of *Ecce Homo* (cf. p. 217 above). The philosophical struggle to embrace a universe of connections and reduce them to a cipher has broken down; agony has been transformed into brash facileness; and as the troublesome object has been set aside, the subject has become an obedient object that allows its story to be told.

The *Dionysus Dithyrambs* are the final product of this inversion. Now that truth has been abandoned, the way is open — exactly in line with Nietzsche's perspective — for the lie of poetry. And now that Nietzsche's person takes the place of all other objects, a lyrical form of expression is inevitable; however, it is a lyricism conditioned by the event described above, meaning that what is communicated is not primarily concerned with the poet's psychological states but the "aspect" the latter acquire in the eyes of an onlooker viewing the person of Nietzsche-Zarathustra. This letting go, this looking at oneself in the mirror, suspended in the twilight, also lends itself well to the unusual lyric form of the *Dithyrambs*, where "you" {*du*} is used where one would expect an "I," and where spurious dialogues intersect, almost as though the lyrical context should be lent a dramatic semblance. And who is it that mockingly or compassionately addresses the figure of Nietzsche-Zarathustra with admonishments and warnings? Certainly not Nietzsche himself, but rather a voice speaking out of him, the voice of the god whose name the *Dithyrambs* bear: Is it perhaps the dark, superhuman presence that Nietzsche also senses menacingly close in other moments in his life? Yet in the *Dithyrambs*, the excitement occasionally flows back to the dreamlike, and the cause of the above-mentioned defeat, imperceptible at first, must now find expression — not just in the sounds of melancholy, the agony of loneliness, and the premonition of impending doom, but also sometimes in the anxious sensation of one who — in the search for the truth — has fallen into a deadly, hopeless trap.

All this makes it difficult to view the *Dithyrambs* merely as a cycle of poems. They lack adequate organization in terms of form and content. The content appears frayed on all sides, and as to form, one has the impression that Nietzsche did not put every last effort into it. The foundation consists of improvised material, a series of firsthand sketches of psychological states, but one will not see here the immense struggle for abstraction otherwise so characteristic of Nietzsche. The verse form, treated with great freedom — albeit within a rhythmic frame reliant on the Greek model — still fails to reach that final closure in the weightlessness of abstraction. In *Zarathustra*, where the immense wealth of abstract thoughts leads back to the immediacy where they first took root, the expressive result had greater force, since the communication of what lay within indicated a final departure from rational preconditions, and the mystical cadence expressed the creative flowing back, the artistic abstraction. Here, in the *Dithyrambs*, where rational content does not make an appearance, where the connection with abstract thought is concealed, the opposite ought to happen, and the abstraction, through a flight from inwardness, should take on a shape. Yet Nietzsche succeeds only partially in this, apart from isolated expressive peaks like the grotesque digressions in "Among Daughters of the Desert" (which, incidentally, was written a few years earlier). True, the mask, the lie of the poet, is promised, but it is not delivered, for that which ought to be masked — the awfulness of a human destiny, the anxiety of a lacerated individual who writes poems — on the contrary, steps even more clearly into the foreground.

Translated by Adrian Del Caro,
Duncan Large, and Alan D. Schrift

Afterword

Andreas Urs Sommer

Nietzsche spent the winter of 1887/88 in Nice, from where, on 3 February 1888 (*KGB* III:5, 242), he contacted Franz Overbeck in Basel. In his letter, he saw, on the one hand, "the outlines of an unquestionably immense task before me," while complaining, on the other hand, about "whole days and nights [. . .] when I did not know any longer how to go on living and when a black despair attacked me, worse than I have ever known before." Furthermore, he writes, "No more 'beautiful things' are to be expected of me: no more than one should expect a suffering and starving animal to attack its prey *gracefully*. The year-long lack of a truly refreshing and healing *human* love, the absurd isolation which it entails, making almost any remnant of a connection with people only something that causes wounds: that is all very bad indeed and has only one right in itself, the right to be necessary."[1] Indeed, in 1888 Nietzsche did not write "beautiful things" anymore, with the exception, perhaps, of some of the *Dionysus Dithyrambs*.

No matter how revealing passages from letters such as this one may be, they tempt us into belittling the products of Nietzsche's last creative year as the results of a desolate physical and mental condition and, at best, into considering them to be of only biographical and pathographical relevance. But

1. Here as elsewhere in what follows, when available, I have used the language from *Selected Letters of Friedrich Nietzsche,* ed. and trans. Christopher Middleton (Chicago: University of Chicago Press, 1969).

this misses the real issues — world- and morality-shaking in Nietzsche's eyes — that these writings raise and intend to cope with. The "right to be necessary" that he evokes in his letter to Overbeck means precisely that it is not the individual situation that is to determine these writings, but rather that which is necessary to the world as a whole. Nietzsche interpreted his own propensity to illness and sufferings of all kinds as a kind of hypersensitivity — due to *décadence* — to the secret sufferings of culture. Without doubt, in early 1889 Nietzsche descended into a pathological state that soon showed features of irreversible dementia. Nevertheless, the onset of this illness does not change the fact that Nietzsche's works and notes of 1888/89 deserve the most serious *philosophical* attention.

On 13 February 1888 (*KGB* III:5, 252), Nietzsche told Heinrich Köselitz: "I have finished the first draft of my 'attempt at a revaluation': it was, all in all, sheer torture, and I am not yet courageous enough for it. Ten years from now, I will do better." This "attempt" is found in *Nachlass* Notebooks W II 1, W II 2, and W II 3. However, the project would not have to wait ten years. On 2 April, Nietzsche left Nice for Turin, but he did not arrive until 5 April because he had gotten on the wrong train. About Turin, he wrote in a letter to Köselitz on 7 April 1888 (*KGB* III:5, 285): "This is really the city that I can *now* use!" In early June, Nietzsche went to the Engadine, to Sils-Maria, for the seventh and last time. He was to stay there until 20 September, before he again returned to Turin, where he remained until his collapse.

The Case of Wagner: A Musicians' Problem

After having ended his personal relationship with Wagner in the late 1870s, Nietzsche seemed to be done with this issue, although occasionally — with polemical intent — he still commented on the composer with whom he had once been such a close friend. So it was somewhat surprising that between April and August 1888, Nietzsche, at first in Turin, then in Sils-Maria, wrote a new work that, like the fourth *Unfashionable Observation* of 1876, dealt with Wagner and, as before, was written with the intention of shedding light on various trends of the time by way of the example of a single individual. But this time the situation was reversed: if earlier Wagner had been portrayed in a favorable light, as a positive guiding figure of cultural renewal, now dark shadows were laid upon him as the exemplary representative of general cultural decline. Nietzsche's brother-in-law, the professional anti-Semite Bernhard Förster, had published, as a second edition of his *Parsifal-Nachklänge* ("Parsifal reverberations"), a book titled *Richard Wagner in seiner nationalen Bedeutung und in seiner Wirkung auf das deutsche Culturleben* ("Richard Wagner in his national significance and in his effect on German cultural life"),[2] which provoked a sharp defensive reaction from Nietzsche, as becomes obvious from a draft letter to his sister, dated the end of December 1887 (*KGB* III:5, 218): "Would you like to get a catalogue of those attitudes I consider antipodean? You will find them, nicely placed next to each other, in your husband's 'Nachklänge zu P⟨arsifal⟩' {'Echoes to P⟨arsifal⟩'}; when I read them, the most hair-raising idea dawns on me that you have understood nothing, nothing of my illness, nor my most painful and astonishing experience — that the man I had most adored, in the course of a disgusting degeneration, transformed into what I had always most despised, into the swindle of moral and Christian ideals."

Exactly here, despite all the aesthetic issues that are also discussed, lies the passionate core of his new book, *The Case of Wagner*. After some back-and-forth between author and publisher concerning new additions to the text that Nietzsche supplied later, the book was published in September 1888, privately financed by Nietzsche himself with donations from acquaintances and admirers.

Following a foreword, the main part of this work consists of a "Letter from Turin of May 1888" divided into twelve numbered

2. (Leipzig: Fock, 1886).

sections that, although signed by Nietzsche, has no explicit
addressee. This is followed by two short postscripts and an epilogue. Initially, Georges Bizet's *Carmen* is recommended as an
antidote to Wagner. This lovely and light-footed music,
Nietzsche writes, completely lacks the Wagnerian pose; it does
completely "without the *lie* of grand style!" (*WA* 1, p. 6). Music,
he says, has the task of liberating the soul — and Bizet's work
seems to meet this criterion. Then *Carmen* provides an opportunity to insert some short remarks on love, which is by no means
as selfless as Wagner claims. Wagner is presented as a master of
self-aggrandizement who, Nietzsche says, inflates everything
with the jingling of virtue so that it appears sublime. Accordingly, Wagner constantly varies the problem of redemption — a
problem, Nietzsche says, that would really only be a problem for
a *décadent*. *Parsifal* is presented as sufficient proof that one is
threatened by "suffocation by ruminating on ethical and religious absurdities" (*WA* 3, p. 10), as Nietzsche redirects a statement by Goethe that referred to the Romantics. As concerns
The Ring of the Nibelung, he observes how Wagner had replaced
his belief in revolution with Schopenhauer's pessimism. "Only
the *philosopher of décadence* gave to the artist of *décadence his
own self.*" (*WA* 4, p. 12)

Wagner's music, Nietzsche states, represents the "degenerescence" of the present while at the same time being one of its
causes. "Intermingled in his art in the most seductive way is
what the whole world most needs today — the three great
stimulantia of the exhausted: the *brutal*, the *artificial* and the
innocent (idiotic)" (*WA* 5, p. 14). As a symptom of *décadence*,
Nietzsche attacks Wagner's tendency toward the chaotic and
his denial of simple melody. The typical feature of *décadence*,
Nietzsche says, is that life no longer determines the whole and
that therefore the particular can no longer be integrated into
the whole. In this context, Wagner is said to be a talented
"miniaturist" (*WA* 7, p. 18) who, by his pursuit of large form,
must in some way have erroneously chosen the wrong genre.
He was interested only in the effect but not in substance; "as a

musician he was still a rhetorician" (*WA* 10, p. 25). Thus, Wagner represents the prevalence of the actor in music. Accordingly, at the end of his open letter Nietzsche demands

> *That the theater should not gain control of the arts.*
> *That the actor should not lead the sincere astray.*
> *That music should not become an art of lying* (*WA* 12, p. 28).

The second postscript makes obvious that not even Johannes Brahms is an alternative to Wagner, whereas the epilogue once again aims at the fundamental, that is, at a "*diagnosis of the modern soul*" (p. 39) whose "instinctive contradiction" (p. 39) can be exemplarily demonstrated in the case of Wagner.

When addressing this work in his correspondence, Nietzsche never failed to praise himself, as we see, for example, in a letter of 4 October 1888 (*KGB* III:5, 447) to Malwida von Meysenbug: "This writing, a declaration of war *in aestheticis*, as it could not be imagined more radically, seems to stir some important movement [. . .] You will see that during this duel I have *not* lost my good mood. To be honest, *to get rid of* a *Wagner* is, in the midst of facing the difficult task of my own life, sheer recreation. I wrote this little text here in Turin, in spring: meanwhile the first book of my *Revaluation of All Values* has been completed — the greatest philosophical event of all times, making the history of humanity fall apart into two halves . . ." This contraposition is effective: "good mood," "recreation" — and all this in the face of the capital world-historical task, that is, the "Revaluation of All Values," of which the manuscript of the first book — *The Antichrist* — had been completed at the time of writing this letter. On the one hand, Nietzsche plays down the significance of the occasional writing *The Case of Wagner* compared to his forthcoming major work; but on the other hand, he still assigns it a crucial role in the diagnosis and therapy of the present: even a minor work by Nietzsche is said to be a great step forward for humanity.

Also in terms of auto-therapy, however, the effect of this small book, which sold remarkably well compared to Nietzsche's other recent books, was significant, and he told his sister in mid-November 1888 (*KGB* III:5, 473–74) that it was a "real blessing" "in the midst of the enormously tense situation I am experiencing." The generally warm reception of *The Case of Wagner* was then interpreted by its author as a sign of the everywhere rampant Nietzsche enthusiasm among the public: "Now," he wrote to Overbeck on 17 December 1888 (*KGB* III:5, 531), "I have got readers — and, fortunately, all of them are *selective* intelligences by whom I am honored — *everywhere*, most of all in Vienna, St. Petersburg, Paris, Stockholm, New York. My forthcoming works will at once be published in several languages."

The Case of Wagner makes use of the composer as a telling example of decadence, which Nietzsche understands to be an overarching phenomenon of his time. The French writer Paul Bourget had given Nietzsche substantial inspiration for this approach. "I am," he says candidly in *The Case of Wagner*, "the child of these times just as much as Wagner, in other words a *décadent*: except that I realized this, except that I fought against it. The philosopher in me fought against it" (*WA* Foreword, p 3). The narrating self considers himself somebody who has recovered from the decline, whereas Wagner represents the illness by which Europe is plagued, thus justifying his treatment as a "case."

The Case of Wagner is not meant to present Nietzsche's insights on Wagner, on his time, and on *décadence* as a dry proclamation; rather, the author clearly attempts a lively literary composition. The work oscillates between seriousness and cheerfulness. Yet the final verdict on Wagner remains deadly serious: "He makes everything he touches sick — *he has made music sick* —" (*WA* 5, p. 12).

The Case of Wagner is an occasional writing that Nietzsche certainly did not want to be considered one of his main works. Nevertheless, in *Ecce Homo* he dedicates a chapter to this work that is longer than his reflections on *Beyond Good and Evil*, *On the Genealogy of Morality*, and *Twilight of the Idols* together. Furthermore, *The Case of Wagner* is the only work in *Ecce*

Homo that is not treated according to the chronology of its writing and publication but instead comes last, after *Twilight of the Idols*, which was in fact written and prepared for publication after *The Case of Wagner* (*EH* III *WA* 1–4, pp. 298–304). In his remarks in *Ecce Homo* on *The Case of Wagner*, Nietzsche neither comments directly on this writing nor gives any further explanation of his criticism of Wagner. Instead, he takes the *case* of Wagner as an opportunity to expound upon the abominations that the Germans, in his opinion, have been guilty of in the history of European culture.

This talking around Wagner and *The Case of Wagner* indicates that *The Case of Wagner* is only superficially concerned with personal reckoning but is actually a case study of a revaluation for which Wagner and his music are only a trigger. Thematically, the arguments against Wagner presented in *The Case of Wagner* are well known from Nietzsche's earlier writings, but only in their polemical tightening in *The Case of Wagner* do they appear as elements of an overall strategy of prescribing to the present new values, namely those of the antidecadent affirmation of life.

On the one hand, *The Case of Wagner* has its significance as an application of a "revaluation of all values." On the other hand, one crucial intention of *The Case of Wagner* (and later of *Nietzsche Contra Wagner*) is to rule out any possible confusion that would mistake Nietzsche for Wagner and the latter's ideas of cultural renewal. The fear of being mistaken for someone else is one particular feature of the writings of 1888 (see, e.g., *EH* Foreword 1, p. 212). Only a ruthless rhetoric of foreclosure seems to be helpful for Nietzsche in this case. By the time *The Case of Wagner* appeared, there is no doubt that Nietzsche had succeeded in moving out from Wagner's shadow. The immediate and intense reception of *The Case of Wagner* makes this writing an important milestone in Nietzsche's reception history. *The Case of Wagner* pursues an exoteric intention, namely, a sharp criticism of the present that forces readers to listen to the new and unprecedented things Nietzsche wants to say.

Unlike Nietzsche's earlier works, *The Case of Wagner* immediately attracted public attention. The first reviews already pointed to the discrepancy between Nietzsche's earlier, Wagner-panegyrical statements in *The Birth of Tragedy* and *Richard Wagner in Bayreuth* and his now harsh anti-Wagnerianism. For instance, the famous music critic Eduard Hanslick wrote in a review of *The Case of Wagner*: "Much of Nietzsche's arguments against Wagner is doubtless absolutely correct; it is also nothing new, it is new only from the mouth of Nietzsche, the most important and ingenious Wagnerian of the past" (*KGB* III:7/3, 2, 1037). Particularly sensitive to this attack were the convinced Wagnerians, most of all Richard Pohl, who in *Musikalisches Wochenblatt* of 25 October 1888 (*KGB* III:7/3, 2, 1026–33), reverses the "Case of Wagner: A Musicians' Problem" into a "Case of Nietzsche: A Psychological Problem." Carl Spitteler takes a quite different approach in the Berne daily newspaper *Der Bund*, presenting a very positive review including a number of excerpts from *The Case of Wagner*: "We have to announce to our readers an aesthetic event: one of the first champions of Wagnerianism, the philosopher Friedrich Nietzsche, has now sided with the opponents, and not only tacitly but, as befits such an influential spokesman, publicly, with substantiated explanation in the form of a protest" (*KGB* III:7/3, 2, 1038). This was not, of course, the last word in the *Bund*, for Viktor Widmann, the head of the editorial staff, believed that Spitteler's statement should not pass unchallenged, and in the *Bund* of 20–21 November 1888 he dedicated a long, critical article to "Nietzsche's Desertion from Wagner," in which he denounced in particular Nietzsche's tendency toward megalomania. "No! it is impossible; no longer are we able to deal with this pamphlet by Nietzsche, shimmering in all colors of the bristling chameleon; we are disgusted by it" (*KGB* III:7/3, 2, 1054). "Nietzsche, who in the past we believed had to be respected and paid attention to, is now dead for us" (*KGB* III:7/3, 2, 1055).

Nietzsche's loyal assistant Heinrich Köselitz, aka Peter Gast, beat the drum for his master's writing in November 1888 in the magazine *Kunstwart*. As Nietzsche's real discovery, Köselitz emphasizes: "Of extraordinary significance for judging Wagner is what, prior to Nietzsche, nobody has clearly seen and emphasized: the actor in him" (*KGB* III:7/3, 2, 1073). And then he completely embraces Nietzsche's self-appraisal: "His anti-romantic, anti-Christian, anti-revolutionary, anti-democratic culture, in short his nobility, will separate (and has always separated) him from Wagner's cause" (*KGB* III:7/3, 2, 1075). *Kunstwart* editor Ferdinand Avenarius added to this hymn of praise a few critical remarks, according to which Nietzsche was indeed "one of the most brilliant and profound thinkers of our time" (*KGB* III:7/3, 2, 1076), but the judgments in *The Case of Wagner* were neither refutable nor could they be proven. "For only errors in thinking can be logically refuted, not errors of perception." Nietzsche did not argue, he only decreed; therefore he, Avenarius, "in contrast to Peter Gast," had been embarrassed by the work "as a very unpleasant thing": "[I]n the end, there is the regret that this time Friedrich Nietzsche wrote like ⟨a⟩ columnist" (*KGB* III:7/3, 2, 1077). Nietzsche took the occasion of these remarks to intervene himself, for the first and only time by way of a newspaper article, in the debate on his work, namely via two letters to Avenarius, demanding on a postcard of 10 December 1888 that they be "published verbatim in the 'Kunstwart'" (*KGB* III:5, 519). Indeed, these open letters, with which Nietzsche seemed to want to authenticate Avenarius's judgment that now he was going to work as a columnist, were published in the second December volume of the *Kunstwart* (*KGB* III:5, 516–18).

Nietzsche's unusual intervention in the debate about his own writing is an expression of the intensified self-marketing tendencies that become obvious in his work of 1888. With respect to *The Case of Wagner*, these tendencies correlate with the actual public attention Nietzsche had almost completely lacked with his previous writings. Accordingly, now for the first time Nietzsche interacts with his own reception — not only by writing the two letters to the *Kunstwart*, but also by reworking the list, published in the second letter of 10 December (*KGB*

III:5, 518), of relevant anti-Wagner passages from earlier works into his own collage-work, *Nietzsche Contra Wagner*.

Beyond its immediate reception, the aftermath of Nietzsche's criticism of Wagner was surprisingly extensive. The keyword *décadence* became a leitmotif of contemporary cultural criticism. As much as Nietzsche, at the time of writing *The Case of Wagner*, was part of the Wagner-critical context of the time, so was his name associated with the radical departure from Wagner's art paradigm with which not only those in the environment of Bayreuth were struggling. As examples, we can refer to authors Robert Musil (1880–1942) and Thomas Mann (1875–1955), as well as the philosopher Theodor W. Adorno (1903–69), as all being positively inspired by *The Case of Wagner*. Musil made use of his reading of *The Case of Wagner* in his novel *The Man Without Qualities*[3] when criticizing the narcotic effect of (Wagner's) music or its "visual restlessness" (*WA* 7, p. 17). Thomas Mann, on the other hand, wrote in "The Sorrows and Grandeur of Richard Wagner" (1933) that he "always regarded Nietzsche's immortal criticism of Wagner [. . .] as a panegyric in reverse, another form of eulogy. It was an expression of love-hate, an act of self-mortification"; but he still wants to accept it as a criticism that "serves to stimulate [his] enthusiasm rather than deaden it."[4] This holds as well for Adorno, although the latter in his *In Search of Wagner* (1952) underlines the fact that Nietzsche's finding "Wagner formless shows that even he still heard him with the ears of the Biedermeier listener."[5]

3. Robert Musil, *Der Mann ohne Eigenschaften,* 3 vols. (Berlin: Rowohlt, 1930, 1933; Lausanne: Rowohlt, 1943); *The Man Without Qualities,* 2 vols., trans. Sophie Wilkins (New York: Knopf, 1995).

4. Thomas Mann, "Leiden und Größe Richard Wagners," in *Gesammelte Werke in dreizehn Bänden* (Frankfurt am Main: Fischer, 1990), 9:373; Thomas Mann, "The Sorrows and Grandeur of Richard Wagner," *Pro and Contra Wagner,* trans. Allan Blunden (London: Faber and Faber, 1985), 100–101.

5. Theodor W. Adorno, *Versuch über Wagner* (Frankfurt: Suhrkamp, 1952), 66; *In Search of Wagner,* trans. Rodney Livingston (London: New Left Books, 1981), 55.

*Twilight of the Idols, or, How to Philosophize
with a Hammer*

Twilight of the Idols is the result of a number of preliminary
drafts and plans that, in 1887/88, were initially titled "The Will
to Power." Nietzsche's *Nachlass* (cf. *CW* 17 and 18) allows us to
clearly comprehend how individual topics that later were to
crystallize as chapters of *Twilight of the Idols* were initially placed
in other contexts in the plans and drafts of "The Will to Power."
The notes provide evidence of the continuous revision, reuse,
and relocation of individual passages. *Twilight of the Idols* arose
from the same preliminary drafts in the *Nachlass* that also contained the passages that would later become the first twenty-
four sections of *The Antichrist*. The *Twilight of the Idols* chapters
"The Problem of Socrates," "'Reason' in Philosophy," "How the
'True World' Finally Became a Fable," "Morality as Anti-Nature,"
"The Four Great Errors," and "The 'Improvers' of Humanity"—
all of them short treatises — have their origin in material
Nietzsche had already compiled in the first half of 1888 for his
planned work "The Will to Power." When he abandoned his
plans for this work, these texts from the *Nachlass* thus became
available for use in another work — *Twilight of the Idols*.

   In early September 1888, Nietzsche decided to have "Idleness of a Psychologist" printed while he, at the same time, also
decided to prepare a new main work with the title "The Revaluation of All Values." On 7 September 1888, he wrote to his
publisher, Constantin Georg Naumann (*KGB* III:5, 411–12):
"Right now you are being sent the cleanest manuscript I have
ever sent to you. It is a writing that, in terms of design, shall be
a perfect twin of 'The Case of Wagner.' Its title is: *Idleness of a
Psychologist*. I need to publish it even now because at the end
of the coming year we will probably have to print my main
work, the *Revaluation of All Values*. As the latter is very strict
and serious, it cannot be followed by something cheerful and
graceful. On the other hand, there must be some time *between*
my latest publication and this *serious* work."

The actual writing of the initial draft of *Twilight of the Idols* took place between the end of June and 3 September 1888, and the initial manuscript was mailed to Naumann on 9 September. At the end of September, the title was changed from "Idleness of a Psychologist" to "Twilight of the Idols"; the chapter "What the Germans Lack" was sent to Naumann on 18 September 1888; §§32–44 of "Forays of an Untimely One" followed in the first half of October 1888; and finally, at the end of October, there followed "What I Owe the Ancients." While writing *Twilight of the Idols* in July and August 1888, Nietzsche was additionally occupied with completing *The Case of Wagner*, so that, after having received the first copies of *Twilight of the Idols* on 24 November 1888, he proudly wrote the following day to Heinrich Köselitz (*KGB* III:5, 489): "You could not spend 10 days more usefully, for that was all the time I needed for the book." Although the work was completed, Nietzsche and his publisher had come to an agreement (cf. N's letter to Naumann of 27 December 1888, *KGB* III:5, 552) that the publication of *Twilight of the Idols*, whose first edition gives 1889 as the year of publication, should be delayed, so at the time of Nietzsche's collapse, at the beginning of 1889, this work was still not available. The distribution and selling of *Twilight of the Idols* started only after consultation with Franz Overbeck, who had fetched the invalid Nietzsche from Turin. The work was first made available in bookstores at the end of January 1889.

On 12 September 1888, in a letter to Köselitz (*KGB* III:5, 417), Nietzsche defined the nature of *Twilight of the Idols* as follows: "[A] very bold and exact sketch of my most essential philosophical heterodoxies: so that this writing [. . .] may serve as an initiation into and appetizer for my *Revaluation of Values*." And in a letter to Georg Brandes on 20 October 1888 (*KGB* III:5, 457), Nietzsche presented himself as being intellectually aggressive: "This writing is my philosophy *in nuce* — radical to the point of crime . . . " The claim to radicalism — as an intensification of political radicalism, which in the nineteenth century appeared throughout Europe in the form of anticlericalism, antinationalism, and in support of the emancipation of the individual — is found in many of Nietzsche's judgments on his new work.

The thematic variety and stylistic polyphony of *Twilight of the Idols* is reflected by the great number of sources Nietzsche made use of. When, in *EH* II 3 (p. 235), he claims, "I have to count back half a year to catch myself with a book in my hand," this cannot alter the fact that Nietzsche in his last creative years was still immensely engaged in intensive readings, although these were always selective and oriented to his own intentions. Doing so, he covered a wide variety of fields. Relevant for *Twilight of the Idols* is his reading of contemporary literary and cultural-critical authors, particularly from France (e.g., Paul Albert,[6] Émile Bérard-Varagnac,[7] Paul Bourget,[8] Georg Brandes,[9] Ferdinand Brunetière,[10] Louis Desprez,[11] Émile Faguet,[12]

6. Paul Albert, *La littérature française au dix-neuvième siècle*, vol. 2 (Paris: Hachette, 1885). *NL*.

7. Émile Bérard-Varagnac, *Portraits littéraires* (Paris: Lévy, 1887). *NL*.

8. Paul Bourget, *Essais de psychologie contemporaine* (Paris: Lemerre, 1883); *Nouveaux essais de psychologie contemporaine: M. Dumas fils, M. Leconte de Lisle, MM. de Goncourt, Tourguéniev, Amiel* (Paris: Lemerre, 1886). *NL*.

9. Georg Brandes, *Die Litteratur des 19. Jahrhunderts in ihren Hauptströmungen*, vol. 2: *Die romantische Schule in Deutschland* (Leipzig: Veit, 1887), *NL*; *Moderne Geister: Literarische Bildnisse aus dem neunzehnten Jahrhundert*, 2nd ed. (Frankfurt am Main: Ruetten & Loening, 1887). *NL*.

10. Ferdinand Brunetière, *Le roman naturaliste* (Paris: C. Lévy, 1884), *NL*; *Études critiques sur l'histoire de la littérature française: Troisième série: Descartes – Pascal – Le Sage – Marivaux – Prévost – Voltaire et Rousseau – Classiques et Romantiques* (Paris: Hachette, 1887). *NL*.

11. Louis Desprez, *L'évolution naturaliste: Gustave Flaubert – Les Goncourt – M. Alphonse Daudet – M. Émile Zola – Les poètes – Le théatre* (Paris: Tresse, 1884). *NL*.

12. Émile Faguet, *Dix-neuvième siècle: Études littéraires: Chateaubriand, Lamartine, Alfred de Vigny, Victor Hugo, A. de Musset, Th. Gautier, P. Mérimée, Michelet, George Sand, Balzac* (Paris: Boivin & Cie., 1887); *Les grands maîtres du dix-septième siècle: Études littéraires et dramatiques*, 4th ed. (Paris: Lecène et Oudin, 1888); *Dix-septième siècle: Études littéraires: Descartes, Malebranche, Corneille, Pascal, La Rochefoucauld, La Fontaine, Molière, Racine, Boileau, Madame de Sévigné, Bossuet, Fénelon, Madame de Maintenon, La Bruyère, Saint-Simon* (Paris: Lecène, Oudin, et Cie., n.d.).

Paul Foucher,[13] the Goncourt brothers,[14] Jules Lemaître,[15] Edmond Schérer,[16] Ludwig Nohl on Wagner,[17] Viktor Hehn on Goethe[18]), as well as literary texts themselves (e.g., Dostoevsky[19]). Other works that Nietzsche already knew open up a general cultural-historical horizon, such as the works of Jacob Burckhardt,[20] Friedrich von Hellwald,[21] and William Edward

13. Paul Foucher, *Les coulisses du passé* (Paris: E. Dentu, 1873).

14. Edmond and Jules Huot de Goncourt, *Journal des Goncourt: Mémoires de la vie littéraire,* 3 vols. (Paris: Charpentier, 1887–88), vols. 2 and 3 in *NL.*

15. Jules Lemaître, *Les contemporains: Études et portraits littéraires: Première série: Théodore de Banville – Sully-Prudhomme – François Coppée – Edouard Grenier – Madame Adam – Madame Alphonse Daudet – Ernest Renan – Ferdinand Brunetière – Émile Zola – Guy de Maupassant – J.-K. Huysmans – Georges Ohnet* (Paris: Lecène et Oudin, 1886), *NL; Les contemporains: Études et portraits littéraires: Deuxième série: Leconte de Lisle – José-Maria de Heredia – Armand Silvestre – Anatole France – Le Pere Monsabré – M. Deschanel et le romantisme de Racine – La comtesse Diane – Francisque Sarcey – J. J. Weiss – Alphonse Daudet – Ferdinand Fabre,* 2nd ed. (Paris: Lecène et Oudin, 1886), *NL; Les contemporains: Études et portraits littéraires: Troisième série: Octave Feuillet – Edmond et Jules de Goncourt – Pierre Loti – H. Rabusson – J. de Glouvet – J. Soulary – Le duc d'Aumale – Gaston Paris – Les femmes de France – Chroniqueurs (Parisiens – Henry Fouquier – Henri Rochefort – Jean Richepin – Paul Bourget,* 2nd ed. (Paris: Lecène et Oudin, 1887).

16. Edmond Schérer, *Études sur la littérature contemporaine* VIII (Paris: Lévy, 1885). *NL.*

17. Ludwig Nohl, *Musiker-Biographien: Fünfter Band: Wagner,* 2nd ed. (Leipzig: Reclam, n.d.).

18. Viktor Hehn, *Gedanken über Goethe,* pt. 1, 2nd ed. (Berlin: Gebrüder Borntraeger, 1888). *NL.*

19. Fyodor Dostoevsky, *Les possédés,* trans. Victor Derely, 2 vols. (Paris: Plon, n.d. [1886]); *L'esprit souterrain,* trans. and adapted by E. Halperine and Ch. Morice (Paris: Plon-Nourrit, n.d. [1886]); *Souvenirs de la maison des morts,* trans. M. Neyroud (Paris: Plon-Nourrit, n.d. [1886]).

20. Jacob Burckhardt, *Der Cicerone: Eine Anleitung zum Genuss der Kunstwerke Italiens,* 2nd ed., Bd. 1: *Architektur,* Bd. 2: *Sculptur,* Bd. 3: *Malerei* (Leipzig: Seemann, 1869), *NL; Die Cultur der Renaissance in Italien: Ein Versuch,* 2nd ed. (Leipzig: Seemann, 1869), *NL; Die Zeit Constantin's des Grossen* (Basel: Schweighauser, 1853).

21. Friedrich von Hellwald, *Culturgeschichte in ihrer natürlichen Entwicklung von der ältesten Zeit bis zur Gegenwart* (Augsburg: Lampart, 1874);

Hartpole Lecky,[22] as well as Ferdinando Galiani's letters,[23] or books he had recently been reading, such as works by Émile Gebhardt[24] and Emanuel Herrmann.[25] Obviously, he read some works for a second time, such as those by Arnobius (on Dionysus) [26] and Afrikan Spir.[27] Nietzsche also spent time reading contemporary medical-physiological, psychological, and biological literature (e.g., works by Charles Féré,[28] Francis Galton,[29] Harald Høffding,[30] Henri Joly,[31] Carl von Nägeli,[32]

2nd ed., 2 vols. (Augsburg: Lampart, 1876–77); 3rd ed., 2 vols. (Augsburg: Lampart, 1883–84); *Die Erde und ihre Völker: Ein geographisches Hausbuch,* 2 vols. (Stuttgart: W. Spemann, 1877–78). *NL.*

22. William Edward Hartpole Lecky, *Geschichte des Ursprungs und Einflusses der Aufklärung in Europa,* 2nd ed., trans. H. Jolowicz, 2 vols. (Leipzig: Winter, 1873), *NL; Sittengeschichte Europas von Augustus bis auf Karl den Grossen: Nach der zweiten verbesserten Auflage mit Bewilligung des Verfassers,* trans. H. Jolowicz, 2 vols. (Leipzig: Winter, 1879). *NL.*

23. Ferdinando Galiani, *Lettres à Madame d'Épinay, Voltaire, Diderot, Grimm, le Baron d'Holbach, Morellet, Suart, D'Alembert, Marmontel, la Vicomtesse de Belsunce etc.,* 2 vols. (Paris: Charpentier, 1882). *NL.*

24. Émile Gebhart, *Études mériodionales: La Renaissance italienne et la philosophie de l'histoire: Machiavel – Fra Salimbene – Le roman de don Quichotte – La Fontaine – Le palais pontifical – Les Cenci* (Paris: Cerf, 1887). *NL.*

25. Emanuel Herrmann, *Cultur und Natur: Studien im Gebiete der Wirthschaft,* 2nd ed. (Berlin: Allgemeiner Verein für Deutsche Literatur, 1887). *NL.*

26. Arnobius, *Sieben Bucher wider die Heiden,* trans. Franz Anton von Besnard (Landshut: Vogel, 1842). *NL.*

27. Afrikan Spir, *Denken und Wirklichkeit: Versuch einer Erneuerung der kritischen Philosophie* (Leipzig: J. G. Findel, 1877). *NL.*

28. Charles Féré, *Sensation et mouvement: Études expérimentales de psychomécanique* (Paris: Alcan, 1887); *Dégénérescence et criminalité: Essai physiologique* (Paris: Alcan, 1888). *NL.*

29. Francis Galton, *Inquiries into Human Faculty and Its Development* (London: Macmillan, 1883). *NL.*

30. Harald Høffding, *Psychologie in Umrissen auf Grundlage der Erfahrung,* trans. F. Bendixen (Leipzig: Fues, 1887). *NL.*

31. Henri Joly, *Psychologie des grands hommes* (Paris: Hachette, 1883). *NL.*

32. Carl von Nägeli, *Mechanisch-physiologische Theorie der Abstammungslehre: Mit einem Anhang: 1. Die Schranken der naturwissenschaftlichen Erkenntniss, 2. Kräfte und Gestaltungen im molecularen Gebiet* (Munich: Oldenburg, 1884). *NL.*

Charles Richet,[33] William Henry Rolph,[34] and Georg Heinrich
Schneider[35]). With respect to philosophical literature, he refers
both to books he had long been familiar with, such as works
by Eugen Dühring,[36] Eduard von Hartmann,[37] Friedrich Albert
Lange,[38] Otto Liebmann,[39] Leopold Schmidt,[40] Arthur Schopenhauer,[41] and Gustav Teichmüller,[42] and to recent readings,
such as works by Victor Brochard,[43] James Anthony Froude,[44]

33. Charles Richet, *L'homme et l'intelligence: Fragments de physiologie et de psychologie* (Paris, 1884), *NL*; *Essai de psychologie générale* (Paris: Alcan, 1887). *NL.*

34. William Henry Rolph, *Biologische Probleme zugleich als Versuch zur Entwicklung einer rationellen Ethik,* 2nd ed. (Leipzig: Engelmann, 1884). *NL.*

35. Georg Heinrich Schneider, *Der thierische Wille: Systematische Darstellung und Erklärung der thierischen Triebe und deren Entstehung, Entwickelung und Verbreitung im Thierreiche als Grundlage zu einer vergleichenden Willenslehre* (Leipzig: Abel, n.d. [1880]), *NL*; *Der menschliche Wille vom Standpunkte der neueren Entwicklungstheorien* (des "Darwinismus") (Berlin: Dümmler, 1882). *NL.*

36. Eugen Dühring, *Der Werth des Lebens: Eine philosophische Betrachtung* (Breslau: Trewendt, 1865). *NL.*

37. Eduard von Hartmann, *Philosophie des Unbewussten: Versuch einer Weltanschauung* (Berlin: Duncker, 1869). *NL.*

38. Friedrich Albert Lange, *Geschichte des Materialismus und Kritik seiner Bedeutung in der Gegenwart.* Wohlfeile Ausgabe (Iserlohn: Baedeker, 1887). *NL.*

39. Otto Liebmann, *Zur Analysis der Wirklichkeit: Eine Erörterung der Grundprobleme der Philosophie,* 2nd ed. (Strassburg: Trübner, 1880), *NL*; *Gedanken und Thatsachen: Philosophische Abhandlungen, Aphorismen und Studien: Erstes Heft: Die Arten der Nothwendigkeit, Die mechanische Naturerklärung, Idee und Entelechie* (Strassburg: Trübner, 1882). *NL.*

40. Leopold Schmidt, *Die Ethik der alten Griechen,* 2 vols. (Berlin: Hertz, 1882). *NL.*

41. Arthur Schopenhauer, *Sämmtliche Werke,* ed. Julius Frauenstadt, 6 vols. (Leipzig: Brockhaus, 1873–74). *NL.*

42. Gustav Teichmüller, *Die wirkliche und die scheinbare Welt: Neue Grundlegung der Metaphysik* (Breslau: Koebner, 1882).

43. Victor Brochard, *Les sceptiques grecs* (Paris: Imprimerie Nationale, 1887). *NL.*

44. James Anthony Froude, *Das Leben Thomas Carlyles,* trans. Th. A. Fischer, vols. 1–2 (Gotha: Perthes, 1887).

Jean-Marie Guyau,[45] Ernst Mach,[46] and Eugène de Roberty.[47]
In the theological and historical fields, his readings also cover
a broad range: in addition to Ernest Renan,[48] he engaged in
particular with the work of Louis Jacolliot[49] and Julius Wellhausen.[50] Finally, it must also be noted that Nietzsche, despite
his comments to the contrary ("an uneducated person like me,
who never reads 'journals'!" — to Overbeck, 23 February 1887
[*KGB* III:5, 27]), also took regular notice of daily newspapers
such as the *Journal des Débats* and magazines such as the *Revue
des Deux Mondes*, some of which finds its way into his works.

   Twilight of the Idols is a challenging text for readers, owing
to its chameleon-like diversity in terms of both style and topics.
As concerns style, Nietzsche tries out every possible literary genre,
from the epigram and the maxim to the aphorism, from the treatise to the essay, from narration to short drama, from the autobiographical report to the prose poem. There is also great variety
at the levels of rhetoric and authorial voice.

   Twilight of the Idols does without any single clear philosophical doctrine toward which the reader might take either a negative or affirmative attitude, thus clearly relating herself to the
text and its author. Instead, the reader is constantly confronted
with new challenges. There is no common thread allowing the

   45. Jean-Marie Guyau, *L'irréligion de l'avenir: Étude sociologique,* 2nd ed.
(Paris: Alcan, 1887). *NL.*

   46. Ernst Mach, *Beiträge zur Analyse der Empfindungen* (Jena: Fischer,
1886). *NL.*

   47. Eugène de Roberty, *L'ancienne et la nouvelle philosophie: Essai sur les
lois générales du développement de la philosophie* (Paris: Alcan, 1887). *NL.*

   48. Ernest Renan, *Vie de Jésus,* 3rd ed. (Paris: Michel Lévy Frères, 1867).

   49. Louis Jacolliot, *Les législateurs religieux: Manou, Moïse, Mahomet:
Traditions religieuses comparées des lois de Manou, de la Bible, du Coran, du
rituel égyptien, du Zend-Avesta des Parses et des traditions finnoises* (Paris:
Lacroix, 1876). *NL.*

   50. Julius Wellhausen, *Prolegomena zur Geschichte Israels,* 2nd ed. of
Geschichte Israels, vol. 1 (Berlin: Reimer, 1883), *NL; Skizzen und Vorarbeiten,*
Erstes Heft: 1. *Abriss der Geschichte Israels und Juda's,* 2. *Lieder der Hudhai-
liten, arabisch und deutsch* (Berlin: Reimer, 1884), *NL; Skizzen und Vorarbeiten.* Drittes Heft: *Reste arabischen Heidentumes* (Berlin: Reimer, 1887). *NL.*

reader to situate herself once and for all; there are at best groups of motifs providing for a certain degree of orientation. *Twilight of the Idols* treats the reader like a guinea pig: it can be understood as experimenting with the reader to find out how she reacts to certain stimuli, how "hollow" she sounds, and in what way she might work as a resonating body when being struck with a tuning fork. In this respect, this text lives on its ever-renewed provocative power of surprise that compels the reader to continually question and redefine her point of view.

Apart from the Foreword and a passage quoted from *Thus Spoke Zarathustra* at the end, titled "The Hammer Speaks," the text consists of ten unnumbered chapters of different length and design. The first chapter, "Sayings and Arrows," is a compilation of forty-four very short sentences that resemble the writings of the French moralists. Thematically, they cover a wide range and aim to provoke the most extreme intensification. The first sentence begins with reflection on psychology and its morally subversive dimension, while the fourth problematizes the simplicity of truth. In sentence 13, the wife appears as a projection of male idealism, and sentence 36 asks if immoralism could harm virtue.

The second chapter, on other hand, titled "The Problem of Socrates," is treatise-like. It renews the criticism of Socrates already articulated in *The Birth of Tragedy*, as Socrates now appears as a representative not only of the "mob" but also of *décadence*, of one in physiological decline whose "instincts were in anarchy " (*TI* "Socrates" 9, p. 55). Thus the philosophers — with help from reason and dialectics — had from then on turned toward fighting the instincts instead of, as with an enhanced life, identifying instinct with happiness. Introduced early, *décadence* will prove to be one of *Twilight of the Idols*'s main themes.

In the third chapter, "'Reason' in Philosophy," the critique of reason is generalized and radicalized. The philosophers, says Nietzsche, suffer from a "lack of historical sense" (*TI* "Reason" 1,

p. 57), meaning that they at the same time want to negate both becoming and sensuality. Furthermore, Nietzsche says, "They put what comes at the end — unfortunately! for it should not come at all — the 'highest concepts,' in other words the most general, emptiest concepts, the last fumes of a vaporizing reality, at the beginning, *as* beginning" (*TI* "Reason" 4, p. 59). This way, he states, the most unreal, that is, the merely conceptual, is hypostatized as actual reality. At the same time, Nietzsche demonstrates the considerable seductive and deceptive power of language: it misleads people into errors of reason by suggesting that concepts such as "ego," "being," or "will" actually exist. But these are nothing other than products of language. We might not even get rid of God, he writes, because we still cling to our belief in grammar. The previous chapters had used psychology and physiology to sound out the idols. Here, on the contrary, it is the critique of language that is the means.

The fourth chapter, "How the 'True World' Finally Became a Fable," condenses the insights gained from the critiques of language and reason into a six-theses narrative: Plato appears as the inventor of a true spiritual world beyond the merely "apparent" sensual world. This "true world" is then transformed through a process of being first Christianized and then Kantianized, before it can finally be discarded as superfluous.

The fifth chapter, "Morality as Anti-Nature," takes up the fight against a morality that suppresses passions, desires, and in general all sensuality. In contrast, Nietzsche says, "every *healthy* morality" (*TI* "Morality" 4, p. 67) must be dominated by "the instincts of life" (p. 67), whereas up to this point all morality has been serving the "*condemnation* of these instincts" (p. 67). This condemnation had been obedient to the interest of sick life, that is, the life of the priest-type.

The sixth chapter, titled "The Four Great Errors," emphasizes that the "*error of confusing cause and consequence*" (*TI* "Errors" 1, p. 69) becomes immediately visible in morality and religion.

The "*error of a false causality*," he says, consists in not knowing what a cause really is and believing, for example, in such causes as "inner facts" (*TI* "Errors" 3, p. 71). According to the "*error of imaginary causes*" (*TI* "Errors" 4, p. 72), Nietzsche writes, a cause is imagined when there is none at hand, which happens both in physiological sensation and in religion and morality. The "*error of free will*" (*TI* "Errors" 7, p. 75) completes the series of errors, before the chapter ends in an atheist manifesto: "The concept 'God'" has hitherto been the greatest *objection* to existence . . . We repudiate God, we repudiate responsibility in God: only *with that* do we redeem the world. —" (*TI* "Errors" 8, p. 76).

In the seventh chapter, "The 'Improvers' of Humanity," this aggressive tone is moderated. The quest for morality to "improve" human beings (*TI* "Improvers" 2, p. 77) could take shape both as the "*taming* of the human beast" (p. 77) and as the "*breeding* of a certain category of human" (p. 78). The classic example of taming by way of weakening is Christianity, whereas *The Laws of Manu*, with its rigid caste order, is understood as a breeding program.

The "*eternal* idols" (*TI* Foreword, p. 44) retreat in the eighth chapter behind the political-cultural diagnosis of the present: the chapter "What the Germans Lack" recalls many of the invectives that one is familiar with from Nietzsche's earlier writings as he seeks to expose the decline of culture in Germany.

The ninth chapter, "Forays of an Untimely One," gathers fifty-one partly formulaic reflections on a variety of subjects. Here, the stylistic proximity to Nietzsche's aphorism-books from the early 1880s is most noticeable. Harsh literary-critical judgments on European intellectuals from Seneca to John Stuart Mill, from Jean-Jacques Rousseau to George Sand, are preceded by reflections on the psychology of the artist, on the beautiful, on the opposition of the Apollonian and the Dionysian, and on intellectual conscience. Arthur Schopenhauer, the "*natural value of egoism*" (*TI* "Forays" 33, p. 105), and the close relation of anarchism and Christianity are also discussed.

Beyond all "liberal institutions" (*TI* "Forays" 38, p. 112), Nietzsche wants to develop a *"concept of freedom"* (*TI* "Forays" 38, *KSA* 6, pp. 112–13) — "as something that you have and have *not*, that you *want*, that you *conquer . . .*" (*TI* "Forays" 38, p. 113). Goethe, with his "naturalness of the Renaissance" (*TI* "Forays" 49, p. 122), is, for the genius-aesthetics of the final paragraphs, a paradigmatic shining light which is outshone only by Nietzsche's own ego.

The tenth chapter, "What I Owe the Ancients," which was inserted at a late stage, seems to choose an autobiographical theme but wants most of all to show that, since *The Birth of Tragedy*, the "revaluation of all values" has been the crucial motif of Nietzsche's life. The final sentence of the chapter also marks this "return" of a vital subject, where the authorial voice confesses to being "the teacher of the eternal recurrence" (*TI* "Ancients" 5, p. 131). The "eternal recurrence" as an ontological or ethical "doctrine" appears nowhere else in *Twilight of the Idols*, and moreover, it is only of marginal significance in Nietzsche's late work that he published or prepared for publication. "What I Owe the Ancients" emphasizes its being influenced by the Roman style (Sallust and Horace), whereas the authorial voice, which otherwise presents itself as being so Graecophile, now claims that "I do not owe the Greeks anything like such strong impressions" (*TI* "Ancients" 2, p. 126); instead, the alien nature of original Hellenism is worked out and emphasized against the "preexistent-Christian" Plato (*TI* "Ancients" 2, p. 126). Thucydides, on the other hand, is said to be helpful. Finally, Nietzsche addresses the Dionysian, which he claims had been rediscovered by him.

For the original draft of the text, the two compilations of aphorisms — "Sayings and Arrows" and "Forays of an Untimely One" — were placed respectively at the beginning and end of the book, thus providing a frame. The compilation of maxims at the beginning served to build up tension; then the longer aphorisms of the "Forays" at the end, which view many contemporary issues from an untimely perspective, served to gradually moderate the tension. In October 1888, when Nietzsche decided to write *Ecce Homo*, he added the chapter "What I Owe the Ancients" to *Twilight of the Idols*. This addition broke up the unity of *Twilight of the Idols* being framed by the two compilations of aphorisms. But this chapter also promises autobiographical information. This extension of the genre repertoire underlines the impression of a "complete overall introduction": the reader of *Twilight of the Idols* is not only provided with a survey of Nietzsche's mountain of thought but also of his landscapes of style and writing.

By his constant breaks in the text of *Twilight of the Idols*, by constantly changing the style, the speech melody, and the mood, Nietzsche refuses any kind of defining speech that, according to *TI* "Reason" 1 (pp. 57–58), has been characteristic of philosophers so far. A way of philosophizing that privileges becoming can at best be adequately expressed by statements that are countered by their opposites. Also in view of the fundamental critique of language articulated particularly in *TI* "Reason" 5 (pp. 59–60) and *TI* "Forays" 26 (p. 103), this constraint of self-dissolution applies: a critique of language can articulate itself only linguistically. Therefore, the language in *Twilight of the Idols* must repeatedly suspend all assertions that point to the possibility of a reality beyond the linguistic constraints of thought.

For a long time *Twilight of the Idols* was overshadowed by other works of Nietzsche — particularly as long as one believed some major work — "The Will to Power" or "The Revaluation of All Values" — to be hidden somewhere in the literary *Nachlass*. Indeed, as a matter of fact, in view of this major work still to come, Nietzsche defined *Twilight of the Idols* as a preparatory and serious yet secondary writing. Since 1884, Nietzsche had been extensively working on a major work that was repeatedly redesigned and repeatedly announced in his published works and unpublished notebooks. He constantly changed, multiplied, and reformulated his plans for a major work — only to reject them. Frequently such plans became concrete in certain works, whereas the so-called magnum opus was again and again postponed into the future. Therefore, most of Nietzsche's late works may be understood as the splitting and decaying results of the plans for a major work. This, however, does not reduce their significance but instead highlights these late works, as it is not appropriate to try to reconstruct any major work or system from the literary remains.

Twilight of the Idols itself is crucial for Nietzsche's oeuvre, because, like a compendium, this writing compresses Nietzsche's thought in his late period and protreptically provides a synthesis as well as a general overview of his ways of thinking and writing. The abandonment of "main doctrines" in this work is not the result of any incapacity but is instead programmatically intended.

In early 1889, the first public perception of *Twilight of the Idols* occurred under the aura of Nietzsche's mental collapse. Nietzsche's friend Franz Overbeck, confronted with the question of which of Nietzsche's literary remains were to be published and in what way, wrote to Erwin Rohde on 22 January 1889 that *Twilight of the Idols* does not show "any trace of madness, at most in a few places the threat of megalomania; otherwise as violent as ever, but intellectually sparkling and everywhere lucid, wonderfully lucid, and strictly oriented to the goal to which the author is heading."[51] The spectrum of contemporary reviews ranged from scorn and rejection to unreserved enthusiasm. The critics were increasingly ready to take Nietzsche's self-characterizations at face value and to spin his metaphors. A notice for *Twilight of the Idols* by "Fritz Hammer" (pseudonym for Michael Georg Conrad), for example, says: "Now Nietzsche's writings are coming one after the other, like the thunderbolts of a great, beautiful thunderstorm — Nietzsche is such a thunderstorm on the dull horizon of Europe's culture."[52] The early reception of

51. Franz Overbeck and Erwin Rohde, *Briefwechsel,* ed. Andreas Patzer (Berlin: de Gruyter, 1990), 133.

52. Quoted in Richard Frank Krummel, *Nietzsche und der deutsche Geist: Ausbreitung und Wirkung des Nietzscheschen Werkes im deutschen Sprachraum bis zum Ende des Zweiten Weltkrieges: Ein Schrifttumsverzeichnis der Jahre 1867–1945* (Berlin: de Gruyter, 1998), 1:169.

Twilight of the Idols shows all those signs of the Nietzsche cult that developed in the 1890s and adapted the exaltation inherent in Nietzsche's late writings.

The Antichrist: Curse upon Christianity

In the summer of 1888, Nietzsche stayed in Sils-Maria until 20 September and then went on an adventurous journey back to Turin. There, on 30 September, the manuscript of the first book of the planned "Revaluation of All Values," *The Antichrist*, was completed. "It is full of energy and clarity," Nietzsche says in a letter to Overbeck on 14 September 1888 (*KGB* III:5, 434), "that perhaps no other philosopher has ever achieved. It seems to me as if suddenly I have learned how to *write*. As for the content, the passion of the problem, this work cuts through the millennia — [. . .] and I want to swear that every critique of Christianity that has ever been thought or spoken is nothing but child's play compared to it."

In the autumn, there is still talk of four books of the "Revaluation" — "they will be published individually," Nietzsche writes to Overbeck on 18 October (*KGB* III:5, 453). On 30 October (*KGB* III:5, 462), Nietzsche announces *Ecce Homo* to Heinrich Köselitz, while telling about its completion in several letters from 13 and 14 November (*KGB* III:5, 466–72). "The whole thing is the prelude to the *Revaluation of All Values*, the work *I have readily at hand*: I swear to you that two years from now we will see all the world in convulsions," Nietzsche told Georg Brandes on 20 November 1888 (*KGB* III:5, 482). Both from this letter and from the one to Paul Deussen on 26 November (*KGB* III:5, 492), it becomes obvious that from this point on, Nietzsche considered the "Revaluation of All Values" completed; instead of four books, now it was supposed to be only one, the completed *Antichrist*: "My *Revaluation of All Values*, with the main title 'The Antichrist,' is finished. In the next two years I will have to take care that the work will be translated into 7 languages; the first edition in each language c. one million copies." In the postscript to these lines to Deussen, it says again: "My health is now wonderful, I have grown the strongest" (*KGB* III:5, 493).

In early December, Nietzsche increasingly saw himself in the role of political agitator. For instance, in the draft of a letter to Georg Brandes of early December 1888 (*KGB* III:5, 500–501), we read:

> We have entered great politics, even the greatest . . . I am preparing an event which will most likely split history into two halves, to the point that we will have a new calendar: starting with 1888 as Year One. Everything which is up today, Triple Alliance, the social question, will completely be transformed into an antagonism between individuals: we are going to have wars like never before, but *not* between nations, *not* between classes: everything is burst apart — I am the most terrible kind of dynamite there is. — In 3 months I want to give orders for the production of a *manuscript* edition of |"The *Antichrist*. Revaluation of All Values"|, it remains completely secret: it will serve as my agitation edition. [. . .] As this is an *extermination blow* against *Christianity*, it is obvious that the only international power having an instinctive interest in the annihilation of Christianity is the *Jews* — here there is an instinctive enmity, not something "imagined" like with any "free spirits" or socialists — I do not care about free spirits. Consequently, we must be sure about all the crucial potentials of that race in Europe and America — furthermore, such a movement needs high finance. Here is the only natural ground for the greatest decisive war in history: other supporters can be considered only *after* the strike. This new power which is going to develop here may in less than no time be the first *world power*: granted, at first the *ruling* classes will take Christianity's part, thus the axe will be ⟨laid⟩ at their roots insofar as indeed all strong and living individuals *will inevitably leave* them. That all intellectually unhealthy races within Christianity will feel the faith of their

rulers on this occasion, and *consequently* take part in the lie,
guessing this does not require one to be a psychologist. The
result is that here the dynamite will explode all army organization, all constitution: that the enemy embodies nothing else
and stands unprepared for war. All in all, the officers by their
instincts will be for us: that to the highest degree it is *dishonor-
able, cowardly, impure* to be a Christian, this judgment one
will inevitably take with oneself from my "Antichrist."

It seems, however, that Nietzsche never sent such a letter to
Brandes, as was also the case with the letters dating from the
same time to Otto von Bismarck and Emperor William II (*KGB*
III:5, 503–5). Obviously, the passage critical of Jewry in *The
Antichrist* did not change Nietzsche's belief that "the *whole Jewish* high finance" (to Köselitz, 9 December 1888, *KGB* III:5, 515)
would join his movement. Nevertheless, Nietzsche did not consider the immediate publication of *The Antichrist* qua "Revaluation"; first, translations were to be started. According to *EH* III
WA 4 (p. 304), the "shattering lightning bolt of the *Revaluation*"
was intended first for 1890, which is also clearly indicated by the
letters to Naumann of 7 September (*KGB* III:5, 411), 18 September (*KGB* III:5, 441), and 6 November 1888 (*KGB* III:5, 463–64).
After Nietzsche's collapse in early 1889, however, a publication
of *The Antichrist* was for some years out of the question.

The Antichrist, in contrast to Nietzsche's aphorism books as
well as *Twilight of the Idols*, is thematically very clearly structured, and the main sources that Nietzsche drew from can be
clearly associated with individual parts of the work, even though
Nietzsche, as was his habit, recontextualized and amalgamated
those sources without revealing them. For his criticism of the
Jewish-Christian concept of God in §§16–19, Wellhausen's *Prolegomena zur Geschichte Israels* as well as Dostoevsky's *The Possessed* supply important catchwords. The depiction of Buddhism
in §§20–23 is indebted to Hermann Oldenberg's *Buddha: Sein
Leben, seine Lehre, seine Gemeinde*.[53] For sketching the history
of Israel, for Jewry, and for early Christianity, Nietzsche drew

from Wellhausen's *Prolegomena zur Geschichte Israels*, and for
his idea of Jesus, despite all his polemics, he borrowed from
Renan's *Vie de Jésus*. Tolstoi's *Ma religion*[54] was also somewhat
influential. The characterization of Jesus as an idiot was likely
due to Nietzsche's probably secondhand knowledge of Dostoevsky's novel *The Idiot*. Renan's *Origines du Christianisme* as
well as Julius Lippert's *Christenthum, Volksglaube und Volksbrauch*[55] provided the material for shaping the prehistory and
early history of Christianity. For his presentation of *The Laws of
Manu*, Nietzsche referred to Jacolliot's 1876 edition *Les législateurs
religieux: Manou, Moïse, Mahomet*, which even in his day had
been largely discredited.[56] The image of the Renaissance in §61 is
much influenced both by Burckhardt's *Die Cultur der Renaissance in Italien* and by Taine.[57] Nietzsche's psycho-physiological
information goes back to Féré's *Sensation et mouvement* and
Dégénérescence et criminalité, while Guyau's *L'irréligion de l'avenir*
contributed specific information about the psychology of religion, and Lecky[58] contributed cultural-historical information.

In contrast to *Twilight of the Idols* and *Ecce Homo*, *The Antichrist* is composed as a continuous polemical treatise consisting of a foreword and sixty-two paragraphs. The subtitle, initially "Attempt at a Critique of Christianity" in the draft
versions, was changed to "Curse upon Christianity"; finally
Nietzsche also deleted the reference to the "Revaluation of All
Values" which originally had also been used as a subtitle.

53. Hermann Oldenberg, *Buddha: Sein Leben, seine Lehre, seine Gemeinde*
(Berlin: Hertz, 1881). *NL*.

54. Leo Tolstoi, *Ma religion* (Paris: Fischbacher, 1885).

55. Julius Lippert, *Christenthum, Volksglaube und Volksbrauch: Geschicht-
liche Entwicklung ihres Vorstellungsinhaltes* (Berlin: Hofmann, 1882). *NL*.

56. Cf. *AC* note 236, p. 532.

57. Hippolyte Taine, *Geschichte der englischen Literatur,* vol. 1: *Die Anfänge
und die Renaissance-Zeit der englischen Literatur,* trans. Leopold Katscher
(Leipzig: Ernst Julius Günther, 1878). *NL*.

58. Lecky, *Geschichte des Ursprungs und Einflusses der Aufklarung in Europa*
and *Sittengeschichte Europas von Augustus bis auf Karl den Grossen.*

By way of several theoretical attempts, *The Antichrist* wants to
prove that Christianity is a product of nihilism that is hostile to
all natural life events. Although the Foreword rejects the ordinary reader — "This book belongs to the very few" — it is a
work that Nietzsche, according to his own written evidence,
intended for a broad audience. His criticism, whose principles
are explained in §§1–7, is stated from the "we"-perspective of
"Hyperboreans" who consider everything good "that heightens
the feeling of power, the will to power, power itself in humans"
(p. 135), and who consider everything to be bad that comes from
weakness. While the Christian (as well as Schopenhauer's) virtue of compassion as suffering-with (*Mit-Leiden*) the weak is
sharply criticized, the breeding of a higher type of human is
advocated. Christianity has initiated a *"war to the death"* (p. 136)
against these strong humans who do not care about traditional
morals. The values of *décadence* have gained the upper hand in
modern times, for which Christianity is directly held responsible. Precisely by compassion, says Nietzsche, Christianity persuades to nothingness, it denies life.

Sections 8–14 denounce Western philosophy as an enterprise
that has thoroughly been ruined by theology. This becomes
particularly obvious in German philosophy, dominated as it is
by Protestantism, especially in Kant. The philosopher appears
almost everywhere as the "further development of the priestly
type" (p. 143), whereas the newly proclaimed philosophy should
be skeptical, scientifically methodical, and modest — modest
in particular when it comes to anthropology, as human beings
are nothing more than the sickest animal, albeit also the most
interesting one. The idea of a mind that is independent of the
body is also subjected to ridicule.

Section 15 marks the transition to a more detailed analysis of
Christianity, first by attesting to its complete blindness to reality
in the service of a negation of the world. This is followed, in
§§16–19, by a "critique of the *Christian concept of God*" (p. 146).
Disparaging God, from a god of the people embodying the fullness of life "in good and bad alike" to a god only of the good, is

outlined in the Jewish-Christian history. Then, in Christianity, God appears as acting against life. It is worrying, Nietzsche says, that the "strong races of northern Europe" (p. 148) did not succeed with offering stronger opposition to this god. §§20–23 compare two "*décadence*-religions" (p. 149), Christianity and Buddhism. In this comparison, Buddhism frequently comes off better, as it is only interested in the fight against suffering and does not care about imaginary things like sin. It refrains from any coercion as well as prayer and asceticism; *ressentiment* is as alien to Buddhism, as the product of the higher classes, as is the fight against dissidents. Christianity, on the other hand, wants to tame the barbarians by making them sick.

With §24 there starts the discussion of the history of the origin, development, and effects of Christianity, which continues, with occasional interruptions, through to §61. First, the development of Christianity is presented as a logical consequence of Judaism, in the context of which the latter's history is depicted as a continuous "*denaturalization* of natural values" (p. 155) that establishes a "*ressentiment*-morality" (p. 154) against an originally dominant "*noble* morality" (p. 154). Christianity appears as an anarchistic continuation of Judaism, with the "psychological type of the Redeemer" deriving completely from the *décadence* schema (§§28–35): *The Antichrist* puts forward Jesus as an "idiot" (p. 161) who is incapable of heroism; who, due to an exaggerated capacity for suffering, gives up all detachment; and who, as a "great symbolist" (p. 166), is completely undone by love. Thus, the basis of its self-legitimation is consistently withdrawn from Christianity.

The example of Jesus, Nietzsche says, was completely misunderstood by the early Christians; in particular, Paul is denounced as a "genius in hatred" (p. 174). The theory of the sacrifice and of immortality are the tools with which the moral falsification of Christianity has become world-historically effective (§§37–46). Christianity in particular maintains a radically negative attitude toward the sciences (§§44–49). Sections 50–55 sketch a "psychology of belief," according to which beliefs are prisons, against which one can arm oneself with skepticism and philology. As a countermodel to Christianity and as an example of the socially healthy use of the "holy lie," §§56 and 57 provide an insight into *The Laws of Manu*, whose caste order is explicitly endorsed in *The Antichrist* (in contrast to highly critical notes by Nietzsche on *Manu* in the notebooks, cf., e.g., *CW* 18, 14[203–4] = *KGW* IX 8, W II 5, 13). According to §§58–61, Christianity undermined the Roman Empire, destroyed the cultural heritage of antiquity, was hopelessly inferior to Islam, and finally, in the form of the Reformation, stifled the auspicious anti-Christian tendencies of the Renaissance. The final paragraph once again summarizes these accusations in the form of a judgment, whereas the attached "Law Against Christianity" lists some of its representatives and representations as being damnable.

The Antichrist, which comes along as a decree tolerating no dissent, seems to confirm Nietzsche's exit from the circle of philosophers, just as he had left the circle of philologists with *The Birth of Tragedy*: the "Law Against Christianity" appended to the work designates the philosopher as the "criminal of criminals." Up to the present, according to the assessment underlying this condemnation, philosophy has been in the service of that kind of morality — hostile to life — by way of which Christianity had determined the fate of the world. At the same time, Nietzsche continues the critical business he had been doing already in the works of his free spirit phase: the "Revaluation," as contained in *The Antichrist*, is most of all a demolition project that only hints at what a new kind of morality might look like that is not hostile to life — that key category Nietzsche continues to advocate.

"Everything else follows from this" (p. 209) says the "Seventh Sentence" of the "Law Against Christianity." We may suppose that in the same way that the reader was supposed to conclude that the revaluation of all values "follows" from this exemplary critique of Christianity, this conclusion was supposed to happen in the practice of life. This writing, masterfully applying different methods of unmasking (psychological, "physiological," philological, historical) and bringing new points of view to bear, is also significant because here Nietzsche's so-called main doctrines either do not play any role at all (eternal return), are only discussed in passing (superhuman), or are rendered problematic (will to power, a quality that the Redeemer-type obviously lacks). Despite his intensified tone and message, Nietzsche's *Antichrist* shows signs of a shift of emphasis — such as when emphatically speaking out in favor of a new form of skepticism (§54). It should be noted that this shift of focus has in most cases been neglected in the reception history of *The Antichrist*, which has usually been motivated either by apologetics or polemics. The unprecedented sharpness of the tone, it must also be noted, has provoked and continues to provoke strong defensive reactions on the part of *The Antichrist*'s exegetes.

After Nietzsche had slipped into madness, the publication of *The Antichrist* was initially postponed. But it did get published — in contrast to *Ecce Homo* — in November 1894, with 1895 as its official year of publication, in the context of the first complete edition by Fritz Koegel, under the supervision of Elisabeth Förster-Nietzsche. Nietzsche's sister withheld four passages (discussed in the notes on p. 509) that seemed to her to be particularly disreputable: where Jesus was directly addressed as an "idiot" (p. 161); where Nietzsche insulted the reigning Kaiser William II (p. 170); which raised doubts about Nietzsche's knowledge of the Bible (p. 167); and which might possibly suggest his delusions of grandeur (p. 207). Although from 1895 on, *The Antichrist* was again and again reprinted in complete editions of Nietzsche's works, the first German individual edition appeared only in 1932, while individual editions of the work in French, English, and Spanish translation were available much earlier.

In the reception history of *The Antichrist*, reactions of shock and rejection were numerous, and not just among theologians. This strand of the reception of *The Antichrist* is dominated by the motif of psychopathologizing Nietzsche's late works. The thesis is that these writings already reveal Nietzsche's madness and that in particular *The Antichrist* cannot be taken seriously as a philosophical text. An opposite strand of Nietzsche reception, on the other hand, keeps its distance from any pathologizing tendencies and looks for the philosophical content of Nietzsche's late works. This strand was supported by Mazzino Montinari, who provided evidence that Nietzsche finally abandoned his plan for a "main work in prose" with the title "The Will to Power."[59]

The Antichrist is particularly significant for Nietzsche's reception in the fields of religion and religious criticism. On the one hand, the writing had a catalytic effect in terms of the founding of a "Nietzschean religion"[60] in so far as, with the example of Christianity, it sketches the most drastic antithesis to what religious Nietzscheans considered desirable. Nevertheless, *The Antichrist* was hardly suitable for developing the positive utopia of a new religion: despite the comparably positive judgments on Israel before the period of exile, Buddhism, Hinduism according to Manu, and Islam, Nietzsche's anti-Christian critique of Christianity leaves not one positive religion untouched, so that only a one-sided reading that ignored those features that were straightforwardly hostile to religion itself could make *The Antichrist* a text that would serve to support a Nietzschean religion.

On the other hand, friends and defenders of Christianity felt their self-image to be put into question. Theological attempts to deal with Nietzsche's fundamental criticism, and in particular with *The Antichrist*, range from rugged self-assertion by way of retreating to dogmatic core beliefs to grand gestures

59. See "Nietzsche's Unpublished Writings 1885–1888 and the 'Will to Power'" above and republished in *CW* 17; see also Mazzino Montinari, "Nietzsche's Unpublished Writings from 1885 to 1888; or, Textual Criticism and the Will to Power," in *Reading Nietzsche*, trans. Greg Whitlock (Urbana: University of Illinois Press, 2003), 80–102; Werner Stegmaier, "Nietzsches Kritik der Vernunft seines Lebens: Zur Deutung von 'Der Antichrist' und 'Ecce homo,'" *Nietzsche-Studien* 21 (1992): 163–83; Andreas Urs Sommer, *Friedrich Nietzsches "Der Antichrist": Ein philosophisch-historischer Kommentar* (Basel: Schwabe, 2000).

60. Steven E. Aschheim, *The Nietzsche Legacy in Germany, 1890–1990* (Berkeley: University of California Press, 1993), 201.

of incorporation. Demonizing Nietzsche as an eschatological figure or as a demonic liquidator of Christian truths, which has dominated the theological Nietzsche literature for a long time, has in many cases been replaced by domesticating him as an unfortunately unredeemed seeker of God. This pattern of re-theologizing Nietzsche became common as early as around 1900, leading to sharp protest from Nietzsche's friend Franz Overbeck.[61]

Among some people it has become an established idea that Nietzsche had only aimed at those wrong developments in the history of Christianity, so that as a Christian one might definitely agree with his objections, in order to defend a reformed or reforming Gospel. But Peter Köster's diagnosis has thus far not been refuted: "*One* idea seems to cause serious difficulties for theological authors and to affect their sense of self: that is the idea that Nietzsche might have grasped some essential features of Christianity very critically and yet accurately — and could nevertheless still have negated it."[62]

Authors with an interest in theology found it particularly difficult to cope with Nietzsche's reconstruction of Jesus, with his "psychology of the Redeemer" in *The Antichrist*. Eugen Biser, in his numerous publications on the topic, never ceased to emphasize Nietzsche's "never completely abandoned connection" to Jesus.[63] But as Ulrich Willers responds: "Taken out of their context, these texts [in *The Antichrist*] may possibly give the impression that Nietzsche wanted to support the true Gospel of Jesus against Paul's 'dysangel,' the Church, indeed Christianity. But it is only true that Nietzsche in his fight against

61. Cf., e.g., Franz Overbeck, *Werke und Nachlass,* vol. 7/2: *Autobiographisches: "Meine Freunde Treitschke, Nietzsche und Rohde,"* ed. Barbara von Reibnitz and Marianne Stauffacher-Schaub (Stuttgart: J. B. Metzler, 1999), 195–96.

62. Peter Köster, "Nietzsche-Kritik und Nietzsche-Rezeption in der Theologie des 20. Jahrhunderts," *Nietzsche-Studien* 10/11 (1981/82): 684.

63. Eugen Biser, "Nietzsches Verhaltnis zu Jesus: Ein literarisch-psychologischer Vergleich," *Concilium: Internationale Zeitschrift fur Theologie* 17 (1981): 405.

Christianity is able to use even Jesus as a weapon, which he consequently does. False, on the other hand, is the idea that Nietzsche is some kind of a teacher of an imitatio Christi."[64]

Ecce Homo: How One Becomes What One Is

Already as a gymnasium and university student, Nietzsche several times wrote reflections on his own life and gave account of its course, as if wanting to provide the contingency of his existence with a touch of necessity. We can, therefore, speak of a constant autobiographical interest that finally culminates in *Ecce Homo*, a writing Nietzsche started on his forty-fourth birthday, 15 October 1888. However, considering *Ecce Homo* a conventional autobiography would be an overly narrow interpretation of the book's intention and content. Friedrich Kittler[65] and Sarah Kofman[66] have both rightly pointed to the fact that this seemingly autobiographical text actually undermines the genre of authobiography. Werner Stegmaier considers the work a narrative depiction of the "living condition of his thought."[67] Against this background, Enrico Müller and I speak of an "autogenealogy" instead of an autobiography.[68]

In a letter to his publisher Naumann of 6 November 1888 (*KGB* III:5, 464), Nietzsche wrote: "In this way, I have *completed* an *extremely heavy* task — that of narrating myself, my

64. Ulrich Willers, *Friedrich Nietzsches antichristliche Christologie: Eine theologische Rekonstruktion* (Innsbruck: Tyrolia, 1988), 275.

65. Friedrich Kittler, "Wie man abschafft, wovon man spricht: Der Autor von 'Ecce homo,'" *Literaturmagazin* 12 (1980): 153–78.

66. Sarah Kofman, *Explosion I: De l'"Ecce homo" de Nietzsche* (Paris: Galilée, 1992).

67. Werner Stegmaier, "Nietzsches Kritik der Vernunft seines Lebens: Zur Deutung von 'Der Antichrist' und 'Ecce homo,'" *Nietzsche-Studien* 21 (1992): 163–83, 168.

68. Enrico Müller and Andreas Urs Sommer, "Einleitung zur Werkstatt [über Nietzsches Ecce homo]," in *Nietzscheforschung: Jahrbuch der Nietzsche-Gesellschaft 12: Bildung – Humanitas – Zukunft bei Nietzsche* (Berlin: Akademie, 2005), 127–31, 130.

books, my opinions and, piecemeal where necessary, *my life* — between 15 October and 4 November." According to this written statement, in *Ecce Homo* the narration of Nietzsche's life is subordinated to explaining the "books," the "opinions," and the "self." The actual autobiographical element is only functionally related to the exposition of the work, its main ideas, and the character of its creator. In fact, this writing in its final version does not offer any chronological account of Nietzsche's life, but instead makes use of biographical information in the discussion of several questions ("Why I Am So Wise," "Why I Am So Clever," etc.) when he believes this information to be useful for answering these questions. This biographical information, inserted bit by bit, thus has a subsidiary function: it serves to verify, support, or illustrate, but it is not told for its own sake.

Someone not familiar with Nietzsche's biography would hardly be able to gain any coherent picture of the course of his life from this autobiographical information. Indeed, it does not follow any chronological narrative but offers only some biographical details of his life or about certain particularities of the person Friedrich Nietzsche when these are helpful for emphasizing the productivity of Nietzsche's thought and the significance of his revaluation project. This kind of information has a verifying function: a specific kind of thought proves its worth in the life of the thinker; and vice versa, this life, by overcoming the threat of *décadence*, must produce an antidecadent, thus anti-Christian and immoralistic, kind of thought. *Ecce Homo* does not propagate any simple causal relation between thought and life, such that thought can simply shape a life or that life must necessarily produce a specific kind of thought. Rather, in a variety of ways, *Ecce Homo* illustrates the interconnectedness of thought and life.

Even before *Ecce Homo*, Nietzsche's autogenealogical reflections revolved around the conditions under which his works developed. Characteristic of this are the prefaces Nietzsche attached to the new editions of 1886 and 1887 of *The Birth of Tragedy, Human, All Too Human, Dawn,* and *The Joyful Science.*

They provide a specific reading of these writings, namely, one that views Nietzsche's oeuvre as a coherent, consistent unity. At the same time, the propagandist-protreptic intent of these new prefaces is unmistakable: they were supposed to invite a new way of philosophizing (one radically different from anything that precedes it), while at the same time making a case for why the books, some of which were several years old, are still — and now more than ever — worth reading. *Ecce Homo* as a whole serves a similar propagandist function as do these prefaces in so far as it points to Nietzsche's "Revaluation of All Values" (see *EH* Foreword, p. 212). In contrast to these prefaces, *Ecce Homo* is not primarily retrospective but is both prospective and retrospective: prospective when it comes to the announced "Revaluation of All Values," retrospective when it comes to the course of his thought thus far. This prospective-retrospective double view concerns not only Nietzsche's own origins and future but also the course of world history as a whole: *Ecce Homo* looks back on a history of cultural decline and means to open the prospect of a promising future that will be determined by the revaluation of all values to come. In the exemplary "I" that speaks in *Ecce Homo*, not only do individual past and future consolidate into one Dionysian present, but world history as a whole comes to its peripety in this "I" who, according to the final chapter, believes itself to be "a destiny."

It is not quite clear whether Nietzsche really intended to incorporate the entire original version of *Ecce Homo* into the text of *Twilight of the Idols*, as he finally did with the *Twilight of the Idols* chapter "What I Owe the Ancients," even if Montinari states definitively: "*Ecce Homo* had initially been intended as an appendix of *Twilight of the Idols*."[69] In the same context of the literary remains, we find some draft titles making clear that the thematic reorientation of the developing text went in different directions: "*Fridericus Nietzsche / de vita sua. /*

69. Mazzino Montinari, "Nietzsche lesen: Die Götzen-Dämmerung," *Nietzsche-Studien* 13 (1984): 69–79, 72.

Translated into German." (*CW* 18, 24[4]) sounds like a conventional title for an autobiography and, by way of being written in Latin, is obviously supposed to underline the "very serious attempt at the *Roman* style" (*TI* "Ancients" 1, p. 125). "*The Mirror /* Attempt / at a Self-Evaluation." (*CW* 18, 24[5]) aims at a critical self-assessment, whereas "*Vademecum.* / On the Reasonability of My Life." (*CW* 18, 24[8]) makes us rather expect a handbook on self-inspiration. Finally, "*Ecce Homo /* Notes / of a Multitude." (*CW* 18, 24[3]) opens the horizon of a dazzling array of possible self-interpretations that should correspond to the diversity of Nietzsche's work and personality. However, this multiplicity is not really helpful for the intention, articulated later in *Ecce Homo*, to be a work preparing and controlling the reception of the "Revaluation of All Values," because multiplicity refuses any attempt to unify into a single particular effect. Nevertheless, this final version of *Ecce Homo* still depicts a multiplicity and thus only conditionally obeys a linear intention to propagate a singular effect on its readers.

On 24 October 1888, Nietzsche received, from Leipzig, the galleys of the *Twilight of the Idols* chapter "What I Owe the Ancients." The title of the new autogenealogical writing was fixed on or before 30 October 1888 (*KGB* III:5, 462), when Nietzsche wrote to Köselitz: "The weather is so beautiful that it is not difficult at all to do something *well*. I began something new again on my birthday, which seems to be turning out well and is already considerably advanced. It is called **Ecce homo**. Or *How One Becomes What One Is*. With great audacity, it is about myself and my writings: it was not just intended to introduce myself *before* the quite uncanny, solitary act of the *Revaluation* — I would like to try out *how much* I could really risk, given the German ideas of *freedom of the press*." Indeed, in the autumn of 1888, the manuscript underwent numerous revisions and new versions, even after Nietzsche had sent a version to Naumann, his publisher. After Nietzsche's collapse, Köselitz took charge of the printer's manuscript, still in Naumann's possession, in early

1889, made a copy, and forwarded it to Overbeck on 27 February, together with the remark: "I just wanted that you, dear Professor, should learn about this writing first based on my copy, that is *without* those passages that give even me the impression of too great self-intoxication or of going too far in their contempt and injustice — thus so as to provide you with *the* impression that I am not really capable of having myself, as I bring to mind the eccentric passages too easily."[70] According to Montinari's observations, Köselitz's copy (with the exception of some minor differences) is textually congruent with the text of the preserved printed copy that Nietzsche had revised himself. From this, Montinari concludes that one must assume "that at that time there still existed further passages of the text that Nietzsche probably sent to the printer in the form of single sheets, but that were deliberately left out by Köselitz in his copy."[71] At the same time, Montinari rules out that Köselitz himself had unilaterally destroyed any manuscripts left by Nietzsche.

On the other hand, Franziska Nietzsche and Elisabeth Förster-Nietzsche may well have destroyed some manuscript pages after Köselitz had handed over the complete printer's copy. In her Nietzsche biography, Elisabeth Förster-Nietzsche openly admits the destruction of complete documents: "At that time [early January 1889], he also wrote a few sheets with strange fantasies in which the myth of Dionysus-Zagreus merged with the Passion of the Gospel and with personalities closest to him from the present: torn apart by his enemies, the god wanders newly resurrected along the banks of the Po and now sees everything he has ever loved, his ideals, the ideals of the present in general, far below him [. . .] In the first years after my brother's illness, when we were still clinging to the false hope

70. Franz Overbeck and Heinrich Köselitz, *Briefwechsel,* ed. David Marc Hoffmann, Niklaus Peter, and Theo Salfinger (Berlin: de Gruyter, 1998), 241.
71. Karl Heinz Hahn and Mazzino Montinari, *Kommentar: Friedrich Nietzsche: Ecce homo: Faksimileausgabe der Handschrift* (Leipzig: Edition Leipzig, 1985), 66.

that he might recover, these sheets were mostly destroyed. It would have hurt my brother's loving heart and his good taste most deeply if he had ever caught sight of such writings afterwards."[72] Today no one can tell what exactly fell victim to the family's censorship.

By 1895, the other writings of Nietzsche's last year of work not published by Nietzsche himself — *Twilight of the Idols, Nietzsche Contra Wagner,* and *Dionysus Dithyrambs,* as well as *The Antichrist* — had all found their way into print. But when it came to *Ecce Homo,* Elisabeth Förster-Nietzsche took her time — almost twenty years, in fact. She exploited the work as a goldmine for her own publications on her brother — in particular for her voluminous biography. These publications were consecrated and authenticated by Nietzsche's otherwise unedited original passages.

When Förster-Nietzsche finally brought herself to have *Ecce Homo* printed, this was also supposed to result in financial gain: edited by the Leipzig philosophy professor Raoul Richter, who also contributed a postface, published by Insel-Verlag in Leipzig in 1908 with its layout designed by the famous Belgian artist Henry van de Velde, the first edition of *Ecce Homo* consisted of 1,100 copies on ordinary paper and another 150 copies printed on Japanese paper in "black and gold inks." The price of the common edition was 20 Reichsmark, that of the luxury edition was 50 Reichsmark — no wonder that this first edition of *Ecce Homo* was called the "bank director's edition."[73]

The final structure of *Ecce Homo* only emerged during the course of writing the text. It was a long process of restructuring and differentiation, from the October version to the intermediate draft to the versions of mid-November and the end of November to the revisions of early December and finally the

72. Elisabeth Förster-Nietzsche, *Das Leben Friedrich Nietzsche's,* vol. 2, pt. 2 (Leipzig: C. G. Naumann, 1904), 921.

73. William H. Schaberg, *The Nietzsche Canon: A Publication History and Bibliography* (Chicago: University of Chicago Press, 1995), 185.

end of December 1888.[74] The list of contents of the manuscript
of the final version (p. 216) mentions six actual chapter titles
— as well as, inserted after the third chapter title and indented
on new lines, the titles of ten of Nietzsche's books. Given the
vehement self-apotheosis of the "I" speaking in *Ecce Homo*, the
restriction to ten books (*The Antichrist* is not mentioned, nor
are the philologica) may be associated with the Mosaic Deca-
logue, and the six chapter titles with the six days of creation in
Genesis. However, this framework was ultimately passed over,
for the final two texts announced by chapter titles — "Declaration of War" and "The Hammer Speaks" — were finally abandoned (or perhaps destroyed by the family). Thus it might seem
as if *Ecce Homo* — apart from the list of contents and the
inserted "On this perfect day" (p. 217) — consists of only four
chapters, if the sections on the individual works, as is often
done, are considered subchapters of *Ecce Homo* "Books." However, the printer's manuscript includes this instruction for the
printer: "*End of the* chapter '*Why I Write Such Good Books*'" at
the end of *EH* III 6 (p. 587, note 34). Thus, the individual commentaries on Nietzsche's own books should not be considered
subchapters but chapters in their own right, which seems plau-
sible, given their respective lengths and the fact that they no
longer answer the question of *why* Nietsche writes such good
books but are rather dedicated to these books that have in themselves been declared good. In any case, the discussion of the history, intent, and idiosyncrasy of Nietzsche's own works is placed
at the center of *Ecce Homo*, while at the center of *The Antichrist*
stood the "psychology of the Redeemer" Jesus, who indeed produced no works of his own.

In its final version, the work is roughly structured into three
parts: first, Nietzsche wants to explain who he is. "Why I Am
So Wise" and "Why I Am So Clever" are dedicated to this
textual self-constitution of the speaking "I." This is followed

74. See Montinari's discussion of the construction of *Ecce Homo* above,
pp. 542–62.

by "Why I Write Such Good Books" and its second part, on the revolutionary creations of the exemplary "I," that is, on a selection of his writings that are named as the chapters' individual titles. It is not sufficient to present a genealogical and psychological-physiological analysis of this speaking "I," as Nietzsche had analyzed Jesus in *The Antichrist*, for what makes Nietzsche essentially different from Jesus is his work, which is to say, his books. Thus the books have to be placed at the center.

Finally, "Why I Am a Destiny" is the third part of this rough outline. In this chapter, what has thus far been kept separate — the person and the work — are brought together under the threatening and hopeful setting of destiny: unlike Jesus, the speaking "I" is not merely a world-historical destiny as a person; instead, the speaking "I" is a world-historical destiny because it stages a work — and indeed a work that will become reality in the form of the "Revaluation of All Values" and thereby cease to be mere literature. *Ecce Homo* as a work is supposed to prevent the obfuscation, obscuring, and annihilation of this work of destiny — something that, according to *The Antichrist*, happened to Jesus's "practice" in the form of Pauline Christianity. With the third part and last chapter of *Ecce Homo*, Nietzsche wants to impose himself on the world as destiny.

In its fine-tuning, the work shows itself as follows: *Ecce Homo* "Wise" discusses the familial-physiological conditions for the wisdom the "I" attributes to itself. It is essential in this context that it has experienced *décadence* itself but has overcome it, and that, at its core, this "I" was actually always healthy. The opposition of what has been inherited from father and mother respectively is reflected by this opposition of *décadence* and health; Nietzsche sees his own philosophy rising from the "will to health, to *life*" (p. 220). Despite its illness, the "I" feels "freedom from *ressentiment*" (p. 224) and believes that "attack" is one of its "instincts" (p. 226). As a final feature of its "nature," "a completely uncanny sensitivity of the instinct for cleanliness" (pp. 227–28) is mentioned, thanks to which Nietzsche also feels threatened by disgust toward humans.

Ecce Homo "Clever" makes the seemingly everyday matters of Nietzsche's existence — his diet, his whereabouts, the climate, and his ways of recreation — topics that are supposed to contribute to clarifying the question raised by the chapter's title. On the other hand, he claims that he never had to struggle with any metaphysical and religious problems; instead of idealities, he has kept reality in view, which is the reason for his particular cleverness.

Ecce Homo "Books" shifts attention from Nietzsche's wisdom and cleverness to his works, whose as yet limited reception invites reflections on being understood and misunderstood. Whoever satisfies the highest intellectual demands and is related to the speaking "I" "by the *loftiness* of their desire" (p. 251) will experience these writings with a pleasure of the highest degree — they are nothing less than the best books ever written, standing out because of their "*art of style*" (p. 252) and their psychological impact.

Then Nietzsche traces his creative path, discussing in individual chapters *The Birth of Tragedy, Unfashionable Observations, Human, All Too Human, Dawn, The Joyful Science, Thus Spoke Zarathustra, Beyond Good and Evil, On the Genealogy of Morality, Twilight of the Idols,* and *The Case of Wagner,* in that order and sometimes with several subsections, thereby presenting them as a unity. The writings are dealt with in chronological order, with the exception of *Twilight of the Idols* and *The Case of Wagner,* both of which were written in 1888 but treated in *Ecce Homo* in reverse order of creation. *The Antichrist* is not mentioned at all, for *Ecce Homo* as a whole was supposed to prepare for the "Revaluation of All Values," that is, for *The Antichrist.* The chapters dedicated to each work may be read as instructions for reading, retrospectively not only suggesting that the works form a single unit but overemphasizing certain traits while at the same time pointing out the circumstances under which each of them was written. Thus, when interpreting these writings, one is well advised not to follow the reading instructions given in *Ecce Homo,* for otherwise one will inevitably adopt

Nietzsche's unifying perspective of 1888 in anticipation of the "Revaluation of All Values," thereby reading each work teleologically as pointing to this single goal. *That* the reader should do this is undoubtedly Nietzsche's intention; however, the reader who is interested in each work's inherent nature is not obligated to follow this intention.

Ecce Homo "Destiny" provides a view of the "I" in its world-historical mission. This mission, it says, will soon be obvious to everybody, that is, by way of "a crisis such as the earth has never seen" (p. 305), the apocalyptic conflict between the old and the new world order. Only from this "I" determining the destiny of the world "will the earth have *grand politics*" (p. 306). The figure of Zarathustra is inaugurated as the prophet of the new age — the "I" understands itself as an immoralist whose task is the unmasking of previous morality, including Christianity. Life- and world-affirmation should replace the negation of world and denial of life. "*Dionysus versus the Crucified*" (p. 313) is the formula according to which the version of *Ecce Homo* that we know comes to an end.

The position of *Ecce Homo* among Nietzsche's corpus is unique. For the first and only time, Nietzsche molds in a book what, in his *Nachlass* as well as in the drafts and variants of his other books, has already become clear, namely, making himself the topic of discussion as a unique thinker-individual. Autogenealogical considerations are indeed frequently found among Nietzsche's works, but only and exclusively in *Ecce Homo* do they take shape as an independent work. Indeed, the genealogical method does not, as in *On the Genealogy of Morality*, serve to delegitimate — in *Genealogy* for delegitimating some fundamental values of the Christian occident — but in *Ecce Homo*, on the contrary, it serves to legitimate, to self-legitimate the speaking "I" as the Revaluer of All Values. If we understand *Ecce Homo* as Nietzsche wanted us to understand the work, as a preparation for the "Revaluation of All Values" that, from November 1888 on, he believed to have been literarily realized by *The Antichrist*, we easily recognize the completely opposite use Nietzsche makes of genealogical methods: if, in *The Anti-christ*, tracing back the pre-, early, and main history of Christianity, serves to unmask it as reprehensible, that same method, that is, bringing to light the pre-, early, and main history of the revaluating "I," creates the opposite effect: the effect of enobling. Thus, *Ecce Homo* demonstrates that the genealogical method does not work only in a negative way, as a strategy of unmasking, but can also work in a positive way, as a strategy of underpinning and elevation.

The significance of *Ecce Homo* is due less to the reader being provided with certain information about Nietzsche's life and work, and the genesis of his thought — all this information, if taken as historical facts, must be treated with the utmost caution. Its significance lies rather in the novelty of a positive genealogy. The revaluating "I," which so far has been critically-genealogically struggling with so many things, is provided in *Ecce Homo* with the only ultimately worthy subject, namely, itself. This is less due to madness than to method. This method consists not only of presenting one's own thought by its destructive power but, performatively, by its positivity. This can only be shown by example. This example is the speaking "I," deifying itself.

Nietzsche's intention is that the method practiced in *Ecce Homo* not be supposed to demonstrate desperate and fruitless self-reflection and intellectual exhaustion, as Giorgio Colli believed (cf. above, pp. 651–52) , but to disclose the first steps toward a positive kind of philosophy. This is underlined by the many quotations from *Thus Spoke Zarathustra*, especially from what Zarathustra himself says, which, on the one hand, support and counter any refutation of what is said in *Ecce Homo*, while, on the other hand, constantly drawing attention to what is affirmative in this work of Nietzsche's. Retrospectively, Nietzsche declares *Zarathustra* his main work whose appropriate reception is said to be the necessary precondition for the "shattering lightning bolt of the *Revaluation*, which is destined to send the earth into convulsions" (*EH* III WA4, p. 304). *Ecce Homo* is to prepare for this lightning bolt while, at the same time, providing an example of the new, positive world order: the autogenealogy presents an "I" that is committed to saying and doing "yes" instead of staying with the gesture of negation. And despite all threats of suffering, *décadence*, and Christian-nihilist values, this "I" presents itself as being fundamentally positive toward this world and this life; thus it wants to refute all apostles of negation and preachers of the Beyond. In other words, *Ecce Homo* is supposed to demonstrate the practical, the life-practical potential of Nietzsche's philosophy, by one example: Nietzsche's own life and work. Not only the *Zarathustra* quotations but *Ecce Homo* itself is supposed to substantiate Nietzsche's thought as a "practice" (*AC* 33, p. 165) suitable for the great individual. *Ecce Homo* is supposed to demonstrate what living according to Nietzsche's ideas actually looks like and how necessary for each individual is the implementation of her own revaluation of values in order to achieve an emphatically positive, "Dionysian" relation to herself and the world. Nietzsche publishes himself and intends to become an example of the future revaluations the readers are supposed to carry out in themselves and in their world.

When *Ecce Homo* was published in 1908, Nietzsche was already a well-established figure in Germany's cultural and academic realms. Thus it does not come as a surprise that the first edition of the work sold out on the first day of its publication. Accordingly, the contemporary reviews are numerous, covering the whole range of possible attitudes toward Nietzsche, from diagnosing psychopathology to enthusiastic adoration. At that time, as well as in subsequent years, the work could hardly be read without attending to Nietzsche's condition, which was generally known by 1908, so that soon there developed heated debates on the question of whether and how far *Ecce Homo* gave expression to Nietzsche's madness. Shortly after the publication of *Ecce Homo*, Sigmund Freud went on record, at the Wednesday Society of the Psychoanalytical Association of Vienna, as saying: "Where great minds have been befallen by paralysis, extraordinary achievements have been made until shortly before the illness

(Maupassant). The indication that this work by Nietzsche [i.e., *Ecce Homo*] must be considered full-fledged and serious is the fact that formal mastery has been maintained."[75] The circle around Stefan George, on the other hand, was rather reserved toward *Ecce Homo*, at least if we believe Ernst Gundolf: "A testimony of madness is also the book *Ecce Homo*."[76] *Ecce Homo* also had a deep impact on the fate of artist Adrian Leverkühn in Thomas Mann's *Doctor Faustus*. The idea, however, that "*Ecce Homo* [is] one of Nietzsche's best books," as Oscar Levy remarked in the introduction to the English edition of 1927,[77] did not seem to be a majority view even among Nietzsche enthusiasts, as the radical immodesty of its tone could hardly be accepted in an educated bourgeois context. Walter Kaufmann, in his Nietzsche account of 1950, lamented that *Ecce Homo* had insufficiently been taken into consideration in the philosophical literature on Nietzsche.[78] Later, Jacques Derrida, in his *Otobiographies*,[79] a conference text of 1976, made a productive philosophical use of *Ecce Homo* by contrasting it to the American Declaration of Independence. For Derrida, Nietzsche's text documents an alternation of masks and personal names in the service of vital self-constitution. Sarah Kofman follows Derrida's

75. Herman Nunberg and Ernst Federn, eds., *Protokolle der Wiener Psychoanalytischen Vereinigung*, 4 vols. (Frankfurt am Main: Psychosozial-Verlag, 1976–81), 2:56.

76. Ernst Gundolf and Kurt Hildebrandt, *Nietzsche als Richter unsrer Zeit* (Breslau: Ferdinand Hirt, 1923), 54.

77. Oscar Levy, *Nietzsche verstehen: Essays aus dem Exil 1913–1937*, ed. Steffen Dietzsch and Leila Kais = *Gesammelte Schriften und Briefe* (Berlin: Parerga, 2005), 1:155.

78. Walter Kaufmann, *Nietzsche: Philosopher, Psychologist, Antichrist*, 4th ed. (Princeton, NJ: Princeton University Press, 1974), 408.

79. Jacques Derrida, *Otobiographies: L'enseignement de Nietzsche et la politique du nom propre* (Paris: Galilée, 1984); English translation: "The Teaching of Nietzsche and the Politics of the Proper Name," trans. Avital Ronell, in *The Ear of the Other: Otobiography, Transference, Translation: Texts and Discussions with Jacques Derrida*, ed. Christie V. McDonald (New York: Schocken Books, 1985), 1–38.

approach in *Explosion I* and *II* (1992/93[80]), her own detailed commentary on *Ecce Homo*, although it is not free of a number of factual errors. Kofman understands *Ecce Homo* not as an autobiography but, like Derrida, as a textual masquerade in the midst of mirrors and competing self-descriptions, as a textual explosion of exuberant life forces. Of course, these do not exhaust the scope of possible interpretations.

Dionysus Dithyrambs

Shortly after having completed *Ecce Homo* in the late fall of 1888, and immediately before his collapse in Turin in the first days of January 1889, Nietzsche wrote the print version of his *Dionysus Dithyrambs* (a facsimile of the original manuscript can be found in the first volume of Wolfram Groddeck's *Friedrich Nietzsche "Dionysos-Dithyramben,"*[81] where the genesis of *Dionysus Dithyrambs* is meticulously reconstructed). Nietzsche based this work on a number of earlier texts, some of which were as yet unpublished or fragmentary, whereas others belonged to the fourth part of *Thus Spoke Zarathustra*, which he had shared with a small circle in the form of a private publication. Beginning in the summer of 1888, Nietzsche had composed five poems based on earlier drafts: "Among Birds of Prey," "The Beacon," "The Sun Is Sinking," "Fame and Eternity," and "On the Poverty of the Richest Man." Together with the poem "Last Will," which dates back to 1883, Nietzsche in a preliminary version of the prologue to *Ecce Homo* called these poems "the first 6 songs of Zarathustra" (*KGW* IX 9, W II 6, 6, 54). When he chose the title *Dionysus Dithyrambs* immediately before his collapse, to these six poems he added three more from *Zarathustra* IV: under the new title "Just a Fool! Just a Poet!," which was still described as a song of

80. Sarah Kofman, *Explosion I* (cf. note 66 above) and *Explosion II: Les enfants de Nietzsche* (Paris: Galilée, 1993).

81. Wolfram Groddeck, *Friedrich Nietzsche "Dionysos-Dithyramben,"* vol. 1: *Textgenetische Edition der Vorstufen und Reinschriften* (Berlin: de Gruyter, 1991), 255–308.

melancholy (its title in *Z* IV), he opened the *Dionysus Dithy-rambs*; he included the chapter "Among Daughters of the Des-ert" from *Z* IV (*CW* 7) together with the text that preceded the poem, but to which he added further verses following the line "*The desert grows: woe to those who harbor deserts.*" Finally, "Ariadne's Lament" is from *Z* IV "The Magician," where not Ariadne but the "penitent of the mind," fraudulently played by the magician, is the one who complains. And unlike *Z* IV, Dionysus himself appears at the end, fulfilling Ariadne's request.

As we know from a statement to Cosima Wagner, the printer's manuscript of *Dionysus Dithyrambs* was ready on 3 January 1889: "I am told that a certain divine buffoon has recently completed the Dionysus Dithyrambs . . . " (*KGB* III:5, 572). Owing to Nietzsche's collapse, however, the printing was post-poned. In 1890, Köselitz and Naumann decided to publish this compilation of poems together with *Z* IV, which, at that time, only existed as a very small and private print edition. Indeed, three out of the nine poems came from the *Zarathus-tra* text, although in different versions, so that now, as an appendix to *Z*, only the remaining six were supposed to be published as the *Dionysus Dithyrambs*. The printing of the vol-ume was completed by November 1890 and was supposed to be delivered in spring 1891, on the occasion of the Leipzig Book Fair. Then, however, Nietzsche's mother, urged by her daughter, intervened with the publisher and demanded that publication be suspended. Only after Elisabeth had been granted the complete copyright of her brother's writings and had wrested an additional fee from Naumann, one thousand copies of the volume, which had been printed long before, were finally delivered in March 1892.[82] The first complete edition of the *Dionysus Dithyrambs*, that is, all nine poems in the sequence of their clean copies of early January 1889, was published in 1898, in the context of the edition Elisabeth Förster-Nietzsche had

82. Friedrich Nietzsche, *Also sprach Zarathustra: Ein Buch für Alle und Keinen,* including an incomplete version of *Dionysos-Dithyramben* (Leipzig: C. G. Naumann, 1891); on the details, see Schaberg, *The Nietzsche Canon,* 173–77.

organized of her brother's *Gedichte und Sprüche* ("Poems and sayings").[83]

Some striking motifs permeate the *Dionysus Dithyrambs* — some that frequently appear in Nietzsche's writings, others that he adopted from contemporary *décadence* literature, and last of all, motifs that are latent but now are openly expressed by the lyrical "I." Three motifs are particularly striking, namely, death, truth, and loneliness.

The style of the *Dionysus Dithyrambs* betrays Nietzsche's preference of a sharply pointed style of writing that also characterizes his other writings after the *Zarathustra* period but is now taken to the extreme.

The *Dionysus Dithyrambs* have seldom been seriously and extensively appreciated as an independent work. Readers of Nietzsche usually pick individual poems and make use of them, each according to their own needs. Occasionally, the *Dionysus Dithyrambs* appear as being almost symptomatic of an epoch, as is the case in Oswald Spengler's *The Decline of the West* (1918/23), which treats them as representative of the downfall of occidental culture. There it is the motif of longing for distance which signals decadence: "The very words of distance possess, in the lyric poetry of all Western languages, a plaintive, autumnal accent that one looks for in vain in the Greek and Latin. It is there [. . .] in Nietzsche's Dionysus-Dithyrambs."[84] Only recently has the *Dionysus Dithyrambs* become a topic of independent research in its own right. A milestone in the history of this research is the two-volume work by Wolfram Groddeck,[85] which meticulously reconstructs the genesis of the texts and analyzes each dithyramb in detail.

83. Friedrich Nietzsche, *Gedichte und Sprüche* (Leipzig: C. G. Naumann, 1898), 133–68.

84. Oswald Spengler, *The Decline of the West,* trans. Charles Francis Atkinson (Oxford: Oxford University Press, 1991), 127.

85. Wolfram Groddeck, *Friedrich Nietzsche "Dionysos-Dithyramben,"* vol. 1: *Textgenetische Edition der Vorstufen und Reinschriften;* vol. 2: *Die "Dionysos-Dithyramben": Bedeutung und Entstehung von Nietzsches letztem Werk* (Berlin: de Gruyter, 1991).

Nietzsche Contra Wagner: Documents of a Psychologist

In September 1888, *The Case of Wagner* was published and soon attracted some attention, and not only among Nietzsche's friends and acquaintances. The editor of the *Kunstwart*, Ferdinand Avenarius, remarked that concerning Wagner, Nietzsche was showing a sudden change of heart, after having celebrated him so enthusiastically in the past. This made Nietzsche write him on 10 December 1888 (*KGB* III:5, 517–18):

> Please allow me, with all cheerfulness, a postscript: it seems as if in the case of Wagner it cannot be without a postscript.
> — Why, after all, did you deprive your readers of the *main thing*? That my "change of heart," as you call it, is not recent? I have been waging war against the *corruption* of Bayreuth for ten years now — since 1876, Wagner has regarded me as his real and only adversary, his later writings are full of the traces. The opposition of a décadent and a nature creating from an overabundance of power, that is, a *Dionysian* nature, for whom the most difficult is just a *game*, is palpable between us [. . .]. We are as different from each other as rich and poor. Among *musicians*, indeed there is no doubt about Wagner's poverty; before me, even the most obstinate people become honest, even the most extreme partisans of his cause have become honest about this point.

This is followed by some passages that are supposed to prove that Nietzsche's opposition to Wagner had been expressed in his works since 1876. Then on the following day, in a letter to Carl Spitteler (*KGB* III:5, 524), Nietzsche suggested the publication — printed in the same way as "The Case of Wagner" — of a volume of "8 extended, carefully selected pieces from my writings, under the title: Nietzsche *contra* Wagner. / Documents / from Nietzsche's Writings." This again is followed by a list of possible selections. As early as 12 December, however, Nietzsche decided to publish this writing himself, as he now told Spitteler (*KGB* III:5, 525): "Behind such a publication as I suggested yesterday I would anyway be assumed as the publisher — there are too many *private* matters mentioned in the pieces which have to be printed." Nietzsche made another plan (p. 634) which intended the aphorism "Astral Friendship" (*JS* 279) to come first. The version of the writing he sent to his publisher Naumann, on 15 December, no longer included this aphorism.

After some further changes, the writing — now titled "Nietzsche Contra Wagner. Documents of a Psychologist" — consisted of the following pieces: a newly written Foreword, the sections "Where I Admire" (reworked from *JS* 87), "Where I Object" (from *JS* 368), "Intermezzo" (from *EH* II 7), "Wagner as Danger 1" (from *MM* 134), "Wagner as Danger 2" (from *WS* 165), "A Music with No Future" (from *MM* 171), "We Antipodes" (from *JS* 370), "Where Wagner Belongs" (from *BGE* 254 and 256), "Wagner as Apostle of Chastity 1" (from *BGE* 256), "Wagner as Apostle of Chastity 2" (from *GM* III 2), "Wagner as Apostle of Chastity 3" (from *GM* III 3), "How I Freed Myself from Wagner 1 and 2" (from *HAH* II Preface 3 and 4), "The Psychologist Has His Say 1–3" (from *BGE* 269 and 270), and "Epilogue 1 and 2" (from *JS* Preface 3 and 4), followed by the poem "On the Poverty of the Richest Man" (which also concludes the *Dionysus Dithyrambs* completed in early 1889).

Nietzsche prepared and completed this writing in the course of only a few days in December 1888. However, he sent a note to his publisher Naumann, dated 2 January 1889 (*KGB* III:5, 571), in which it appears that he wanted to delay publication of the work, even as he had already been reading and approving galley proofs: "Events have completely overtaken the little writing Nietzsche Contra W." When Franz Overbeck arrived in Turin on 8 January 1889 to fetch Nietzsche, who had obviously gone mad, he met him, as he later wrote to Köselitz on 15 January: "cowering on a sofa corner and reading — as it turned out, the final proof of Nietzsche contra Wagner."[86] Accordingly, in the weeks to follow, in the correspondence between Köselitz

---

86. Overbeck and Köselitz, *Briefwechsel,* 205.

and Overbeck, they discussed how to proceed with those of
Nietzsche's manuscripts that were ready for printing, among
them the manuscript of *Nietzsche Contra Wagner*. Finally,
against what had been agreed to with Köselitz and Overbeck,
Constantin Georg Naumann produced one hundred instead
of fifty copies of *Nietzsche Contra Wagner* as a private edition
for friends, which was indeed criticized by Overbeck in his
letter to Naumann of 15/16 February 1889.[87] In fact, the work
was not delivered to bookstores until November 1894,[88] with
1895 as the year of publication, as volume VIII of the first complete edition of Nietzsche's works, edited by Fritz Koegel,
which also included the first edition of *The Antichrist*.

Being a collage and thus an experiment in form, *Nietzsche
Contra Wagner* is unique among Nietzsche's works. Although
Nietzsche, when working on different writings at the same
time, frequently regrouped material and finally published it
somewhere other than where it was originally intended, sometimes even in the form of self-citations, prior to *Nietzsche Contra Wagner* he had never compiled a complete manuscript from
material previously published elsewhere. A thorough comparison of what was published in *Nietzsche Contra Wagner* with
their original versions shows not only that quite a few passages
were orthographically and stylistically polished by Nietzsche,
but also that on the whole — as already indicated by some of
the programmatic new titles of the selected sections — they
were reworked toward enhancing his original intentions. The
collage technique, with its rearrangement and recontextualiza-
tion of originally isolated passages, allowed for a harmoniza-
tion of what was meant. That the selected passages were "above
all, shortened" (*NCW* Foreword, p. 385) is an important indication of a method Nietzsche chose for his late works, namely,

---

87. Franz Overbeck, *Werke und Nachlass,* vol. 8: *Briefe,* in collaboration
with Andreas Urs Sommer, ed. Niklaus Peter, et al. (Stuttgart: Metzler,
2008), 269–75.

88. Schaberg, *The Nietzsche Canon,* 179.

the technique of trenchant abbreviation, in order to express the respective meaning in each case more clearly and less ambiguously.

The broadside against the Germans and the allusions to the Triple Alliance of Germany, Austria, and Italy as well as to Italian prime minister Francesco Crispi in the Foreword signals that *Nietzsche Contra Wagner* is by no means just a private settling of scores with Wagner but, as a counterpoint of the revaluation of all values, is intended to expose a decidedly political dimension, thereby losing some of its (pseudo-)documentary nature: Wagner should not only be discredited as the *décadence*-type but also as a despicable moral-aesthetic embodiment of all that Nietzsche's new "great politics" wanted to overcome. Nietzsche was ready to admire Wagner only where the latter presented himself as a "*master* of the miniature" (*NCW* "Where I Admire," p. 389), which, however, he had in most cases forgotten in his presumptuous striving for the great. The physiological point of view demanded by the speaking "I" requires music to provide for "*relief*" for the "body" (*NCW* "Where I Object," p. 390), whereas Wagner wants the theatrical, the attitude that makes sick. By way of producing "*chaos* in place of rhythm," Wagner "overturned the previous physiological precondition of music" (*NCW* "Wagner as Danger" 1, pp. 392–93). Nietzsche accuses Wagner of only aiming at an effect on the masses. The section "We Antipodes," where suffering "from the *superabundance* of life" is distinguished from suffering "from the *impoverishment* of life" (p. 395), attributes the latter to Wagner (as well as to Schopenhauer), whereas the speaking "I" claims the former for itself and further develops the contrast between Nietzschean life-affirmation and the nihilistic negation of life. Wagner appears as a representative of a pan-European *décadence* movement to which, in particular, the chastity ideology of *Parsifal* fits perfectly. As a "psychologist," Nietzsche opposes compassion, and in the epilogue he speaks in favor of "*Amor fati*" (*NCW* Epilogue 1, p. 405), while in the concluding poem (pp. 409–12) he speaks in favor of the virtue of giving oneself away.

The collage method of *Nietzsche Contra Wagner* might itself be understood as a typical piece of *décadence* art that reaches back to hackneyed ideas. Such considerations are found, for example, in a note titled *"Unter Musikern"*: "We are late musicians. We have inherited an immense past. Our memories quote constantly. When being among ourselves, we may make allusions in an almost scholarly way: we understands [*sic*] ourselves already. Even our audience love our allusions: it flatters them, they feel by it intellectual" (*KGW* IX 8, W II 5, 154, 1–6). According to such an interpretation, Nietzsche in *Nietzsche Contra Wagner* deliberately decides for a decadent principle of composition in order to illustrate *décadence*. Of course, then the point would be that the citations do not come from some other source, which would be less fruitful, but that the source and the epigone are one and the same, thereby revealing that Nietzsche and his work only *seem* to be *décadent*. Seen this way, *Nietzsche Contra Wagner* could be understood as an ironic adaptation to the expectations of a decadent audience to which one must answer, and answer with the appropriate artistic means.

Striking is the gesture of self-justification that, despite all the self-aggrandizement in *Nietzsche Contra Wagner* as well as in *Ecce Homo*, is at least the occasion for each of these literary undertakings. Obviously, even a revaluator must legitimize himself for what he is doing — even if in *Nietzsche Contra Wagner* he attempts to demonstrate that he has (almost) always done something different from what the audience attributes to him. In the case of *Nietzsche Contra Wagner*, he says, he had been criticizing Wagner for a long time without the readers taking notice.

Nietzsche Contra Wagner is considered a compilation of different passages from Nietzsche's earlier writings that have been hastily pieced together, for the sole purpose of showing that it was not in *The Case of Wagner* that he had first turned away from his former spiritual mentor. This, however, underestimates this work. *Nietzsche Contra Wagner* belongs with Nietzsche's attempts to subordinate his own biography — as in *Ecce Homo* — to a radical teleology and to see world-historical necessity at work everywhere along the path of his thought. In *Nietzsche Contra Wagner*, Wagner is only a vehicle for emphasizing, *ex negativo*, the indispensability of a complete renewal of human valuation. Thus, according to Nietzsche's own testimony, his long struggle with Wagner has a tragic character (cf. his letter to Naumann of 15 December 1888, *KGB* III:5, 525). Here the "revaluation of all values" is tested on an actual phenomenon of the present — Wagner — while at the same time suggesting to the readers that this revaluation has always been Nietzsche's project.

Translated by Mirko Wittwar and Alan D. Schrift

Index of Persons

Page numbers followed by n and nn indicate notes.

classical poet, novelist,
playwright, and natural
philosopher, 10, 39, 84, 97,
100, 122–23, 129, 142, 285,
396, 399, 451n8, 453nn23–30,
454n32, 454nn35–36, 455n46,
462n22, 470n4, 472n13,
484n11, 489n22, 506n93,
507n99, 508n7, 508n9, 513n4,
532n240, 554, 566n9, 596n73,
607n148, 609n159, 628n7,
632n3, 645n69, 664, 674, 681

Gogol, Nikolai (1809–52),
Russian writer, 403

Goldmark, Karl (1830–1915),
Hungarian composer whose
opera *The Queen of Sheba*
premiered in Vienna in
1875, 36, 464n8

Goncourt, Edmond (1822–
96), and Jules (1830–70),
French sibling authors, 18,
88, 92, 431, 457n66, 469n22,
486n7, 487n13, 489n31, 674

Gordius, mythological king of
Phrygia, father of Midas,
588n46

Gottsched, Johann Christoph
(1700–1766), German
philosopher, author, and
critic who exercised
enormous influence on
German literature from
1725 to 1740, 508n10

Gretchen, Faust's love in
Goethe's tragic play, 454n35

Gutzkow, Karl (1811–78),
German writer, 455n51

Guyau, Jean-Marie (1854–88),
French philosopher, 677,
687

Gyp (pen name of Sibylle
Riqueti de Mirabeau,
comtesse de Martel de
Janville) (1849–1932),
French writer, 235, 572n19

Hafiz, pen name of Shams
ud-din Mohammed (ca.
1327–90), Persian poet, 399,
646n67

Hamlet, eponymous character
in Shakespeare's play, 238,
405, 568n19, 588n50

Hammer, Fritz (one of several
pseudonyms of Michael
Georg Conrad, 1846–1927),
author of a positive review
of *Twilight of the Idols* in the
literary journal *Die
Gesellschaft* (April 1889), 683

Handel, Georg Friedrich
(1685–1759), German-En-
glish baroque composer, 15,
36, 194, 241, 391, 456n57

Hanslick, Eduard (1825–1904),
influential 19th-century
Austrian music critic, 668

Hart, Heinrich (1855–1906),
German writer who wrote
to N about *The Birth of
Tragedy*, 587n37

Subject Index

Page numbers followed by n and nn indicate notes. Page numbers in boldface indicate primary texts.

310–12; morality as anti-
nature, 64–67; morality of
improvement, 56; as
nihilistic religion, 518n77;
Pascal and, 502n74; Paul's
interpretation of, 174–77,
183; political agitation
against, 685–86; as psychological corruption, 177–79;
psychology of belief,
186–87; psychology of the
Redeemer, 160–61; as
question mark, 168; Renan
and ruination of reason,
88–89; Schopenhauer and,
100; sexuality and, 130,
208–9, 311; sickness, need
for, 187–90; the socialist
and the Christian, 499–
500n70; superior humans,
war against, 136–37; true vs.
apparent in, 61; virtues,
Christian, 74; waging war
on, 227; Wagner and, 9, 31.
See also Church(es)
Church(es): cause vs. consequence and, 70; erected out
of opposite of Gospel, 168;
as menagerie, 78; negated
by Christianity, 159;
passion, battle against,
64–65, 475n1; Plato and,
127; power and, 169. See also
Christianity
Cleverness, 230–46 passim;
Socrates and, 56; Wagner
and, 14, 24

Climate, 6, 150, 233–35, 241,
245, 479n3, 702
Commanding: authority and,
471n12; backward inference
and, 396; Christian morality
as command, 90; communal
instinct and, 476n7; giving
reasons vs., 53; instinct of,
234, 390; organizing idea
and, 244; priests and, 194;
through dying, 341; Wagner
and, 28; war and, 227
Communication: art of style
and, 252; commentary on,
659–60; the Dionysian
human and, 94; revelation
and, 197; tragic artist and,
102; vulgarized, 103
Compassion: Christian, on
show, 17; commentary on,
688, 713–14; contagious,
514n26; cooling down, 268;
the Dionysian and, 130–31;
the educated and, 403; free
will and, 75; the impersonal
and, 103; life denied through,
138–39; morality of, 110–11,
497n70; as more harmful
than vice, 136; overcoming
of, 223; physiologists and,
275; poets and, 403–4;
psychologists and, 402–3;
tragedy and, 259; Wagner
and, 19; Zarathustra and, 290
Competition: erotic, Plato's
philosophy as, 101; secret, in
Christianity, 151

Psychology: of belief, 186–87;
cleanliness or uncleanliness
of a race and, 301–2; of
conscience, 293; of conviction, 192–94; of error,
73–75; the Galilean type,
154; Germans, psychological
tact of, 97; of the Gospel,
165–66; imaginary, 145;
leisure and, 45; none before
me, 310; as not-yet-science,
58; of the orgiastic, 130–31;
of the priest, 185–86; of the
Redeemer, 160–61; of
tragedy, 258–59

Punishment: concealing
ruling power, 529n192;
corruption of souls and,
201; for deep spirit, 406;
error of free will and,
75–76; "God will punish,"
480n7; in history of Israel,
157; misfortune as, 156;
psychology of the Gospel
and, 165; psychology of the
priest, 185; sin and, 74

Purpose(s): art and, 101–2;
beauty and, 100; commen-
tary on, 599n94; conscience
and, 170; higher, 525n157; of
holy lies, 198; as lacking, 76;
morality translated into,
307; reality shorn of, 213; of
religious legislation, 200;
selfishness and, 107; will of
God and, 157; Zarathustra
and, 564n10

Race(s), 236; beauty of, 120;
breeding of, 78–79;
Buddhism and, 152;
Christianity and, 148–49,
177, 188–89; dilettantes and,
482n10; estimating value of,
237; German, 303; Jews as,
482n6; kingdom of, 145;
morality and, 70, 80;
pessimism and, 109; Polish
nobility, 221–22, 566n9,
567n9; psychology and
cleanliness or uncleanliness
of, 301–2; refinement of, 5;
strong, 148, 241, 391;
stronger, remnants of, 36;
Voltaire, Sainte-Beuve, and,
488n16

Rationality: Greeks, Socrates,
and, 55–56; against instinct,
257; modern marriage and,
114, 504n80; revelation and,
197. See also Reason

Reading: Ecce Homo as
instructions for 702; the
Gospels, 178; Hugo over
Homer, 486n9; Nietzsche's,
during last creative years,
673–77; Nietzsche reading
own works, 434, 440;
Nietzsche reading nothing,
270; the New Testament,
181, 526n163; Petronius after
Paul, 181; philology as art of
reading well, 190; as
recreation, 235; Shake-
speare, 238; well, 202

idiocy and, 38, 188; idleness,
160; Indian, 149, 481n6;
pouring over books, 242;
without intellect, 82
Schopenhauer as Educator
(Nietzsche), 265–66
Science and scientists:
barbarizing, 262; character,
scientific, 119, 143, 404,
516–17n64; cheerfulness
and, 404; Christianity and,
183; God's fear of science,
183–84; happiness and, 185;
imaginary natural science,
145; philosophers and, 58;
priests and, 143; reward and
punish *vs.*, 529n192;
scientism, 143, 150, 516n64
Seduction, 398, 629n9;
décadence and, 12, 274, 313;
ecclesiastical, 164–65; to
existence, 399; to false
conclusions, 404; good
people and, 602n114;
Gospels and, 178; idealists
and, 139–40; integrity and,
584n22; by Leibniz and
Kant, 610n163; martyrs and,
191; masters in, 584n22; of
minds, 25, 122; Renan and,
89; by revolution as spectacle, 122; through morality,
178; Wagner and, 31–32;
Zarathustra and, 214, 630n15
Self-contempt, 501n74
Selfishness, 622n118; altruism
and atrophy of, 107; art of,

243; casuistry of, 245; laws
of nature and, 176; of the
loafer, 525n156, 525n158;
national, 134; natural value
of egoism, 105–6; refined,
234; shameful, 168; strict,
311; Unfashionables and, 262
Selflessness, 622n118; Christian
morality and, 311; cult of,
499n70; forgetting one's
distance, 234–35; life *vs.*,
270; morality and, 275;
neutrality of the stomach
and, 299; Pascal, Flaubert,
and, 396
Self-overcoming, 83, 103;
continual, 228; Germans
and, 610n163; of intellect,
170, 191; of morality
through truthfulness, 307,
564n10, 600n94; Renais-
sance and, 122; Wagner
and, 3–4; will to power and,
416
Self-preservation: art of, 243;
décadence and, 155; genius
and, 117–18; instinct of, 98,
162, 241–43; intellect's
instinct for, 82; Jews, Jewish
Christians, and, 179;
opposing strength and, 66;
radicalism and, 477n7;
Socrates and, 55; theolo-
gian-instinct and, 140
Self-sacrifice, 118
Sensations: denying validity of
sense-experience, 472n5;

The Complete Works of Friedrich Nietzsche

Library of Congress Cataloging-in-Publication Data

Names: Nietzsche, Friedrich Wilhelm, 1844–1900, author. | Del Caro,
  Adrian,
  1952– translator. | Diethe, Carol, 1943– translator. | Large, Duncan,
  translator. | Leiner, George H., translator. | Loeb, Paul S.,
  translator. | Schrift, Alan D., 1955– translator. | Tinsley, David
  Fletcher, translator. | Wittwar, Mirko, translator. | Sommer, Andreas
  Urs, writer of afterword. | Nietzsche, Friedrich Wilhelm, 1844–1900.
  Works. English. 1995 ; v. 9.
Title: The case of Wagner, Twilight of the idols, The antichrist, Ecce homo,
  Dionysus dithyrambs, Nietzsche contra Wagner / Friedrich Wilhelm
  Nietzsche ; translated by Adrian Del Caro, Carol Diethe, Duncan Large,
  George H. Leiner, Paul S. Loeb, Alan D. Schrift, David F. Tinsley and
  Mirko Wittwar ; with an afterword by Andreas Urs Sommer.
Description: Stanford, California : Stanford University Press, 2021. |
  Series: The complete works of Friedrich Nietzsche ; volume 9 | Includes
  bibliographical references and index.
Identifiers: LCCN 2019046793 | ISBN 9780804728829 (cloth) |
  ISBN 9781503612549 (paperback)
Subjects: LCSH: Philosophy.
Classification: LCC B3312.E5 D45 2021 | DDC 193—dc23
LC record available at https://lccn.loc.gov/2019046793

Typeset by Classic Typography in 10.5/12 Adobe Garamond

CPSIA information can be obtained
at www.ICGtesting.com
Printed in the USA
JSHW020229090123
35924JS00001B/1